Introduction to
Real Estate Law

Second Edition

Introduction to

Real Estate Law

Second Edition

Deborah Flynn

West Publishing Company
St. Paul • New York • Los Angeles • San Francisco

Copyediting   Barbara Hodgson
Composition   Graphic World, Inc.

Library of Congress Cataloging-in-Publication Data

Flynn, Deborah.
  Introduction to real estate law.

  Rev. ed. of: Introduction to real estate law/by
the Institute for Paralegal Training. 1978.
  1. Real property—United States.   2. Vendors and
purchasers—United States.   3. Mortgages—United States.
I. Title.
KF570.F58   1986   346.7304′6   85–7301
ISBN 0–314–77984–1
1st Reprint—1987   ∞

This book is dedicated to my brother and sister,
Thomas Flynn and Karin Flynn-Rodden.

Summary of Contents

Introduction   xxxv

Chapter 1   **Introduction to Real Property**   1

    I. Introduction   2
   II. Basic Concepts of Real Property Rights   3
  III. Public Control Over Land Use   7
  IV. Determination of Ownership   9
   V. Summary   9

Chapter 2   **Titleholders**   10

Part One   INTRODUCTION TO TITLEHOLDERS   10
    I. Introduction   10
   II. Title in the Name of an Individual   10
  III. Title in Joint Names   11
  IV. Partnerships and Joint Ventures   15
   V. Corporations   18

Part Two   INCOME TAX CONSEQUENCES OF
              PARTNERSHIP *vs.* CORPORATION   19
    I. Introduction to Federal Income Taxes   19
   II. The Concept of Tax Deductions   19
  III. Concept of Tax Loss and Tax Shelter   21
  IV. Comparison of Partnerships and Corporations   22
   V. Choice of Entity   24

Part Three *STRAW PARTIES*   24
   I. Introduction   24
  II. Individuals as Nominees or Straw Parties   25
 III. Corporations as Nominees   27

Chapter 3 **Buying and Selling Real Estate**   **29**

    I. Introduction   29
   II. Terms Common to Agreements of Sale for All Types
      of Real Estate   33
  III. Typical Additional Provisions of Agreements of Sale
      for New Single Family Residences (Existing Building)   66
  IV. Typical Additional Provisions of Agreements of Sale
      for Newly Constructed Single Family Residences   77
   V. Typical Additional Provisions of Agreements of Sale
      for Raw Land to be Developed   89
  VI. Typical Additional Provisions of Agreements of Sale
      for Commercial Improved Real Estate   91
 VII. Discussion of Other Types of Real Estate
      Agreements of Sale   97
VIII. Checklist for Purchase and Sale of Real Estate   99

Chapter 4 **Surveys and Legal Descriptions**   **105**

   I. Introduction   105
  II. Surveys   106
 III. Types of Legal Descriptions   111
 IV. Checking the Legal Description for Accuracy   116
  V. Interpretation of Legal Descriptions   117
 VI. Conclusions   118

Chapter 5 **Deeds of Conveyance**   **120**

   I. Introduction   120
  II. The Elements of a Deed   121
 III. Statutory Form of Deed   148
 IV. Delivery of Deeds   149
  V. Special Deeds and Deed Clauses   149

Chapter 6 **Title Abstracting and Title Insurance** **161**

    I. Introduction   161
    II. Title Search   164
    III. The Abstract   166
    IV. Title Report   169
    V. Summary   175

Chapter 7 **Real Estate Mortgages** **186**

Part One   *RESIDENTIAL MORTGAGES*   186
    I. Introduction   186
    II. Residential Mortgages   188

Part Two   *COMMERCIAL-INDUSTRIAL*
      MORTGAGES   201
    I. The Application for a Commercial-Industrial Mortgage   201
    II. Issuance of Commitment   205
    III. Preparation of Documents   209
    IV. Closing   209
    V. Post Closing   210

Part Three   *CONSTRUCTION MORTGAGES*   210
    I. Introduction   210
    II. Construction Loans and Permanent Loans   211
    III. Title   214
    IV. Preparation of Documents   214
    V. Preparation for Closing   226
    VI. Mechanics' Liens   226
    VII. Construction Loan Closing   227
    VIII. Post Closing   227
    IX. Permanent Loan Closing   228

Part Four   *FEDERAL HOUSING ADMINISTRATION*
      (FHA) MORTGAGES   229
    I. Introduction to the FHA   229

Part Five   *INDUSTRIAL DEVELOPMENT*
      AUTHORITY LOANS   233
    I. Mortgage Loan From the Bank to the Industrial
      Development Authority   234
    II. Lease with the Industrial User   234
    III. Agreement of Purchase   234

Part Six FORM AND SUBSTANCE OF THE NOTE
       AND MORTGAGE   235
    I. Drafting Notes   235
    II. Drafting Mortgages   241

Part Seven ASSIGNMENT, SATISFACTION AND
       RELEASE OF MORTGAGES   260
    I. Assignment of Mortgages   260
    II. Satisfaction of Mortgages   260
    III. Release of Mortgages   262
    IV. Sales Under and Subject to Mortgages   263
    V. Subordination of Mortgages   264

Part Eight MORTGAGE FORECLOSURE   266
    I. Introduction   266
    II. Action on Note or on Mortgage   266
    III. The Default   267
    IV. The Complaint   267
    V. Execution Sale   270
    VI. Conclusion   270

Chapter 8 **Settlements and Closings**   **271**

    I. General Information   271
    II. Preparation for Settlement—Purchase—Sale
         of Property   271
    III. Settlement for the Purchase and Sale of Property 282
    IV. Post Closing—Purchase—Sale of Property   288
    V. Construction Loan Closing   289
    VI. Permanent Loan Closing   295
    VII. Disclosure and the Real Estate Settlement
          Procedures Act of 1974   298
    VIII. Summary   310

Chapter 9 **Recording Statutes**   **328**

    I. Introduction   328
    II. Recording Statutes   329
    III. The Torrens System   341
    IV. Summary   342

Chapter 10 **Leasing**   **343**

Part One *BASIC ELEMENTS OF A LEASE*   343
    I. Introduction   343
    II. Essential Elements of a Lease   344
    III. The Need for a Written Lease   348
    IV. Additional Provisions Common to All Types of Leases 348

Part Two *SPECIAL TYPES OF LEASES*   374
    I. Commercial and Shopping Center Leases   374

Part Three *OFFICE BUILDING LEASES*   391
    I. In General   391
    II. Net and Ground Leases   394
    III. Surety or Guaranty Agreement   400
    IV. Assignment or Subletting   401

Chapter 11 **Condominiums, Planned-Unit Developments, and Cooperatives**   **408**

    I. Introduction   408
    II. Condominiums   408
    III. Planned-Unit Developments   418
    IV. Cooperative Apartments   420

Glossary   **425**
Index   **434**

Contents

Introduction   **xxxv**

Chapter 1 **Introduction to Real Property**   **1**

  I. INTRODUCTION 2
  II. BASIC CONCEPTS OF REAL PROPERTY RIGHTS 3
    A. Physical Characteristics 3
    B. A Bundle of Rights 3
      1. Fee 3
      2. Lease 4
      3. Mineral Interest or Air Rights 4
      4. Easements, Rights of Way 5
      5. Life Estate 5
      6. Future Interests 5
    C. Methods of Acquiring Title to Real Estate 6
      1. Purchase 6
      2. Inheritance and Gift 6
      3. Adverse Possession 6
    D. Legal Interests of a Spouse 7
      1. Dower 7
      2. Curtesy 7
  III. PUBLIC CONTROL OVER LAND USE 7
    A. Nuisance 8
    B. Zoning 8
    C. Private Restrictions 8
    D. Liens 8
  IV. DETERMINATION OF OWNERSHIP 9
    A. Title Searching 9
    B. Documents 9
  V. SUMMARY 9

Chapter 2 **Titleholders** **10**

Part One INTRODUCTION TO TITLEHOLDERS 10
 I. INTRODUCTION 10
 II. TITLE IN THE NAME OF AN INDIVIDUAL 10
 III. TITLE IN JOINT NAMES 11
  A. Tenants in Common 11
  B. Joint Tenants 12
  C. Tenants by the Entirety 13
  D. Commercial Practices Regarding Title in Joint Names 14
 IV. PARTNERSHIPS AND JOINT VENTURES 15
  A. General Partnerships 15
   1. Nature of a Partner's Interest 15
   2. General Characteristics of a Partnership 15
    (a) Personal Liability 15
    (b) Control 16
    (c) Tax Implications 16
   3. Form in Which Title is Held 16
  B. Limited Partnerships 16
   1. Classes of Partners 16
   2. Liability 16
   3. Control 17
  C. Joint Ventures 17
 V. CORPORATIONS 18
  A. General Characteristics of Corporate Ownership 18
  B. Advantages of Corporate Ownership 18
  C. Disadvantages of Corporate Ownership 18

Part Two INCOME TAX CONSEQUENCES OF
     PARTNERSHIP *vs.* CORPORATION 19
 I. INTRODUCTION TO FEDERAL INCOME TAXES 19
 II. THE CONCEPT OF TAX DEDUCTIONS 19
  A. Generally 19
  B. Depreciation or Cost Recovery 20
 III. CONCEPT OF TAX LOSS AND TAX SHELTER 21
 **IV. COMPARISON OF PARTNERSHIPS AND
   CORPORATIONS** 22
  A. Taxation of Partnerships 22
  B. Taxation of a Corporation 23
 V. CHOICE OF ENTITY 24

Part Three STRAW PARTIES 24
 I. INTRODUCTION 24
  A. Use of a Straw Party Simplifies the Transfer of Title 24
  B. Use of a Straw Party May Avoid Possible Title Problems 25

C. Use of a Straw Party May Secure Anonymity of Ownership   25
D. Use of a Straw Party May Avoid Personal Liability on Mortgage
    Obligations   25

II. **INDIVIDUALS AS NOMINEES OR STRAW PARTIES**   25
A. Common Practice   25
B. Declaration of Trust   26
C. Control of Nominee Required   26
D. Problems Created by the Use of Individuals as Nominees   26

III. **CORPORATIONS AS NOMINEES**   27
A. Benefits of Using Corporate Nominees   27
B. Income Tax Problems Created by the Use of Corporate
    Nominees   27

Chapter 3 **Buying and Selling Real Estate**   29

I. **INTRODUCTION**   29
A. The Need for an Agreement of Sale   30
B. The Need for a Written Agreement of Sale   31
C. Legal Consequences of Executing an Agreement of Sale
    for Real Estate   32

II. **TERMS COMMON TO AGREEMENTS OF SALE FOR ALL
    TYPES OF REAL ESTATE**   33
A. Date   34
B. Parties   34
    1. Seller   36
       (a) Agent as Seller   36
       (b) Joinder of Spouse   36
    2. Purchaser   37
C. Description of Property Being Sold   37
    1. Methods of Description   37
       (a) Description by Reference to a Plan   37
       (b) Legal Description   38
       (c) Recorded Plan, Street Number   38
    2. Items to be Included in Description   38
       (a) Reference to Buildings   38
       (b) Acreage   39
       (c) Reference to Public Streets   39
       (d) Condemnation Awards   39
       (e) Other Property Included in Sale   39
D. Purchase Price and Payment Terms   40
    1. Standard Provision   40
    2. Escrow Account   41
E. Condition or Quality of Title to be Conveyed   43
    1. Good and Marketable Title   46
    2. Insurable Title   47

F. Time and Place of Settlement 48
G. Possession 49
H. Apportionments 51
I. Real Estate Transfer Taxes 53
J. Municipal Improvements and Violations of Laws,
    Ordinances or Regulations 53
K. Condemnation 55
L. Defaults and Remedies 56
    1. The Law Absent Agreement by the Parties 56
        (a) Default by the Purchaser 56
        (b) Default by Seller 56
    2. Agreement of the Parties 57
        (a) Purchaser's Default 57
        (b) Seller's Default 58
M. Zoning 58
N. Purchaser's Right of Inspection 60
O. Brokers 61
P. Miscellaneous Provisions 61
    1. Merger (Survival after Settlement) 61
    2. Recording the Agreement of Sale 62
    3. Notices 62
    4. Parties Bound 63
        (a) Assignment Permitted 63
        (b) Assignment Not Permitted 63
    5. Captions 63
    6. Integration (Entire Agreement) 64
    7. Negation of Representations by the Seller 64
    8. Preparation of Documents 65
Q. Signatures 65
    1. In General 65
    2. Co-Owners 65
    3. Partners 65
    4. Corporation 66
    5. Agent 66
III. TYPICAL ADDITIONAL PROVISIONS OF AGREEMENTS OF
    SALE FOR SINGLE FAMILY RESIDENCES (EXISTING
    BUILDING) 66
A. Mortgages 67
    1. Purchase Subject to Existing Mortgage 67
        (a) No Personal Liability 68
        (b) Purchaser Personally Liable to Seller 69
        (c) Purchaser Personally Liable to Seller and
            Mortgagee 69
    2. Purchase Money Mortgage from Purchaser to Seller 70
    3. Mortgage Contingency 71

B. Fire or Other Casualty and Risk of Loss 72

C. Termite Inspection and Certificate 73

D. Condition of the Premises 74

E. Fixtures and Articles of Personal Property Included in the Sale 75

IV. **TYPICAL ADDITIONAL PROVISIONS OF AGREEMENTS OF SALE FOR NEWLY CONSTRUCTED SINGLE FAMILY RESIDENCES** 77

A. Additional Protection Which the Buyer Requires When Purchasing a Newly Completed Residence 78

  1. Description of Property 78

  2. Warranties From Seller Relating to the Premises Themselves 78

    (a) Subdivision Approval 78

    (b) Water and Sewer Hooked-Up 78

    (c) Mechanics' Liens 79

  3. Warranties From Seller With Respect to Construction and Equipment 79

  4. Uncompleted Items 80

B. Additional Provisions to Protect the Purchaser of Residences to be Constructed or in the Process of Construction at the Time the Agreement of Sale Is Executed 88

  1. Description 88

  2. Deposit 88

  3. Settlement Date 89

V. **TYPICAL ADDITIONAL PROVISIONS OF AGREEMENTS OF SALE FOR RAW LAND TO BE DEVELOPED** 89

A. Subdivision Approvals 89

B. Municipal Approval; Streets, Water Service and Sewer Service 90

C. Right to Inspect Premises and Make Test Thereon 90

D. Building Permits 91

VI. **TYPICAL ADDITIONAL PROVISIONS OF AGREEMENTS OF SALE FOR COMMERCIAL IMPROVED REAL ESTATE** 91

A. Description of Fixtures and Personalty Included in the Sale 91

B. Possession 92

C. Zoning and Licensing 92

D. Existing Leases 92

E. Warranty as to Income and Expenses Generated by Premises 95

F. Service Contracts 95

G. Apportionments 96
   1. Percentage Rentals 96
   2. Maintenance and Service Contracts, etc. 96
   3. Lease Brokerage and Managing Agent's Commission 97

VII. **DISCUSSION OF OTHER TYPES OF REAL ESTATE AGREEMENTS OF SALE** 97
  A. Option Agreements 97
  B. Installment Sale Agreements 97
  C. Sale Leaseback Agreements 98

VIII. **CHECKLIST FOR PURCHASE AND SALE OF REAL ESTATE** 99
  A. Preparation of Agreement of Sale 99
    1. Parties 99
    2. Description of Property 99
    3. Purchase Price 99
    4. Conditions 100
    5. Settlement 101
    6. Title 101
    7. Assessments, Notices, etc. 101
    8. Items Included in Sale 101
    9. Apportionments and Expenses 102
   10. Remedies 102
   11. Risk of Loss 102
   12. Miscellaneous 102
  B. Additional Checklist for Residence Under Construction or to be Constructed 103
  C. Additional Checklist for Raw Land 103
  D. Additional Checklist for Commercial Improved Real Estate 103

Chapter 4 **Surveys and Legal Descriptions** **105**

I. **INTRODUCTION** 105
II. **SURVEYS** 106
  A. Background 106
  B. Mechanics of the Survey 107
    1. Point of Reference 107
    2. Metes and Bounds Survey 107
    3. Government or Rectangular Survey Systems 108
      (a) Background 108
      (b) Mechanics of the System 108
      (c) Reference Points 111
III. **TYPES OF LEGAL DESCRIPTIONS** 111
  A. Street Number or Name 111
  B. Monuments 111

C. Subdivision Plot Plan 112
D. Metes and Bounds 112
   1. No Compass Reference Necessary 112
   2. Compass References Necessary 114
   3. Surveys Containing Curved Lines 115
IV. **CHECKING THE LEGAL DESCRIPTION FOR ACCURACY** 116
A. Survey 116
B. Where There is no Survey 116
V. **INTERPRETATION OF LEGAL DESCRIPTIONS** 117
A. Width of Boundaries 117
B. Inconsistency in the Description 118
VI. **CONCLUSIONS** 118

Chapter 5 **Deeds of Conveyance** **120**

I. **INTRODUCTION** 120
A. The Indenture 121
B. The Deed Poll 121
II. **THE ELEMENTS OF A DEED** 121
A. Standard Language and Forms 121
B. Parts of Deed 122
C. Premises 122
   1. Date 122
   2. Names of the Parties 123
   3. Consideration 124
   4. Granting Clause 124
      (a) Implied Warranty 125
      (b) Words of Inheritance 125
      (c) Nature of the Estate Granted 126
   5. Description 127
   6. Recital 128
      (a) Deed to the Grantor Signed by an Attorney-in-Fact 129
      (b) Grantor Received Sheriff's Deed 129
      (c) Name of Corporate Grantor Changed 129
      (d) Real Estate Being Conveyed Was Assembled in Multiple Transfers 130
      (e) Entireties Property Where One Spouse Has Died 130
   7. Encumbrance Clauses 130
   8. Use of the Encumbrance Clause for Creation of New Restrictions 132
      (a) Purposes 132
      (b) Covenants Running with the Land 132
      (c) Limitations on Restrictions 133
      (d) Drafting 133

9. Encumbrance Clause for Mortgage Liens   133
    (a) *Personal Liability of Grantee to Mortgagee*   134
    (b) *Indemnification of Grantor*   135
    (c) *Effect Upon Statement of Consideration*   135
10. Encumbrance Clause for Easements   136
11. Exceptions and Reservations   136
    (a) *Drafting Easements*   137
    (b) *Deed of Grant*   137
    (c) *Declaration of Easements and Reciprocal Easement Agreement*   138
    (d) *Creation of Easements by Other Means*   139
12. Appurtenances   139
D. Habendum   140
    1. "To Have and To Hold" Clause   140
    2. Warranty Clause   141
        (a) *Covenants in General*   141
        (b) *Covenants for Title*   141
        (c) *General Warranty*   142
        (d) *Special Warranty*   142
        (e) *Fiduciary's Warranty*   143
        (f) *Quitclaim Deed without Warranty*   144
        (g) *Reference to Encumbrance Clauses*   144
E. Conclusion   144
    1. Execution Clause   144
        (a) *Individual*   144
        (b) *Corporation*   144
    2. Signatures   145
        (a) *Individual*   145
        (b) *Corporate*   145
        (c) *Attorney-in-Fact*   145
    3. Receipt   146
    4. Certification of Grantee's Address   146
    5. Acknowledgment   146
III. **STATUTORY FORM OF DEED**   148
IV. **DELIVERY OF DEEDS**   149
A. Delivery in Escrow   149
B. Acceptance of Delivery by Grantee   149
V. **SPECIAL DEEDS AND DEED CLAUSES**   149
A. Sheriff's Deed   149
B. Deed of Confirmation or Correction   150
C. Condominium Deed   150
D. Coal and Other Mineral Severance Clauses   150

Chapter 6 Title Abstracting and Title Insurance 161

I. **INTRODUCTION** 161
  A. General Introduction 161
  B. Marketability of Title 162
  C. Types of Title Examination 163
    1. Attorney Direct Search and Opinion 163
    2. Abstract and Opinion 163
    3. Torrens System 163
    4. Title Insurance 164
II. **TITLE SEARCH** 164
  A. Recording Systems 164
  B. The Index Systems 165
    1. The Grantor-Grantee Index 165
    2. The Tract Index 166
  C. Differences 166
III. **THE ABSTRACT** 166
  A. In General 166
  B. Chain of Title 167
  C. Search for Related Conveyances and Encumbrances 167
    1. Related Conveyances 168
    2. Mortgages 168
    3. Judgments 168
    4. Tax Liens 168
    5. Federal Search 169
    6. State and Local Court Matters 169
    7. Corporate Matters 169
IV. **TITLE REPORT** 169
  A. In General 169
  B. Analysis of Alta Title Report 170
    1. Heading 170
    2. Schedule A: Caption 171
    3. Schedule B-1: Matters Affecting Title 171
      (a) Taxes, Sewer, and Water Rents 171
      (b) Mechanics' and Municipal Liens 171
      (c) Mortgages and Judgments 172
      (d) Objections 172
    4. Schedule B-11: Exceptions and Objections Pertaining to the Land 172
      (a) Property-Specific Exceptions 172
      (b) Party-Specific Objections 173
    5. Legal Description 173
    6. Endorsements 173
V. **SUMMARY** 175

Chapter 7   **Real Estate Mortgages**   **186**

Part One   RESIDENTIAL MORTGAGES   186
  I. INTRODUCTION   186
  II. RESIDENTIAL MORTGAGES   188
     A. Methods of Repayment   188
         1. Interest   188
         2. Principal   189
     B. The Application for a Mortgage   191
     C. Issuance of Commitment Letter   195
     D. Preparation for Settlement   197
         1. Mortgage Documents   197
         2. Title Search   197
         3. Termite and Other Certificates   198
         4. Insurance   198
         5. Closing   198
            *(a) Interest to the First Day of the First Regular Interest
                Period*   199
            (b) Escrow Funds   199
            (c) Miscellaneous Charges   200
     E. Post Closing   201

*Part Two   COMMERCIAL-INDUSTRIAL
            MORTGAGES*   201
   **I. THE APPLICATION FOR A COMMERCIAL-INDUSTRIAL
      MORTGAGE**   201
     A. The Mortgagee's Concerns   201
     B. The Mortgagor's Concerns   202
  II. ISSUANCE OF COMMITMENT   205
     A. Title and Title Insurance   205
     B. Lease on Premises   206
         1. Rights of Tenant versus Mortgagee   206
         2. Attornment and Non-Disturbance   207
     C. Compliance with Laws   208
     D. Easements   209
 III. PREPARATION OF DOCUMENTS   209
 IV. CLOSING   209
  V. POST CLOSING   210

Part Three   CONSTRUCTION MORTGAGES   210
  I. INTRODUCTION   210
  II. PERMANENT LOANS AND CONSTRUCTION LOANS   211
     A. The Permanent Loan   211
     B. The Construction Loan   212
 III. TITLE   214

IV. **PREPARATION OF DOCUMENTS** 214
    A. Construction Loan Agreement 214
    B. Note 219
    C. Mortgage 219
    D. General Construction Contract 219
    E. Completion Bond 220
    F. Corporate Resolutions 220
    G. Insurance 220
    H. Survey 220
    I. Building Permit 220
    J. Buy-Sell Agreement 220
    K. Declaration of Cross Easements 223
    L. Security Agreement and Financing Statement 223
V. **PREPARATION FOR CLOSING** 226
VI. **MECHANICS' LIENS** 226
VII. **CONSTRUCTION LOAN CLOSING** 227
VIII. **POST CLOSING** 227
IX. **PERMANENT LOAN CLOSING** 228
    A. Declaration of No Set-Off 228
    B. Tenant's Estoppel Certificate 229
    C. Corporate Resolutions 229

Part Four FEDERAL HOUSING ADMINISTRATION
        (FHA) MORTGAGES 229
I. **INTRODUCTION TO THE FHA** 229
    A. The Role of the FHA 229
    B. The Function of Mortgage Insurance 230
    C. The Organization of the FHA 231
    D. Types of Projects on Which the FHA Will Insure the
       Mortgage 231
    E. Types of Mortgages Which the FHA Will Insure 232
    F. FHA Mortgage Subsidies and Rent Supplement
       Programs 232
       1. Interest Subsidy 232
       2. Rent Supplements 233

Part Five INDUSTRIAL DEVELOPMENT AUTHORITY
        LOANS 233
I. **MORTGAGE LOAN FROM THE BANK TO THE
INDUSTRIAL DEVELOPMENT AUTHORITY** 234
II. **LEASE WITH THE INDUSTRIAL USER** 234
III. **AGREEMENT OF PURCHASE** 234

Part Six FORM AND SUBSTANCE OF THE NOTE AND
            MORTGAGE 235
I. DRAFTING NOTES 235
   A. Parties 235
   B. Payment 237
   C. Prepayment Privilege 238
   D. Acceleration 239
   E. Special Clauses in Construction Loan Notes—Advance
      Money Obligations 239
II. DRAFTING MORTGAGES 241
   A. Parties 242
   B. Conveyance—Description 242
   C. Property Included 243
   D. Habendum 243
   E. Taxes 244
   F. Insurance 245
   G. Maintenance 246
   H. Condemnation 247
   I. Financial Statements 247
   J. Mortgagee's Performance for Mortgagor 247
   K. Default—Remedies 248
   L. Warranty of Title 250
   M. Payment of Sums Secured 250
   N. Security Agreement 250
   O. Transfer of Title 251
   P. Construction Mortgage 252
   Q. Limitation of Liability 252
   R. Second Mortgage Clause 252
   S. Execution 254
   T. Acknowledgments 254

Part Seven ASSIGNMENT, SATISFACTION, AND
             RELEASE OF MORTGAGES 260
  I. ASSIGNMENT OF MORTGAGES 260
 II. SATISFACTION OF MORTGAGES 260
III. RELEASE OF MORTGAGES 262
 IV. SALES UNDER AND SUBJECT TO MORTGAGES 263
   A. Purchaser Assumes Debt 263
   B. Purchaser Indemnifies Seller 263
   C. No Liability Assumed by Purchaser 264
  V. SUBORDINATION OF MORTGAGES 264

Part Eight   MORTGAGE FORECLOSURE   266
  I. INTRODUCTION   266
 II. ACTION ON NOTE OR ON MORTGAGE   266
III. THE DEFAULT   267
 IV. THE COMPLAINT   267
   A. Plaintiff   268
   B. Defendant   268
   C. Defenses and Counterclaims   269
       1. Performance and/or Waiver   269
       2. Invalidity of Mortgage   269
       3. Technical Defenses Regarding Foreclosures   269
       4. Counterclaims and Offsets   269
  V. EXECUTION SALE   270
 VI. CONCLUSION   270

Chapter 8   **Settlements and Closings**   **271**

  I. GENERAL INFORMATION   271
 **II. PREPARATION FOR SETTLEMENT—PURCHASE—SALE
      OF PROPERTY**   271
   A. Preparation by Seller   272
       1. Deed   272
       2. Objections and Exceptions in the Title Report   272
          *(a) Mortgage Pay-off Statement and Satisfaction
               Piece*   272
          (b) Real Estate Taxes   273
          (c) Water and Sewer Rents   273
          (d) Judgments   273
          (e) Miscellaneous Title Objections   274
       3. Documents Needed for Special Situations   274
          (a) Corporation as Seller   274
          (b) Leased Property   275
          (c) Purchaser Money Mortgage   275
          (d) New Construction   275
          (e) Conveyance Where Record Owner is Deceased   276
          (f) Residential Property   277
          (g) Commercial or Industrial Properties   278
   B. Preparation by the Purchaser   278
       1. Title Report   279
       2. Deed   279
       3. Survey   279
       4. Inspection of Property   279

5. Mortgage   279
6. Fire Insurance   280
7. Public Utilities   280
8. Advance Calculation of Funds Needed to Complete Settlement   280
9. Notice of Settlement   281
10. Special Situations   281
   (a) Purchaser as Corporation   281
   (b) Property Subject to Lease   281

III. **SETTLEMENT FOR THE PURCHASE AND SALE OF PROPERTY**   282
A. Place of Closing   282
B. Settlement Clerk   282
C. Mechanics of the Settlement   282
   1. Record of Parties Present   283
   2. Execution and Exchange of Documents   283
   3. Conforming Copies of the Documents   283
   4. Computation of the Amount to be Paid by Purchaser   283
      (a) Purchase Price   283
      (b) Apportionments   284
      (c) Expenses of Settlement   285
   5. Payments by the Seller   288
   6. Settlement Sheet   288
   7. Escrow Accounts   288
   8. Marked-Up Title Report   288

IV. **POST CLOSING—PURCHASE—SALE OF PROPERTY**   288
A. Recording   288
B. Title Policy   289
C. Escrow   289
D. Tenant Letter   289
E. Binder   289

V. **CONSTRUCTION LOAN CLOSING**   289
A. Preparation for Closing   289
   1. Note and Mortgage   290
   2. Plans and Specifications   290
   3. General Construction Contract   290
   4. Corporate Resolutions   290
   5. Survey   290
   6. Insurance   290
   7. Completion or Performance Bond   290
   8. Construction Loan Agreement   291
   9. Building Permit   291
   10. Security Agreement and Financing Statements   291

11. Declaration of Cross Easements or Declaration of Reciprocal Easements 291
12. Buy-Sell Agreement 291
13. Leases 291
14. Assignment of Lease 291
15. Subordination Agreement 292
16. Attornment/Nondisturbance Agreement 292
17. Waiver of Mechanics' Lien 292
18. Letter of Permanent Lender Approving Documents 292
19. Title Report 292
20. Letter Confirming Date of Closing 292
21. Rehearsal for Closing 292
B. Closing 293
1. Place of Closing 293
2. Closing Report 293
3. Mechanics of Closing 293
(a) *Expenses of the Borrower* 293
(b) *Settlement Sheet* 294
(c) *Marked-Up Title Report* 294
C. Post Closing 294
1. Recordation of the Mortgage and Other Documents 294
2. Issuance of Title Policy 294
3. Binder 294
VI. PERMANENT LOAN CLOSING 295
A. Preparation for Closing 295
1. Assignment of Mortgage 295
2. Certificate of Occupancy 295
3. As-Built Survey 295
4. Rent Roll 295
5. Estoppel Certificates 295
6. Declaration of No Set-Off 295
7. Security Agreements and Financing Statements 295
8. Corporate Resolutions 296
9. Advance Arrangements for Pay-Off of Construction Lender 296
10. Title Bring Down 296
11. Notice to Parties 296
B. Closing 297
1. Place of Closing 297
2. Parties Present 297
3. Mechanics of Closing 297
(a) *Exchange of Money* 297
(b) *Settlement Sheet* 298
(c) *Marked-Up Title Report* 298
C. Post Closing 298

VII. DISCLOSURE AND THE REAL ESTATE SETTLEMENT PROCEDURES ACT OF 1974 298

A. Introduction 298

B. Scope of RESPA 300
1. Transactions Covered 300
2. Prohibition Against Kickbacks and Unearned Fees 300
3. Limitations on Escrows 300
4. Uniform Settlement Sheet 300

C. Disclosures 301
1. Booklet 301
2. Finance Charges and Annual Percentage Rate 301
3. RESPA Disclosures 302

D. Settlement Sheet 302
1. Block J. Summary of Borrower's Transaction 305
   (a) Section 100 305
   (b) Section 200 306
   (c) Section 300 306
2. Block K. Summary of Seller's Transaction 306
   (a) Section 400 306
   (b) Section 500 307
   (c) Section 600 307
3. Block L. Settlement Charges 307
   (a) Section 700 307
   (b) Section 800 307
   (c) Section 900 308
   (d) Section 1000 308
   (e) Section 1100 308
   (f) Section 1200 308
   (g) Section 1300 309
   (h) Section 1400 309

VIII. SUMMARY 310
A. Closing Agenda 310
1. Personae 310
2. Documents 310
3. Status and Responsibility 310
4. Disposition 310
B. Closing Report and Binder 311

Chapter 9 **Recording Statutes**   **328**

I. INTRODUCTION 328
II. RECORDING STATUTES 329
A. Types of Statutes 329
1. "Race" Statutes 329
2. "Notice" Statutes 330
3. "Race-Notice" Statutes 331

B. Other Time Limits Under Recording Statutes   332

C. What Classes of Persons Are Protected by Recording Statutes   333

D. What Instruments May be Recorded   333
   1. Judgments and Judgment Notes   334
   2. Lis Pendens   335
   3. Agreements of Sale   335
   4. Leases and Memoranda of Leases   336
   5. Assignments of Mortgages   337
   6. Satisfaction of Mortgages   337

E. How to Record Documents   338
   1. The Index   338
      (a) Tract Indices   338
      (b) Name Indices   338
   2. Acknowledgments   339
   3. Recording Costs   340
      (a) Filing Fees   340
      (b) Transfer, Recording, and Intangible Taxes   340

III. **THE TORRENS SYSTEM**   341

IV. **SUMMARY**   342

Chapter 10 **Leasing**   **343**

Part One   BASIC ELEMENTS OF A LEASE   343

  I. **INTRODUCTION**   343

 II. **ESSENTIAL ELEMENTS OF A LEASE**   344

A. Date   344

B. Parties   344
   1. Landlord   344
      (a) Individual as Landlord   344
      (b) Partnership as Landlord   344
      (c) Corporation as Landlord   345
      (d) Fiduciaries   345
      (e) Agents   345
   2. Tenant   345

C. Statement of Demise   345

D. Description of Premises   346

E. Term of Lease   346

F. Rental   347

G. Execution   348

III. **THE NEED FOR A WRITTEN LEASE**   348

IV. **ADDITIONAL PROVISIONS COMMON TO ALL TYPES OF LEASES**   348

A. Use Clause   349

B. Repairs 350
    1. Generally 350
    2. Areas Outside Building 351
    3. Compliance with Requirements of Public Authorities 351
C. Alterations and Improvements 351
D. Fire 353
    1. Obligation to Pay Rent and Make Repairs 353
    2. Liability for Damage Caused by Fire 354
E. Other Casualty 355
F. Condemnation 355
G. Assignment and Subletting 356
H. Entry and Inspection 357
I. Default Provisions 358
    1. Default of Tenant 358
        (a) Landlord's Remedies 358
        (b) Landlord's Enforcement of Remedies 358
        (c) Tenant's Right to Cure Default 361
    2. Default by Landlord 362
J. Renewals 362
K. Notices 363
L. Recording of Leases; Acknowledgments 363
M. Inability to Give Possession 364
N. Additional Rent 364
O. Services and Utilities 365
P. Liability and Indemnification Provisions 366
    1. Injury to Tenant or Damage to Tenant's Property 366
    2. Injury to Third Persons or Damage to their Property 366
Q. Subordination 367
R. Security Deposits 368
S. Option to Purchase 369
    1. Purchase Price 369
    2. Manner of Exercising Option and Time of Exercise 369
    3. Time of Settlement 370
    4. Condition of Title 370
    5. Other Provisions 370
T. Rights of First Refusal 370
U. Rules and Regulations 371
V. Affirmative Covenants 372
W. Negative Covenants 372
X. Miscellaneous Provisions 372
    1. Waiver of Custom 372
    2. Integration Clause 373
    3. Heirs and Assigns 373
    4. Captions 373

Part Two *SPECIAL TYPES OF LEASES* 374
I. COMMERCIAL AND SHOPPING CENTER LEASES 374
  A. Trade Fixtures 374
  B. Percentage Rent 375
    1. Straight Percentage Rent 376
    2. Minimum or Basic Rent Plus a Percentage 376
    3. Definition of "Sales" 377
    4. Record of Gross Sales 377
    5. Time for Payment of Percentage Rent 377
    6. No Partnership 378
    7. Other Considerations Applicable to Percentage Rent 379
      (a) Active Operation 379
      (b) Diversion of Sales 380
  C. Common Areas 380
    1. Use, Location, and Control 380
    2. Common Area Maintenance Expenses 380
    3. Heating, Ventilation, and Air Conditioning 381
    4. Merchants' Association 381
  D. Commencement of the Term and Rent 382
    1. If the Shopping Center is in Existence 382
    2. If the Shopping Center is Not Completed 382
      (a) Payment of Rent 382
      (b) Fixturing Period 382
      (c) Indemnification 382
      (d) Store Openings 382
  E. Insurance 383
    1. Fire and Extended Coverage Insurance 383
    2. Liability Insurance 384
  F. Work to be Done by Landlord 384
  G. Exclusives 385
  H. Tax Escalation 385
    1. Tenant's Share of Escalation 386
    2. Base Year 386
    3. Deduction of Tax Escalation from Percentage Rental 387
    4. Tenant's Right to Contest Increased Taxes 387
    5. Tax Escalation Due to Additional Construction 388
    6. Caps 388
    7. Tenants Pay All Taxes and Operating Costs 388
  I. Parking 389
  J. Estoppel Certificates 389
  K. Clauses of Concern to Mortgagee 390

Part Three *OFFICE BUILDING LEASES* 391
I. IN GENERAL 391
  A. Services 391
  B. Consumer Price Index Escalation 392

C. Actual Cost Escalation   393
D. Landlord's Work   393
II. **NET AND GROUND LEASES**   394
A. Intent Clause   394
B. Impositions   395
C. Insurance   395
D. Repairs   396
E. Ground Leases and Leasehold Mortgages   396
   1. Defaults Which May Be Cured by Payment of Money   397
   2. Defaults Consisting of a Failure to Repair   398
F. Alterations   398
G. Casualty   398
H. Condemnation   399
I.   Sale and Leaseback Transactions   399
J. Close Corporation—Partnership Net Lease   399
III. **SURETY OR GUARANTY AGREEMENT**   400
IV. **ASSIGNMENT OR SUBLETTING**   401

Chapter 11 **Condominiums, Planned-Unit Developments,
and Cooperatives**   **408**

I. **INTRODUCTION**   408
II.**CONDOMINIUMS**   408
A. The Legal Basis of Condominium Ownership   409
   1. Declaration   410
      (a) General Information   410
      (b) Description of Units   410
      (c) Common Expenses and Limited Common Expenses   411
      (d) Managing Body   411
      (e) Plans   412
   2. Articles of Incorporation   412
   3. Bylaws or Code of Regulations   412
   4. Rules and Regulations   412
   5. Public Offering Statement   413
   6. Management Contract   414
B. Fire Insurance   414
C. Assisting a Condominium Purchaser   415
   1. The Condominium Documents   415
   2. Common Expenses and Percentage Interests   416
   3. Reserved Rights of the Declarant   417

III. **PLANNED-UNIT DEVELOPMENTS** 418
   A. The Legal Basis of PUD Ownership 419
      1. Declaration of Covenants, Restrictions, and Easements 419
      2. Articles of Incorporation 420
      3. Bylaws 420
      4. Book of Resolutions 420
   B. Assisting a PUD Purchaser 420
IV. **COOPERATIVE APARTMENTS** 420
   A. The Legal Basis of Cooperative Ownership 421
   B. Assisting a Prospective Co-op Member 422

Glossary 425
Index 434

Introduction

This text is especially designed to reach the broad spectrum of real estate professionals. Paralegals will use this text as a basis for acquiring the essential substantive and practical skills necessary to participate effectively in real estate transactions. General practitioners and real estate specialists will find that the text serves as a handbook which deals with the pragmatics, rather than the esoterics, of real estate practice. Other professionals, such as lending officers, real estate agents, mortgage brokers, property managers, developers, and real estate investment advisors will discover that the text focuses on a variety of matters relevant to their respective areas of expertise.

While each chapter is a fairly self-contained treatment of its subject matter, the book reinforces throughout the concept that knowledge of the entire transaction, as well as each of its component parts, is essential to a legal assistant's effective participation in a particular real estate transaction. The first two chapters introduce the reader to basic real property concepts. Chapters Three through Nine follow a typical real estate transaction, which involves entering into an agreement of sale for a particular piece of property, identifying the property in a legally sufficient manner, preparing the deed by which the property will be conveyed, addressing the property's state of title, dealing with the financing of the property's acquisition, conducting the settlement or closing, and making the transaction part of the public record. Chapter Ten deals with leasing and Chapter Eleven discusses some of the more typical development alternatives utilized in current land planning.

In using this book as a text for scholastic instruction in real estate law, I urge that lecturers apply an informal Socratic method in the classroom. For students, this method requires preparation sufficient to produce a level of understanding which permits a flow of creative thought. For lecturers, it entails eliciting these thoughts, encouraging their interaction and directing their course. I have found that this method can be as edifying for the lecturer as it is for the student.

As the paralegal profession continues to gain, and merit, greater credibility within the real estate community, the depth and breadth of legal matters in which paralegals become involved continues to expand. It is important for paralegals as well as other real estate professionals to be sensitive to the corresponding ethical considerations which accompany the expanding scope of paralegal practice. Each paralegal, together with the attorney with whom he or she is working, should continually monitor the appropriateness of his or her role in a given transaction in light of the Code of Professional Responsibility governing the legal profession.

The contributions, criticisms, and support of many colleagues are reflected throughout this edition. These colleagues include Peter Schwartz, Marty Macartney, Terry Allgier Garfinkel, Tom Flynn, Frank Ferro, Nina Segre, Jim Koller, Tom Thompson, Chuck Johnson, and Lyn Coyne, most of whom are my colleagues at Dechert Price & Rhoads. A great deal of credit belongs to my legal assistants, Lori Campbell and Chris Arfaa, who dedicated endless hours of detailed review and pragmatic feedback to this text. Many thanks also to my close friend and colleague, Patti Alleva, whose eloquence and intellectual creativity are an infinite source of inspiration, and to my family, whose love is a perpetual source of support.

Philadelphia, PA   **Deborah Flynn**
December, 1985

Introduction to
Real Estate Law

Second Edition

Chapter 1

Introduction to Real Property

This book has two major purposes. The first is to develop in the prospective legal assistant an understanding of the basic information, concepts, and language necessary to perform in any phase of a real estate transaction in the United States. The second is to develop certain skills and techniques, some of which, such as drafting skills, are of general application to a legal assistant's career and others of which, such as preparing a deed, are of particular application for a real estate paralegal.

The scope of this book is limited to basic real estate transactions for which a legal assistant may expect to be given some measure of responsibility. Such basic transactions include the purchase and sale of real estate, mortgage loans, and leasing. Component transactions are composed of two or more basic transactions, such as the sale of property financed by a mortgage loan. A legal assistant must be familiar with the individual basic transactions, the integration of the component transactions, and the language used by lawyers and clients in the real estate field.

This text treats the major component transactions of a comprehensive real estate development in logical sequence. In actual practice, not all real estate transactions will involve every aspect of the materials provided in this book. However, an understanding of at least the basics of real estate is necessary to comprehend the forces that shape even the most elemental of transactions, such as the purchase of a house for cash.

The first important concept that must be understood fully by a legal assistant is the definition of the term "real estate."

1

I. INTRODUCTION

"Real estate" or, as it is referred to in technical terms, "real property," is defined as land and all structures permanently affixed to land. All other property, such as automobiles, jewelry, stocks, and cash, is called "personal property" or "personalty." From a legal standpoint, therefore, all property is classified as either real property or personal property. The distinction is important because in many situations the law governing or affecting real property is different from the law governing personal property, and a different result will be obtained depending on whether the property in question is real property or personal property.

In some instances, it is difficult to determine whether a given item of property is real or personal. For example, a window air conditioner that has been built into the window frame could be viewed as being either permanently affixed to a building, and therefore considered real property, or not permanently affixed, and therefore considered personal property.

Historians and sociologists may debate the reasons, but no one will deny that the desire of human beings to possess and control land has been a dominant force in the development of civilization. Among various cultures, the need to use land for survival has resulted in strikingly different social and legal patterns. Our own concepts of ownership and property rights are by no means the necessary or logical result of such desire and need. Many societies, including many American Indian tribes, have had no concept of "ownership" of land, but only of rights of use, often common to an entire tribe. Other societies have stressed the stewardship concept, which assumes that the present user of the land has an obligation to society and to future users to maintain the property and not permit it to go to waste.

Our system of property law, as well as most of our other laws, is derived most directly from the English principles of law that existed during the colonial period. The derivation is not pure, and in various parts of our country, Spanish and French laws have had considerable influence. More remotely, many of our legal principles go back to Roman civil law, and some concepts extend even further back.

Most of the English law that existed during the colonial period was decreed by judges and was not legislatively enacted. There were few statutes, and those that existed were subject to significant judicial interpretation. Courts and judges make laws by deciding actual cases and by announcing in an opinion the legal principles on which they have based their decision. In order that the law be consistent, prior decisions and principles are generally followed by later judges, such prior cases being called "precedents." The resultant body of law, consisting of precedents and stated principles, is called the common law. Although English common law continues to be a source of precedents for American judges, each American state also has developed its own state common law. Since the Industrial Revolution, however, the common law in America has been increasingly supplemented, and sometimes supplanted, by statutory law.

II. BASIC CONCEPTS OF REAL PROPERTY RIGHTS

We generally think of land and real estate only in the physical sense. Certainly land does have measurable physical characteristics, and these must be ascertained with considerable precision in order to avoid disputes. However, lawyers also think of real estate as consisting of a bundle of rights, both actual and potential. Broadly, four aspects of real property are included in the bundle of rights, elements of which might be separated from the bundle and granted to different persons. The four elements are (1) ownership, which is the core element of the bundle; (2) possession, which may be granted to another (usually by a lease) and which involves the *general* right to use the property during the period of possession; (3) use, which may be separate from possession in the case of an easement or other *limited* right of use; and (4) control, which may be granted to another by means of private agreement or to society by law. We shall briefly review some of these elements, all of which are discussed in greater detail in the various chapters.

A. PHYSICAL CHARACTERISTICS

The first object of real estate law is to define a parcel of land so that it can be precisely identified and distinguished from other parcels of land. In order to distinguish various parcels of land, each is said to have certain boundaries that define where one parcel ends and another begins. Boundaries are generally defined in relation to some established landmark. The landmark in an urban area may be a street. In the country, it may be a stone fence, an unusual tree, or a boulder. Using surveyor's instruments and starting at a particular landmark as a point of reference, a parcel of land can then be defined.

B. A BUNDLE OF RIGHTS

There are various interests that one may own in a piece of land.[1] The rights in and to real estate that a person owns are sometimes referred to as that person's "interest in the real estate." Some examples of these interests are listed below:

1. Fee

The ultimate core of ownership is called the "fee." If one person has the entire ownership interest, and if such interest cannot be taken from that person or his or her heirs and assigns without consent (subject to the

---

1. A further semantic confusion is that one who possesses an interest in real estate is sometimes said "to own that interest," even though the interest itself is not an ownership interest in the land. Thus, one who holds a possessory interest in land, such as a tenant under a lease, may be said to "own that possessory interest."

right of the state of eminent domain), then that person is said to have title in "fee simple absolute" or in "fee."

More than one person may own a share of a fee interest in land. Persons having an undivided[2] fee interest are said to be co-owners and to own the property as tenants-in-common.

2. Lease

A person[3] may not own the fee, but still have the right to use the land, a portion of the land, or a portion of a building located on the land for a specific period. Such a person may be called a tenant or lessee. A tenant's right to possession may be derived from the fee owner or from an existing tenant. A person giving such rights is referred to as the landlord or lessor.

3. Mineral Interest or Air Rights

A person may have merely the right to mine or drill for and remove minerals from a parcel of land. Such right is usually derived from the fee owner, who, according to legal principles, owns the subsurface of his or her land to the center of the earth and the airspace above his or her land (subject to the public's right to use the airways for transportation). When the owner of the entire fee grants a right to remove minerals or timber from real property, such a right is called a profit, from the Norman term *profit à prendre*. This should be distinguished from the practice common to many mining areas in the United States of horizontal division of a property into different strata, with different persons having fee ownership of different strata. In some coal mining regions, for example, a town may be built on surface ownership of the ground, with one or more coal companies holding fee title to the ground beneath the surface. The coal companies may mine the subsurface property that they own with no restrictions except an obligation to the owner of the surface rights to provide physical support to the surface of the ground, and sometimes they do not even have any obligation to provide physical support.

A landowner can also grant air rights from any level above the surface of the ground. One purpose of acquiring air rights is to prevent the blockage of light and air to an individual's property. For example, a person owning land may want to acquire air rights above a level of 50 feet on adjoining property to preclude the construction of high buildings on the adjoining property. A second purpose is to obtain the right to build. For

2. Undivided means that each person has an interest in the whole property, and not merely an interest in a portion of the property.

3. The word "person" can refer to individuals, whether male or female, or to people in a nonindividual capacity, such as trustees or executors, or to entities, such as corporations, associations, or partnerships. The term "individual" refers only to people acting in their own capacity.

example, in New York City, the Pan Am Building is built in the air over Grand Central Station. In such an instance, the person acquiring the air rights would also need an easement of support.

4. Easements, Rights of Way

One may merely own the right to travel over a piece of property, or to string and maintain a wire over the property, or to use a portion of the land in some other limited way. Such a right may be referred to as an easement or right of way.

At common law, only seven kinds of easements could be created, and there were special conditions to their creation. With the development of modern recording statutes, many other kinds of easements have been developed. For example, the owner of a large residential tract may develop it in separate stages of midrise apartments, each of which may ultimately be owned by a separate entity. There may be common security systems, woods, and recreational facilities throughout the residential tract. In order to tie the development into a single project for purposes of using the roads, sidewalks, parking, and other facilities and in order to allocate the costs of maintaining these facilities, the developer may record a declaration of easements covering the entire project and granting cross-easements throughout.

The holder of an easement and the owner of the land subject to the easement have certain mutual obligations with respect to the use and maintenance of the property and the easement area. Unlike a lease situation, the grantor of an easement does not usually grant possession or exclusive use, but merely a right of use.

5. Life Estate

A life estate in realty is the right of a person (called the "life tenant") to use real property until death. This right cannot be passed on to an heir, but terminates at the death of the user. A variation of a life estate is a life estate *par autre vie,* which means that the life by which the term of the estate is measured is the life of someone other than the user. There is a substantial amount of common law dealing with the specific rights that pertain to a life estate, such as whether the holder of the life estate can cut and remove timber, and with the rights and duties of the person to whom the property will come on the expiration of the life estate (called a "remainderman"). There is also considerable law dealing with the valuation of the respective interests of a life tenant and a remainderman in the event of a forced sale, such as a condemnation.

6. Future Interests

Future interests are present rights in real property that give the right to future possession or use. There are many kinds of future interests. For example, the remainderman who has a right to use or possession of real property on the expiration of a life estate possesses a future interest. Remaindermen have certain present rights in the property, such as the right to certain protections against the commission of waste by the life tenant.

C. METHODS OF ACQUIRING TITLE TO REAL ESTATE

1. Purchase

Our system of law permits and protects the right to transfer interests in real estate, including the right to sell such interests. There are relatively few restrictions on these rights. One restriction requires the owner of a parcel of land to obtain approval of the local government prior to such owner's sale of a portion of that parcel. The approval required is called "subdivision approval," because the owner is proposing to divide his or her land. The type of subdivision that requires approval and the body whose approval must be obtained are matters of state law. Generally, such powers of approval are constitutionally limited to a determination that the subdivision will not violate local requirements with regard to parking, lot size, setback restrictions, and the like. The local authority would not have the power to disapprove arbitrarily or for a prohibited reason, such as dislike of the proposed grantee.

2. Inheritance and Gift

Interests in real estate may be transferred from one person to another as a gift. In addition, a person may transfer interests in real property at death by a will. If no will exists, the interests will be transferred to certain heirs of the deceased owner as directed by state intestacy[4] law. Again, free rights of transfer by gift or by will are protected rights, subject, of course, to tax laws such as federal gift taxes and federal and state estate and inheritance taxes.

3. Adverse Possession

The doctrine of adverse possession was derived from the English common law, although many states have enacted statutes governing the subject. The doctrine provides that one may obtain ownership of real estate interests by taking possession for a certain period of time and holding it in a manner adverse to the legal owner. The term "adverse" includes a requirement that the party claiming title by adverse possession shall not have been in possession by permission of the legal owner.

---

4. The term "intestacy" relates to the local law governing distribution of the property of a person who dies "intestate," that is, without having left a valid will.

D. LEGAL INTERESTS OF A SPOUSE

1. Dower

At common law, on the death of her husband, a widow was entitled to receive a one-third interest in all real property owned by her husband in fee at the time of and after their marriage, whether or not the property was owned by her husband at the time of his death. In most states this right, known as the "right of dower," has either been abolished or changed by statute. In jurisdictions in which the right of dower or a statutory substitute exists, conveyances of real property by a husband, even though held in his name alone, would be made subject to his wife's dower or similar statutory rights. Therefore, a person who purchases the husband's property would not own the entire "bundle of rights" with respect to it, and the wife, on her husband's death, could claim her dower or similar statutory rights in the property. The wife's joinder in the deed, however, would permit her husband to transfer the property free and clear of her dower or similar statutory rights.

2. Curtesy

The common law also provided that a widower receive, on the death of his wife, a life estate in all real property owned by his wife in fee at any time during their marriage. This right was called the right of curtesy. The general principles governing dower applied also to curtesy. Most states have also abolished or revised the common law right of curtesy. As in the case of dower rights, the joinder of the husband in the deed would release his curtesy or similar statutory rights in the property being transferred.

The rights of dower and curtesy, and their statutory equivalents, apply to property owned by a spouse in his or her own name and to which the other spouse has no present rights of use. In states in which dower and curtesy or similar statutory rights still exist, a person taking an interest in real estate from a married person without the joinder of the other spouse in the document transferring the interest is gambling that the spouse transferring the interest will be the survivor of the two.

III. PUBLIC CONTROL OVER LAND USE

The right of an owner of real estate to use the land is not absolute. Society, acting through various government agencies, often has a voice in the way the land may be used. The use that an owner makes of his or her land can have a definite affect on neighbors, sometimes to their serious detriment. In order to control such situations, the common law of nuisance, and its statutory counterpart, zoning, has been developed.

A. NUISANCE

In general terms, the law of nuisance regulates the use of land so as to prevent uses that unduly interfere with a neighbor's use and enjoyment of the neighbor's own land. For example, a storage facility might not be permitted to store explosive or otherwise hazardous materials that could harm residents of adjoining properties. Usually common law nuisance cases involve a balancing process by the courts, which try to balance the harm caused against the economic benefit and property rights of the alleged offender.

B. ZONING

Many communities have enacted zoning laws that dictate the manner in which land within the community can be used and developed. As a general proposition, such laws, although clearly infringing on rights of private ownership, have been held to be constitutional. However, many specific zoning laws, patterns, practices, and even motivations have been declared constitutionally invalid. Exclusionary zoning, which is designed to exclude particular economic or social groups, is not legally permissible. The permissible rationale underlying zoning is that certain uses of land are not compatible with other uses.

C. PRIVATE RESTRICTIONS

In addition to zoning laws and the common law of nuisance, it is possible to restrict the use of land by agreement among the individual owners. An owner or group of owners of land may voluntarily agree in writing to restrict the use of their land. Such restrictions may affect and bind future owners.[5] Examples of private restrictions would be those that prohibit building within a certain distance from roads, prohibit nonresidential use, or prohibit certain uses, such as raising livestock. Some of these private restrictions will be enforced by courts of law. For example, restrictions on sale to, or ownership by, persons of a particular religion or race are unenforceable.

D. LIENS

Under certain circumstances, one who is owed money can protect his or her position as a creditor by acquiring an interest in the real estate or personal property of his or her debtor. Such an interest is called a lien. An example of a type of lien is a "mortgage lien," which is a lien voluntarily given on an interest in real estate to secure performance of an obligation,

---

5. When a promise to do something (a "covenant") or to refrain from doing something (a "restriction") is imposed on the ownership of land and binds future owners, then the covenant or restriction is said to "run with the land."

usually the payment of money. Sometimes a creditor can unilaterally obtain a lien on the debtor's property in order to secure repayment, or a lien may be created by statute. For example, a contractor who performs services or supplies materials for construction or repair of a building may be entitled by statute to a lien as security for payments for such services or materials. Having a lien usually gives the holder the right, after following certain procedures, to force a sale of the property subject to the lien to obtain proceeds to pay ("satisfy") the debt.

IV. DETERMINATION OF OWNERSHIP

A. TITLE SEARCHING

The various interests that people hold in a particular parcel of land can be determined by examining public records kept for such purpose. All states have systems for recording interests in land. By reviewing ("searching") such records, it is possible to go back hundreds of years and trace the various interests in a piece of land. In some states, interests in land can be traced back to the time of its colonization. By searching title, a prospective purchaser can determine whether an interest in a parcel of real estate to be acquired is subject to the rights of others. For example, Greene might offer to sell White a parcel of real estate on which Greene lives. A search of the real estate records might reveal the the land is really owned by Rodman, who has merely rented it to Greene. Thus, the search of the records has revealed to White that Greene cannot transfer fee title to the land.

B. DOCUMENTS

Transfers of interests in real estate are normally evidenced by means of formal written documents. The format of such documents is often highly stylized because of their historical origins and the formalities imposed by statutes governing public recording. In some jurisdictions, however, statutes have been enacted requiring that certain documents be drafted in "plain language." As shall be seen, the usual document for a transfer of a fee interest in real property is a deed.

V. SUMMARY

The concepts introduced in this first chapter are the building blocks necessary to function in the real estate field. Out of context, these concepts may seem difficult to understand, easy to forget, and even unimportant. Subsequent chapters provide that context by discussing various kinds of real estate transactions. As you study these chapters, you may find it helpful to reread this chapter.

Chapter 2

Titleholders

Part One
INTRODUCTION TO TITLEHOLDERS

I. INTRODUCTION

Every time real property is to be conveyed from one person or entity to another, a decision must be made by the new owner as to the nature of the entity that will hold the title. Title might be held by one or two individuals; by a group of individuals, as individuals or as a partnership; or by a corporation. The choice is usually determined on the basis of the following considerations: (a) the purpose for which the property will be used; (b) the liabilities incurred on acquisition by the new ownership entity; (c) the ease of transferring or selling the property; (d) possible costs of acquisition and of transfer or sale of the property; (e) the imposition of tax on income derived from the property; and (f) inheritance and estate tax implications. The purpose of this chapter is to explore the different legal forms in which title may be held and the considerations involved in choosing a particular form.

II. TITLE IN THE NAME OF AN INDIVIDUAL

Taking title in the name of one individual does not generally raise any problems or require extensive documentation. The individual titleholder is entitled to all of the rents and profits and need have no agreement with anyone else with respect to the use and operation of the real estate, unless, of course, the individual leases it or grants rights to use it to others. The individual titleholder will be personally liable for claims

10

arising out of ownership and operation of the real estate. The individual owner is taxed on the income from the property and may deduct from his or her income tax any loss generated by the property. In the event the individual wishes to convey the title, no one's consent or joinder is needed unless the individual is married, in which case the joinder of the spouse must be obtained.[1]

III. TITLE IN JOINT NAMES

Property may be held in the names of several individuals or entities. In practice, the choice of an appropriate form of joint ownership is sometimes difficult and usually requires careful analysis. The principal forms of joint ownership are tenancy in common, joint tenancy, and tenancy by the entirety.

A. TENANTS IN COMMON

A tenancy in common exists when two or more persons each owns an undivided interest in the entire property. This means that although there is more than one owner of the property, the interests are not physically distinct, but are fractional interests in the whole. Tenants in common are often referred to as "co-tenants" or "co-owners."

Under the law of most states, a tenancy in common exists when two or more persons own an interest in property and the deed or other document conveying the ownership interest to them does not clearly indicate the form of ownership. For example, if the property were owned by "James Large and Martin Jones" without any additional words indicating the type of interest owned by the parties, they would be deemed to be tenants in common in most states. In most jurisdictions, tenants in common are presumed to own equal undivided interests in the property (except that spouses, if so named, are often treated as one co-owner) unless the deed(s) establishing their interests provide otherwise. If co-tenants are to have disproportionate interests, this should be specified in the granting clause of the deed, as shown in Chapter Five.

Tenants in common should establish among themselves, by written agreement if possible, the precise nature of their relationship with each other. The agreement should set forth the relative rights and obligations of the co-owners with respect to rents, profits, losses, and liabilities arising from the ownership and operation of the real property as well as the rights of the co-owners with respect to management, control, and use of the real property. A tenant in common may convey, mortgage, or devise his or her undivided interest without the consent of the other co-owners, unless, of course, the co-owners have agreed to the contrary. A co-owner's interest passes to his or her heirs, or personal representatives if the co-

1. See Chapter One, subsection II, D, for a discussion of rights of dower and curtesy.

owner dies intestate; it does not pass to the surviving co-tenants. Unless otherwise agreed, a tenant in common who takes possession of the entire property to the exclusion of the other co-tenants must pay those co-tenants their proportionate shares of the rents and profits. A tenant in common must obtain the joinder of his or her spouse, if any, in order to make a transfer or conveyance that is free and clear of dower or curtesy interests (or other statutory rights in lieu of dower or curtesy). All of the co-tenants (or an agent authorized by all of them) must sign leases as joint lessors, if the proposed tenant is to have the exclusive right to possession of the real estate.

B. JOINT TENANTS

A joint tenancy is similar to a tenancy in common in that two or more owners possess an undivided interest in the property. The primary distinction between a tenancy in common and a joint tenancy is that a joint tenancy involves a right of survivorship. This means that if one of the joint tenants dies, the ownership of the entire property automatically passes to the surviving joint tenant or tenants without the necessity of any payment by the surviving joint tenant. Because of this survivorship feature, a joint tenancy will not be presumed. The joint tenancy must be specifically spelled out in the deed or other instrument conveying the property. Accordingly, the deed for a property that was owned jointly by two or more persons would indicate that the property had been conveyed to "James Large and Martin Jones as joint tenants with right of survivorship and not as tenants in common." At English common law, and still in many jurisdictions, a joint tenancy with right of survivorship can be created only if all of the grantees have received their interest in the property at the same time, by the same document, from the same grantor, and in equal shares.[2] As with tenants in common, in most jurisdictions it is presumed that joint tenants have equal rights among themselves, regardless of the amount each actually contributed to the acquisition of the real estate.

Because of the fellow joint tenant's right of survivorship, a joint tenant cannot dispose of his or her interest by will. However, during lifetime, a joint tenant may break the "jointure" and convey the interest to a third party or mortgage or assign the interest. Even without consent, the joint tenant's interest may be sold pursuant to a judgment obtained by creditors, which will also serve to break the jointure. In any of the preceding

2. Suppose Fred Stolz, widower, owned real property in his own name and decided to create a joint tenancy with his daughter Frieda, who is unmarried. At English common law he could not do so by conveying a one-half interest to her, because the tenancy created would not meet the identity of interest test, in that they did not receive their interests at the same time and from the same grantor. Consider the use of an intermediate third party grantee who would act as a common grantor, thus establishing the necessary identity of interest.

cases, the jointure is broken between the new owner and the remaining joint tenant. The new owner becomes a tenant in common with the other former joint tenant or tenants. Thus, if Appley, Bendix, and Cutter all hold as joint tenants, and Appley sells her interest to Davenport, then Bendix and Cutter are still joint tenants between themselves with respect to their interest, although they are tenants in common with respect to Davenport.

Joint tenants are often given special treatment under transfer, estate, and inheritance tax laws because of the right of survivorship. The establishment of a joint tenancy does not of itself create a new entity, and thus does not have any affect respecting income tax or personal liability for debts that arise in connection with the property.

C. TENANTS BY THE ENTIRETY

With one significant difference, a tenancy by the entirety is a joint tenancy in which the owners of the property are husband and wife. In many jurisdictions, the conveyance of real property to a husband and wife automatically creates in them a tenancy by the entirety, rather than a joint tenancy or tenancy in common. This is because, at common law, husband and wife were considered to be one legal entity, even though that entity consisted of two natural persons. The law treated them as though they could not acquire individual, undivided interests but only a single interest in the entire estate. Accordingly, they could not be deemed tenants in common or joint tenants.

The fundamental difference between tenants by the entirety and joint tenants is that neither tenant by the entirety owns an undivided share. The notable feature of a joint tenancy is the ease with which the jointure may be broken, either voluntarily by one joint tenant, even without the consent of the other, or involuntarily by the actions of a creditor of one of the joint tenants. A tenancy by the entirety may not be broken by either spouse without the consent of the other. In most of the jurisdictions that recognize the entirety estate, a creditor of only one spouse may not execute on the property, because in legal theory the debtor spouse has no individual interest in the property, present or future. Rather, the property is owned by the legal entity of husband and wife. Similarly, neither spouse alone may transfer or mortgage any interest in the property because neither has any legal interest to convey or mortgage. If two individuals hold property as joint tenants, and on marriage wish to hold the property as tenants by the entirety, a new deed creating the desired tenancy must be executed and recorded. Divorce, on the other hand, has the legal effect of converting the status of tenants by the entirety to tenants in common.

Another difference is that tenants by the entirety do not have to account to each other for rents from the real property. It is presumed that such rents will be used for the benefit of both.

As in the case of joint tenancy, at the death of one of the tenants by the entirety, the surviving tenant becomes the sole owner of the entire estate.

There are two principal benefits gained by holding property as tenants by the entirety. Creditors of one spouse cannot claim such property while both spouses are alive unless the consent of the other spouse has been obtained. Additionally, in many states, state inheritance taxes are not imposed on such property when a spouse dies if he or she is the first to die. Property held by the entirety, however, may be subject to the federal estate tax on the estate of the first spouse to die, and income tax and personal liability are imposed as in the case of other property interests owned by individuals. In practice, tenancies by the entirety are not often created, except with respect to family residences. Other forms of joint ownership involving husbands and wives are usually more useful and convenient when commercial property is involved.

D. COMMERCIAL PRACTICES REGARDING TITLE IN JOINT NAMES

For various reasons, it is relatively uncommon for a group of individuals to take title to commercial real estate in joint names as tenants in common, joint tenants, or tenants by the entirety. Joint tenancies are rare in a commercial setting, both because the jointure is so easy to break that it is ineffective and because the joint tenancy, if not broken, may deprive the deceased joint tenant's estate of a valuable asset and grant to the surviving joint tenant a windfall.

The only fairly common situation in which tenancy in common is used is for a joint venture, which will be discussed in greater detail later. One should understand that joint venturers will not rely on the common law regarding tenants in common to govern their relationship. The common law principles regarding tenancy in common arose in the context of English agricultural life, and those principles would be insufficient, and often incorrect, if applied as the sole guiding force in the typical commercial joint venture situation. Thus, in practice, tenants in common will enter into an extensive co-owners' agreement or joint venture agreement. The result is that a joint venture is more like a partnership in terms of the economic relationships among the parties, and therefore will be discussed together with partnerships later.

PROBLEM

Rita and Jimmy are engaged and plan to be married next June. They have executed an Agreement of Sale on their dream house that calls for settlement next April. How should Rita and Jimmy take title to the property? In your jurisdiction, will Rita and Jimmy need to take any steps to convert their title to a tenancy by the entirety after they are married?

IV. PARTNERSHIPS AND JOINT VENTURES

The most common choice to be made by a group of individuals about to acquire real property for business purposes is whether to form a corporation, a partnership, or a joint venture to take title.[3] The following discussion is intended only to familiarize the student with the general characteristics of partnerships and joint ventures, and to discuss the relative advantages of each form.

A. GENERAL PARTNERSHIPS

1. Nature of a Partner's Interest

An interest in a partnership is personal property. It is the partnership entity that holds title to the real property, not the individual partners. The partners have no separate interest in the real property itself. Real estate acquired with partnership funds is deemed to be partnership property, unless a contrary intent is specified.

Because an interest in a partnership is personal property, the spouse of a partner has no dower right or other interest in partnership property acquired with partnership funds. Accordingly, a spouse need not join in any deed to be executed by the partnership. Similarly, a creditor having a judgment against one partner cannot enforce it against any partnership property per se. The creditor can only enforce the judgment against the partner's interest in the partnership, which, if the partnership were dissolved and liquidated, would entitle the creditor to the debtor partner's share in the assets of the partnership remaining after all partnership debts have been paid.

2. General Characteristics of a Partnership

Although the law may differ from state to state, partnership property may generally be conveyed on behalf of the partnership by any general partner. In the event a partnership dissolves without being reformed,[4] the former partners become tenants in common in the real property previously owned by the partnership.

(a) Personal Liability

Partners have unlimited personal liability as individuals for the debts and obligations of the partnership. If the partnership incurs debts or liabilities that exceed the value of the property owned by the partnership, the assets of the individual partners are subject to claims by creditors. Partners will be required to meet these claims out of their personal assets

---

3. As indicated above, it is incorrect to say that the joint venture takes title. The joint venturers take title as tenants in common.
4. A partnership may be technically dissolved and immediately reformed on the happening of certain events. Usually when lawyers speak of a partnership's dissolving, they are referring to a decision to terminate the partnership form, and not to a technical dissolution.

without regard to the proportion of capital that each contributed to the partnership or to the proportion of their partnership interest.

(b) Control

All partners have a legal right to take part in the management of the partnership. Partners can, however, relinquish or limit this right in a partnership agreement signed by all the partners.

(c) Tax Implications

Federal income tax considerations will be discussed in Part Two of this chapter.

3. Form in Which Title Is Held

If title to real property is to be held by a partnership, it is necessary to determine whether title will be taken in the name of the partnership itself (e.g., "Bluestone Company, a co-partnership") or in the names of the individual partners (e.g., "Adam Bell and Ella Johnson, co-partners trading as Bluestone Company, for the uses and purposes of such partnership"). If there is a transfer tax imposed upon the recording of deeds reflecting changes in the membership of the partnership, it may be preferable to keep title in the name of the partnership entity rather than in the names of the individual partners so that transfers of individual partnership interests (which are personal property) will not require the recording of deeds. The important thing to understand is that even if title is taken in the names of the individual partners, as partners, the real property is owned by the partnership as an entity and not by the partners in their individual capacity.

B. LIMITED PARTNERSHIPS

Limited partnerships are quite similar to general partnerships with three exceptions:

1. Classes of Partners

Limited partnerships consist of at least one general partner and at least one limited partner. The general partner (or general partners) is responsible for the management of the partnership.

2. Liability

Although the general partner is personally liable for partnership debts (as are all the partners in a general partnership), the liability of a limited partner is limited to that partner's investment (which is called that partner's capital contribution) in the partnership. This limitation on the limited partner's liability gives this form of partnership its name.

3. Control

The other major distinguishing characteristic of a limited partnership is that only the general partners have the legal right to manage the partnership. The limited partners have no management authority. A limited partner who exercises any control in the management of the partnership will lose that partner's status as a limited partner and thereby have the same exposure for liability as a general partner.

In all other regards, for purposes of this chapter, you may consider general partnerships and limited partnerships to be identical.

C. JOINT VENTURES

The term "joint venture" is often used fairly loosely to describe a typical real estate transaction where two or more parties come together to acquire or develop real estate. More specifically, a joint venture has been characterized as a partnership established for a single business venture (usually not the only business venture of the joint venturers) rather than a partnership that encompasses all or most of the business ventures of the partners. The joint venturers normally agree on the rules for ownership and operation of the real property to be owned by the joint venture, including the formula for sharing the profits and losses, and set forth their decision in a joint venture agreement.

Although case law may vary from state to state, the individual joint venturers are generally deemed to be tenants in common with respect to the real estate, and the joint venture is not considered to be an entity that can hold title itself. Accordingly, the venturers' spouses must sign the deed in order to convey the real estate. Because a joint venturer's interest in a joint venture that owns real estate is a real property interest, and not a personal property interest as in a partnership, a judgment against one joint venturer will be a lien against the venturer's undivided interest in the real property.

The usual reason for electing to form a joint venture rather than a general partnership is that the venturers desire to insulate themselves as much as possible from the open-ended liability of a general partnership. A partner of a general partnership has very broad powers to bind the partnership to various contractual relationships, even though the other partners do not consent and even though the contract may be outside the intended scope of the partnership. By use of the joint venture form, the investors hope that they will not be liable for any contract that only one of the venturers has signed on behalf of the venture, or at least that they will not be liable unless the contract in question is clearly within the scope of the single business of the venture.

PROBLEM

Identify at least ten issues you would expect prospective partners to resolve prior to their execution of a partnership agreement.

V. CORPORATIONS

A. GENERAL CHARACTERISTICS OF CORPORATE OWNERSHIP

Corporations are entities that are formed pursuant to a specific state (or federal) statute. There is no such thing as a common law corporation, and one cannot be formed in the absence of an enabling statute. The major characteristics of a corporation are that it is considered to be a separate person (but not an individual) distinct from its directors, officers, and shareholders; that it may have perpetual existence; that it has centralized control and management; that the interests in the corporation are transferrable; and that the shareholders have limited liability.

B. ADVANTAGES OF CORPORATE OWNERSHIP

Corporate ownership has several benefits. The stockholders will have no personal liability with respect to corporate debts, contracts, or other liabilities. Because a corporation's life is perpetual, the corporation and the surviving shareholders do not incur any federal estate tax, local inheritance tax, or real estate transfer tax on the death of a stockholder. The shareholders do not have any direct interest in the real property of the corporation, and therefore there are no problems with rights of dower or curtesy. Also, property owned by a corporation may be conveyed by action of the board of directors and officers without the necessity of having a deed executed by all of the shareholders.

C. DISADVANTAGES OF CORPORATE OWNERSHIP

Some factors (other than federal income tax factors) to consider in using the corporate entity as a titleholder are the additional expenses of forming and maintaining the corporation; additional taxes or higher tax rates imposed on the corporation by state and/or local authorities; the need to qualify to do business in the jurisdiction in which the real estate is located if the corporation is not organized under the laws of that state; and the possible requirement of special approval by the stockholders of the corporation, in addition to the usual authority from the board of directors, to sell real estate owned by a corporation if it is the principal asset or only asset of the corporation.

Part Two
INCOME TAX CONSEQUENCES OF PARTNERSHIP vs. CORPORATION

I. INTRODUCTION TO FEDERAL INCOME TAXES

The federal government, through the Internal Revenue Service (IRS), imposes a tax on net income earned by all taxable individuals and entities in the United States. This means that each individual or taxable entity must add up all of its income that is subject to tax (gross taxable income), subtract all items that the Internal Revenue Code permits it to deduct (tax deductions), and then pay tax on the remaining amount (net taxable income). For individuals, this net taxable income is taxed on the basis of a progressive rate. That is, the first level of net taxable income is taxed at the lowest rate (e.g., in 1985, 11% for single taxpayers)[5] and the next level is taxed at a higher rate (e.g., 13%) and so on until a 50% tax is reached. With regard to corporations, however, net taxable income is taxed in steps. Presently, that is 15% on the first $25,000 of net taxable income, 18% on the second $25,000 of net taxable income, 30% on the third $25,000 of net taxable income, 40% on the fourth $25,000 of net taxable income, and 46% on any amount over $100,000. The graduated rates are phased out for corporations with taxable income over $1,000,000, so that corporations with taxable income of $1,405,000 or more pay, in effect, a flat tax at the rate of 46%.

II. THE CONCEPT OF TAX DEDUCTIONS

A. GENERALLY

Anyone who has filled out a personal tax return knows the fact that only a very limited number of expenses qualify as tax deductions (e.g., under current law, interest, certain medical expenses, certain state and local taxes, and charitable contributions). The more payments a taxpayer makes that can qualify as tax deductions, the lower will be the net taxable income, and thus the lower the tax.

5. Tax rates and other tax information are all as of June 30, 1985. The information and discussion are greatly simplified and should not be considered as instructions for completing tax returns. In addition, various tax reform proposals now under active consideration would dramatically change this discussion.

B. DEPRECIATION OR COST RECOVERY

Depreciation is a special kind of tax deduction. Most of the business expenses a taxpayer incurs are for items or services used up either immediately or within a short time. For example, if a taxpayer pays wages, it is for work already performed; if cleaning supplies are purchased, they will be used up quickly. However, some items are intended to be used over a long period. For example, a taxpayer who operates a shoe business may purchase a cash register. One would expect the register to last perhaps ten years. If the taxpayer could take a tax deduction for the full cost of the cash register in the year he or she purchased it, that would not be a true reflection of the costs of doing business in that year. For example, assume that the cash register costs $1,000. At the end of the first year of use the cash register may have lost only $100 of value and still be worth $900. Thus the true cost of the cash register for that year is only $100, and that is all that should be allowed as a tax deduction. Of course, as the cash register loses value in the ensuing years, the taxpayer can take a tax deduction for those costs. The loss of value each year is called depreciation.

To attempt to determine the true economic depreciation of an item for any one year would be time-consuming and difficult. Hence, the tax law allows depreciation deductions (or cost recovery allowance) to be computed by set formulas. There are a number of such formulas, most of which are beyond the scope of this book. The one often used for real estate is the straight line method. To compute the depreciation deduction for any one year using the straight line method, a taxpayer takes the cost of the item (called the "basis") and divides the resulting number by the number of years over which the cost of the property may be recovered. In 1985, the costs of improvements to real property generally are able to be recovered over an eighteen-year period. Notice that the actual expenditure of money occurs only in the year of acquisition. In each succeeding year, the cost recovery or depreciation deduction is taken without any further expenditure of money. That is why depreciation is often called a "non-cash" deduction. Also notice that a taxpayer gets the deduction without having to prove the actual loss in value. Hence, the depreciation deduction can be taken even if the asset is actually *increasing* in value, as is often the case with buildings and other improvements to real estate.

One final note on depreciation. A taxpayer can take a depreciation deduction only if the item can lose value from *use*. That is, the item must be susceptible to wearing out. Thus a share of stock owned by a business may lose value, but it cannot be depreciated because it does not lose value by use (only business assets may be depreciated). So too, if a taxpayer owns real estate, only the building can be depreciated, because land theoretically does not wear out.[6]

6. A taxpayer who farms the land or takes the minerals out of it is entitled to a different deduction for this loss in value which is called "depletion."

III. CONCEPT OF TAX LOSS AND TAX SHELTER

As discussed earlier, a taxpayer computes his or her net taxable income by subtracting tax deductions, including depreciation, from gross taxable income. It should be noted at this point that a taxpayer must compute his or her net taxable income (or loss) derived from each and every business in which that taxpayer has an interest. For example, assume a taxpayer, Mr. X, has a job from which he earns a wage and receives interest from bank accounts and dividends from shares of stock he owns. In addition, the taxpayer has an antique business and owns a small apartment building. When the taxpayer prepares his tax return, he first segregates his personal income (wages, interest, and dividends) and subtracts from that his personal tax deductions (such as medical expenses, interest paid, state and local taxes, and contributions) to get his net taxable personal income. The taxpayer then does the same thing for each of his businesses. At that point, he combines all net taxable incomes to determine his total net taxable income. The major reason tax returns are designed that way is to make it easier for the IRS to understand and check on the items reported.

In computing the net taxable income for a business, it is not at all unusual for the tax deductions to exceed the gross taxable income. When this occurs, the taxpayer is said to have suffered a tax loss, which is the opposite of net taxable income. In some cases, this results from actually paying out in wages and other costs of doing business, more than the taxpayer takes in.[7] In many cases, however, particularly if the business has substantial depreciable property, the taxpayer actually takes in more than his or her cash expenses but has a tax loss because of non-cash depreciation deductions.

A brief example may make this clearer. Assume that an individual taxpayer owns a small apartment building from which $10,000 of rent is collected in a given year. In the same year, the taxpayer paid out $2,500 in real estate taxes, $3,000 in interest on the mortgage, and another $2,500 for maintenance of the property and other miscellaneous expenses (e.g., repairs, cleaning, wages, utilities, and accounting fees). If the taxpayer computed his or her net taxable income at this point, it would look like the following:

Gross Taxable Income	
Rents	$10,000
Tax Deductions	
Real Estate Taxes $2,500	
Interest on Mortgage $3,000	
Maintenance and Miscellaneous Expenses $2,500	$ 8,000
Net Taxable Income	$ 2,000

---

7. Even a business that is actually losing money may be generating some cash, because loans to the business are not counted as income.

However, the taxpayer has a depreciable asset—his or her apartment building. Assume it cost the taxpayer $110,000 for the land and building. Also assume that the cost of the building will be recovered over a eighteen-year period on a straight line basis. Finally, assume that the taxpayer reasonably allocates the $110,000 between land and building as follows: $20,000 to land value and $90,000 to the value of the building. (Remember, only the building can be depreciated, not the land.) The depreciation deduction can be computed as follows:

$$\frac{\$90,000}{18 \text{ years}} = \$5,000 \text{ per year}$$

If the taxpayer takes into account this $5,000 depreciation deduction, the business tax computation would be as follows:

Gross Taxable Income		
Rents		$10,000
Tax Deductions		
Real Estate Taxes	$2,500	
Interest on Mortgage	$3,000	
Maintenance and Miscellaneous Expenses	$2,500	
Depreciation Deduction	$5,000	
		($13,000)
Tax Loss		($ 3,000)

Notice that the taxpayer has a tax loss and thus has no tax liability from this business even though the taxpayer actually has $2,000 in cash left over at the end of the year. We say that the depreciation has given the taxpayer a "tax shelter." In other words, it has sheltered the $2,000 from being taxed and thus the taxpayer can keep all $2,000 for the taxpayer's own use rather than pay some of it in taxes. But also notice that our taxpayer has an additional advantage. In our example, the depreciation deduction sheltered the remaining $2,000 of gross taxable income from the apartment house business. There is an additional $3,000 of loss, however, that was not used in sheltering the income from this business. The amount, which is shown above as being a tax loss, is excess tax shelter. When the individual taxpayer combines personal tax computations with business tax computations, the $3,000 tax loss from the apartment house business will be used to shelter from taxes the $3,000 of income from other sources that otherwise would have been taxed. This excess tax shelter is the main attraction for many real estate investors.

IV. COMPARISON OF PARTNERSHIPS AND CORPORATIONS

A. TAXATION OF PARTNERSHIPS

Partnerships, although entities for purposes of holding title to real estate, are not entities for purposes of paying taxes. That is, a partnership pays no federal income tax. Any net taxable income or tax loss that a partnership has is divided among the partners, according to the percentage interest each owns in the partnership, and accounted for on the individual tax return of each partner. Being a partner in a partnership is identical, for tax purposes, to the operation by a single taxpayer of a business in the earlier discussion. For example, assume that two taxpayers form a fifty–fifty partnership to own the apartment building used as an example in the preceding section. Each year the net taxable income or tax loss of the partnership would be computed and divided between them. Thus, if there were $1,000 of net taxable income, each taxpayer would show an additional $500 of net taxable income on his personal tax return. If, however, there were a $1,000 tax loss, each taxpayer would have $500 to use to shelter other taxable income on his or her personal tax return.

B.   TAXATION OF CORPORATIONS

Corporations are different from partnerships in that they are taxable entities as well as titleholding entities. This means that corporations must directly and separately account to the IRS for any net taxable income or tax loss. Assume, again, two taxpayers who form a corporation to hold the apartment building. If the corporation has net taxable income, it is taxed at the corporate rate (15% on the first $25,000, etc.). If the shareholder taxpayers are to get any of this money, however, the corporation would have to pay it to them as dividends. When each shareholder taxpayer receives the dividends, they are taxable income to the shareholder. This means that to get income to a shareholder it must be taxed twice, once on the corporate level and once again to the shareholder when received as a dividend. This is the first major tax disadvantage of a corporation as opposed to a partnership. Partnership income to each partner is only taxed once on the individual partner level, whereas corporate income to each shareholder is taxed twice.

The other major tax advantage of the partnership over the corporation occurs when the entity holding the real estate has a tax loss or excess tax shelter created by the depreciation deduction. If the entity is a partnership, each partner can use his or her proportionate share of the tax loss to shelter other personal income. If the titleholding entity is a corporation, however, the tax loss belongs to the corporation in its capacity as a taxable entity, and there is no way to pass through any of the loss to the shareholders. This results from the corporation's tax entity status. Thus, there is no way a shareholder can use the excess tax shelter to shelter other personal income. The corporation must retain the loss and can make use of it only by carrying it forward to succeeding years or backward to prior years to shelter taxable income of the corporation, if any, in those years. Using the same assumptions as to revenue and deductible items set forth under Part Two, section III of this chapter, a corporation that owned the property would realize the same $2,000 of "sheltered" income and $3,000 of "excess" tax shelter as would an individual or partnership. In order to benefit its shareholders directly, which is taxable. Assuming that the shareholders pay 50% of their income in taxes, the $2,000 cash generated would yield a total of $1,000 to the shareholders after payment of the dividend. The "excess" shelter has no direct value to the shareholders. By way of comparison, the partners of the partnership could not only receive the $2,000 tax free, but they also receive the benefit of the $3,000 excess shelter directly. If the partners are in the 50% tax bracket, the excess shelter will save them $1,500 in taxes on other income. Thus it may be said that the partners would benefit directly by the sum of $3,500, whereas the shareholders' direct benefit from the same investment is only $1,000.

V. CHOICE OF ENTITY

In the overwhelming majority of cases the use of a partnership to own income producing real estate is preferable to the use of a corporation. This is particularly true because the limited partnership can be used to get the limited liability characteristic of the corporation, at least for the limited partners. In some situations it would be advantageous, from a tax point of view, to use a corporation as the titleholding entity rather than a partnership. These situations generally occur when the following three characteristics exist:

1. The entity will show a net taxable income rather than a tax loss.
2. The net taxable income is intended to be reinvested in the property. That is, it will remain in the entity and will not be paid out to the owners of the entity.
3. The owners of the entity would pay taxes at a higher individual rate than the corporate rate on the same amount of net taxable income.

Part Three
STRAW PARTIES

I. INTRODUCTION

A straw party or nominee is one who holds title to property on behalf of the actual or beneficial owner. It is sometimes desirable to have title to real estate and related personal property held in the name of a straw party or nominee. Some of the reasons follow:

A. USE OF A STRAW PARTY SIMPLIFIES THE TRANSFER OF TITLE

When real estate will be owned by a relatively large group of people as tenants in common, joint tenants, or partners, it will often be time-consuming and difficult to locate all of those needed to sign deeds, leases, and other legal documents on behalf of all of the real owners. One solution is to have title held by an agent (called a "straw party") for all of the real owners, having the authority to sign specific documents, such as mortgages and leases, on behalf and at the direction of the real owners.

B. USE OF A STRAW PARTY MAY AVOID POSSIBLE TITLE PROBLEMS

When the beneficial owners of property are individuals and one of them dies, there is a "cloud" on title until the administration of the deceased owner's estate is begun. In the interim it would be very difficult to sell, lease, or mortgage the property.

C. USE OF A STRAW PARTY MAY SECURE ANONYMITY OF OWNERSHIP

In various circumstances, the owners of real estate do not want the general public to know that they have acquired the property. This occurs frequently when a well-known individual, partnership, corporation, or other institution seeks to assemble numerous small parcels of real estate. If the developer's intention becomes public, the owner of each small parcel needed to assemble the project may try to hold out for a higher price.

D. USE OF A STRAW PARTY MAY AVOID PERSONAL LIABILITY ON MORTGAGE OBLIGATIONS

In some jurisdictions the beneficial owner of the real estate will not be personally liable on a mortgage note or bond executed by his or her agent if the beneficial owner is an undisclosed principal. If the note and mortgage is executed by a straw party, then the straw party, and not the beneficial owner, will be personally liable on the note. If the straw party has no liquid assets, the mortgage lender will look to the real estate in satisfaction of the mortgage loan. Therefore, the liability of the beneficial owner of the real estate will be limited to the loss of his or her interest in the land.

II. INDIVIDUALS AS NOMINEES OR STRAW PARTIES

A. COMMON PRACTICE

It has long been customary for individuals to act as straw parties. Real estate brokers often sign agreements to purchase land on behalf of undisclosed principals, particularly when anonymity is important. Some individuals serve as professional nominees and, for a fee, will sign mortgage notes and mortgages for beneficial owners who wish to avoid personal liability. The documents used in such cases are prepared in exactly the same form as they would be if the straw party were the real owner or mortgagor of the real property.

B. DECLARATION OF TRUST

There should always be written evidence of the agency or trust relationship between the beneficial owner and his or her nominee. Such an agreement should be signed by the parties prior to, or simultaneously with, the acquisition of record title by the straw party. In most cases it is sufficient for the straw party to execute a statement acknowledging that the straw party holds title merely as trustee, nominee, or agent for the specifically named beneficial owner. It is advisable to have such a document acknowledged by the signing parties so that it can be recorded, thereby giving constructive notice of the agency relationship either simultaneously with the conveyance of record title to the straw party or at some later time if the beneficial owner so desires. Without such an agreement, the heirs or successors of the individual straw party may claim that the straw party was, in fact, the real owner of the real estate. A declaration of trust will always contain a statement by the straw party (trustee) to the effect that the straw party is holding title for another and will deed the property to the beneficial owner, or do any other act with regard to the property, on the request of the beneficial owner.

C. CONTROL OF NOMINEE REQUIRED

Needless to say, the real owner's choice of an individual straw depends to a great extent on the confidence the real owner has in his or her ability to control the activity of the straw party in connection with the real estate. The real owner must be sure that the straw party will not (a) violate the agency relationship and disclose the identity of the real owner, (b) sign documents without authority, or (c) convey record title to another person. The owner must also be able to obtain from the straw party, on request, a deed conveying the real estate to him or her or to someone else, at his or her direction. The straw party must be readily available to sign, at the real owner's request, those documents that must be signed by the holder of record title, such as deeds to parts of the real estate, leases, and other agreements. It is a wise practice to obtain from the straw party, simultaneously with the conveyance of nominal title to the straw party, a signed and acknowledged deed conveying the real estate to the real owner. Such a deed can then be held by the real owner and used when the occasion for its need arises.

D. PROBLEMS CREATED BY THE USE OF INDIVIDUALS AS NOMINEES

Although it has been customary to use individuals as straw parties, this practice sometimes results in problems. For example, the straw party may die while holding title to the real estate. In that case it would be necessary to subject the property to the administration of the straw titleholder's estate until such time as the personal representative is willing to execute a deed to a new straw or the real owner. Additionally, the personal representative may be unwilling to sign documents on behalf of the real owners at least until he or she is fully aware of the obligations of the deceased straw titleholder.

In some jurisdictions, use of an individual nominee may protect the real owner from personal liability on mortgage notes, bonds, or contracts, but the straw party is not similarly protected and is therefore exposed to such liability. Accordingly, the straw party must be and remain "judgment proof" or impecunious. An individual straw party should hold title only to a single piece of property at any one time, because judgments against the straw party will be record liens against all properties of which the straw party is the titleholder of record. Individual nominees should also be single persons who have never married. Otherwise, future grantees and others will require proof that it is not necessary to have the straw party's spouse join in the conveyance or other instrument.

II. CORPORATIONS AS NOMINEES

A. BENEFITS OF USING CORPORATE NOMINEES

The problems that may arise out of the use of an individual as a nominee are eliminated when the straw party is a corporation. A corporation can have perpetual existence. A new and different corporation can be used as a straw for each different parcel of real estate, thereby insulating each property from the liabilities of others. A corporation can be easily and quickly formed, and can be controlled by individuals whom the real owner trusts, such as attorneys, accountants, or brokers. A corporation can be kept judgment-proof and impecunious simply be keeping its assets at a nominal level. Finally, a corporation acts through its officers, and it may have as many authorized officers as the board of directors determines, thus making it relatively easy to have documents signed.

B. INCOME TAX PROBLEMS CREATED BY THE USE OF CORPORATE NOMINEES

There should be no conceptual difference between the use of an individual as a nominee and agent for a real owner and the use of a corporation as a nominee and agent. However, the case law dealing with income tax issues in this area has created a confusing situation. If nominal title to real estate is held in the name of an individual straw, there is no doubt that it is the real owner who is taxable on the income from the real estate and not the straw party. For example, assume a real estate broker, Jane Smith, signs an agreement of sale and takes nominal title to an income producing property on behalf of her principal, the real owner, pursuant to a declaration of trust requiring her to forward all rents and other income from the property to the real owner. The burden of the income tax (and all other taxes and carrying costs) should and does fall on the real owner, the one who receives the benefit of such income. The real however, the corporation must pay a dividend, estate broker, who is merely a straw party and conduit for transmittal of the funds, is only the agent of the real owner. In such cases, the IRS looks to the real owner to pay the applicable tax on the income from the property, even though record title is in Jane Smith's name.

Unfortunately, in several cases involving corporate agents as straw parties, the IRS has persuaded the tax courts to impose an income tax on the corporate straw on the theory that the corporate straw itself is the real owner because it was formed and organized for the sole purpose of serving as a vehicle for the acquisition of title for its shareholders (who are sometimes the real owners). In fact, some courts have held that, for tax purposes at least, because the corporation is an entity formed for the benefit of the real owner and owned by the real owner, it must be deemed an independent entity rather than a mere agent and nominee, and therefore the real recipient of the income from the property. Such cases often allow the IRS to tax the corporate straw on the income at corporate rates and then impose a second tax on the income distributed by the straw corporation to its shareholders as dividends paid by the straw corporation.

Contrary to the position of the IRS, many tax lawyers argue that the corporate straw is no different from the individual straw. The corporation is in the business of acting as an agent and nominee and is not in the business of owning real estate for its own benefit. However, to prove that the corporation is merely an agent of the real owner and not a real owner itself, it becomes imperative that the underlying documentation of the relationship corroborate the agency theory. It is also important to maintain the independent nature of the corporate straw during the entire period when the straw is in title. The documents involved must be carefully drafted and the corporate straw must operate strictly in accordance with the applicable rules of agency law.

Chapter 3

Buying and Selling Real Estate

I. INTRODUCTION

A contract for the sale and purchase of real estate is customarily called an agreement of sale. For reasons that will be discussed later, an agreement of sale for an interest in real estate is almost always embodied in a written document signed by both the seller and the purchaser. Execution of the agreement of sale by both parties fixes the relative rights and obligations of the seller and purchaser. For this reason, the agreement of sale is a critical document in a transaction involving a sale and purchase of real estate.

Although the legal assistant will rarely represent a client in negotiating the terms of an agreement of sale, he or she may be given responsibility for preparing an agreement of sale for a supervising attorney either (a) as an initial proposal prior to negotiation, or (b) as an initial draft subsequent to the negotiation of the major business and legal terms. Even if the paralegal is never given the responsibility for preparing a draft of an agreement of sale, he or she must be able to comprehend the legal terms of an agreement of sale in order to be able to prepare for settlement. For these reasons, this chapter is written as if you, as a paralegal, would be first negotiating and then drafting an agreement of sale. You may receive the impression that every provision of every agreement of sale is both subject to negotiation and actually negotiated in every transaction. In many transactions, however, and especially in residential transactions, few or none of the provisions are negotiated, and standard form agreements are used virtually unchanged. Indeed, in many cases the client does not even seek legal counsel until after he or she has executed an agreement of sale and thus already fixed his or her rights and obligations. If the client seeks legal counsel before executing the agreement of sale, the decision as to which provisions to negotiate is properly the decision of the attorney, using professional judgment.

The purpose of this chapter is to familiarize you with some of the negotiating and drafting considerations that may arise in connection with agreements of sale for various types of real estate. One of this chapter's techniques is to identify the rights and responsibilities of each party when an agreement of sale did not deal with an issue or if a typical form agreement of sale was used. That result is then contrasted with the rights and responsibilities of each party which would result if a provision were used favoring either the seller or the purchaser. This will help to illustrate the first rule of negotiating and drafting: Consider every issue with regard to the position and requirements of your present client, either purchaser or seller. A provision that you may insist on when your client is the seller of real estate may lose its charm when your client is the purchaser.

A. THE NEED FOR AN AGREEMENT OF SALE

As previously indicated, an agreement of sale for real estate is a contractual undertaking by the owner of real estate to sell his or her interest in the real estate to another party, and an undertaking on the part of the purchaser to acquire the real estate, usually for the payment of a stated purchase price.[1]

Parties usually enter into an agreement of sale to be consummated at a future date instead of exchanging title and the purchase money immediately on reaching an agreement. The principal reason for the delay in time is that there are many matters that both the purchaser and seller must attend to between the time they agree on the terms of the sale and the time the actual exchange of title for purchase money can be made. Such matters include establishing the "marketability of title" (discussed in section II(E) of this chapter) and arranging for a loan to pay for the purchase price (purchase money financing). The agreement allocates responsibility between the parties to ensure that these and other matters to be resolved prior to, or as a condition of, consummation of the sale (referred to as the "settlement" or "closing") are accomplished in a satisfactory manner.

Because both parties normally invest considerable time and expense in making arrangements for settlement, both purchaser and seller want to be assured that they have an agreement that is legally enforceable against the other party. Furthermore, without a legal commitment the seller would not want to agree to refrain from seeking another purchaser for his or her real estate and the purchaser would not want to cease looking at other properties.

---

1. In this chapter we shall assume that the purchaser is paying money and/or assuming a mortgage in exchange for the real estate. There are many other items of value, the promise of which will be legally sufficient to act as consideration for the promise to convey real estate.

B. THE NEED FOR A WRITTEN AGREEMENT OF SALE

One of the oldest statutes in Anglo-American jurisprudence is the "Statute of Frauds," which deals with the problem of the enforceability of various agreements and instruments by establishing minimum requirements that must be met before the courts will enforce the agreement or instrument. Every state has enacted some version of the Statute of Frauds. Generally, modern versions of the Statute of Frauds contain the requirement that in order for a party to compel specific enforcement of an agreement to convey real estate, or to recover remedies for loss of bargain, the essential terms of the agreement must be contained in a writing signed at least by the party against whom enforcement is sought (and in some jurisdictions by the party seeking enforcement as well).

The lawsuit for enforcement of an agreement of sale for real estate is called an action for specific performance. The remedy of specific performance means that a court will compel the recalcitrant party to perform that party's obligations under the contract. Normally, if one party breaches a contract, the remedy of the other party would be to receive damages to compensate for any loss occasioned by the breach. Although money damages usually satisfies a disappointed seller, money fully cannot satisfy a disappointed purchaser because each parcel of land is unique. Through the remedy of specific performance, a court can force an unwilling seller to sell, and an unwilling purchaser to buy the property under an agreement of sale that complies with the Statute of Frauds. The terms of many agreements of sale specifically deny this remedy to one or both parties.

Without a writing that satisfies the Statute of Frauds, a purchaser is not able to recover damages from the seller for the purchaser's loss of bargain, which is the difference between the purchase price and the market value of the property (often determined by what a new purchaser is willing to pay for the property). Some relief from the harshness of the nonenforceability consequences of the Statute of Frauds is provided, however, if the purchaser can prove that there was an oral agreement of sale for the real estate. Most jurisdictions permit the buyer to recover from the seller payments made to the seller and reimbursement for expenses that the purchaser incurred on the strength of an oral agreement.

The Statute of Frauds is intended to protect the owners of real estate from fraudulent claims. With this in mind, there are a number of common exceptions to the Statute of Frauds. In many states if the seller can prove the existence of a written agreement signed only by the purchaser but accepted orally by the seller, the courts will force the purchaser to complete the transaction or to pay the seller's damages, notwithstanding the fact that the seller's agreement is oral. The seller's damages equal the amount the purchaser agreed to pay less the sum of money paid by a new purchaser, which again is the concept of "loss of bargain." In addition, the seller is entitled to recover the expenses incurred in obtaining a new purchaser. In such jurisdictions, the purchaser can help to protect himself or herself against enforcement of an oral contract by providing in any agreement of sale he or she executes that the offer to purchase contained in the agreement may be accepted only in writing by executing and delivering a copy of the agreement of sale to the purchaser within a specified period of time.

Another exception is that an informal writing signed by the party against whom enforcement is sought, which sets out sufficient details of the agreement so that the court can ascertain the essential terms of the transaction, is deemed to be a sufficient writing to satisfy the requirements of the Statute. The party seeking enforcement will be entitled to specific performance even though no formal agreement of sale was ever signed. Thus, an initialed memorandum of proposed agreement of sale can sometimes bind a party. Such memoranda and similar "agreements to agree" can be dangerous to those who believe that they are protected until they sign a formal document labeled "Agreement of Sale."

When property is owned by more than one person, or more than one person has a legal interest in the property (such as the spouse of a married owner), all of those persons must sign a writing before a court will compel a conveyance. If one of the co-owners of the property does not sign the alleged "agreement," the courts of most states will not compel a conveyance of any interest in the property, not even the interests of those persons who have signed the agreement.

PROBLEM

1. Find the Statute of Frauds of your jurisdiction relating to the sale of real estate.

2. What are the essential terms that the Statute of Frauds for your jurisdiction requires to be contained in a writing in order to enforce an agreement of sale for an interest in real estate?

C. LEGAL CONSEQUENCES OF EXECUTING AN AGREEMENT OF SALE FOR REAL ESTATE

An extensive body of law has developed over the years concerning the legal consequences of executing an agreement of sale. Many jurisdictions have held that the execution of an agreement of sale causes the immediate transfer of beneficial (or "equitable") ownership of the real estate to the purchaser, leaving the seller with mere legal title which he or she holds as trustee for the purchaser and as security for the balance of the purchase price due from the purchaser. The important legal consequences that flow from this event can best be illustrated by the use of several examples:

(a) As soon as an agreement of sale has been executed, the law views the purchaser as having an interest in the real estate. If the purchaser dies before the transaction is consummated, his or her rights (and obligations) under the agreement of sale would pass to his or her heirs in the same manner as his or her other real estate interests, and not in the manner provided for in other contract rights dealing with personal property.[2] As with other real estate interests, the purchaser's interest in the property described in the agreement of sale may be mortgaged, may become subject to a lien for unpaid debts of the purchaser, and, absent agreement between the purchaser and the seller to the contrary, may be transferred to other parties in the same manner as real estate is normally transferred.

(b) In the absence of an agreement to the contrary, upon execution of the agreement of sale, the risk of loss of the real estate passes from the seller to the purchaser, giving the purchaser an insurable interest in the property. This means that if, for example, the property that the purchaser has just agreed to buy were to be damaged or destroyed by fire between the time the agreement is executed and settlement, the seller can still compel the purchaser to purchase the property at the full price stated in the agreement of sale, notwithstanding the damage to or destruction of the property.

(c) Absent an agreement to the contrary, if the seller remains in possession of the property between the date of execution of the agreement and settlement (which is the usual case), the law imposes on him or her an obligation to use reasonable efforts to maintain and protect the property on behalf of the purchaser until settlement.

It should be noted, however, that the execution of an agreement of sale does not normally affect rights in the real estate of persons who are not parties to the agreement of sale. Consequently, a seller cannot object to the entry of a lien filed by one of his or her creditors against the real estate between the date of execution of the agreement and settlement by claiming that he or she is no longer the equitable owner of the real estate. Similarly, the title that the purchaser would receive at settlement would be subject to the rights granted to an innocent or "bona fide" third party (such as a tenant) by the seller in the period between execution of the agreement and settlement. The concept of an innocent or bona fide third party without notice will be discussed at greater length in Chapter Nine.

II. TERMS COMMON TO AGREEMENTS OF SALE FOR ALL TYPES OF REAL ESTATE

This section focuses on terms of agreements of sale that are essential terms to the transaction and are therefore common to all purchase-sale transactions. Unless specified to the contrary, it will be assumed in this

---

2. At common law, the property of a person who died intestate (without a will) would be distributed in certain shares to the closest relatives of the deceased. The relatives to whom the property would go and the shares of the property they would get differed de-pending on whether the property in question was real property or personal property. Most jurisdictions have specific intestacy distri-bution statutes, and in many of them the distinction between real and personal prop-erty has been eliminated.

chapter that the parties will be following the order of events customary to most transactions involving the sale of real property. Typically, a prospective purchaser makes an offer by signing an agreement of sale prepared either by a real estate broker or by his or her attorney. This signed agreement as presented to the seller constitutes an offer to purchase the property on the terms contained therein. The seller may accept the offer, usually by executing and delivering to the purchaser a copy of the agreement, although the seller may also accept orally, unless the offer requires written acceptance. After review by the seller or his or her attorney, the seller may object to certain terms and provisions of the offer, instead of accepting the offer. Negotiation may follow. Once the parties have agreed on all of the terms and conditions to be included in the written agreement, then either the existing offer is changed accordingly and executed by the seller, with both parties initialing the changes, or a new agreement embodying the agreed terms and conditions is submitted by one party or the other. Although the new agreement of sale contains all the terms and conditions that both parties have agreed to orally, the new agreement is technically only an offer being submitted by a party. The other party is not legally bound to accept the offer and is not bound by the agreement until he or she does accept the offer.

A. DATE

The date is usually the first item appearing on the agreement of sale. We have noted that the purchaser becomes the equitable owner of the property on the date of the agreement. If there is damage to the premises by fire, or a taking by eminent domain, the precise date on which the purchaser became the equitable owner may be of great importance. When an agreement is to be signed by all parties, the best practice is to date the agreement on the date of execution by the last party to execute.

There is sometimes a question as to when a party has actually executed an agreement of sale. Some forms of printed agreements of sale contain a signature line where the broker signs the agreement as agent for the owner. If the agent has legal authority to bind the owner to the agreement, the agreement would be effective on the date on which it is signed by the agent and the purchaser. If, however, the agent lacks such authority, the effective date of the agreement would be the date on which the owner approved the agreement of sale. The rules that govern the appointment of an agent for purposes of entering into an agreement of sale on behalf of either the purchaser or the seller are discussed in detail in subsection B.

B. PARTIES

It is important that the nature and status of all parties to an agreement of sale be described fully and accurately in the agreement. For example, the seller or the purchaser may be co-tenants, a partnership, limited partnership, corporation, trust, or estate. The parties should be identified carefully and the status in which they are to execute should be delineated. In the case of a party that is not a natural person, e.g., a corporation, the capacity of the person executing the agreement on behalf of the entity should be stated. The student will recall from the discussion of the Statute of Frauds that if the property is owned by more than one person, each co-owner should be named as a seller and should execute the agreement.

Care must be taken when dealing with any party other than an individual to obtain all the signatures necessary to bind the party. Thus, for a corporation, one commonly requires the signature of one officer plus the attesting signature of another officer with a clear indication that they are signing on behalf of the corporation in their capacity as officers. You should be careful to understand that the signature of a person to an agreement in one capacity does not bind that person in any other capacity, and another signature by that same person may be required. For example, if Joan Smith Buggy Whip, Inc., a corporation, is selling property to Herman and Joan Smith, husband and wife, the agreement should contain the following signature lines:

                                        Seller
Attest: JOAN SMITH BUGGY WHIP,
                                            INC.

                                        By: _____
_____   Joan Smith, President
Fred Brown, Secretary
[Corporate Seal]

Witnesses: Purchaser

_____   _____ [Seal]
                                        Herman Smith

_____   _____ [Seal]
                                        Joan Smith

PROBLEM

Greenacre is co-owned by (1) Wanda Wylie, Sanford Tunney, and Decedent's Bank and Trust Company, Executors of the Estate of Robert Wylie, Deceased, and (2) Sanford Tunney and Ida Tunney, his wife. The owners have agreed to sell Greenacre to Greenacre Associates, a general partnership consisting of Wanda Wylie, Ida Tunney, and Jack Parris. Please prepare the signature lines necessary and appropriate to bind all of the parties to the agreement.

1. Seller

For the protection of the purchaser, it is advisable that the seller or sellers be named in the agreement of sale in precisely the same way that the grantee is described in the deed by which title is held. The drafter can obtain this information from the seller's deed, a copy of which should be inspected, if possible, prior to preparing the agreement. Information concerning the title holder is also reflected in the title report ordered by the buyer (if title insurance is used), but typically a title report is not available until after the agreement of sale has been signed.

(a) Agent as Seller

Some printed form agreements of sale name the seller's real estate agent as the seller. This is not a desirable practice from the purchaser's point of view because even though the agent may produce written evidence of his or her authority, the purchaser has no way of knowing whether that authority has been revoked by a later act. Therefore, the purchaser should require that the actual owner of the property be named as the seller and that the seller also execute the agreement.

(b) Joinder of Spouse

As discussed in Chapter Two, the laws of some states give one spouse an automatic contingent property interest in any real estate owned or acquired by the other spouse, as an individual, during the period of the marriage, notwithstanding the fact that only one spouse is named in the deed as grantee of the property. In order for the purchaser to receive good title to the real estate in such a jurisdiction, it is necessary for the spouse of the seller to join in the deed, thereby conveying his or her contingent interest to the purchaser. In those jurisdictions granting the spouse an interest in real estate, it is imperative that the purchaser ascertain prior to executing the agreement of sale whether any of the sellers is or has ever been married. Based on this information, the purchaser's attorney can decide whether it is necessary for the spouse or former spouse of the seller to join in the execution of the deed. If it is determined that the joinder of a spouse is needed, then it is important to the purchaser that the spouse agree in writing to join in the deed. Otherwise, the purchaser will have no right to compel the seller's spouse to join in the deed. One way of requiring the spouse to join in the deed is to make him or her a party to the agreement of sale, and this procedure is often followed. However, naming the spouse as a party would make the spouse responsible for all of the seller's obligations under the agreement of sale, which may not be the intended result. The purchaser will be adequately protected if the spouse simply obligates himself or herself to join in the deed if settlement is consummated. This can be done by having the spouse sign a short statement below the signatures on the agreement of sale, substantially as follows:

For good and valuable consideration, and intending to be legally bound, the undersigned wife (husband) of the seller in the above agreement, without becoming a party thereto, hereby joins in the sale for purposes of approving the sale and agreeing to join her (his) husband (wife) in executing and acknowledging the deed.

2. Purchaser

The purchaser of the property should be named and described in the agreement in the same way in which he or she will take title to the property. This ensures that the seller will deliver a deed that correctly describes the purchaser and the nature of the tenancy by which title is to be held. Assume that an agreement of sale were signed by John Smith intending to acquire the property for his business, John Smith, Inc. If John Smith subsequently requested the seller to name John Smith, Inc. as grantee in the deed, the seller could legitimately (and should) refuse to deliver the deed in the name of anyone other than John Smith. Absent proof of proper assignment of the agreement of sale by the named purchaser, the seller would act at his or her legal peril in conveying the property to anyone else, even an apparently related party. In the event that the agreement permits the purchaser to assign his interest in the agreement, the purchaser should be described as "John Smith, or his nominee or assignee."[3]

C. DESCRIPTION OF PROPERTY BEING SOLD

In order to comply with the Statute of Frauds, the property intended to be conveyed must be identified with sufficient detail to preclude confusion as to which property is involved in the transaction.

1. Methods of Description

There are several ways customarily used to describe the real property that is subject to an agreement of sale.

(a) Description by Reference to a Plan

One way of describing property is by reference to a plan of the property, which plan is then attached as an exhibit to the agreement of sale. An example of a provision setting forth this type of description follows:

All that certain parcel of land with the buildings and improvements thereon and the appurtenances thereto, situate in Bellfield Township, Lakes County,

3. A party having legal rights set forth in an agreement or contract generally has the right to convey those benefits to another party. The conveyance is called an "Assignment", the conveyor an "assignor" and the recipient an "assignee". Usually an assignment also conveys to the assignee the assign-or's responsibilities and obligations in the agreement or contract. Not all contracts or agreements are assignable. Some are not assignable because the agreement itself so specifies, and this is often the case with agreements of sale for real estate.

Illinois as outlined in red on the plan attached hereto as Exhibit "A" and hereby made a part hereof.

(b) Legal Description

The agreement of sale may contain a full legal description of the property as taken from a recent survey or the seller's deed, either written out in its entirety or incorporated into the agreement of sale by reference to an attached exhibit. If the survey plan from which the legal description was taken was not prepared in connection with this particular conveyance, or if the legal description is taken from a prior deed or title report, the parties must carefully verify that the property intended to be conveyed by the agreement of sale is indeed identical to that described in the legal description.

(c) Recorded Plan, Street Number

If neither a plan nor a legal description of the property is available for inclusion in the agreement of sale, it may be adequate to identify the real estate merely by reference to a recorded plan, a lot number, a prior conveyance, a street name and number, or even by the name by which the property has been popularly known for an extended period. Chapter Four deals at greater length with forms of legal descriptions and their use in an agreement of sale.

2. Items to Be Included in Description

(a) Reference to Buildings

Regardless of the method chosen to identify the property, it is a good practice to include with the description of the land certain additional references to improvements on the property, such as "together with the buildings and improvements thereon and the appurtenances thereto." To the extent that improvements, air rights, or subsurface rights are not being conveyed, it is imperative that the agreement of sale specifically exclude the property or rights that the parties do not intend to convey. If the principal improvement being purchased is a commercial or industrial building, it is desirable to identify the building by its commonly used name, or by a reference to the number of floors and present use of the building:

> All that certain parcel of land situate in the County of Philadelphia, Pennsylvania, bounded and described as follows: Beginning at a point in the intersection of the north side of Walnut Street (50 feet wide) and the west side of Fourth Street (50 feet wide); thence in a westerly direction along the north side of Walnut Street One Hundred (100') Feet to a point; then in a northerly direction, parallel to Fourth Street, Two Hundred (200') Feet to a point; thence in an easterly direction, parallel to Walnut Street, One Hundred (100') Feet to a point on the westerly side of Fourth Street; thence along said westerly side of Fourth Street a distance of Two Hundred (200')

Feet to the point and place of beginning. Being No. 401 Walnut Street. Together with the 15 story office building erected thereon known as the "Stern Electronics" building.

(b) Acreage

When representing the purchaser, it is usually a good practice, if the information is available, to include at the end of the description a statement identifying the approximate number of acres contained in the tract to be conveyed. If there is a misunderstanding between the parties as to the property being sold, this device often brings the disagreement into the open at an early stage.

(c) Reference to Public Streets

When one or more of the boundaries of the real estate lie along a public thoroughfare, a prudent draftsperson will include in the agreement of sale and in the deed a clause stating that the conveyance includes all rights of the seller in and to the beds of streets, highways, and alleys abutting the property. This is done to make it clear that the conveyance includes all the property rights of the seller, a fact that would be relevant if some time in the future the course of the street is changed or the street is closed to traffic or stricken as a street.

(d) Condemnation Awards

For reasons discussed in subsection II(K) of this chapter, if there is any possibility that the property or any part of the property has been condemned prior to the conveyance to the purchaser, the purchaser's attorney should add to the description of the property a clause substantially as follows:

> and all awards in condemnation, or damages of any kind, to which Seller may have become entitled or may hereafter be entitled, by reason of any exercise of the power of eminent domain with respect to, or for the taking of, the premises sold hereunder or any part thereof.

If such a provision is not included, the purchaser could end up with a condemned property and the seller would have the right to the proceeds of the condemnation.

(e) Other Property Included in Sale

Just as it is important to describe adequately the real estate that is the subject of the agreement of sale, it is equally important to describe any property intended to be included in the sale that is not, or might not, be considered part of the real estate and, conversely, to describe property not intended to be covered by the sale, such as "fixtures." As discussed in Chapter One, "fixtures" is a legal term that includes such items as plumbing, electrical wiring, heating and sprinkler systems, television antennas, curtain rods, and lighting fixtures. Unless specifically excepted in the agreement of sale, fixtures are automatically included in the conveyance of the real estate to which they are attached. Often, however, it is unclear whether a particular item is a fixture. Especially when it is important to one party or the other that a particular item be included or excluded from the sale, an express provision should state whether the item is or is not intended to be included in the sale. The problem of fixtures is discussed in more detail in section VI of this chapter, dealing with agreements of sale for commercial improved real estate.

PROBLEM

Prepare a short provision for an agreement of sale for a residence indicating that the Lalique chandelier in the dining room is not included in the sale, and the washer and dryer are.

D. PURCHASE PRICE AND PAYMENT TERMS

1. Standard Provision

The agreement of sale should set forth the amount of the purchase price and the method of payment. Often, part of the purchase price is paid at the time the agreement of sale is executed and the balance is paid at settlement. The following is a typical provision setting out the purchase price and payment terms in a cash transaction[4]:

> The total consideration or purchase price for the premises shall be $ ____, and shall be paid as follows:
>
> (a) $_____ on the signing of this agreement in cash or by plain check to be held in escrow by Agent, and
>
> (b) $_____ at settlement in cash, by certified check, or by check of the title insurance company.

In order to satisfy the Statute of Frauds, the purchase price for the property must be ascertainable from a writing signed by the seller. The writing may simply state the purchase price or may give a formula from which the purchase price may be derived, as when the purchase price is stated in terms of a specified number of dollars to be paid per acre of land.

In the absence of language to the contrary, it is presumed that the purchase price is payable in cash. It is rare, however, that the seller insists on payment in cash. The initial deposit at the signing of the agreement of sale is often paid by purchaser's plain check (as distinguished from a

---

4. In this chapter, a cash transaction is one in which the seller receives the purchase price entirely in cash. This is in contrast to transactions in which the seller receives the purchase price partly in cash and partly by a purchase money note and mortgage at settlement. The purchaser in a cash transaction may well have obtained the cash needed to complete settlement from a mortgage loan made by a third party.

certified check). To protect the buyer, the seller should acknowledge receipt of the check, and to protect the seller, the acknowledgment should be subject to collection.[5] The seller will not normally, however, accept the balance of the purchase price in the form of purchaser's plain check because of the possibility that the check might be dishonored, leaving the seller with nothing more than a large money claim against the purchaser, who has received and probably recorded the deed. In some parts of the United States where settlements are customarily held at the offices of a title insurance company, the title company acts as the collection and disbursing agent. In such areas, one form of acceptable payment of the balance of the purchase price is for the title insurance company to issue its check to the seller. The title insurance company is normally willing to issue its check if it first receives a certified check from the purchaser. If the title insurance company and the bank on which the title insurance company's check is drawn are financially solvent, there is little danger that the title insurance company's check will be dishonored. If there is some doubt as to the financial stability of either the title insurance company or its bank, the seller should insist that payment be made by the bank, or by cashier's check of a reliable bank. Once such a check has been issued and delivered to the seller, the purchaser has no right to stop payment on the check.

The use of purchase money mortgages and installment sales agreements is more common in commercial real estate transactions, and the discussion of their use and the drafting and negotiating considerations attendant to their use are reserved for later sections of this chapter.

2. Escrow Account

An extremely desirable practice followed in many parts of the United States is to provide in the agreement that deposit monies paid by the purchaser will be placed in an escrow account, the control over which will be in the hands of a neutral party, frequently an attorney, a real estate broker, or a title insurance company, who has been designated by the parties to act as the escrow holder or "escrowee." Payment to an escrowee negates the obvious advantage in the seller's position if a substantial downpayment has been received and a dispute arises before settlement. The duties of the escrowee and the conditions on which the monies will be paid over to one party or the other should be set forth in the agreement or in a separate letter.

The concept of an escrow is to have a trusted neutral party hold the deposit monies until the occurrence of specified events, such as settlement, in which case the escrowee pays the deposit monies to the seller, or a default by the seller, in which case the escrowee pays the deposit monies to the buyer. Some agreements merely state that the deposit monies shall be held in escrow, without identifying the events on which the deposit

---

5. This can be accomplished by the following language with reference to the purchaser's check in payment of the deposit: "receipt whereof, subject to collection, is hereby acknowledged."

monies should be released from escrow and to whom they should be paid. In such a case, the release of the deposit monies would be determined by other provisions of the agreement of sale and by the state laws that deal with escrows. In the great bulk of real estate transactions that are concluded successfully, the role of the escrowee would not require any greater definition. However, because the very idea of requiring an escrow suggests that some dispute may arise, the drafter of an escrow provision should consider dealing with some of the following issues:

The first and most basic question is to whom the escrowee should pay the deposit monies if nothing goes wrong and the transaction is consummated. The following provision might be used:

> At settlement under this Agreement of Sale, the escrowee shall pay all deposit monies to Seller, who shall apply them towards the purchase price to be paid to Seller by Purchaser hereunder.

The next concern for the escrowee is the question of what to do with the deposit monies if either party shall clearly default:

> If Seller fails, refuses or is unable to make settlement, and Purchaser elects not to sue for specific performance or is precluded from suing for specific performance by the terms of this agreement, in addition to Purchaser's remedies other than specific performance, Purchaser shall, upon giving written notice thereof to escrowee and Seller, become entitled to the return of all deposit monies held by escrowee pursuant to this agreement. If Purchaser fails, refuses or is unable to make settlement, upon giving written notice thereof to escrowee and Purchaser, in addition to Seller's other remedies, seller shall, upon giving written notice thereof to escrowee and Purchaser, become entitled to receive all monies held by escrowee pursuant to this agreement.

Because an escrowee does not want the responsibility of deciding whether one party or the other is in default, especially if both claim the money, the following language should be added to the foregoing provision:

> Escrowee shall pay the monies held in escrow to the party making a demand for payment of the escrow as above provided, unless within five (5) days after receiving notice of the demand for payment of the monies, escrowee shall have received notice in writing from the other party that such other party denies the right of the demanding party to receive such monies. The objecting party shall set forth in his or her notice, under oath, the reason(s) why such party denies the right of the demanding party to receive these monies. In the event escrowee receives conflicting demands for the monies held in escrow or in the event the parties do not agree in writing as to whom the monies belong, escrowee shall have the right to hold the monies until escrowee has received a written agreement between the parties as to its disposition. If escrowee is sued, escrowee shall have the right to interplead the parties and deposit the money in a court of competent jurisdiction.[6]

6. On the other hand, escrowee might want to interplead the parties and deposit the escrow monies in court after a dispute as to the release of the monies arises in order to avoid the likelihood of being sued by a party insisting that the escrowee has wrongfully withheld the monies.

It is advisable to state what compensation, if any, the escrowee will receive and from whom. In addition, the escrowee may insist on the inclusion of a provision indemnifying the escrowee against liability, costs, and expenses incurred as escrowee. The following sample provision may be added to deal with the above problems:

> In any action taken relative to this Agreement, escrowee shall not be liable for any mistake of fact or error of judgment, or for any acts or omissions of any kind unless caused by its own willful mistake, gross negligence or bad faith. Escrowee may act in reliance upon the advice of counsel satisfactory to it in reference to any matter connected with the escrow and shall not incur any liability for any action taken in accordance with such advice. The parties agree to pay escrowee its fee for acting as such, the amount of which fee shall be $_____, and to indemnify and hold harmless escrowee from and against any and all damages, costs and expenses, including attorneys' fees, incurred by escrowee, except such as result from its own breach of this Agreement, and escrowee shall have a security interest in the subject matter of this escrow for the payment of all such costs, expenses and fees.

If the sum being held by the escrowee is large, it may be advantageous to deposit it in an interest-bearing account, such as a savings account, in a money market account, or in short-term certificates of deposit. However, because no investment is entirely risk free, unless insured (and then only to the extent insured), the escrowee might want specific authorization to deposit the money in one of these interest-bearing accounts. If this is done, the agreement must clearly indicate who is entitled to the interest earned on the money both in the situation where the transaction is completed and when there is a default.

PROBLEM

Draft a clause of the escrow provision authorizing the escrowee to deposit the deposit monies in an interest-bearing account at any local commercial bank or savings and loan association, or in a money market account, and providing that interest will be paid to the party entitled to receive the deposit monies (but note that if the seller receives the interest, the amount of the interest is not credited toward the purchase price).

E. CONDITION OR QUALITY OF TITLE TO BE CONVEYED

The escrow provision was the first truly lawyerly term that we have so far discussed. Any intelligent layperson would probably include in an agreement a brief description of the parties, the purchase price, and the property being sold. Few laypersons would think to include an escrow provision. As few or fewer would think to include a provision dealing with the quality of title. Yet this is one of the most important terms of an agreement of sale. The description of the premises indicates the physical boundaries of what is being conveyed. The quality of title indicates the legal boundaries of the real estate interest being conveyed. As you will recall from Chapter One, many kinds of interests or estates in real property can be conveyed, and real property can be subject to a virtually limitless number of interests, including estates, rights, powers, restrictions, easements, liens, and encumbrances. Each state has decided according to its own state laws what quality of title the seller must convey and the purchaser must accept if the agreement of sale is silent as to quality of title. The state law in this respect could vary all the way from requiring the seller to provide title in fee simple absolute, subject to no easements, restrictions, agreements, liens, or encumbrances whatsoever, to requiring the purchaser to accept only a quitclaim deed conveying whatever interest (if any) the seller has, subject to all existing easements, restrictions, agreements, liens, and encumbrances.

The drafter of the quality of title provision must be aware of this range of possibilities. A quality of title provision that is poorly drafted from the seller's standpoint can be so restrictive in terms of what the seller must provide that the purchaser, in effect, has an option to buy or reject the property at settlement. On the other hand, a provision that is poorly drafted from the purchaser's standpoint might require the purchaser to complete the transaction and pay the full purchase price for a piece of real estate that a title search reveals to be worth but a fraction of what the purchaser has agreed to pay for the property. Each of the following five provisions deals with the problem in a different way.

EXAMPLE 1

The Premises are to be conveyed free and clear of all liens, encumbrances and easements, excepting, however, the following: mortgage encumbrances as above mentioned, existing building restrictions, ordinances, easements of roads, privileges or rights of public service companies, and all other restrictions or conditions of record, if any, otherwise title to the Premises shall be good and marketable or such as will be insured by a reputable Title Insurance Company in the City of Chicago or the adjacent counties, at its regular rates.

EXAMPLE 2

Title to the Premises shall be good and marketable and free and clear of all liens, restrictions, easements, leases, tenancies and other encumbrances and title objections, and shall be insurable as such at regular rates by any reputable title insurance company selected by Buyer.

EXAMPLE 3

Title to the Premises shall be good and marketable and free and clear of all liens, covenants, restrictions, easements, leases and tenancies, and other encumbrances and title objections excepting, however, those encumbrances and title objections set forth on Exhibit "A" attached hereto and made a part hereof; and shall be insurable as such by any reputable title insurance company selected by Buyer at its regular rate.

EXAMPLE 4

Title to the Premises shall be good and marketable and free and clear of all liens, encumbrances and easements, excepting, however, the following: existing building restrictions, ordinances, easements of roads, privileges or rights of public service companies, and other restrictions of record, if any; provided, however, that the present use of and improvements to the Premises are not in violation of any of the above and none of the above shall restrict or prevent the use of the Premises as a single-family dwelling or impose any monetary or maintenance obligations (except in the case of ordinances) upon the owner of the Premises; otherwise, title to the Premises shall be good and marketable and insurable as such by First National Land Title Insurance Company at its regular rates.

EXAMPLE 5

Title to the Premises shall be good and marketable and such as will be insured by First National Land Title Insurance Company at its regular rates; excepting only existing covenants, restrictions, easements and agreements of record that do not unreasonably interfere with the use, occupancy, enjoyment or marketability of the Premises.

Very narrow — must go to 1st Nat'l

Example 1 of the condition of title clause is so broad as to impose hardly any obligation on the seller, other than to pass title. *Example 2,* on the other hand, is so narrow that few owners of real estate in urban or suburban areas could comply with it. *Examples 3, 4,* and *5* are fairly typical of quality of title provisions that have been negotiated by the attorneys for the purchaser and seller.

Let us now examine the language of these provisions more closely to determine how the language of each is advantageous to one party or the other. Ideally, a purchaser wants title to his or her property to be free and clear of all encumbrances, easements, and restrictions. If the purchaser has no alternative but to take title to certain relatively minor title objections, as is normally the case in a populated area, he or she would like to know, prior to committing to purchase the property, precisely what those title objections will be. In that manner the purchaser can make an informed judgment as to the price he or she is willing to pay for the property or whether the purchaser wants the property at all. Because it permits "all other restrictions or conditions of record" on the title, thereby leaving the purchaser vulnerable to an almost limitless number of title restrictions, the language in *Example 1* dealing with liens, encumbrances, and easements may not be acceptable to a purchaser. Most sellers, when confronted by a knowledgeable purchaser, are willing to obligate themselves to deliver a title that is free and clear except for a certain number of limited objections to the title that are impossible or impractical to remove and that either are specifically enumerated in the agreement of sale and agreed to by the parties, as in *Example 3,* or will not restrict the purchaser in his or her intended use of the property, as in *Examples 4* and *5.*

If a title search on the property has been completed shortly before the agreement of sale is executed, both parties can decide prior to executing the agreement which of the title objections appearing on such a report will be acceptable. Frequently, however, a title search is not available prior to execution of the agreement of sale. If the seller obtained title insurance when he or she bought the property, the parties can refer to that title insurance policy for the purpose of enumerating the acceptable title objections. Of course, that title insurance policy will not show any encumbrances, easements, or restrictions that may have arisen while the seller was the owner of the property. It is important, therefore, when representing a seller, to question the seller closely to determine whether anything has happened during the seller's ownership of the property to encumber or restrict the title and, if something has occurred, to add that to the list of objections obtained from the seller's title insurance policy.

In some circumstances the seller will not know what title objections, if any, exist. In such instances the approach demonstrated in *Examples 4* and *5* is often used as a substitute for the more exact, and therefore preferable, approach shown in *Example 3*.

1. Good and Marketable Title

Each of the sample provisions quoted above refers to a good and marketable title. What does this term mean? In exploring the meanings of good and marketable title in Chapter Six, you may find the definition hard to grasp. It is a term that legal writers also have found difficult to define in a noncircular manner. One authority defined marketable title as follows:

> [The term marketable title] was coined by the equity courts to designate a title which, although it may be clouded by some uncertainties or defects, is sufficiently free from all fair or reasonable doubt, so that they would compel a purchaser to accept it in a suit for specific performance. Conversely, an unmarketable title, although not necessarily bad, is one that has apparent defects or encumbrances which will cause such a doubt in the mind of a reasonable, prudent, and intelligent person that he will refuse to take the property, or to take it at its full value. In fact, it has frequently been held that a doubt sufficient to impair a title's quality of marketableness must be such as to affect the selling value of the property or to interfere with the marketing of a sale. The good title which a purchaser may require need not be free from all clouds or suspicions; it need only be such a title as prudent men, well advised as to the facts and their legal bearings, would be willing to accept. . . . [It is generally conceded that for title to be good and marketable the following elements must be established:]
> 1. Rightful ownership of the entire property, or of the entire interest or estate contracted for, free from all fair or reasonable doubts . . . [which in some states, as a matter of law, and under most agreements of sale, is satisfied by production of appropriate record evidence of ownership].
> 2. Freedom of the estate or interest involved from liens, charges or other encumbrances.
> 3. Rightful possession of the property.[7]

7. American Law of Property § 18.7 (A.J. Casner ed. 1952). Reprinted by permission of Little, Brown and Co.

2. Insurable Title

A second test stated in the sample provisions for determining the condition of title to the premises is the requirement that the title will be insurable. Title insurance simply indemnifies the holder against damages resulting from failure of the title as stated in the title insurance policy or from the existence of encumbrances, easements, or restrictions against the property not discovered by the title insurance company and excepted from title. In order to forestall any arguments as to whether the requirement is satisfied if at least one title company will issue or whether every title company must be willing to issue title insurance, the parties can specify a particular title company. The seller may agree to let a single designated title insurance company be the arbiter if that company also issued the seller's policy. If this approach is used and the Real Estate Settlement Procedures Act of 1974 applies (this Act, also known as RESPA, is discussed in detail in Chapter Eight), the agreement of sale should make it clear that the purchaser chose the particular title company or that the company is being referred to only as the judge of quality of title, with no requirement that the purchaser obtain title insurance from that company.[8] Failure to make this clear may subject the seller to substantial penalties under RESPA. Because the title insurance company that insured the seller when he or she bought the property is already obligated to pay for unexcepted defects in the title occurring prior to the seller's ownership, it will often insure the purchaser's title in circumstances where other title insurers would not. The reason for this is that by so doing the title insurance company may avoid having to pay damages to the seller under the seller's policy, although it might have liability to the purchaser at a later time.

The purchaser will not be adequately protected if the agreement of sale merely states that the title will be insurable. It is necessary to add the words "at regular rates." If paid a sufficient premium, some title insurance companies can be induced to assume an unusually high risk. If this short phrase were omitted, the purchaser could be required to purchase a property with a serious defect and, if the purchaser desired title insurance, be subject to payment of an extremely high premium.

If you read again the five provisions quoted above, you will note that four of them provide that title is to be good and marketable *and* such as will be insurable at regular rates, whereas *Example 1* provides that title is to be good and marketable *or* such as will be insurable at regular rates. There is a meaningful difference between the two phrases. In the one case the title must be both good and marketable *and* meet with the approval of the title company. In the second the title could be unmarketable but insurable by some title insurance company, or it could be good and marketable but not insurable by any title insurance company.

---

8. The provision is included in response to the restriction in RESPA forbidding a seller or financer from requiring a purchaser to employ a certain title company. It is essentially an anti-kickback provision.

If the purchaser is to be adequately protected, he or she should insist that the quality of the title meet both tests.

F. TIME AND PLACE OF SETTLEMENT

Chapter Eight contains a detailed description of what transpires at a "settlement" or "closing." For purposes of this chapter, you need only understand that it is at settlement that the seller delivers an executed deed to the purchaser in exchange for the purchase price (which may include a purchase money note and mortgage), and the other obligations contained in the agreement of sale are also generally satisfied.

The courts will interpret an agreement of sale that does not specify the time and place of settlement as meaning that the parties intended settlement to be held within a reasonable time after execution of the agreement, at a place reasonably convenient to the parties. However, the time and place of closing should be specified in the agreement of sale in order to avoid the delay and risk of litigation.

Many standard forms of agreement of sale attempt to cover time of settlement by merely providing that settlement shall be made on or before a certain date, without specifying the time of day or place where the settlement is to be held. If the parties cannot agree as to the time and place of settlement, one party might have a difficult time establishing that the other party breached the agreement by failing to complete settlement. Of course, the fact that a time and place of settlement is expressly stated in the agreement does not preclude the parties from changing the time and place of settlement. For this reason, a good agreement of sale will normally contain a provision similar to the following:

> Settlement will be made at the offices of _____, [insert address] _____, at _____ o'clock on _____, 19 __, or at such other definite place and time and prior date as Seller and Purchaser (or their respective attorneys) may agree upon in writing.

By specifying a time and place for settlement, either party can properly "make tender" in the event the other party breaches the agreement of sale. "Tender" is a legal term meaning that one party produces and offers the requisite money or property to the other party as required by the agreement of sale. Tender is usually followed by a demand that the other party meet its corresponding obligations. In most jurisdictions, unless the agreement of sale provides for a waiver of formal tender of the deed, the seller must appear at the time and place designated for settlement with a signed, sealed, and acknowledged deed before the seller has the right to declare the buyer in default under the agreement of sale. The above rule would apply even if the purchaser declared bankruptcy or fled the country the week before settlement. Similarly, in the absence of the agreement of sale providing a waiver of formal tender of the purchase money, the purchaser must appear at the time and place designated for settlement with the balance of the purchase price in hand (in the form specified in the agreement of sale) if the purchaser is to have the right to declare the seller in default. Many standard agreements of sale now provide that formal tender of both the deed and the purchase money is waived.

Many agreements of sale provide that the times set for the performance of various obligations (such as the obligation to pay the purchase price or to deliver the deed) are "of the essence" of the agreement. This phrase is used to designate those obligations which are sufficiently important to the parties so that if they have not been satisfied by the designated time, the resulting default will be deemed a material breach of the entire agreement. Such a breach entitles the nondefaulting party to obtain rescission of the agreement, which is a judicial concellation of the agreement accompanied by a return to the *status quo ante*. In the absence of an express stipulation that time is of the essence, the general rule is that courts will grant a defaulting party a reasonable time in which to cure his or her default and will not grant a nondefaulting party rescission of the agreement if the breach is cured in a reasonable time. If the defaulting party does cure his or her breach, then a court will limit the nondefaulting party's remedies to compensation for damages caused by the delay.

When the parties wish to provide that the failure on the part of either to perform punctually all of the obligations under the agreement shall be deemed to be a material breach of the contract, a provision such as the following should be used:

> The time set for settlement hereunder and all other times referred to for performance of any of the obligations of this agreement shall be of the essence.

G. POSSESSION

The final act in consummating a real estate transaction is for the seller to surrender possession of the property to the purchaser. Because the seller cannot deliver possession of a piece of real estate by handing it to the purchaser, a symbolic form of delivery of possession takes place at settlement. A fairly typical provision relating to symbolic delivery states:

> Possession of the Premises shall be given to Purchaser at the time of settlement (the Premises being then unoccupied and free of any leases, claims to or rights of possession) by delivery of the keys to the Premises and Seller's special warranty deed (with release to dower, curtesy and homestead rights, if any) duly executed and acknowledged by Seller, and in proper form for recording.

The foregoing provision requires delivery of the premises "unoccupied and free of any leases, claims to or rights of possession." If the property or part of the property is under lease at the time of sale and the buyer desires to purchase the property subject to the lease(s), the language would have to be amended so to provide. In addition, the agreement should then obligate the seller to assign all of the leases to the purchaser at the settlement and produce a signed notice to each tenant, directing the tenant to make future rental payments to the purchaser. Furthermore, because the purchaser will be responsible for returning the security deposits to the tenants, a provision is normally included allowing the amount of these deposits as a credit to the purchaser. The seller should insist that the purchaser agree to assume all of the obligations of landlord under the leases being assigned.[9]

There is a particular problem when real estate is being sold to the tenant of the property. Pennsylvania courts have held that the execution of an agreement of sale by a tenant, or a tenant's exercise of an option to purchase, terminates the landlord-tenant relationship.[10] This is seldom the intended result as far as a seller is concerned, and it is therefore necessary to state specifically that the lease survives until settlement.

Sometimes the purchaser wishes to take possession of the real estate prior to the date scheduled for settlement or, conversely, the seller wishes to remain in possession of the property after settlement has been completed. Both of these conditions are normally undesirable from the standpoint of the party out of possession. The problem is that the party out of possession may experience difficulty getting the party in possession to vacate the premises at the appointed time. When it is necessary to permit the nonowner of the property to have possession, the rights of the parties should be defined by a written lease that contains appropriate legal remedies if the nonowner fails to vacate on time. If the seller desires to remain in possession until a specified date, the purchaser will normally be well advised to insist on postponing settlement for the period the seller needs to remain in possession rather than to complete settlement and have the seller as a tenant. Problems such as deterioration of the property between the date of settlement and the date of possession become more difficult to remedy if settlement has occurred.

If the purchaser is to take possession of the property prior to settlement, both the agreement of sale and the lease for the property for the interim period prior to settlement should provide that the purchaser's possession is governed exclusively by the terms of the lease and that he or she is not a purchaser in possession under an agreement of sale. Furthermore, the lease should provide that its term expires on the date set for settlement, so that if the purchaser fails to complete settlement, the seller will have the right to evict the purchaser. Frequently, the lease incorporates liquidated damages provisions, which make it extremely onerous for a defaulting purchaser to remain in possession after a default.

9. The other side of an assignment of an agreement or contract is the agreement of the assignee to perform all of the assignor's obligations under the agreement being assigned. When an assignee agrees to become personally and primarily responsbile for assignor's obligations, then the assignee is said to have "assumed" the agreement.
10. This is the doctrine of "merger," which states that the leasehold interest of a tenant "merges into" his or her equitable interest in the property acquired on the execution of an agreement of sale, or legal title to the property acquired on the recordation of the deed to the property. Whether merger occurs on the transfer of equitable or legal title depends on the laws of the state in which the property is located.

H. APPORTIONMENTS

At the settlement for almost all real estate sales, certain expenses relating to the property must be apportioned between the parties. The apportionments arise because of charges that must be paid by the owner of the property at a specified time, but that relate to the use of the premises during a period spanning ownership by seller and purchaser. It would not be equitable to expect one party or the other to bear the entire amount of these expenses, depending on the mere chance of which party is in possession at the time the charge is payable. It is customary, therefore, for the purchaser and seller to allocate the charges between themselves on the basis of the percentage of the period for which the charge is imposed that each one of them is in possession of the property.

A typical standard form of agreement of sales deals with this apportionment problem in the following manner:

> Taxes, rents, water and sewer rents, and interest on mortgage encumbrances, if any, shall be apportioned pro rata as of the date of settlement, which apportionments shall be based upon the actual fiscal period for which the charges are assessed or levied.

The proper way to handle the apportionment problems and the safeguards that are necessary to protect the purchaser and seller will depend greatly on the law and practices of the jurisdiction governing the transaction. In any case, the first steps are to determine the period for which the charge is imposed and whether the charge is imposed in arrears, in advance, or partly each. Taxes often are assessed for a twelve-month period, but the twelve-month period does not always coincide with the calendar year. If, for example, the taxes are for a July 1–June 30 fiscal year and settlement is held on August 1, for purposes of apportioning this particular charge, the seller has been in possession of the property for only $\frac{1}{12}$th of the year, not $\frac{7}{12}$ths. By this example the seller would be responsible for $\frac{1}{12}$th of that annual tax and the purchaser would be responsible for $\frac{11}{12}$ths. If the tax is payable in advance and has been paid by the seller, then the seller is entitled to receive compensation from the purchaser for $\frac{11}{12}$ths of the tax. If the tax is not yet due or is due but has not yet been paid by the seller,[11] then the purchaser is entitled to a credit for $\frac{1}{12}$th of the tax.

In some areas one set of taxes is imposed for one twelve-month period and a second set is imposed for a different twelve-month period. For example, a tax imposed by a school district may be based on a fiscal year starting July 1, while a tax to support general municipal services is based on a calendar year. Sometimes both taxes are assessed in one bill, in which case various portions of the bill will be treated differently in regard to apportionments. Some charges are imposed for periods of less than twelve months, such as quarterly or semiannually.

11. A properly drafted clause should impose on the seller the full burden of any penalties due for taxes that are overdue.

Another variation is that in some areas taxes are paid by one or more estimated installments during the taxable period. The estimated tax is usually based on the final tax for the previous tax period. A final reckoning is made at the end of the tax period based on the actual budgetary expenses of the taxing authority. Taxpayers are entitled to a credit if the final tax is less than the estimated tax they have paid. However, the usual experience in the recent inflationary times is for taxing authority expenses to increase, and the taxpayer in such areas usually must anticipate an increase every year. For purposes of apportionments, the paralegal in such areas must realize that the actual tax to be paid for the entire tax period is attributable to the entire period. Thus, at settlement in areas using estimated tax payments, the ultimate tax liability of the seller for the period prior to settlement may not be known until several months after settlement. Local practice will usually make some accommodation for this fact, by way of escrows or estimated increases.

PROBLEM

How many local taxes are imposed on real estate in your area? What taxing periods do the taxing authorities use? Are taxes paid in advance or in arrears? Are taxes paid in installments and, if so, are they estimated installments?

It is advisable to determine whether the charge creates a personal liability against the owner of the property or whether it merely results in a lien against the property. In some states, for example, real estate taxes are assessed and become liens as of the time the rate is determined or as of the beginning of the tax fiscal year. In those states where the liens are effective as of the date the rate is determined, the owner of real estate becomes personally liable for payment of taxes as of the day of assessment, regardless of the fact that he or she sells the property the next day and has no interest in the property for the balance of the year. Because of the personal liability aspect, the seller must be sure not only that real estate taxes assessed against the property during his or her ownership are apportioned, but also that both the seller's share and the purchaser's share of the taxes are paid in full to the taxing authority at settlement even though they are not yet due. If any particular charge does not result in personal liability to the seller, his or her only real concern is that it is properly apportioned.

Apportionment of rents payable under leases on the property is discussed in section VI of this chapter. Apportionment of interest on mortgages that are remaining on the property after the property is conveyed is discussed in Chapter Eight and is discussed further in subsection III(A) of this chapter.

I. REAL ESTATE TRANSFER TAXES

Many states and municipalities tax the transfer of real estate or the recording of a deed. These taxes are similar in some respects to sales taxes imposed on the sale of personal property.[12] The name by which the tax on the transfer of real estate is known and the amount of the tax varies with the jurisdiction.

The statute enacting a transfer or recording tax may specify that the purchaser, the seller, or both are responsible for payment of the tax. Local custom may also dictate who is responsible for its payment. In Pennsylvania, for example, it is customary for the burden of the realty tax to be split evenly between the purchaser and the seller. In New Jersey, on the other hand, it is customary for the seller to pay the full amount of the transfer fee. Notwithstanding the prevailing law or custom, it is perferable for the agreement of sale to fix responsibility for payment of a transfer or recording tax.

J. MUNICIPAL IMPROVEMENTS AND VIOLATIONS OF LAWS, ORDINANCES, OR REGULATIONS

Normally, assessments that have been made for municipal improvements, such as street paving and curbing and installation of water and sewer lines, are encumbrances on the property and must be removed as title objections before the seller can convey title that is free and clear of all liens and encumbrances.

The problem is that occasionally assessments have not been made by the time of settlement for improvements that have been completed or that are close to completion. If the purchaser has not adequately provided for this eventuality in the agreement of sale, he or she may be in the unpleasant position of receiving an unexpected assessment after he or she takes possession of the property. Consequently, the purchaser should question the seller as to whether the local authorities have contemplated making, are in the process of making, or have recently made any improvements that might result in an assessment against the property. In addition, the subject should be covered in the agreement of sale. If the seller is willing to pay for improvements begun before the agreement is executed and the purchaser, as the equitable owner, is willing to bear the burden thereafter, the following provision might be included in the agreement of sale:

> Seller warrants and represents that, as of the date hereof, no assessments for public improvements have been made against the Premises which remain unpaid. Seller shall be responsible for the payment of any assessment

---

12. One difference between transfer taxes and sales taxes relates to the federal income tax consequences of the tax. Unlike most state sales taxes, transfer taxes may not be included on Schedule A of an itemized income tax return in the category of "taxes paid." Transfer taxes are a cost of selling or purchasing real estate and are included within the tax basis of the property for purposes of determining gain or loss on sale.

or charge hereafter made for any public improvement begun before the date hereof. Purchaser shall be responsible for the payment of any assessment or charge hereafter made for any public improvement begun after the date hereof.

If the seller refuses the above, the purchaser may be willing to settle for the following type of provision, although in that case the purchaser should make a particularly close inspection of the property to determine whether any recent municipal improvements have been made:

Seller warrants and represents that the Premises will not be assessed for any street improvements, or installation of or connection to sewer or water lines heretofore made. Purchaser will be responsible for any public improvements, no matter when begun, which have not yet been completed.

The purchaser must also be careful that he or she will not be burdened with the costs of bringing the property into compliance with the health, building, safety, zoning, and related laws of the jurisdiction in which the property is located. The purchaser might request that an inspection of the property be made by the appropriate officials or require the seller to produce at settlement certificates from the local authorities stating that the property is in compliance with all applicable laws. The seller will often refuse to agree to provisions of this type, either because the seller knows that there are violations, or for fear that an inspection will reveal one or more technical violations of the law. If the seller is unwilling to have the property inspected or to produce certificates of compliance at settlement, a clause substantially similar to the one that follows is often used:

Seller covenants and represents that, prior to the execution of this agreement, no notice from any governmental authority has been served upon the Premises, or upon Seller, or Seller's agent, requiring or calling attention to the need for any work, repairs, construction, alterations or installations on or in connection with the Premises, which have not been complied with. If Purchaser takes title to the Premises, Purchaser will be responsible for the cost of all such work, repairs, construction or installations which may be required or called attention to, by any notice served by any of the said authorities at or after the execution of this agreement.

The problem with such a provision is that because the purchase is not being presented with a certificate from the local authorities, he or she may not learn of a violation of covenant until sometime after settlement. At such time the purchaser's only remedy will be a lawsuit against the seller (who may be unavailable or without assets) to recover the cost of correcting the violations. Indeed, unless the warranty "survives" the settlement, it is possible that the warranty will not be operative after settlement, in which case the purchaser will have no remedy. (See subsection P, 1 of this section.)

K. CONDEMNATION

Under certain circumstances, federal and state governments, political subdivisions thereof, and some public utilities have the power (referred to as the power of condemnation or eminent domain) to acquire interests in real estate without the consent of the owner or the possessor of the property affected. The taking may be accomplished with little or no notice to the owner of the property or the party in possession. The Fifth Amendment to the U.S. Constitution requires that the condemning authority compensate the owner for the interest taken. In most jurisdictions the identity of the owner is determined as of the date of the condemnation, which is sometimes prior to the actual taking of possession by the condemning authority. A possible result is that if property subject to an agreement of sale is condemned prior to settlement, the purchaser will ultimately suffer the loss, but the condemning authority will pay the condemnation award to the seller, as the owner of record, even if the award is not paid until after settlement is made.

If the agreement of sale is silent as to the respective rights of the parties in the event of a condemnation, the purchaser in most jurisdictions would have the right to rescind the transaction or, if the taking was of only a part of the property, to obtain a reduction of the purchase price if the purchaser discovered the condemnation prior to settlement. However, if the purchaser does not discover the condemnation prior to the time of settlement and pays the full purchase price and accepts the deed, in most jurisdictions the purchaser will have no right to recover anything from the seller unless the seller delivered a deed of general warranty rather than special warranty or "quitclaim."

For the purchaser to be fully protected in this situation, the drafter must include in the agreement of sale an assignment of any condemnation award received or receivable by the seller. The agreement should also provide that any award received by the seller will be credited to the purchase price if settlement is concluded. From the purchaser's standpoint it is advisable, notwithstanding the assignment of any award, also to reserve the right, at the purchaser's option, to terminate the agreement in the event of a condemnation of all or part of the property.

Many standard forms of agreement of sale do not contain any provision dealing with the condemnation problem. It is necessary, therefore, when using such a standard form, to add a condemnation clause. One suggested provision is as follows:

> In the event of the taking of all or any part of the Premises by condemnation or eminent domain proceedings or the commencement of any such proceedings prior to settlement, Purchaser shall have the right, at Purchaser's option, to terminate this agreement by giving written notice thereof to Seller on or before the date fixed for settlement hereunder. If Purchaser does not so terminate this agreement, the purchase price for the Premises shall be reduced by the total of any awards or other proceeds received by Seller at or prior to settlement with respect to any taking, and

at settlement Seller shall assign to Purchaser all rights of Seller in and to any awards or other proceeds payable by reason of any taking. Seller agrees to notify Purchaser of any condemnation or eminent domain proceedings within five days after Seller learns thereof. Notwithstanding the fact that neither Purchaser nor Seller knows of the taking of all or any part of the Premises by condemnation or eminent domain proceedings at the time of settlement, Seller shall execute, acknowledge and deliver at settlement an assignment of all the rights of Seller in and to any awards to other proceeds payable by reason of any such taking, whether known or unknown. At Purchaser's option, such assignment may be included in the deed from Seller to Purchaser or may be in the form of a separate assignment.

L. DEFAULTS AND REMEDIES

1. The Law Absent Agreement by the Parties

The statutory and common law of each state provides for certain rights and remedies to a party to an agreement of sale upon the default of the other party, whether or not the agreement itself specifies any such rights or remedies. The following are typical categories of remedies available in some form in most states.

(a) Default by the Purchaser

In most jurisdictions, if the purchaser fails to complete settlement, the following remedies are available to the seller:[13]

(i) Suit for Damages

The seller may sue the purchaser for damages suffered by the seller, of which one measure would be the difference between the purchase price stated in the agreement of sale and the amount (less costs of the sale) received by the seller at a subsequent fair sale of the property, sometimes with interest on such damages.

(ii) Specific Performance

In lieu of a suit for damages, the seller may maintain an action for specific performance of the agreement of sale in order to obtain from the purchaser the balance of the purchase price.

(b) Default by Seller

In most jurisdictions, if the seller fails to complete settlement, the following remedies are available to the purchaser:

(i) Suit for Damages

The purchaser can bring a suit for damages suffered by the purchaser in

---

13. Remember that the seller may have to tender a deed, as discussed earlier in this chapter.

an amount equal to any unreturned deposit made by the purchaser in addition to his or her actual expenses (such as cost of a title search and preparing a survey), plus interest.

(ii) Specific Performance

The purchaser may maintain an action for specific performance of the agreement of sale to compel the seller to sell the property in accordance with the agreement of sale. The purchaser may be given a reduction in the purchase price to compensate for the damages suffered by the purchaser by reason of the delay (one measure of such damages being the amount by which the net income produced by the property during the period of the delay exceeds the interest on the balance of the purchase price during that period).

(iii) Loss of Bargain

If the seller willfully breaches the agreement or is guilty of bad faith in an attempt to escape his or her obligations under the agreement, such as by conveying or agreeing to convey the property to a second purchaser, the purchaser may be able to recover not only the deposit money paid, plus interest and expenses, but also damages for loss of the bargain.[14]

2. Agreement of the Parties

Often the parties wish to alter the respective rights and liabilities of the parties that the state law would provide on default of a party. This may be done by specifying in the agreement what their respective rights will be in the event of breach. Within certain broad limitations, the parties to an agreement of sale can agree to expand on or limit the remedies that would otherwise be available to them.

(a) Purchaser's Default

The following is an example of a typical provision dealing with default by a purchaser:

> Should Purchaser violate or fail to fulfill and perform any of the terms or conditions of this agreement, then and in that case all sums paid by Purchaser on account of the purchase price or consideration herein may be retained by Seller, either on account of the purchase price, or as liquidated damages for such breach, as Seller shall elect, and in the latter event Seller shall be released from all liability or obligation and this agreement shall become null and void.

The above provision is largely declaratory of the law in the absence of a default clause in the agreement. An attorney representing the purchaser will want to amend the provision to eliminate the right of the seller to

14. See subsection P of this section regarding loss of bargain damages.

bring suit for the purchase price. That will leave the seller with damages equal to the down payment made by the purchaser. The change may be accomplished by the following language:

> Should Purchaser violate or fail to fulfill and perform any of the terms or conditions of this agreement then and in that case all sums paid by Purchaser on account of the purchase price or consideration herein shall be retained by Seller as liquidated damages. In such event both parties shall be released from all liability or obligation to the other under this agreement and this agreement shall become null and void. The retention of such damages shall be Seller's sole remedy in the event of default by Purchaser; and Seller hereby waives any right to recover the balance of the purchase price or any part thereof not already paid by Purchaser.

(b) Seller's Default

The following provision (also favorable to the seller) limits the usual state law remedies to which the purchaser would be entitled in the event of the seller's default:

> In the event Seller is unable to give good and marketable title or such as will be insured by any reputable title insurance company, as above set forth, Purchaser shall have the option of taking such title as Seller can give without abatement of price, or of being repaid all monies paid on account by Purchaser to Seller and Purchaser shall also be reimbursed for any Title Company charges incurred; and in the latter event there shall be no further liability or obligation by either of the parties hereunder and this agreement shall become null and void.

The attorney for the purchaser might want to restore most or all of the purchaser's usual state law remedies as previously set forth.

M. ZONING

Zoning is the generic name for municipal ordinances that regulate the use of real property within a municipality by restricting a landowner in a particular zone to certain specified classes of use. The issue of zoning raises some problems to which the parties might wish to address themselves in an agreement of sale. The purchaser may attempt to include in the agreement of sale a provision by which the seller warrants to the purchaser that the present use is permitted under the existing zoning classification, and that conditions settlement on continued legality of use. A provision to that effect follows:

> Seller hereby represents and warrants that the zoning classification of the premises is _____, that the present use of the premises as _____ is in compliance with the zoning laws and all ordinances pertaining thereto, and that Purchaser's intended use of the premises as _____ is also in compliance therewith. If, prior to settlement, an amendment to the zoning ordinances or any other law, ordinance or regulation comes into effect which prohibits the operation of _____ upon the premises, Purchaser shall have

the right, upon giving written notice thereof to Seller at or before settlement, to cancel this agreement and to recover all monies paid to Seller on account of the purchase price.

Normally, if the agreement of sale contains no representation or warranty as to zoning or legality of use, then the purchaser is wholly subject to the zoning laws and any changes in the zoning laws, and may not refuse to make settlement because the purchaser discovers that his or her intended use is not permitted. However, as a safeguard, the seller should negate any warranty or representation as follows:

> Buyer hereby acknowledges that Buyer has ascertained the zoning classification of the Premises and the legality of the present use thereof Buyer further acknowledges that Seller has made no representation or warranty relating to zoning or use, notwithstanding any statute or customs to the contrary.

If the purchaser knows that the property cannot be put to his or her intended use without first obtaining a variance or special exception under the zoning code, the obligation to complete the sale should be conditioned upon the purchaser's ability to obtain whatever approval of local authorities is needed. Because of the possibility of appeals and other delays, it may take a long time to obtain and finalize such approval. Therefore, the purchaser wants to provide ample time to obtain the approvals. The seller, on the other hand, does not want the property removed from the market for a long period. Accordingly, it is advisable in this type of situation for the parties to establish an outside date at which time the agreement will become null and void and the purchaser's purchase money will be returned if the necessary approvals have not been received and the possibility of appeal has been eliminated. The agreement should make clear which of the seller and the purchaser will be responsible for obtaining the necessary zoning approval. If the seller is to obtain the approval, the purchaser should make provision for the right to take over and carry on the procedure if the seller fails to pursue the matter diligently, which might occur if the seller receives a better offer for the property. A provision dealing with the problem of zoning approval from the viewpoint of the purchaser follows:

> Purchaser's obligation to complete settlement under this agreement is conditioned, in accordance with the provisions hereinafter stated, upon the issuance to Purchaser by the duly constituted public authorities of such permits, certificates, variances, exceptions, licenses, authorizations, approvals and changes (including, by way of illustration and not limitation, zoning variances, zoning exceptions, subdivision approval and building permits) (collectively referred to herein as the "Permits") as may be required or desired by Purchaser to permit the use of the Premises as a _____. Seller agrees to cooperate with Purchaser in obtaining the Permits and prosecuting any appeals in connection therewith and to execute any documents submitted by Purchaser with respect thereto. If at the time of settlement hereunder all of the Permits are not validly issued and received

by Purchaser or the time within which an appeal may be taken from the issuance of any Permit has not elapsed or an appeal has been taken from the issuance of a Permit and for any reason has not been finally determined in favor of the applicant for the Permit, then, in any such event, Purchaser shall have the right, at its option, to terminate this agreement by giving written notice thereof to Seller.

The attorney for the seller would want to make sure that the purchaser makes a good-faith effort to obtain the necessary permits; otherwise, the purchaser might attempt to get out of a "bad deal" simply by not going forward with the necessary efforts needed to obtain such permits.

PROBLEM

Add the necessary language to the above provision requiring the purchaser to make a good-faith effort to obtain the permit, including a waiver of the condition and a reiteration of the obligation to complete settlement if the purchaser fails to make the requisite effort.

N. PURCHASER'S RIGHT OF INSPECTION

Shortly before the time scheduled for the settlement, the purchaser should inspect the premises in order to verify that they are in the condition required by the agreement, that all fixtures that the seller has agreed to leave on the property have indeed been left and that they are in good operating condition.[15] It may be desirable for the purchaser to have the property inspected prior to settlement by experienced inspectors. However, unless the purchaser has reserved the right to come onto the property for the purpose of conducting such inspections, the seller can legally bar the purchaser's entry until after settlement. A provision granting the purchaser a right of inspection follows:

> Pending consummation or termination of this Agreement, Purchaser and Purchaser's authorized representatives are hereby granted the free right and privilege, at Purchaser's sole risk and expense, at reasonable times and after notice to Seller, to enter upon the Premises from time to time for the purpose of inspecting the same. Purchaser shall repair any damage caused thereby and shall indemnify and hold Seller harmless from and against any and all liability, obligation, loss, cost and expense resulting therefrom.

---

15. Please note that there is no legal requirement that the fixtures or any personalty included in the sale be in good operating condition unless the agreement of sale specifically imposes such a requirement.

O. BROKERS

A real estate broker is usually engaged by a prospective buyer to assist in locating a desirable piece of property, and by a prospective seller to assist in locating a desirable purchaser. The real estate broker normally helps the buyer and the seller to consummate the sale and receives a commission equal to a certain percentage of the purchase price. It is common practice for the agreement between the broker and the party who engaged the broker to be set forth in a separate document and not made part of the agreement of sale. However, occasionally serious disputes arise over the questions of whether a particular broker is entitled to a commission and who is to pay the commission. Therefore, it is often advisable for the parties to state whether any broker has become involved in the transaction and to allocate the responsibility for compensating the broker. In addition, the agreement of sale should contain a representation from each party that no other broker has been engaged, and each party should indemnify the other against any claim for broker's commissions resulting from a breach of such representation.

PROBLEM

1. Draft a broker's commission provision for an agreement of sale regarding which the seller has agreed to pay XYZ Realty a 6% commission.
2. Draft a broker's commission provision for an agreement of sale regarding which no broker has been involved.

P. MISCELLANEOUS PROVISIONS[16]

1. Merger (Survival After Settlement)

The "merger doctrine" provides that, unless the parties indicate a contrary intent, the delivery of the deed at settlement in exchange for the purchase money terminates all covenants in the agreement of sale that are inconsistent with the parties' actions in completing settlement. This doctrine may be grounded on the theory that, by their acts at settlement, the parties demonstrate their intention to modify the agreement of sale by waiving all covenants, representations, and warranties not also contained in the deed. For all practical purposes, therefore, absent express agreement to the contrary, agreements of sale expire once the settlement is concluded, and all provisions in such an agreement are considered to have merged into the deed, and the convenants and warranties contained in the deed.

---

16. In lawyer's jargon, fairly standard provisions of agreements and other legal documents are often referred to as "boiler plate."

Therefore, the benefits to a seller or purchaser of real estate of a well-negotiated, well-drafted agreement of sale can be lost after settlement by virtue of the merger doctrine unless proper precautions are taken. As to most matters, it is the attorney's responsibility to protect his or her client adequately by insisting at settlement that all provisions of the agreement be strictly complied with as a prerequisite to his or her client's concluding settlement. However, some agreements of sale contain warranties and representations that are of such a nature that a breach of the warranty is not likely to be discovered until after settlement, or that the party benefitting from the warranty desires the effect of the warranty to continue after settlement. In some cases a covenant contained in the agreement can be preserved by inserting a similar covenant in the deed itself, but this is not appropriate in all cases. If it is important to the client that a particular covenant survive settlement and it is an inappropriate convenant to include in the deed, then the drafter should rebut the presumption of merger by specifically providing in the agreement of sale that a particular covenant is intended by the parties to survive settlement. Alternatively, the drafter may wish to include a general survival provision affecting all the covenants, representations, and warranties contained in the agreement. The survival provision may limit the survival to a specified period after settlement.

2. Recording the Agreement of Sale

The agreement of sale does not have to be recorded to be effective as between the parties. However, as discussed in Chapter Nine, in most jurisdictions an unrecorded agreement of sale is ineffective as against third parties who acquire an interest in the real estate by purchase, by operation of law, or otherwise, without having received notice of the existence of the outstanding agreement of sale. It is to the advantage of the purchaser, therefore, to record the agreement of sale, especially when a long period will elapse between the execution of the agreement of sale and the scheduled date for settlement. The seller, however, has a strong interest in not recording. The seller's principal objection to recording the agreement of sale is that it creates a cloud on title that might be difficult and expensive to remove if the purchaser defaults and does not complete settlement. For this reason, many form agreements of sale expressly prohibit the purchaser from recording the agreement.

3. Notices

Agreements of sale frequently require the delivery of certain papers and provide for various notices to be given by one party to the other. For example, the data fixed for settlement may be changed by notice from either party to the other. It is a good practice to specify the acceptable method by which delivery of notice and other papers is to be made. The following is an example of one such notice provision:

All notices to be given by either party to the other shall be in writing and shall be mailed by Registered or Certified United States mail, postage prepaid, return receipt requested, addressed to Seller at _____ with a copy to _____, and to Purchaser at _____ with a copy
    (Seller's attorney)
to _____; or to such other address as either party may
    (Purchaser's attorney)
designate by written notice to the other given pursuant to this section. Notice will be considered to have been given upon the postmark date of mailing. The title report, form of deed or other papers which either party desires or is required to deliver may be mailed in the same manner.

The requirement that the notices be sent by registered mail, return receipt requested, is desirable because the return receipt provides a simple and effective method of ascertaining that the addressee has indeed received a communication sent to him. Some notice provisions go further and provide that a return receipt is the only acceptable evidence that a notice has been sent.

4. Parties Bound

Most agreements of sale include a provision, largely declaratory of the law, stating that neither the death of a party nor an assignment of the agreement shall affect the obligations under the agreement.

(a) Assignment Permitted

If the agreement of sale does not by its terms prohibit assignment, the drafter can use a clause similar to the following:

> This agreement shall be binding upon the parties hereto and their respective heirs, personal representatives, successors, and permitted assigns.

(b) Assignment Not Permitted

If, on the other hand, there is a restriction on the right of the purchaser to assign the agreement, the following clause would be more appropriate:

> Subject to the foregoing provision regarding assignment by Purchaser this agreement shall extend to and bind the heirs, successors, and assigns of the respective parties hereto.

5. Captions

If an agreement contains captions or headings at the beginning of the various provisions, the drafter might consider indicating in the agreement that the captions themselves are not part of the agreement. This will preclude someone from later trying to support a particular interpretation of the agreement based on language found in a caption. For this purpose, a clause similar to the following is appropriate:

> The captions contained herein are not a part of this agreement, are intended solely for the convenience of the parties, are not relevant in the construction of this agreement, and do not in any way modify, amplify, or give full notice of any of the terms, covenants, or conditions of this agreement.

6. Integration (Entire Agreement)

Although it is also largely declaratory of the law, the prudent drafter should include a provision that attempts to preclude one party or the other from claiming that various oral covenants had been made regarding the sale in addition to or modifying those contained in the written agreement. Such a clause is commonly called an "integration clause." The following is typical of the type of integration clause used in agreements of sale:

> This Agreement and the Exhibits hereto set forth all of the promises, covenants, agreements, conditions, and undertakings between the parties hereto with respect to the subject matter hereof, and supersede all prior and contemporaneous agreements and undertakings, inducements or conditions, express or implied, oral or written, except as contained herein. This Agreement may not be changed orally but only by an agreement in writing, duly executed by or on behalf of the party against whom enforcement of any waiver, change, modification, consent, or discharge is sought.

7. Negation of Representations by the Seller

In seller's forms of agreement of sale it is not uncommon to find, in addition to an integration clause, a provision expressly negating any representation or warranty by the seller that is not expressly stated in the agreement of sale. A typical provision of this kind reads as follows:

> It is understood and agreed that Purchaser has inspected the Premises and that Purchaser has agreed to purchase the same as a result of such inspection and not because of or in reliance upon any representation by Seller or any agent of Seller. It is also understood and agreed that Seller shall not be responsible or liable for any agreement, condition or stipulation not expressly set forth herein relating to or affecting the physical condition of the Premises, or otherwise.

Of course, if the purchaser is indeed relying on a representation made by the seller or a real estate agent, it is incumbent on the purchaser's attorney to include that representation in the agreement of sale and expressly to negate the above provision. In recent years some jurisdictions have developed doctrines that imply by law certain warranties as to the condition of the property, especially regarding the sale of newly constructed residences. These warranties exist even though no express statement of condition has been made by the seller. Many seller's forms of agreements of sale attempt to negate the implied warranties, with more or less success.

8. Preparation of Documents

Although both attorneys should try to include clauses protecting their clients in the various instruments involved in real estate transactions, absent express agreement to the contrary, the custom of the particular community usually dictates whether the seller's or buyer's attorney will draw the deed, and the various debt instruments if the seller is taking back a purchase money mortgage. If it is intended that the prevailing custom in the community will not be followed in this regard, express language in the agreement of sale will be needed in order to negate the custom. Even when the custom is to be followed, however, it is good practice to include a short statement allocating the responsibility for the preparation of the various instruments needed at the closing.

Q. SIGNATURES

1. In General

The signature lines of the agreement should provide a place for signatures of all of the parties to the agreement of sale. As mentioned previously in subsection II(B), the signatures should be obtained both of all persons who have any interest in the real estate and of all persons who will be taking title. In addition, there should be signature lines provided for the witnesses to the signing of the agreement by the parties.

2. Co-Owners

The student will recall that if property is owned by more than one person as co-owners, an agreement of sale that lists all of the co-owners but does not include the signatures of all of the co-owners will not, in most jurisdictions, bind any of the co-owners.[17] Consequently, it is important for the purchaser to verify that all co-owners of the property have signed the agreement of sale as sellers.

3. Partners

Although partnership law in most jurisdictions permits any general partner to execute an agreement and thereby bind the entire partnership, it is wise to require that all of the general partners execute the agreement. Otherwise, the attorney representing the other party might be compelled to examine the partnership agreement in order to determine whether the partnership agreement itself places restrictions on the ability of a single partner to sign an agreement of sale on behalf of the partnership.

17. The signature of one or more, but less than all, of the co-owners might give rise to a lawsuit for damages against the executing co-owners under some circumstances.

4. Corporation

The signature of a corporation is made by the signature of its president or one of its vice-presidents, with an attestation by its secretary, treasurer, assistant secretary, or assistant treasurer to the effect that the president or vice-president is authorized to sign the agreement on behalf of the corporation. In addition, the corporate seal is generally affixed next to the signature of the officers by the secretary or assistant secretary of the corporation. Although the use of a corporate seal is no longer mandatory in some states, it is typically used in executing documents relating to real estate.

5. Agent

As discussed previously, the practice of permitting a person to be a party to an agreement solely in the capacity of an agent for another is to be avoided. When it is necessary, however, for an agent to execute the agreement on behalf of the principal, it is important that a provision be added requiring the principal to ratify the act of the agent in writing, preferably by signing the agreement itself, within a specified time from the date of the agreement. This provision should also state that failure to ratify within the time limit specified will cause the agreement to be null and void, in which event all deposit monies, together with any interest earned thereon, will be returned to the purchaser.

6. Joinder by Escrow Agent

In most instances the broker will also act as the escrow agent for the deposit monies. The parties should require the escrow agent to join in the agreement of sale in order to bind the escrow agent to the terms of the escrow agreement. On the other hand the escrow agent will not want to become a party to the entire agreement. A typical provision of this kind reads as follows:

> First Title Company, the Escrow Agent, has joined in the execution of this agreement of sale solely for the purposes of (a) acknowledging receipt from Buyer of deposit monies hereunder in the amount of $_____, and (b) agreeing to perform its obligations as the Escrow Agent as provided in paragraph 10 hereof.

III. TYPICAL ADDITIONAL PROVISIONS OF AGREEMENTS OF SALE FOR SINGLE-FAMILY RESIDENCES (EXISTING BUILDING)

Because of the vast number of sales of single-family residences and the relatively small amount of money usually involved in these transactions, it is uncommon for a "custom-made" agreement of sale to be used. In most instances the real estate broker representing the seller will present the prospective purchaser with a standard form of agreement of sale on which the blanks have been filled in and perhaps several other minor changes have been made to reflect any special terms of the transaction. The typical standard form of agreement of sale for residential real estate is prepared for use by the seller's broker. Therefore, the form can be expected to provide fairly adequate protection for the seller while seldom providing necessary protection for the purchaser. It is usually up to the purchaser's attorney, if the purchaser consults an attorney prior to executing the agreement, to modify, supplement, and, in some cases, delete the standard provisions of the agreement of sale so that the agreement includes more adequate protection for the purchaser.

Most of the provisions of a typical agreement of sale for a single-family residence that will require the particular attention of the purchaser's attorney have already been discussed in detail in section II of this chapter. This section will be devoted to a study of additional provisions that are needed to protect sellers and purchasers of single-family "used" dwellings and that are peculiar to this type of transaction.

A. MORTGAGES

Most real estate purchases are financed, partially or entirely, by some form of time payments. Generally, the financing takes the form of a note or bond secured by a mortgage or a deed of trust, all of which is discussed at greater length in Chapter Five. The discussion that follows deals with a mortgage as the form of security instrument. The deed of trust form of security instrument has virtually the same effect as a mortgage, and consequently, the provisions discussed in this section would apply with little change if a deed of trust were used in lieu of a mortgage.

There are basically three types of provisions dealing with the subject of mortgages that may be found in agreements of sale. If the property being purchased is already encumbered by a mortgage, and if the mortgage so permits, the seller and purchaser may agree to transfer the property subject to the lien of the mortgage. The effect of this is that the amount of cash that the purchaser is required to pay at the settlement will be reduced by the principal balance of the mortgage, and the purchaser will be obligated to pay off that balance over the life of the mortgage. A second alternative method of financing is for the seller to agree to accept as part of the purchase price a purchase money mortgage. A purchase money note and mortgage constitute an extension of credit by the seller to the purchaser for a portion of the purchase price. The third form of financing is for the purchaser to obtain a mortgage loan from an outside source, such as a bank, a savings and loan association, or other lending institution. These three alternatives are discussed below:

1. Purchase Subject to Existing Mortgage

As discussed in Chapter Seven, a mortgage lender ("mortgagee") who loans money to a borrower ("mortgagor") and takes a mortgage on real estate as security for the repayment of the loan, has several remedies in the event that the mortgagor defaults on the mortgage (fails to repay the loan). The mortgage lender can sell the property at what is commonly referred to as a "foreclosure sale," or "sheriff's sale," and use the proceeds of the sale to pay off the outstanding balance of the mortgage. If the proceeds of the sale are greater than the outstanding indebtedness, the difference would be paid to the mortgagor. If the proceeds of the sale are less than the outstanding indebtedness, the mortgage lender could institute a judicial proceeding to recover the difference. If successful, the mortgage lender would obtain a deficiency judgment against the mortgagor and would then be able to come against other assets of the mortgagor to satisfy the judgment.

The parties can agree, however, that the mortgage lender will look only to the property to satisfy the repayment of the indebtedness in the event of a default. This is referred to as "nonrecourse indebtedness" because the mortgage lender agrees to waive the right to a deficiency judgment and therefore its recourse against the personal assets of the mortgagor. A mortgagor who has signed a nonrecourse note and mortgage has no personal liability for the mortgage debt, and the only recourse a mortgage lender has is against the real estate.

The purchaser's liability for payment of the principal and interest owing on a mortgage that will remain on the property can be any one of three types, and it is important to state in the agreement of sale what liability, if any, the purchaser will bear with respect to the existing mortgage.

(a) No Personal Liability

If the existing mortgage is nonrecourse, the seller of the property will not be assuming any risk if he or she agrees that the purchaser will not be personally liable, either to the seller or to the mortgagee, for the payment of the mortgage debt. A sample provision for this situation is set forth below. The sample provision assumes a total purchase price of $100,000.

> The total consideration to be paid by Buyer shall be One Hundred Thousand Dollars ($100,000), payable as follows:
>
> (a) Ten Thousand Dollars ($10,000) shall be paid to the Escrowee at the signing of this agreement by Purchaser's check, receipt of which check, subject to collection, is hereby acknowledged;
>
> (b) Ninety Thousand Dollars ($90,000) shall be paid to Seller by Purchaser at settlement as follows:
>> (i) Forty Thousand Dollars ($40,000) shall be paid in cash, certified check, or check of ABC Title Insurance Company,
>> (ii) The balance, being Fifty Thousand Dollars ($50,000) shall be paid by Purchaser's accepting the Premises encumbered by the lien of a certain mortgage on the Premises granted by Seller to XYZ Bank on April 5, 1980, and recorded in Mortgage Book PHL 479, page 1024,

which, as of the date of settlement, shall have an outstanding principal balance of Fifty Thousand Dollars ($50,000). Purchaser will not indemnify Seller against such mortgage obligation nor will Purchaser assume the aforementioned mortgage.

The last sentence of clause (b)(ii) makes it clear that the purchaser will have no personal liability to either the seller or the mortgage lender. In the event that the seller is personally liable for the mortgage, this clause would prevent the mortgage lender from obtaining a deficiency judgment against the purchaser but not the seller.

(b) Purchaser Personally Liable to Seller

If the terms of the existing mortgage are such that the seller is personally liable under the mortgage in the event of a default, the seller normally will be unwilling to sell the property with the existing mortgage on it unless the seller extracts from the purchaser an agreement to indemnify the seller in the event of the purchaser's default under the mortgage. In many states all that need be done to accomplish this result is to provide in the deed that the purchaser shall take the premises "under and subject" to the mortgage. The following provision can be utilized:

> The total consideration to be paid by Buyer shall be One Hundred Thousand Dollars ($100,000) payable as follows:
>
> (a) Ten Thousand Dollars ($10,000) shall be paid to the Escrowee at the signing of this agreement by Purchaser's check, receipt of which, subject to collection, is hereby acknowledged;
>
> (b) Ninety Thousand Dollars ($90,000) shall be paid to Seller by Purchaser at settlement as follows:
>
>> (i) Forty Thousand Dollars ($40,000) shall be paid in cash, certified check, or check of ABC Title Insurance Company,
>>
>> (ii) The balance, being Fifty Thousand Dollars ($50,000), shall be paid by Purchaser accepting the Premises under and subject to a certain mortgage on the Premises granted by Seller to XYZ Bank on April 5, 1980, and recorded in Mortgage Book PHL 479, page 1024, which as of the date of settlement shall have an outstanding principal balance of Fifty Thousand Dollars ($50,000).

Use of the phrase "under and subject" to the existing mortgage does not make the purchaser personally liable to the mortgagee for such payments. The courts have construed that phrase to obligate the purchaser to indemnify the seller against any loss actually suffered by the seller. Of course, unless and until the seller suffers such a loss, the seller has no cause of action against the purchaser.

(c) Purchaser Personally Liable to Seller and Mortgagee

A seller who is personally liable for the payment of an existing mortgage debt may want more protection than a mere indemnity from the purchaser against actual loss. In some jurisdictions the seller can get this added protection by using the phrase "assumes and agrees to pay" wherever the existing mortgage is referred to. In such a case, clause (b)(ii) would read as follows:

(ii) The balance, being Fifty Thousand Dollars ($50,000), shall be paid by Purchaser's accepting the Premises under and subject to a certain mortgage on the Premises granted by Seller to XYZ Bank on April 5, 1980, and recorded in Mortgage Book PHL 479, page 1024, which Purchaser hereby assumes and agrees to pay and which as of the date of settlement said mortgage shall have an outstanding principal balance of Fifty Thousand Dollars ($50,000).

The purchaser's agreement to "assume and pay" the mortgage debt has the effect of making the purchaser personally liable for payment of the debt, regardless of whether the seller suffers any actual loss and regardless of whether the purchaser is still the owner of the property at the time the mortgage is in default. The agreement to "assume and agree to pay" has the additional effect, at least in some jurisdictions, of permitting the mortgagee to sue the purchaser directly on the note. The mortgagee does not have this right if the purchaser has only agreed to accept the premises under and subject to the mortgage.

An extremely cautious seller may not be willing to convey the property with the mortgage on it, even though the purchaser has agreed to assume and pay the mortgage debt, unless the seller has obtained from the mortgagee a release of the seller's personal liability under the mortgage. Agreements of sale for residences are seldom conditioned on the ability of the seller to obtain a release of personal liability under the mortgage, for the reason that few mortgagees are willing to grant such a release. In the absence of such a release, the seller must rely on the value of the real estate and the financial ability of the purchaser to pay off the mortgage debt as security for the mortgagee.

When an existing mortgage is to remain a lien on the property after conveyance, it is common to add to the section of the agreement of sale dealing with apportionments that interest payable on the mortgage will be apportioned between the seller and the purchaser as of the date of settlement. No such apportionment is made with respect to payments on account of principal, because the parties have presumably already considered what the amount of the unpaid balance of the mortgage would be at the time of settlement when they fixed the purchase price. If, however, settlement is not held as scheduled and the seller is thereby relieved from making a mortgage payment or is required to make an additional mortgage payment, provision should be made in the agreement of sale to either decrease or increase the amount of cash the purchaser must pay in order to complete settlement.

2. Purchase Money Mortgage from Purchaser to Seller

When a purchase money mortgage is used, the purchaser gives the seller a note, secured by a mortgage on the property, in lieu of cash for all or a portion of the purchase price. It is often advisable to agree on the terms of the note and mortgage at the time the agreement of sale is negotiated. The form of note and mortgage can then be attached to the agreement as an exhibit. If this degree of completeness is not practicable, then the essential terms of the note and mortgage should be spelled out in the agreement.

3. Mortgage Contingency

If the purchaser intends to finance part of the purchase price by obtaining a mortgage loan from someone other than the seller, the purchaser will want to be able to regain the deposit in the event that he or she is unable to obtain a mortgage on satisfactory terms and conditions. Therefore, it is important from the purchaser's standpoint that the agreement of sale contain a provision (often called a mortgage contingency clause) making the purchaser's obligations contingent on obtaining a commitment for a satisfactory mortgage. On the other hand, before the seller will agree to take the property off the market, the seller will want some assurance that the purchaser will make a good-faith effort to obtain a mortgage.

The mortgage contingency clause should state which of the two parties is obligated to attempt to obtain the mortgage. Furthermore, the provision should set forth the more important terms of the mortgage, such as the principal sum, the interest rate, the maturity date, the amount and frequency of installments, the number of points[18] to be paid, the absence of personal liability on the part of the mortgagor, if applicable, and the source of the mortgage funds, such as "any reputable bank, trust company, insurance company, or pension fund." Although the source of the funds may seem to be an immaterial fact to the purchaser, he or she has a definite interest in knowing that the lender, with whom the purchaser is likely to have a long association, is reputable and reasonable to deal with.

Often the parties provide that the purchaser will be given a fixed period of time in which to try to obtain mortgage financing, and if the purchaser is unable to obtain financing, the seller will have the opportunity for a fixed period to obtain it for the purchaser. If such a scheme is used, the agreement should spell out specific time periods during which the respective parties may act and provide for giving notice to each other not later than the end of their respective time periods as to whether they have been successful in obtaining financing.

PROBLEM

Incorporate the above comments into a mortgage contingency clause that provides that the agreement is contingent on the purchaser's obtaining

---

18. A "point" is 1% of a specific amount. Thus if a lender is charging a commitment fee of 3½ points, then the commitment fee on a $200,000 loan would be $7,000 ($200,000 × 0.035).

within forty-five days an institutional self-amortizing[19] mortgage of $80,000 at 13% interest payable monthly over a term of thirty years and having a service or commitment fee of not more than 2½%. Do not forget to provide for proper notices and for the results if the mortgage is not obtained in time.

B. FIRE OR OTHER CASUALTY AND RISK OF LOSS

As discussed in section I of this chapter, in some jurisdictions, absent an express agreement by purchaser and seller to the contrary, the purchaser has the risk of loss of the property commencing with the date of execution of the agreement of sale. As a consequence, the purchaser is deemed to have an insurable interest in the property from that date. Having an "insurable interest" means that the purchaser benefits or will benefit financially from the property and would sustain financial harm if it were destroyed. Having established an insurable interest, the purchaser may obtain an insurance policy on the property prior to settlement, even though the purchaser has not taken possession and is not yet the record owner of the property. Furthermore, if the real estate is damaged between execution of the agreement of sale and settlement, and the seller, as record owner of the property, receives proceeds as compensation for the damage, the seller must hold the proceeds in trust for the purchaser and as security for the purchaser's performance of the agreement. As a consequence, the purchaser is entitled to have the proceeds paid over to him or her at settlement.

To avoid duplication of costs, the seller and purchaser often agree between themselves that the seller will maintain his or her insurance in force until settlement. If such an arrangement is made, the agreement should require that the seller add the purchaser to the existing policy as an insured, "as his or her interest may appear," to ensure that the seller fulfills his or her obligation to pay any insurance proceeds to the purchaser. A clause similar to the following can be used:

Insurance against fire and extended coverage risks is now carried by Seller in the amount of One Hundred Thousand Dollars ($100,000). Such insurance shall be maintained by Seller, and forthwith upon the execution of this agreement all such policies shall be endorsed or amended to make the proceeds payable to Seller and Purchaser, as their interests may appear, in regard to any damage occurring between the date hereof and conveyance of the Premises to Purchaser. A certificate to that effect issued by the insurance company will be delivered to Purchaser within ten (10) days after the date hereof. This agreement will not be cancelled or affected by reason of damage or destruction due to fire or other casualty. The net proceeds of

19. Self-amortizing means that the combined installment payments of principal and interest are such that the loan will be fully repaid during the term of the loan. This is distinguishable from a negative amortization loan or a loan with a "balloon payment," both of which are discussed in Chapter Seven.

any insurance collected prior to settlement will be paid or credited to Purchaser on account of the purchase price at settlement. All unpaid claims and rights in connection with losses under any policies will be assigned to Purchaser at settlement but will not be credited to Purchaser. If this agreement is cancelled or becomes void for any reason, Purchaser hereby authorizes Seller to sign any letter or instrument or do any other thing necessary to cancel the amendment or endorsement under which Purchaser was named as a party in interest in such insurance.

If there is fire or other insured damage to the property after the purchaser has been added as a named insured, the proceeds of the insurance will be payable to both seller and purchaser. If, for some reason, settlement is not held, the seller may have a difficult time getting the purchaser to endorse the proceeds of the insurance check over to the seller. The purchaser, on the other hand, is obligated to complete settlement regardless of whether the premises have been destroyed by fire or other casualty, and some kinds of casualties, such as floods, are not covered by even an "extended coverage" insurance policy. If the purchaser is concerned about the property being damaged or destroyed by such casualties, he or she should obtain insurance coverage for these risks.

The amount of insurance carried by the seller may be substantially less than the present value of the property. This is particularly likely to be true if the seller has owned the property for a long period. If this is the case, the seller will rarely agree to increase the existing amount of insurance coverage. Thus the purchaser in this situation should obtain his or her own policy for an appropriate amount.

C. TERMITE INSPECTION AND CERTIFICATE

The purchaser of residential real estate is, of course, concerned that the house is in as good condition as it appears from visual inspection. One condition that is not always readily apparent is infestation and damage caused by termites and other wood-boring insects. The following type of provision is intended to provide the purchaser with protection in this regard:

> At settlement Seller shall, at Seller's expense, provide Purchaser with a certificate from a reputable exterminator (a) certifying that the building on the Premises is free and clear of infestation and any resulting wood damage caused by termites and other wood-boring insects, and (b) guaranteeing the same for at least one (1) year after the date of settlement. Should such infestation or damage be found, Seller, at Seller's expense, shall promptly have any infestation cured and/or repair and restore any damage caused to the Premises by termites or other wood-boring insects.

There can, of course, be many variations on this provision, including the requirement that the purchaser obtain the certificate at his or her own expense, but with the obligation of the seller to repair if damage is discovered. Another alternative would be to require the seller to repair all damage up to a certain dollar amount of damage. If the repairs would cost more than the dollar limit, the seller might retain the option of terminating the agreement rather than expending the funds to make the repairs.

D. CONDITIONS OF THE PREMISES

The purchaser may have particular concerns about other conditions, including the condition of the roof and the plumbing system, the condition of mechanical and electrical equipment such as the heating and air conditioning systems, and, in those houses that have basements, possible water leakage or excessive moisture in the basement. If the purchaser's bargaining position is strong enough, he or she may be able to get the seller to agree to a provision similar to the following:

> Seller covenants, represents, and warrants that the plumbing, heating, air conditioning, and electrical systems serving the building on the Premises are in good working order and condition and shall be in good working order and condition at the time of settlement. In the event that Seller is unable to make the foregoing warranty as of the time of settlement, Purchaser shall be entitled to an abatement of the purchase price in the amount which the parties agree is reasonably required to restore the defective equipment to good working order and condition, and in the absence of such agreement the provisions of the foregoing sentence shall survive and continue after settlement and shall not merge therein so that Purchaser shall be entitled to pursue all legal and equitable remedies available to Purchaser. Seller covenants that the Premises will, at the time of settlement, be in substantially as good condition as on the date hereof, and Seller agrees, at Seller's expense, to make any and all repairs required to maintain such condition between the date hereof and the time of settlement.

By allowing the purchaser an abatement of the purchase price equal to the amount needed to restore the defective equipment, a provision such as the one above puts the seller "on the hook" for any deficiencies in the condition of the equipment listed in the provision. A seller is therefore likely to resist such a provision and force a buyer to rely on his or her own examination of the property, and will sometimes insist that a provision be included in the agreement that negates any warranties of any kind. Such a provision is often referred to as an "as is" clause, and provides that the premises are being purchased "as is," or without any warranty, express or implied.

PROBLEM

Prepare an "as is" clause for an agreement of sale.

E. FIXTURES AND ARTICLES OF PERSONAL PROPERTY INCLUDED IN THE SALES

One of the most frequent disputes occurring at settlement between the parties to a residential real estate transaction arises as a result of verbal understandings as to what items of personal property are included in the sale. In order to eliminate or minimize these disputes, it is highly desirable that the parties reduce these understandings to writing in as much detail as possible. The following is an example of one such provision:

> All plumbing, heating, ventilating, air conditioning, mechanical, electrical, and lighting fixtures and systems appurtenant thereto and forming a part thereof, and all other fixtures of whatever nature or description now in or located on the Premises, including, without limitation, all ranges, ovens, refrigerators, sinks, tubs, toilets, garbage disposals, vanities, laundry tubs, dishwashers, TV antennas and rotors, shades, awnings, venetian blinds, couplings for automatic washers and dryers, window air-conditioners, radiator covers, cornices, kitchen cabinets, wall-to-wall carpeting in living room and front bedroom, draperies and drapery hardware, valances, door, curtain rod hardware including traverse rod hardware and fixtures, if any, screen and storm windows and doors, mailboxes, any remaining heating and cooking fuels stored on Premises, and all presently existing trees, shrubbery, and plantings (except interior plants) in or on the Premises on the date of this Agreement, unless specifically excepted herein, are included in the sale and purchase price. None of the foregoing shall be removed (or permitted to be removed) by Seller from the Premises after the date of this Agreement, and Seller hereby agrees to maintain their present condition, ordinary wear and tear excepted. If Purchaser so requests, Seller shall execute a bill of sale in form satisfactory to counsel for Purchaser, enumerating all or any part of said personal property, fixtures, and equipment to be included in the conveyance.

Items that the seller wants to remove, and that are even arguably includable among the above, should be listed with an indication that they are not included in the sale and that the seller has the right to remove them. Depending on the items and the difficulty of removal, the purchaser may want to insist on replacement of certain items (e.g., lighting fixtures) to be removed.

An example of an agreement of sale for residential property follows in *Example 3-1.*

PROBLEM

The standard form of agreement of sale for residential property set forth on the following pages is seller oriented. What modifications to this form would you make if you were representing a buyer?

Example 3-1   **Agreement of sale for residential property**

COPIES
1. White . . . . . Seller
2. Yellow . . . . . Agent
3. Pink . . . . Buyer
4. Blue . . . .Mortgagee
5. Gold . . . .
6. Green . . . . . Buyer's
copy at time of signing.

AGREEMENT FOR THE SALE OF REAL ESTATE

This form recommended and approved for, but not restricted to, use by members of the Pennsylvania Association of REALTORS®

COPYRIGHT PENNSYLVANIA ASSOCIATION OF REALTORS® 1973

—— **AGENT FOR THE SELLER** ——

S 1969A
(Rev. 1-81)
(Modified 3-84)

PA. LICENSED BROKER

This Agreement, made this........................day of .......................A.D. 19.............

1. PRINCIPALS *(1-78)* Between ....

.... (residing at

.... Zip......................) hereinafter called Seller, and

.... (residing at

....Zip......................) hereinafter called Buyer.

2. PROPERTY *(1-78)* Witnesseth: Seller hereby agrees to sell and convey to Buyer, who hereby agrees to purchase: ALL THAT CERTAIN lot or piece of ground with buildings and improvements thereon erected, if any, known as:...

....

.... in the .... of ....

County of .... State of ...., Zip ....

3. TERMS *(1-78)* (a) Purchase Price ....

.... Dollars

which shall be paid to the Seller by the Buyer as follows:

(b) Cash or check at signing this agreement: $........................

(c) Cash or check to be paid on or before:........................ 19 .... $........................

(d) .... $........................

(e) Cash or certified check at time of settlement: $........................

                    TOTAL $........................

(f) Written approval of Seller to be on or before: ....19....

(g) Settlement to be made on or before: ....19....

(h) Conveyance from Seller will be by fee simple deed of special warranty.

(i) Payment of Transfer taxes will be divided equally between Buyer and Seller.

(j) The following shall be apportioned pro-rata as of and at time of settlement: Taxes as levied and assessed, rents, interest on mortgage assumptions if any, water and or sewer rents if any, together with any other lienable municipal services.

4. MORTGAGE CONTINGENCY *(5-80)* This sale and settlement hereunder are NOT conditional or contingent in any manner upon the sale or settlement of any other real estate NOR subject to any mortgaging or financing except as hereinafter provided.

(a) Term and amount of mortgage loan required by Buyer: ....years, $........................

(b) Type mortgage and interest rate required by Buyer: Type...................................... Interest rate.................... %
HOWEVER, BUYER AGREES TO ACCEPT THE INTEREST RATE AS MAY BE COMMITTED BY THE MORTGAGE LENDER.

(c) Commitment date for approval of the mortgage:.................................... 19 ....

(d) Mortgage loan application shall be made through the office of ....
who for the purpose of negotiating for the said mortgage loan, shall be considered the agent for the Buyer, and if said mortgage loan cannot be obtained, this agreement shall be NULL AND VOID and all deposit moneys shall be returned to the Buyer on or before date for settlement as provided herein, subject however to the provisions in paragraphs #4(e) and #4(f).

(e) Buyer shall make a completed application to a responsible mortgage lending institution for the aforementioned mortgage loan, through the office of the agent named in paragraph #4(d), within ten (10) days from the Seller's approval hereof. Should the Buyer fail to make such completed application within the specified ten (10) days, it shall be at the option of the Seller, within five (5) days thereafter to:
     (1) Declare this agreement NULL AND VOID, at which time, all moneys paid on account will be forfeited to Seller as liquidated damages, or
     (2) In absence of written notice to the Buyer, by the Seller, declaring this agreement, NULL AND VOID, the condition and contingency herein provided for in paragraphs #4(a) through #4(f) together with any other mortgage loan contingencies that may be herein or endorsed hereto, shall no longer prevail, and this agreement shall remain effective according to its terms in the same manner as if the condition and contingency were not a part hereof.

(f) Seller or Agent must receive a written commitment, valid until the date of settlement, for the mortgage loan, on or before the date as specified in paragraph #4(c). If the said commitment is not furnished with the terms as specified herein, or on other terms accepted in writing by the Buyer, on or before the specified date, Seller shall have the option, at that date, or any other time thereafter, during the term of this agreement, until, but not beyond the date of receipt of the commitment by the Seller, or Agent, to declare this agreement NULL AND VOID, by written notice to the Buyer of his decision to cancel, at which time all deposit moneys paid on account shall be returned to the Buyer, subject to the payments required, if any, provided for in paragraph #7(b), 1, 2 and 3.

(g) Seller hereby agrees to permit inspections by authorized appraisers, reputable certifiers and/or Buyer as may be required by the lending institution or insuring agencies.

5. SPECIAL CLAUSES

6. ASSESSMENTS *(3-70)* Seller covenants and represents as of the approval date of this agreement of sale, that no assessments for public improvements have been made against the premises which remain unpaid and that no notice by any governmental or other public authority has been served upon the Seller or anyone on the Seller's behalf, including notices relating to violations of housing, building, safety or fire ordinances which remain uncorrected unless otherwise specified herein. Buyer will be responsible for any notices served upon the Seller after the approval date of this agreement and for the payment of any assessments and charges hereafter made for any public improvements, if work in connection therewith is hereafter begun in or about said premises and adjacent thereto. Seller will be responsible for any such improvements, assessments or notices received prior to the date of this agreement, unless the improvements consist of sewer or water lines not in use on or prior to the date of approval hereof.

7. TITLE & COSTS *(1-78)*

(a) The premises are to be conveyed free and clear of all liens, encumbrances, and easements, EXCEPTING HOWEVER, the following: Mortgage encumbrances, as aforementioned, if any; existing building restrictions, ordinances, easements of roads, privileges or rights of public service companies, if any; agreements or like matters of record or easements or restrictions visible upon the ground, otherwise the title to the above described real estate shall be good and marketable or such as will be insured by a reputable Title Insurance Company at the regular rates.

(b) The Buyer will pay for the following:
     (1) The premium for mechanics lien insurance and/or title search, or fee for cancellation of same, if any.
     (2) The premiums for flood insurance and/or fire insurance with extended coverage, insurance binder charges or cancellation fee, if any.
     (3) Appraisal fees and charges paid in advance to mortgagee if any.
     (4) Buyer's normal settlement costs and accruals.

(c) Any survey or surveys which may be required by the Title Insurance Company or the abstracting attorney, for the preparation of an adequate legal description of the premises (or the correction thereof), shall be secured and paid for by the Seller. However, any survey or surveys desired by the Buyer or required by his mortgagee shall be secured and paid for by the Buyer.

(d) In the event the Seller is unable to give a good and marketable title or such as will be insured by a reputable Title Company, subject to aforesaid, Buyer shall have the option of taking such title as the Seller can give without abatement of price or of being repaid all monies paid by Buyer to the Seller on account of the purchase price and the Seller will reimburse the Buyer for any costs incurred by the Buyer for those items specified in paragraph 7(b) items (1), (2), (3), and in paragraph 7(c); and in the latter event there shall be no further liability or obligation on either of the parties hereto and this agreement shall become NULL AND VOID and all copies will be returned to Seller's agent for cancellation.

8. **FIXTURES, TREES, SHRUBBERY, ETC. (1-81)** All existing plumbing, heating and lighting fixtures (including chandeliers) and systems appurtenant thereto and forming a part thereof, and other permanent fixtures, as well as all ranges, laundry tubs, T.V. antennas, masts and rotor systems, together with wall to wall carpeting, screens, storm sash and/or doors, shades, awnings, venetian blinds, couplings for automatic washers and dryers, etc., radiator covers, cornices, kitchen cabinets, drapery rods, drapery rod hardware, curtain rods, curtain rod hardware, all trees, shrubbery, plantings now in or on property, if any, unless specifically excepted in this agreement, are included in the sale and purchase price. None of the above mentioned items shall be removed by the Seller from premises after date of this agreement. Any remaining heating and/or cooking fuels stored on the premises at time of settlement are also included under this agreement. Seller hereby warrants that he will deliver good title to all of the articles described in this paragraph, and any other fixtures or items of personalty specifically scheduled and to be included in this sale.

9. **PAYMENT OF DEPOSIT (1-81)** Deposits or hand monies shall be paid to agent for Seller, who shall retain the same until consummation or termination of this agreement in conformity with all applicable laws and regulations. Agent for the Seller may, at his sole option, hold any uncashed check tendered as deposit or hand monies, pending the acceptance of this offer.

10. **POSSESSION AND TENDER** (1-77)

  (a) Possession is to be delivered by deed, keys and physical possession to a vacant building (if any) at day and time of settlement, or by deed and assignment of existing lease(s) at time of settlement if premises is tenant occupied at the signing of this agreement, unless otherwise specified herein. Buyer will acknowledge existing lease(s) by initialing said lease(s) at time of signing this agreement of sale if tenant occupied.

  (b) Seller will not enter into any new leases, written extension of existing leases, if any, or additional leases for the premises without expressed written consent of the Buyer.

  (c) Formal tender of an executed deed and purchase money is hereby waived.

  (d) Buyer reserves the right to make a pre-settlement inspection of the subject premises.

11. **RISK OF LOSS** (5-73) Any loss or damage to the property caused by fire, or loss commonly covered by the extended coverage endorsements of reputable insurance companies between the date of this Agreement and the time of settlement, shall not, in any way, void or impair any of the conditions or obligations hereof unless the required mortgaging or financing, as specified herein, cannot be obtained because of such loss or damage. Seller shall maintain existing fire and extended coverage or homeowners' type insurance policies, if any, until the time of final settlement. Buyer is hereby notified that it is his responsibility to insure his interest in the said premises at his own cost and expense. Seller shall maintain the property (including all items mentioned in paragraph #8 herein) and any personal property specifically scheduled herein in its present condition, normal wear and tear excepted.

12. **REPRESENTATIONS** (2-69) It is understood that Buyer has inspected the property, or hereby waives the right to do so and he has agreed to purchase it as a result of such inspection and not because of or in reliance upon any representation made by the Seller or any other officer, partner or employee of Seller, or by the agent of the Seller or any of the latter's salesmen and employees, or by a cooperating Broker, if any, or any of his salesmen and employees and that he has agreed to purchase it in its present condition unless otherwise specified herein. It is further understood that this agreement contains the whole agreement between the Seller and the Buyer and there are no other terms, obligations, covenants, representations, statements or conditions, oral or otherwise of any kind whatsoever concerning this sale. Furthermore, this agreement shall not be altered, amended, changed or modified except in writing executed by the parties hereto.

13. **RECORDING** This agreement shall not be recorded in the Office for the Recording of Deeds or in any other office or place of public record and if Buyer shall record this agreement or cause or permit the same to be recorded, Seller may, at his option, elect to treat such act as a breach of this agreement.

14. **ASSIGNMENT** This agreement shall be binding upon the respective heirs, executors, administrators, successors and, to the extent assignable, on the assigns of the parties hereto, it being expressly understood, however, that the Buyer shall not transfer or assign this agreement without the written consent of the Seller being first had and obtained.

15. **AGENT** It is expressly understood and agreed between the parties hereto that the herein named agent, his salesmen and employees or any officer or partner of agent and any cooperating broker and his salesmen and employees and any officer or partner of the cooperating broker are acting as agent only and will in no case whatsoever be held liable either jointly or severally to either party for the performance of any term or covenant of this agreement or for damages for the nonperformance thereof.

16. **DEFAULT** (1-79) The said time for settlement and all other times referred to for the performance of any of the obligations of this agreement are hereby agreed to be of the essence of this agreement. Should the Buyer:

  (a) Fail to make any additional payments as specified in paragraph #3,

  (b) Furnish false or incomplete information to the Seller, the Seller's agent, or the mortgage lender, concerning the Buyer's legal or financial status, or fail to cooperate in the processing of the mortgage loan application, which acts would result in the failure to obtain the approval of a mortgage loan commitment, or

  (c) Violate or fail to fulfill and perform any of the terms or conditions of this agreement,

then in such case, all deposit money and other sums paid by the Buyer on account of the purchase price, whether required by this agreement or not, may be (1) Retained by the Seller on account of the purchase, or

  (2) As moneys to be applied to the Seller's damages, or

  (3) As liquidated damages for such breach,

as the Seller may elect, and in the event that the Seller elects to retain the moneys as liquidated damages in accordance with paragraph #16 (3), the Seller shall be released from all liability or obligations and this agreement shall be NULL AND VOID and all copies will be returned to the Seller's agent for cancellattion.

APPROVAL BY BUYER

IN WITNESS WHEREOF, the parties hereto, intending to be legally bound hereby, have hereunder set their hands and seals the day and year first above written.

BUYER ....(SEAL)

WITNESS AS TO BUYER ....

BUYER ....(SEAL)

WITNESS AS TO BUYER ....

BUYER ....(SEAL)

APPROVAL BY SELLER

Seller hereby approves the above contract this .... day of .... A.D. 19........ and in consideration of the services rendered in procuring the Buyer, Seller agrees to pay to the named Agent a commission of .... of the herein specified sale price. In the event Buyer defaults hereunder, any monies paid on account shall be equally divided between Seller and Agent, but in no event will the sum paid to the agent be in excess of the above specified commission.

WITNESS AS TO SELLER ....

SELLER ....(SEAL)

WITNESS AS TO SELLER ....

SELLER ....(SEAL)

SELLER ....(SEAL)

AGENT BY: ....(SEAL)

TO: ....(Agent) Date ....19............

In conjunction with the purchase of the premises described in the agreement of sale attached hereto, I/We hereby authorize your firm to perform the services as indicated below by my/our initials.

A. Order Title insurance in any reputable title insurance company ....(INITIALS)

B. Order insurance in the amount of $ .... ☐ Homeowners ☐ Fire & Extended Coverage ☐ Flood ....(INITIALS)

C. ....(INITIALS)

IV. TYPICAL ADDITIONAL PROVISIONS OF AGREEMENTS OF SALE FOR NEWLY CONSTRUCTED SINGLE-FAMILY RESIDENCES

An agreement of sale for residential real estate entered into at a time when the house is not yet completed is substantially the same as that for completed homes. However, certain additional provisions must be added, especially provisions describing the obligations of the seller as the builder.

This section deals with some additional agreement of sale provisions relating to the construction of new homes.

Often in the purchase of newly constructed or under-construction housing, especially when the house being purchased is part of a larger development, the purchaser is handed a printed agreement of sale prepared by the seller. The agreement is likely to be extremely favorable to the seller. Depending on the relative bargaining power of the two parties, changes can sometimes be made to these agreements that make them less biased in favor of one party or the other.

A. ADDITIONAL PROTECTION THAT THE BUYER REQUIRES WHEN PURCHASING A NEWLY COMPLETED RESIDENCE

1. Description of Property

It is important for the purchaser of a new-construction residence that the agreement of sale require the seller to produce at or prior to settlement an "as built" survey plan of the premises prepared after all construction has been completed. Such a survey will show (a) any encroachments of the buildings and other improvements on a neighbor's land or encroachments by a neighbor's buildings on the land being sold, (b) possible easements and other physical conditions that the surveyor has observed, (c) the exact location and dimension of the buildings, (d) the location of buildings and improvements with respect to setback and side yard and rear yard restrictions, (e) party walls and openings therein, (f) the boundaries including adjoining properties and streets, (g) the courses and distances of the boundaries, and (h) the locations of markers on the boundaries, if any.

2. Warranties from Seller Relating to the Premises Themselves

(a) Subdivision Approval

The seller might be requested to warrant that the house was erected in compliance with the zoning requirements and that all necessary subdivision approvals, building permits, and certificates of occupancy have been obtained. If new streets have been opened, the seller should be required to warrant that the streets have all been completed or that a bond to ensure completion of such streets has been posted with the local government. The seller should also covenant to dedicate the streets and maintain them until such dedication has been accepted by the local municipality.

(b) Water and Sewer Hooked-Up

The seller should identify the source of the fresh water supply to the premises and warrant that such water service has been installed, connected, and fully paid for by the seller, and that the water is potable. Similarly, if applicable, the seller should warrant that the premises are served by a sanitary sewer system that has been installed and connected and that all charges in connection with the system have been paid by the seller.

(c) Mechanics' Liens

Most state legislatures have created statutory remedies for unpaid contractors or material suppliers in connection with any kind of real estate development and construction. The remedies vary from state to state but are commonly referred to as mechanics' liens. These statutes permit a lien to be filed on the property and in many states such mechanics' liens are granted a priority based on the date of the visible commencement of any work on the property, rather than the date of filing of the lien. The effect of this priority is that a grantee taking title prior to the filing of a mechanics' lien could find at a later time that the property is subject to mechanics' liens filed by contractors who had performed work for the grantor. A purchaser should require the seller to include in the agreement of sale a warranty that at the settlement the seller will have paid all monies due the general contractor and all subcontractors and material suppliers. The condition-of-title clause should make it clear that the title delivered by the seller must be free and clear of all mechanics' and material suppliers' liens.

By the same statutory priority, a mechanics' lien might become superior to a mortgage. Consequently, many mortgage lenders will insist on having a mortgagee's title policy issued without an objection relating to mechanics' liens. Title insurers will often remove the objection for mechanics' liens on payment of an additional premium. Because the purchaser usually pays for all title insurance, including that for the mortgagee, if the seller is to pay any additional premium for mechanics' lien insurance, this obligation should be specifically set forth in the agreement of sale. In addition, the title company may require some form of assurance from the builder that all contractors and material suppliers have been paid or have waived their right to file a lien.

3. Warranties from Seller with Respect to Construction and Equipment

The purchaser would like to obtain from the seller as many warranties as possible, which may include a one-year guarantee by the seller against defects in workmanship and material and an assignment of all manufacturer's warranties on equipment. Some builders include in their agreements of sale warranties of the kind described above, and some provide their standard warranty booklet at settlement. The entire area of new-home warranties is undergoing change, coming in part from the courts, which have sometimes held builders to have made implied warranties. Additionally, passage of the Magnuson-Moss Act regarding consumer warranties and the development of group warranty plans, such as the current Home Owners Warranty plan developed by the National Association of Home Builders, have created impetus for change. Care should be taken in reviewing warranties proposed by a seller, because they often attempt to limit the obligations of the seller that would otherwise be imposed under state law.

4. Uncompleted Items

If, at the time the agreement of sale is executed, the house has not been fully completed, it is desirable from the purchaser's standpoint to attach to the agreement of sale a list of all uncompleted work that is to be done by the seller prior to settlement. The agreement should specify that it will be a condition precedent[20] to the purchaser's obligation to complete settlement that the specified work has been completed. The purchaser should not sign any instruments certifying that the work has been completed until an inspection of the property has been made that verifies the completion, and the agreement should provide for a pre-settlement inspection by the purchaser accompanied by an agent of the seller authorized to sign a "punch list" of items that remain to be completed and corrected after settlement. The punch list should contain appropriate time limits and remedies.

An agreement of sale for a newly completed residence follows in *Example 3-2*.

Example 3-2:   **Agreement of sale for a newly completed residence**

AGREEMENT FOR THE SALE OF REAL ESTATE

THIS AGREEMENT FOR THE SALE OF REAL ESTATE (the "Agreement") is made this   day of July, 1986 between Smith Development Co., Inc., ("Seller"), and William White and Brenda White, husband and wife, (together, "Buyer"),
WITNESSETH:

PROPERTY AND TERMS   1. Seller hereby agrees to sell and convey to Buyer, who hereby agrees to purchase, ALL THAT CERTAIN lot or piece of ground, together with improvements and buildings thereon erected situate, known and numbered as 781 Smith Terrace, Upper Merion Township, Montgomery County, Pa., according to a plan made for Smith Development Co. by Jones Engineering Co., dated May 15, 1985, together with a building completed thereon in a good and workmanlike manner. Being all the real property owned by Seller at such location, and which shall be more fully described in the legal description which is to be contained in a Deed which will be executed and delivered from Seller to Buyer at time of Final Settlement, and containing

20. When an agreement is contingent upon the satisfaction of a particular item, then that item is a condition precedent to the obligations of the parties under the agreement; that is, the satisfaction of the condition must occur before (precede) the settlement under the agreement. This is to be distinguished from conditions subsequent, which indicate that the status of the parties, having been settled by a closing, may be altered if something occurs at a later time (subsequently).

0.509 acres (the "Premises"), for the sum of Seventy-four Thousand Five Hundred Forty-five Dollars ($74,545.00) which shall be paid to Seller by Buyer as follows:

Cash at the signing of this Agreement	$ 1,000.00
Cash to be paid on or before July 30, 1986	$ 6,454.50
Cash at Settlement	$67,090.50
TOTAL	$74,545.00

SETTLEMENT　　2. Settlement shall be made on September 30, 1986. The said time for settlement and all other times referred to for the performance of any of the obligations of this Agreement are hereby agreed to be of the essence of this Agreement.

TITLE　　3. The Premises are to be conveyed free and clear of all liens, encumbrances, restrictions, easements, and other matters of record, EXCEPTING, HOWEVER, the following: existing building restrictions, ordinances, easements of roads, privileges or rights of public service companies, if any; or easements or restrictions visible upon the ground, otherwise the title to the Premises shall be good and marketable and such as will be insured by any reputable title insurance company at the regular rates. See Rider Section M.

In the event that Seller is unable to give a good and marketable title and such as will be insured by any reputable title company, subject as aforesaid, Buyer shall have the option of taking such title as Seller can give without an abatement of the purchase price, or of being repaid all monies paid by Buyer and held in escrow on account of the purchase price together with such title company charges as Buyer may have incurred; and in the latter event there shall be no further liability or obligation on either of the parties hereto and this Agreement shall become null and void.

If any surveys are necessary or desired, they shall be secured and paid for by Buyer. Seller shall provide stakes at all corners of the property.

Seller covenants and represents as of the approval date of this Agreement, that no assessments for public improvements have been made against the Premises which remain unpaid and that no notice by any governmental or other public authority has been served upon Seller or anyone on Seller's behalf, including notices relating to violations of housing, building, safety, or fire ordinances which remain uncorrected unless otherwise specified herein. Buyer will be responsible for any notices served upon Seller after the approval date of this Agreement and for the payment of any assessments and charges hereafter made for any public improvements, if work in connection therewith is hereafter begun in or about Premises or adjacent thereto. Seller will be responsible for any such improvements, assessments, or notices received prior to the date of this Agreement, unless the improvements consist of sewer or water lines not in use on or prior to the date of approval hereof, provided settlement shall be completed hereunder.

POSSESSION　　4. Possession is to be delivered by special warranty deed, keys, and physical possession at day and time of settlement, and the Premises will be vacant, unoccupied, and in broom-clean condition.

TAXES AND ADJUSTMENTS　　5. All apportionable debits and credits, including taxes, rents, interest on encumbrance (if any), and sewer rent (if any) for the current term shall be calculated as levied and pro-rated as of date of settlement. (School taxes are levied on a fiscal year basis; Township and County taxes are levied on a calendar year basis.) All real estate transfer taxes imposed by any governmental authority shall be divided equally between Buyer and Seller.

Continued.

Example 3–2 **Agreement of sale** *continued*

TENDER

6. Formal tender of an executed deed and purchase money is hereby waived.

PAYMENT OF DEPOSIT

7. Deposit or hand monies shall be paid to Seller who shall retain the same in escrow until consummation or termination of this Agreement as required in accordance with the Act of Assembly of Pennsylvania of July 9, 1957, Public Law 608, Section 4.

FIXTURES, TREES, SHRUBBERY, ETC.

8. All plumbing, heating, and lighting fixtures and systems appurtenant thereto, and forming a part thereof, as well as all ranges, laundry tubs, dishwashers, disposals, TV antennas, mailboxes, door knockers, and other permanent fixtures, together with screens, storm sash and doors, shades, awnings, venetian blinds, valances, curtain rods, drapery rods, or traverse rods, radiator covers, and all trees, shrubbery, and plantings now in or on the Premises, unless specifically excepted in this Agreement, are to become the property of Buyer and are included in the purchase price. None of the above-mentioned items shall be removed by Seller from the Premises after the date of this Agreement. Seller hereby warrants that Seller has good legal title free and clear of any claim and encumbrance to all the articles described in this paragraph. It is further agreed that all fuel oil remaining in the tank at final settlement shall become the property of Buyer and is included in the purchase price.

Seller agrees to remove all rubbish and debris from the Premises and garage and leave broom-clean prior to settlement, or to accept the liability for its removal.

INSURANCE

9. Any loss or damage to the property caused by fire, or loss commonly covered by the extended coverage endorsement of reputable insurance companies between the date of this Agreement and the time of settlement shall not in any way void or impair any of the conditions and obligations hereof. It is Buyer's responsibility, at Buyer's own cost and expense, to carry such insurance on the Premises as he or she may deem desirable.

DEFAULT

10. Should Buyer fail to make any additional payments as specified in Paragraph 1 hereof, or violate or fail to fulfill and perform any of the terms or conditions of this Agreement, then and in that case all deposits and other sums paid by Buyer on account of the purchase price, whether required by this Agreement or not, may be retained by Seller, as liquidated damages for such breach, and Seller and Buyer shall be released from all liability or obligation and this Agreement shall become null and void. The foregoing shall be Seller's sole remedy.

REPRESENTATIONS

11. It is understood that Buyer has inspected the Premises and that Buyer has agreed to purchase it as a result of such inspection and not because of or in reliance upon any representation made by Seller or by any agent of Seller and that Buyer has agreed to purchase it in its present condition unless otherwise specified herein. It is further understood that Seller agrees to maintain the grounds and the improvements and buildings thereon in the same condition as prevails at the time of the signing of this Agreement. This Agreement contains the whole agreement between Seller and Buyer and there are no other terms, obligations, covenants, representations, statements, or conditions, oral or otherwise, of any kind whatsoever concerning this sale. Any changes or additions to this Agreement must be made in writing and executed by the parties hereto.

RECORDING   12. This Agreement shall not be recorded in the Office for the Recording of Deeds or in any other office or place of public record, and if Buyer shall record this Agreement or cause or permit the same to be recorded, Seller may, at Seller's option, elect to treat such Act as a breach of this Agreement.

ASSIGNMENT   13. This Agreement shall be binding upon the respective heirs, executors, administrators, successors, and, to the extent assignable, on the assigns of the parties hereto, it being expressly understood, however, that Buyer shall not transfer or assign this Agreement without the written consent of Seller being first obtained. This Agreement is to be construed and interpreted in accordance with the laws of the Commonwealth of Pennsylvania.

14. Buyer and Seller each hereby represents to the other that neither has dealt with any broker other than _____. It is expressly understood and agreed between the parties hereto that such broker is (are) acting as agent(s) only and will in no case whatsoever be held liable to either party for the performance of any terms or covenants of this Agreement or for damages for the nonperformance thereof. Seller agrees to pay to such agent(s) a real estate commission in the amount of $_____ for services rendered.

DESCRIPTIVE CAPTIONS   15. The descriptive captions used herein are for convenience of reference only and they shall have no effect whatsoever in determining the rights or obligations of the parties.

16. See Mortgage Contingency Addendum attached and made a part hereof.

17. See Description of Materials and Specifications Addendum attached and made part hereof.

18. See Rider attached hereto and made a part hereof containing Sections A through L.

IN WITNESS WHEREOF, the individual parties hereto have hereunto set their hands and seals, and the corporate parties hereto have caused these presents to be executed and their corporate seal to be attached by their proper officers thereunto duly authorized, the date first above written.

Attest: SELLER
                            SMITH DEVELOPMENT CO., INC.

_____   By: _____
                Secretary   President
[Corporate Seal]

Witnesses: BUYER

_____   _____ [Seal]
                             William White

_____   _____ [Seal]
                             Brenda White

MORTGAGE CONTINGENCY

1. It is mutually understood and agreed that, within five (5) days from the date hereof, Buyer will prepare and file an application with any repu-

Example 3–2 **Agreement of sale** *continued*

table lending institution for a direct reduction first mortgage loan to be secured upon the property in the amount of $85,000.00 for a term of not less than 30 years at an interest rate not to exceed prevailing rate to enable Buyer to finance the purchase of the Premises.

2. Should Buyer be unable to obtain a written commitment for a mortgage loan on the terms set forth above, Buyer shall advise Seller in writing, by certified mail on or before August 23, 1986, of such condition and Seller shall thereupon have twenty (20) days from date of receipt of such notice within which to obtain such a mortgage commitment for and on behalf of Buyer. Buyer agrees to execute any reasonable and customary application at Seller's request and Buyer agrees to pay a service charge not in excess of 1% of the loan amount plus $75.00 to the lender.

3. If Buyer fails to make application for such mortgage loan or to notify Seller of their inability to obtain a written commitment as herein set forth or fails to execute any application for such mortgage loan at Seller's request, the condition and contingency provided for shall no longer prevail and this Agreement shall be and remain in full force and effect according to its terms in the same manner as if the condition and contingency were not a part hereof.

4. Should neither Buyer nor Seller be able to obtain such a mortgage commitment on the terms set forth above within the above-referred period, Buyer, at Buyer's election, may (a) proceed with consummation of this contract without regard to the failure of the condition, or (b) cancel this Agreement, in which event all monies paid hereunder by Buyer on account of the purchase price will be returned to Buyer upon receipt by Seller of (1) Buyer's written notice of intention to cancel, and (2) return to Seller of all copies of this Agreement in Buyer's possession. Thereafter, all rights and liabilities of these parties shall cease and determine, anything herein contained to the contrary notwithstanding. Buyer shall notify Seller in writing by certified mail of Buyer's election under (a) or (b) within three (3) days after being notified by Seller that a mortgage loan commitment was not obtained. In the event that Buyer fails to notify Seller of their election to cancel the contract under (b) above within the prescribed time limit, Buyer shall be obligated to proceed with consummation of the Agreement.

Attest:

SELLER
SMITH DEVELOPMENT CO., INC.

_____
                     Secretary

By: _____
                     President

[Corporate Seal]

Witnesses:

BUYER

_____

_____ [Seal]
William White

_____ [Seal]
Brenda White

UPPER MERION TWP., MONTGOMERY CO., PA

DESCRIPTION OF MATERIALS AND SPECIFICATIONS

1. CHIMNEYS—Material—Brick; Flue lining—terra cotta; Heater flue size 8½ × 8½.
2. SIDING—⅝" Texture III, stained at factory, Olympic stain Color #718.
3. FIREPLACES—Fireplace flue, size 9 × 12; Brick, full wall, raised hearth with 2" × 8" wood mantel.
4. FLOORS—Basement floor: concrete slab, mix 1–2–4 3" thick; Garage: concrete slab, mix 1–2–4 4" thick; Finished floor: center hall, living room, dining room, family room, all bedrooms and center hall upstairs and closets will be ⁵⁄₁₆ hardwood floors, #2 oak 2"-width resin, top nailed paper, filled and sanded, finished natural throughout with 2 coats of shellac.
5. GUTTERS & DOWNSPOUTS—Aluminum 4" (white) Gutter; Aluminum 3" (white) Downspout; 1' × 2' splash block.
6. INTERIOR WALLS—½" drywall, joint treatment taped; 2 coats white latex (prime & finish); 2 coats white latex enamel (prime & finish) on interior trim and windows.
7. DOORS—type: Hollow core mahogany 1¾", finished natural throughout, Main entrance door—1¾" × 36" wood (frame wood); other entrance doors, wood 2' 8" wide. Attic louvered, aluminum 14" × 18".
8. WINDOWS—Anderson casement style. Storm panels & screens available at extra cost.
9. CABINETS & INTERIOR DETAIL—Kitchen cabinets & wall units by Triangle Pacific Liberty style. Approximately 13 cabinets. Counter top—Spanish Oak #344, Wilson Art Series.
10. STAIRS—Basement & main—wood 1" thick, strings 2 × 10, handrail 2 × 3.
11. SPECIAL FLOORS—2nd floor bathrooms: Hall bath—ceramic in wet bed (floor only); Master bedroom bath—ceramic in wet bed (floor only). Ceramic tile to be chosen at John Trevisan, 390 E. Pembroke Ave., E. Lansdowne, Pa., 626–6793. Kitchen and laundry rooms ¹⁄₁₆" vinyl asbestos to be chosen at Fred Callaghan's, 555 Abbott Dr., Broomall, Pa., 544–2644.
12. PLUMBING—Hall bathroom: Fixtures will be Kohler Wellworth—water closet #K3510, color Cerulean Blue, tub #K715 Villager, color Cerulean Blue. Master bedroom bath: Fixtures will be Kohler, water closet #K3510, color Mexican Sand. Powder room: Fixture will be Kohler: water closet #K3510, color Fresh Green. Total extra cost for Kohler fixtures will be $310.00. 80-gallon electric hot water heater, Bradford glass-lined or equal. House drain: inside, copper; outside, cast iron.
13. HEATING—Bryant 85,000 furnace, model #390A048125; air conditioner: 3-ton Bryant or equal, same quality as heat model.
14. ELECTRIC—Service: overhead circuit breaker, 200 amp service. Wiring: nonmetallic cable. Special outlet: range, dryer, and heating system. Door bell: push bell, location—front door.
15. LIGHTING FIXTURES—$75.00 allowance at builder's supplier—David Tori, 60 Old State Road, Media, Pa., 566–1972.
16. INSULATION—Ceiling, 6" blown fiberglass; Walls, 3" batts, exterior walls only.

Example 3–2 **Agreement of sale** *continued*

17. APPLIANCES—GE J767 Americana Double-Oven Range vented or equal $525.00 extra, color Avocado. Dishwasher—GE #SD281, 2-cycle sound-insulated or equal, color Avocado. Disposal—GE–FC110 or equal.
18. GARAGE DOOR—7 × 16 wood composition, installed by Buranich.
19. VANITIES—Two 30 × 22 Bellwood vanities to be selected from Knock on Wood, 3721 West Chester Pike, Newtown Square, Pa., 353–3333.
20. FINISH GRADE & SEED—All disturbed ground and planting of 6 shrubs.
21. DRIVEWAY—Asphalt—9′ entrance, 2-car width in front of garage. Concrete walk from drive to entrance.
22. Deck in rear of house to be extended to 10′ width at extra charge of $610.00. See Rider Section G.
23. Wood handrail installed on hall stairs in lieu of wrought iron.
24. Seller shall transfer, assign, and deliver to Buyer at settlement all warranties and guarantees that Seller has received or may then have received and/or which may thereafter be received.
25. Seller shall furnish at its sole cost and expense the labor, materials, and equipment required to make repairs and to correct any and all poor workmanship or defective materials installed in or on the property, for a period of one year following settlement. Seller shall not be responsible for normal wear and tear or repairs made necessary by the negligence on part of Buyer. See Rider Section C.
26. Seller is not responsible for shrinkage of lumber, trim, millwork, and hardwood floors or the results thereof including drywall cracks, which are normal in new-house construction. Buyer understands and is aware that shrinkage and results thereof may not be an indication of poor workmanship or defective materials, and Buyer understands that the repairs thereof may be maintenance and therefore the responsibility of Buyer. However, Seller agrees to repair at its own expense in the one-year warranty period all nail pops, cracked seams, and swollen or shrunken doors.
27. Buyer and their authorized representatives have the right of continuing inspection after reasonable notice.
28. Seller is given the option, at Seller's discretion, to make substitutions of material of equal or better quality and structural strength whenever Seller shall find it necessary or expedient to do so. It is understood that no changes in construction or in completion ordered by Buyer will be made unless authorized in writing by Buyer at a cost agreed upon and approved by Seller in writing. The cost of any such changes requested by Buyer and so approved by Seller shall be added to the total cost named herein and will be paid in cash by Buyer prior to the commencement of such changes. Seller may, at Seller's option, require additional deposit money to be paid under this Agreement in the event that Seller agrees to any such changes in construction requested by Buyer.
29. Seller extends new home guarantee by Home Owners Warranty Corp. to Buyer at time of final settlement.

SELLER _____   BUYER _____

RIDER TO AGREEMENT OF SALE ("AGREEMENT") BETWEEN SMITH DEVELOPMENT CO., INC. ("SELLER") AND WILLIAM WHITE AND BRENDA WHITE, HUSBAND AND WIFE ("BUYER") PREMISES: 781 SMITH TERRACE, GULPH MILLS, UPPER MERION TOWNSHIP

A. Seller represents and warrants that all construction has been or will have been performed in compliance with, and that the completed Premises are or will, at settlement, be in compliance with all applicable zoning ordinances, building codes, and other governmental requirements. Seller will obtain and deliver to Buyer at settlement all necessary governmental permits or certificates of occupancy.

B. Seller shall, prior to the date of settlement, complete the Premises in all respects in accordance with the Description of Materials and Specifications attached. In the event that any substitutions of material shall be deemed necessary or expedient by Seller, as provided in Section 28 of the Description of Materials and Specifications, said substitutions shall be of equal or better quality to those materials set forth on said Description of Materials and Specifications. Seller shall give Buyer at least three (3) days prior notice of any substitutions which are contemplated. In the event that the Premises shall not be completed prior to the date scheduled for settlement hereunder, Buyer shall have the right to extend such date for an additional thirty (30) day period.

C. Seller shall and does hereby unconditionally guarantee the work and materials and equipment furnished hereunder against defects in materials and workmanship for a period of one (1) year from the date of settlement. Seller shall, within a reasonable time after receipt of notice thereof, correct any defects in materials, equipment, and workmanship which may develop within such period for which said materials, equipment, and workmanship are guaranteed and also correct, at Seller's expense, any damage to other work caused by the repairing of such defects.

D. In addition to all of the guarantees referred to herein, Seller shall deliver to Buyer, at settlement, all guaranties extended by manufacturers or suppliers, including, without limitation, heating and air-conditioning equipment, appliances, roofing shingles, and hot water heater.

E. Seller represents and warrants, on the date hereof and on the date of settlement, that all utilities and street improvements (including streets, curbs, sidewalks, water and sewer lines) and all other installations at or abutting the Premises have been completed and paid for by Seller.

F. In the event that the Premises are substantially damaged or destroyed prior to settlement, Buyer shall have the option, exercisable by notice in writing to Seller, of terminating this Agreement. In the event of such termination, all deposit money paid by Buyer pursuant to this Agreement shall be returned to Buyer and neither party shall have any further liability hereunder.

Continued.

Example 3–2 **Agreement of sale** *continued*

Seller shall maintain full fire and extended coverage insurance for the Premises up to the date of settlement and shall make the proceeds of any such insurance available to Buyer in the event of loss or damage to the Premises, provided that Buyer shall not have elected to terminate this Agreement as provided in the first paragraph of this Section G.

G. The deck to be constructed in the rear of the house as specified in Section 22 of the Description of Materials and Specifications shall be _____ feet in length.

H Seller shall, prior to settlement hereunder, install a fence across the entire rear of the premises at such location as shall be designated by Buyer, which fence shall be of the following material _____ .

I. At settlement, Seller shall provide Buyer with a certification and an assignable one (1) year service warranty from a reputable exterminating company certifying that there is no infestation by wood-destroying or wood-boring insects (including termites) and that there is no uncorrected damage from prior infestation, if any.

J. In the event of any conflict or inconsistency between this Rider and the printed portion of this Agreement, the provisions of this Rider shall be controlling.

K. All provisions, agreements, representations, and warranties hereof shall survive settlement hereunder.

L. Seller shall provide Buyer and Buyer's mortgagee with mechanics' liens insurance from Gulph Title Insurance Company, insuring against mechanics' liens and the possibility thereof.

Attest: SELLER
                                                 SMITH DEVELOPMENT CO., INC.

_____   By: _____
                    Secretary   President
[Corporate Seal]

Witnesses: BUYER

_____   _____ [Seal]
                                                 William White
_____   _____ [Seal]
                                                 Brenda White

B. ADDITIONAL PROVISIONS TO PROTECT THE PURCHASER OF RESIDENCES TO BE CONSTRUCTED OR IN THE PROCESS OF CONSTRUCTION AT THE TIME THE AGREEMENT OF SALE IS EXECUTED

In addition to the provisions discussed in the preceding section with respect to the purchase of recently completed residential real estate, there are several types of provisions that should be added to an agreement of sale in order to protect a purchaser of a residence that is to be constructed or is in the process of construction.

1. Description

In the portion of the agreement dealing with the description of the property, the land should be identified either by legal description, by lot identification on a filed subdivision plan or on a survey plan, or by reference to the lot's area, front footage (length of the side of the property abutting a street), and its location with respect to streets and other lots. The buildings and improvements should be described not merely by reference to a particular model house, but rather to a specific set of plans and specifications showing all the details of construction.

2. Deposit

To protect against the loss of the deposit money in the eventuality that the builder becomes bankrupt or insolvent during the course of construction of the building, it is important to the purchaser that the deposit be placed in escrow with a reputable real estate broker, attorney, or title company, rather than paid directly to the seller.

3. Settlement Date

Because of the vagaries of the construction business, sellers of homes to be constructed or under construction are frequently loath to include a firm settlement date in the agreement of sale. In order to help protect the purchaser, the agreement of sale should recite the dates by which construction must commence and be completed and give the purchaser the option to terminate the agreement and receive back all monies paid on account of the purchase price in the event that either of these deadlines is not met. A sample provision follows:

> Construction of the dwelling to be built on the Premises shall commence on or about August 15, 1986, and shall be completed on or before March 15, 1987. The parties agree that such time shall be of the essence; provided, however, that Seller shall not be responsible for, and is hereby relieved and discharged from all liability by reason of any delay in completion of the Premises or of settlement if such delay is caused by conditions beyond the control of Seller. In any event, if the Premises are not completed by April 15, 1987, or, due to no fault of Purchaser, settlement is not held by April 15, 1987, Purchaser may cancel this Agreement by giving notice thereof to Seller no later than April 16, 1987. In the event Purchaser cancels this Agreement persuant to this paragraph, all deposit monies paid by Purchaser shall be forthwith returned to Purchaser and this Agreement shall be null and void and of no further force or effect.

V. TYPICAL ADDITIONAL PROVISIONS OF AGREEMENTS OF SALE FOR RAW LAND TO BE DEVELOPED

If a purchaser is interested in purchasing raw land for development purposes, certain terms should be added to the agreement of sale. These relate to conditions of the land that are peculiar to undeveloped real estate and that, if not adequately provided for in the agreement, could make the buyer's proposed development of the real estate impossible or burdensome. The ability to develop the land and to use it as the purchaser desires may hinge on such factors as zoning approval, subdivision approval, building permits, and mortgage commitments.

A. SUBDIVISION APPROVALS

Many jurisdictions have legislation that provides that no one may divide a parcel of land, or erect a building on land in a subdivision, unless a subdivision plan has been approved by a designated authority, usually a county or local governmental authority. If the purchaser's proposed use of the tract in question will eventually necessitate obtaining subdivision approval, the purchaser should make the obligation to complete settlement conditional on obtaining such approval. As in the case of zoning approval, it is important to specify (a) which party has the obligation to prepare and submit to the appropriate authorities the subdivision plan on which subdivision approval may be based, and (b) which party is to pay the cost therefor. Each party requires the same conditions as those discussed in section II(M) of this chapter. If the purchaser is purchasing a tract of land that is part of a subdivision, the agreement of sale should provide that an approved subdivision plan will be filed of record not later than the date of settlement. This requirement is important because many subdivision ordinances prohibit the sale of land in a subdivision before such a plan has been approved. In any event, the parties should agree who will be responsible for making any improvements to, or for the benefit of, the premises (such as the installation of streets and specified utility lines) that are required by the local officials as conditions of obtaining final subdivision approval.

B. MUNICIPAL APPROVAL; STREETS, WATER SERVICE, AND SEWER SERVICE

In order to protect the buyer, the agreement of sale should contain either a warranty by the seller that the premises have direct access to designated public thoroughfares, or an agreement by the seller to provide the purchaser with access to public thoroughfares over private roads or other easements. The purchaser will also need a representation or warranty from the seller as the the present availability of water service, storm and sanitary sewer service, and perhaps gas service, at the boundaries of the premises. Such warranty or representation should include a statement that these facilities will be adequate for the purchaser's intended use of the property and should specify what "tap in" or connection charges, if any, are payable in order to make use of these facilities and which party is to bear the expense.

C. RIGHT TO INSPECT PREMISES AND MAKE TESTS THEREON

Land on which improvements are to be constructed must have certain support characteristics lest the cost of construction be prohibitive. A purchaser will want to have the right to test the land for these characteristics and will want to condition settlement on their presence.

> Seller hereby grants to Purchaser, and designated representatives of Purchaser, the right at any time after execution of this Agreement, and from time to time, to enter upon the Premises to inspect, appraise and make surveys of the Premises and to make borings, drive test piles and make soil bearing or other tests to determine the suitability of the Premises for building foundations and other improvements which Purchaser may wish to make for the purpose of constructing or erecting a ten-story concrete office building on the Premises; provided, however, that said tests shall not be so conducted as to damage materially Seller's property or substantially interfere with Seller's use of the Premises. Purchaser shall have the right, at any time prior to the time of settlement, to terminate this Agreement by giving written notice to Seller in the event that such tests indicate the presence of rock or other adverse conditions which, in Purchaser's judgment, will preclude the economic installation of building foundations or other improvements, or both, on or in the Premises.

D. BUILDING PERMITS

Before a builder can commence construction of buildings and improvements on real property, most jurisdictions require the builder to obtain building permits or approvals of plans from the appropriate county or municipal authorities.

PROBLEM

Using the formats previously discussed in sections II(M) (Zoning) and V(A) (Subdivision Approvals) of this chapter, prepare a provision making the agreement of sale contingent on purchaser's obtaining necessary building permits for a ten-story office building.

VI. TYPICAL ADDITIONAL PROVISIONS OF AGREEMENTS OF SALE FOR COMMERCIAL IMPROVED REAL ESTATE

Commercial improved real estate is usually acquired either as an investment or for use in the purchaser's business, or both. There are additional provisions that are appropriate in an agreement of sale for the purchase of commercial improved real estate.

A. DESCRIPTION OF FIXTURES AND PERSONALTY INCLUDED IN THE SALE

You will recall from section III(E) of this chapter that it is important to list the fixtures and personalty to be included in a sale. For several reasons, it is even more important in a commercial transaction. One is that the purchaser may be purchasing an ongoing business that includes most, if not all, items of furniture, inventory, machinery, and equipment. This contrasts with the typical residential transaction, in which it is unusual for much personalty to remain. A second reason is that the seller of a commercial building may not be the owner of everything contained in the building. The seller may lease equipment, or it may be that most non-fixture items belong to tenants of the building. Thus, if the parties are not more specific, the purchaser might be unpleasantly surprised by a general reference to "the premises and all of Seller's property located therein." A third reason is simply the magnitude of the sums involved. A $95,000 house is likely to retain its value even though an attractive lighting fixture is removed. However, the personalty involved in a commercial transaction can represent a substantial portion of the value of the property. A provision similar to that discussed in section III(E) is suitable. However, some further protections are useful:

> Seller hereby represents and warrants to Buyer that, at the time of settlement, Seller will have clear title to all of the aforesaid fixtures, machinery, apparatus and equipment; that Seller shall have full power, right and authority to sell the same to Buyer; and that the same shall be delivered to Buyer in the same condition as they now are, ordinary wear and tear alone excepted, and free and clear of all liens, encumbrances, security interests and rights of possession of others therein.

B. POSSESSION

Because all or part of the property may be occupied by tenants at the time of the conveyance, a provision of the following type dealing with the problem of delivery of possession may be appropriate:

> Possession of the Premises shall be given by Seller to Purchaser by delivery of a special warranty deed and keys to the Premises, and by the execution, acknowledgment, and delivery of a written assignment of the existing leases as listed in Exhibit "B" and any leases given by Seller between the date hereof and the time of settlement and approved by Purchaser in accordance with the provisions of this agreement, which assignment shall be in form and substance acceptable to Purchaser. All unrented parts of the building on the Premises shall be delivered at settlement in broom-clean condition and free of all personal property not conveyed to Purchaser under this agreement.

C. ZONING AND LICENSING

The provisions relating to zoning and licensing discussed earlier in this chapter are also applicable in the case of commercial real estate. In addition, items such as the adequacy of off-street parking should be investigated, if such items are relevant to the purchaser's intended use of the property. In those parts of the country in which municipal authorities issue certificates of occupancy or other documents certifying that the buildings on the property have been built in accordance with the plans and specifications approved at the time the building permits were issued, the seller should be required to produce that document at settlement. Similarly, when the agreement covers land in a municipality that issues certificates to the effect that a specified use of the property conforms to its zoning classification, the purchaser should request a provision in the agreement requiring the seller to furnish such a certificate at settlement.

D. EXISTING LEASES

If all or part of the property is leased to tenants and the parties intend that these leases will continue in effect after the conveyance to the purchaser, the purchaser will be concerned about the terms of the various leases. The purchaser's attorney should inspect the leases prior to execution of the agreement of sale in order to ascertain the terms of the leases, including the anticipated rental income from the property and the obligations the purchaser will assume as landlord (such as return of security deposits). In addition to inspecting the leases, the purchaser will want assurance that the leases inspected are true and correct copies of all of the leases and that no changes in the leases will be made prior to settlement without the consent of the purchaser.

As an example, if the purchaser has adequate bargaining power, he or she may be able to obtain provisions similar to the ones that appear below. Carefully examine those provisions and suggest any way in which a seller would seek to have these provisions modified.

(a) *Lease Provisions.* Various parts of the Premises are presently occupied under written leases. Seller warrants that Exhibit "C" represents a complete schedule of all leases in effect at the date hereof accurately showing, for each such lease, inter alia, the name of the tenant, the date of the lease, the space leased, the rental, any security deposited by the tenant, the commencement date of the term, the length of the term or the expiration date thereof, the provisions with respect to renewal or extension of the term, the right, if any, of the tenant to assign his lease and sublet the space he or she leases, and the right, if any, of the tenant to purchase the Premises or any part thereof. Seller and Purchaser have this day initialled Seller's copies of said leases. Seller warrants that there is no right of possession to any part or all of the Premises which is not set out in the leases described in Exhibit "C."

(b) *Covenants, Representations and Warranties.* Seller covenants, represents, and warrants with, and to, Purchaser with respect to the leases listed in Exhibit "C" that, as of the date hereof and as of the time of settlement:

(i) Said leases are in full force and effect and are the only leases affecting the Premises;

(ii) Neither the landlord nor the tenant is in default under any of the provisions of any of the leases;

(iii) The information relating to said leases as set forth in Exhibit "C" is accurate;

(iv) No amendments, oral or written, have been made with respect to said leases other than those listed in Exhibit "C," and all of the terms of each of said leases are in writing;

(v) None of the tenants under said leases have made any security deposits thereunder other than as set forth in Exhibit "C" or prepayments of rent, and there are no sums to be credited to the tenants by reason of alterations, or other rental allowances, reductions in rent, or for free rental periods;

(vi) There are no rights of use or occupancy for any portions of the Premises now in effect or hereafter to come into effect except the tenancies under the leases listed in Exhibit "C";

(vii) No notices have been given to or by any of the tenants under said leases; and

(viii) No claim of any nature has been made by any tenant under any of said leases.

(c) *Seller's Inability to Make Covenants, Representations, and Warranties as at Time of Settlement.* In the event that Seller is unable to make all of the foregoing covenants, representations, and warranties as at the time of settlement and Purchaser has not theretofore given written approval of whatever action, if any, Seller may have taken in connection with the cause of Seller's inability so to covenant, represent, and warrant, Purchaser shall have the right to cancel and terminate this Agreement.

(d) *Execution of Leases Prior to Settlement.* Seller agrees that, after the execution of this Agreement, no additional leases, licenses, easements, or rights will be executed or given for any portion or portions of the Premises, nor will any existing leases be extended, cancelled, modified, added to, or amended in any respect, or any assignment or subletting approved for any leases, without in each instance first obtaining the written approval of Purchaser.

(e) *Termination of Leases Prior to Settlement.* Seller agrees that, after the execution of this Agreement, no action will be taken with respect to the termination of any of said leases without having obtained the prior written approval of Purchaser.

(f) *Performance of Landlord's Obligations.* Seller agrees that all of the obligations of the landlord under said leases accruing to the date of settlement or arising from conditions existing prior thereto will be performed by Seller, and Seller hereby indemnifies and agrees to hold Purchaser harmless from and against any and all claims, losses, damages, set-offs, or counterclaims arising from the failure of Seller to fulfill said obligations.

(g) *Assignment of Security Deposits.* The total sum of all security deposits, as listed in Exhibit "C," shall be given as a credit to Purchaser at settlement.

(h) *Assignment of Landlord's Interest in Leases.* Seller agrees that at settlement Seller will, in a writing satisfactory to counsel for Purchaser, assign, transfer, and set over to Purchaser all of Seller's right, title, and interest in and to the leases listed in Exhibit "C" and such other leases as shall hereafter be entered into with the approval of Purchaser as aforesaid, and to deliver to Purchaser, Seller's fully executed copy of each of said leases. The said assignment of leases shall be free and clear of any right, title, or interest of real estate brokers or other persons in the rents, whether or not such brokers or other persons negotiated the said leases or have contracted with Seller, or anyone else, for the collection of said rents. At or before settlement, Seller will pay the balance of the compensation in full owing to all brokers who negotiated or obtained leases for any part of the Premises, and will produce releases to that effect at settlement. The aforesaid assignment of leases shall contain Seller's warranty of title to said leases and shall contain an assumption of all of Seller's duties and obligations thereunder by Purchaser.

(i) *Notifying Tenants of Lease Assignments.* Seller agrees to execute at settlement letters to be prepared by Purchaser for transmission to the tenants of the Premises informing said tenants of the assignment of said leases to Purchaser.

(j) *Collection of Rents After Settlement.* Except as set forth in paragraph _____ hereof, all rents and other sums collected by Purchaser, after settlement, up to the respective amounts currently due Purchaser from time to time, will be retained and applied by Purchaser on account of the rents and other sums to become due to Purchaser, notwithstanding that there may be rents and other sums due to Seller for any period prior to settlement. If and when any tenant shall pay to Purchaser a sum in excess of all rents and other sums which have accrued to Purchaser, and which sums are on account of arrearages which became due prior to settlement, Purchaser will remit such excess to Seller to be applied on account of the indebtedness due to Seller. Purchaser assumes no obligation to collect or enforce the payment of any such moneys which may be owing to Seller. Any broker collecting rents for the Premises shall have the right to deduct and retain from Seller's share of such rent and other sums, compensation at the same rate payable to such broker in connection with rents collected from similar space in the Premises.

(k) *Survival.* All of the provisions of this Section shall survive and continue after settlement and shall not merge therein.

The student should recognize that paragraph (j) touches on several problems. If a tenant's rent is in arrears at the time of settlement, paragraph (j) makes clear that the purchaser will not apply future rental payments to the arrearage (which would be rightfully the seller's money) until the tenant has first paid the purchaser all sums that have accrued after settlement. The paragraph leaves open the question of the treatment of rental payments that relate to periods prior to settlement but which are not due as of the date of settlement. Because rent is normally prepaid, this problem should not occur with respect to rent. However, it will commonly arise in regard to items of additional rent, such as increased taxes or sums due because of an escalator provision relating to operating expenses. These items are normally billed to the tenant at the end of a rental or calendar period. The provision does not deal with apportionment of rent already paid to seller for periods that extend beyond the date of settlement. That item is normally handled in a separate provision devoted to all types of apportionments.

E. WARRANTY AS TO INCOME AND EXPENSES GENERATED BY PREMISES

If the property is being acquired solely or partially for investment purposes, the purchase will want an accurate financial history of the premises in order to make projections as to what kind of income the property will generate in the future. Therefore, he or she will want to require the seller to produce, and warrant the accuracy of, financial statements relating to the operation of the property and to permit inspection of books and records containing the relevant financial data.

F. SERVICE CONTRACTS

The operation of most commercial or industrial buildings requires various kinds of management and service contracts. For example, janitorial service may be supplied by an independent contractor, rather than being performed by employees of the owner of the building. It is desirable that there be no interruption in the services at settlement. Provisions dealing with the assignment of various service and management contracts (which are usually assignable to succeeding owners of the property) are similar in form and nature to the foregoing provisions dealing with leases.

PROBLEM

Prepare proper provisions dealing with service contracts, including contracts for janitorial services and for servicing the heating and air conditioning systems.

G. APPORTIONMENTS

In addition to the usual apportionments that should be covered in an agreement of sale, a commercial transaction may involve apportionment of percentage rentals, payment under maintenance and service contracts, and commissions for lease brokerage and managing agents, and others, depending on the particular situation presented.

1. Percentage Rentals

Many leases of commercial property provide, in addition to a fixed rental payment known as "minimum rent," that the tenant will share with the landlord a percentage of the receipts or profits the tenant derives from his or her business. This latter payment, usually referred to as "percentage rental," is usually calculated by a method or formula contained in the lease.[21] Whether and how much percentage rent is payable depend on the volume of tenant's business during a specified period for which the percentage rent is payable. The percentage rent is either payable in estimated installments, with an adjustment made at the end of the lease year, or no installments are made and the computation of percentage rent due is made at the end of the lease year.

---

21. Percentage rental is discussed in detail in Chapter Ten.

If a lease of all or part of the property to be sold has a percentage rent provision, the purchaser and seller would normally agree on a method for apportionment of the percentage rent. Because the total percentage rent to be paid will usually not be determined or collected until after settlement, the parties must anticipate making a post-settlement adjustment. Normally, the purchaser will receive the money from the tenant and account to seller for the seller's share. If, however, the seller does not trust the purchaser, or the seller is worried about the financial condition of the purchaser, payment could be made to an escrowee. Note that if in any situation the tenant is to pay percentage rent directly to an escrowee, the seller will have to notify tenant, in writing, that payment of percentage rent should be made to the escrowee through the balance of the current lease year and thereafter to the purchaser.

2. Maintenance and Service Contracts, Etc.

In those instances in which the owners of a commercial building have entered into employment contracts with personnel who operate the building and contracts for cleaning, elevator maintenance, burglar alarm service, and the like, the contracts will frequently be assigned to the buyer. If so, a method of apportioning the credits due or amounts owing under these contracts should be specified in the agreement of sale. An apportionment may also be necessary with respect to vacation and other fringe benefits under employment contracts. A sample of a provision relating to the above-mentioned apportionments follows:

> At settlement, in accordance with paragraph _____ hereof, Seller shall assign to Purchaser all existing contracts concerning maintenance, personnel, and supplies used in operating the Premises. Any pre-payment made by Seller pursuant to such contracts, as well as any payments which will be made by Purchaser, part of which will apply to periods prior to the settlement, shall be apportioned by the parties. An apportionment shall also be made with respect to wage and vacation pay, for the year in which the Premises are conveyed to Purchaser, due or paid to personnel directly employed by Seller for work on the Premises. Seller hereby represents to Purchaser that such contracts are assignable.

3. Lease Brokerage and Managing Agent's Commission

Often, when a real estate broker is entitled to a commission for obtaining a tenant and negotiating a lease, the broker's commission will be a certain percentage of the rents to be paid to the broker as rent is paid by the tenant. This type of arrangement is common when the broker is also the collection agent for the landlord. Frequently the agreement with the agent will contain a provision for a lump sum payment of the balance of the commission if the collection arrangement is terminated. The seller would want the agreement to provide that the purchaser will idemnify and hold the seller harmless against all lease brokerage claims accruing after settlement and against any liability for the lump sum payment due if the broker's rent collection authority is terminated.

VII. DISCUSSION OF OTHER TYPES OF REAL ESTATE AGREEMENTS OF SALE

A. OPTION AGREEMENTS

An option is a contract, whereby the owner of property (the "optionor") is bound to sell the property on specified terms to the purchaser (the "optionee"), but the purchaser has no corresponding obligation to purchase the property unless he or she exercises the option by electing to make the purchase on the terms set forth in the option agreement. The optionee normally pays a price to obtain the option (the "option price"). The option price might vary from one dollar to thousands of dollars, depending on the value of the option and the amount of time the optionee has to exercise his or her option. Upon the exercise of the option, the optionee is deemed to have the same interest in the property as a purchaser who has signed an agreement of sale for the property on the date the option was granted.

Because the option becomes a full-fledged agreement of sale once the option is exercised, and because neither party thereafter has any unilateral right to change the terms of the agreement, it is important that the option agreement contain the same essential provisions as an agreement of sale, in addition to the grant of the option and the provision dealing with the procedure for exercise of the option. One way of preparing an option agreement would be to prepare a simple document setting forth the terms of the option with an agreement of sale attached as an exhibit.

The option should state that the notice of exercise of the option will be in writing and should set out in detail the manner and place of delivery and even the exact text of the notice. Unless the optionee has already paid a substantial amount of money as consideration for the option, he or she should be required, on exercise of the option, to pay a sum of money as a deposit. Option agreements usually provide that the consideration for the option will be retained by the optionor in the event the option is not exercised, but that, if it is exercised, the consideration will be credited to the optionee on account of the purchase price. It is not uncommon, however, for the optionor to receive a substantial sum of money merely as the price of the option, and in such a case there is no credit toward the purchase price. Often, as discussed in Chapter Ten, an option to purchase is granted to a tenant in his or her lease.

B. INSTALLMENT SALE AGREEMENTS

An installment sale agreement is one method of financing a purchase of property in lieu of obtaining a mortgage loan. The instrument itself is really a combination of an agreement of sale and a purchase money mortgage. It contains all of the essential provisions of a typical agreement of sale plus many typical mortgage provisions, such as the payment terms and the rights and remedies of the installment seller in the event of a breach of the agreement by the purchaser. Unlike the usual methods of financing a purchase, however, legal title to the property does not pass to the purchaser until all installment payments have been made.

C. SALE LEASEBACK AGREEMENTS

The sale leaseback transaction is a financing technique whereby an owner of real estate can retain possession and use of the property while freeing his or her investment in the property for other use. The transaction itself consists of a sale of the premises by the owner to another entity for a specified purchase price, followed immediately by a lease of the property from the purchaser to the seller. Consequently, agreements relating to the future sale and leaseback of a piece of real estate usually take the form of an agreement of sale containing all the usual provisions for the particular type of real estate to be conveyed, to which is added one or more provisions obligating the parties to enter into a lease of the premises. A sample of such a provision follows:

> This Agreement, and the obligation of the parties to complete settlement hereunder, is expressly conditioned upon the parties executing the lease attached hereto as Exhibit "A" and executing and acknowledging the memorandum of lease attached hereto as Exhibit "B," both of which are hereby made part hereof.

The principal provisions of the lease should be agreed on prior to the execution of the "agreement of sale," and they should either be set out verbatim in the agreement or, as provided in the above sample provision, a completed but unsigned copy of the lease should be attached to the "agreement of sale" as an exhibit. A discussion of the leasing aspects of sale leaseback may be found in Chapter Ten.

VIII. CHECKLIST FOR PURCHASE AND SALE OF REAL ESTATE

The following is a checklist that will be useful to the legal assistant in connection with the purchase and sale of real estate.

A. PREPARATION OF AGREEMENT OF SALE

1. Parties

    (a) Individuals: Identify full names and addresses and determine competence.

    (b) Domestic corporations, foreign corporations, and partnerships:

        (1) Identify exact names, addresses, and states of incorporation or formation.

        (2) Arrange for any necessary shareholder or partner vote or other ownership approval.

        (3) Arrange for any necessary corporate or partnership resolutions and other evidence of authority (e.g., corporate seal).

    (4) Arrange for production of charter or articles of incorporation and (if a foreign corporation) certificate of authority; or partnership agreement and partnership certificate of formation.

  (c) Fiduciaries: Identify names and addresses and arrange for production of evidence of appointment.

2. Description of Property

  (a) Procure legal description from former deed or title policy.

  (b) Identify buildings, structures and other improvements, fixtures, equipment, and personal property, if any, that are included in the sale.

  (c) Identify any easements and appurtenances.

  (d) Arrange for preparation of survey, if necessary.

3. Purchase Price

  (a) Identify aggregate consideration.

  (b) Determine amounts and timing of downpayments.

  (c) Determine identity of escrowee and arrange for the establishment of escrow account, if necessary.

  (d) Determine whether deposits are to be made into interest bearing or non–interest bearing account and how interest is to be paid at settlement or on earlier termination of the agreement.

  (e) Assumption of existing mortgage:

    (1) Secure copies of note and mortgage (check amount, interest rate, term, events of default, mortgagor's liability).

    (2) Obtain consent of mortgagee.

    (3) Procure a representation by seller and certificate from mortgagee as to absence of defaults and outstanding balance of the note (at time of agreement and at settlement).

    (4) Arrange for release of seller from mortgage obligation, if permitted by mortgage.

  (f) Creation of purchase money mortgage:

    (1) Determine amount, interest rate, and term.

    (2) Attach forms of proposed note and mortgage papers, or, at minimum, identify major provisions with particularity.

4. Conditions

  (a) Specify any special conditions which are conditions precedent to obligations of seller or buyer to go forward with agreement:

    (1) Mortgage financing: type (conventional, FHA, VA), amount, term, rate (fixed, variable), payment terms (self-amortization, negative amortization, balloon), lending institution, prepayment penalties, and fees and expenses in connection with loan.

    (2) Termite certification.

(3) Operating condition of appliances and heating, air conditioning, plumbing, mechanical, and electrical systems.

(4) Condition of structural components and roof.

(5) Satisfactory report of professional home inspection company.

(6) Condition and capacity of any on-site sewage disposal systems, availability of sewer connections.

(7) Condition, capacity, and potability of any on-site water system.

(8) Zoning or subdivision approvals; variances.

(9) Delivery of use and occupancy (or similar) certificate.

(10) Delivery of certificate evidencing absence of any uncorrected violations of applicable housing, building, safety, and fire or other ordinances.

(11) Validity, existence, and assignment of any leases at settlement.

(12) Ability of buyer to assume existing mortgage.

(13) Satisfactory results of any test borings, subsurface soil tests, or percolation tests on the property.

(14) Creation of any easements, reservation of any rights.

(15) Availability of utility services (electric, telephone, gas) at boundaries of or within a specified distance of property.

(16) Completion of any work on or about the property.

(17) Applicable environmental approvals.

(b) Identify which party has obligation to secure satisfaction of conditions and what such obligation entails (e.g., good faith and diligent effort, notice to other party of satisfaction of obligations, and payment of costs and expenses).

(c) Specify time period within which conditions must be satisfied, and who, if anyone, has the right to waive their fulfillment.

5. Settlement

(a) Establish outside data for settlement and its location.

(b) Establish who should determine exact date, time, and place for settlement.

(c) Specify whether settlement should be stepped up on fulfillment of a condition or conditions.

6. Title

(a) Secure, if possible, a recent title report or seller's existing title policy, and review each exception and objection.

(b) Ascertain from title company what it requires to remove objections.

(c) Identify in agreement exceptions to title that buyer will accept.

(d) Determine whether buyer's contemplated use of property will violate any matters of record or existing or proposed zoning ordinances.

7. Assessments, Notices, Etc.

(a) Determine existence of any outstanding notices of uncorrected violations, or any notices of unpaid assessments for public improvements.

(b) Determine existence of any condemnation proceedings or proposed road widening.

(c) Check whether locality requires statement in agreement of sale and delivery of certificate as to notices of uncorrected code violations.

8. Items Included in Sale

(a) Identify with particularity any borderline items that are intended to be included or excluded from the sale.

9. Apportionments and Expenses

(a) Identify methods of apportioning real estate taxes, water and sewer rentals, rental payments, and interest on mortgage, and of allocating realty transfer taxes, recording taxes, and the like.

(b) Identify party to bear cost and expense of special items, particularly surveys and fulfillment of zoning, subdivision, termite inspection, and other contingencies.

10. Remedies

(a) Identify seller's remedies if buyer breaches:

(1) Seller can retain deposit monies and all other sums paid on account of purchase price as liquidated damages.

(2) Seller has right of specific performance.

(3) Seller has right to sue for damages.

(b) Identify buyer's remedies if seller breaches:

(1) Buyer has right to return of deposit monies and all other sums paid on account of purchase price (with interest), and other expenses in connection with obtaining title and mortgage commitments.

(2) Buyer has right to sue for specific performance.

(3) Buyer has right to sue for damages.

11. Risk of Loss

(a) Determine who bears risk of loss between date of agreement and settlement.

(b) Determine who will maintain or obtain, and who will be the beneficiary of, insurance on property.

12. Miscellaneous

(a) Check whether buyer has right to inspect property immediately before settlement.

(b) Identify whether there are any brokerage commissions, to whom they are payable, by whom they are payable, and include an indemnity provision.

(c) Check "bulk sales" considerations in states which have statutory requirements on transfer of a substantial portion of a corporation's assets.

(d) Determine whether buyer can assign agreement of sale.

(e) Check whether there are any warranties concerning condition of property.

(f) Determine apportionments as to:

    (1) Lease brokerage.

    (2) Payments on supply and maintenance contracts.

    (3) Salary, vacation pay, and fringe benefits of building personnel.

(g) For purposes of completing the FIRPTA Affidavit,[22] seller's employer identification number.

B. ADDITIONAL CHECKLIST FOR RESIDENCE UNDER CONSTRUCTION OR TO BE CONSTRUCTED

(a) Check whether plans and specifications are included in agreement.

(b) Determine items to be added to plans and specifications or, if construction is completed, items to be added to structure.

(c) Check whether agreement includes Builder's Warranty and Architect's Warranty.

(d) Provide for assignment of roof and appliances warranties.

(e) Determine completion date.

(f) Determine payment schedule and method of payment.

(g) Check for warranty that streets, sewers, and utilities will be installed and paid for.

(h) Provide for allocation of premium to insure against mechanics' liens.

C. ADDITIONAL CHECKLIST FOR RAW LAND

(a) Check whether there is provision concerning zoning and/or subdivision approval and issuance of building permits.

(b) Check whether there is warranty relating to streets, sewers, and utilities.

22. The Foreign Investors Real Property Tax Act ("FIRPTA") requires that a buyer withhold tax from the purchase price of a U.S. real property interest if the seller is a foreign person. If the seller is not a foreign person, it must certify that fact to the buyer in an affidavit which also contains its U.S. employer identification number (or, if an individual, his or her social security number).

(c) Check whether there is right to inspect premises and conduct tests to determine feasibility of construction.

(d) Determine whether there is provision concerning continuity, if more than one parcel of land.

(e) Determine whether seller will guarantee permissibility of buyer's intended use.

D. ADDITIONAL CHECKLIST FOR COMMERCIAL IMPROVED REAL ESTATE

(a) Determine whether there will be leases on the premises, and if so:

    (1) Describe leases.

    (2) Determine apportionments of rent.

    (3) Check provision for security deposits.

    (4) Check lease brokerage provision.

    (5) Provide for assignment of leases, security deposits, and letters to tenants.

(b) Check whether agreement contains warranty as to income and expenses of property.

(c) Determine whether sale will be conditioned on obtaining permit giving evidence of permissibility of use.

(d) Determine whether there are private restrictions against use intended by buyer.

(e) Determine apportionments as to:

    (1) Lease brokerage.

    (2) Payments on supply and maintenance contracts.

    (3) Salary, vacation pay, and fringe benefits of building personnel.

Chapter 4

Surveys and Legal Descriptions

I. INTRODUCTION

A real estate transaction concerns a particular parcel of land. "Surveys" and "legal descriptions" are used in defining parcels of land. A survey is a graphic representation of the property, similar to a map. Like a map, a survey can simply show the boundaries of the property, or may show a variety of other facts concerning the property, such as the existence and location of buildings and other improvements, easements, encroachments, or improvements to be built. In contrast to deeds and mortgages, a survey is not normally a required part of most residential real estate transactions. Surveys are often necessary in connection with transactions involving a large tract of land, particularly in cases where a tract is being divided into several smaller tracts. Legal documents that usually necessitate a survey include a subdivision plan,[1] a declaration of condominium,[2] a declaration of easement,[3] or a declaration of covenants, easements, and restrictions.[4]

A legal description is simply a written description that is deemed to

---

1. The subdivision (dividing up) of a larger tract often necessitates local approval, and is often accomplished by recording an approved survey as a subdivision plan.

2. Many state condominium statutes require the recording of a form of survey showing the location of the units and common elements of the condominium.

3. It is fairly common to record a declaration of easements in connection with a tract that is to be developed in stages, and perhaps for multiple use, and which is to have certain common areas and cross-easements. Such a declaration of easements often contains, or refers to, a recorded survey.

4. A declaration of covenants, easements, and restrictions is often used to establish a mandatory homeowners' association and may contain, or refer to, a recorded survey.

be legally sufficient to define a parcel of real estate in connection with a particular transaction. Although English and American courts have often found untechnical descriptions to be legally sufficient (such as a reference to the south forty acres), a legal description usually entails a much more technical description.

The purpose of this chapter is to teach the student how to read a survey and a legal description and how to compare the two in order to find any inconsistencies. In addition, a legal assistant should be able to prepare a legal description from a survey and to sketch out a rough survey from a legal description.

II. SURVEYS

A. BACKGROUND

A surveyor[5] is an individual who, by the use of a transit and other land measurement instruments, is able to locate and measure land and thereafter to draw a map-like diagram of a parcel of land. In jurisdictions where surveyors are officials of the local government, only those surveys produced by the official surveyor will be acceptable for some purposes.

For historical, geographical, economic, and topological reasons, there are very different practices with respect to surveys in different areas of the country. Even within an area, practices have changed as different uses have been made of the land. As you read this chapter you should consider the different surveying needs and practices in various areas, such as an urban area, a new suburban development, a farming district, and a mineral-rich mountain region.

Although it is always useful to have a survey made when one is buying, leasing, or taking a mortgage on land, it is not always economically feasible or worthwhile. This is particularly true in circumstances where a legal description of the land exists, the land is located in an urban area in which boundary lines are easily identified, the boundary lines of the land are not in dispute, and there is no reason to believe that a survey would disclose any additional information about the land. Additionally, a new survey is generally not required by a title insurance company when an existing survey has been prepared within the last ten years and the original surveyor executes an affidavit certifying that the survey is correct and has not been changed. A new survey is, however, usually required in situations where there has been a change in boundary lines or existing structures, or where new structures have been constructed on the land. In any case, when a survey is not required, a depiction of the land can be sketched from the legal description with the aid of a protractor.

---

5. George Washington was a surveyor, as were Mason and Dixon, whose survey settled a boundary dispute between Pennsylvania and Virginia.

B. MECHANICS OF THE SURVEY

1. Point of Reference

Surveys must have a starting point, preferably one that relates to some identifiable physical object, often called a monument. A monument might be a street, a body of water, a rock, or a tree. The more permanent a monument is, as to both time and location, the more useful it is for purposes of a survey. A stream whose course shifts from time to time, for example, is not a good reference point.

2. Metes and Bounds Survey

After locating a point of reference, the surveyor will choose a starting point along the boundary of the property to be surveyed by going along one or more lines from the point of reference, and from there the surveyor will describe the boundary itself as consisting of several lines. There are two things that must be known about any line shown on a survey: (1) the direction in which the line runs (its "bound") and (2) the length of the line in that direction (its "mete"). The mete can be precisely determined by use of a tape measure. In order to determine the bound the surveyor uses a transit, which is a sophisticated compass. The compass is divided into 360 degrees (360°); each degree is divided into 60 minutes (60'); and each minute is divided into 60 seconds (60"). A bearing (which gives the direction of one point or object with respect to another) will therefore include degrees, minutes, and seconds in a given direction. (For example, South 18° 20' 3" East.) Figure 1 represents the face of a compass.

Figure 1

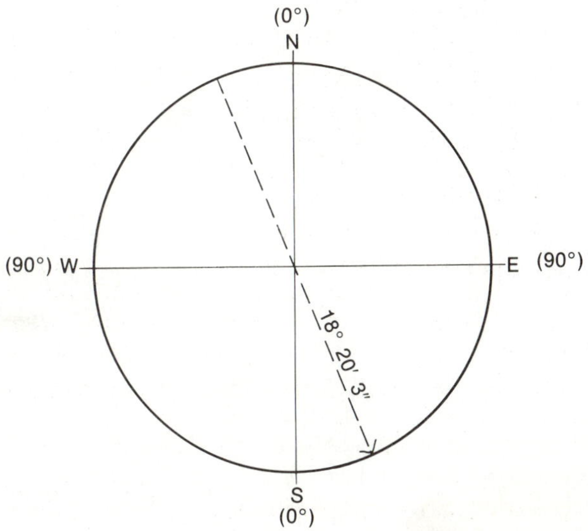

The face of the compass is divided in half from left to right; the upper half is north and the lower half is south. The first direction mentioned indicates whether, as the surveyor sights along a line, the compass needle points somewhere in the upper half (north) or in the lower half (south). The numbers that follow indicate how far from due north or due south the line crosses the compass. Rather than using 360°, the surveyor divides the compass into 90° quadrants. Therefore, South 18° 20' 3" indicates that the line crosses the south half of the compass 18° 20' 3" to the east or west (right or left) of due south (see Figure 1). The addition of the direction "East" (South 18° 20' 3" East) indicates that the line crosses to the east (right). It would appear on the compass as shown in Figure 1. Of course, if the surveyor had started from the other end of the line, it would be equally accurate to say the line is North 18 degrees (18°), 20 minutes (20'), 3 seconds (3") West.

Therefore, a metes and bounds survey consists of defining the boundaries in terms of their compass direction and length.

3. Government or Rectangular Survey Systems

(a) Background

In 1785 the federal government recognized the difficulty of locating a beginning point for a metes and bounds description in most rural areas and the then unexplored regions of the West. In that year the rectangular survey system was adopted. It applied to all lands other than the original thirteen states. Today the system is used in thirty states, including all those west of the Mississippi River except Texas, and all states (except for the original thirteen) north of the Ohio River, including Alaska. In addition, the system is used in Mississippi, Alabama, and Florida.

Even states using the rectangular survey system have need of a metes and bounds description, as many of the original parcels have been divided or sold in smaller units. The rectangular survey system, in that event, is used merely to fix the starting point for a metes and bounds description, especially in some of the more densely populated areas of states using the rectangular survey system. The system provides precise fixed beginning points.

(b) Mechanics of the System

The rectangular survey system is based on "meridians," which are imaginary surveying lines running north and south, and "base lines," which are imaginary surveying lines running east and west. The principal meridians and base lines are fixed by a government survey and relate to longitudinal and latitudinal measurement. Thirty-four principal meridians have been established and are identified by number. At intervals of 24 miles on each side of principal meridians, "guide meridians" have been established. They are referred to as "first guide meridian east," "third guide meridian west," etc. Similarly, at intervals of 24 miles on each side of a base line, "standard parallels" have been fixed.

The area bounded by two meridians (one principal meridian and one guide meridian) and two base lines (one base line and one standard parallel or two standard parallels) is a square block consisting of 24 miles on each side of the square. Each 24-mile square block is further divided into sixteen square blocks that are called townships. Each township is 6 miles on every side of the square. A line of townships running north and south is called a range. Each range is assigned a number (1, 2, 3, 4, and so on) based on its position in relation to the nearest principal meridian. A line of townships running east and west is called a tier and is assigned a number (1, 2, 3, 4, and so on) based on its position in relation to the nearest base line. Therefore, the diagonally marked township in Figure 2 would be known as Township Tier 2 North (i.e., north of the base line) Range 2 West of the 2nd Principal Meridian (Township T. 2N, Rge. 2W of 2nd P.M.). The cross-hatched township would be Township T. 2N, Rge. 2E of 2nd P.M.

Each township is further divided into thirty-six square blocks called sections. Sections are squares of 1 mile on each side. They are numbered consecutively starting with the upper right-hand section of the township

Figure 2

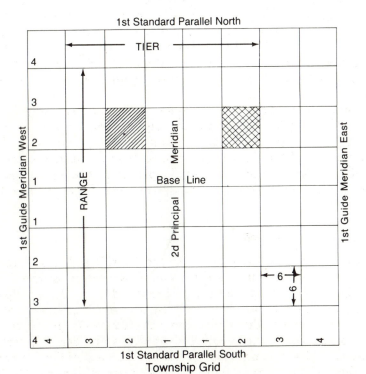

1st Standard Parallel North

Township Grid

Figure 3

6	5	4	3	2	1
7	8	9	10	11	12
18	17	16	15	14	13
19	20	21	22	23	24
30	29	28	27	26	25
31	32	33	34	35	36

Township Sections

Figure 4

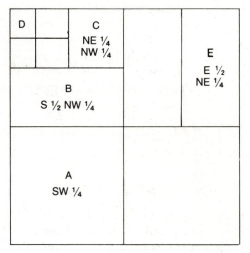

Section 1

and continuing first right to left, then left to right, and so on until all the sections are numbered, as shown in Figure 3.

With this system the section in the uppermost right-hand corner of the cross-hatched township of Figure 2 would be known as Section 1, Township Tier 2 North, Range 2 East of the 2nd Principal Meridian, or, by shorthand, Section 1, Township T. 2N, Rge. 2E of 2nd P.M. Finally, each section can be divided into even smaller parcels. The parcel delineated as A on Figure 4 is called the Southwest (SW) quarter (¼) of Section 1; parcel B is the South (S) half (½) of the Northwest (NW) ¼ of Section 1; parcel C is the Northeast (NE) ¼ of the NW ¼ of Section 1; parcel D is the NW ¼ of the NW ¼ of the NW ¼ of Section 1, and parcel E is the East (E) ½ of the NE ¼ of Section 1. The full description of parcel D of Section 1 is NW ¼ of the NW ¼ of the NW ¼ of Section 1, Township T. 2N, Rge. 2E of 2nd P.M.

(c) Reference Points

It is possible to use the governmental survey system to arrive at a corner of a government unit and to use that corner, or a point that can be defined in relation to that corner, as the starting point for a metes and bounds survey.

III. TYPES OF LEGAL DESCRIPTIONS

A. STREET NUMBER OR NAME

Property may be described merely by referring to the name and number of the street on which it is located, or by its name in the case of a farm or estate (e.g., "Forsyth Manor"). Although such descriptions are adequate for most nonlegal purposes, they are the poorest form of legal description because boundaries of the property are omitted. The use of a street number may clearly designate a particular structure, but it would not make clear the boundaries of the lot on which the structure is located. Street numbers or property names should never be used as the sole legal description in deeds or mortgages,[6] although for purposes of leasing space in office or apartment buildings, or for agreements of sale where no legal description is yet available, reference to land by street number may be justified. On the other hand, because of the nature of condominium ownership, a legally sufficient description of a condominium unit is its unit number.

B. MONUMENTS

In areas and transactions where the cost of a survey necessary for an accurate description (which could be several hundred dollars for a large parcel of land) would be disproportionate to the amount of money involved in the transaction, a description by monuments alone may be warranted. An example of this type of description follows:

> The farm of Jeffrey Scott located at Childsville, Potter County, Alabama, bounded and described as follows: Beginning at the large dead oak tree on Lee Road where the farms of Brian Alan and Jeffrey Scott are divided by a fence. Then along Lee Road to the point where Lee Road meets Roberta Creek. Then along Roberta Creek to a point where the creek is met by the fence dividing the farms of Brian Alan and Jeffrey Scott. Then along said fence to the large dead oak tree, the point of beginning.

6. Despite the admonition, it is nevertheless true that a deed or mortgage with a bare street number or property name may be a legally effective conveyance or encumbrance.

The difficulties of such a description are obvious. Fences are not permanent, and creeks shift courses and dry up. Therefore, whenever possible and financially feasible, a description based on a survey should be utilized.

C. SUBDIVISION PLOT PLAN

In most instances a builder or real estate developer will buy a parcel of land with the idea of dividing it into smaller parcels and erecting homes or other buildings on these smaller parcels, a process known as subdivision. The builder cannot do this without receiving consent from the appropriate local authorities. In order to have the authorities consider the application for subdivision, the builder must provide them with a subdivision plot plan in the form of a map that is a survey of the entire subdivision. In addition, the plan will depict every lot and will contain measurements so that the location of the lots can be determined. Each lot will be assigned a reference number.

The legal description for any one lot may be obtained by referring to the plot plan and then to the particular lot by number. An example of such a description is as follows:

> All that certain lot, piece or parcel of land, shown upon a map or plot plan of land at Lyndora, Montgomery County, Maryland, surveyed by John Doe, dated July 8, 1943; as and by the lot number 205.

Because the plot plan is on file with the recorder of deeds in Montgomery County, the exact location of the lot referred to can always be determined.

D. METES AND BOUNDS

Metes and bounds is the most accurate method of legal description. Such a description is created from a survey of the land and merely reproduces in words the lengths of boundaries and compass directions. A description by metes and bounds, however, is only valuable if the starting point of the description is readily and permanently ascertainable. This means that a metes and bounds description is more useful in urban and suburban areas, where starting points such as the intersections of streets can be located with accuracy.

1. No Compass Reference Necessary

Metes and bounds descriptions can be relatively simple or extremely complicated, depending on how regular the lot is, whether there are any curved lines, and whether or not the land is located in an area where there is easy reference to streets or other physical monuments. For example, if the area surveyed is bounded by fronting and intersecting streets, the metes and bounds description is relatively uncomplicated, as the following survey and legal description indicate.

A description of lot "A" in Figure 5, a perfectly rectangular or "regular lot," would read as follows:

Figure 5

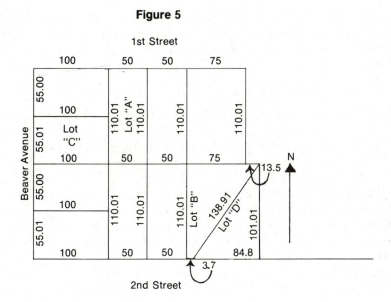

Beginning at a point on the southerly side of First Street, 100 feet in an easterly direction from the intersection of the southerly side of First Street and the easterly side of Beaver Avenue; thence along the southerly side of First Street, 50 feet; thence southerly parallel to the easterly side of Beaver Avenue, 110.01 feet; thence westerly parallel to the southerly side of First Street, 50 feet; thence northerly parallel to the easterly side of Beaver Avenue, 110.01 feet to the point and place of beginning.

A description of the "irregular lot," "B," in Figure 5 is not much more complicated:

Beginning at a point on the northerly side of Second Street, 200 feet in an easterly direction from the intersection of the easterly side of Beaver Avenue and the northerly side of Second Street; running thence northerly and parallel to the easterly side of Beaver Avenue, 110.01 feet; thence easterly parallel to the northerly side of Second Street, 88.50 feet; thence southwesterly, 138.91 feet to a point on the northerly side of Second Street, which point is 3.70 feet easterly from the point and place of beginning; and thence westerly along the northerly side of Second Street, 3.70 feet to the point and place of beginning.

PROBLEM

Using the legal descriptions for Lot "A" and Lot "B" as examples, draft the legal descriptions for Lot "C" and Lot "D" in Figure 5. Review your legal descriptions in class.

Figure 6

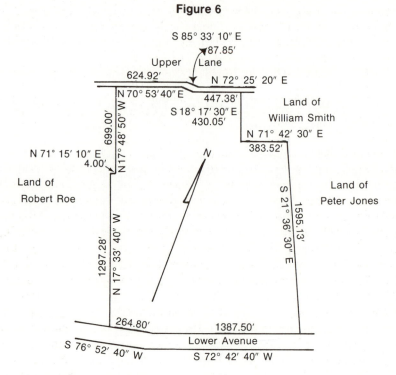

2. Compass References Necessary

When there are no fronting or intersecting streets, or the side lines are not parallel, it is necessary to refer to compass directions. An example of a lot where compass directions are necessary is shown in Figure 6. A description of this parcel of land would read as follows (note the difficulty in locating a "good" starting point):

All that tract or parcel of land beginning at the junction of the westerly line of the land now or late of William Smith and the southerly side of Upper Lane and running thence along the land of said William Smith South 18 degrees 17 minutes 30 seconds East 430.05 feet; thence along the land of said William Smith North 71 degrees 42 minutes 30 seconds East 383.52 feet to a point where the land of the said William Smith intersects with the land now or late of Peter Jones; thence along the land of said Peter Jones South 21 degrees 36 minutes 30 seconds East 1595.13 feet to the intersection of the land of Peter Jones and the northerly side of Lower Avenue; thence along said northerly side of Lower Avenue South 72 degrees 42 minutes 40 seconds West 1387.50 feet; thence continuing along said northerly side of Lower Avenue South 76 degrees 52 minutes 40 seconds West 264.80 feet to the point of intersection of the northerly side of Lower Avenue and the land now or late of Robert Roe; thence along the land of said Robert Roe North 17 degrees 33 minutes 40 seconds West 1297.28 feet; thence North 71 degrees

15 minutes 10 seconds East 4 feet; thence continuing along the land of said Robert Roe North 17 degrees 48 minutes 50 seconds West a distance of 699 feet to the intersection of the land of said Robert Roe and the southerly side of Upper Lane; thence along said southerly side of Upper Lane North 70 degrees 53 minutes 40 seconds East 624.92 feet; thence continuing along said southerly side of Upper Lane South 85 degrees 33 minutes 10 seconds East 87.85 feet; thence continuing along said southerly side of Upper Lane North 72 degrees 25 minutes 20 seconds East 447.38 feet to the point and place of beginning.

Notice that the description runs clockwise around the lot. It is customary that a legal description name the boundaries in a consistent manner, whether it be clockwise or counterclockwise. Sometimes a surveyor is not consistent. In that event, the person writing the legal description should reverse the bearings where necessary, so that the description reads consistently clockwise or counterclockwise. In the survey, for example, the surveyor may have first surveyed the Lower Avenue boundary starting from the west and continuing in an easterly direction along Lower Avenue. The first bearing along Lower Avenue would then have read N 76° 52′ 40″ E. If a person prepared a legal description without reversing the Lower Avenue description or, alternately, all other bearings, the description would not be consistently clockwise or counterclockwise. In order to reverse a bearing one simply imagines that the line runs in the opposite direction on a compass face. Therefore, a line that is North 85° East becomes South 85° West; a line that is South 18° 20′ 3″ East is, from the other vantage point, North 18° 20′ 3″ West (see Figure 1).

3. Surveys Containing Curved Lines

A complication that one might encounter in a metes and bounds survey is a lot that has curved boundaries. In order to describe a curve one must become familiar with several basic terms; (a) the "arc" is the length of the curving line that is part of the lot description (the distance between A and B on the curved line); (b) the "chord" is the length of a straight line drawn from the start of the arc to the end of the arc (the distance between A and B on a straight line); and (c) the "radius" is the length of an imaginary line drawn from any point on the curved line to the center of an imaginary circle that would be formed by extending the curved line all the way around until it closed.

In a metes and bounds description, the curved line in Figure 7 extending from A to B would be described as "thence extending along the arc of a circle curving to the left having a radius of 231.097 feet, the arc distance of 40 feet (the chord of said arc extending South 27 degrees 25 minutes 30 seconds East, 89.42 feet) to a point." If it were necessary to describe the same curved line from the opposite direction (that is, the curved line extending from B to A), it would be described as "thence extending along the arc of a circle curving to the right having a radius

Figure 7

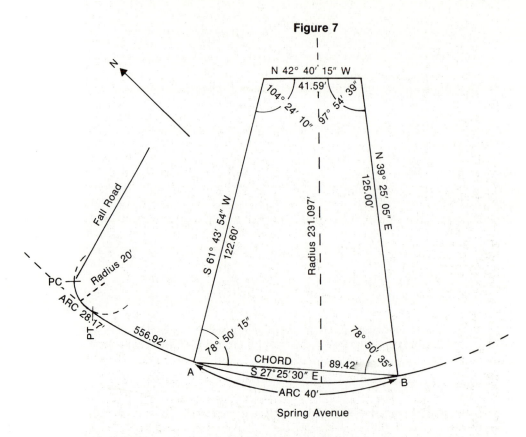

of 231.097 feet, the arc distance of 40 feet (the chord of said arc extending North 27 degrees 25 minutes 30 seconds West, 89.42 feet) to a point."

IV. CHECKING THE LEGAL DESCRIPTION FOR ACCURACY

A. SURVEY

When there is a survey, one should always verify the accuracy of a legal description by comparing the metes and bounds with those shown on the survey. When proofreading a legal description against a survey, one should always check the accuracy of easements, surrounding streets, and landmarks described in the legal description.

B. WHEN THERE IS NO SURVEY

If no survey exists and it is not feasible to obtain a new one, a cursory check of the accuracy of a legal description is still possible. This is done by drawing, in scale, the boundary lines described in the legal description to see whether they start and end at the same point.

Figure 8

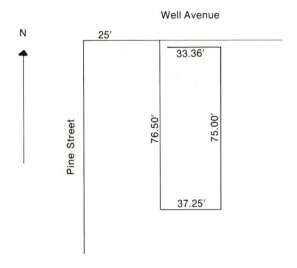

If, for example, you prepare a drawing of the following legal description, you would find that the description is incorrect (see Figure 8):

> Beginning at a point on the southerly side of Well Avenue 25 feet easterly from the corner formed by the intersection of the southerly side of Well Avenue and the easterly side of Pine Street; thence southerly parallel to the easterly side of Pine Street 76.50 feet; thence easterly parallel to the southerly side of Well Avenue 37.25 feet; thence northerly parallel to the easterly side of Pine Street 75.00 feet to the southerly side of Well Avenue; thence westerly along the southerly side of Well Avenue 33.36 feet to the point and place of beginning.

Under these circumstances it would be necessary to have a survey made so that a correct legal description could be prepared. Absent such a survey there is no way of knowing the size of the lot.

V. INTERPRETATION OF LEGAL DESCRIPTIONS

A. WIDTH OF BOUNDARIES

Legal descriptions often refer to streets, streams, railroad rights of way, or other natural boundaries. Such monuments have certain widths. It is important to know, therefore, if the land being described extends only to the nearer edge, the middle, or the more distinct edge of the boundary. This issue is sometimes resolved by a clear-cut statement in the instrument itself. However, if no such statement exists, the usual rule is that the land described extends to the middle of the boundary.

B. INCONSISTENCY IN THE DESCRIPTION

On occasion, a legal description will contain more than one descriptive reference. For example, a particular metes and bounds description may read in part, "365.50 feet to a point where an iron fence meets Wilson Road." If on survey it turns out that the point of intersection of the fence and road is really 372.60 feet, there is an internal inconsistency in the description that must be resolved. Another fairly common inconsistency, particularly with large tracts, is between a metes and bounds description and quantity statements (e.g., "containing 64 acres").

Although every jurisdiction has its own methods of resolving inconsistencies, points of reference are generally considered reliable and, as a consequence, determine the size and legal description of the lot, in the following order of priority:

1. Monuments
2. Map References (e.g., meridians)
3. Metes and Bounds
4. Quantity Statements (containing 64 acres)
5. Lot Numbers

A monument that is referred to in a legal description will generally prevail as a boundary marker rather than a stated distance. The paramount importance and interpretive priority given to monuments by the law, in addition to the fact that people often think of what they own or will buy by reference to monuments, have caused lawyers and surveyors to make common mention of monuments in surveys and legal descriptions.

VI. CONCLUSIONS

You will probably not be called on to prepare a survey, or perhaps even a legal description. However, a paralegal must be able to compare a survey with a legal description and to ascertain whether there are any inconsistencies.

PROBLEM

Using a protractor, please diagram the following legal description:

ALL THAT CERTAIN lot or piece of ground situate in West Deptford, Gloucester County, New Jersey, described according to an Amended Final Subdivision Plan for Green Balm Development made by Thompson and Johnson, Inc., Engineers and Surveyors, Woodbury, New Jersey, dated October 10, 1979, and last revised June 16, 1981, and recorded in Plan Book A-43 Pages 45, 46, and 47, as follows, to wit:

BEGINNING at a point of curve on the northwesterly side of Morris Drive (50 feet wide), which point is measured North 26 degrees 36 minutes

00 seconds East, 160.432 feet from the intersection of the said northwesterly side of Morris Drive with the northeasterly side of Ferro Avenue; thence extending from the said point and place of beginning leaving Morris Drive and along Lot 17 on said Plan, North 30 degrees 28 minutes 55 seconds West, 266.155 feet to a point in line of lands now or formerly of Frank and Nina Frenetic; thence along same North 81 degrees 37 minutes 59 seconds East, 140.000 feet to an iron post (found), a corner of Lot 18 on said Plan; thence along the said lot 18 South 59 degrees 06 minutes 06 seconds East, 217.648 feet to a point on the said northwesterly side of Morris Drive; thence along same the three following courses and distances: (1) on the arc of a circle curving to the right having a radius of 325.000 feet, the arc distance of 142.929 feet (the chord of said arc extending South 49 degrees 05 minutes 54 seconds West, 141.780 feet) to a point of tangency; (2) South 61 degrees 41 minutes 50 seconds West, 76.273 feet to a point of curve; (3) on the arc of a circle curving to the left having a radius of 481.000 feet, the arc distance of 18.296 feet (the chord of said arc extending South 60 degrees 36 minutes 27 seconds West, 18.295 feet) to the first mentioned point and place of beginning.

CONTAINING 42,942 square feet, more or less.

BEING Lot 17 on said Plan.

Chapter 5

Deeds of Conveyance

I. INTRODUCTION

Title to real property is normally transferred by signing and delivery of a legal instrument called a deed of conveyance. The body of laws, rules, procedures, and customs relating to the transfer of title to real property is known as conveyancing.

The rules regarding the transfer of real property differ greatly from those dealing with transfers of personal property. Most items of personal property, such as clothes, books, and furniture, are able to be delivered in a physical sense. Title to such personalty can and does pass from one person to another by mere physical delivery, although formal documents evidencing title are sometimes prepared and used to make a written record of the transaction. On the other hand, real property cannot be moved[1] and therefore cannot be physically delivered. During the earliest days of the common law, title to real estate was transferred without written documentation. Instead, the seller of medieval times simulated the physical delivery of title to the real estate by meeting the purchaser on the land to be conveyed and delivering a symbol of the land, such as a clod of earth or a twig. It was necessary to have witnesses present at the ceremony so that, if challenged, the purchaser could prove the terms of the oral conveyance. Such a method of conveyancing was satisfactory when transfers of title were infrequent and actual possession was the best evidence of ownership. However, the constant subdividing of land into small parcels, more complex family arrangements for the descent of

---

1. Indeed, on being removed, it ceases to be real property. Thus, felled timber or mined ore becomes personal property.

land, and the rise of more modern forms of commercial enterprise required more permanent records of land transactions.

Two basic forms of written records of the transfer of title to real property developed—the indenture and the deed poll.

A. THE INDENTURE

An indenture was originally a deed between two or more parties written out twice on the same long piece of paper. The duplicate copies were separated by cutting or tearing along a jagged or indented line. Each party signed both halves and received one of the counterpart copies. The reason the grantee signed the deed was to prove that the grantee had accepted the property and the deed, including the grantor's covenants contained in the deed.[2] The grantee could not enforce the covenants unless he or she had signed the deed. If the authenticity of the deed was ever questioned, the issue could be resolved by fitting together the two indented counterparts and comparing them. Although we no longer prepare deeds by cutting one piece of paper into two parts, the most common modern form of deed is still called an "indenture." However, in the modern form the indenture deed does not require the signature of the grantee.

B. THE DEED POLL

The other early form of deed, the deed poll, was distinguished from the indenture by the fact that it was not executed in counterpart. It was signed only by the grantor, and its top was "polled" (i.e., shaved or cut straight), not indented. If there were no covenants contained in the deed that the grantee was required to accept, only the grantor had to sign, and a deed poll could be used. The deed poll survives today in the typical form of sheriff's deed, which is discussed later in this chapter.

II. THE ELEMENTS OF A DEED

A. STANDARD LANGUAGE AND FORMS

The common law form of deed of conveyance was developed to perform a relatively simple task. It served to memorialize the intent of the grantor to transfer to the grantee title to a certain interest in a particular parcel of real estate. Although modern deeds are sometimes long and complex, they contain only a few essential elements that can be simply expressed.

A deed should recite that the grantor intends, by delivery of the deed, to transfer to the named grantee title to a specific interest in a described piece of real estate. By custom, particularly when the grantee is to pay a price for the real estate, the grantor warrants to the grantee that (a) the grantor owns the real estate, (b) the grantor has the right to transfer

---

2. The party conveying the property is called the grantor and the party to whom the property is being conveyed is called the grantee.

it, (c) that no one has any claim against the real estate or any other interest therein, and (d) that the grantor will defend the title being transferred if any adverse claimant attacks it.

As the modern form of deed of conveyance developed during the past few hundred years, the words lawyers used to describe the grantor's intentions to convey and warrant have been construed by countless courts and, in the tradition of the common law, have been given precise meanings. Because of the certainty gained by use of these words, the forms of deed commonly used today have a rather quaint flavor and style of language. Each state has developed standard forms that are almost universally used by the lawyers of that jurisdiction. In fact, the forms are so well defined and widely accepted that they are printed by local legal stationers with blank spaces for the names of the parties, the price, and the description of the real estate. At this point you should review the sample deed set forth on page 151, which has been prepared on a form customarily used in Pennsylvania.

B. PARTS OF DEED

The three main parts of the typical common law indenture are the premises, the habendum, and the conclusion. The *premises* includes the date; the names of the parties; a recital of the consideration; the grant; the legal description; exceptions and reservations, if any; the recital; the encumbrance clauses, if any; and the appurtenance clause. The *habendum* includes the "to have and to hold" clause; a reference to or repetition of the exceptions, reservations, and encumbrances, if any; and the covenants and warranty. The *conclusion* consists of the execution clause, a receipt for the consideration (in some cases), and the acknowledgment (for recording purposes). We will now consider each of the sections of the deed in detail.

C. PREMISES

1. Date

Title to real estate passes on the delivery of a deed, rather than on the date of its execution. Nevertheless, good conveyancing dictates that the date of execution be inserted in the heading of the deed. Unless other evidence is brought forth, it will be presumed that the deed was delivered to the grantee on the date of execution as indicated in the heading. In order for the deed to be recorded, it cannot be dated after the date on which the grantor gave his or her acknowledgment before a notary public. (The acknowledgment is discussed later.) In drafting a deed for use at a settlement that will take place in the future, it is best to leave blank the day and the month. This can be filled in by hand at settlement, when the deed is executed.

2. Names of the Parties

After the date, the names of the grantor(s) and grantee(s) appear as follows:

> ALAN L. BURNS AND MARY R. BURNS, husband and wife, of 100 Black-acre Lane, Philadelphia, Pennsylvania (hereinafter called the Grantors), of the one part, and ROBERT B. DAVIS, singleman, of 642 Greenacre Road, Philadelphia, Pennsylvania (hereinafter called the Grantee), of the other part,

Names should be stated with the greatest possible accuracy and completeness. If an individual party has a middle initial or uses a title such as "Jr.," it should be included as part of his or her name. Nicknames should be avoided. It is a wise practice to indicate the marital status of the grantor (e.g., Mary R. Burns, singlewoman (if never married); or Mary Brennan, unmarried woman (if divorced); or Mary S. Bell, widow; or Joseph P. Dobbs, singleman; or Peter Brandon, unmarried man; or Frank R. Green, widower). If the parties are husband and wife, their relationship should be indicated. Such information helps those who search the chain of title to determine whether it is necessary for a spouse to join in the deed. If a corporation is a party to a deed, its official name should be used and its state of incorporation mentioned to avoid confusion with other entities having similar names (e.g., BCP Associates, Inc., a Pennsylvania corporation).

Before preparing a deed it is helpful to obtain a copy of the deed by which the grantor acquired title to be sure that he or she is using the same name in conveying title. If a copy of the deed cannot be obtained from the grantor, the grantee may obtain a copy of the previous deed by searching the recorders' office in the county in which the property is located. The grantee-grantor index is organized chronologically according to the year in which the property was purchased and alphabetically according to the grantor's name. One should remember that the grantor who is now selling the property will be listed as a grantee in the index under the year in which he or she purchased the property. Of course, in many cases the named grantee in the last recorded deed will not be the titleholder, or the titleholder's name will have changed since the last recorded deed. For example, when real estate has passed at the death of the record titleholder to an heir, the property records may contain no evidence of such transfer. Other examples are when the grantor was an unmarried woman when she acquired title, but has since remarried and changed her name, and when a corporation merges into another corporation or changes its name after taking title. In such cases a brief explanation is necessary to keep the recording officials from misindexing the deed. Consider, for example: "Jane B. Doe, widow (formerly Jane A. Burns)"; or "RCA Corporation (formerly known as Radio Corporation of America)"; or "ITT Corporation (successor by merger to The Sheraton Company)."

Similar care should be taken to designate the grantee in precisely the name in which title is intended to be taken. For example, when the grantee is to be a partnership, it is necessary to determine whether title is to be held in the name of the partnership without mention of the names of the individual partners, or whether title is to be held in the individual names of the partners.

3. Consideration

Consideration is a legal term for the payment or inducement that one gives in exchange for a promise or for services, goods, or real estate. At common law there had to be consideration given for a deed. The consideration clause of the model deed set forth on page 151 is as follows:

> WITNESSETH that the said Grantors for and in consideration of the sum of Ninety Thousand Dollars ($90,000.00) lawful money of the United States of America, unto them well and truly paid by the said Grantee, at or before the sealing and delivery hereof, the receipt whereof is hereby acknowledged,

Traditionally, the amount of the consideration or price is not important so long as the deed recited that the grant or had received some consideration. When the actual consideration for the transfer of title is something other than money (e.g., an unrelated contractual undertaking), or when the price is substantial, but the parties wish to avoid disclosing the real price, it has become the custom to insert "one dollar" as the consideration. A recital of one dollar is also used when the grantor intends to make a gift of the real estate to the grantee.

For most purposes the recital of the consideration is merely a formality and not conclusive. It may be contradicted and the real consideration established by other evidence. In many states, however, taxes are imposed on the transfer of real estate or the recording of the deed. Such taxes are based on the actual consideration paid for the real estate or, in the case of a gift, on the market value of the real estate. In such cases, the actual consideration or the market value is usually established by an affidavit that accompanies or is attached to the deed.

4. Granting Clause

The granting clause follows the recitation of the consideration. In the deed set forth on page 151 the granting clause is as follows:

> have granted, bargained and sold, released and confirmed, and by these presents do grant, bargain and sell, release and confirm unto the said Grantee, his heirs and assigns, . . .

The purpose of the granting clause is to state the grantor's intention to convey title to the grantee. The words above have been construed many times by the courts of Pennsylvania, and their meaning is now well defined by the case law. In fact, the legislature has defined the meaning of some of the words by statute. For example, the phrase "these presents" has come to signify the instrument in which it is written; in the above example, it refers to the deed itself. It should be pointed out that although these are the customarily used words of grant in Pennsylvania, in other jurisdictions other words of grant have the same effect. Similarly, in other jurisdictions variations on this formula have become sacred over the years as a result of their continual use and interpretation by the courts.

PROBLEM

In your jurisdiction what are the customarily used words of grant? How do they differ from the Pennsylvania format?

(a) Implied Warranty

In many states, the courts have construed the words used in the granting clause to imply certain covenants, promises, and warranties by the grantor in favor of the grantee. In other states, the legislature has affirmatively defined by statute the customarily used words of the granting clause to include certain covenants and warranties. For instance, in Pennsylvania, the words "grant, bargain, sell" have been defined to be an express covenant to the grantee that the grantor holds a title that cannot be defeated by another, that the land is unencumbered (i.e., not subject to claims of the mortgagee or other creditors), and that the grantee shall not be disturbed or evicted from the premises by the grantor or his or her heirs.

Certain kinds of deeds for limited purposes require the words of the standard granting clause to be changed. For example, when the grantor wishes to negate any implications of covenants or warranties, the grantor delivers a "quitclaim" deed. Such a deed is in reality a "release" in favor of the grantee of whatever interest the grantor may have in a parcel of real estate. A quitclaim contains no representation as to quality of title and no express warranty clause in the habendum (to be discussed later); it simply "remises" (remits or gives up) the grantor's interest in the property. Such a deed would not include the words "grant, bargain, sell" in the granting clause, or the warranties sought to be avoided would arise by implication. Accordingly, the quitclaim deed uses the following form of granting clause:

> has remised, released and quitclaimed, and by these presents does remise, release and quitclaim unto the said party of the second part, and to his heirs and assigns forever,

(b) Words of Inheritance

The words "his heirs and assigns" that appear at the end of the granting clause had great significance in the early days of the common law. If such words were not used, the grantee did not obtain a fee simple estate, but only a life estate (that is, the right to ownership of the real estate was limited to the duration of the grantee's life), which the grantee could not pass on to his or her heirs after death. For that reason, the words "his heirs and assigns" are called words of "inheritance." In most states today either court decisions or statutes have made words of inheritance superfluous and therefore unnecessary. Nevertheless, attorneys are reluctant to tamper with time-revered language, and words of inheritance continue to be used in nearly all forms of deeds.

(c) Nature of the Estate Granted

In Chapter Two, the various forms in which title to real estate may be held are discussed. Conveyancing puts into action the decision respecting the choice of a titleholder. At the end of the granting clause the conveyancer inserts words that indicate the nature of the estate granted to the grantee or grantees. If no estate is expressly stated, the law of most jurisdictions will imply a particular estate depending on the nature of the grantees. If the grantees are husband and wife and the nature of their estate is intended to be a tenancy by the entirety, the words "as tenants by the entirety" should be added at the end of the granting clause. Some states have held as a matter of law that the designation of the grantees as husband and wife creates the legal implication that they hold as "tenants by the entirety" unless some other tenancy is specified, such as tenants in common. Other jurisdictions hold directly to the contrary, and tenancy by the entirety will not be implied but must be specified. If individual grantees intend to hold title as joint tenants, the phrase "as joint tenants with right of survivorship and not as tenants in common" should be used. If there is more than one grantee, and they are not husband and wife, it will be assumed that they hold title as tenants in common in *equal* shares. If that is not the case, it is extremely important to indicate the fractional share that each tenant receives. For example:

> in the undivided portions or shares of one-third to A, his heirs and assigns, one-ninth to B, his heirs and assigns, two-ninths to C, her heirs and assigns, and one-sixth each to D and E and their respective heirs and assigns.

It is particularly important to describe the nature of the estate conveyed to tenants in common when two of them are husband and wife. In such a case in many jurisdictions there is a strong legal presumption that the husband and wife are intended to take one share as tenants by the entirety as between themselves. Therefore, if B and C are husband and wife, a conveyance to A, B, and C may be construed to be a conveyance of a one-half interest to A and the other one-half interest to B and C (who will hold their one-half interest as tenants by the entirety), rather than a conveyance of one-third interests to A, B, and C each. If a father wishes to convey a one-third interest in the family home to his wife, "A," and the remaining two-thirds interest to his son and daughter-in-law, "B" and "C," the granting clause should indicate that the grantees hold their unequal share as follows:

> in the undivided portions or shares of one-third to A, her heirs and assigns, and two-thirds to B and C, his wife, their heirs and assigns, as tenants by the entirety as between B and C, his wife, and as tenants in common as between them as such tenants by entirety, and A.

When real estate is to be conveyed to A and B, who are to be business partners and not merely tenants in common or joint tenants, it is important to indicate that they will hold "as tenants in co-partnership for the uses and purposes of the co-partnership."

In the rare case in which a conveyance is limited to a life estate, the granting clause should indicate that the grantee holds "for the term of his natural life only."

5. Description

In a practical sense the legal description of the real estate being conveyed is the most crucial part of the deed and requires the greatest accuracy in drafting. As we have seen, legal descriptions are usually prepared by surveyors, title insurance companies, or other experts. They are often based on professional surveys, official city plans, or prior conveyances. Because this subject is dealt with in Chapter Four, only a few points need be mentioned here.

The legal description must be sufficiently clear and precise to enable a surveyor (but not necessarily a layperson) to locate and identify the property to the extent that the surveyor is able to place boundary markers at each corner of the parcel of land and at any other point along the entire perimeter. This does not mean that a full metes and bounds description is necessary. In many cases, although the real estate has not been surveyed, the boundary lines are ascertainable by reference to visible and reasonably permanent markers or other boundaries, such as roads, streams, or party walls.[3]

Occasionally, the legal description is based on an official plan of survey or a plan of survey prepared by a registered surveyor or civil engineer. Some attorneys and title insurance companies refer to such a survey in the introduction to the legal description even when the survey has not been recorded among the official local land records. The practice is based on the theory that a future purchaser or interested party will be able to obtain a copy of the plan either from the grantor or from the surveyor who drew the plan. When it is permitted by the rules and practices of

---

3. Party walls are walls that are located on the common boundary of two parcels of land. Such walls are generally shared by buildings on the adjoining properties. Party walls are especially common in the older cities of the east and in modern townhouse developments. There is a considerable amount of common law regarding the rights, duties, and obligations of the owners of party walls.

the local recording office, it is becoming common to attach to the deed a copy of the plan referred to in the legal description.

In some jurisdictions, recording offices maintain a "map file" in which original copies of survey plans may be filed or recorded. When residential communities are created in accordance with an officially approved plan of subdivision, the plan is normally filed or recorded and the deeds to the purchasers of subdivision lots contain a reference to that plan. In other jurisdictions (for example, New York City) it is the practice not to refer to any plan of survey, on the contrary theory that the deed should stand on its own and not depend on, or even suggest that, reference to another document or plan is necessary to locate accurately the land referred to in the legal description.

Whenever possible, the legal description to be used in the deed should be checked against any plan of survey to which it refers, as errors in transferring information from a survey are common.

6. Recital

The recital is a clause that follows the legal description and serves to explain how the grantor acquired title to the real estate. The deed on page 151 contains the following recital:

> BEING the same premises which Charles Clark and Dorothy Clark, husband and wife, by Indenture dated July 8, 1945 and recorded in the Office for Recording of Deeds in and for the County of Philadelphia (now the Department of Records of the City of Philadelphia) in Deed Book J.M.H. No. 2286, page 354, granted and conveyed unto the said Alan L. Burns and Mary R. Burns, husband and wife, in fee, as tenants by the entirety.

The recital is not a legally necessary part of the deed. However, it is a valuable aid to conveyancers and those who search the land records to examine the chain of title. It also may provide evidence of the grantor's intention in certain respects. For example, the recital may indicate that the premises being conveyed are "the same premises" that the grantor acquired by a specific prior deed or that they are only "a part of" certain premises that the grantor acquired by a certain deed.

In cases in which the granting clause of the deed leaves the extent of the grant uncertain or vague, the recital may be deemed to reveal the grantor's true intent. A court may construe the recital to restrict general words to a narrower meaning if the intent to do so is clear. In most states, however, it cannot enlarge a clearly defined grant. If the operative words of the granting clause and the recital conflict, the operative words of the granting clause will prevail, so long as they are certain and definite.

Recitals can be concisely drafted whenever the grantor obtained title by one deed and there have been no subsequent changes in the grantor's name or the nature of the title. However, there are many situations that require more complex recitals, such as the following:

(a) Deed to the Grantor Signed by an Attorney-in-Fact

Often a grantor will not be available to execute a deed. In such situations the grantor may appoint another as attorney-in-fact with power to execute deeds on his or her behalf. When the deed to the present grantor was signed by an attorney-in-fact for the previous grantor, a recital such as the following must be inserted in the new deed:

> BEING a part of the same premises which James P. Monroe, III by his attorney-in-fact, William C. Hamilton (by virtue of a power of attorney given by the said James P. Monroe, III, dated April 8, 1984, and recorded in the Office for Recording of Deeds in and for the County of Montgomery, Pennsylvania, in Miscellaneous Book No. 4331 at page 24) by Indenture dated April 20, 1984, and recorded in said Office in Deed Book No. 778 at page 578, &c., granted and conveyed unto George Q. Andrews, in fee.

(b) Grantor Received Sheriff's Deed

When the deed to the grantor was given by the sheriff or other judicial officer after a foreclosure sale, a recital such as the following should be employed in a new deed given by the grantor:

> BEING the same premises which William M. Lennox, Sheriff of the County of Philadelphia, by deed-poll dated February 10, 1977 and recorded in the Department of Records of the City of Philadelphia for the consideration therein mentioned, by virtue of a certain Writ of Execution therein recited, granted and conveyed unto Donald L. Stone and Susan B. Stone, his wife, in fee, as tenants by the entirety.

(c) Name of Corporate Grantor Changed

When the corporate grantor has changed its name or has merged into another company since acquiring title, language such as the following should be inserted in the deed:

> BEING the same premises which Clyde Hanson by Indenture dated September 4, 1969 and recorded in the Office for the Recording of Deeds in and for the County of Montgomery, Pennsylvania, in Deed Book No. 345 at page 765, &c., granted and conveyed unto Atlas Harness and Buggy Whip Manufacturing Company, a Pennsylvania corporation, in fee.
>
> AND on October 10, 1970, a Certificate of Merger evidencing the merger of Atlas Harness and Buggy Whip Manufacturing Company, a Pennsylvania corporation, with and into Aberfoyle Petroleum Refining Co., Inc., a Pennsylvania corporation, was issued to the said corporation by the Secretary of the Commonwealth of Pennsylvania, changing its name and corporate title from Atlas Harness and Buggy Whip Manufacturing Company to Atlas Corporation.
>
> (AND on October 10, 1970, a Certificate of Merger evidencing the merger of Atlas Harness and Buggy Whip Manufacturing Company, a Pennsylvania corporation, with and into Aberfoyle Petroleum Refining Co., Inc., a Pennsylvania corporation, was issued by the Secretary of the Common-

wealth of Pennsylvania to the surviving corporation, the name and corporate title of which is Atlas Corporation.)

(d) Real Estate Being Conveyed Was Assembled in Multiple Transfers

When the real estate being conveyed has been assembled by several conveyances to the grantor, several recitals are required to show the prior conveyance of each piece, each beginning:

BEING, AS TO A PART THEREOF, the same premises which . . .

When several grantors own separate interests that they are conveying together, but that they acquired at different times, several recitals are again necessary to give the history of each piece. Each such recital would begin as follows:

BEING THE SAME PREMISES which A . . . granted and conveyed unto B, in fee, as to a one-third interest therein.

(e) Entireties Property When One Spouse Has Died

When the real estate was acquired by husband and wife as tenants by the entirety, but one spouse has since died, the following clause is added to the normal form of recital:

AND the said Frank D. Bennett died on November 21, 1984, and title to the property passed to the said Emma J. Bennett by operation of law.

PROBLEM

Prepare a deed recital for the following fact situation: on January 21, 1958, BCR Associates, Inc., an Iowa corporation, conveyed certain property to Frank Z. Conn and Mary R. Conn, his wife, as tenants by the entirety. The deed was recorded in Blackhawk County in Deed Book 113, page 272. On November 15, 1969, Frank Z. Conn died, leaving Mary as his widow. On October 19, 1972, Mary R. Conn married Joseph W. Moore, and she is now known as Mary Conn Moore. Mary, joined by her husband, is now conveying the property to the grantee.

---

7. Encumbrance Clauses

A deed may convey property that, on agreement of the buyer, is subject to various encumbrances, such as pre-existing mortgages, restrictions created by prior deeds, or other liens, easements, exceptions, and reservations. Such encumbrances are each set forth in one or more clauses referred to as the "encumbrance clause" or, more commonly, the "under and subject" clause. The latter phrase is derived from the introductory words commonly used in such a clause, an example of which follows:

UNDER AND SUBJECT, nevertheless, to certain conditions and restrictions as appear of record in Deed Book W.S.M. No. 231, page 253, &c.

The grantee will acquire title subject to all encumbrances that actually exist, whether or not the deed mentions them or lists them in the encumbrance clauses. However, by mentioning and listing encumbrances the grantor gives the grantee notice of their existence and thereby limits the scope of his or her covenants and warranties of title to encumbrances not mentioned. Accordingly, the grantor should attempt to list all the encumbrances on title of which he or she has knowledge. Good conveyancing practice calls for inclusion of the full text of each encumbrance to be included in the text of the deed. However, such text may be many pages in length. It is usual, therefore, merely to refer to each encumbrance by setting forth the recording data, which will enable the grantee, his or her attorney, or the title searcher to locate in the local land records the document creating the encumbrance. Such a reference to the encumbrance is sufficient to limit the grantor's warranty of title with respect to a particular encumbrance.

If the grantor is not certain of the particular encumbrances that remain in a chain of title, the grantor may attempt to limit the scope of his or her covenants and warranties by using a general encumbrance clause such as the following:

UNDER AND SUBJECT to all agreements, covenants, liens, reservations, exceptions, restrictions and other encumbrances of record.

The grantor may also limit his or her warranties by use of a "special warranty deed" or deed with covenants only "against the acts of grantor," both of which shall be examined in section D(2) (d).

In some cases the grantee may object to reference being made in the deed to obsolete restrictions and encumbrances that may have expired by passage of time or may be extinguished by other circumstances. Such an objection is especially pertinent when restrictions or encumbrances are referred to by a catch-all provision referring to all encumbrances of record. Many lawyers feel that mention of such obsolete restrictions might be viewed as evidence that the parties wish to revive them or continue to treat them as binding and enforceable. A compromise solution is achieved by changing the wording of the catch-all encumbrance clause to the following:

UNDER AND SUBJECT to all agreements, covenants, liens, reservations, exceptions, restrictions and other encumbrances of record, to the extent still valid, subsisting, and enforceable.

A similar change in language can be used at the end of a provision listing specific encumbrances and restrictions.

Reference to existing encumbrances should appear both in the "under and subject" clause in the premises portion of the deed and again, by reference, in the habendum. It is also good practice to refer to encumbrances a third time, in the warranty clause. Reference to encumbrances in the habendum and warranty clauses are discussed later.

8. Use of the Encumbrance Clause for Creation of New Restrictions

In addition to conveying subject to former encumbrances, the grantor may wish to create new restrictions by his or her own conveyance.

(a) Purposes

Restrictions are most often created by residential developers who, for the benefit of all homeowners, impose limitations on the use of each lot in their subdivision. Limitations might relate to the kind and quality of buildings and improvements that may be constructed and to the amount of lot area and the location or placement of the building on the lot. Such restrictions serve as private zoning and building codes and attempt to prevent the establishment of any nuisances in the subdivision community. Customarily, these restrictions appear in the developer's deed for each lot and are enforceable by and against each lot owner in the subdivision.

Restrictive covenants are also used when a business, such as a retail furniture store, moves from its original location to a nearby location and wishes to prohibit its grantee and future owners of the original location from opening a competitive retail furniture enterprise. Gasoline companies use such restrictive covenants to limit the number of service stations in prime areas.

Another common use of deed restrictions is to assure the seller of a portion of a large tract of land that the land conveyed will be used for purposes compatible with the use of the remainder of the grantor's land. For example, a farmer may be willing to have the purchaser of his or her south 60 acres develop that land for residential purposes, but not for commercial or industrial uses. The farmer is protected by inserting a restrictive covenant in the deed to the purchaser.

(b) Covenants Running with the Land

Restrictions may be of two types: those for the personal benefit and protection of the grantor only and those for the protection of others (such as neighbors in a subdivision), including the grantor's successors in title. A restriction of the first type is enforceable only by the grantor who creates it, whereas a restriction of the second type is intended to be of continual benefit to the original grantor as well as his or her heirs and successors in title. Such a restriction is known as a "covenant running with the land."

In order to determine whether a particular covenant is the type that runs with the land, a prospective purchaser, and the courts, if necessary, must determine the intent of the parties who created the restriction. Books are filled with legal theory and precedent on this subject. However, good drafting will forestall many disputes. By adding a clause such as the following to the deed restrictions, any question about the grantor's intention will be eliminated:

And the Grantee, for himself, his heirs and assigns, by acceptance of this indenture, agrees with the Grantor, his heirs and assigns, that the restrictions and conditions set forth above shall be covenants running with the land, and that in any deed of conveyance of the above-described premises or any part thereof to any person or persons, such restrictions and conditions shall be set forth therein or shall be incorporated by reference to this indenture and the record hereof.

(c) Limitations on Restrictions

Even though the grantor may want his or her restriction to be a covenant running with the land, the grantor may not wish it to be a perpetual restriction. In such cases the grantor must indicate a time limitation, such as ten, twenty, or fifty years. This is becoming an advisable practice because courts are more frequently holding restrictions to be unenforceable in light of changing circumstances. For example, if the adjoining neighborhoods become commercial or industrial, land located in or near the heart of a city that was originally restricted for dwelling purposes only, may become undesirable for such use. If there is no time limit on the restriction for dwelling purposes imposed on such land, courts are likely to hold that the restrictions have become obsolete and are unenforceable. Restrictions limited to twenty or thirty years have a much greater chance of being upheld as reasonable until they expire by their own terms.

In most jurisdictions today deed restrictions that impose limitations on the use of real estate based on race or national origin have been held unconstitutional and unenforceable. When such restrictions appear in a chain of title, they may safely be ignored.

(d) Drafting

When there is any doubt as to the meaning of a restriction, a court will construe the language in a manner most unfavorable to the grantor.[4] Therefore, restrictions must be drafted carefully, lest either the restriction be construed in an unintended manner, or be completely unenforceable because of its ambiguity. For example, it is important in drafting a restriction to make clear whether you are trying to limit the kind of building that may be erected or the use to which a building may be put, or both, e.g., a restriction intending to prohibit construction of any dwelling other than a dwelling house for commercial or quasi-commercial purposes, such as a real estate broker's office or a doctor's office.

9. Encumbrance Clause for Mortgage Liens

If the grantor has borrowed money and created a mortgage debt during his or her ownership of the real estate to be conveyed, his or her title is

---

4. The theory on which such a rule is based is that when the language of a restriction is unclear, it is better to leave the land unencumbered.

burdened with another type of encumbrance, a mortgage lien. Often the grantee will be willing to receive the property subject to the mortgage lien. In such a case the grantee would take a credit against the purchase price in an amount equal to the unpaid balance of the mortgage debt.[5] If the grantee is willing to take title subject to the mortgage, the grantor will certainly want to limit the granting clause and his or her warranties by adding to the deed an "under and subject" clause such as the following:

> ALSO UNDER AND SUBJECT to the lien of a certain mortgage debt created by David G. Metropolis in favor of East Kalamazoo Savings and Loan Association by Mortgage dated January 6, 1971 and recorded in the Office of the Recorder of Deeds in and for Montgomery County, Pennsylvania in Mortgage Book No. 3168 at page 405, in the original principal amount of $35,000.00 but since reduced by payments on account to $33,600.00, with interest thereon as the same may become due and payable.

Such an encumbrance clause should be inserted in the premises section of the deed and referred to again in the "to have and to hold" clause and in the warranty clause of the habendum.

(a) Personal Liability of Grantee to Mortagee

As discussed in Chapter Seven, under the terms of some mortgage loans the debtor's liability is personal, whereas liability under certain other mortgage loans is limited to the land. In the latter case the holder of the mortgage can satisfy his or her debt only from the value of the mortgaged real estate.

It is important to determine whether, under the law of the local jurisdiction, the words chosen to refer to the existence of the mortgage lien create any personal liability on the grantee for payment of the mortgage debt. The grantee may be willing to take title subject to the likelihood that if he or she does not pay the sums due on the mortgage debt, the mortgagee will foreclose and cause the real estate to be sold at foreclosure sale. However, the grantor may not be willing to risk personal liability for the payment of any balance due on the mortgage if the foreclosure sale does not produce sufficient funds to satisfy the mortgage debt. In Pennsylvania, for example, the use of the words "under and subject" have been statutorily defined to eliminate the implication that the grantee has assumed personal liability for the mortgage debt. In some cases, however, the grantor may insist that the grantee become personally liable to the mortgagee, and the grantee may agree. In such cases it is necessary to add the phrase "which the grantee hereby assumes and agrees to pay" to the above form of encumbrance clause referring to an existing mortgage debt.

---

5. Please refer to Chapter Seven for a discussion of financing the purchase of real property by taking under and subject to an existing mortgage.

(b) Indemnification of Grantor

In the event the grantee assumes the mortgage of the grantor, the grantor will be concerned about being protected in the event the grantee fails to perform his or her obligations under the mortgage. Such a problem, of course, need only concern a grantor who will remain personally liable for the mortgage debt. The protection normally desired by a grantor is indemnification from the grantee.

In choosing the wording for a mortgage encumbrance clause, one must consider whether the law of the state implies any right of indemnification by the grantee in favor of the grantor in the event the mortgagee sues the grantor on the original mortgage note (following a default by the grantee). Because the grantor allowed the grantee a credit against what would otherwise have been the purchase price on the understanding that the grantee would pay the installments on the mortgage debt, the grantor ordinarily expects to have such a right of indemnification; and in many states, including Pennsylvania, the law implies one. If the parties agree that the grantee will not indemnify the grantor, it is necessary to negate the implication of such a right of indemnification in those jurisdictions in which it would otherwise be implied by law. The following sentence, when added to the encumbrance clause (omitting, of course, the words "assume and agree to pay"), accomplishes that aim:

> But it is expressly agreed that the grantee herein shall not be held liable to indemnify or reimburse the grantor for any loss which the grantor may sustain by being required to pay the mortgagee or its successors in interest, or the grantor's predecessors in title or any of them, in satisfaction of such mortgage debt or any part thereof for which such mortgage was given as security, and that any and all such liability which may arise by operation of law is hereby expressly released.

Such an agreement could be the subject of a separate agreement, but it is preferable to include it in the deed immediately after the mortgage encumbrance clause that would otherwise give rise to the implied right of indemnity.

(c) Effect on Statement of Consideration

Whenever an encumbrance clause refers to a judgment, mortgage lien, or other obligation payable in money, it is best not only to refer to the relevant recording data, but also to indicate the original principal amount of the debt and the outstanding principal balance thereof as of the date of conveyance. This latter sum is the amount of the "credit" that the grantor allows the grantee in reduction of what would be the purchase price if the real estate were to be sold free and clear of the lien of the debt. Some lawyers prefer to state the amount of this credit in the consideration clause of the deed to avoid confusion. In such cases the consideration clause may be phrased as follows:

for and in consideration of the sum of One Million, Two Hundred Thousand Dollars ($1,200,000.00) lawful money of the United States of America, Two Hundred Thousand Dollars ($200,000.00) of which has been paid in cash and the balance of which, One Million Dollars ($1,000,000.00), is the outstanding principal balance of a certain mortgage lien hereinafter referred to.

In some localities it is customary to state in the consideration clause only the amount of cash and other consideration (such as a purchase money mortgage note) paid to the grantor.

10. Encumbrance Clause for Easements

Another form of encumbrance on title is the easement. If the grantor's title was subject to an easement when he or she acquired it, the encumbrance clause referring to it is drafted in a manner similar to that for restrictions:

ALSO UNDER AND SUBJECT to an easement of a certain 25-foot-wide driveway, as set forth in an Easement Agreement between Potter M. Brenner and Mary R. Burns dated January 8, 1971, and recorded in the Office of the Recorder of Deeds of Norfolk County, Massachusetts, in Deed Book Volume XV at page 91.

Of course, if the actual text creating the easement is not unduly long and complicated, it is preferable to repeat it in full in the deed. As is the case of other encumbrances, the "to have and to hold" and warranty clauses should also refer to the encumbrance of the easement.

11. Exceptions and Reservations

Often the grantor wishes to create a new easement for his or her own purposes across the lands being conveyed. Creation of such an easement may be accomplished by "excepting" or "reserving" such easement from and out of the interest in the real estate being conveyed. An "exception" is created by withholding from the operation of the deed some existing right that would otherwise normally pass to the grantee. A "reservation" creates a new right that had no previous existence. An exception does not require words of inheritance to be used in order to survive for the benefit of the grantor's heirs and assigns because title to that which is excepted was part of what the grantor and his or her heirs and assigns owned prior to the present conveyance. It continues to be held by the grantor and his or her heirs. A reservation, however, does require words of inheritance, since it is a newly created right and not part of an existing estate of inheritance. Obviously, it is difficult in practice to distinguish between exceptions and reservations. Conveyancers may avoid the problem by referring to the grantor's right as both an exception and reservation and by using words of inheritance. Such a clause may be drafted as follows:

EXCEPTING AND RESERVING unto the grantor, his heirs and assigns, the full, free liberty and right at all times hereafter forever, in common with the grantee, his heirs and assigns, to have and use as a passageway and driveway that certain strip of land twenty-five feet (25') in width, extending in a northerly direction for a distance of one hundred fifteen feet (115') from the northerly right-of-way line of State Highway 100 (50 feet wide), across the premises herein conveyed to the grantee, to the southerly boundary of other premises of the grantor on the north; the centerline of such twenty-five-foot-wide passageway and driveway being parallel to and at a distance of twelve and one-half feet (12½') from the easterly sideline of the premises herein conveyed to the grantee.

(a) Drafting Easements

When drafting such easements it is important

(1) to specify the limited purposes for which the easement is granted, for example:

as a driveway and parking lot for pedestrian and vehicular traffic.

(2) to state whether or not the easement is to be perpetual or limited in duration, for example:

for a period of twenty-five (25) years from the date of this indenture or at all times hereafter forever.

(3) to indicate whether the easement is an exclusive right of the grantor or whether the grantor must use it in common with the grantee (or with the grantee and also his or her heirs and assigns), for example:

unto the grantor, and his heirs and assigns, including future owners, mortgagees, tenants and their respective customers, invitees, and permitees, in common with the use thereof by the grantee, his heirs and assigns.

(4) to describe the land to be burdened by the easement (using a full metes and bounds description or other form of legal description where necessary);

(5) to describe, when appropriate, the lands to be benefitted by the creation of the easement (e.g., if the grantor has retained a large tract of land, but the grantee is willing to have the easement benefit only a small portion of that retained land); and

(6) to list any conditions imposed by the grantee on the exception and reservation, for example:

subject to the duty and obligation of maintaining such passageway and driveway in good order and repair, including maintaining a smooth, hard surface thereon with curbs and adequate drainage.

(b) Deed of Grant

Easements may be created by a document that does not convey any other interest in the burdened real estate, such as when one neighbor grants an easement for driveway purposes to another neighbor years after the parties acquired their respective lots. Such a document is identical in form to an indenture but is called a "Deed of Grant" or "Deed of Easement"; instead of conveying the fee title to the described real estate, only an easement therein is granted.

(c) Declaration of Easements and Reciprocal Easement Agreement

Occasionally, the owner of a tract of ground anticipates its subdivision for resale or for mortgage purposes and wishes to impose certain reciprocal rights and easements on each part of his or her land for the benefit of every other part. For example, the owner of a garden apartment complex may want to assure future owners of sections of the complex the right to use recreational facilities, roads, and a common entrance gate. This may be done by a unilateral "Declaration of Easements." Such a Declaration of Easements might be used in a rental garden apartment project either because different sections will be syndicated to different limited partnership, thus creating different ownerships immediately, or because different sections will be separately financed, creating the possibility of different ownerships in the future because of foreclosure on one or more sections.

The establishment of a condominium creates certain reciprocal easements as well as common ownership of the common area within the condominium. If a complex is to contain several separate condominium sections, then the entire complex may first be subjected to a Declaration of Easements, for the same reason as described earlier.

A Declaration of Covenants and Easements is sometimes used to create mandatory homeowners' associations. Such a Declaration might be used in a development of single-family residences to create certain reciprocal easements. However, a Declaration of Covenants, Restrictions and Easements for a homeowners' association goes beyond a simple Declaration of Easements, for it would contain the affirmative covenant of each homeowner to join an association. The association would own certain common use areas, including perhaps roads and recreational facilities, and would have the power to assess the homeowners for a share of the costs of maintaining the common-use areas. In addition, such a Declaration would ordinarily also include a variety of restrictions, such as a restriction against non-residential use. The association is a form of self-government, with the right to regulate certain aspects of life within the complex, such as policies covering fences, pets, and plantings. In many ways a Declaration of Covenants, Restrictions and Easements is analogous to the creation of a condominium, but without benefit (and restrictions) of an enabling statute.

If two or more neighbors wish to join in dedicating a portion of their respective real estate for common use by all of them, they may do so by joining in a "Reciprocal Easement Agreement." Reciprocal Easement

Agreements are common in connection with the development of shopping centers. Each major department store may obtain title to the land on which its store is constructed but dedicates a large portion of it for use as a part of the common system of driveways and parking lots.

(d) Creation of Easements by Other Means

Easements may arise by operation of law rather than by express language in an indenture or deed of grant. For example, a "way of necessity" is an easement that arises by implication when a portion of a larger parcel of land is conveyed without any express grant of an easement, but the land conveyed is so situated that access to it from a public highway can be had only by passing over the retained land of the grantor. Such an easement is known as an "easement by implication." Easements by implication also arise when an owner of land subjects part of it to an open, visible, permanent, and continuous easement in favor of another party and then conveys either part. The purchaser's title is subject to the easement or is benefitted by it, as the case may be, even though it is not referred to in the deed.

Easements "by prescription" arise in a manner similar to the acquisition of title by adverse possession, where continuous, open, visible, hostile, and adverse use of a right continues for twenty-one years or more. Even though no written document may ever have existed, the law presumes that at some time in the remote past such a right or easement was granted. Whenever an easement is known to exist, even though it was not created by express language in a deed and is not of record, the prudent grantor will insert a reference to it in an encumbrance clause when he or she conveys title.

12. Appurtenances

As a matter of law in most jurisdictions, all easements, rights, and incidents that belong to the property conveyed and are necessary to its full enjoyment, will pass with the conveyance of that property as "appurtenances" without specific mention of them in the deed. But those that are merely "convenient" and not "necessary," will not pass unless they are apparent at the time of conveyance and are not expressly excepted or reserved. Therefore, it is important to determine, for example, whether, under the law of the jurisdiction, a conveyance of the surface of the land will include, without specific mention, title to the gas, oil, and minerals beneath the land. Note that the model Pennsylvania deed, pages 151–154, includes the following clause, beginning with the words "together with," following the encumbrance clauses in the deed:

> TOGETHER with the free and common use, right, liberty, and privilege of the aforesaid alley as and for a passageway and watercourse at all times hereafter forever.

If the tract of land conveyed acquired the benefit of an easement by a prior deed or by a deed of grant made after the grantor acquired the original tract, care should be taken to refer to the recording data of such instrument and, if possible, the full text of the easement should be set forth.

Because of the complex rules and common law precedents that determine which of the grantor's rights will pass to the grantee and which will not, the legislatures of some states have statutorily defined the rights and interests that are deemed to pass. Although Pennsylvania has such a statutory definition, nearly all printed forms of deed continue to contain a general appurtenance clause with language nearly identical to the statutory definition (requiring only the insertion of a reference to any buildings or other improvements that may be situated on the land). The model deed for Pennsylvania contains the following clause:

> TOGETHER with all and singular the buildings, improvements, ways, streets, alleys, driveways, passages, waters, water-courses, rights, liberties, privileges, hereditaments and appurtenances, whatsoever unto the hereby granted premises belonging, or in any wise appertaining, and the reversions and remainders, rents, issues, and profits thereof; and all the estate, right, title, interest, property, claim and demand whatsoever of them, the said Grantors, as well at law as in equity, of, in, and to the same.

The general appurtenance clause is unnecessary because it follows the language of the Pennsylvania statute, but it is advisable to use it because lawyers expect it to appear in the deed. The general appurtenance clause usually follows all of the encumbrance clauses and precedes the habendum portion of the deed.

D. HABENDUM

1. "To Have and To Hold" Clause

The second section of the deed, the habendum, begins with the "to have and to hold" clause, which, in our model form of Pennsylvania deed, reads as follows:

> To have and to hold the said lot or piece of ground above described with the buildings and improvements thereon erected, hereditaments and premises hereby granted, or mentioned, and intended so to be, with the appurtenances, unto the said Grantee, his heirs and assigns, to and for the only proper use and behoof of the said Grantee, his heirs and assigns forever.

Strictly speaking, the purpose of the foregoing clause is to designate the quantity of the estate that is to pass to the grantee. The "to have and to hold" clause may be used to explain, limit, qualify, or vary the estate granted by the granting clause. For example, it may provide that the grantee is to have and to hold the real estate only "as long as it is used as a church or other place of worship" or "as long as it is used for residential purposes." The effect of such limiting language is to create an estate in the grantee that may terminate on the violation of the condition imposed. If the estate is terminated, title to the real estate will revert back to the grantor who imposed the condition or to his or her heirs and assigns. In the early days of the common law it was a common practice to impose limitations to keep title to the family domain in the hands of the direct male descendants of the grantor. Today, however, the "to have and to hold" clause is generally used to merely suggest to the grantee the purpose for which the grantor *hopes* the grantee will use the real estate. For example, the provision may say, "as and for a school for the training of doctors, nurses, and other medical personnel." In such cases the words of grant are not legally limited by the words of the habendum, and title does not revert to the grantor or to his or her heirs when the real estates ceases to be used for the desired purpose. In some instances, however, the habendum clause is used to create conditions, subsequent to which, if broken, will either provide for a reversion back to the grantor or to a grant over to a third party.

The "to have and to hold" clause serves no useful purpose that could not be fulfilled by the premises portion of the deed. Therefore, it could be eliminated, thereby preventing disputes about inconsistencies between the granting clause and habendum. Nevertheless, in Pennsylvania, as well as elsewhere, it continues to be perpetuated by lawyers who revere its ancient common law history. Most printed forms continue to contain the "to have and to hold" clause.

It is necessary to limit the effect of the "to have and to hold" clause when the grant itself is limited, such as when there are encumbrance clauses referring to restrictions, mortgage liens, or exceptions and reservations. In such cases it is customary not to repeat the entire text of the encumbrance clauses, but only to refer to them by adding at the end of the "to have and to hold" clause the words "under and subject as aforesaid." If the estate is conveyed to more than one grantee, such as a conveyance to tenants-in-common, the "to have and to hold" clause should make reference to that tenancy by adding the phrase "as tenants-in-common" at the end of the clause.

2. Warranty Clause

(a) Covenants in General

A "covenant" has been defined as any writing under seal whereby a party guarantees the truth of certain facts or agrees to perform or give something to another. Covenants can be of many kinds and used for many purposes. General covenants can be expressed in or implied from the grant.

(b) Covenants for Title

Although general covenants do not appear in most deeds, covenants for title have been and continue to be of great importance. Naturally, the grantee wishes to obtain as much assurance as possible that the grantee is getting that title to the real estate for which he or she has bargained. For hundreds of years, grantees have required grantors to include in deeds of conveyance specific covenants whereby the grantor personally guarantees certain facts and agrees to protect the grantee if the title is attacked by others.

Historically, covenants for title dealt with six subjects: seisin, the right to convey, freedom from encumbrances, warranty, quiet enjoyment, and further assurances. The grantor covenants that the grantor is lawfully "seised of" (owns) the premises he or she purports to convey, and that the grantor has a "right to convey" the described premises. The grantor also guarantees that the premises conveyed are "free and clear of all encumbrances." The meaning of such a covenant in any particular jurisdiction depends on the meaning there of the term "encumbrance." "Encumbrances" usually include unpaid tax liens, assessments, mortgage liens, building restrictions, encroachments, and easements. The grantor's covenant for warranty is an agreement to compensate the grantee for any loss that the grantee may sustain by virtue of the failure of the title that the deed purports to convey. This form of covenant is the most important today. A similar covenant is that of quiet enjoyment, whereby the grantor guarantees that the grantee will not be disturbed by the holder of a paramount title. The covenant for "further assurances" binds the grantor to do those things that may be required to perfect the grantee's title.

(c) General Warranty

In many states the meaning of the ancient covenants has been defined by statute. These covenants are implied from the words of grant and do not have to be set forth in full. However, in most jurisdictions at least the warranty of title is still set forth. The so-called "general" warranty is the grantor's assurance that neither the grantor nor any predecessor of his or her title, nor anyone else, will disturb the grantee's use and enjoyment of the real estate by reason of any superior title or encumbrance. This form of warranty is closest to the original medieval form of covenant and is still widely used. In Pennsylvania deeds it is worded as follows:

> AND the said Grantor, for himself, his heirs, executors and administrators, does covenant, promise and agree, to and with the said Grantee, his heirs and assigns, by these presents, that he the said Grantor and his heirs, all and singular the hereditaments and premises hereby granted or mentioned and intended so to be, with the appurtenances, unto the said Grantee, his heirs and assigns, against him, the said Grantor and his heirs, and against all and every person and persons whomsoever lawfully claiming or to claim the same or any part thereof, shall and will, warrant and forever defend.

(d) Special Warranty

In areas where real estate is reconveyed every few years, such as in residential sections of our large cities, grantors have developed a reluctance to give such a broad warranty when their predecessors in title were not family members. In order to feel comfortable about giving such a warranty, the grantor would have to have a search made of his or her title. Indeed, in many jurisdictions it is still the obligation of the grantor to present to the grantee, before the closing, an attorney's certificate evidencing the state of title. Sometimes grantors simply refuse to make such broad warranties and agree to give only "special" warranties. A special warranty, also known as a "covenant against the grantor's acts," is limited to an assurance that the grantor did not create any encumbrances during his or her period of ownership to which the conveyance will be subject. Use of such a limited warranty is customary in most large cities today. The availability of owner's title insurance, issued by large and financially responsible corporations, has minimized the grantee's risk of relying on so limited a warranty.

In our model form of Pennsylvania deed a special warranty is established by the following language:

> AND the said Grantors, for themselves, their heirs, executors and administrators do covenant, promise and agree, to and with the said Grantee, his heirs and assigns, by these presents, that they, the said Grantors and their heirs, all and singular the hereditaments and premises hereby granted or mentioned and intended so to be, with the appurtenances, unto the said Grantee, his heirs and assigns, against them, the said Grantors and their heirs, and against all and every person whomsoever lawfully claiming or to claim the same or any part thereof, by, from or under him, her, them, or any of them, shall and will, warrant and forever defend.

The critical words that distinguish the special warranty from the general warranty appear in the limitation of the grantor's obligation to defend title to only those actions that may be brought by the grantor and his or her heirs or any other person lawfully claiming *"by, from or under her, him, them or any of them."* If those "magic" words are omitted from the warranty clause, the deed becomes a general warranty deed, and except for any listed encumbrances, the grantor must defend the grantee's title against all humankind. Before preparing a deed for any transaction it is imperative to determine whether the agreement of sale requires the delivery of a general warranty deed.

(e) Fiduciary's Warranty

The warranty normally required of a trustee, executor, or administrator of the grantor's estate is limited in much the same manner as a special warranty. A fiduciary covenants only that *the fiduciary* did nothing to encumber title during the time of his or her ownership. In Pennsylvania, a fiduciary's deed contains the following covenant:

> AND the said Grantors, for themselves and their respective executors, administrators and successors, do covenant, promise and agree, to and with the said Grantee, his heirs and assigns, by these presents, that they, the said Grantors, have not done, committed, or knowingly or willingly suffered to be done or committed, any act, matter or thing whatsoever whereby the

premises hereby granted, or any part thereof, is, are, shall or may be impeached, charged or incumbered, in title, charge, estate, or otherwise howsoever.

(f) Quitclaim Deed

The grantor, for many reasons, may not wish to give the grantee the benefit of any warranty. Title to a particular piece of real estate may be quite complicated and confused, and the grantor may not be sure what interest he or she really owns or how free of encumbrances the title may be. However, for a given price, the grantor is willing to sell and convey whatever estate and title he or she has. In such cases the grantor delivers a deed without warranty, also called a "quitclaim" deed, which is similar to a release. Quitclaim deeds are often used when purported heirs or adjoining property owners wish to convey and release any rights that they may have in property, the title to which is disputed.

(g) Reference to Encumbrance Clauses

As indicated elsewhere, if any encumbrance, exception, or reservation is referred to in the granting clause and the "to have and to hold" clause, it is wise to refer to it again in order to expressly limit the scope of the warranty. In Pennsylvania deeds it is sufficient to insert the words "subject as aforesaid" or "excepting and reserving as aforesaid" prior to the words "warrant and forever defend" or at some other appropriate place at the end of the warranty clause.

E. CONCLUSION

1. Execution Clause

The first clause appearing in that part of the deed called the conclusion is the clause beginning "In witness whereof." It is known as the "testimonium" or "execution" clause. The exact language used is not critical.

(a) Individual

When individuals are the grantors, the following form is appropriate:

> IN WITNESS WHEREOF, the parties of the first part, (the Grantors), have hereunto set their hands and seals on the date first above written.

(b) Corporation

The customary form of testimonium for corporate grantors is as follows:

> IN WITNESS WHEREOF, the party of the first part, (Grantor), has caused this Indenture to be signed by its President, duly authorized thereunto, and has caused its corporate seal to be hereunto affixed and attested by its Secretary on the date first above written.

2. Signatures

(a) Individual

The signature lines for individual grantors usually call for witnesses:

SEALED AND DELIVERED
in the presence of us:
Witness:

_____   _____ [Seal]
                                     John Q. McDonald

_____   _____ [Seal]
                                     Alexa S. McDonald

(b) Corporate

The typical form of corporate signature calls for the signature of the president or vice-president to be witnessed or "attested" by the secretary or assistant secretary, who also impresses the seal of the corporation:

Attest: AJAX CORPORATION

_____   By: _____
Alexa S. McDonald, Secretary   John Q. McDonald, President
[Corporate Seal]

The officers signing and attesting the signing of the deed on behalf of the corporation or other entity must be authorized to do so by the board of directors or other managing body. The signing officer may be a president, vice-president, trustee, partner, chief executive officer, dean, or other authorized representative. Because local laws vary, it is wise to check with the local recording office to determine whether a deed signed by such an officer or attested by an officer other than a secretary (such as a cashier, treasurer, or clerk) will be accepted for record.

(c) Attorney-in-Fact

If an individual signs by his or her attorney-in-fact, it should be indicated thus:

Witness:

_____   _____ [Seal]
                                     Alexa S. McDonald, by her attorney-
                                     in-fact, John Q. McDonald, duly
                                     authorized and constituted by Power
                                     of Attorney dated November 13, 1986.

3. Receipt

In some jurisdictions a clause may be inserted after the execution clause to serve as a receipt for the consideration paid to the grantor. Such a provision need not be included when the consideration is only nominal.

> Received on the date of the above Indenture, from the above-named grantee, the full consideration above mentioned.

Witnesses:

_____   _____ [Seal]
                                     John Q. McDonald

_____   _____ [Seal]
                                     Alexa S. McDonald

4. Certification of Grantee's Address

With the growing complexity of our local taxing systems, it has become common for local authorities to require all deeds to contain a certification of the address of the grantee so that notices and tax bills may be forwarded to him or her. The signing party need not be the grantee. In Pennsylvania the following form is used on the back of the deed or following the signatures:

> The address of the above-named Grantee is:
>
> 642 Greenacre Road
> Philadelphia, PA
> /S/
> On behalf of the Grantee

5. Acknowledgment

The final clause of the deed is the acknowledgment. The grantor must appear before an officer qualified by law to take acknowledgments and "acknowledge" that he or she signed the deed or other instrument. The officer, who is usually a notary public, must sign the acknowledgment clause in the required manner. Although the execution and the delivery of the deed and its acceptance by the grantee is sufficient to vest title in the grantee, the acknowledgment is a critical part of the deed. Without it, the deed will not be accepted by the local recording officer and the grantee will not obtain the benefits of the recording system. At one time every state had its own required form of acknowledgment. The Uniform Acknowledgment Act has eliminated some of the technical difficulties in this regard and those states subscribing to the Uniform Acknowledgment Act will accept deeds acknowledged in other jurisdictions in the form provided by that Act, even when it varies from the preferred form. If, however, the jurisdiction in which the deed will be recorded has not adopted the Uniform Acknowledgment Act, the acknowledgment form used must be the one acceptable to the recording state. In the model form of Pennsylvania deed, the acknowledgment (in the form adopted by the Uniform Acknowledgment Act) appears as follows:

Commonwealth of Pennsylvania ⎫
County of Philadelphia   ⎬ ss.
                                          ⎭

On this, the 26th day of May, 1986, before me, a Notary Public in and for the Commonwealth of Pennsylvania, the undersigned Officer, personally appeared ALAN L. BURNS and MARY R. BURNS, husband and wife, known to me (satisfactorily proven) to be the persons whose names are subscribed to the within instrument, and acknowledged that they executed the same for the purposes therein contained.

IN WITNESS WHEREOF, I hereunto set my hand and official seal.

_____
Notary Public

[Notarial Seal]   My commission expires:

The important elements to be set forth in the acknowledgment are:

(a) The *venue,* or place where the acknowledgment is taken, in our example, in the Commonwealth of Pennsylvania and County of Philadelphia;

(b) The *date* on which the acknowledgment is made and taken. An acknowledgment may be made at any time after execution of the deed. An acknowledgment cannot be made before execution of the deed, because it is impossible to acknowledge an act that has not yet been performed. Although the acknowledgment need not be made on the same day that the deed is signed, it is best to have the deed signed in the presence of the notary public, usually a settlement clerk, who may immediately complete the taking of the acknowledgment.

(c) The *name* of the person taking the acknowledgment and

(d) his or her *official position* (e.g., "Notary Public").

(e) The location of the *office* of the officer (that is, the state and county, city, township, or borough that the officer serves);

(f) the *date of expiration* of the officer's commission. Of course, the officer must sign the acknowledgment and impress the officer's official seal next to his or her signature.

Depending on the jurisdiction, there may be limitations on those who are qualified to take acknowledgments. For example, a Pennsylvania notary public may not act as such for any bank of which he or she is a director or an officer. Therefore, when a bank officer's signature is to be acknowledged, the notary public should certify below the acknowledgment as follows:

> I certify that I am not an officer or director of the above-named bank, banking institution or trust company.

In some jurisdictions the corporate acknowledgment takes the form of a deposition and requires the attesting officer of the corporate grantor to sign the acknowledgment in addition to the notary public. The following is a form widely employed in New Jersey:

STATE OF NEW JERSEY ⎫
COUNTY OF CAMDEN ⎬ ss.
                  ⎭

BE IT REMEMBERED, that on this 26th day of May in the year of our Lord one thousand nine hundred and eighty-six before me, a Notary Public, personally appeared ALAN L. BURNS who being by me duly sworn, on his oath saith, that he is the Secretary of COUNTRY VILLAGE, INC., the grantor within named, and that WAYNE EMERSON is the President; that deponent knows the common or corporate seal of said grantor and that the seal annexed to the within Deed of Conveyance is such common or corporate seal; that the said Deed of Conveyance was signed by the said President and the seal of said grantor affixed thereto in the presence of deponent; that said Deed of Conveyance was signed, sealed and delivered as and for the voluntary act and deed of said grantor for the uses and purposes therein expressed, pursuant to a resolution of the Board of Directors of said grantor; and at the execution thereof this deponent subscribed his name thereto as witness.

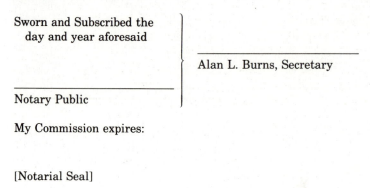

Sworn and Subscribed the
 day and year aforesaid

_____
Alan L. Burns, Secretary

_____
Notary Public

My Commission expires:

[Notarial Seal]

III. STATUTORY FORM OF DEED

Many jurisdictions have attempted to shorten, simplify, and standardize the language and forms of deeds by adopting a statutory form. One of the purposes of such legislation is to eliminate the verbosity that the old common law deed forms perpetuate. However, as is the case in many fields, lawyers and conveyancers have felt more comfortable with the tried and true common law forms and have been reluctant to use the statutory form.

IV. DELIVERY OF DEEDS

The final requirement for the effectiveness of a deed is that it be delivered to and accepted by the grantee. No special ceremony is necessary to deliver the deed so long as it is the intention of the grantor that the deed be passed from his or her control into the hands of the grantee or the grantee's agents. Even though the grantor may have signed a deed, it is not sufficient delivery if it is stolen and delivered to the grantee.

A. DELIVERY IN ESCROW

Delivery may be made to a third person, such as an escrow holder. When a lawyer, real estate broker, or title insurance company holds the document in escrow, the condition precedent to the delivery of the deed to the grantee is that the grantor or grantee comply with specific conditions established by mutual agreement. Such conditions should be clearly spelled out in the escrow agreement so that there will be no dispute as to whether the escrow holder should return the deed to the grantor or deliver it to the grantee. In such cases, delivery to the escrow holder is complete delivery so far as the grantor is concerned.

B. ACCEPTANCE OF DELIVERY BY GRANTEE

A grantor cannot unilaterally convey title to real estate to an unwilling grantee. (This could occur when the property is worth less than its annual taxes.) Acceptance by the grantee is a necessity. Such acceptance may, however, be implied from the acceptance by the grantee of the benefits of the deed.

V. SPECIAL DEEDS AND DEED CLAUSES

A. SHERIFF'S DEED

When real estate is sold at a public auction sale, pursuant to the law and procedural rules of the jurisdiction, in execution on a judgment for money damages or a judgment in mortgage foreclosure, or on a lien for unpaid taxes, the sheriff or other authorized judicial officer delivers a deed conveying title to the successful bidder at the sale. The former owners of the real estate sold at the sale are not required to sign the deed. The sheriff's deed resembles the common law form of the deed poll. It recites the consideration paid to the sheriff by the successful bidder, but it does not contain the customary granting clause. However, it does use the words "grant and convey," and in Pennsylvania, those words are statutorily defined to mean that the purchaser obtains the entire estate that the former owner held. The sheriff makes no warranties. The deed contains an explanation of the basis for the judicial sale; it refers to the court, term, and number of the case that led to the judgment on which execution was held at the public auction sale.

B. DEED OF CONFIRMATION OR CORRECTION

The purpose of a deed of confirmation is to correct an error in a prior deed of conveyance and thereby confirm the grantee's title. The deed of confirmation may take the form of an ordinary indenture with a special recital to indicate that the purpose of the deed is to confirm title already held by the grantee and to convey to the grantee any outstanding interest or claim against his or her title that may exist by reason of a defect in the original conveyance, such as a typographical error in the legal description or improper recording; in some cases it is wise to explain the error in the recital. Such deeds are also used when an owner desires to record a perimeter legal description of a number of lots that he or she has acquired by numerous separate deeds containing overlapping or otherwise inconsistent legal descriptions. In such cases the owner "conveys" to himself, and the recital explains how each part of the entire described premises was acquired and that the purpose fo the deed is to describe the same properties in accordance with a new perimeter description. This form of deed is usually exempt from recording or transfer taxes because its purpose it not to convey any additional real estate.

C. CONDOMINIUM DEED

In most states where condominiums have been developed there are special statutes that prescribe how a condominium may be established and how the fee title to a part or unit of the condominium may be conveyed. Condominium deeds are not necessarily any different from ordinary indentures, except that the legal description does not usually refer to metes and bounds that can be traced on the ground. Instead, the deed incorporates by reference the description of the condominium unit as set forth in the Declaration of Condominium that must be recorded prior to any sale of a condominium unit. Also, in some jurisdictions, by statute or by practice, the grantee of a condominium unit deed signs the deed agreeing to be liable for condominium maintenance assessments. Condominiums are discussed more fully in Chapter Eleven.

D. COAL AND OTHER MINERAL SEVERANCE CLAUSES

Some jurisdictions, by statute, require deeds conveying the surface of land where there is or has been a severance of the underlying coal or other minerals or a severance of the right to surface support, to include a prescribed form of notice or warning that such document (a) may not, or does not, include or insure title to underlying minerals and right of support under the surface; (b) that the owner of the minerals may or does have the right to remove such; and (c) that damage to the surface and any buildings thereon may result therefrom. Such a clause is appropriately inserted before the general appurtenance clause.

The following are examples of fee simple, sheriff's, and quitclaim deeds.

Example: **Fee Simple Deed (Pennsylvania)**

Printed for and Sold by John C. Clark Co., 1326 Walnut St., Phila.

This Indenture **Made the** 26th **day of**

May **in the year of our Lord one thousand nine hundred and** eighty-six **(19**86 **)**

Between ALAN L. BURNS and MARY R. BURNS, husband and wife, of 100 Blackacre Lane, Philadelphia, Pennsylvania

(hereinafter called the Grantor S **), of the one part, and**

ROBERT B. DAVIS, single man, of 642 Greenacre Road, Philadelphia, Pennsylvania

(hereinafter called the Grantee   ), of the other part,

Witnesseth **That the said Grantor**s

for and in consideration of the sum of

Ninety Thousand Dollars ($90,000.00) **lawful money of the United States of America, unto** them **well and truly paid by the said Grantee , at or before the sealing and delivery hereof, the receipt whereof is hereby acknowledged,** have **granted, bargained and sold, released and confirmed, and by these presents** do **grant , bargain and**

sell, release and confirm unto the said Grantee , his heirs **and assigns,**

ALL THAT CERTAIN lot or piece of ground with the buildings and improvements thereon erected, bounded and described in accordance with an official survey and plan thereof by Adam Smith, Surveyor and Regulator for the First District, dated April 10, 1971, as follows:

SITUATE on the North side of Blackacre Lane at the distance of three hundred sixty-eight feet (368') westward from the West side of Bond Street in the Tenth Ward of the City of Philadelphia;

CONTAINING in front or breadth on the said Blackacre Lane fifty feet (50') and extending of that width in length or depth northward between parallel lines at right angles with the said Blackacre Lane eighty-one feet, six inches (81' 6") to the middle of a certain three feet (3') wide alley leading eastward and westward from Bond Street to Abbey Road.

BEING known as No. 100 Blackacre Lane.

BEING the same premises which Charles Clark and Dorothy Clark, husband and wife, by Deed dated July 8, 1945 and recorded in the Office for Recording of Deeds in and for the County of Philadelphia (now the Department of Records of the City of Philadelphia) in Deed Book J.M.H. No. 2286, Page 354 granted and conveyed unto the said Alan L. Burns and Mary R. Burns, husband and wife, in fee, as tenants by entirety.

Continued.

Example: **Fee Simple Deed (Pennsylvania)** *continued*

UNDER AND SUBJECT, nevertheless, to certain conditions and restrictions as appear of record in Deed Book W.S.M. No. 231, Page 253.

TOGETHER with the free and common use, right, liberty and privilege of the aforesaid alley as and for a passageway and water-course at all times hereafter forever.

AND

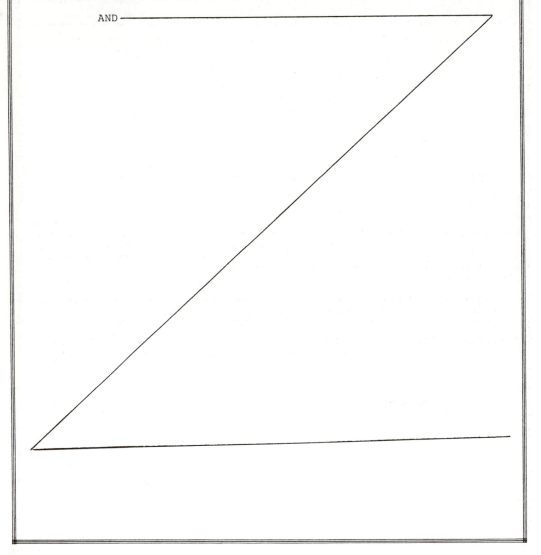

𝕿𝖔𝖌𝖊𝖙𝖍𝖊𝖗 with all and singular the buildings, improvements, ways, streets, alleys, driveways, passages, waters, water-courses, rights liberties, privileges, hereditaments and appurtenances, whatsoever unto the hereby granted premises belonging, or in any wise appertaining, and the reversions and remainders, rents, issues, and profits thereof; and all the estate, right, title, interest property, claim and demand whatsoever of them

the said Grantor s, as well at law as in equity, of, in, and to the same.

𝕿𝖔 𝖍𝖆𝖛𝖊 𝖆𝖓𝖉 𝖙𝖔 𝖍𝖔𝖑𝖉 the said lot or piece of ground above described with the buildings and improvements thereon erected, hereditaments and premises hereby granted, or mentioned, and intended so to be, with the appurtenances, unto the said Grantee , his heirs and assigns, to and for the only proper use and behoof of the said Grantee , his heirs and assigns forever.

UNDER AND SUBJECT, as aforesaid. ─────────────────────

𝕬𝖓𝖉 the said Grantors, for themselves, and their

heirs , executors and administrators do covenant, promise and agree, to and with the said Grantee , his heirs and assigns, by these presents, that they , the said Grantors and their heirs, all and singular the hereditaments and premises hereby granted or mentioned and intended so to be, with the appurtenances, unto the said Grantee , his heirs and assigns, against them, the said Grantors and their

heirs, and against all and every person and persons whomsoever lawfully claiming or to claim the same or any part thereof, by, from or under him, her, them or any of them, shall and will SUBJECT as aforesaid, WARRANT and forever DEFEND.

𝕴𝖓 𝖂𝖎𝖙𝖓𝖊𝖘𝖘 𝖂𝖍𝖊𝖗𝖊𝖔𝖋, the parties of the first part have hereunto set their hands and seals . Dated the day and year first above written.

𝕾𝖊𝖆𝖑𝖊𝖉 𝖆𝖓𝖉 𝕯𝖊𝖑𝖎𝖛𝖊𝖗𝖊𝖉
IN THE PRESENCE OF US:

_____(SEAL)
Alan L. Burns

_____(SEAL)
Mary R. Burns

Continued.

Example: **Fee Simple Deed (Pennsylvania)** *continued*

Commonwealth of Pennsylvania
County of Philadelphia   } **ss:**

On this, the   26th   **day of**   May   , 19**86, before me,**   a Notary Public in and
for the Commonwealth of Pennsylvania,
                                                                    the undersigned Officer,
personally appeared   ALAN L. BURNS and MARY R. BURNS, husband and wife,

known to me (satisfactorily proven) to be the person s **whose names** ~~is~~ **(are) subscribed to the
within instrument, and acknowledged that** t h e y **executed the same for the purposes therein contained.**

In Witness Whereof, I hereunto set my hand and official seal.

                                        Notary Public
(Notarial Seal)   My Commission Expires:

Deed.

ALAN L. BURNS and MARY
R. BURNS, husband and wife

TO

ROBERT B. DAVIS, single man

Dated: May 26, 1986
Premises:

No. 100 Blackacre Lane
10th Ward
Philadelphia, Pa.

753-S   John C. Clark Co., Phila.   1977

After recording, please
send to:

The address of the above-named Grantee
is   642 Greenacre Road,
Philadelphia,   PA
          On behalf of the Grantee

Example: **Quitclaim Deed (Pennsylvania)**

Quit-claim Deed No. 664/S   Printed for and Sold by John C. Clark Co., 1326 Walnut St., Phila.

12th   *day of*   April   *in the year of our*

Lord one thousand nine hundred   eighty-six (1986)

Between VILLAGE GREENE, INC., a Pennsylvania corporation, having an office at 13th Floor, 401 Walnut Street, Philadelphia, Pennsylvania, party of the first part, and

P E S ASSOCIATES, a Pennsylvania partnership, having an office at 1001 Wilmington Pike, Dover, Delaware, party of the second part,

Witnesseth, *That the said party*   *of the first part, for and in consideration of the* **sum of** Two Thousand Five Hundred Dollars ($2,500.00)

lawful money of the United States of America, to   it   *well and truly paid by the said* *part* y   *of the second part, at and before the sealing and delivery of these presents, the receipt whereof is hereby acknowledged,* has   **remised,** *released and quit-claimed, and by these presents,* does   **remise,** *release and quit-claim unto the said part* y   *of the second part, and to* its successors

and assigns forever, ALL THAT CERTAIN tract of land SITUATE in the Township of Upper Gwynedd, County of Montgomery, Commonwealth of Pennsylvania, bounded and described according to a Plan of Survey made for Village Greene, Inc. by Urwiler and Walter, Inc., dated April 1, 1986 , as follows, to wit:

    (Legal description and recital, although the recital is
      sometimes omitted.)

    CONTAINING, five and five hundred seventy-four one-thousandths (5.574) acres of land, more or less.

Continued.

Example: **Quitclaim Deed (Pennsylvania)** *continued*

Together *with all and singular, the tenements, hereditaments and appurtenances thereunto belonging, or in any wise appertaining, and the reversions, remainders, rents, issues and profits thereof:* **And** *also, all the estate, right, title, interest,*

                           property, claim and demand whatsoever, as well in law as in equity, of the said part y *of the first part, of, in, or to the above-described premises, and every part and parcel thereof, with the appurtenances.*

To have and to hold *all and singular the above-mentioned and described premises, together with the appurtenances, unto the said part* y *of the second part,* its successors

and assigns forever.

     In Witness Whereof, the party of the first part, by its proper officers thereunto duly authorized, has caused its name and corporate seal to be hereunto affixed on the date first above written.

     Sealed and Delivered ⎫
         IN THE PRESENCE OF US: ⎬

Attest: VILLAGE GREENE, INC.

                                    By : _____
_____
Albert F. Greene, Secretary   Albert F. Village, President

(Corporate Seal)

Commonwealth of Pennsylvania ⎫
County of ⎬ *SS.*

On this, the   *day of*   *, 19*   *, before me, the undersigned Officer,*

                            , personally appeared

                              known to me (satisfactorily proven) to be the person whose name is (are) subscribed to the within instrument, and acknowledged that **he** *executed the same for the purposes therein contained.*

In Witness Whereof, *I hereunto set my hand and official seal.*

Commonwealth of Pennsylvania
County of Philadelphia   } SS.

On this, the   12th   *day of* April   *19* 86   *before me*, a Notary
Public, in and for the Commonwealth of Pennsylvania,
the undersigned Officer, personally appeared ALBERT F. VILLAGE
who acknowledged himself to be the   President *of* VILLAGE GREENE, INC.
                    , a corporation, and that   he as such President
            , being authorized to do so executed the foregoing instrument for the purposes
therein contained by signing the name of the corporation by himself (herself) as   President.

In Witness Whereof, I hereunto set my hand and official seal.

Notary Public

(Notarial Seal)   My Commission Expires:

Deed.

VILLAGE GREENE, INC.

TO

P E S ASSOCIATES

Dated: April 12, 1986
Premises:
± 5.574 acres
Upper Gwynedd Township
Montgomery County
Pennsylvania

1976   John C. Clark Company, Philadelphia.   664/S

After recording, please
send to:

The address of the above-named Grantee
is 1001 Wilmington Pike,
Dover, Delaware
On behalf of the Grantee

Example: **Sheriff's Deed (Pennsylvania)**

Printed for and Sold by John C. Clark Co., 1326 Walnut St., Phila.

Know all Men by these Presents

THAT I,   WILLIAM M. LENNOX,   ***Sheriff of the County of***   Philadelphia,
in the Commonwealth of Pennsylvania, for and in consideration of the sum of   six
hundred ($600.00)

dollars, to me in hand paid, do hereby grant and convey to   HARDCASH SAVINGS
BANK, a Pennsylvania corporation, its successors and assigns,

ALL THAT CERTAIN lot or piece of ground with the two-story
brick building thereon erected, SITUATE on the East side of 50th
Street at the distance of four hundred thirty-nine feet (439')
northward from the North side of Main Street in the Thirty-fourth
Ward of the City of Philadelphia;

CONTAINING in front or breadth on said 50th Street fifteen
feet (15') and extending of that width in length or depth eastward
between parallel lines at right angles to said 50th Street ninety
feet (90') to a certain three feet (3') wide alley extending northward
and southward between Main Street and Rosetree Lane.

BEING known as No. 159 North 50th Street.

TOGETHER with the free and common use, right, liberty and
privilege of the aforesaid alley as and for a passageway and water-
course at all times hereafter forever;

the same having been sold by me to the said grantee , *on the* 3rd *day of*

May *Anno Domini one thousand nine hundred and* eighty-six *after due*

advertisement, according to law, under and by virtue of a writ of Execution

issued ~~*Decree entered*~~☆ *on the* 25th *day of* April *Anno Domini*

one thousand nine hundred and eighty-six *out of the* Court of Common Pleas of

Philadelphia County, Trial Division *as of* April *Term, one thousand nine*

hundred and eighty-six *Number* 734 *at the suit of* Hardcash

Savings Bank v. Alan L. Burns and Mary R. Burns, his wife, Real

Owners.

𝕴𝔫 𝔴𝔦𝔱𝔫𝔢𝔰𝔰 𝔴𝔥𝔢𝔯𝔢𝔬𝔣, *I have hereunto affixed my signature, this* 27th

day of May *Anno Domini one thousand nine hundred and* eighty-six.

SEALED AND DELIVERED
IN THE PRESENCE OF

WILLIAM M. LENNOX, SHERIFF

By: _____
James Browne, Chief Deputy *Sheriff*

☆ Eliminate which not applicable.

Continued.

Example: **Sheriff's Deed (Pennsylvania)** *continued*

Commonwealth of Pennsylvania

County of Philadelphia   } *SS.*

On this, the   27th   *day of*   May,   19 86 , *before me*

the undersigned Officer, personally appeared   JAMES BROWNE, Chief Deputy
Sheriff of the County of   Philadelphia , *known to me (or satisfactory proven) to be the person described in the foregoing instrument, and acknowledged that he executed the same in the capacity therein stated and for the purposes therein contained.*

In Witness Whereof, *I hereunto set my hand and official seal.*

Prothonotary

Writ No. 232/73.

Deed-Poll.

WILLIAM M. LENNOX,   **Sheriff.**

TO.

HARDCASH SAVINGS BANK,
a Pennsylvania corporation,
its successors and assigns

Hardcash
Savings Bank   C.P.

                              } Apr. T. 19 86

vs.   No. 734.

Alan L. Burns
Mary R. Burns.

Premises:

159 North 50th Street
34th Ward
Philadelphia, PA

2-69 John C. Clark Company, Philadelphia.

After recording, please
send to:

The address *of the within-named*
Grantee is 620 E. Spring Road,
Philadelphia, PA.

On behalf of the Grantee

Chapter 6

Title Abstracting and
Title Insurance

I. INTRODUCTION

A. GENERAL INTRODUCTION

In Chapter Nine recording systems and statutes are discussed. The philosophy behind recording statutes is to promote certainty with respect to interests in real property. Recording systems uphold the claims of those who comply with the requirements of public recording and deny support to those who fail to comply.

In this chapter the concepts of "title" and "good and marketable title" are briefly discussed. When used in connection with real estate, the word "title" means the ownership of an interest, and usually a fee interest, in real property.

Title abstracting is simply the gathering of information from various public records concerning the title to particular real property. Traditionally, title abstracting has been performed by lawyers, who then render opinions as to title. An opinion is neither a guaranty nor an insurance of title. Increasingly since 1876,[1] purchasers and lenders have instead sought insurance of title from title insurance companies. This has particularly been so in certain large metropolitan areas, and in large commercial transactions throughout the United States.

The purpose of this chapter is to teach the student how to understand and work with title insurance reports and policies. In order to review,

---

1. Commonwealth Land Title Insurance Company, which is headquartered in Philadelphia, was founded in 1876 and claims to be the oldest title insurance company in America.

understand, and negotiate title insurance reports, a paralegal must have some understanding of the abstracting procedure. This chapter offers that understanding but does not purport to train the student to be an abstracter.

B. MARKETABILITY OF TITLE

The goal of an examination of title is to determine whether the title is "marketable." A marketable title is one that is free from liens and other encumbrances[2] and free from all reasonable doubt or controversy. Conversely, an unmarketable title is one that is encumbered or has such serious defects that there is a reasonable chance that it would subject a buyer to the hazards of adverse claims or litigation.

Many defects in title may come to light in the examination. Some of these defects are serious and some are not. The ultimate determination is not whether title is free of all defects and doubt, but whether the apparent defects affect marketability. The trend in modern real estate transactions seems to be that a marketable title is one without any legitimate adverse claims that will enable a purchaser to hold title peacefully during his or her period of ownership.

Obviously, it is difficult to apply the vague notion of marketability to every case. Some titles appear to be marketable from the public land records and yet may not be marketable because a grantor's signature in one deed in the chain of title[3] may have been forged. Marketability is sometimes a question of law, sometimes a question of fact, and sometimes an issue of both law and fact. If a will or a deed in the chain of title has to be interpreted by a court, then marketability would be a question of law. If a party claims title by adverse possession, then marketability would be a question of fact (e.g., did the claimant have possession or use for the required period) or a mixed question of fact and law (e.g., was the possession or use of a kind that is adverse).

In order to determine whether a title is marketable, the history of the title must be summarized. A history of title will disclose not only the chain of title, but also all easements, restrictions, and encumbrances affecting the property. An examination of the complete history should reveal whether the chain of title to the present owner is clear and unbroken. The history of a title is then compiled by an abstracter (commonly referred to as a "title examiner") into a document called an "abstract" or a "title report." The abstract contains a complete summary, including recording and docket information, of all documents and entries in the public records pertaining to the property.

In addition to a review of the public records, it is also usually incumbent on a purchaser to examine the property before the purchase. Title

2. Examples of encumbrances (also known as "objections" or "clouds on title") are liens, mortgages, leases, and tenancies.

3. The chain of title is the succession of conveyances of a parcel of land dating from the original source of the title.

to the property may be subject to matters that would be revealed by such an inspection, such as tenants in possession, claimants by adverse possession, utility easements visible on the site, and stream or water rights.

C. TYPES OF TITLE EXAMINATION

There are several types of title examinations and forms of assurance regarding the state of title: the attorney direct search and opinion, the abstract and opinion, the Torrens registration, and title insurance. The choice in any case usually relates to the custom in effect in the area in which the property is located, and the type of transaction in question.

1. Attorney Direct Search and Opinion

Under the direct search system, an attorney usually makes a title examination directly from the records at the recorder's office. After compiling an abstract of title, the attorney analyzes it and renders an opinion as to whether or not the title is marketable. The formal opinion sets forth all pertinent items and also may call for additional information in order to clear up possible clouds or encumbrances. The attorney search and opinion system is still in wide use throughout the United States, especially outside metropolitan areas. The purchaser of property relies on the skill and integrity of the lawyer who examines the title. In the event the lawyer has made a mistake through negligence and the title turns out to be defective, the purchaser may sue the lawyer. Lawyers who render title opinions generally carry insurance against this risk well in excess of their normal malpractice coverage. In many law firms the legal assistant will conduct a title search and prepare a title abstract that will be reviewed by the attorney who renders the opinion.

2. Abstract and Opinion

Under the abstract system a search is made by a title examiner, who then prepares an abstract showing all recorded instruments affecting the land in question. The title examiner certifies that the abstract is a complete and accurate copy of all record items. The abstract is kept up-to-date by a further search at the time of each transfer of ownership and is delivered to each new owner. The purchaser's attorney reviews the abstract and renders an opinion after completing an examination of the abstract. This method of title examination is used primarily in certain Western states and in Florida.

3. Torrens System

As mentioned in Chapter Nine, under the Torrens or land registration system the applicant files a request for registration of land with a court in the county where the land is located. If the court finds that the applicant has good title, it issues a certificate of title to the county land registrar and the owner. The certificate of registration contains all pertinent data as to the particular parcel of land, such as the names of the owners, description of the property, mortgages, liens, easements, or other encumbrances, and any other facts pertinent to the title. Every time there is a transfer of title (or a change in title ordered by a court decree), the registrar will cancel the old certificate of registration and issue a new one. To determine the validity of each registration, a search can be made in the Torrens registrar's office of all the facts endorsed on the owner's certificate.

4. Title Insurance

A major source of conceptual confusion respecting title insurance is the word "insurance." In contrast to most forms of insurance, which provide protection against loss caused by future events, title insurance insures against loss based on claims that derive from the past. The title insurance policy is really a financially backed opinion of the state of title immediately after recordation of the instrument creating the interest being insured. It is important to remember that there are different types of title insurance policies provided to insure different interests, including the interests of owners of fee simple and leasehold estates, lenders, and construction lenders.

Title insurance companies are specifically incorporated as such and are regulated by the insurance departments of the various states. One way in which they operate is to have employees or agents prepare abstracts in the usual manner. The company then issues a title report and subsequent insurance policy on the basis of the abstract.

In certain areas, however, title companies do not rely wholly on abstracts from the public records. Instead, the title companies maintain their own separate system of records, often using a tract index system rather than the grantor/grantee system maintained in the public records. The title insurance company can conduct a search of these files at its own facilities. However, it will have to search the public records for the period of time between the last transfer on the title company's records and the date of the report.[4] A title report is then issued based on the search.

II. TITLE SEARCH

A. RECORDING SYSTEMS

The recording system, as it exists with variations from state to state, establishes a public repository for transcriptions (or copies) of original

---

4. The search for information appearing on the public records since the title company's last entry is called a "bringdown."

documents that have a bearing on land titles. All states have laws known generically as the "Statute of Frauds," which, among other things, requires documents transferring title to or other interests in real estate to be in writing. The written document, which is then "recorded," preserves evidence of ownership and gives notice to all persons who may wish to acquire an interest in the property. The public land records should be examined before land is purchased or a loan is made in which land is used as collateral. In addition, the records should sometimes be examined before land is leased.

As mentioned in Chapter Nine, recording acts are now in force in all states. The stated purposes of these acts are (a) protection of a claimant who properly and timely records a claim against the property, (b) protection of subsequent purchasers against secret or unknown conveyances, and (c) preservation of accessible histories of each title so that anyone needing information may find it and rely on it.

In order to accomplish the purposes of recording, the maintenance of land records is required by law, usually in the courthouse building of the county in which the land is located. Therefore, an examination of the title to a particular property will often begin in the county in which the land is situated. Some records outside the county that may also have to be consulted (such as state and federal records disclosing judgments against the property) are discussed in Section III, C of this chapter.

Access to the various documents on record depends on an index system. The title examiner must consult the index to locate the instruments so that he or she can examine and appraise them and evaluate the title.

B. THE INDEX SYSTEMS

There are basically two kinds of index systems: the grantor-grantee index, which indexes by the names of the parties, and the tract index, which indexes by reference to parcels of land.

1. The Grantor-Grantee Index

In the grantor-grantee index each deed, easement, lease, mortgage, or other instrument is indexed both under the name of the grantor and under the name of the grantee.[5]

The theory of a recording system is that a purchaser is chargeable with notice of all matters affecting the title that are expressly set forth in any instrument forming an essential link in the title, and in legal proceedings affecting the property, such as judgments against the owner, tax assessment proceedings, condemnation proceedings, and bankruptcy proceedings. The grantor-grantee index system is based on the "chain of

---

5. If leases, mortgages, and other documents are included in the same books, then the grantor index will include the other "or" words, such as "mortgagor" and "lessor." The "or" search will tell you what someone who has an interest in the land is doing to the land, such as leasing it, mortgaging it, or deeding it.

title" theory, which states that all recorded instruments not within the direct chain of title to a particular parcel are irrelevant to the examination and do not give constructive notice of an interest to the prospective purchaser. Recording acts extend the doctrine of constructive notice to title records, with the result that a purchaser is bound by all facts that can be disclosed from an examination of all instruments in the chain of title.

The grantor-grantee index systems of some states use a separate set of books and separate indices for recording deeds, mortgages, judgments, attachments, mechanics' liens, leases, tax liens, and other miscellaneous documents.

2. The Tract Index

The tract index is compiled by parcels of land rather than by the parties to the instrument of conveyance. Tracts vary in size from government survey system "sections," which give legal descriptions of large sections of the United States, to a city block or lots of a subdivision. Instruments affecting property in a particular tract are indexed on the pages assigned to that tract. In order to use a tract index, you first locate the parcel of land on the recorder's map. The map shows an identification number for each parcel. The starting point is normally a series of large maps that break a city or region into large sections using separate identification numbers for each section. Depending on the size of the parcel and the refinement of the system in that area, there might be further references to maps showing an even smaller, and therefore more detailed, area. Eventually, an identification number is obtained, and that number will lead to all instruments relevant to that parcel, whenever and by whomever filed.

C. DIFFERENCES

The major difference between the two systems is that a tract index gives the title examiner all of the relevant instruments by one reference number. The examiner then must arrange the instruments and try to complete a chain of title. In searching a grantor-grantee index, the examiner first searches backward from the present titleholder to the original source of title (such as the U.S. government) and then searches forward along the chain to discover all relevant documents.

III. THE ABSTRACT

A. IN GENERAL

An abstract has two basic components. The first component is the chain of title to the present owner. The second is the discovery of encumbrances and other matters of record that relate to the property being abstracted.

B. CHAIN OF TITLE

Following the caption, which contains a description and a survey reference, the first part of an abstract is the compilation of all recorded instruments to form the chain of title. This compilation is done in chronological order from the first deed in the abstract down to the most current. The abstract contains a summary of the important facts from each recorded instrument.

The synopsis of each deed in the chain of title should contain the following:

(a) Full names of grantors and their marital status (if individuals);

(b) Full names of grantees and their marital status (if individuals);

(c) Date of deed;

(d) Consideration stated in deed;

(e) Date of acknowledgment;

(f) Date of recording;

(g) Deed book volume and page references;

(h) Reference to payment of any documentary stamps or transfer taxes;

(i) Statement of whether the description in the deed corresponds to the description in the caption to the abstract;

(j) Recitation of the preceding deed or other facts in the preceding title; and

(k) Recitation of all exceptions, reservations, restrictions, conditions, covenants, encumbrances, or other pertinent fact affecting title.

The purpose of compiling this information is to establish an unbroken chain of valid transfers of title from the last indisputable holder of title to the current holder. As we shall see, a title report sometimes requires certain documents or other proofs to be produced in order to verify or complete the unbroken chain.

C. SEARCH FOR RELATED CONVEYANCES AND ENCUMBRANCES

The search for related conveyances and encumbrances is begun by placing all of the names of the parties in chronological order. The examiner must check the index for the names of all the parties in the chain of title. As to adverse conveyances and creation of mortgages, each party need only be checked for the period during which he or she owned the property. Judgments against a particular party must be checked for the period prior to ownership as well as the time during which a party held title to the property.[6]

---

6. This is because judgments are usually a lien on property acquired after the date of the judgment.

1. Related Conveyances

The examiner must check the name of each party in the grantor index. If any prior grantor conveyed any property during the party's ownership of the property in question other than the conveyance to the next party in the chain of title, the examiner must review the conveyance in order to determine whether it purported to convey any part of or interest in the property being examined. Conveyances granting easements would be indicated in the abstract.

2. Mortgages

The examiner must go to the mortgagor index and determine whether any mortgages were created by any of the named parties during their period of ownership of the property. If they were, the examiner must check the terms of each such mortgage and determine whether it affected the subject property. If a mortgage were created that affected the subject property, the examiner must look at the record to determine whether the mortgage has been satisfied. If the mortgage has been satisfied, then the examiner makes note of that fact and can disregard the mortgage. If the mortgage has not been satisfied, it will appear as a lien or encumbrance on the abstract.

3. Judgments

A judgment that is recorded is a lien against all of the judgment debtor's real estate in the county where the judgment is recorded. Judgments last only for a specified period in each jurisdiction, after which they may be renewed for a fixed period and in that manner renewed again and again. The examiner must check the judgment indexes for each of the parties who held title to the real estate during the appropriate period while judgments could still be effective. If any party had a judgment on record against him or her during the period while he or she was in title, that judgment would be a lien against the subject property unless the examiner could determine that the judgment had been satisfied or had expired, or the lien had been released.

4. Tax Liens

Local real estate taxes, special tax assessments (such as for construction of sidewalks or sewer lines), and water and sewer rents that are unpaid are liens against the real estate against which they are assessed, in some cases with priority over an existing mortgage. The tax lien records are normally indexed by reference to the premises rather than the owner. Therefore, the examiner need only search the subject property in the tax lien records.

5. Federal Search

In addition to the search that is made at the county land records and courthouse, a search must be made of the records in the federal courthouse in the judicial district in which the land is located. This search is to determine whether any judgments or federal tax liens that could still be effective have been filed and to see whether the grantor has been adjudged bankrupt (in which case the grantor may not be able to transfer the property without leave of court).

6. State and Local Court Matters

State court records must also be searched to determine whether any judgments or state tax liens that could still be effective have been filed. If necessary, the records of the probate court (the court that administers the estates of deceased persons) must be searched for transfers of title through persons now deceased.

7. Corporate Matters

The records of the state corporate offices must be examined if a party is a corporation, or limited partnership, to confirm the status of the entity and, in the case of corporations, to obtain corporate tax information.

IV. TITLE REPORT

A. IN GENERAL

If it has been decided that title insurance will be obtained, the abstract will be in the form of a title report. Such preliminary reports, sometimes called commitments for title insurance or interim binders, advise the prospective purchaser or lender as to the status of title before the transaction is closed and assure the prospective purchaser or lender that on compliance with the requirements set forth in the commitment, the title insurance company will issue the policy. In some cases it is the legal assistant's role to explain to the client the concept of title insurance as well as the specific coverage of the policy. Therefore, it is important for the legal assistant to have a complete understanding of title insurance, as well as the title report and the subsequent policy. Although the format and layout of the title report vary from company to company, most title reports and policies are based on forms developed by the American Land Title Association (ALTA), which contain certain basic elements.[7] A title

---

7. New York, Texas, and California generally do not use ALTA forms, although their standard forms provide substantially similar coverage. The legal assistant should also be aware that the Attorney Guaranty Fund, which is comprised of title insurance companies consisting of practicing attorneys operating in approximately forty states, now performs title examinations and issues policies that are similar to ALTA forms.

report issued by Commonwealth Land Title Insurance Company (which is the ALTA Owner's Form B-1970)[8] has been reprinted at the end of this chapter and is discussed in detail later. Although most title companies use "standard forms," it is important for the legal assistant to review the title report carefully so that he or she can competently assess the report and the coverage and discuss it with the client or the attorney handling the matter. It is equally important for the legal assistant to review the title insurance policy (which is issued by the title insurer either at the closing or a short time thereafter) to be sure it reflects the same coverage stated in the title report.[9]

B. ANALYSIS OF ALTA TITLE REPORT

1. Heading

The heading of the title report contains the title number and the date of the report. The title company maintains its internal records by reference to the title report number. The number can be used as a reliable shorthand reference to the policy in drafting corporate resolutions or agreements of sale. The date is important because insurance policies do not insure against loss or damage on account of matters arising subsequent to the date of the report and policy.

The heading also contains the amount of the policy. The title insurance coverage is limited to the amount of the policy stated in the title report, plus certain fees and expenses related to the cost of defending the title. The legal assistant should pay particular attention to the amount of insurance and discuss its adequacy with the attorney handling the matter. The amount of coverage is often subsequently adjusted if the value of the property increases or the interest insured is a leasehold.[10] Financing

8. The most widely used owner's policy is the ALTA Owner's Form B-1970, which provides affirmative coverage with respect to loss related to the vesting of title; undisclosed defects, liens, or encumbrances; lack of access; and unmarketability of title. ALTA Owner's Form A-1970 encompasses the same coverage as Owner's Form B except the marketability coverage. ALTA Residential Title Insurance Policy-1979 is similar to Owner's Form B except that this type of policy is in plain language and includes an owner's information sheet, a table of contents, and an expanded list of coverages. ALTA Loan Policy-1970 includes the matters covered in Owner's Form B as well as coverage of the validity, enforceability, and priority of the mortage lien.

9. The standards of title evidence acceptable to the U.S. government, or its agencies,

when it acquires an interest in real estate by purchase, condemnation, dedication, or exchange, are different from those policies and certificates ordinarily issued to private insureds. A certificate of title covering fee simple title that guarantees only against matters of record or matters known to the title insurance company is usually issued prior to acquisition. A final certificate is issued after the United States takes title. There is also a United States Policy Form-1963, which again is issued prior to acquisition and acts as an interim binder. After taking title, the title insurance company issues a "date down" endorsement, which amends the effective date of the policy and shows title in the United States.

10. This adjustment is usually effected pursuant to an Endorsement 500 discussed in Section IV (B)(6) of this chapter.

techniques such as negative amortization, share of cash flow, and shared appreciation create additional considerations for the lender in determining the amount of insurance necessary to cover its risks in the transaction.

2. Schedule A: Caption

The caption just below the heading gives a brief description of the interests to be insured. If the transaction is a purchase being financed by a mortgage loan, then the caption will indicate that the instruments to be produced include a deed from the seller to the purchaser and a mortgage from the purchaser to the lender. The caption should be reviewed immediately on receipt of a report to ensure that the full interest is included and that all the parties are correctly named. The caption is where most errors are made and any discrepancies should be reported quickly.

The recital section of the caption is a summary of the relevant information concerning the most recent recorded conveyance of the property in question. Inclusion of recitals in deeds and mortgages will be of great assistance to future title searchers attempting to trace a chain of title.[11]

3. Schedule B-1: Matters Affecting Title

This section of a title report lists items that affect title to the property. The individual items must be removed, discharged, or compiled with by producing necessary documentation, such as a mortgage pay-off statement or tax receipts, to the title company. It is the paralegal's responsibility to identify from the title report those items which affect title and to coordinate and assemble the required documentation prior to the closing. Set forth below are the various items usually listed on Schedule B-1.

(a) Taxes, Sewer and Water Rents

In this section the title company will list the tax receipts and water and sewer receipts (where supplied by municipal authorities) that must be produced as a requirement of closing to evidence that real estate taxes and water and sewer assessments that are then due have been paid. The title insurance company will then insure title against the lien of past real estate taxes. It will not, of course, insure title against the lien of future real estate taxes, as payment of those taxes is in the control of the owner and not the title insurer.

(b) Mechanics' and Municipal Liens

A mechanics' lien is a statutorily created remedy that gives laborers and suppliers of materials a right to create a special priority lien on real estate that their labors or materials have improved. Mechanics' liens laws vary, but often the state law permits the priority of the lien to "relate

---

11. See Chapter Five, *Deeds of Conveyance.*

back" to a time earlier than the filing of the lien, and usually from the commencement of the work. Thus the section marked "Mechanics' and Municipal Claims" might or might not have actual filed claims listed, but in either event it will also have an objection for *unfiled* claims. This objection may sometimes be removed by an affidavit from the owner that no work has been performed by any contractors within a specified period. The problem of title insurance respecting mechanics' liens when work *has* recently been done is a difficult one that has received considerable attention from large lenders and from the title insurance industry. As a legal assistant, you should be aware of this potential problem area.

(c) Mortgages and Judgments

The next item listed is the necessary reference data for mortgages and judgments that appear in the public record. Most title companies list any judgments found in the county in which the property is located that are docketed against anyone with a name similar to that of the owner. If a judgment is against someone other than the owner, then the judgment may be removed from the list of objections by an affidavit of the owner stating that the listed judgments are not against him or her. In the case of a mortgage on the property or a judgment that is really against the owner, the lawyer or paralegal for the owner will have to have the judgment and mortgage satisfied, either prior to or at settlement. If the judgment or mortgage is to be paid out of the proceeds of settlement, then usually all that is needed is a form of pay-off statement from the mortgagee or judgment creditor stating that the mortgage or judgment will be satisfied on payment of a certain sum.

(d) Objections

Title companies often have already printed on their reports certain objections to its title insurance coverage that are standard for every transaction, no matter what the property is or who the parties are. General standard objections are not completely uniform throughout the nation or from company to company, but they generally include (i) an exclusion for tenants under unrecorded leases and (ii) an exclusion against any easements or encroachments that would be visible from an inspection of the property or that a proper survey would disclose. Standard objections are sometimes removed and sometimes not, depending on the particular transaction.

4. Schedule B-II: Exceptions and Objections Pertaining to the Land

(a) Property-Specific Exceptions

Certain exceptions are added for specific properties. These exceptions might be standard for the type of property, e.g., property abuting water, or might be specific easements, restrictions, and rights of way that have been shown to affect the property. These exceptions would also include recorded leases or other rights that have also been shown to affect the property. These exceptions normally remain unless something affirmative is done, such as producing a termination of a lease. Usually attached to the title report is a copy of each of the recorded documents listed on this schedule.

(b) Party-Specific Objections

Certain objections appear because of the nature of the parties involved or because of peculiarities in the chain of title. Again, some of these objections are standard for certain parties, e.g., a corporate seller must usually show that its board of directors authorized the transaction, and an estate must show that proper authority was granted to the representatives of the estate and that state and federal estate and inheritance taxes have been taken care of. Other objections are included if there are gaps in the chain of title. Let us suppose, for example, that the last recorded deed for a parcel shows title to have been conveyed to Diogenes Corp., in 1982. In 1984 Diogenes Corp. merged with Lampco, Inc., and Lampco., Inc. was the surviving corporation. No deed was recorded, and the title passed automatically to Lampco, Inc. In 1986 Lampco, Inc. dissolved at a time when its sole shareholders were Xerxes and Darius, each owning 5,000 shares of stock. No deed was recorded, and the title passed automatically to Xerxes and Darius as tenants in common. A title company would want satisfactory evidence of all this, including at least a certificate of merger from the state corporate bureau respecting the 1982 merger and a certificate of dissolution for the 1986 dissolution. Additionally, the title company might require corporate resolutions showing that the merger and the dissolution were both duly authorized.

5. Legal Description

The last section of a title report is the legal description of the property to be insured. Usually the title insurer obtains the description from the last recorded deed or most recent survey. It is extremely important that this section be checked for accuracy.

6. Endorsements

In evaluating a policy, a legal assistant should also remember that a standard form can be tailored to a particular transaction by the use of endorsements. An endorsement is an amendment to the policy that provides some affirmative coverage, e.g., some express insurance against a particular loss that would otherwise be excluded from the coverage. Two commonly utilized endorsements granted to a lender pursuant to a mortgagee's policy are Endorsement 100, which insures that certain covenants, conditions, and restrictions have not been violated and that a future violation will not cause a forfeiture or reversion of title, and Endorsement 300, which removes the title policy exception of discrepancies or conflicts in boundary lines, unrecorded easements, encroachments, or area content that a complete and accurate survey would disclose. Endorsement 300 is usually issued by a title company only after the title examiner's review of a recent survey. Endorsement 500, reprinted below from an owner's policy, provides coverage to both owners and mortgagees in the event of an inflationary increase in the value of the land being insured. Endorsement 800, issued to both owners and mortgagees of condominium units, insures that the condominium was properly created.

Endorsement 500

The Company, recognizing the current effect of inflation on real property valuation and intending to provide additional monetary protection to the Insured Owner named in said Policy, hereby modifies said Policy, as follows:

Notwithstanding anything contained in said Policy to the contrary, the amount of insurance provided by said Policy, as stated in Schedule A thereof, is subject to cumulative annual upward adjustments in the manner and to the extent hereinafter specified.

"Adjustment date" is defined, for the purpose of this Endorsement, to be 12:01 a.m. on the first January 1 which occurs more than six months after the Date of Policy, as shown in Schedule A of the Policy to which this Endorsement is attached, and on each succeeding January 1.

An upward adjustment will be made on each of the Adjustment Dates, as defined above, by increasing the maximum amount of insurance provided by said Policy (as said amount may have been increased theretofore under the terms of this Endorsement) by the same percentage, if any, by which the United States Department of Commerce Composite Construction Cost Index (base period 1967) for the month of September immediately preceding exceeds such Index for the month of September one year earlier; provided, however, that the maximum amount of insurance in force shall never exceed 150% of the amount of insurance stated in Schedule A of said Policy, less the amount of any claim paid under said Policy which, under the terms of the Conditions and Stipulations, reduces the amount of insurance in force. There shall be no annual adjustment in the amount of insurance for years in which there is no increase in said Construction Cost Index.

In the settlement of any claim against the Company under said Policy, the amount of insurance in force shall be deemed to be the amount which is in force as of the date on which the insured claimant first learned of the assertion or possible assertion of such claim, or as of the date of receipt by the Company of the first notice of such claim, whichever shall first occur.

PROVIDED, HOWEVER, this endorsement shall be effective only if one of the following conditions exists at Date of Policy:

a. The land described in this policy is a parcel on which there is only a one-to-four family residential structure, including all improvements on the land related to residential use, in which the Insured Owner resides or intends to reside; or,

b. The land consists of a residential condominium unit, together with the common elements appurtenant thereto and related to residential use thereof, in which the Insured Owner resides or intends to reside.

This endorsement is made a part of said policy and is subject to Exclusions, Schedules, Conditions and Stipulations thereto, except to the extent as modified by the provisions hereof. Nothing herein contained shall be construed as extending or changing the effective date of said policy. This Endorsement shall not be valid or binding until countersigned by an authorized signature as designated below.

V. SUMMARY

In minimizing the risks of issuing title insurance policies, title companies perform services and functions that overlap the traditional functions of a lawyer in a real estate transaction. For example, an attorney representing a client purchasing from a corporation would want to make sure that the corporation was authorized to convey the property. The title company has the same concern and is likely to seek the same proof, such as certified resolutions of the board of directors (and, in some instances, of the shareholders as well).

The role of the title insurer and the measures that the company takes to minimize its risks shape the format and function of the title report itself. Thus, the report states what a search of the public records has disclosed about the status of title as it relates to the contemplated transaction, and further describes what gaps must be filled in and what documents and proofs must be produced in order for the title insurer to issue a policy insuring that the title on settlement day is as stated in the title report. The policy is not prospective or predictive; it is just a description of title as of one fixed moment in time.

The function of the title report shapes its utility. As a legal assistant, you can use the title report as a guide to the agenda of documents that must be produced in order to complete a settlement. The title report gives advance notice of certain problems and an opportunity for the parties to allocate responsibility for solving those problems.

Reprinted in *Example 6-1* is an example of a title report prepared for a specific transaction and a title policy issued to the owner of the property following the transaction.

PROBLEM

1. You are working in a law firm in an area where title insurance is generally available, and where the title insurers are equipped to conduct their own searches. New clients, who have come to your firm for representation in connection with their proposed home purchase, note the cost of title insurance on the estimate of settlement costs prepared for them by the real estate agent connected with the transaction. "We'd prefer that your firm conduct a title search," they tell you, "we trust your competence." How would you respond?

2. After a title commitment (or title report) is issued but before settlement occurs, your firm's client becomes aware of a $10,000 judgment affecting the property she proposes to purchase. The judgment does not appear

on the title commitment. Should she proceed with settlement and then attempt to collect under her owner's title policy?

3. Your firm's client is about to purchase a home with a newly installed swimming pool. Does this present any special problems with respect to title insurance? Could the agreement of sale have been drafted to avoid potential problems in this regard?

Example 6-1 **Title Report and Title Policy**

NO.   TITLE REPORT   DATE

Commonwealth Land Title Insurance Company

Home Office: 1510 Walnut Street, Philadelphia, Pennsylvania 19102

COMPANY WILL ISSUE ITS CURRENT A.L.T.A. POLICY OF TITLE INSURANCE WITH RESPECT TO THE PREMISES ENDORSED HEREON, UPON SETTLEMENT OF THE TRANSACTION, RECORDATION OF THE INSTRUMENTS AND COMPLIANCE WITH ALL OF THE REQUIREMENTS SET FORTH HEREIN, IN CONFORMITY WITH THIS TITLE REPORT.

AMOUNT OF POLICY

alfred I. Mackler

Asst. Vice President

MORTGAGEE $ _____ OWNER $ _____

SCHEDULE A INSTRUMENTS TO BE PRODUCED AND RECORDED	*See Last Page for description and recital as to premises:*– 810 South 9th Street, Darby Boro. Del. Co DEED: James Freeport and Dorothy Freeport, his wife TO: John Hannahan and Thelma M. Hannahan DATED RECORDED MORTGAGE: $_____ John Hannahan and Thelma M. Hannahan TO: Sharon Federal Savings and Loan Association DATED RECORDED
SCHEDULE B-1	*UPON SATISFACTORY EVIDENCE OF DISCHARGE, SATISFACTION OR COMPLIANCE WITH THE FOLLOWING ITEMS AFFECTING TITLE TO THE SUBJECT PREMISES, SUCH ITEMS WILL BE REMOVED AND THE POLICY WILL BE ISSUED WITHOUT EXCEPTION THEREFOR.* ADDITIONAL EXCEPTIONS BASED ON A CONTINUATION OF TITLE SEARCHES WILL BE ADDED IF NOT DISPOSED OF TO SATISFACTION OF COMPANY. Possible unfiled mechanics liens and municipal claims. Terms of any unrecorded lease or rights of parties in possession. Proof that all natural persons in this transaction are of full age and legally competent. Proof of identity of parties as set forth in Recital. Payment of State and local Real Estate Transfer Taxes, if required. Possible additional assessments for taxes for new construction or for any major improvements pursuant to provisions of Acts of Assembly relating thereto.
TAXES	Receipts for all taxes for the years 1984 to 1985 inclusive to be produced. Due for current year 1986.
WATER RENTS	Receipts to be produced for years 1982 to 1985 inclusive. Due for current year 1986. Possible charge for water pipe installation and connection.
SEWER RENTS	**Receipts to be produced for years 1982 to 1985 inclusive.** Due for **current year 1986.** Possible charge for sewer installation and connection.
MECHANICS AND MUNICIPAL CLAIMS	NONE
MORTGAGES	$9,200.00 James Freeport and Dorothy Freeport, his wife to Sharon **Federal Savings and Loan Association dated February 29th, 1978 and** recorded March 1st, 1978 in Mortgage Book 2749 page 942.
JUDGMENTS	Public Consumer Discount Company vs James Freeport and Dorothy Freeport, C.P. 72-1489 filed 4-1-1972 DSB $4,000.00 Docket 369 page 542.

PA 2
725-99-2005

Continued.

Example 6-1 **Title Report and Title Policy** *continued*

SCHEDULE B-II *THE PREMISES ENDORSED HEREON ARE SUBJECT TO THE FOLLOWING ITEMS WHICH, TOGETHER WITH ITEMS NOT REMOVED IN SCHEDULE B-I, WILL BE EXCEPTED IN THE POLICY. ITEMS MARKED "SUBORDINATE" WILL APPEAR IN THE POLICY BUT COMPANY WILL INSURE THAT SUCH ITEMS ARE SUBORDINATE TO THE INSURED MORTGAGE (MORTGAGE POLICY ONLY).*

EXCEPTIONS

1. Discrepancies or conflicts in boundary lines, easements, encroachments, or area content that a satisfactory survey would disclose.

2. Easement of 9 feet wide driveway on Southwest, and subject to the proportionate part of keeping said driveway in good order and repair.

3. Restrictions affecting title as in Deed Book K-6 page 542 and Deed Book 2483 page 601.

4. Rights granted to the Philadelphia Electric Company and Bell Telephone Company in Deed Book 1243 page 609, and Deed Book 1234 page 1024.

ENDORSEMENTS   The following endorsements will appear in Policy if indicated.

Endorsement 100 _____ Endorsement _____

Endorsement Pa. 300 _____ Endorsement _____

Endorsement Pa. 500 _____ Endorsement _____

Endorsement Pa. 800 _____ Endorsement _____

TITLE INSURANCE SERVICES AVAILABLE

THROUGH THIS COMPANY, ITS SUBSIDIARIES, AGENTS, & APPROVED ATTORNEYS, IN:

Alaska	Kansas	New Jersey	Utah
Alabama	Kentucky	New Mexico	Vermont
Arizona	Louisiana	New York	Virginia
Arkansas	Maine	North Carolina	West Virginia
California	Maryland	North Dakota	Wisconsin
Colorado	Massachusetts	Ohio	Wyoming
Connecticut	Michigan	Oklahoma	
Delaware	Minnesota	Oregon	◆
Florida	Mississippi	Pennsylvania	
Georgia	Missouri	Rhode Island	
Hawaii	Montana	South Carolina	Bahamas
Idaho	Nebraska	South Dakota	District of Columbia
Illinois	Nevada	Tennessee	Puerto Rico
Indiana	New Hampshire	Texas	Virgin Islands

DESCRIPTION and RECITAL

ALL THAT CERTAIN brick messuage and lot or piece of land SITUATE on the Northwesterly side of Ninth Street, in the Borough of Darby, County of Delaware and State of Pennsylvania, and described as Lot No. 12, according to a certain survey and plan made by Alonzo H. Yocum, Surveyor, dated the 27th day of May A.D. 1922 and recorded in the Office for the Recording of Deeds, &c., in and for the County of Delaware aforesaid, in Deed Book 701 page 462 &c. as follows:

BEGINNING at a point in the Northwesterly side of Ninth Street at the distance of 208.84 feet Southwestwardly from a point in the corner formed by the intersection of the Southwesterly side of Willow Street and the Northwesterly side of Ninth Street; thence extending South 22 degrees 6 minutes West 22 feet to a point; thence extending North 67 degrees 46 minutes West 108 feet to a point; thence extending North 22 degrees 6 minutes East 22 feet to a point; thence extending South 67 degrees 46 minutes East passing through the center of the party wall of the messuage hereby conveyed and the messuage adjoining on the Northeast 108 feet to a point in the Northwesterly side of Ninth Street, the first mentioned point and place of beginning.

BEING No. 810 South Ninth Street.

TOGETHER with the right and subject to a corresponding right in the owner or owners of the adjoining property on the Southwest of using as and for a passageway and driveway forever, a certain 9 feet wide driveway and extending in length 88 feet and shown on said plan and laid out half on the property hereby conveyed and half on the property adjoining on the Southwest for the common use and benefit of each of the said properties.

BEING the same premises which Howard J. Elkins and Mildred E. Elkins, his wife by Deed dated February 29, 1978 and recorded in Deed Book 2849 page 180 conveyed unto James Freeport and Dorothy Freeport, his wife, in fee.

Continued.

Example 6-1 **Title Report and Title Policy** *continued*

SPECIMEN

POLICY
OF
TITLE
INSURANCE

PA 10 ALTA Owner's Policy
1970-Form B (Amended 10/17/70)

Issued by

COMMONWEALTH LAND
TITLE INSURANCE COMPANY

Title Insurance Since 1876

HOME OFFICE
1510 WALNUT STREET
PHILADELPHIA, PA. 19102

POLICY OF TITLE INSURANCE

COMMONWEALTH LAND
TITLE INSURANCE COMPANY

(a stock company)
PHILADELPHIA, PENNSYLVANIA

SCHEDULE A

POLICY NO.	DATE OF POLICY: *The date shown below or the date of recording of the instrument referred to in Item 3 whichever is the later.*	AMOUNT OF INSURANCE
C-842-785-D		$40,000

1. Name of insured: John Hannahan and Thelma M. Hannahan, Husband and Wife

2. The estate or interest in the land described herein and which is covered by this policy is:

Owners in fee.

3. The estate or interest referred to herein is at Date of Policy vested in:

insured, by deed from James Freeport and wife to insured, dated
January 28, 1986 and recorded January 29, 1986 in Deed Book 4216
page 379 at Media, Pennsylvania

4. The land referred to in this policy is described in the said instrument and identified as follows:

ALL THAT CERTAIN brick messuage and lot or piece of land SITUATE on
the Northwesterly side of Ninth Street, in the Borough of Darby,
County of Delaware and State of Pennsylvania, and described as Lot
No. 12, according to a certain survey and plan made by Alonzo H.
Yocum, Surveyor, dated the 27th day of May A.D. 1922 and recorded
in the Office for the Recording of Deeds, &c., in and for the
County of Delaware aforesaid, in Deed Book 701 page 462 &c. as
follows:

Countersigned:

....
Authorized Officer or Agent

PA 10 ALTA Owner's Policy-1970-Form B (Amended 10/17/70)
810-35-1349

Sched. A

Continued.

Example 6-1   **Title Report and Title Policy** *continued*

COMMONWEALTH LAND
TITLE INSURANCE COMPANY

OWNER'S TITLE INSURANCE POLICY

SUBJECT TO THE EXCLUSIONS **FROM COVERAGE**, THE EXCEPTIONS CONTAINED IN SCHEDULE B AND THE PROVISIONS OF THE CONDITIONS AND STIPULATIONS HEREOF, COMMONWEALTH LAND TITLE INSURANCE COMPANY, a Pennsylvania corporation, herein called the **Company**, **insures**, **as of Date** of Policy shown in Schedule A, against loss or damage, not exceeding the amount of insurance stated in **Schedule A**, and **costs**, attorneys' fees and expenses which the **Company** may become obligated to pay hereunder, sustained or incurred **by the insured** by reason of:

1. Title to the estate or interest **described** in Schedule A being vested otherwise than as **stated** therein;

2. Any defect in or lien or **encumbrance** on such title;

3. Lack of a right of access to **and** from the land; or

4. Unmarketability of such title.

IN WITNESS WHEREOF the Company has caused this Policy to be signed and sealed, to be valid when Schedule A is countersigned by an authorized officer or agent of the Company, all in accordance with its By-Laws.

COMMONWEALTH LAND TITLE INSURANCE COMPANY

By _____
                                    ent

Attest: _____
                                    Secretary

EXCLUSIONS FROM COVERAGE

The following matters are expressly excluded from the coverage of this policy:

1. Any law, ordinance or governmental regulation (including but not limited to building and zoning ordinances) restricting or regulating or prohibiting the occupancy, use or enjoyment of the land, or regulating the character, dimensions or location of any improvement now or hereafter erected on the land, or prohibiting a separation in ownership or a reduction in the dimensions or area of the land, or the effect of any violation of any such law, ordinance or governmental regulation.

2. Rights of eminent domain or governmental rights of police power unless notice of the exercise of such rights appears in the public records at Date of Policy.

3. Defects, liens, encumbrances, adverse claims, or other matters (a) created, suffered, assumed or agreed to by the insured claimant; (b) not known to the Company and not shown by the public records but known to the insured claimant either at Date of Policy or at the date such claimant acquired an estate or interest insured by this policy and not disclosed in writing by the insured claimant to the Company prior to the date such insured claimant became an insured hereunder; (c) resulting in no loss or damage to the insured claimant; (d) attaching or created subsequent to Date of Policy; or (e) resulting in loss or damage which would not have been sustained if the insured claimant had paid value for the estate or interest insured by this policy.

SCHEDULE B

Policy No._____

This policy does not insure against loss or damage by reason of the following:

1. Discrepancies or conflicts in boundary lines, easements, encroachments, or area content that a satisfactory survey would disclose.

2. Easement of 9 feet wide driveway on Southwest, and subject to the proportionate part of keeping said driveway in good order and repair.

3. Restrictions affecting title as in Deed Book K-6 page 542 and Deed Book 2483 page 601.

4. Rights granted to the Philadelphia Electric Company and Bell Telephone Company in Deed Book 1248 page 609, and Deed Book 1234 page 1024.

Continued.

Example 6-1 Title Report and Title Policy *continued*

SPECIMEN

CONDITIONS AND STIPULATIONS

1. DEFINITION OF TERMS

The following terms when used in this policy mean:

(a) "insured": the insured named in Schedule A, and, subject to any rights or defenses the Company may have had against the named insured, those who succeed to the interest of such insured by operation of law as distinguished from purchase including, but not limited to, heirs, distributees, devisees, survivors, personal representatives, next of kin, or corporate or fiduciary successors.

(b) "insured claimant": an insured claiming loss or damage hereunder.

(c) "knowledge": actual knowledge, not constructive knowledge or notice which may be imputed to an insured by reason of any public records.

(d) "land": the land described, specifically or by reference in Schedule A, and improvements affixed thereto which by law constitute real property; provided, however, the term "land" does not include any property beyond the lines of the area specifically described or referred to in Schedule A, nor any right, title, interest, estate or easement in abutting streets, roads, avenues, alleys, lanes, ways or waterways, but nothing herein shall modify or limit the extent to which a right of access to and from the land is insured by this policy.

(e) "mortgage": mortgage, deed of trust, trust deed, or other security instrument.

(f) "public records": those records which by law impart constructive notice of matters relating to said land.

2. CONTINUATION OF INSURANCE AFTER CONVEYANCE OF TITLE

The coverage of this policy shall continue in force as of Date of Policy in favor of an insured so long as such insured retains an estate or interest in the land, or holds an indebtedness secured by a purchase money mortgage given by a purchaser from such insured, or so long as such insured shall have liability by reason of covenants of warranty made by such insured in any transfer or conveyance of such estate or interest; provided, however, this policy shall not continue in force in favor of any purchaser from such insured of either said estate or interest or the indebtedness secured by a purchase money mortgage given to such insured.

3. DEFENSE AND PROSECUTION OF ACTIONS—NOTICE OF CLAIM TO BE GIVEN BY AN INSURED CLAIMANT.

(a) The Company, at its own cost and without undue delay, shall provide for the defense of an insured in all litigation consisting of actions or proceedings commenced against such insured, or a defense interposed against an insured in an action to enforce a contract for a sale of the estate or interest in said land, to the extent that such litigation is founded upon an alleged defect, lien, encumbrance, or other matter insured against by this policy.

(b) The insured shall notify the Company promptly in writing (i) in case any action or proceeding is begun or defense is interposed as set forth in (a) above, (ii) in case knowledge shall come to an insured hereunder of any claim of title or interest which is adverse to the title to the estate or interest, as insured, and which might cause loss or damage for which the Company may be liable by virtue of this policy, or (iii) if title to the estate or interest, as insured, is rejected as unmarketable. If such prompt notice shall not be given to the Company, then as to such insured all liability of the Company shall cease and terminate in regard to the matter or matters for which such prompt notice is required; provided, however, that failure to notify shall in no case prejudice the rights of any such insured under this policy unless the Company shall be prejudiced by such failure and then only to the extent of such prejudice.

(c) The Company shall have the right at its own cost to institute and without undue delay prosecute any action or proceeding or to do any other act which in its opinion may be necessary or desirable to establish the title to the estate or interest as insured, and the Company may take any appropriate action under the terms of this policy, whether or not it shall be liable thereunder, and shall not thereby concede liability or waive any provision of this policy.

(d) Whenever the Company shall have brought any action or interposed a defense as required or permitted by the provisions of this policy, the Company may pursue any such litigation to final determination by a court of competent jurisdiction and expressly reserves the right, in its sole discretion, to appeal from any adverse judgment or order.

(e) In all cases where this policy permits or requires the Company to prosecute or provide for the defense of any action or proceeding, the insured hereunder shall secure to the Company the right to so prosecute or provide defense in such action or proceeding, and all appeals therein, and permit the Company to use, at its option, the name of such insured for such purpose. Whenever requested by the Company, such insured shall give the Company all reasonable aid in any such action or proceeding, in effecting settlement, securing evidence, obtaining witnesses, or prosecuting or defending such action or proceeding, and the Company shall reimburse such insured for any expense so incurred.

4. NOTICE OF LOSS—LIMITATION OF ACTION

In addition to the notices required under paragraph 3(b) of these Conditions and Stipulations, a statement in writing of any loss or damage for which it is claimed the Company is liable under this policy shall be furnished to the Company within 90 days after such loss or damage shall have been determined and no right of action shall accrue to an insured claimant until 30 days after such statement shall have been furnished. Failure to furnish such statement of loss or damage shall terminate any liability of the Company under this policy as to such loss or damage.

5. OPTIONS TO PAY OR OTHERWISE SETTLE CLAIMS

The Company shall have the option to pay or otherwise settle for or in the name of an insured claimant any claim insured against or to terminate all liability and obligations of the Company hereunder by paying or tendering payment of the amount of insurance under this policy together with any costs, attorneys' fees and expenses incurred up to the time of such payment or tender of payment, by the insured claimant and authorized by the Company.

6. DETERMINATION AND PAYMENT OF LOSS

(a) The liability of the Company under this policy shall in no case exceed the least of:

(i) the actual loss of the insured claimant; or
(ii) the amount of insurance stated in Schedule A

(b) The Company will pay, in addition to any loss insured against by this policy, all costs imposed upon an insured in litigation carried on by the Company for such insured, and all costs, attorneys' fees and expenses in litigation carried on by such insured with the written authorization of the Company.

(c) When liability has been definitely fixed in accordance with the conditions of this policy, the loss or damage shall be payable within 30 days thereafter.

Conditions and Stipulations Continued on Cover

SPECIMEN

CONDITIONS AND STIPULATIONS

(Continued)

7. LIMITATION OF LIABILITY

No claim shall arise or be maintainable under this policy (a) if the Company, after having received notice of an alleged defect, lien or encumbrance insured against hereunder, by litigation or otherwise, removes such defect, lien or encumbrance or establishes the title, as insured, within a reasonable time after receipt of such notice; (b) in the event of litigation until there has been a final determination by a court of competent jurisdiction, and disposition of all appeals therefrom, adverse to the title, as insured, as provided in paragraph 3 hereof; or (c) for liability voluntarily assumed by an insured in settling any claim or suit without prior written consent of the Company.

8. REDUCTION OF LIABILITY

All payments under this policy, except payments made for costs, attorneys' fees and expenses, shall reduce the amount of the insurance pro tanto. No payment shall be made without producing this policy for endorsement of such payment unless the policy be lost or destroyed, in which case proof of such loss or destruction shall be furnished to the satisfaction of the Company.

9. LIABILITY NONCUMULATIVE

It is expressly understood that the amount of insurance under this policy shall be reduced by any amount the Company may pay under any policy insuring either (a) a mortgage shown or referred to in Schedule B hereof which is a lien on the estate or interest covered by this policy, or (b) a mortgage hereafter executed by an insured which is a charge or lien on the estate or interest described or referred to in Schedule A, and the amount so paid shall be deemed a payment under this policy. The Company shall have the option to apply to the payment of any such mortgages any amount that otherwise would be payable hereunder to the insured owner of the estate or interest covered by this policy and the amount so paid shall be deemed a payment under this policy to said insured owner.

10. APPORTIONMENT

If the land described in Schedule A consists of two or more parcels which are not used as a single site, and a loss is established affecting one or more of said parcels but not all, the loss shall be computed and settled on a pro rata basis as if the amount of insurance under this policy was divided pro rata as to the value on Date of Policy of each separate parcel to the whole, exclusive of any improvements made subsequent to Date of Policy, unless a liability or value has otherwise been agreed upon as to each such parcel by the Company and the insured at the time of the issuance of this policy and shown by an express statement herein or by an endorsement attached hereto.

11. SUBROGATION UPON PAYMENT OR SETTLEMENT

Whenever the Company shall have settled a claim under this policy, all right of subrogation shall vest in the Company unaffected by any act of the insured claimant. The Company shall be subrogated to and be entitled to all rights and remedies which such insured claimant would have had against any person or property in respect to such claim had this policy not been issued, and if requested by the Company, such insured claimant shall transfer to the Company all rights and remedies against any person or property necessary in order to perfect such right of subrogation and shall permit the Company to use the name of such insured claimant in any transaction or litigation involving such rights or remedies. If the payment does not cover the loss of such insured claimant, the Company shall be subrogated to such rights and remedies in the proportion which said payment bears to the amount of said loss. If loss should result from any act of such insured claimant, such act shall not void this policy, but the Company, in that event, shall be required to pay only that part of any losses insured against hereunder which shall exceed the amount, if any, lost to the Company by reason of the impairment of the right of subrogation.

12. LIABILITY LIMITED TO THIS POLICY

This instrument together with all endorsements and other instruments, if any, attached hereto by the Company is the entire policy and contract between the insured and the Company.

Any claim of loss or damage, whether or not based on negligence, and which arises out of the status of the title to the estate or interest covered hereby or any action asserting such claim, shall be restricted to the provisions and conditions and stipulations of this policy.

No amendment of or endorsement to this policy can be made except by writing endorsed hereon or attached hereto signed by either the President, a Vice President, the Secretary, an Assistant Secretary, or validating officer or authorized signatory of the Company.

13. NOTICES, WHERE SENT

All notices required to be given the Company and any statement in writing required to be furnished the Company shall be addressed to its Home Office, 1510 Walnut St., Phila., Pa. 19102.

—Valid Only If Schedules A and B Are Attached

PA 10 ALTA Owner's Policy · 1970 · Form B (Amended 10/17/70)
295-00-1352

Chapter 7

Real Estate Mortgages

Part One
RESIDENTIAL MORTGAGES

I. INTRODUCTION

A mortgage is a means by which a creditor can obtain security interest in a debtor's real property. The use of mortgages as security devices in connection with the lending of money began with the breakup of the feudal system and the inception of a money economy in England. Pursuant to the earliest known form of mortgage, a creditor (the "mortgagee") was granted possession of the land of his or her debtor (the "mortgagor") and was permitted to keep any rents or profits without applying them to the reduction of the debt. The rents or profits took the place of interest[1] on the debt, and the mortgagor was expected to repay the debt out of his or her other resources. Mortgages in their modern form became more common as the capitalist system began to develop between 1200 and 1450. Under the modern form of mortgage, the mortgagor retains possession and use of the property.

A mortgage may be defined as "any form of written instrument whereby a lien is created on real estate or whereby title to real estate is reserved or conveyed to a mortgagee as security for the payment of a debt or fulfillment of other obligations." Some states adhere to a "title theory" of mortgages. In such states a mortgage is considered to be a technical

---

1. Interest in the form of money was considered usury during that era and was unlawful.

186

conveyance or transfer of real estate by the mortgagor to the mortgagee, given to secure performance of an obligation, most commonly repayment of a debt. If and when the debt has been paid, the conveyance becomes null and void and the property reverts to the debtor. In other states, known as "lien theory" states, the creation of the mortgage does not constitute a technical conveyance, but simply creates an immediate lien against the mortgaged real estate. The practical differences between the two theories are of little significance. In either case the mortgagee holds an interest in the land only as security for the debt and must surrender that interest when the debt has been repaid.

If the debtor's obligations are not discharged, the mortgagee may obtain title to the real estate[2] or sell it to others. Nevertheless, to protect debtors from the loss of their lands because of technical or insignificant defaults, English courts of equity intervened on behalf of debtors. To redress the harsh and technical treatment sometimes imposed by creditors, courts of equity began to force reconveyance by the creditors even when the debtor had failed to perform completely or promptly. The equity courts gradually developed as a remedy for debtors a right to reacquire or "redeem" the real estate, notwithstanding incomplete or imperfect performance. Even now a mortgagor's rights in mortgaged real estate are referred to as the "equity" or "equity of redemption."

Although a mortgagor is entitled to protection against harsh and unreasonable remedies, the mortgagee must be able at some point to extinguish or "foreclose" the mortgagor's right to redeem his or her "equity of redemption." The practice developed whereby a mortgagee, after a default had occurred, would file suit in a court of equity to obtain a decree foreclosing the mortgagor's right to redeem the property. Once that decree had been entered, the mortgagee was free to sell the property to anyone it might choose. The foreclosure sale is the direct lineal descendant of the English decree in equity foreclosing the borrower's right to redeem.

In some states, particularly in the South and the West, deeds of trust are used instead of mortgages. There are several technical differences of form between a mortgage and a deed of trust. However, the purposes of the two instruments are the same. Under a deed of trust, the debtor transfers the property to a trustee who holds title to the real estate in trust until the debt is paid, whereupon the trustee reconveys the property to the debtor. If the debt is not repaid in accordance with its terms, the trustee will either sell the property and pay the proceeds to the creditor, or transfer title to the creditor.

The purpose of the following sections of these materials is to outline for the student the basic transactions and situations for which mortgages are created, and to review the documentation and activity involved in

---

2. In a title theory state the mortgagee technically has title from the outset and could evict the mortgagor from its premises.

different kinds of mortgage transactions. The basic mortgage documents for residential, industrial-commercial and construction mortgages have many similarities, but each also has many distinguishing characteristics. The greater risks in commercial and construction mortgages result in more complex documentation of the transactions. In this chapter we will discuss residential, commercial-industrial, construction, and industrial development authority mortgages, and also the subject of foreclosure.

II. RESIDENTIAL MORTGAGES

The purchase of a home is the largest single investment most people ever make. It is not surprising to find that in most cases the buyer of a home does not have all of the funds required to complete the purchase. Normally, he or she will have to finance part of the cost by borrowing the money, usually from a bank, insurance company, or savings and loan association. Accordingly, most home buyers will insist that the agreement under which they purchase a home contain a provision that makes their obligation to purchase contingent on being able to obtain a satisfactory mortgage loan. Such mortgage contingency clauses were discussed in Chapter Three of these materials.

A. METHODS OF REPAYMENT

1. Interest

When a borrower borrows money to finance the purchase of real property, he or she must repay the amount of money borrowed, usually called the "principal," and pay the lender an amount, usually known as "interest," for use of the money for the period that it has been borrowed. The total dollar amount of interest that will be paid by the borrower over the life of a loan depends on the interest rate, the length of time for which the money is borrowed, and the amount of the loan.

The interest rate charged by a lender is traditionally stated as a percentage charge for use of money for one year. Therefore, if one borrows $1,000 at 9% interest, he or she would pay $90 per year in interest (.09 × $1,000). If the loan were paid in six months, $45 of interest would be payable (.09 × $^6/_{12}$ × $1,000). The interest is stated on an annual basis but is recalculated for shorter time periods. The interest can be calculated on a monthly basis by multiplying the rate by $\frac{1}{12}$ or on a daily basis by multiplying by $\frac{1}{365}$.[3]

---

3. Because of the varying lengths of months and also because of leap years, certain conventions have been generally adopted concerning the calculation of interest. Often, for example, the year is treated as if it consisted of 12 months of 30 days each, and banks often charge daily interest by multiplying annual interest by $\frac{1}{360}$ rather than by $\frac{1}{365}$. A 360-day year is often called a "banker's year."

PROBLEM

1. **What is the interest on $1,500 at 13¾% for one year?**
2. **What is the interest on $2,500 at 12% for nine months?**

---

2. Principal

It is possible to borrow money for a specified period (the "term" of the loan) and repay the principal as a lump sum at the end of the term of the loan. Such a loan is said to have a "balloon payment" at the end because the final payment is so much larger than the period payments of interest only that it is like a balloon on the end of a string. Interest-only balloon loans[4] were the usual type of mortgage loan, both residential and commercial, until the Depression. Many lenders found during the Depression that balloon loans did not afford them sufficient security on default, especially in a time of declining real estate values, because they had to look to the mortgaged property for recovery of the entire principal sum of the loan. Therefore, lenders sought a form of loan that would involve gradual repayment of principal during the term of the loan, thus reducing their dependence on the value of the mortgaged property as the loan was paid off. Presently, full or partial balloon loans are used more frequently in a commercial context. Residential mortgages are usually structured to include periodic payments of portions of the borrowed principal as well as interest.

There are many possible methods of repaying principal. For example, the same amount of principal could be repaid with each installment. A twenty-year loan of $65,000 could be repaid in 360 monthly installments of $180.56 each plus interest on the then outstanding principal balance. With this method of payment the interest payments will change each month and payments will be large in early years and decline in later years. For homeowners, that is often a serious problem if earnings are expected to rise in the future.

Most homeowners would prefer to make a constant monthly payment of principal and interest combined over the life of a loan. In order to accommodate that desire, financial institutions have developed the "level payment" loan. Other names such as "level monthly payment," "self-amortizing," or "self-liquidating" loan are often used to describe this loan. The amount of the level payment is calculated so that if the payment is first applied to interest with the remainder reducing principal, the loan will reduce to $0 by 360 equal payments. For example, the level payment

---

4. Also known as "standing" loans because the principal stands the same throughout the term of the loan.

necessary to repay a $65,000 loan at 13% per annum interest over thirty years is $719.02 per month. That portion of the $719.02 payment that is necessary to cover the interest for the prior month is paid first and the balance is applied to the principal. The interest due after the first month of this loan is $704.17 ($65,000 × .13 = $8,450; $8,450 ÷ 12 = $704.17). Thus $704.17 of the first month's payment will be applied to interest and $14.85 to principal. In the second month the borrower will have an outstanding principal balance of $64,985.15 ($65,000 − $14.85). The interest due this month is $704.01 (64,985.15 × 13% = $8,448.06; $8,448.06 ÷ 12 = $704.01). The $704.01 is paid first and $15.01 is applied to principal. Each month the interest portion of the payment decreases and the principal portion increases. By the end of the term of the loan, the interest portion is very small and the principal portion is almost the whole level payment.

The amortization table in *Example 7-1* shows the portion of each installment payment that is applied to principal and interest during the life of a thirty-year, $65,000 mortgage at 13%.

Example 7-1 Amortization Table

AMORTIZATION OF LOAN

AMOUNT OF LOAN $65,000.00
TERM   30.00 YEARS
NO. OF PAYMENTS PER YEAR   12
ANNUAL RATE   13.0000
INSTALLMENT AMOUNT $719.02

MOS	TIME YRS	PERIODS	PAYMENT ON INTEREST	PAYMENT ON PRINCIPAL	TOTAL PAYMENT	INTEREST TO DATE	PRINCIPAL TO DATE	PAYMENT TO DATE	BALANCE OF LOAN
5	1985	1	704.17	14.85	719.02	704.17	14.85	719.02	64985.15
6	1985	2	704.01	15.01	719.02	1408.18	29.86	1438.04	64970.14
7	1985	3	703.84	15.18	719.02	2112.02	45.04	2157.06	64954.96
8	1985	4	703.68	15.34	719.02	2815.70	60.38	2876.08	64939.62
9	1985	5	703.51	15.51	719.02	3519.21	75.89	3595.10	64924.11
10	1985	6	703.34	15.68	719.02	4222.55	91.57	4314.12	64908.43
11	1985	7	703.17	15.85	719.02	4925.72	107.42	5033.14	64892.58
12	1985	8	703.00	16.02	719.02	5628.72	123.44	5752.16	64876.56
1	1986	9	702.83	16.19	719.02	6331.55	139.63	6471.18	64860.37
1	1987	21	700.59	18.43	719.02	14751.26	348.16	15099.42	64651.84
1	1988	33	698.05	20.97	719.02	23142.18	585.48	23727.66	64414.52
1	1989	45	695.16	23.86	719.C2	31500.35	855.55	32355.90	64144.45
1	1990	57	691.86	27.16	719.02	39821.25	1162.89	40984.14	63837.11
1	1991	69	688.11	30.91	719.02	48099.73	1512.65	49612.38	63487.35
1	1992	81	683.85	35.17	719.02	56329.92	1910.70	58240.62	63089.30
1	1993	93	678.99	40.03	719.02	64505.16	2363.70	66868.86	62636.30
1	1994	105	673.47	45.55	719.02	72617.89	2879.21	75497.10	62120.79
1	1995	117	667.18	51.84	719.02	80659.47	3465.87	84125.34	61534.13
1	1996	129	660.03	58.99	719.02	88620.05	4133.53	92753.58	60866.47
1	1997	141	651.88	67.14	719.02	96488.47	4893.35	101381.82	60106.65
1	1998	153	642.62	76.40	719.02	104252.03	5758.03	110010.06	59241.97
1	1999	165	632.07	86.95	719.02	111896.23	6742.07	118638.30	58257.93
1	2000	177	620.07	98.95	719.02	119404.61	7861.93	127266.54	57138.07
1	2001	189	606.41	112.61	719.02	126758.41	9136.37	135894.78	55863.63
1	2002	201	590.87	128.15	719.02	133936.30	10586.72	144523.02	54413.28

1	2003	213	573.18	145.84	719.02	140914.00	12237.26	153151.26	52762.74
1	2004	225	553.05	165.97	719.02	147663.84	14115.66	161779.50	50884.34
1	2005	237	530.14	188.88	719.02	154154.41	16253.33	170407.74	48746.67
1	2006	249	504.06	214.96	719.02	160349.92	18686.06	179035.98	46313.94
1	2007	261	474.39	244.63	719.02	166209.61	21454.61	187664.22	43545.39
1	2008	273	440.63	278.39	719.02	171687.16	24605.30	196292.46	40394.70
1	2009	285	402.20	316.82	719.02	176729.81	28190.89	204920.70	36809.11
1	2010	297	358.47	360.55	719.02	181277.55	32271.39	213548.94	32728.61
1	2011	309	308.70	410.32	719.02	185262.06	36915.12	222177.18	28084.88
1	2012	321	252.06	466.96	719.02	188605.56	42199.86	230805.42	22800.14
1	2013	333	187.60	531.42	719.02	191219.58	48214.08	239433.66	16785.92
1	2014	345	114.25	604.77	719.02	193003.46	55058.44	248061.90	9941.56
1	2015	357	30.77	688.25	719.02	193842.60	62847.54	256690.14	2152.46
2	2015	358	23.32	695.70	719.02	193865.92	63543.24	257409.16	1456.76
3	2015	359	15.78	703.24	719.02	193881.70	64246.48	258128.18	753.52
4	2015	360	8.16	753.52	761.68	193889.86	65000.00	258889.86	.00

B. THE APPLICATION FOR A MORTGAGE

Once the purchaser and seller have signed a residential agreement of sale, the purchaser will apply to a lending institution for a loan. The lender will insist on obtaining certain information from the purchaser before considering the request for a loan, including the purchase price of the property; the percentage of the purchase price that the purchaser desires to borrow; the purchaser's income (to determine whether it is sufficient to pay the normal expenses and make the monthly payment on the mortgage); the purchaser's reputation and credit standing in the community; and the purchaser's other financial resources. The lender will require the purchaser to complete an application form and, usually, to pay fees for a credit report and for an appraisal of the property. A form of residential loan application is reprinted as *Example 7-2* at the end of this section B.

On receipt of an application the lender will obtain a report on the borrower's credit from an independent credit-investigating agency, and will have an appraisal made to ascertain the approximate fair market value of the property. The lender will also require a signed copy of the agreement of sale to confirm the existence and terms of the agreement of sale.

In most conventional residential mortgage loan situations, the purchaser wishes to borrow from 50% to 80% of the purchase price. However, there are cases in which the buyer finds it necessary to borrow as much as 95% of the purchase price. Obviously, the less "equity"[5] in the purchase, the greater the lender's risk, because the lender has less assurance that

---

5. When mortgage lenders speak of "equity" they mean the difference between the value of the property and the principal sum of the mortgage. If the mortgaged property has a value equal to the purchase price, then the purchaser's equity will initially be that portion of the purchase price that the purchaser pays out of his or her own pocket.

it will be able to sell the property, in the event of a default, at a price that will pay all expenses of foreclosure, unpaid interest, and the balance due on the loan. In addition, the less equity a borrower has in the mortgaged property, the less incentive a borrower has to prevent a foreclosure by the mortgage lender.

To assist purchasers of modest means who lack funds for a substantial down payment, certain governmental or quasi-governmental agencies, such as the Federal Housing Administration (FHA) or the Veterans Administration (VA) will, under certain circumstances, issue a guarantee of repayment to the lender.[6] On application by a qualified borrower, the FHA or VA will agree to guarantee repayment to a lender of a substantial portion of the loan. The credit backing of the U.S. government makes such loans much more attractive to institutional lenders, who might otherwise be prevented by regulation or banking policy from making such loans. You should be aware that, as a condition to issuing a guarantee, both the FHA and the VA impose certain requirements. For example, the FHA and VA may insist that the real estate meet certain minimum standards pertaining to quality and safety of construction. The VA and FHA also have qualifying requirements as to the maximum amount of money that an applicant may earn and the maximum amount of the loan. The FHA and VA also require that the interest rate to be charged the borrower not exceed certain specific rates that the FHA and VA from time to time determine.[7] If the maximum interest rate the FHA will allow on a mortgage is less than the then prevailing market rate of interest, the lender, as a condition for making the FHA-insured loan, may require a lump sum payment at the outset in addition to the periodic payments of interest. Making a lump-sum payment is referred to as paying "points." A point equals 1% of the amount of the mortgage.[8] The points are calculated to provide the lender with the same "yield" or income on the loan that it would have received over the period of the loan if the loan had been made at the market rate of interest rather than the FHA rate. The applicable law usually provides that points must be paid by the seller rather than the purchaser, because the points are additional interest and, if the purchaser were to pay them, the loan would be in violation of the

6. The programs of other agencies, such as the Federal National Mortgage Association ("FNMA" or "Fanny Mae"), the Government National Mortgage Association ("GNMA" or "Ginny Mae"), and the Federal Home Loan Mortgage Corporation ("FHLMC" or "Freddy Mac") are usually programs by which the agencies agree to purchase mortgages that are not in default rather than to insure mortgages.

7. State laws regulating interest rates typically exempt VA and FHA loans.

8. A $900 lump-sum payment on a $30,000

mortgage is a payment of 3 points. Even in a conventionally financed transaction a lender may require a payment of a "placement fee" or "origination fee" as a consideration for making the loan. Lawyers often refer to such fees as points. Ostensibly, these fees are intended to cover the expenses of the lender in considering the application. In fact, in many cases the charging of a placement fee is simply a way of increasing the net income that the lender will realize on the transaction.

Example 7-2 Residential Loan Application

RESIDENTIAL LOAN APPLICATION

MORTGAGE APPLIED FOR	☐ Conventional ☐ FHA	Amount	Interest Rate	No. of Months	Monthly Payment Principal & Interest	Escrow/Impounds (to be collected monthly)
	☐ VA	$	%		$	☐ Taxes ☐ Hazard Ins. ☐ Mtg. Ins.

Prepayment Option

SUBJECT PROPERTY

Property Street Address	City	County	State	Zip	No. Units

Legal Description (Attach description if necessary)	Year Built

Purpose of Loan: ☐ Purchase ☐ Construction-Permanent ☐ Construction ☐ Refinance ☐ Other (Explain)

Complete this line if Construction-Permanent or Construction Loan ☞	Lot Value Data Year Acquired _____ $	Original Cost $	Present Value (a) $	Cost of Imps. (b) $	Total (a + b) $	ENTER TOTAL AS PURCHASE PRICE IN DETAILS OF PURCHASE.

Complete this line if a Refinance Loan   Purpose of Refinance _____   Describe Improvements ( ) made ( ) to be made
Year Acquired _____ Original Cost _____ Amt. Existing Liens _____ $_____   Cost: $_____

Title Will Be Held In What Name(s)	Manner In Which Title Will Be Held

Source of Down Payment and Settlement Charges

THIS APPLICATION IS DESIGNED TO BE COMPLETED BY THE BORROWER(S) WITH THE LENDER'S ASSISTANCE. THE CO-BORROWER SECTION AND ALL OTHER CO-BORROWER QUESTIONS MUST BE COMPLETED AND THE APPROPRIATE BOX(ES) CHECKED IF ☐ ANOTHER PERSON WILL BE JOINTLY OBLIGATED WITH THE BORROWER ON THE LOAN, OR ☐ THE BORROWER IS RELYING ON INCOME FROM ALIMONY, CHILD SUPPORT OR SEPARATE MAINTENANCE OR ON THE INCOME OR ASSETS OF ANOTHER PERSON AS A BASIS FOR REPAYMENT OF THE LOAN, OR ☐ THE BORROWER IS MARRIED AND RESIDES, OR THE PROPERTY IS LOCATED, IN A COMMUNITY PROPERTY STATE.

BORROWER			CO BORROWER		
Name	Age	School Yrs.	Name	Age	School Yrs.
Present Address No. Years _____ ☐ Own ☐ Rent			Present Address No. Years _____ ☐ Own ☐ Rent		
Street _____			Street _____		
City/State/Zip _____			City/State/Zip _____		
Former address if less than 2 years at present address			Former address if less than 2 years at present address		
Street _____			Street _____		
City/State/Zip _____			City/State/Zip _____		
Years at former address ☐ Own ☐ Rent			Years at former address ☐ Own ☐ Rent		
Marital Status ☐ Married ☐ Separated (incl. single, divorced, widowed) ☐ Unmarried	DEPENDENTS OTHER THAN LISTED BY CO BORROWER NO. AGES		Marital Status ☐ Married ☐ Separated (incl. single, divorced, widowed) ☐ Unmarried	DEPENDENTS OTHER THAN LISTED BY CO BORROWER NO. AGES	
Name and Address of Employer	Years employed in this line of work or profession? _____ years Years on this job _____ ☐ Self Employed*		Name and Address of Employer	Years employed in this line of work or profession? _____ years Years on this job _____ ☐ Self Employed*	
Position/Title	Type of Business		Position/Title	Type of Business	
Social Security Number***	Home Phone	Business Phone	Social Security Number***	Home Phone	Business Phone

GROSS MONTHLY INCOME				MONTHLY HOUSING EXPENSE**			DETAILS OF PURCHASE	
Item	Borrower	Co-Borrower	Total	Rent	$ PRESENT	PROPOSED	Do Not Complete if Refinance	
Base Empl. Incom	$	$	$	First Mortgage (P&I)		$	a. Purchase Price	$
Overtime				Other Financing (P&I)			b. Total Closing Costs (Est.)	
Bonuses				Hazard Insurance			c. Prepaid Escrows (Est.)	
Commissions				Real Estate Taxes			d. Total (a + b + c)	$
Dividends/Interest				Mortgage Insurance			e. Amount This Mortgage	( )
Net Rental Income				Homeowner Assn. Dues			f. Other Financing	( )
Other †(BEFORE COMPLETING, SEE NOTICE UNDER DESCRIBE OTHER INCOME BELOW.)				Other:			g. Other Equity	( )
				Total Monthly Pmt.	$	$	h. Amount of Cash Deposit	( )
				Utilities			i. Closing Costs Paid by Seller	( )
Total	$	$	$	Total			j. Cash Reqd. For Closing (Est.)	$

DESCRIBE OTHER INCOME

	NOTICE: †Alimony, child support, or separate maintenance income need not be revealed if the Borrower or Co-Borrower does not choose to have it considered as a basis for repaying this loan.	Monthly Amount
B—Borrower C—Co-Borrower		$

IF EMPLOYED IN CURRENT POSITION FOR LESS THAN TWO YEARS COMPLETE THE FOLLOWING

B/C	Previous Employer/School	City/State	Type of Business	Position/Title	Dates From/To	Monthly Income
						$

THESE QUESTIONS APPLY TO BOTH BORROWER AND CO BORROWER

If a "yes" answer is given to a question in this column, explain on an attached sheet.	Borrower Yes or No	Co-Borrower Yes or No	If applicable, explain Other Financing or Other Equity (provide addendum if more space is needed).
Have you any outstanding judgments? In the last 7 years, have you been declared bankrupt?			
Have you had property foreclosed upon or given title or deed in lieu thereof?			
Are you a co-maker or endorser on a note?			
Are you a party in a law suit?			
Are you obligated to pay alimony, child support, or separate maintenance?			
Is any part of the down payment borrowed?			

* FHLMC/FNMA require business credit report, signed Federal Income Tax returns for last two years, and, if available, audited Profit and Loss Statements plus Balance sheet for same period.
** All Present Monthly Housing Expenses of Borrower and Co-Borrower should be listed on a combined basis.
*** Neither FHLMC nor FNMA requires this information.

FHLMC 65 Rev. 8/78   Banking Forms Supply Co.   (313) 364-5000   STOCK ITEM #1 FR   FNMA 1003 Rev. 8/78

Continued.

Example 7-2 Residential Loan Application *continued*

This Statement and any applicable supporting schedules may be completed jointly by both married and unmarried co-borrowers if their assets and liabilities are sufficiently joined so that the Statement can be meaningfully and fairly presented on a combined basis; otherwise separate Statements and Schedules are required (FHLMC 65A/FNMA 1003A). If the co-borrower section was completed about a spouse, this statement and supporting schedules must be completed about that spouse also. ☐ Completed Jointly ☐ Not Completed Jointly

ASSETS		LIABILITIES AND PLEDGED ASSETS			
		Indicate by (*) those liabilities or pledged assets which will be satisfied upon sale of real estate owned or upon refinancing of subject property			
Description	Cash or Market Value	Creditors' Name, Address and Account Number	Acct. Name If Not Borrower's	Mo. Pmt. and Mos. left to pay	Unpaid Balance
Cash Deposit Toward Purchase Held By	$	Installment Debts (include "revolving" charge accts)		$ Pmt./Mos.	$
Checking and Savings Accounts (Show Names of Institutions/Acct. Nos.)				/	
Stocks and Bonds (No./Description)				/	
				/	
Life Insurance Net Cash Value Face Amount ($)		Other Debts Including Stock Pledges		/	
SUBTOTAL LIQUID ASSETS	$			/	
Real Estate Owned (Enter Market Value from Schedule of Real Estate Owned)		Real Estate Loans			
Vested Interest in Retirement Fund					
Net Worth of Business Owned (ATTACH FINANCIAL STATEMENT)					
Automobiles (Make and Year)		Automobile Loans		/	
Furniture and Personal Property		Alimony, Child Support and Separate Maintenance Payments Owed To		/	
Other Assets (Itemize)					
		TOTAL MONTHLY PAYMENTS		$	
TOTAL ASSETS	A $	NET WORTH (A minus B) $		TOTAL LIABILITIES	B $

SCHEDULE OF REAL ESTATE OWNED (If Additional Properties Owned Attach Separate Schedule)

Address of Property (Indicate S if Sold, PS if Pending Sale or R if Rental being held for income)		Type of Property	Present Market Value	Amount of Mortgages & Liens	Gross Rental Income	Mortgage Payments	Taxes, Ins. Maintenance and Misc.	Net Rental Income
			$	$	$	$	$	$
TOTALS →			$	$	$	$	$	$

LIST PREVIOUS CREDIT REFERENCES

B—Borrower C—Co-Borrower	Creditor's Name and Address	Account Number	Purpose	Highest Balance	Date Paid
				$	

List any additional names under which credit has previously been received _____

AGREEMENT: The undersigned applies for the loan indicated in this application to be secured by a first mortgage or deed of trust on the property described herein, and represents that the property will not be used for any illegal or restricted purpose, and that all statements made in this application are true and are made for the purpose of obtaining the loan. Verification may be obtained from any source named in this application. The original or a copy of this application will be retained by the lender, even if the loan is not granted. The undersigned ☐ intend or ☐ do not intend to occupy the property as their primary residence.

I/we fully understand that it is a federal crime punishable by fine or imprisonment, or both, to knowingly make any false statements concerning any of the above facts as applicable under the provisions of Title 18, United States Code, Section 1014.

_____ Date _____   _____ Date _____
Borrower's Signature   Co-Borrower's Signature

INFORMATION FOR GOVERNMENT MONITORING PURPOSES

The following information is requested by the Federal Government if this loan is related to a dwelling, in order to monitor the lender's compliance with equal credit opportunity and fair housing laws. You are not required to furnish this information, but are encouraged to do so. The law provides that a lender may neither discriminate on the basis of this information, nor on whether you choose to furnish it. However, if you choose not to furnish it, under Federal regulations this lender is required to note race and sex on the basis of visual observation or surname. If you do not wish to furnish the above information, please initial below.

BORROWER: I do not wish to furnish this information (initials) _____   CO-BORROWER: I do not wish to furnish this information (initials) _____

RACE	☐ American Indian, Alaskan Native ☐ Asian, Pacific Islander	RACE	☐ American Indian, Alaskan Native ☐ Asian, Pacific Islander
NATIONAL	☐ Black ☐ Hispanic ☐ White ☐ Female	NATIONAL	☐ Black ☐ Hispanic ☐ White ☐ Female
ORIGIN	☐ Other (specify) _____ ☐ Male	ORIGIN	☐ Other (specify) _____ ☐ Male

FOR LENDER'S USE ONLY

(FNMA REQUIREMENT ONLY) This application was taken by ☐ face to face interview ☐ by mail ☐ by telephone

_____   _____
(Interviewer)   Name of Employer of Interviewer

FHLMC 65 Rev. 8/78   REVERSE   FNMA 1003 Rev. 8/78 legally permitted limit. As a result, the seller who is selling his or her property under an FHA-insured loan will seek a somewhat higher price to offset the points the seller will have to pay.

The FHA and VA guarantee is like an insurance policy for the lender. The borrower pays a premium equal to an extra ½% in interest per year, which goes to the FHA or VA to finance the program. Of late, private companies have entered the field of mortgage insurance. These companies operate in similar fashion to the FHA or VA. However, they do not require that the property meet the same sort of standards, nor do they limit the amount of interest that may be charged by the lender. In many cases the private mortgage insurance only applies until the borrower has repaid a portion of the loan, usually 20% of the purchase price of the property.

C. ISSUANCE OF COMMITMENT LETTER

If the lender is satisfied with the property and with the credit standing of the borrower, and if the lender is willing to make the loan on the terms contained in the application, it will issue to the borrower a letter, commonly known as a "commitment letter." In the commitment letter the lender will agree to lend a specific amount of money to the borrower on terms and conditions set out in the commitment letter. A commitment letter is technically an offer to make a loan on the conditions set forth in the letter. The lender will require the borrower to countersign the commitment letter and return a copy to the lender, indicating the borrower's acceptance of the offer. Once the offer has been accepted, the commitment constitutes a contract both to lend and to borrow, provided the conditions imposed on the borrower are met. These conditions are discussed in subsection D. See *Example 7-3* below.

Example 7-3: **Commitment Letter (Residential Mortgage)**

```
                    XYZ Bank
             12 S. 12th Street
          Philadelphia, PA   19107


             CONVENTIONAL MORTGAGE
                March 1, 1986
```

Premises:

Mortgagor:

Amount: $ Int. Rate: % Term: years   Monthly Payment
                                                           Int. & Prin.
                                                           $

Philadelphia, Pennsylvania 19116

Continued.

Example 7-3 Commitment Letter (Residential Mortgage) *continued*

Dear

Your application for a first mortgage loan on the terms outlined above has been approved subject to the following provisions.

The following must be submitted to this office at least five working days before settlement.

1.   The prepared mortgage papers on the enclosed forms.

2.   A "marked-up" report of title issued by a title insurance company approved by XYZ indicating that the mortgage will be insured as a first lien, free and clear of all encumbrances, subject only to such objections as meet with our approval. The title report must include copies or abstracts of all recorded public utility agreements, restrictions, and easements.

Please direct the mortgage papers to our SETTLEMENT SUPERVISOR and inform him or her of the settlement date with the Title Company. The approved papers will then be forwarded directly to the Title Company, together with our check and letter of instructions.

At settlement, we must be furnished a fire insurance policy (not a binder) with extended coverage in the full amount of the loan. The policy shall be for a term of not less than three years in a company acceptable to XYZ and include a standard mortgagee clause in favor of XYZ Bank.

Our commitment to make this loan will expire May 31, 1986.

If the property to be mortgaged is located in New Jersey a new survey must be submitted and fire insurance coverage must specifically protect outbuildings and garages (if any). Settlement for New Jersey properties must be held in Pennsylvania.

If you decide to accept this commitment, you may do so only by signing and returning one copy of the enclosed DISCLOSURE STATEMENT REQUIRED BY FEDERAL LAW so that it is received by XYZ, Mortgage Department, 12 South 12th Street, Philadelphia, Pennsylvania, 19107, within 10 days of the date of this letter, in which case the commitment will become a contract binding both on you and on XYZ in accordance with its terms. If you do not sign and return the Statement, this commitment will lapse.

Prepayment of the principal balance may be made in whole or in part at any time without penalty.

At the time of settlement, a fee of $100.00 will be charged the purchaser representing the balance of our 1% service charge for this loan.

Sincerely,

Assistant Mortgage Officer

D. PREPARATION FOR SETTLEMENT

Having received the commitment letter, the borrower and his or her attorney must begin to prepare for settlement. As discussed in Chapter Three, the settlement is the time when the purchaser will acquire the new home, partially with funds obtained from the lender. It will often be the task of the legal assistant to prepare for settlement in accordance with the commitment letter and the agreement of sale. Some of the usual requirements of the commitment are as follows:

1. Mortgage Documents

In connection with a mortgage loan it is usually necessary to create two documents. The first is a mortgage note, or bond, that evidences the debt and that sets forth the terms for repayment. The second is a mortgage that grants a security interest in the mortgaged property in case the debt is not repaid. In most instances the mortgage documents are prepared by the lender on its own forms. In some localities it is customary for the borrower's attorney to prepare the mortgage documents, but normally, they are prepared on forms furnished or approved by the lender. The form and content of the mortgage documents are considered more fully in part VI of this chapter.

2. Title Search

As discussed in Chapter Six, the lender will require that a competent person, who may be a title examiner or an attorney, search the public records to ascertain who now owns the property and what persons, if any, other than the record owner, have any interests in the property. In this manner the lender will be assured that at settlement the borrower can grant the lender a mortgage that will constitute a first lien on the property. In many localities, lenders require that the borrower purchase title insurance. Under this procedure an insurance company issues an insurance policy to the lender, not insuring repayment of the mortgage loan, but insuring the validity and priority of the mortgage lien. For instance, the title insurance company will protect the mortgagee against economic loss in the event that the borrower does not own the property because of some technical defect in title or if the mortgage is defective and cannot be foreclosed because of a defect in the execution or recording of the mortgage instrument.

In the typical residential transaction the seller has the legal obligation to convey good and marketable title, and thus has the burden of clearing title. This involves presenting to the lender or to the title company, as the case may be, various documents required to remove from the public records any lien for judgments, unpaid taxes, unpaid water or sewer rent, prior mortgages, and the like, that might take priority over the lien of the mortgage being created.

3. Termite and Other Certificates

In some instances, particularly in an FHA-insured mortgage, the lender may require the borrower to produce a certificate with respect to the condition of the premises being purchased, such as the roof, the plumbing, or the electrical work. Such certificates may be obtained, for a fee, from reputable roofers, plumbers, and electricians. The lender may also require the borrower to produce a certificate from a termite-exterminating company to the effect that the premises are free of termites and other wood-boring insects and free of damage that was caused by such insects.

4. Insurance

Because the lender is depending to a large extent on the value of the real estate as security for repayment of the debt, the lender will want to be protected in the event any buildings on the property are destroyed or damaged by fire, wind, or other casualty. Accordingly, the lender will normally require that the borrower deliver at settlement a fire insurance policy in an amount equal to the mortgage loan, and in a form and with a company approved by the lender. The lender will also require that the policy have a "mortgagee loss payable" clause, the effect of which is to require the insurance company, in the event of loss, to prepare its check for the amount of the loss to the order of the lender.[9] This insurance fund, at least temporarily, takes the place of the destroyed structure as security for the loan. The mortgage documents will normally contain provisions for the disbursement of the insurance funds once they are received from the insurance company. The insurance company is also required to give notice to the lender in the event the policy is to be cancelled.

5. Closing

If the borrower is using borrowed funds to purchase real estate, the closing[10] on the mortgage loan will usually take place at the same time as the closing on the purchase of the real estate. This combined closing is discussed in detail in Chapter Eight. At closing, the borrower will sign the note and the mortgage and deliver them to the lender, together with the first insurance policy and any required certificates concerning the condition of the property. The lender will in turn deliver its check to the borrower, or to the title company that is going to insure the borrower's

---

9. A mortgagee could alternatively become an additional insured under the title policy. This is less protective of a mortgagee because, as an additional insured, any check for the insurance proceeds is made payable jointly to the borrower and the mortgagee. In the event of a dispute respecting the dis-tribution of the insurance proceeds, it is more difficult for a mortgagee to obtain access to the insurance proceeds when it has to obtain the co-signature of the borrower.
10. Remember that "closing" and "settlement" are synonymous.

title and the lender's lien, for disbursement to the seller. The title company, or the attorney, if no title company is employed, will then make up a settlement sheet showing the amount advanced by the lender and the charges due the lender. In connection with this, the lender will sometimes require that the following sums be paid at the closing:

(a) Interest to the First Day of the First Regular Interest Period

Occasionally, lenders charge interest in advance so that interest paid May 1 will be for the period May 1 to May 31. Most lenders, however, charge interest in arrears, so that interest paid on May 1 will be for the period April 1 to April 30. Most lenders have a standard due date for all their loans, usually on the first or the fifteenth of each month, regardless of the day that closing takes place. Each of the monthly payments, including the first, is equal to all the others. It is therefore usually necessary at settlement to collect a certain amount of interest in advance in order to reconcile all of the above. For example, suppose a lender charges interest in arrears and requires payment on the first of each month. If settlement takes place on March 20, the first payment will be due May 1 and will include interest for the month of April. At settlement, the lender would collect interest for the eleven days from (and including) March 20 to (and including) March 31. Thus, even a lender who normally charges in arrears will typically require this payment of advance interest at settlement.

PROBLEM

Assume that a lender charges interest in advance and requires payment on the fifteenth of each month. Settlement takes place on October 20 and the first payment is due November 15. If the loan is for $20,000 at the interest rate of 8% per annum, what interest charge will be made at settlement?

(b) Escrow Funds

(i) Real Estate Taxes

In some jurisdictions, unpaid real estate taxes and other municipal charges, such as sewer rent, will become a lien on property that is prior to the lien of the mortgage. Normally, liens take priority only from the time that they are recorded in a public place. However, there are exceptions to this rule, and real estate taxes are often among the exceptions. These taxes may become a first lien on the property, ahead of all mortgages, even though the taxes arise in years subsequent to the year in which the mortgage was created and recorded. To prevent a loss of priority to unpaid real estate taxes, the lender may require the borrower to pay to the lender with each monthly mortgage payment an amount equal to $\frac{1}{12}$th of the annual tax payment, as estimated by the mortgagee. The tax fund accumulated is held in escrow by the mortgagee. We have discussed the escrow concept in previous chapters. In this context it means that the mortgagee does not own the money, but is merely holding it for distribution to a third party, the tax collector. The mortgagee will apply the escrow fund each year to pay the real estate taxes due on the property. Normally, the borrower will readily agree to this because it is a convenient way for him or her to pay real estate taxes. However, unless the first mortgage payment is due on the first day of the tax year, the taxes will be due before borrower has made twelve payments. Accordingly, the lender will not have collected enough money out of the monthly payments to pay the full tax bill. To prevent this, the lender will require that the borrower pay in advance at closing a sum of money that, when added to the regular tax payments made during the remainder of the year, will be sufficient to pay the tax bill.

(ii) Insurance Premiums

Some lenders will also require that the amount needed to pay fire insurance premiums on the mortgaged property be paid into escrow with each monthly payment. Therefore, it may be necessary to pay an initial amount into escrow for insurance premiums at settlement, just as in the case of taxes. However, this is far less common because insurance premiums are normally paid one year in advance at the time the policy is purchased, which should be near the time of settlement. Accordingly, if the lender collects $\frac{1}{12}$th of the annual premium commencing with the first payment, it will have the right amount for the next year's premium at the time it is due.

(c) Miscellaneous Charges

The mortgagee will collect at settlement any sums still due it for a credit report, appraisal fees, mortgage placement fees, "points," or the like.

Normally, the representative of the lender will take from the closing the original note or bond and warrant, a copy of the mortgage, a settlement sheet, and checks for any amounts due the lender as set forth above. The original mortgage will remain with the title insurance company or the lender's attorney, who will immediately have it recorded in the recording office in the county (or other proper jurisdiction) in which the real estate is located. The borrower will normally take from closing a copy of the note, a copy of the mortgage, and a copy of the settlement sheet. If the closing is also to purchase real estate, the proceeds of the loan will be used to pay the seller the purchase price of the property. If the loan is for some other purpose and the borrower is using already-owned real estate as security, the proceeds will be given to the borrower.

E. POST CLOSING

After the recorder has made a copy of the mortgage and entered the name of the mortgagor and the mortgagee in the appropriate indices in the recorder's office, the original will be returned to the title company or the lender's attorney for forwarding to the lender, to be kept in its vault until the mortgage has been paid, assigned,[11] or foreclosed. Anyone subsequently searching title to the real estate will find that the owner has subjected it to the lien of this particular mortgage and will find a copy of the mortgage in the recorder's office.

Part Two
COMMERCIAL-INDUSTRIAL MORTGAGES

Now let us consider the use of mortgage loans for the financing of a commercial development (e.g., a shopping center) or an industrial building (e.g., a factory). In this chapter we will consider a situation in which the prospective borrower owns a fully improved piece of real estate, that is, one on which a completed building has been constructed. We will also assume that the building is about to be leased to a business tenant. We will consider later in this chapter the special problems that arise when an owner of undeveloped land wishes to use a mortgage loan to finance the construction of a new building for its own use or for use by a tenant.

I. THE APPLICATION FOR A COMMERCIAL-INDUSTRIAL MORTGAGE

A. THE MORTGAGEE'S CONCERNS

As in the case of a residence, the mortgage transaction begins with the borrower's application for a loan to the mortgage lender. In this case the mortgagee is concerned not only with the integrity and credit rating of the borrower, and the value of the real estate offered for security, but also with the credit rating and integrity of the tenant and with the amount of rent to be paid by the tenant. The reason for this should be apparent; the building will be occupied by the tenant and the rents will provide the owner with the primary source of funds required to pay principal and interest on the mortgage,[12] as well as taxes, insurance, and maintenance. The mortgagee, therefore, wants to know (a) that the tenant is in possession and prepared to pay rent; (b) that the tenant has no legal claim against the landlord or anyone else that would permit the tenant to refuse to pay rent; (c) that the amount of the rent is sufficient to pay the debt

---

11. Assignment of mortgages is discussed in Chapter Eight.

12. Annual payments of principal and interest due on a mortgage loan are sometimes referred to as "debt service."

service and other operating costs; (d) that the tenant has a good credit rating and is likely to pay the rent; and (e) the term of the lease.

In many commercial-industrial transactions the amount of the loan is so substantial that the mortgagee cannot realistically expect to receive payment solely from the borrower's assets. Therefore, the mortgagee is very much concerned with the quality and condition of the real estate and the quality of the tenant and terms of the lease. It is from these sources, rather than from the borrower's other income and assets, that the mortgage payments will come. As we shall see, there are many commercial mortgages in which the mortgagor's liability is limited to its interest in the mortgaged property, and the mortgagee is not permitted to look to the mortgagor's other income and assets.

Before making the loan, the lender wants to know what the operating costs are, including the taxes, the insurance costs, the maintenance and repair costs, and the water and sewer and utility charges, and it also wants to know whether it is the owner or the tenant who has the responsibility to pay them. Finally, it wants to know that after payment of all these charges (whether by the owner or the tenant) and after debt service there will be sufficient funds from the rent to provide some kind of profit, generally referred to as "cash flow" for the owner. Unless there is some cash flow for the borrower, the borrower may lose interest in the project and fail to maintain the property, and may even default under the mortgage. Conversely, if there is substantial cash flow, the borrower is going to work very hard to avoid any possible default under the mortgage through which he or she could lose the entire project.

Example 7-4 shows the contents of an application for a commercial or industrial mortgage and *Example 7-5* is a sample mortgage loan application.

B. THE MORTGAGOR'S CONCERNS

There are also items that are of special concern to a mortgagor in addition to those involved in a residential transaction. If the value of the building is substantially in excess of the amount the borrower seeks to borrow, the rent is sufficient to pay debt service and all expenses and carrying charges, and the tenant is a large substantial company with excellent credit (sometimes referred to as a "triple A" tenant), the borrower may ask the lender not to look to the borrower for repayment, but to rely entirely on the value of the real estate and the lease. As discussed in Chapter Two, this can be accomplished through the use of a "straw" to make the application and sign the mortgage documents. Another method of accomplishing the same result is simply to insert in the mortgage documents a statement to the effect that liability under the documents will be enforced only out of the real estate. Specific clauses "limiting liability to the land" are considered in section VI of this chapter.

Frequently, the mortgagor may own more property than it wishes to subject to the lien of the mortgage. For example, a mortgagor may have a shopping center and parking area, with an adjacent tract of undeveloped

Example 7-4: **Mortgage Application (Commercial or Industrial)**

Name of Bank	Account Officer	Address & Branch of Bank

LOCATION AND PHYSICAL DESCRIPTION OF SECURITY

Street Address

between what major cross streets

City	County	State

LAND: Dimensions   Sq. Ft. Area

BUILDING: Type, Use, Size and Stories:

YEAR BUILT: REMODELED (YR. & COST):

(The property is to be insured as required by New York Life Insurance Company and the policies will be delivered to the Company with mortgagee loss clauses attached.)

MORTGAGOR'S STATEMENT OF COST

Existing construction: Date purchased   Cost $

Proposed construction: Starting date   Est. completion date   Cost $

Land: Date purchased or optioned   Purchase price $

Est. Current Value: Land $ Improvements $ Total $

Are there any mortgages against the property at this time? If none, so state. If so, give mortgagee, interest rate, maturity, loan balance, payments and prepayment options.

Are there any other mortgage application(s) or mortgage loan commitment(s) presently outstanding against this security; (If none, so state):

ATTACHMENTS: ☐ Legal Description and Survey showing location and description of all easements. ☐ Plot Plan. ☐ Building Plans and Specifications. ☐ Owner's Financial Statements. ☐ Operating Statements. ☐ Pro-Forma Statements. ☐ Photos. ☐ Cost Breakdown. ☐ Owner's Detailed Statement of Equity Source. ☐ Copy of Ground Lease. ☐ Rent Roll showing name of tenant, designation of space, square foot area, minimum annual rental, renewal options, date of lease, dates of commencement and expiration and conditions which permit tenant to cancel for any reason other than landlord's breach. ☐ Copies of principal Leases.

Accompanying this application is check of the undersigned in the amount of $. It is agreed that if you issue a commitment for the loan (or the purchase thereof) as applied for herein and such commitment is not accepted in writing within 10 days from the date of such commitment, you will retain $ as an application fee, and return the balance (if any) of the above amount. It is further agreed that upon the acceptance of such commitment, the above amount (first mentioned) shall be applied toward the required commitment fee and/or security deposit.

Concurrently, with the acceptance of your commitment as applied for, the undersigned will deposit with Life Insurance Company, an additional $ as a security deposit on account of liquidated damages, which deposit shall not bear interest. If and when the loan is funded,   Life will refund the security deposit.

The undersigned further agrees that the form and substance of each and every document evidencing the loan or the purchase thereof and the security therefor and title and evidence thereof must be satisfactory to the Company, and any and all obligations incurred by the Company by reason of commitment issued for the loan shall be subject to such approval. The undersigned further agrees to pay all fees and expenses incurred in connection with closing the loan or purchase thereof including fees and expenses of local counsel, if any, employed by the Company in connection therewith, title insurance charges, cost of survey, recording and filing fees, documentary stamps and other taxes payable in connection with the closing of the loan. The undersigned will arrange with the occupants of the premises for full inspection by the Company's appraisers.

Broker's Signature	Signature of individual, partnership, corporation, etc. to whom commitment is to be issued.
Address	Address
Date	Date

Example 7-5: Mortgage Loan Application

MORTGAGE
LOAN APPLICATION
(INCOME PROPERTY)

LIFE INSURANCE COMPANY

Please sign and submit in triplicate. All questions must be answered.

The undersigned hereby applies for: ☐ a direct loan from   Life Insurance Company or ☐ a loan to be purchased by assignment by   Life Insurance Company upon the terms and conditions set forth below,

To be secured by:

☐ a first mortgage or deed of trust on the marketable fee simple title to the property described below:

☐ a first mortgage or deed of trust on the lessee's interest in the following leasehold estate:
   (Give lessor, lessee, annual ground rent, initial term, renewal options, lease maturity date, contingent rental)

and on the easements appurtenant thereto and on all improvements to the property, free of prior mechanics, or materialmen's liens or special assessments for work completed or under construction on the date of the closing, and, if the Company requires, as additional security, it shall receive a chattel first mortgage (free of title retention agreements) on all fixtures and articles of personal property now or hereafter attached to or used in connection with the management, maintenance, and operation of the property, and an assignment of the lessor's interest in each occupancy lease of or affecting any part of the said property as additional security for the loan, which assignment shall be recorded and copy of which shall be served on the tenant; as to each lease to be assigned, the lease shall be in full force and effect, there shall be no offsets or defenses to enforcement of the lease, the tenant shall have accepted its premises, confirmed the commencement of its lease term, be in occupancy and paying rent on a current basis, evidence of which shall be furnished the Company.

L O A N

Amount: $ Interest Rate: %   Term

Repayable in monthly installments of $ due on the 10th of the month to be applied first to interest and then to principal, and monthly deposits for real estate taxes and hazard insurance.

Additional compensation to   Life:

Non-refundable commitment fee:

Rental requirement for loan advance(s):

Prepayment Privilege:

Estimated Funding Date:

Liquidated Damages: $ to be paid to   Life, if, after acceptance of the commitment, the loan fails to close for any reason whatsoever except default by   Life.

MORTGAGOR

Give name and address of borrower, (if borrower is a partnership or a corporation, give name and addresses of partners or stockholders and their respective interests. If borrower is a trust, give full designation thereof, and identify beneficiary(s) with address(es).

ground. The mortgagor may not wish to subject the undeveloped ground to the lien of the mortgage because it may wish to sell the ground or build on it at a later time. Accordingly, it is important to consider precisely what area is to be mortgaged in preparing the mortgage application. If less than all of the area owned by the borrower is going to be covered by the mortgage, the mortgagor needs to consider the advisability of creating cross-easement rights between the tracts that will be superior in right to the mortgage.

II. ISSUANCE OF COMMITMENT

Assuming the borrower's mortgage application is approved, a commitment will be issued by the lender. Although the terms and conditions of the commitment are often quite complicated, the effect is the same as in the case of a residential mortgage. In many instances, because of the expense incurred by the lender in analyzing an application for a commercial or industrial mortgage, a substantial commitment fee will be charged.

Once accepted by the borrower, along with the payment of any fee that may be due, the commitment letter forms a contract pursuant to which the mortgagee is legally bound to make the loan and the borrower is legally bound to borrow the money on the terms and conditions set forth in the commitment letter.

The commitment letter indicates some of the primary concerns of the mortgagee.

A. TITLE AND TITLE INSURANCE

In the usual case the mortgagee expects a first lien for the mortgage. Moreover, as in the case of a residential mortgage, the mortgagee will want a title insurance policy insuring that the mortgagee's lien is a valid lien (not subject to attack for forgery, improper recording, defective title in the borrower, or the like) and that it is a first lien. A first lien means that, in the event of a judicial sale of the property, the first funds payable from the proceeds of sale (after real estate taxes and certain expenses of sale) will be payable to the mortgagee up to the full amount of the mortgage debt plus interest and costs incurred by the mortgagee. Because of the large dollar amount of the insurance, a complication concerning title insurance may arise in the case of a large commercial-industrial transaction. Many institutional lenders are reluctant, in the case of large mortgages, to have only one title insurance company underwrite the entire risk of a defective title because the title insurance company itself may not have sufficient financial strength to assure that it will be able to pay such a large potential loss. Customarily, title insurance companies reinsure such risks; that is, they will take part of the risk, for example, the first $500,000 and then they will in turn reinsure the balance of the risk with another company or companies. If the lender is concerned with this problem, there are various ways in which the problem might be covered in the commitment letter. For example, the lender may insist on the right to approve the title insurance company, the right to require reinsurance with acceptable companies, and the delivery of copies of the reinsurance agreements at closing.

B. LEASE ON PREMISES

1. Rights of Tenant versus Mortgagee

If the lender is depending on rental from the lease for repayment of the debt, it may also require in the commitment letter that the lease be either presently or collaterally assigned to it as additional security for the loan. A present assignment requires the landlord-borrower to transfer to the lender the landlord's right to collect rents due under the lease. To the extent the periodic rent exceeds the mortgage payment, the excess will be turned over to the landlord by the mortgagee. In most instances the lender will accept a collateral assignment, which means that so long as the borrower is not in default of the loan, the borrower will collect the rents and remit the amount required for the mortgage payment. Only on default would the lender exercise its rights to require that rents be paid directly to it.

An important question arises with respect to the relative priorities of the lease and the mortgage. For example, if the mortgagee forecloses or takes possession, can the mortgagee terminate the lease, in the belief that the property would be more valuable without being burdened by the lease? On the other hand, can the tenant terminate the lease by reason of the mortgagee's foreclosing? According to common law and the laws of most jurisdictions, the answers to these two questions depend on whether the mortgage or the lease was recorded first. The answers are rooted in the title theory of mortgages. The courts reason that once a borrower has leased the property to a tenant, the borrower's rights in the property are limited to the right to regain possession of the property at some future time (on expiration or termination of the lease) and the right to collect rent in the interim. Because the borrower cannot transfer to the mortgagee any greater rights than the borrower has, the borrower can transfer to the mortgagee only the right to get the property back at some future time and the right to collect rent in the interim. Accordingly, if the mortgagee had legal notice of the existence of the lease before the mortgage was created,[13] then, in the event of a foreclosure, the mortgagee (or any other purchaser at the sheriff's sale) acquires title subject to the rights of the tenant. The purchaser at a foreclosure sale can purchase only what the mortgagee has to sell: a lien on the borrower's rights to

---

13. As discussed in Chapter Nine, the mortgagee will have legal notice of the existence of the lease if (a) it actually knows of the existence of the lease, (b) the tenant is in possession of the premises, or (c) the lease (or a memorandum of the lease) has been recorded.

get the property back at some future time and to collect rents in the interim. So long as the tenant fulfills his or her obligations under the lease, the purchaser cannot dispossess the tenant, increase the rent, or change any of the terms and conditions of the lease. Likewise, the tenant's condition is unaffected by activity respecting an inferior interest in the property. The tenant, therefore, has no right to claim a default in the lease or otherwise to terminate the lease simply by reason of the foreclosure.

Conversely, once the mortgage has been signed, acknowledged, and recorded, all the borrower has left is a right to get the property back from the mortgagee at some future time, if and when he or she pays the mortgage debt. Technically, the mortgagor does not have even the right to possession of the premises. The mortgagee has the right to possession, although such right is rarely, if ever, exercised in the absence of a default. It follows that a tenant whose lease begins after the mortgage is recorded can obtain his or her right to possession only subject to the prior right of possession of the mortgagee. In such a case the mortgagee (or any other purchaser at a foreclosure sale) will acquire the property free of the lease. Another way of expressing this is that once the mortgagee's rights (including its unexercised right to possession) have become fixed, such rights cannot be diminished by a subsequent act of the landlord and a third party, the tenant. In such a case, the tenant's rights have been cut off by the foreclosure, and therefore the tenant no longer has any obligations under the lease. Thus, on a foreclosure of a superior mortgage, a tenant is free to vacate the property and cease paying rent and will have no further obligation on account of the lease. This may be a desirable result for a tenant if, as is often the case, the reason that the mortgagor defaulted was that the project (for example, a shopping center) is an economic failure.

2. Attornment and Non-Disturbance

In a case in which the mortgage is prior in right to the lease, a foreclosure will terminate the rights of the tenant. This occurs because the tenant's rights depend on the rights of the landlord, which were extinguished by the foreclosure sale. This could be a problem for the mortgagee. For example, in a shopping center in which the mortgagee is depending on rental payments pursuant to a lease signed by a good tenant, the tenant might now like to avoid the terms of the lease. In the event of foreclosure on a prior mortgage, the inadvertent extinguishment of the lease would allow the tenant to leave the premises with no further obligations under the lease. The mortgagee will want to be certain that such a lease will not be extinguished by a foreclosure.

The mortgagee's problem can most easily be avoided if the tenant is in possession of the premises prior to the mortgage or if the lease is recorded prior to the mortgage. However, even if the lease came before the mortgage, it may have provided that it is subordinate to any mortgage, no matter when created. In addition, some mortgagees may require the tenant to execute a subordination agreement[14] declaring the lease subordinate to the mortgage, because they want it clear that their mortgage has priority over all other recorded interests.

Where the lease is subordinate, or is subordinated, the mortgagee may require the borrower to obtain a separate agreement with the tenant requiring the tenant to "attorn"[15] to the mortgagee. In practical terms, this means that the tenant agrees that, in the event of a foreclosure, the lease will not be extinguished but will continue as a lease between mortgagee and tenant, and that the tenant will thereupon pay rent directly to the mortgagee.

Where the lease is subordinate, the tenant is concerned that, even though he or she may pay rent promptly, the landlord may for one reason or another fail to comply with the terms of the mortgage, resulting in a foreclosure that could extinguish the lease. The risk of premature termination of the lease is particularly threatening when the tenant is investing substantial amounts of money in improvements that become part of the real estate, such as air conditioning, heating systems, and other types of fixtures that would be difficult and expensive to remove. To be protected from this problem, the tenant will want to have an agreement from the mortgagee, called a "non-disturbance agreement."[16] A non-disturbance agreement contains the agreement of the mortgagee that, in the event of foreclosure, the tenant may remain on the property so long as he or she continues to comply with the terms of the lease. Mortgagees are frequently willing to give such agreements. However, a mortgagee may be concerned that rent may be paid far in advance, leaving the mortgagee with a tenant who cannot be dispossessed and who has already paid rent to the defaulting mortgagor, who is probably completely insolvent. To prevent such a problem, the non-disturbance agreement may include a provision prohibiting the tenant from making advance rental payments.

C. COMPLIANCE WITH LAWS

In a commercial-industrial situation the mortgagee will frequently want to be certain that the premises are in compliance with the myriad laws and regulations pertaining to building safety, fire, health, zoning, subdivision, and the like. The mortgagee may require evidence of such com-

14. A subordination agreement is an agreement by which a party having a superior right in the property (such as a first lien mortgage) agrees with someone having an inferior right (such as a lease entered into after the mortgage was recorded) that, as between the two of them, the inferior right shall be treated as if it were superior.

15. To "attorn" is to agree to recognize that

another party, who would not otherwise have privity, may enforce a contract as though it were originally a beneficiary of the contract.

16. Usually a non-disturbance agreement is the cost to lender of an attornment agreement, and they are frequently combined into one document.

pliance at settlement. Mortgagees are more concerned about this in a commercial context than a residential context because (a) larger amounts of money are involved; (b) the regulations and ordinances pertaining to commercial-industrial buildings are more complex and often stricter than those applied to single-family residential properties; and (c) the ordinances and regulations are frequently more stringently enforced respecting commercial and industrial properties. The mortgagee must look at the property as though to purchase it. A mortgagee would probably not want to purchase a property in which it may have to invest substantial additional funds to effect compliance with local codes.

D. EASEMENTS

The mortgagee will want to be sure that the property has the benefit of easements for access to public roads, and that the mortgaged premises are served by water, sewer, electric, gas, and other utilities. The borrower may have to create these easements over other property that it owns. If the property that would provide access is itself subject to a mortgage, then the other mortgagee will have to consent in writing to the easements. Without such consent, the easements would be extinguished by a foreclosure on the other mortgage because the easement was an interest subordinate to the mortgage.

III. PREPARATION OF DOCUMENTS

Frequently in a commercial-industrial transaction, the responsibility for the preparation of documents will be divided between counsel for the borrower and counsel for the lender. The lender's council will want to examine the lease and to prepare the note, mortgage, and assignment of lease on forms satisfactory to the lender. Lender's counsel will also want to examine the title report to make sure there are no easements, liens, or other title objections that could adversely affect the value of the property and/or the priority or validity of the lien. It will be the burden of the borrower's counsel, generally, to review the documents prepared by the lender's counsel and to furnish surveys, corporate resolutions authorizing the loan (if the borrower is a corporation), receipts evidencing payment of taxes, water charges, and sewer rents. The borrower's counsel may also prepare subordination, attornment, and/or non-disturbance agreements and any easement agreements that may be required.

IV. CLOSING

As in the case of the residential mortgage, at closing all the necessary papers referred to above will be executed, acknowledged before a notary public where necessary, and delivered to the appropriate parties. The documents that are to be recorded (which may include, in addition to the mortgage an assignment of leases, a subordination, a non-disturbance and attornment agreement, and an easement agreement) will be delivered to the party responsible for recording them.

V. POST CLOSING

After closing, the documents that have been recorded will be returned to the mortgagee, or to the mortgagor in the case of any easement agreement. After the closing, both the mortgagor and the mortgagee will want a complete set of original or conformed closing documents showing the recording data of any recorded documents.

PROBLEM

It is often the task of a legal assistant to follow up on post-closing requirements including the furnishing of copies of all documents to the client. What format might you follow as a paralegal after a commercial mortgage closing which included twenty-three documents executed or provided by your client?

Part Three
CONSTRUCTION MORTGAGES

I. INTRODUCTION

Now let us consider a situation in which a corporation decides to construct a new building and finance the construction through a mortgage. We will be considering construction financing in the context of the following fact situation:

SAMPLE FACT SITUATION

Cen Tenn Realty Co., Inc. has purchased a partially occupied shopping center, together with a large tract of adjacent vacant ground. The purchase price was $4 million, which was paid partly in cash and partly by accepting title to the premises subject to an existing mortgage in favor of First Mortgagee Insurance Company. Cen Tenn would like to construct a large store on the adjacent vacant ground and lease that store to Xerxes Department Store Co., which is a well-known operator of discount department stores across the United States. Being a well-known chain, Xerxes will probably draw a great deal of extra traffic to the shopping center. If Cen Tenn can build that store, it believes that it can find tenants at favorable rents for the vacant stores, and also receive increased rents in existing stores (most of which pay rent based at least in part on a percentage of gross business).[17]

Cen Tenn approaches Xerxes and makes tentative arrangements for construction and leasing of a store containing 80,000 square feet of floor space at a rental of $160,000 per year, plus a certain amount for increases in taxes and maintenance. Cen Tenn must now ascertain the cost of building the store. It must also determine whether it can borrow the money required to construct the store, on terms that would make the rent payable by Xerxes sufficient to pay the interest and principal on the mortgage loan plus real estate taxes, insurance, and miscellaneous expenses in connection with the building (to the extent that Xerxes has not agreed to pay these items) and leave some profit for Cen Tenn. Cen Tenn and Xerxes meet with their respective architects and engineers to decide on what kind of building will be required. This involves not only size and height, but also building materials, store front, fixtures, air conditioning, electrical equipment, and the like, all of which are important items of cost. After this Cen Tenn approaches several general building contractors and asks for bids based on the preliminary plans and specifications prepared by the architects. It finds from the bids that the total cost of construction will be approximately $1 million. In addition, Cen Tenn will have to be prepared to pay certain fees to the construction lender (discussed below), legal fees, settlement costs, interest during the construction period (during which period no rent is collected from Xerxes), surveys, engineering, insurance, and miscellaneous costs. Cen Tenn computes these at approximately $100,000, making the aggregate cost of the new building $1.1 million.

II. CONSTRUCTION LOANS AND PERMANENT LOANS

Lending institutions include commercial banks, savings banks, savings and loan associations, insurance companies, pension trusts, and real estate investment trusts. Most lending institutions specialize in making either construction loans or permanent loans, to the general exclusion of the other. Commercial banks, as a rule, are most likely to make construction loans, and to have construction loan departments skilled in processing and supervising construction loans. Insurance companies are much more likely to make permanent loans. The following is a brief description of these two kinds of loans and the different risks attendant to them.

A. THE PERMANENT LOAN

The application for a permanent mortgage for property to be constructed is substantially the same as in the case of any commercial-industrial mortgage.

---

17. The concept of rent based on a percentage of gross business is considered in detail in Chapter Ten. At this point, it is sufficient to understand that in addition to a fixed monthly amount, the rental will include a percentage of the dollar amount of the tenant's sales at the leased premises. Therefore, the higher the tenant's sales, the greater its rent.

The prospective permanent mortgagee will consider basically the same factors, including the value of the building, the financial standing of the tenant, and the integrity of the mortgagor. However, the permanent lender is agreeing to make a loan based on the security of a lease with a tenant who is not yet in possession for a building that is not yet constructed. The lender will want to make its obligation to lend the money contingent on (a) the building being constructed in accordance with the plans and specifications presented to it with the application and (b) the lease being in full force. If all the conditions are met, then the permanent loan will be funded and will be like any long-term mortgage. In our example, let us suppose that a commitment has been obtained from New Hampshire Mutual Life Insurance for a loan of $1,000,000 with interest at 11% per annum having a term of twenty-five years and being fully self-amortizing. Having obtained its permanent loan commitment, Cen Tenn must now seek a source of financing during the construction period.

B. THE CONSTRUCTION LOAN

New Hampshire Mutual is willing to lend on the condition that the improvements will be constructed according to the plans and specifications. However, New Hampshire Mutual, like many insurance companies and pension trusts, does not have the personnel or the knowledge to oversee the actual construction. Also the improvements are being constructed in a location far from the main office of New Hampshire Mutual. Therefore, New Hampshire is not willing to lend any money until the improvements are completed. However, Cen Tenn will need money to pay a general contractor periodically as the construction proceeds, which may take a year or longer. The general contractor must pay its own workers, subcontractors, and material costs as they are supplied. Because most developers do not maintain sufficient capital to finance the construction of large projects, the mortgagor needs to borrow money to meet these payments until the building is complete and New Hampshire Mutual funds its permanent loan. The gap is filled by a construction lender, often a bank in the vicinity of the construction site. The construction lender, which, in our example, is The Second Centralia National Bank of Centralia, Tennessee, will lend the mortgagor up to $1,000,000, which will be advanced over a period of a year or two as the money is needed to meet payments on the construction. In our example, the construction loan is for up to $1,000,000 for a term of one year, with monthly payments of interest only[18] during the term of the loan calculated on the basis of the outstanding principal from time to time advanced.

---

18. Why would you think the loan would be for interest only with no repayment of principal until the maturity date of the loan?

The Second Centralia either knows of or has on its own staff trained architects, engineers, and inspectors who can check the construction and can verify that the bills for labor and materials are proper, that the value of the work is consistent with the amount of the bill, and that the plans and specifications, which have been approved by New Hampshire Mutual, are being followed. A construction lender will seldom advance 100% of the value of the work as it is done. Instead, the construction lender will advance a lesser percentage (often 90%) so that the value of the construction, which is the security for the loan, will always exceed the amount outstanding on the loan. Second Centralia also has the bookkeeping facilities to keep track of how much has been advanced at any given time and to compute interest from month to month on the constantly changing principal. Because of the extra expense involved in construction lending, construction lenders will normally make a "supervision" or "inspection" charge, or some other commitment fee or charge, of 1% to 2% of the total amount of the loan, payable at the settlement on the construction loan. In addition, the interest rate on construction loans will normally be higher than on permanent loans.

Second Centralia knows that Cen Tenn cannot possibly pay back $1,000,000 on completion of construction out of its own funds. Second Centralia and Cen Tenn expect that the construction loan will be repaid out of the proceeds of the permanent loan. Indeed, as we shall see, often the actual technique used is to have the permanent lender purchase the construction loan from the construction lender for the full amount of the loan. In the jargon of the business, it is said that the construction lender wishes to be "taken out" of the loan by the permanent lender. For this reason the permanent loan commitment is often referred to as a "take-out."

The construction lender is also concerned with the financial stability and integrity of the general contractor. If the general contractor cannot live up to its commitment to build the improvements for $1,000,000, Second Centralia may be forced to hire another contractor, usually at a higher price, to complete the improvements in order to be in a position to satisfy the conditions of the permanent loan commitment. Even the "cushion" produced by paying less than 100% of each bill may not be enough to cover the extra expense of bringing in a new contractor. In addition, a construction lender must analyze the plans and specifications carefully to ascertain whether the general contractor will be able to construct the building within the time allotted in the permanent loan commitment and for the amount of money available in the construction loan.

A construction lender is also concerned with the availability of water, sewer, and other utilities, with access, and with zoning and building laws because it wants to be sure that the building, when constructed, will be complete, usable, and in compliance with the law. Otherwise, the tenant may refuse to take possession, and the permanent lender may refuse to close the permanent loan.

To summarize, the construction lender must at every stage of construction consider what its situation would be if the borrower defaulted and it had to take over the borrower's position. In such a case the construction lender would act as a developer and would coordinate and balance the requirements of the general contractor, the tenant, and the permanent lender.

Examples 7-6 and *7-7* show a construction and permanent loan commitment that might be used in the transaction described in the sample fact situation.

III. TITLE

A construction lender will take a different view of easements and restrictions than will a mortgagee of property that has already been developed. A mortgagee taking a mortgage on an existing building will often assume that any building restrictions or easements on the property do not adversely affect the building, particularly if the building has been there and in use for a number of years. However, a construction lender taking a mortgage on vacant ground has no such comfort from a fact situation that has survived the passage of time. The construction lender will, therefore, require that the title report contain the full text of any restrictions or easements (including utility company rights-of-way) and that such easements and restrictions be clearly located on a current survey of the property.

IV. PREPARATION OF DOCUMENTS

There are several parties who may be involved in a construction loan, including the developer, permanent lender, construction lender, general contractor, and one or more major tenants. As a result, usually more documents are required than in the case of the other types of loans we have reviewed. Among the documents that may be necessary for a construction loan closing are the following:

A. CONSTRUCTION LOAN AGREEMENT

The basic understanding between the mortgagor and the construction lender, pursuant to which the construction lender agrees to advance the funds as they are needed for the project, is set forth in the construction loan agreement. The agreement is often prepared on forms supplied by the construction lender. For major transactions the construction loan agreement will be thoroughly negotiated, as it is the single most important agreement between the borrower and the construction lender.

Example 7-6: **Construction Loan Commitment**

SECOND CENTRALIA NATIONAL BANK

November 1, 1985

Cen Tenn Realty Co., Inc.
Centralia, Tennessee

    Re: Route 27 and Swamp Road
          Centralia, Tennessee

Gentlemen:

    Subject to acceptance of and compliance with the following terms and conditions, we have approved your request for a construction mortgage loan in an amount not to exceed One Million Dollars ($1,000,000.00):

Term: Due and payable on or before December 15, 1986.

Interest Rate: 1% in excess of the Prime rate charged by us from time to time but in no event less than 11% per annum.

Non-Refundable Service Charge: $15,000.00, payable from the proceeds of the initial disbursement of the loan.

Documentation: Prior to the initial disbursement of the loan, we shall be furnished with the following documents, which must be acceptable to us at our sole discretion:

    1.   Mortgage Note.

    2.   Mortgage.

    3.   Construction Loan Agreement.

    4.   Buy-Sell Agreement.

    5.   Schedule of Operation.

    6.   Lease between Cen Tenn Realty Co., Inc. and Xerxes Department Store Co.

    7.   Memorandum of Lease.

    8.   Assignment of Lease.

    9.   Report of Title.

   10.   Personal Guarantee of Daniel Developer.

   11.   Declaration of Reciprocal Easements.

Continued.

Example 7-6 **Construction Loan Commitment** *continued*

12. Copy of Construction Contract with Best Builders, Inc. including trade payment breakdown.

13. Final Working Plans and Specifications as approved by Borrower.

14. Copy of Building Permit.

15. Builder's Risk Insurance for the full amount of the loan with extended coverage, vandalism and malicious mischief protection.

16. Approval from New Hampshire Mutual Life Insurance Company on the following items:

    A. Mortgage Note.
    B. Mortgage.
    C. Lease.
    D. Report of Title.
    E. Declaration of Reciprocal Easements.

17. Original accepted commitment of New Hampshire Mutual Life Insurance Company.

18. Other documents which we may reasonably require.

Initial Disbursement: If the initial disbursement of the loan is not made on or before January 1, 1986, our approval will be automatically and fully terminated. The Construction Loan settlement must be held in Centralia.

Please indicate your acceptance hereof by executing and returning the enclosed copy of this letter on or before November 31, 1985.

Second Centralia National Bank

By: _____
                                President

Accepted and agreed to this ____ day of November, 1986.

Cen Tenn Realty Co., Inc.

BY: _____

Example 7-7: **Mortgage Commitment (Permanent Loan)**

NEW HAMPSHIRE MUTUAL LIFE INSURANCE COMPANY

September 1, 1985

Cen Tenn Realty Co., Inc.
Centralia, Tennessee   Re: Route 27 and Swamp Road
                                          Centralia, Tennessee

Gentlemen:

Your application for a mortgage loan covering property above referred to, is approved in the amount of $1,000,000.00 for a term of twenty-five years providing for constant payments of $8,392.00 each month which shall be applied first to interest at the rate of 11% per annum and the balance in reduction of principal, subject to the following terms and conditions:

1.   That either the Note, Mortgage or other suitable instrument shall provide that this company will participate in the annual gross income to the extent of 1% of the minimum rental income of $160,000.00 or 25% of the additional rental income as set forth in paragraph 5A of the lease, whichever is the greater. You will furnish by March 15 of each year, a certified statement for the preceding year, as submitted by the tenant and pay to us the amount due as herein set forth, as additional income.

2.   That you furnish to us by December 1, 1985, a complete set of plans and specifications and an M.A.I. appraisal which shall be satisfactory to us and indicate a value of not less than $1,350,000.00.

3.   The mortgage shall cover a plot of 3 acres, which is adjacent to and joining an existing shopping center known as Centraltown upon which 3-acre plot shall be erected a one-story steel and masonry building having an area of 80,000 square feet.

4.   That a guaranteed survey of the subject property with the improvements located thereon acceptable to our counsel be furnished at your expense.

5.   That a policy of title insurance issued by a title company acceptable to our counsel shall be furnished, which policy shall insure the construction lender as owner and holder of a valid first lien mortgage on the subject premises.

6.   That fire insurance with extended coverage (minimum $100 deductible) shall be furnished for the loan at the time of closing, in a company acceptable to us, properly endorsed in an amount to be determined by us upon receipt of appraisal as required under section #2 herein.

7.   The premises shall be in an undamaged condition at the time of closing.   *Continued.*

Example 7-7 **Mortgage Commitment (Permanent Loan)** *continued*

8.   That the lease between you and Xerxes Department Store Co.
     expiring in 1999 providing for a minimum annual rent of
     $160,000.00 shall be in full force and effect.

9.   Upon acceptance of this commitment you will pay to us the sum
     of $20,000.00 which commitment fee shall be deemed earned by
     us by issuance hereof and shall be non-refundable to you
     whether or not the loan contemplated hereby is actually made.
     However, should the loan close as herein agreed upon, we will
     refund the sum of $10,000.00 at the time of closing.

10. That the construction lender agree not to assign their
     mortgage to any one other than to this company, and you will
     undertake to procure such agreement upon their issuance of a
     commitment.

11. That upon closing of this loan an easement agreement will be
     delivered to us setting forth full parking privileges for the
     entire shopping center which shall remain in effect for the
     full term of our loan or any extension thereof.

12. That either the Note, Mortgage, or other suitable instrument
     provide that the loan cannot be prepaid during the first ten
     year period, that during the eleventh year the obligation
     may be prepaid upon payment of a penalty of 5%, thereafter
     the penalty shall reduce 1/2 of 1% each year until reduced
     to 2%.

13. This commitment shall expire if the loan is not delivered to
     us as herein agreed upon by March 1, 1987.

14. This commitment is subject to a satisfactory site inspection
     which shall be made by us within ten days after our receipt
     of plans, specifications and M.A.I. appraisal. You will be
     advised within five days of our decision.

15. In the event we are not satisfied with the M.A.I. appraisal
     or site inspection, the commitment fee of $20,000.00 shall be
     returned to you within five days.

16. All legal matters and documents shall be subject to the
     approval of our counsel.

17. All costs and charges for title examination and issuance of
     policy, survey, mortgage tax, recording fees, revenue stamps,
     and all other disbursements including legal fees ($1,000)
     of our attorneys in connection with the making of this
     mortgage loan shall be paid by you at the time of closing
     which shall take place at our office in Brooklyn, New York.

18. The obligation shall be limited to the mortgage covering
     the real estate and the lease with Xerxes Department Store Co.
     There shall be no personal liability.

     The terms of this letter may not be waived, modified or in
any other way changed, except as agreed to in writing and signed
by both parties.

If the terms and conditions of this commitment meet with your approval, you will please so indicate by signing the acceptance below and returning to us a properly signed copy of this letter.

This commitment shall become effective upon receipt of your acceptance in Brooklyn, New York, within five days from the date hereof, together with your check in the amount of $20,000.00.

Very truly yours,

New Hampshire Mutual Life
Insurance Company

BY: _____
                 Vice-President

Accepted and agreed to
this ____ day of September, 1985.

Cen Tenn Realty Co., Inc.

BY: _____
                 President

B. NOTE

Generally, the note will be on the form of note used by the permanent lender. Using this form the construction lender will include certain clauses outlining the construction loan arrangements. The considerations for a decision to include such clauses and examples of such clauses appear in section I of Part Six of this chapter.

C. MORTGAGE

The mortgage will be similar to the mortgage required by the lender in the commercial-industrial situation. As in the case of the note, the construction lender will want certain clauses included to reflect the special construction loan arrangements. Drafting considerations for and examples of such clauses appear in section II of Part Six of this chapter.

D. GENERAL CONSTRUCTION CONTRACT

The construction lender will want a copy of the contract between the borrower and the general contractor to be sure that the general contractor has obligated itself to construct the building within the time limit and for the amount of money the construction lender is depending on. The monetary concern may not be met by delivery of a copy of the contract because many construction contracts are not for a fixed sum, but for the general contractor's cost plus a percentage of such cost.

E. COMPLETION BOND

The general contractor has no direct obligation to the construction lender. Nevertheless, the construction lender wants to be sure it can enforce the construction contract directly against the general contractor in the event the construction lender takes the place of the borrower. Accordingly, the construction lender may require the general contractor to sign a bond guaranteeing that it will complete its obligation under the construction contract.

F. CORPORATE RESOLUTIONS

If the mortgagor is a corporation, the construction lender will want a copy of resolutions of the corporation's board of directors authorizing the loan. The copy should be certified by the secretary of the corporation.

G. INSURANCE

The construction lender will require insurance against destruction of the partially completed structure by fire and similar hazards. Such insurance will usually be on a "builder's risk" form that increases in value as the value of the construction increases. In addition, the construction lender will want the general contractor to carry liability insurance and workmen's compensation insurance.

H. SURVEY

As indicated above, a survey is extremely important to the construction lender in order to be sure that the proposed construction will not in any way interfere with any existing easements or rights of way or violate any existing enforceable building restrictions.

I. BUILDING PERMIT

The construction lender wants to be certain that the local municipal authority has issued a valid permit allowing the proposed construction. Generally, such a permit can be obtained only if the proposed building complies with the applicable building code and the zoning and subdivision ordinances.

J. BUY-SELL AGREEMENT

The permanent loan commitment is an agreement between New Hampshire Mutual and Cen Tenn. Second Centralia, which is looking toward that permanent loan commitment to take it out, has no direct right to enforce that permanent loan commitment letter because Second Centralia does not have privity of contract with New Hampshire Mutual. Similarly, New Hampshire Mutual has no control over the construction loan agreement and can neither directly enforce the construction loan agreement against Second Centralia nor require Second Centralia to sell the note to it on completion of the project rather than to some other permanent lender. The only link between New Hampshire Mutual and Second Centralia is Cen Tenn, who may prove to be a weak link indeed, unable or unwilling to conclude the transaction as contemplated. A permanent lender and a construction lender generally forge a new, and direct, link between themselves by entering into a buy-sell agreement. This agreement, which creates the necessary privity of contract, includes the agreement of the permanent lender to purchase the note and mortgage from the construction lender in accordance with the terms of the permanent commitment letter, and the agreement of the construction lender to sell the note and mortgage to the permanent lender. The permanent lender and construction lender each agree to attorn to the other in the event that the other takes over the position of the developer due to a default by the developer.

The buy-sell agreement is also usually signed by the developer. For the developer, it often serves as an opportunity to resolve some of the uncertainties of the permanent loan commitment. That commitment usually reserves the right of the permanent lender and its counsel to approve various aspects of the transaction. A developer often lacks the bargaining power to force the permanent lender to set forth its terms with greater specificity. The construction lender, however, has the same need for certainty, and usually has the necessary bargaining power to gain a larger measure of certainty by obtaining the permanent lender's approval in the buy-sell agreement of a variety of items, such as the state of title and acceptability of exceptions to title.

Example 7-8, a Buy-Sell Agreement, might be used in our sample fact situation.

Example 7-8: Buy-Sell Agreement

```
               SECOND CENTRALIA NATIONAL BANK
                  CENTRALIA, TENNESSEE

                                    December 1, 1985

New Hampshire Mutual Life Insurance Co.
Rocky Falls, New Hampshire

Gentlemen:

     With reference to your commitment dated September 1, 1985
wherein you agree to make or purchase a first mortgage loan to Cen
Tenn Realty Co., Inc. of not exceeding $1,000,000.00, we agree to make
a construction loan up to that amount using papers to be submitted to
and approved by you that will contain the terms of the permanent loan
and be acceptable to you for later purchase.

     In consideration of your agreeing to purchase such papers from
us, without recourse, subject to the conditions of your commitment
```

Continued.

Example 7-8 Buy-Sell Agreement *continued*

having been met, we agree to hold such papers available for such purchase and to cooperate with you in all reasonable ways in connection therewith. The foregoing is subject to the following understanding becoming applicable in the event of default or expiration of your commitment.

We agree to take no action (by taking steps to enforce the terms of the papers or otherwise) which would give anyone the right to prepay the indebtedness nor to sell or assign the papers to others except with your prior written assent or unless within twenty days after receipt by you of notice from us specifying the nature of a default or advising of the expiration of your commitment you fail to purchase the papers, to extend the term of your commitment or the time for performance of a defaulted condition thereof for a reasonable period of time, to state that the default will not affect your agreement to purchase, or to make such reasonable change in the conditions of your commitment as will remove the default. In the event of default or expiration of your commitment, regarding which no notice as above is given by us, it is agreed that you shall have the right upon reasonable notice to us to purchase such papers. Upon your request, any special collateral held by us solely in connection with the loan shall be assigned and delivered to you if you purchase said papers while a default exists or after the expiration of your commitment.

Very truly yours,

Second Centralia National Bank

By:_____
                    Vice-President

In consideration of your agreement in the above letter, we are pleased to accept the obligations imposed on us therein and agree to be bound thereby.

New Hampshire Mutual Life
Insurance Co.

By:_____
                    Vice-President

We hereby assign to Second Centralia National Bank all of our right, title, and interest in the aforesaid commitment and agree not to prepay the construction mortgage loan.

Cen Tenn Realty Co., Inc.

By:_____
                    President

K. DECLARATION OF CROSS EASEMENTS

In our hypothetical case the property was subject to an existing mortgage in favor of First Mortgagee Insurance Company. First Mortgagee Insurance Company has agreed that the new construction would enhance the overall value of the shopping center. It will therefore release from the lien of its mortgage the area required to construct the new building for the new tenant. This will allow the mortgagor to create a first lien on the property in favor of Second Centralia. However, the fact that different portions of the shopping center will be subject to separate mortgages held by different mortgagees raises the possibility that at some future time, by foreclosure, the two portions of the shopping center might be vested in separate owners. Because the two portions together constitute a single integrated shopping center, each owner will need the right to go on the property of the other for parking, access, and possibly support. Accordingly, prior to recording of the new mortgage, the owner and the holder of the existing mortgage will execute a reciprocal easement agreement granting such easement rights to all present or future owners of either property. The agreement would normally consist of (a) a recital of the relevant background; (b) the actual grant of the easement; (c) a provision concerning responsibility for the expense of maintaining the property subject to the easement; (d) a statement of the duration or term of the easement; and (e) a description of the property benefited and burdened by the easement.

SECURITY AGREEMENT AND FINANCING STATEMENT

The construction lender may wish to obtain a security interest in the mortgagor's personal property at the premises, which will usually be in the form of a security agreement and financing statements. Security agreements and financing statements, because they cover personal property rather than real property, are generally filed in the recorder's office or the prothonotary's office in the county in which the real property to be mortgaged is located. In addition, one copy of the financing statement may have to be filed at the state capital and/or where the borrower has its principal place of business.

Example 7-9 shows a security agreement and financing statement.

Example 7-9: **Security Agreement and Financing Statement**

SECURITY AGREEMENT made this 15th day of December, 1985, between

Cen Tenn Realty Co., Inc., Centralia, Tennessee, a Tennessee corpora-

tion ("DEBTOR"), and Second Centralia National Bank, 1 Central Plaza,

Centralia, Tennessee ("SECURED PARTY");

Continued.

Example 7-9 **Security Agreement and Financing Statement** *continued*

W I T N E S S E T H :

On this date SECURED PARTY will lend to DEBTOR with interest,
all as provided in and evidenced by a Mortgage Note (the "Note")
of even date herewith in the face amount of One Million Dollars
($1,000,000.00), and secured by a Mortgage (the "Mortgage") also of
even date upon the interest of DEBTOR in certain real estate situated
in Central County, Tennessee, as more particularly described in said
Mortgage.

NOW, THEREFORE, to induce the SECURED PARTY to lend the sum of
$1,000,000.00 to DEBTOR, DEBTOR and SECURED PARTY, intending to be
legally bound, hereby agree as follows:

1. DEBTOR hereby grants to SECURED PARTY a security interest
in and mortgages to SECURED PARTY all of the interest of DEBTOR in
the following described property, together with all parts, accessories,
attachments and equipment at any time installed therein or affixed
thereto and all accessories thereto and additions and replacements
thereof and all proceeds of the foregoing (collectively referred to
as the "collateral"):

All furniture, furnishings, fixtures, machinery and equipment and other tangible personal property of whatsoever kind
and nature attached to or located on the real estate of debtor
located in Central County, Tennessee, containing in the aggregate
approximately 3.00 acres, as more particularly described in
"Exhibit A", attached hereto and hereby made a part hereof.

2. This security interest is given as additional security
for the repayment of the aforementioned loan in accordance with the
terms of the Note and the collateral shall be encumbered in the same
manner and on the same terms and conditions to which the premises

covered by the Mortgage are subjected. DEBTOR, for itself and any subsequent owner, will at DEBTOR'S expense execute and deliver for filing all financing and other statements and take or join with SECURED PARTY in taking any other action requested by SECURED PARTY to perfect and continue perfected SECURED PARTY'S secured interest throughout the term of the Mortgage.

3. All of the covenants and agreements in the Note and Mortgage to be performed by DEBTOR thereunder are incorporated herein by reference, and all of the remedies provided for herein may be exercised concurrently with the remedies provided for in the Note and Mortgage.

4. Until default DEBTOR shall be entitled to possession, use and enjoyment of the collateral. A default under either the Note or Mortgage shall also constitute a default under this Agreement. Upon the occurrence of such default, SECURED PARTY may exercise all rights and remedies of a SECURED PARTY under the Uniform Commercial Code of Tennessee.

IN WITNESS WHEREOF, the parties have executed this Agreement as of the day and year first above written.

Attest: CEN TEN REALTY CO., INC.

_____   By:_____
            Secretary   President
(Corporate Seal)

Attest: SECOND CENTRALIA NATIONAL BANK

_____   By:_____
            Secretary   President
(Corporate Seal)

Continued.

Example 7-9 **Security Agreement and Financing Statement** *continued*

Uniform Commercial Code—**FINANCING STATEMENT**—Form DSCB:UCC-1

PRINTED FOR AND SOLD BY JOHN C. CLARK CO. 1326 WALNUT ST., PHILADELPHIA, PA 19107

This FINANCING STATEMENT is presented to a Filing Officer for filing pursuant to the Uniform Commercial Code.		No. of Additional Sheets Presented:	Maturity Date 3. (optional):
1. Debtor(s) (Last Name First and Address(es):	2. Secured Party(ies): Name(s) and Address(es):		4. For Filing Officer: Date, Time, No.-Filing Office
Cen Tenn Realty Co., Inc. Centralia, Tennessee	Second Centralia National Bank 1 Central Plaza Centralia, Tennessee		

5. This Financing Statement covers the following types (or items) of property:	6. Assignee(s) of Secured Party and Address(es)
All furniture, fixtures, machinery and equipment and other tangible personal property of whatsoever kind and nature attached to or located on the real estate of debtor described below.	
☒ Proceeds — ☒ Products of the Collateral are also covered.	7. ☐ The described crops are growing or to be grown on: * ☒ The described goods are or are to be affixed to: * * (Describe Real Estate Below).

8. Describe Real Estate Here:	9. Name(s) of Record Owner(s):	Cen Tenn Realty Co., Inc.
Parcel of ground located in Centralia, Tennessee as described in Exhibit A hereto		
No. & Street Town or City County		Section Block Lot

10. This statement is filed without the debtor's signature to perfect a security interest in collateral (check appropriate box)

☐ already subject to a security interest in another jurisdiction when it was brought into this state, or

☐ which is proceeds of the original collateral described above in which a security interest was perfected:

Cen Tenn Realty Co., Inc.   Second Centralia National Bank

By_____   By_____
    Signature(s) of Debtor(s)   Signature(s) of Secured Party(ies)
(1) FILING OFFICER COPY - NUMERICAL

FORM DSCB:UCC-1 (Rev. 8-72)—Approved by Department of State of the Commonwealth of Pa.

V. PREPARATION FOR CLOSING

In addition to preparation of the documents set forth above, the construction lender will want to obtain the approval of the permanent lender as to (a) the form of the note and mortgage that the permanent lender will purchase by assignment on completion of construction; (b) the form of lease to be used for the tenant or tenants of the property; and (c) the plans and specifications for the store. In many cases the permanent lender either will prepare the note and mortgage, including the clauses concerning the construction loan, or will supply the forms of note and mortgage to be used by the construction lender.

VI. MECHANICS' LIENS

In any large construction project the general contractor will purchase services and materials from other companies and tradespeople. These people are called subcontractors and material suppliers. In the early nineteenth century, when the United States was expanding rapidly and it was considered socially useful to encourage people to go into the building trades and crafts, various states passed statutes giving artisans and mechanics a lien on any real property for which they had furnished labor or material. This lien is effective until the mechanic is paid, in full, for work on the property. The significant concept concerning mechanics' lien statutes is that they also benefit material suppliers, mechanics, and artisans who are subcontractors, and who therefore have no direct contractual relationship with the owner. Thus, even if the owner of the property has paid the general contractor for the work, if the general contractor did not pay the subcontractors, then the subcontractors were entitled to a lien on the property. Like a mortgage, this lien could be executed on to force a judicial sale of the property, and the proceeds of such sale would be paid to the holder of the mechanics' lien, among others. Ultimately, each state passed a mechanics' lien statute, and these laws vary from state to state.

There is also substantial variation from state to state as to what an honest owner, who pays his or her general contractor, can do to be protected against a mechanics' lien attaching to his or her property. The question of who should suffer the loss if the general contractor, having been paid by the owner, is unable or unwilling to pay his or her subcontractor, is a particularly difficult one. The question has been resolved differently in different states. In a few states a waiver by the general contractor of the right to file a mechanics' lien also has the effect of waiving the rights of all subcontractors, provided the waiver is filed in a public place before any work begins. This is not true in most other states, where the question has basically been resolved in favor of subcontractors.

Mechanics' liens present an especially thorny problem for the construction lender and the title insurer. In some states a mechanics' lien has priority over a mortgage lien when the work began before the mortgage was recorded, even if the mechanics' lien is actually filed or recorded after the mortgage. The statutory scheme for priorities varies from state to state. A paralegal must be aware of the problem of mechanics' liens and learn how the problem is handled in the state in which the real estate is located.

VII. CONSTRUCTION LOAN CLOSING

At closing for the construction loan, all of the various documents referred to above will be executed, acknowledged where appropriate, and delivered as in other mortgage settlements. Although there are many more documents than in the ordinary mortgage settlement, the procedure at settlement is basically the same.

VIII. POST CLOSING

After settlement, the owner and the construction lender will proceed in accordance with the construction loan agreement. Usually, the mortgagor or the general contractor will submit periodic requests for advances on account of the loan, on voucher forms supplied by the construction lender. The construction lender will send out its inspectors periodically to ascertain whether the work for which payment has been requested has actually been done and whether the value of the work is consistent with the amount of the payment requested. If the inspectors are satisfied, the construction lender will issue its check to the owner or the general contractor or, in some cases, directly to subcontractors.

IX. PERMANENT LOAN CLOSING

Closing on the permanent loan will be held some time after completion of the building and occupancy by the tenant or tenants, and must be held before the expiration of the term of the permanent commitment. At the closing on the permanent loan, the note and mortgage and collateral assignment of lease and any additional security documents (such as financing statements on personal property) will be assigned to the permanent lender, who will then issue its check to the construction lender. If the permanent lender's check exceeds the sum due the construction lender, the difference will be paid to the mortgagor as a final advance on the construction loan. The permanent lender will also require that the title search be continued down to the date of the permanent closing. This bring-down search will disclose any documents or liens that have been recorded subsequent to the mortgage that might in some way affect the validity or priority of the mortgage or that might indicate that there is some problem with payment of contractors or subcontractors. Interest for the final month of the construction loan will be apportioned and paid.

In some instances the permanent lender may not purchase the existing documents by assignment, but may simply lend the mortgagor the funds to pay the construction lender and then record a new mortgage. The advantage to assignment of the construction mortgage is that, for purposes of determining priority of interests, the lien held by the permanent lender will date back to the date of the construction loan closing.

There are three additional documents that are usually required by the permanent lender at the permanent loan closing.

A. DECLARATION OF NO SET-OFF

If the permanent lender is purchasing the note and mortgage from the construction lender, the permanent lender wants to be sure that the mortgagor does not have some defense to or counterclaim against the construction lender. The defense or counterclaim might arise out of a default by the construction lender in the construction loan agreement, or out of some transaction between the mortgagor and the construction lender completely separate from the loan being sold. To preclude such a problem, the permanent lender will require a statement from the mortgagor that the full amount of the loan is owing and that the mortgagor has no defenses, counterclaims, or set-offs against the face amount of the note and mortgage. This estops the mortgagor from interposing any such defenses against the permanent lender at any time.

B. TENANT'S ESTOPPEL CERTIFICATE

Because the permanent lender is relying on the rent payable by the tenant to pay interest and principal on the loan, the permanent lender wants to be sure (a) that the tenant has taken or is prepared to take possession of the building; (b) that the tenant agrees that the building as constructed complies with the terms of the lease; and (c) that the tenant at the time of settlement on the permanent loan has no defense to any claim for prepaid rent or other allowances. The permanent lender normally requires the mortgagor to obtain from each tenant a certificate or letter to that effect, which is called an "estoppel certificate."

C. CORPORATE RESOLUTIONS

As in the case of the construction loan closing, the permanent lender will want a certified copy of resolutions of the board of directors of a corporate mortgagor authorizing the officers of the corporation to execute the documents necessary to close the permanent loan.

Part Four
FEDERAL HOUSING ADMINISTRATION MORTGAGES

The Federal Housing Administration (FHA) is an administrative part of the Department of Housing and Urban Development (HUD). The FHA is HUD's principal means of implementing HUD's various programs and policies in the housing field, as such programs and policies are determined by the President and the Congress. This chapter is intended only to familiarize the student with elementary FHA terminology and with the kind of programs that the FHA has traditionally administered. The FHA mortgage programs are in a constant state of flux. New programs are adopted and old ones discarded, and new regulations and requirements are formulated continually for existing programs. The programs discussed below are examples of programs that have existed and, in one form or another, will probably continue to exist for some time.

I. INTRODUCTION TO THE FHA

A. THE ROLE OF THE FHA

The FHA's principal business has traditionally been the insurance of mortgages on residential properties. It has also been assigned the responsibility of managing the federal government's programs of subsidizing mortgage payments so as to permit new and rehabilitated housing to be owned or rented by lower-income occupants who would not otherwise be able to afford it. You should understand that the FHA does not act as the mortgagee, but rather insures the mortgagee against loss if there is a default on the mortgage. The insurance takes the form of an agreement by the FHA to purchase the mortgage loan from the holder, thus becoming the mortgage holder itself. Consequently, the owner or developer of an FHA-insured mortgage project must obtain mortgage commitments from lending institutions as if he or she were not using an FHA-insured mortgage, provided that the mortgagee or mortgagees must be approved by the FHA.

B. THE FUNCTION OF MORTGAGE INSURANCE

When the FHA, or any mortgage insurer,[19] insures a mortgage, it guarantees the mortgagee that, if there is a default under the mortgage, the mortgagee will have the right to assign the mortgage in default to the FHA in consideration for the FHA's payment to the mortgagee of the oustanding principal and interest then owed on the mortgage. It is then up to the FHA either to foreclose the mortgage, to obtain a purchaser of the mortgaged property who will attempt to rescue the project, to refinance the mortgage, or otherwise to assist the mortgagor in carrying the property.

This kind of additional security for the mortgagee's loan is obviously beneficial to the mortgagee because it reduces its risk in making the loan. It is also beneficial to the mortgagor because the reduced risk to the mortgagee will permit the mortgagee to make loans that it would not otherwise make. The interest rate for an FHA-insured loan may be lower than the interest rate for a comparable non-insured mortgage because of the lower risk to the mortgagee. Another way in which FHA involvement benefits a borrower is in the amount of the total project cost that can be borrowed through an FHA-insured mortgage loan. Such a mortgage will frequently be made at a higher loan-to-value ratio (or lower loan-to-equity ratio)[20] than the mortgagee would be willing to permit if the loan were

---

19. Private insurance companies have come into existence that also insure all or part of mortgage loans. These companies operate for a profit. Indeed, the stock of the best known of them trade on national stock exchanges.

20. A loan-to-equity ratio is obtained by comparing the amount the lender is willing to lend with the amount the owner has invested in the property (which is referred to as the owner's "equity"). If the mortgagee lends the owner $50,000 to construct a building on property which the owner has previously purchased for $150,000, this is said to be a one-to-three loan-to-equity ratio.

This can also be expressed as a 25% loan-to-value ratio ($50,000 being one-quarter of $200,000, the total value of the land and the building to be constructed thereon). This is a low loan-to-value ratio, and the mortgagee has less exposure if the loan defaults than it would have if the loan-to-value ratio were higher, such as in a three-to-one loan-to-equity transaction in which the loan-to-value ratio would be 75%. A 75% loan-to-value ratio occurs when the mortgagee has loaned $150,000 and the owner has invested only $50,000 in the property. This is a typical loan-to-value ratio.

not so insured. This means that the owner or developer of a project usually needs to invest less equity money to develop an FHA-insured mortgage project than to build a project secured by a conventional mortgage.

C. THE ORGANIZATION OF THE FHA

The student should have some familiarity with the way the FHA is organized in order to know where to obtain necessary information or answers to questions or to submit drafts of documents that must be approved by the FHA. The structure of the FHA is, or course, subject to change; however, a brief description of its present structure may be helpful.

The main office of the FHA is in the HUD Office Building in Washington, D.C. This office is the source of general policy decisions, new and amended regulations, and changes in overall procedures. Questions of an unusual nature relating to a particular project may ultimately have to be referred to Washington for a decision.

A legal assistant is most likely to have contact with the HUD Area Office that has jurisdiction over the project on which an insured mortgage will be placed. Between the HUD Washington Office and the forty area offices there are ten regional offices blanketing the country, each of which has one or more area offices reporting to it. For example, the Philadelphia Regional Office is responsible for all HUD programs in Delaware, the District of Columbia, Maryland, Pennsylvania, Virginia, and West Virginia (including five area offices—Philadelphia, Pittsburgh, Baltimore, Richmond, and Washington, D.C.—and four insuring offices in Wilmington, Delaware, and Charleston, West Virginia). The Philadelphia Area Office, in turn, has jurisdiction over all HUD programs in the state of Delaware and the thirty-eight Pennsylvania counties nearest Philadelphia, with the Pittsburgh Area Office being responsible for the balance of the Pennsylvania counties.

D. TYPES OF PROJECTS ON WHICH THE FHA WILL INSURE THE MORTGAGE

The FHA is authorized to insure mortgages for a vast array of residential projects. Each program is commonly referred to by the section or title of the National Housing Act that authorizes the particular program. The FHA has responsibility for insuring mortgages on such diverse projects as housing designed specifically for the elderly, cooperative and condominium housing, nursing homes, rehabilitation of run-down homes, luxury apartments, experimental housing, and housing for veterans. It is neither possible nor necessary to discuss all these programs in the confines of these materials. Rather, we will consider the Section 236 Program, which is for mortgages on new construction rental apartment projects.

E. TYPES OF MORTGAGES THAT THE FHA WILL INSURE

The FHA has the power to insure several types of mortgages. If the FHA is insuring only the permanent loan, it is said to be insuring the loan on an "Insurance upon Completion" basis. If both the construction loan advances and the permanent mortgage loan are being insured, the insurance is said to be issued on an "Insurance of Advances" basis. Obviously, only the latter method provides insurance protection for the construction lender as well as for the permanent lender. An Insurance of Advances mortgage loan may be the only way to finance the construction or rehabilitation of projects that are located in high-risk areas or that are being undertaken by a developer who lacks substantial experience and a good credit rating.

F. FHA MORTGAGE SUBSIDIES AND RENT SUPPLEMENT PROGRAMS

The FHA administers certain programs by which it provides subsidized mortgages. The Section 236 program was designed primarily for the purpose of encouraging the construction or rehabilitation by private developers of rental housing for low and moderate income families, with a priority going to those families who have been displaced by urban renewal or other governmental actions. The "encouragement" provided by the FHA is in the form of a direct governmental subsidy of the interest payments made on the loan by the mortgagor, as well as the usual federal insurance of the mortgage loans. In addition, in some instances described below, the FHA may make a regular cash payment to the owner to supplement a tenants' rent payments.

1. Interest Subsidy

The mechanics of the interest subsidy operate in the following manner: The mortgagor makes monthly payments to the mortgagee in the amount of the required amortization of the principal of the loan together with interest at the rate of 1% per annum on the unpaid principal balance. The FHA pays directly to the mortgagee the difference between this 1% interest rate and the interest rate set forth on the face of the note.

The owner must pass the benefit of the interest reduction to its low and moderate income tenants in the form of lower rents. A "basic rental" charge is determined for each apartment. The "basic rental" equals the amount of money needed each month to amortize the principal of the mortgage, pay interest on the mortgage at the rate of 1% per annum, cover the estimated operating expenses of the apartment, and give the developer the percentage return on investment permitted by the FHA pursuant to the particular program. Any rental collected by the owner in excess of the "basic rents" must be returned to HUD for deposit in a revolving fund, which is used for making other interest-reduction payments.

The FHA will also determine "fair market rental" for each apartment. This is the amount that would be charged for the apartment if the project were financed conventionally. The landlord will be permitted to rent an apartment either at the basic rental for that apartment or at 25% of the income of the tenant family, whichever is greater. However, in no event may the rent exceed the fair market rental for that apartment. A family's income must be recertified every two years and the rent charged to it adjusted accordingly.

2. Rent Supplements

Mechanically, rent supplements in Section 236 projects work as follows: As previously discussed, a tenant of an apartment in a Section 236 project would normally pay the greater of 25% of income or the basic rent for that apartment computed on the basis of a 1% interest rate mortgage loan. In the case of tenants whose family income is low enough to make them eligible for public housing, the basic rent for their apartment would in fact be about 35% to 40% of the family's income. The rent supplement payment fills the gap between 25% of the tenant's income and the basic rent so that the landlord would receive the full basic rent even though the tenant paid only 25% of the family's income.

Part Five
INDUSTRIAL DEVELOPMENT AUTHORITY LOANS

In order to attract industry, many communities throughout the United States have created industrial development authorities, which grant low-interest mortgages on both old and new industrial and commercial facilities. Interest received from units of state and local government is exempt from the federal income tax. Taxpayers who buy obligations of such a governmental unit need not pay income tax on the interest income produced. This tax exemption allows state and local governments to raise money at a lower interest rate than would otherwise be necessary to attract investors, because a dollar of tax-free interest is worth more to an investor than a dollar of other interest income on which the taxpayer must pay income tax.

Promoters of local industry have utilized these facts by creating a government "authority" in the form of a nonprofit corporation that is a branch of the local government. This authority would borrow money from a bank, use the money to purchase or build an industrial or commercial facility, and then lease the facility to a tenant who would pay enough rent to pay off the mortgage.[21] When the mortgage was paid in full, the authority would sell the facility to the industrial user for a nominal price. The authority in such a case is a mere conduit. The true economic sub-

---

21. The tenant is usually the company that sought to build the industrial or commercial facility and is referred to as the "industrial user."

stance of the transaction is a mortgage loan from the bank to the industrial user of the building. However, because the interest was actually being paid by a branch of the government, the interest income is tax exempt. Banks are therefore willing to lend money at a lower interest rate, and the benefit of this rate is passed on to the industrial user in the form of lower rent. Instead of a lease with rent, the transaction between the authority and the industrial user might be an installment sale contract. In either case the industrial user is fully responsible for the property and all the expenses of operating, repairing, and maintaining it.

While it is beyond the scope of this course to detail the steps of this type of mortgage, we will describe briefly the substance of such a loan.

I. MORTGAGE LOAN FROM THE BANK TO THE INDUSTRIAL DEVELOPMENT AUTHORITY

An industrial development authority loan starts when the authority obtains a mortgage loan from a financial institution on a piece of property that the authority will acquire for an industrial user. In actuality, the industrial user will normally approach the authority after having spotted a property that suits its purposes. The authority will not advance any of its own money. The costs of acquisition, plus construction, if applicable, will be paid from the mortgage loan. The balance, if any, will be supplied by the industrial user. The mortgage will look much like any other mortgage, with the authority as the mortgagor.

II. LEASE WITH THE INDUSTRIAL USER

In order to be assured of the funds necessary to meet the mortgage payments, the authority will lease the premises to the industrial user or will grant possession under an installment sales contract. The rent will normally equal the mortgage payments, fire insurance premiums, and real estate taxes. In some instances the latter two items would not be included in the rent, but would be the direct responsibility of the tenant. The lease would be what is called a "net" or a "net-net lease," meaning that the authority would have no responsibilities as a landlord. All repairs and other expenses would be the obligation of the industrial user as tenant.

III. AGREEMENT OF PURCHASE

It is the intention of the parties that the industrial user will own the property when the mortgage has been paid off. The lease itself could contain the sales agreement in the form of an option to buy the property for nominal consideration, or the whole arrangement might be cast as an installment sale agreement.

Although the mechanics of industrial development authority transactions may differ from one locale to another, they all will resemble the format outlined above.

Part Six
FORM AND SUBSTANCE OF THE NOTE
AND MORTGAGE

I. DRAFTING NOTES

The mortgagor's debt will be evidence by an instrument called a note[22] and secured by a conveyance or lien on real estate called a mortgage. The note will set forth the obligation itself, the interest rate, and the terms and date of repayment.

In preparing a note, the drafter must consider a number of items:

A. PARTIES

The drafter has the usual concerns respecting parties and proper execution. Normally, the signer of the note, who is usually referred to as the "maker" or the "obligor," will be the same person who owns the real estate on which the mortgage is being given. However, this is not always the case, and it is this possibility that can create unusual concerns for the drafter. These situations can arise in a number of different factual settings, most of which are variations on two basic possibilities. The first of these basic situations is one in which the person borrowing the money has some interest in the real property, but there is some other person who also has an interest and who must join in the mortgage in order to grant a mortgage lien on the entire property. The second basic situation is one in which the person borrowing the money has no interest whatsoever in the real property to be mortgaged, and the borrower requests the owner of the real property to grant a mortgage as security for the payment of the debt. The owner may accede to this request either because the owner is a related party to the borrower or because the owner is itself obligated in some way to the borrower.

Let us consider the example of Holly Singer, who wishes to borrow $25,000.00 from Greene National Bank. Holly and her husband Fred are the owners of 2021 Spruce Street, Centre City. Holly has other asseets of her own, and is willing to be personally liable for repayment of the loan. Fred also has other assets of his own. Although he is willing to mortgage 2021 Spruce Street, and to lose it if the loan is not repaid, he is unwilling to risk any of his individual assets. Under these circumstances Holly alone, and not Fred, would sign the note. Both Holly and Fred would sign the mortgage, but the standard language of the mortgage would probably be reworked to make it clear that the obligation that the mortgage secured was not an obligation of both mortgagors, but was only the obligation of Holly. Additionally, Greene National Bank will be concerned that there is sufficient legal consideration for the agreement of Fred to join in the mortgage and it will therefore very likely include in

---

22. In some areas a "bond" is used in place of a note.

the mortgage a recitation that Fred is joining in the granting of the mortgage in order to induce Greene to make the loan to Holly.

Notes signed by persons under eighteen years of age (twenty-one years in some jurisdictions) are voidable[23] in many cases. If the person who has signed the note is less than eighteen at the time the note was signed, he or she can disavow the note and refuse to pay it. There are certain exceptions to this general rule. The drafter should ascertain whether the signatory is under eighteen and if so, should determine whether, under applicable state law, the minor signatory will be bound by the instrument. Similarly, a note signed by a person who is mentally incompetent may be voidable.

If the signatory is a trustee, the drafter will want to examine the document under which the trust has been created to ascertain whether the trustee has the authority to sign notes and subject the trust property to the lien of the mortgage. The same applies to guardians, executors, and administrators.

With reference to partnerships the general rule is that any partner may sign for the partnership if the mortgage is necessary for carrying on the business of the partnership in the usual way. However, the rules relating to partners' authority are not always entirely clear, and there are certain legal limitations on partners' authority. In any event it is generally considered good practice to obtain the signatures of all general partners and to obtain proof, by affidavit or otherwise, that the people who have signed are all of the general partners.

The question of authority to sign also arises in connection with corporations. A corporation is a legal entity and, as such, may sign notes and mortgages. However, the action of the corporation must be authorized by its board of directors, and the documents must be signed by natural persons authorized to do so by the board. Normally, these persons will be the corporation's officers. In some states if all or a substantial portion of the property of the corporation is to be mortgaged, a note and mortgage require the approval of the shareholders in addition to the approval of the directors. This should be checked in each instance.

To satisfy itself as the authority of the people signing the note or mortgage, the lender will want the borrower to provide resolutions of the board of directors (and the shareholders, if necessary) in substantially the following form:

> RESOLVED, that this corporation borrow the sum of $10,000.00 from the First National Bank to be repaid with interest at 10% per annum in 180 equal successive monthly installments of $107.47 each; and on such other terms and conditions as the President may deem proper;
> FURTHER RESOLVED, that to secure payment of the aforesaid loan this

---

23. Lawyers distinguish between agreements that are voidable and those that are void. A voidable agreement may be negated by the active denial of a person entitled to void it. A void agreement is void from its inception, and there is no requirement for anyone to perform an active denial in order for it to be void and unenforceable.

corporation create a first mortgage on its real estate known as 214 Main Street, Hartford, Ohio.

FURTHER RESOLVED, that the President or Vice-President be and they hereby are authorized, empowered and directed to execute, acknowledge, and deliver a mortgage note and mortgage in the foregoing amount, and to execute, acknowledge, and deliver such other documents and take such other steps as may be necessary or desirable to effectuate the foregoing resolutions.

B. PAYMENT

As discussed previously, residential mortgages are normally self-liquidating, level payment loans.[24] That is, the borrower makes identical payments during each month while the loan is being repaid. The payments are applied first to accrued interest at the rate set forth in the note and the remainder of the payment is used to reduce the principal. Because the principal is constantly being reduced, the amount of interest, which is payable only on the outstanding balance of the principal, is also reduced. Each succeeding month, therefore, a smaller amount is applied to interest and a larger amount to principal. The exact allocation of each payment can be determined from amortization schedules, which most lawyers can obtain for a particular loan.

The payment provision, which usually contains the most significant terms of the loan from the borrower's standpoint, should indicate the interest being charged, the number and frequency of payments, the allocation of payments between interest and principal, and the date on which the first payment is due.

An example of a level payment provision for a twenty-year loan of $20,000.00 with interest at the rate of 11% per annum follows:

> The principal, together with interest thereon at the rate of 11% per annum, shall be payable in 360 consecutive equal monthly installments of Two Hundred Thirty-Eight Dollars and Nine Cents ($238.09) each, commencing on the first day of June 1985, and thereafter on the same date of each month until the principal and interest are paid in full. The final payment of the entire indebtedness evidenced hereby, together with all accrued interest thereon, shall be due and payable on May 1, 2015.

Nonresidential mortgage notes often call for other than level payments. For example, a note might provide for principal to be paid in equal quarterly installments over a five-year period with interest payable at the same time on the then remaining balance. The principal payments will always be equal, but the interest payments will decline as the principal balance declines. An example of such a provision in regard to a $1,000,000.00 loan follows:

24. The concept of self-liquidating is also referred to as self-amortizing. When a debt is liquidated or amortized, it has been paid in full. When, by consecutive payments during the term of the loan, the loan is paid in full on the date of maturity, the loan is self-liquidating, or self-amortizing.

Beginning on January 1, 1985, principal shall be due and payable in forty successive quarter annual installments of Twenty-Five Thousand Dollars ($25,000) each, together with interest at the rate of 12% per annum, the final installment to be in the full amount of principal and interest then remaining due and unpaid, shall be due December 1, 2004.

A variation of the above provision is one in which the periodic payments would not be sufficient to liquidate the loan. For example, a $2,000,000.00 loan may call for quarterly principal payments of $50,000.00 during a five-year term of the loan. The final payment will have to include an extra $1,000,000.00. Such a note is said to contain a "balloon," referring to the extra large payment at the end.

PROBLEM

Prepare a repayment clause for a $1,200.00 loan bearing interest at 10% per annum. Payments are semiannual beginning January 1, 1985, with the first two payments being interest only. Beginning with the third payment, payments shall include principal of $100.00 plus interest. Loan matures on July 1, 1992.

C. PREPAYMENT PRIVILEGE

Another item that is frequently included in the note but not in the mortgage is the borrower's right to prepay. Particularly in periods when interest rates are high, lenders may provide either that the borrower may not make any prepayments of principal, or that the borrower may not prepay the entire loan. The borrower wants to reserve the privilege to prepay the loan at any time so that if interest rates should decline, the borrower would have the right to replace the existing loan with one at a lower interest rate. Prepayment is frequently a matter of intense negotiation between borrower and lender. Generally the lender is willing to permit prepayment but only after a number of years have elapsed and even then only on payment of a fee, sometimes called a "prepayment premium" or "prepayment penalty."

The prepayment penalty is generally set forth as a percentage of the amount prepaid, and in many cases the prepayment penalty declines as the loan grows older (and the lender has received most of the interest he or she originally anticipated receiving). For example, it is not unusual for a note in commercial transactions to provide that no prepayment is permitted for a period of ten years; and thereafter prepayment may be made, but only if the loan is paid in full and the prepayment is accompanied by a prepayment penalty that in the eleventh year is equal to 5% of the then outstanding balance. The amount of the prepayment penalty may decline each year thereafter until it is reduced to 1%, or even nothing. In many jurisdictions the failure to include a prepayment clause reserving to the borrower the right to make prepayments has the effect of barring any prepayment without the lender's consent. As a result, the provision permitting prepayment should be included even if no penalty or premium will be charged. In other jurisdictions, if the note is silent with respect to prepayment, the maker is presumed to be entitled to prepay the note. The legal assistant should be familiar with the laws of the jurisdiction that govern the note.

PROBLEM

Prepare a prepayment clause for the situation described in the preceding paragraph.

D. ACCELERATION

A note will generally provide for acceleration to maturity in the event of default. This means that if the borrower fails to pay even one installment when it is due, the lender may immediately declare the entire balance due at one time. Without the right to accelerate, the lender would be able to sue only for the amount then due, and would have to sue each month for the most recent default in payment. The following provision is a form of acceleration provision:

> It is hereby expressly agreed by Maker that, should any default be made in the payment of any installment of principal and/or interest as aforesaid on the date on which it shall fall due, or in the performance of any of the terms, agreements, or covenants contained in this Note, or in the Mortgage,[25] then the entire unpaid balance of such principal sum with interest accrued thereon and all other sums due by Maker hereunder or under the provisions of the Mortgage, shall at the option of Payee and without notice to Maker become due and payable immediately.

E. SPECIAL CLAUSES IN CONSTRUCTION LOAN NOTES— ADVANCE MONEY OBLIGATIONS

When a construction loan is settled the borrower may receive at settlement only funds required to pay certain settlement costs and sometimes the cost of acquiring the land. The borrower receives the remainder of the loan as the work progresses, generally by presenting vouchers or requisitions each month to the lender for work done during the prior month. The construction loan agreement, if one is used, will describe the procedures and contingencies necessary for disbursements of the loan.

---

[25] The provision that a default in the mortgage is a default in the note is called a cross-default provision. There may also be cross-default provisions with a loan agreement, assignment of lease, security agreement, or other collateral for the loan.

The note signed at settlement will normally be in the full amount of the loan, so that the borrower and the lender do not have to prepare and sign new notes every time the borrower wants an advance. In order for the note to reflect accurately the understanding of the parties, there will normally be a reference to the fact that sums are being advanced from time to time by the lender toward the stated principal sum of the note. A note that is accompanied by a construction loan agreement might contain the following type of clause:

> This Note and the accompanying Mortgage are made pursuant to a written Construction Loan Agreement between Maker and Payee, in connection with the construction of certain improvements on the mortgaged premises and the advance, from time to time, of sums evidenced by this Note in payment of labor and materials incorporated into the work, and associated costs, upon terms and conditions therein set forth. Advances under the aforesaid Construction Loan Agreement shall constitute advances of the principal of this Note. . . . Any breach of the aforesaid Construction Loan Agreement shall, at the option of Payee, constitute a default under this Note and the Mortgage, as a result of which Payee shall have all of the rights and remedies it would have in the event of default in the payment of any principal or interest due hereunder.

If a note is to be both a construction loan note and a permanent loan note, then certain other provisions will have to be revised from the normal form. The note will provide for two maturity dates; one if the permanent lender does purchase the note and another, earlier maturity date if the permanent lender does not purchase the note. Similarly, the note will provide for payment of interest only during the construction loan period and for amortized payments of interest (probably at a different rate) and principal if and when the permanent lender purchases the note.

There are various drafting techniques that might be used to prepare the provisions needed to reflect the dual purpose of the note. The most obvious technique, and one which is often difficult to perform well, is straight narrative. A second technique is to draft as if it were a permanent loan note and then to add a proviso as follows:

> Notwithstanding any contrary terms of payment contained herein, no payments of principal but interest only at a rate which is 2% in excess of the prime rate of interest charged by Payee from time to time, shall be paid by Maker on amounts actually advanced by Payee to or for the account of Maker, payable on the first day of each month, until such time as this Note has been assigned to the Permanent Lender. The outstanding principal balance of this Note, together with unpaid accrued interest shall be due and payable to Payee on _____, 19__, unless this Note has been earlier assigned to the Permanent Lender.

A third technique would be to deal with each concept in the alternative as follows:

> This Note shall be repaid as follows:
> a. Until such time as Payee has assigned this Note to the Permanent Lender, then . . .

b. From and after the date that this Note is assigned to the Permanent Lender, then . . .

This Note may be prepaid as follows:

a. Until such time as Payee has assigned this Note to the Permanent Lender, then . . .

b. From and after the date that this Note is assigned to the Permanent Lender, then . . .

A fourth technique would be to define certain terms such as Construction Loan Period, Permanent Settlement Date, and Permanent Loan Period, and then to group together all of the terms that are particular to the different provision of the Note:

Construction Loan Period

During the Construction Loan Period the following terms and conditions shall apply: . . .

Permanent Settlement Date

On the Permanent Settlement Date the following shall occur: . . .

Permanent Loan Period

During the Permanent Loan Period the following terms and conditions shall apply: . . .

The choice of techniques, and combinations thereof, should be based on both stylistic preferences and the particular complexities of the note in question. A careful drafter can employ any of the techniques and still accurately memorialize the intended transaction. A less experienced drafter might find it helpful to adopt some variation of the fourth technique, at least to the extent of defining terms. Errors and inaccuracies can often occur from a failure to define terms. For example, the permanent loan commitment might provide for no right of prepayment for the first ten years. If the prepayment clause is drafted to read, "Maker shall have no right of prepayment for the first ten years of this Note," then it will be inaccurate. The commitment letter undoubtedly intended that the ten-year period commence from the time the *permanent* lender makes its loan, whereas the drafted language causes the ten-year period to run from the date that the *construction* lender commences to make its loan. If terms have been defined, then the drafter could easily write that "Maker shall have no right of prepayment for ten years from the Permanent Settlement Date."

Example 7-10, which appears at the end of Part Six, is the form of note approved by Federal Home Loan Mortgage Corporation (FHLMC) and Federal National Mortgage Association (FNMA) for use nationwide.

II. DRAFTING MORTGAGES

A mortgage is the grant of an interest in real property to secure performance of the borrower's obligations under the note. In addition, the mortgage normally includes the agreement of borrower and lender with respect to various other items, such as payment of taxes, application of fire insurance proceeds, application of proceeds of any eminent domain award, and repairs to the property. An example of a mortgage *(Example 7-11)* is appended at the end of this Part Six. That example is the form of mortgage approved by FHLMC or FNMA for use nationwide.

A. PARTIES

The first part of the mortgage sets forth the date of the mortgage, the names of the parties and the background of the transaction that led to the creation of a mortgage.

> MORTGAGE, made this twenty-first day of June in the year one thousand nine hundred eighty-five between [*insert name of Mortgagor*] (hereinafter called "Mortgagor") (whether one or more than one), of the one part, and NATIONAL BANK, a national banking association organized and existing under the laws of the United States of America, having its principal place of business in the City of Dallas, Texas (hereinafter called "Mortgagee"), of the other part:
>
> WHEREAS, Mortgagor has executed and delivered to Mortgagee a certain promissory note of even date herewith (hereinafter called the "Note"), in favor of Mortgagee in the principal sum of One Hundred Thousand Dollars ($100,000.00) with interest thereon at the rate therein specified, and payable in the manner and at the times therein set forth and under the terms and conditions therein contained, all of which are incorporated herein by reference;[26]
>
> AND WHEREAS, Mortgagee may hereafter make further loans to Mortgagor and it is intended that the same, with interest, shall be secured hereby.[27]

The drafter must take care to use the precise name of the mortgagor and the mortgagor's capacity to execute the mortgage, as such appear in the last deed of record, if mortgagor is the same person as the grantee thereunder. The drafter must also be certain that the mortgagor is in fact the party who holds title to the real estate.

B. CONVEYANCE—DESCRIPTION

Just as with a deed, a precise description of the property is set forth in the mortgage. Generally, there is no disagreement between the parties concerning the description.[28] The drafter should be sure that the descrip-

---

26. The practice in some areas, by force of custom or law, is to recite the exact repayment terms of the note in the mortgage. Where this is not necessary, it is probably undesirable, as it can lead to question of loss of priority of right on a modification of terms of repayment.

27. In many jurisdictions this clause is necessary in order to obtain mortgage security for other funds later advanced to the borrower. This clause does not grant priority to such further loans, but does grant security for them.

28. The most common problems arise when there has been assemblance of a large tract from several smaller tracts and an overall perimeter description is to be used.

tion has been checked against a survey, wherever possible, to be sure that the description accurately represents the property borrower and lender intended to be mortgaged. A survey will also illustrate the location of any buildings on the mortgaged premises so that a review will show whether they are within the boundary lines and therefore subject to the mortgage.

C. PROPERTY INCLUDED

If there is a particular easement or appurtenance that is important to the property, it should be mentioned specifically and described by metes and bounds. In addition, if the lender intends to obtain a lien on certain personal property, the mortgage should describe that property specifically and contain, either here or at some other place in the mortgage, a statement that the mortgage is intended to create a security interest in personal property under the Uniform Commercial Code. Generally, a borrower will not object to this clause, unless the borrower intends to obtain separate financing for some or all of the personal property, or unless the borrower does not have unencumbered title to the personal property in question.

> Together with all and singular the present and future buildings, additions, and improvements as well as any and all fixtures, appliances, and equipment of any nature whatsoever now or hereafter installed in or upon said premises or used in connection with the premises or the operation of the plant, business or dwelling situate thereon, streets, alleys, passages, ways, waters, water courses, rights, liberties, privileges, hereditaments, and appurtenances whatsoever thereunto belonging, or in any wise appertaining, and the reversions and remainders, rents, issues, and profits thereof, now or hereafter accruing.

D. HABENDUM

A mortgage will contain a habendum clause similar to the habendum clause in a deed. Although it is absolute in form, the conveyance will become ineffective as a matter of law when the mortgage debt has been paid.

> TO HAVE AND TO HOLD said property, hereby granted, or mentioned and intended so to be, with the appurtenances (such property and appurtenances being hereinafter referred to together as the "Mortgaged Property"), unto Mortgagee, for its own use forever, in fee.

Even though the mortgage, as a matter of law, will be ineffective when the debt has been paid, the borrower would like to include an additional clause to that effect, called a defeasance clause, substantially as follows:

> If Mortgagor pays to Mortgagee said principal sum and all other sums payable by Mortgagor to Mortgagee as are hereby secured, in accordance with the provisions of said Note and in the manner and at the times therein

set forth, without deduction, fraud, or delay, then and from thenceforth this Mortgage, and the estate hereby granted, shall cease and become void, notwithstanding anything herein contained to the contrary.

E. TAXES

In general, the lien of a mortgage takes priority over any lien that arises subsequent to the time the mortgage has been recorded. There are certain liens, however, such as liens for real estate taxes and taxes owed state and local governments by corporate borrowers, that will take precedence over the lien of the mortgage. This means that on a foreclosure sale, the fund produced at the sale will be paid first to satisfy these prior liens for taxes and then to satisfy the mortgage. To protect itself against this situation, the mortgagee wants to be sure that all of such taxes are paid when due, and are not permitted to accumulate. The mortgagee may only require that the mortgagor present evidence of payment of such taxes before they are due (as in the first provision below) or it may require the mortgagor to deposit in escrow each month $\frac{1}{12}$ of the estimated yearly taxes (as in the second provision below).

> Until the entire indebtedness secured by this Mortgage, including all sums due Mortgagee under the terms of this Mortgage and of the Note, with interest, is fully paid, Mortgagor covenants and agrees:
>
> (1) *No Escrow.*
>
> To pay when due and payable and before interest and penalties are due thereon all taxes, water and sewer rents, assessments and all other charges or claims which may be assessed or levied upon the Mortgaged Property at any time, by any lawful authority, and which by any present or future law may have priority over said indebtedness either in lien or in distribution out of the proceeds of any judicial sale, and to produce to Mortgagee on or before the last day upon which they may be paid without penalty or interest, receipts of the current year for the payment of all such taxes, water and sewer rents, assessments, charges and claims.
>
> (2) *Escrow.*
>
> To pay to Mortgagee, if requested, on each installment due date an additional sum equal to one-twelfth of the annual taxes, assessments and water and sewer charges, if any, on the Mortgaged Property. If the fund so held by Mortgagee shall be insufficient to pay any of the aforesaid items when due, Mortgagor upon demand shall deposit with Mortgagee such additional funds as may be necessary to remove such deficiency. All the sums deposited with Mortgagee may be comingled with Mortgagee's general funds and shall be non-interest bearing. In the event title to the Mortgaged Property passes to another party either voluntarily or by operation of law, all the right, title and interest of Mortgagor in the aforesaid fund shall pass to the new owner of the Mortgaged Property, or at the option of Mortgagee be used to reduce the mortgage debt.

Generally, the mortgagor will not object to clause (1), although the mortgagor may object to clause (2) because it forces the mortgagor to tie up money during the year in a non–interest-bearing account. In either case the mortgagor wants to be in a position to contest real estate taxes if the mortgagor thinks they are excessive, without being in default under the mortgage. Accordingly, the mortgagor will want to include a clause substantially as follows:

> However, if Mortgagor in good faith and by appropriate legal action shall contest the validity of any such item, or the amount thereof, and, if required by Mortgagee, shall have furnished reasonable assurance satisfactory to Mortgagee indemnifying it against any loss by reason of such contest, then Mortgagor shall not be required to pay the item or to produce the required receipts so long as the contest operates to prevent collection, is maintained and prosecuted with diligence, and shall not have been terminated or discontinued adversely to Mortgagor.

F. INSURANCE

The mortgage will contain a provision requiring the mortgagee to keep the premises adequately insured against loss by fire or other casualty. Unlike the sample clause below, the provision may require monthly payment to mortgagee of $\frac{1}{12}$th of the insurance premiums due for a year. In the latter case the mortgagee will use the fund to pay the annual premium.

> Mortgagor shall maintain insurance on the Mortgaged Property of such kinds, in such amounts, and with such companies as are satisfactory to Mortgagee; and if such insurance or any part thereof shall expire, or be withdrawn, or become void by breach of any condition thereof by Mortgagor, or become void or unsafe by reason of the failure or impairment of the capital of any company in which such insurance may then be, or if for any other reason whatsoever such insurance shall become unsatisfactory to Mortgagee, to effect new insurance on the Mortgaged Property satisfactory to Mortgagee; and to pay as they shall become due all premiums for such insurance; and to lodge with Mortgagee, as further security for such indebtedness, all policies therefor, with loss payable clauses in favor of and acceptable to Mortgagee. In event of loss Mortgagor will give immediate notice by mail to Mortgagee, and Mortgagee may make proof of loss if not made promptly by Mortgagor. Mortgagor hereby directs any insurance company concerned to pay directly to Mortgagee any moneys not in excess of the unpaid balance of said indebtedness which may become payable under such insurance, including return of unearned premiums, such moneys, or any part thereof, to be applied at the option of Mortgagee to said unpaid balance or to the repair of the property damaged; and Mortgagor appoints Mortgagee as attorney in fact to endorse any draft therefor.

The provisions of the mortgage relating to insurance are frequently the most difficult in the mortgage. The mortgagor will not object to the requirement that insurance be carried nor to the requirement that the insurance policy bear a standard form of "mortgage clause" that makes losses payable to the mortgagor and mortgagee jointly. The mortgagor can understand the mortgagee's concern that in the event of fire its security may disappear. The mortgagor, however, will want the mortgagee to agree to make the insurance proceeds available to reconstruct the building. Otherwise, the mortgagee may elect to apply the insurance proceeds from a substantial fire to payment of the debt, and the mortgagor may be left with a partially gutted building and no funds with which to reconstruct. The mortgagor, therefore, will want to add a clause substantially as follows:

> All insurance proceeds shall be made available to Mortgagor for repair and restoration of the Mortgaged Property. Such proceeds shall be paid to Mortgagee to be held in trust and disbursed to Mortgagor from time to time as the work proceeds, provided such advances shall not be made more often than twice in each calendar month and shall not exceed 90% of the value of labor and materials for which an advance is requested, with the balance due upon delivery of a certificate of substantial completion from a licensed engineer or architect.

The above clause provides some safeguards for the mortgagee by permitting it to hold the funds and disburse them from time to time as work progresses, much in the manner of a construction lender. In the case of a substantial fire, the mortgagee must be sure that the building as reconstructed will be satisfactory for the balance of the loan.

G. MAINTENANCE

To protect the security, the mortgagee will want a clause requiring the mortgagor to keep the property in repair.

> Mortgagor shall maintain the Mortgaged Property in good repair, order and condition; Mortgagor shall not remove from the Mortgaged Property fixtures, appliances and equipment of any nature covered by the lien of this Mortgage without having obtained the prior written consent of Mortgagee; and Mortgagor shall not make, install, or permit to be made or installed, any alterations, additions, improvements, fixtures, appliances, or equipment of any nature to or in the Mortgaged Property without obtaining the prior written consent of Mortgagee, which consent Mortgagee hereby reserves the right to refuse or grant at its sole discretion.

Although not objecting to maintaining the property in good repair, the mortgagor may object strenuously to the portion of the above clause that prevents the mortgagor from removing fixtures, appliances, and equipment or making any alterations. Such a clause may restrict the mortgagor's freedom of action much more than is really necessary to afford protection to the mortgagee. The mortgagor would much prefer a clause substantially as follows:

> Mortgagor shall maintain the Mortgaged Property in good condition and repair, reasonable wear and tear alone excepted.

H. CONDEMNATION

Governmental agencies have the power, under certain circumstances, to obtain property by condemnation. The holder of a mortgage on land that is condemned will lose its security. The mortgagee, therefore, will want to make certain that the award be first applied to pay off the mortgage. A sample provision follows:

> Mortgagor shall notify Mortgagee promptly upon receiving any notice of commencement of any proceedings for the condemnation of the Mortgaged Property, and shall permit Mortgagee to participate in such proceedings and to receive all proceeds payable to Mortgagor as an award or in settlement up to the amount of the unpaid principal, accrued interest and any other sums due hereunder.

As in the case of loss by fire, the mortgagor will want to have the mortgagee agree to make the proceeds available for reconstruction in the event only a part of the mortgaged premises is condemned, for example, to make way for a road. Accordingly, the mortgagor will want to add the following:

> If only a part of the Mortgaged Property is condemned, Mortgagor shall promptly restore the remaining portion of the Mortgaged Property so that it will constitute a complete architectural unit and upon completion of such work, the condemnation award shall be released to Mortgagor to pay the reasonable cost thereof. If the Mortgaged Property cannot be restored to a complete architectural unit, or if the condemnation is so extensive that the Mortgaged Property would not, after restoration, be suitable for the use to which it was put prior to condemnation, the condemnation shall be considered a total taking.

I. FINANCIAL STATEMENTS

Some Mortgages on income-producing properties will provide for the mortgagor to submit financial statements to the mortgagee periodically.

> Mortgagor shall furnish Mortgagee within sixty (60) days of the close of each fiscal year audited statements prepared by independent certified public accountants satisfactory to Mortgagee, in such detail as Mortgagee may reasonably require.

The mortgagor may want the words "audited" and "independent" deleted from the above clause because preparation of audited financial statements involve greater expense to a mortgagor than do unaudited statements. In addition, engaging an "independent" accountant may also involve additional expense if the mortgagor is a company that has accountants on its own staff.

J. MORTGAGEE'S PERFORMANCE FOR MORTGAGOR

In the event the mortgagor fails to make any payment relating to the property that could jeopardize the mortgagee's first lien or jeopardize the security itself, the mortgagee will want the power to make such payment on behalf of the mortgagor and charge the mortgagor for the same.

> In the event Mortgagor should fail to pay said taxes, water and sewer rents, assessments, charges, claims, costs, expenses or fees or to maintain such insurance, or to make all necessary repairs to the Mortgaged Property, all as herein before provided, Mortgagee may at Mortgagee's sole option and without notice to Mortgagor, advance sums on behalf of Mortgagor in payment of said taxes, water and sewer rents, assessments, charges, claims, costs, expenses, fees, insurance and repairs, which repairs Mortgagor hereby authorizes Mortgagee to make, without prejudice to the right of enforcement of the obligation of the Note, or the other remedies of Mortgagee as herein set forth, by reason of the failure of Mortgagor to make payment of the same; and all such sums so advanced by Mortgagee shall be added to and become a part of the indebtedness secured hereby, and repayment thereof, with interest thereon at the rate set forth in said Note, from the dates of their respective expenditures, may be enforced by Mortgagee against Mortgagor at any time.

From the standpoint of the mortgagor, the main objection to this clause is the phrase "at Mortgagee's sole option and without notice to Mortgagor." The mortgagor will not object to the above clause provided the mortgagor has notice and an opportunity to make the payment. In some cases, the mortgagor may have a good reason for not wanting to make the payment. For example, the mortgagor may wish to contest a tax or assessment. The mortgagor would want to insert, in lieu of the words "at Mortgagee's sole option and without notice to Mortgagor," the words "unless Mortgagor has made such payment within thirty (30) days after written notice from mortgagee to do so," and the mortgagor will also want to add at the end of the clause a statement substantially as follows:

> Mortgagor's obligations to make the payments provided in this paragraph within thirty (30) days after notice as aforesaid are subject to Mortgagor's right to contest taxes, assessments, and other impositions as hereinabove provided.

K. DEFAULT—REMEDIES

In the event of default by the mortgagor or any of his or her obligations under the note or mortgage, the mortgagee desires a full range of legal remedies to protect itself from loss. The remedies desired are (a) foreclosure, (b) the right to take over possession of the mortgaged premises, and (c) the right to sue the mortgagor for the balance of principal and interest due on the note as well as any expenses incurred by the mortgagee as a result of the default.

> When such principal sum or any unpaid balance thereof shall become due and payable, or in case default shall be made in the payment of

any installment of principal and/or interest on the date on which it shall fall due in accordance with the provisions of said Note, or in the performance of any of the terms, agreements or covenants contained in said Note or in this Mortgage, then Mortgagee may forthwith and without further delay:

(a) institute an action of mortgage foreclosure against the Mortgaged Property, or take such other action at law or in equity for the enforcement hereof and realization on the within mortgage security as the law may allow, and may proceed thereon to final judgment and execution thereon for the entire unpaid balance of such principal sum, with interest at the rate stipulated in said Note together with all other sums due by Mortgagor in accordance with the provisions hereof and of the Note, including all sums which may have been loaned by Mortgagee to Mortgagor after the date of this Mortgage, and all sums which may have been advanced by Mortgagee for taxes, water or sewer rents, charges or claims, insurance or repairs to the Mortgaged Property, all costs of suit, together with interest at six percent (6%) per annum on any judgment obtained by Mortgagee from and after the date of any Sheriff's Sale until actual payment is made by the Sheriff of the full amount due Mortgagee and reasonable attorneys' fees. Without any law, usage or custom to the contrary notwithstanding; and/or

(b) enter into possession of the Mortgaged Property, with or without legal action, and by force if necessary; collect all rentals therefrom and, after deducting all costs of collection and administration expense, apply the net rentals to the payment of taxes, water and sewer rents, charges and claims, insurance premiums and all other carrying charges, and to the maintenance, repair or restoration of the Mortgaged Property, or on account and in reduction of the principal and/or interest hereby secured, in such order and amounts as Mortgagee, at Mortgagee's sole discretion, may elect; and for such purpose Mortgagor hereby assigns to Mortgagee all rentals due and to become due under any lease or leases of the Mortgaged Property whether now existing or hereafter created, as well as all rights and remedies provided in such lease or leases for the collection of said rents.

The remedies of Mortgagee as provided herein, or in the Note, shall be cumulative and concurrent, and may be pursued singly, successively, or together against Mortgagor and/or the Mortgaged Property at the sole discretion of Mortgagee, and the failure to exercise any such right or remedy shall in no event be construed as a waiver or release of the same.

Mortgagor hereby waives and releases all errors, defects, and imperfections in any proceedings instituted by Mortgagee under this Mortgage, as well as all benefit that might accrue to Mortgagor by virtue of any present or future laws exempting the Mortgaged Property, or any part of the proceeds arising from any sale thereof, from attachment, levy or sale under execution, or providing for any stay of execution, exemption from civil process, or extension of time for payment.

The words Mortgagor and Mortgagee whenever occurring herein shall be deemed and construed to include the respective heirs, personal representatives, successors and assigns of Mortgagor and Mortgagee; and if there shall be more than one Mortgagor, the obligation of each shall be joint and several. This Mortgage shall be governed by and construed according to the laws of the State of Pennsylvania.

Generally, neither party will object to the inclusion of this clause. Ordinarily, a mortgage will be construed according to the laws of the state in which the mortgaged property is located.[29]

L. WARRANTY OF TITLE

Sometimes the mortgagee will desire the mortgagor to warrant the title of the mortgaged premises.

> Mortgagor warrants and will warrant specially the property hereby conveyed.

The Mortgagor will generally prefer to omit this clause entirely, especially in areas in which the mortgagee obtains title insurance at the mortgagor's expense. The effect of this clause is to make the mortgagor a title insurer. If the mortgagee has a title insurance policy from a title insurance company, it is unnecessary to impose this additional burden on the mortgagor.

M. PAYMENT OF SUMS SECURED

Although it is unnecessary, mortgagees generally like to insert a clause that repeats the provision of the note requiring the various payments to be made to the mortgagee. The mortgagor generally has no substantial objection to such a provision, unless the mortgagor is not the same person as the maker of the note. If this is so, then this clause must be deleted.

> Mortgagor shall pay to Mortgagee the principal of and interest upon the Note according to the terms of the Note secured hereby, reasonable charges fixed by Mortgagee to satisfy and discharge this Mortgage of record, and all other sums hereby secured; and shall keep and perform every other covenant and agreement of the Note and this Mortgage.

N. SECURITY AGREEMENT

As mentioned previously, the mortgagee will often want a lien against the mortgagor's personal property located at the premises, as additional security for the loan. Furthermore, a security agreement may be used to obtain a lien on property that is not clearly real property and not clearly personal property. The security agreement may be a separate document or it may be included within the mortgage.

> This Mortgage creates a security interest in the personal property included in the Mortgaged Premises and constitutes a security agreement under the Uniform Commercial Code. Mortgagor shall execute, file and refile such financing statements or other security agreements as Mortgagee shall require from time to time with respect to property included in the Mortgaged Premises.

---

29. Some large lenders, especially those based in New York, require that New York law shall apply to all transactions because their attorneys believe that the documents are satisfactory if interpreted by New York law.

Such a provision may raise problems where a security interest has already been given in regard to certain items of personal property. For example, a mortgagor that financed with a bank the purchase of office equipment used on the mortgaged property will probably have granted the bank a security interest in the equipment. Even if some personal property is not subject to a security interest, the mortgagor may wish to use that as collateral to secure an additional loan. If either of the above problems is present, the mortgagor may refuse to grant the mortgagee a security interest in the personal property or may wish to limit the interest to specified items of personal property. This result could be accomplished by the following clause:

> This Mortgage creates a security interest and constitutes a security agreement under the Uniform Commercial Code in those items of personal property located at the Mortgaged Premises as set forth in Exhibit A hereto. Mortgagor shall execute, file and refile such financing statements or other security agreements as Mortgagee shall require from time to time with respect to such property located at the Mortgaged Premises.

O. TRANSFER OF TITLE

Often the mortgagee will require a clause providing that a transfer of title to the mortgaged premises is a default of the note and mortgage. The effect of such a provision is that the mortgagor cannot sell the property subject to the mortgage. Selling the property subject to an existing mortgage would be desirable if the prospective buyer is unable to obtain a mortgage as favorable as that presently on the property.

> A transfer by sale, gift, devise, operation of law or otherwise of the fee title interest in all or any portion of the Mortgaged Premises shall have the same consequences as an event of default respecting the indebtedness secured hereby, and upon such transfer, Mortgagee, without prior notice or the lapse of any period of grace or the right to cure, shall have the right to declare all sums secured hereby immediately due and payable, and, upon failure by Mortgagor to make such payment within thirty days of written demand therefor, Mortgagee shall have the right to exercise all remedies provided in the Note, this Mortgage, or otherwise at law.

This is a harsh provision that the mortgagor may resist. A "due on sale" clause gives a mortgagee the right to call the loan and thus prevent a sale on terms that might otherwise be desirable to the mortgagor, particularly if interest rates have risen substantially since the mortgage was obtained. The mortgagor may argue that sale does not really endanger the loan, since the sale does not diminish the personal liability (if any) of the original mortgagor. However, where the property is commercial, the mortgagee may insist that its security is affected by the identity of the owner and by the owner's ability to operate the property on a profitable basis.

P. CONSTRUCTION MORTGAGE

When the mortgage is being used in connection with a construction loan, the mortgagee will often want to include a provision that makes a breach of the construction loan agreement a breach of the mortgage.

> This Mortgage and the accompanying Note are made pursuant to a written Construction Loan Agreement, signed or about to be signed between Mortgagor and Mortgagee, with reference to construction of certain improvements on the Mortgaged Premises. Any breach of the aforesaid Construction Loan Agreement shall, at the option of Mortgagee, constitute a default under the Note and this Mortgage, as a result of which Mortgagee shall have all of the rights and remedies it would have in the event of a default in the payment of any principal or interest due hereunder.

Q. LIMITATION OF LIABILITY

There may be situations in which the lender is willing to rely entirely on the real estate for repayment of the debt, and waive its rights to look also to the other assets of the borrower. As previously discussed, this protects the borrower from personal liability and is referred to as "non-recourse financing." This is commonly done in connection with income-producing property when the mortgagee is satisfied that the income will be more than adequate to cover the debt service, taxes, insurance, and other carrying charges. The mortgagor is willing to accept the risk that he may lose the property if he fails to pay the mortgage debt, but he would certainly prefer not to expose any other assets he may have in the event the value of the mortgaged property turns out to be less than anticipated.

> Enforcement of the debt evidenced by the Note, and the obligation of Mortgagor under this mortgage, shall be limited to the Mortgaged Premises. The lien of any judgment against Mortgagor in any proceeding instituted on, under or in connection with this mortgage or the Note shall not extend to any property now or hereafter owned by Mortgagor other than the Mortgaged Premises, and the judgment index and docket will be so noted.

R. SECOND MORTGAGE CLAUSE

A second mortgagee holds a mortgage subject to the existing first mortgage. In the event of foreclosure on the first mortgage, the funds generated at the sale will not be divided pro rata between the first mortgagee and the second mortgagee, but will be paid entirely to the first mortgagee up to the full amount owed to it. Only the excess, if any, will be paid to the second mortgagee and such foreclosure sale will foreclose the second mortgagee's security interest in the property. In many cases the second mortgagee will bid the amount of the first mortgage at the sheriff's sale unless there is another bidder who is willing to pay the total amount of both mortgages. By acquiring the property, the second mortgagee is in the position of being able to recover the debt if it can resell the property at some future date for a price equal to the purchase price plus the second mortgage.

The second mortgagee is, therefore, concerned that the mortgagor avoid default under the first mortgage, which could give the first mortgagee reason to accelerate the mortgage debt and precipitate a foreclosure. To protect itself, the second mortgagee may require proof of payments on the first mortgage (so it will immediately be aware of any default), and in the event of such a default, it will want the right to accelerate the second mortgage loan to maturity so that the full amount of its mortgage loan will be payable at the sheriff's sale in the event that there are bidders. The second mortgagee increases its security with every payment that is made on the first mortgage because with every payment the debt that has priority over the second mortgage is decreased. Accordingly, the second mortgagee does not want the borrower to be in a position to defer amortization (principal payments) on the first mortgage. To deal with these problems, the second mortgagee will generally insist on a clause similar to the following in the second mortgage:

> This Mortgage is under and subject to the lien of the existing first mortgage in the original principal amount of $_____ which has since been reduced by payments on account to $_____ held by the Savings Bank (the "prior lien"). With respect to the prior lien, Mortgagor agrees as follows:
>
> 1. Mortgagor will pay the principal, interest and all other sums when due and payable under the prior lien no later than their due date, and will comply with all of the other terms, covenants and conditions thereof; and
>
> 2. Mortgagor will, upon written notice, forward to Mortgagee on or before said due date, copies of checks, or receipts or other evidence of payment satisfactory to the Mortgagee, that the aforesaid sums have been seasonably made; and
>
> 3. Mortgagor will not enter into any agreement or arrangement, without the prior written consent of Mortgagee, pursuant to which Mortgagor is granted any forebearance or indulgence (as to time or amount) in the payment of any principal, interest or other sums due in accordance with the terms and provisions of the prior lien. Any default by Mortgagor under the prior lien, by failure to make payment or otherwise to comply with the terms thereof, or any failure by Mortgagor to produce receipts, or Mortgagor's entering into an agreement contrary to the provisions of this paragraph shall constitute a default under this Mortgage, and Mortgagee shall have the right, at its election, to declare immediately due and payable the entire indebtedness secured hereby with interest and other appropriate charges. Mortgagee, at its election, and without notice to Mortgagor, may make, but shall not be obligated to make, any payments Mortgagor has failed to make under the prior lien but such payment by Mortgagee shall not release Mortgagor from Mortgagor's obligations or constitute a waiver of Mortgagor's default hereunder.

The clause set forth above does not really protect the second mortgagee from the possibility of default under the first mortgage; it simply gives it a way of discovering such a default promptly. A much better solution for the second mortgagee is to obtain a letter from the first mortgagee pursuant to which first mortgagee agrees to give the second mortgagee notice of default and a ten-day period within which to cure any default. Second mortgagees customarily ask for such a letter, but first mortgagees are not always willing to give it.

S. EXECUTION

The final section of a mortgage has one or more lines for the mortgagor's signature. This section appears in the usual forms that you have previously seen.

T. ACKNOWLEDGMENTS

In order to be valid as against other creditors of the mortgagor, the mortgage must be recorded in the proper place for the jurisdiction in which the real estate is situated. Once recorded, the mortgage becomes a public record that any other prospective creditor is bound to search for and find. To be recorded, the mortgage must be acknowledged before a proper official. The form for acknowledgments varies from state to state, and the drafter should be sure to use the proper form (individual, partnership, or corporate) for the state in which the real estate is situated. If the mortgage is signed and acknowledged in one state but is to be recorded in another, it must bear the acknowledgment form of the state in which it is to be recorded. Generally, a telephone call to the recording office in the jurisdiction in which the real estate is located can verify that the form is appropriate.

Example 7-10: Note

___

NOTE

...., 19.........			...., ...
						[City]				[State]

....
					[Property Address]

1. BORROWER'S PROMISE TO PAY

In return for a loan that I have received, I promise to pay U.S. $... (this amount is called "principal"), plus interest, to the order of the Lender. The Lender is ....
.... I understand that the Lender may transfer this Note. The Lender or anyone who takes this Note by transfer and who is entitled to receive payments under this Note is called the "Note Holder."

2. INTEREST

Interest will be charged on unpaid principal until the full amount of principal has been paid. I will pay interest at a yearly rate of ....%.

The interest rate required by this Section 2 is the rate I will pay both before and after any default described in Section 6(B) of this Note.

3. PAYMENTS

(A) **Time and Place of Payments**

I will pay principal and interest by making payments every month.

I will make my monthly payments on the .... day of each month beginning on ...., 19.......... I will make these payments every month until I have paid all of the principal and interest and any other charges described below that I may owe under this Note. My monthly payments will be applied to interest before principal. If, on

...., ..., I still owe amounts under this Note, I will pay those amounts in full on that date, which is called the "maturity date."

I will make my monthly payments at ....
.... or at a different place if required by the Note Holder.

(B) Amount of Monthly Payments
My monthly payment will be in the amount of U.S. $..

4. BORROWER'S RIGHT TO PREPAY

I have the right to make payments of principal at any time before they are due. A payment of principal only is known as a "prepayment." When I make a prepayment, I will tell the Note Holder in writing that I am doing so.

I may make a full prepayment or partial prepayments without paying any prepayment charge. The Note Holder will use all of my prepayments to reduce the amount of principal that I owe under this Note. If I make a partial prepayment, there will be no changes in the due date or in the amount of my monthly payment unless the Note Holder agrees in writing to those changes.

5. LOAN CHARGES

If a law, which applies to this loan and which sets maximum loan charges, is finally interpreted so that the interest or other loan charges collected or to be collected in connection with this loan exceed the permitted limits, then: (i) any such loan charge shall be reduced by the amount necessary to reduce the charge to the permitted limit; and (ii) any sums already collected from me which exceeded permitted limits will be refunded to me. The Note Holder may choose to make this refund by reducing the principal I owe under this Note or by making a direct payment to me. If a refund reduces principal, the reduction will be treated as a partial prepayment.

6. BORROWER'S FAILURE TO PAY AS REQUIRED

(A) Late Charge for Overdue Payments
If the Note Holder has not received the full amount of any monthly payment by the end of .... calendar days after the date it is due, I will pay a late charge to the Note Holder. The amount of the charge will be ....% of my overdue payment of principal and interest. I will pay this late charge promptly but only once on each late payment.

(B) Default
If I do not pay the full amount of each monthly payment on the date it is due, I will be in default.

(C) Notice of Default
If I am in default, the Note Holder may send me a written notice telling me that if I do not pay the overdue amount by a certain date, the Note Holder may require me to pay immediately the full amount of principal which has not been paid and all the interest that I owe on that amount. That date must be at least 30 days after the date on which the notice is delivered or mailed to me.

(D) No Waiver By Note Holder
Even if, at a time when I am in default, the Note Holder does not require me to pay immediately in full as described above, the Note Holder will still have the right to do so if I am in default at a later time.

(E) Payment of Note Holder's Costs and Expenses
If the Note Holder has required me to pay immediately in full as described above, the Note Holder will have the right to be paid back by me for all of its costs and expenses in enforcing this Note to the extent not prohibited by applicable law. Those expenses include, for example, reasonable attorneys' fees.

7. GIVING OF NOTICES

Unless applicable law requires a different method, any notice that must be given to me under this Note will be given by delivering it or by mailing it by first class mail to me at the Property Address above or at a different address if I give the Note Holder a notice of my different address.

Any notice that must be given to the Note Holder under this Note will be given by mailing it by first class mail to the Note Holder at the address stated in Section 3(A) above or at a different address if I am given a notice of that different address.

8. OBLIGATIONS OF PERSONS UNDER THIS NOTE

If more than one person signs this Note, each person is fully and personally obligated to keep all of the promises made in this Note, including the promise to pay the full amount owed. Any person who is a guarantor, surety or endorser of this Note is also obligated to do these things. Any person who takes over these obligations, including the obligations of a guarantor, surety or endorser of this Note, is also obligated to keep all of the promises made in this Note. The Note Holder may enforce its rights under this Note against each person individually or against all of us together. This means that any one of us may be required to pay all of the amounts owed under this Note.

9. WAIVERS

I and any other person who has obligations under this Note waive the rights of presentment and notice of dishonor. "Presentment" means the right to require the Note Holder to demand payment of amounts due. "Notice of dishonor" means the right to require the Note Holder to give notice to other persons that amounts due have not been paid.

10. UNIFORM SECURED NOTE

This Note is a uniform instrument with limited variations in some jurisdictions. In addition to the protections given to the Note Holder under this Note, a Mortgage, Deed of Trust or Security Deed (the "Security Instrument"), dated the same date as this Note, protects the Note Holder from possible losses which might result if I do not keep the promises which I make in this Note. That Security Instrument describes how and under what conditions I may be required to make immediate payment in full of all amounts I owe under this Note. Some of those conditions are described as follows:

Transfer of the Property or a Beneficial Interest in Borrower. If all or any part of the Property or any interest in it is sold or transferred (or if a beneficial interest in Borrower is sold or transferred and Borrower is not a natural person) without Lender's prior written consent, Lender may, at its option, require immediate payment in full of all sums secured by this Security Instrument. However, this option shall not be exercised by Lender if exercise is prohibited by federal law as of the date of this Security Instrument.

If Lender exercises this option, Lender shall give Borrower notice of acceleration. The notice shall provide a period of not less than 30 days from the date the notice is delivered or mailed within which Borrower must pay all sums secured by this Security Instrument. If Borrower fails to pay these sums prior to

MULTISTATE FIXED RATE NOTE—Single Family—FNMA/FHLMC UNIFORM INSTRUMENT   Form 3200 12/83

Continued.

Example 7-10 Note *continued*

the expiration of this period, Lender may invoke any remedies permitted by this Security Instrument without further notice or demand on Borrower.

WITNESS THE HAND(S) AND SEAL(S) OF THE UNDERSIGNED.

....(Seal)
-Borrower

....(Seal)
-Borrower

....(Seal)
-Borrower

[Sign Original Only]

Example 7-11: **Mortgage**

——————————— [Space Above This Line For Recording Data] ———————————

MORTGAGE

THIS MORTGAGE ("Security Instrument") is given on ....,
19......... The mortgagor is ....
.... ("Borrower"). This Security Instrument is given to ....
...., which is organized and existing
under the laws of ...., and whose address is ....
.... ("Lender").
Borrower owes Lender the principal sum of ....
.... Dollars (U.S. $...............................). This debt is evidenced by Borrower's note
dated the same date as this Security Instrument ("Note"), which provides for monthly payments, with the full debt, if not
paid earlier, due and payable on .... This Security Instrument
secures to Lender: (a) the repayment of the debt evidenced by the Note, with interest, and all renewals, extensions and
modifications; (b) the payment of all other sums, with interest, advanced under paragraph 7 to protect the security of this
Security Instrument; and (c) the performance of Borrower's covenants and agreements under this Security Instrument and
the Note. For this purpose, Borrower does hereby mortgage, grant and convey to Lender the following described property
located in .... County, Pennsylvania:

which has the address of ...., ...,
                                     [Street]   [City]
Pennsylvania .... ("Property Address");
                  [Zip Code]

TOGETHER WITH all the improvements now or hereafter erected on the property, and all easements, rights, appurtenances, rents, royalties, mineral, oil and gas rights and profits, water rights and stock and all fixtures now or hereafter a part of the property. All replacements and additions shall also be covered by this Security Instrument. All of the foregoing is referred to in this Security Instrument as the "Property."

BORROWER COVENANTS that Borrower is lawfully seised of the estate hereby conveyed and has the right to mortgage, grant and convey the Property and that the Property is unencumbered, except for encumbrances of record. Borrower warrants and will defend generally the title to the Property against all claims and demands, subject to any encumbrances of record.

THIS SECURITY INSTRUMENT combines uniform covenants for national use and non-uniform covenants with limited variations by jurisdiction to constitute a uniform security instrument covering real property.

PENNSYLVANIA—Single Family—**FNMA/FHLMC UNIFORM INSTRUMENT**   Form 3039 12/83

UNIFORM COVENANTS. Borrower and Lender covenant and agree as follows:

1. Payment of Principal and Interest; Prepayment and Late Charges. Borrower shall promptly pay when due the principal of and interest on the debt evidenced by the Note and any prepayment and late charges due under the Note.

2. Funds for Taxes and Insurance. Subject to applicable law or to a written waiver by Lender, Borrower shall pay to Lender on the day monthly payments are due under the Note, until the Note is paid in full, a sum ("Funds") equal to one-twelfth of: (a) yearly taxes and assessments which may attain priority over this Security Instrument; (b) yearly leasehold payments or ground rents on the Property, if any; (c) yearly hazard insurance premiums; and (d) yearly mortgage insurance premiums, if any. These items are called "escrow items." Lender may estimate the Funds due on the basis of current data and reasonable estimates of future escrow items.

The Funds shall be held in an institution the deposits or accounts of which are insured or guaranteed by a federal or state agency (including Lender if Lender is such an institution). Lender shall apply the Funds to pay the escrow items. Lender may not charge for holding and applying the Funds, analyzing the account or verifying the escrow items, unless Lender pays Borrower interest on the Funds and applicable law permits Lender to make such a charge. Borrower and Lender may agree in writing that interest shall be paid on the Funds. Unless an agreement is made or applicable law requires interest to be paid, Lender shall not be required to pay Borrower any interest or earnings on the Funds. Lender shall give to Borrower, without charge, an annual accounting of the Funds showing credits and debits to the Funds and the purpose for which each debit to the Funds was made. The Funds are pledged as additional security for the sums secured by this Security Instrument.

If the amount of the Funds held by Lender, together with the future monthly payments of Funds payable prior to the due dates of the escrow items, shall exceed the amount required to pay the escrow items when due, the excess shall be, at Borrower's option, either promptly repaid to Borrower or credited to Borrower on monthly payments of Funds. If the amount of the Funds held by Lender is not sufficient to pay the escrow items when due, Borrower shall pay to Lender any amount necessary to make up the deficiency in one or more payments as required by Lender.

Upon payment in full of all sums secured by this Security Instrument, Lender shall promptly refund to Borrower any Funds held by Lender. If under paragraph 19 the Property is sold or acquired by Lender, Lender shall apply, no later than immediately prior to the sale of the Property or its acquisition by Lender, any Funds held by Lender at the time of application as a credit against the sums secured by this Security Instrument.

3. Application of Payments. Unless applicable law provides otherwise, all payments received by Lender under paragraphs 1 and 2 shall be applied: first, to late charges due under the Note; second, to prepayment charges due under the Note; third, to amounts payable under paragraph 2; fourth, to interest due; and last, to principal due.

4. Charges; Liens. Borrower shall pay all taxes, assessments, charges, fines and impositions attributable to the Property which may attain priority over this Security Instrument, and leasehold payments or ground rents, if any. Borrower shall pay these obligations in the manner provided in paragraph 2, or if not paid in that manner, Borrower shall pay them on time directly to the person owed payment. Borrower shall promptly furnish to Lender all notices of amounts to be paid under this paragraph. If Borrower makes these payments directly, Borrower shall promptly furnish to Lender receipts evidencing the payments.

Borrower shall promptly discharge any lien which has priority over this Security Instrument unless Borrower: (a) agrees in writing to the payment of the obligation secured by the lien in a manner acceptable to Lender; (b) contests in good faith the lien by, or defends against enforcement of the lien in, legal proceedings which in the Lender's opinion operate to prevent the enforcement of the lien or forfeiture of any part of the Property; or (c) secures from the holder of the lien an agreement satisfactory to Lender subordinating the lien to this Security Instrument. If Lender determines that any part of the Property is subject to a lien which may attain priority over this Security Instrument, Lender may give Borrower a notice identifying the lien. Borrower shall satisfy the lien or take one or more of the actions set forth above within 10 days of the giving of notice.

5. Hazard Insurance. Borrower shall keep the improvements now existing or hereafter erected on the Property insured against loss by fire, hazards included within the term "extended coverage" and any other hazards for which Lender requires insurance. This insurance shall be maintained in the amounts and for the periods that Lender requires. The insurance carrier providing the insurance shall be chosen by Borrower subject to Lender's approval which shall not be unreasonably withheld.

All insurance policies and renewals shall be acceptable to Lender and shall include a standard mortgage clause. Lender shall have the right to hold the policies and renewals. If Lender requires, Borrower shall promptly give to Lender all receipts of paid premiums and renewal notices. In the event of loss, Borrower shall give prompt notice to the insurance carrier and Lender. Lender may make proof of loss if not made promptly by Borrower.

Unless Lender and Borrower otherwise agree in writing, insurance proceeds shall be applied to restoration or repair of the Property damaged, if the restoration or repair is economically feasible and Lender's security is not lessened. If the restoration or repair is not economically feasible or Lender's security would be lessened, the insurance proceeds shall be applied to the sums secured by this Security Instrument, whether or not then due, with any excess paid to Borrower. If Borrower abandons the Property, or does not answer within 30 days a notice from Lender that the insurance carrier has offered to settle a claim, then Lender may collect the insurance proceeds. Lender may use the proceeds to repair or restore the Property or to pay sums secured by this Security Instrument, whether or not then due. The 30-day period will begin when the notice is given.

Unless Lender and Borrower otherwise agree in writing, any application of proceeds to principal shall not extend or postpone the due date of the monthly payments referred to in paragraphs 1 and 2 or change the amount of the payments. If under paragraph 19 the Property is acquired by Lender, Borrower's right to any insurance policies and proceeds resulting from damage to the Property prior to the acquisition shall pass to Lender to the extent of the sums secured by this Security Instrument immediately prior to the acquisition.

6. Preservation and Maintenance of Property; Leaseholds. Borrower shall not destroy, damage or substantially change the Property, allow the Property to deteriorate or commit waste. If this Security Instrument is on a leasehold, Borrower shall comply with the provisions of the lease, and if Borrower acquires fee title to the Property, the leasehold and fee title shall not merge unless Lender agrees to the merger in writing.

7. Protection of Lender's Rights in the Property; Mortgage Insurance. If Borrower fails to perform the covenants and agreements contained in this Security Instrument, or there is a legal proceeding that may significantly affect Lender's rights in the Property (such as a proceeding in bankruptcy, probate, for condemnation or to enforce laws or regulations), then Lender may do and pay for whatever is necessary to protect the value of the Property and Lender's rights in the Property. Lender's actions may include paying any sums secured by a lien which has priority over this Security Instrument, appearing in court, paying reasonable attorneys' fees and entering on the Property to make repairs. Although Lender may take action under this paragraph 7, Lender does not have to do so.

Any amounts disbursed by Lender under this paragraph 7 shall become additional debt of Borrower secured by this Security Instrument. Unless Borrower and Lender agree to other terms of payment, these amounts shall bear interest from the date of disbursement at the Note rate and shall be payable, with interest, upon notice from Lender to Borrower requesting payment.

Continued.

Example 7-11 **Mortgage** *continued*

If Lender required mortgage insurance as a condition of making the loan secured by this Security Instrument, Borrower shall pay the premiums required to maintain the insurance in effect until such time as the requirement for the insurance terminates in accordance with Borrower's and Lender's written agreement or applicable law.

8. Inspection. Lender or its agent may make reasonable entries upon and inspections of the Property. Lender shall give Borrower notice at the time of or prior to an inspection specifying reasonable cause for the inspection.

9. Condemnation. The proceeds of any award or claim for damages, direct or consequential, in connection with any condemnation or other taking of any part of the Property, or for conveyance in lieu of condemnation, are hereby assigned and shall be paid to Lender.

In the event of a total taking of the Property, the proceeds shall be applied to the sums secured by this Security Instrument, whether or not then due, with any excess paid to Borrower. In the event of a partial taking of the Property, unless Borrower and Lender otherwise agree in writing, the sums secured by this Security Instrument shall be reduced by the amount of the proceeds multiplied by the following fraction: (a) the total amount of the sums secured immediately before the taking, divided by (b) the fair market value of the Property immediately before the taking. Any balance shall be paid to Borrower.

If the Property is abandoned by Borrower, or if, after notice by Lender to Borrower that the condemnor offers to make an award or settle a claim for damages, Borrower fails to respond to Lender within 30 days after the date the notice is given, Lender is authorized to collect and apply the proceeds, at its option, either to restoration or repair of the Property or to the sums secured by this Security Instrument, whether or not then due.

Unless Lender and Borrower otherwise agree in writing, any application of proceeds to principal shall not extend or postpone the due date of the monthly payments referred to in paragraphs 1 and 2 or change the amount of such payments.

10. Borrower Not Released; Forbearance By Lender Not a Waiver. Extension of the time for payment or modification of amortization of the sums secured by this Security Instrument granted by Lender to any successor in interest of Borrower shall not operate to release the liability of the original Borrower or Borrower's successors in interest. Lender shall not be required to commence proceedings against any successor in interest or refuse to extend time for payment or otherwise modify amortization of the sums secured by this Security Instrument by reason of any demand made by the original Borrower or Borrower's successors in interest. Any forbearance by Lender in exercising any right or remedy shall not be a waiver of or preclude the exercise of any right or remedy.

11. Successors and Assigns Bound; Joint and Several Liability; Co-signers. The covenants and agreements of this Security Instrument shall bind and benefit the successors and assigns of Lender and Borrower, subject to the provisions of paragraph 17. Borrower's covenants and agreements shall be joint and several. Any Borrower who co-signs this Security Instrument but does not execute the Note: (a) is co-signing this Security Instrument only to mortgage, grant and convey that Borrower's interest in the Property under the terms of this Security Instrument; (b) is not personally obligated to pay the sums secured by this Security Instrument; and (c) agrees that Lender and any other Borrower may agree to extend, modify, forbear or make any accommodations with regard to the terms of this Security Instrument or the Note without that Borrower's consent.

12. Loan Charges. If the loan secured by this Security Instrument is subject to a law which sets maximum loan charges, and that law is finally interpreted so that the interest or other loan charges collected or to be collected in connection with the loan exceed the permitted limits, then: (a) any such loan charge shall be reduced by the amount necessary to reduce the charge to the permitted limit; and (b) any sums already collected from Borrower which exceeded permitted limits will be refunded to Borrower. Lender may choose to make this refund by reducing the principal owed under the Note or by making a direct payment to Borrower. If a refund reduces principal, the reduction will be treated as a partial prepayment without any prepayment charge under the Note.

13. Legislation Affecting Lender's Rights. If enactment or expiration of applicable laws has the effect of rendering any provision of the Note or this Security Instrument unenforceable according to its terms, Lender, at its option, may require immediate payment in full of all sums secured by this Security Instrument and may invoke any remedies permitted by paragraph 19. If Lender exercises this option, Lender shall take the steps specified in the second paragraph of paragraph 17.

14. Notices. Any notice to Borrower provided for in this Security Instrument shall be given by delivering it or by mailing it by first class mail unless applicable law requires use of another method. The notice shall be directed to the Property Address or any other address Borrower designates by notice to Lender. Any notice to Lender shall be given by first class mail to Lender's address stated herein or any other address Lender designates by notice to Borrower. Any notice provided for in this Security Instrument shall be deemed to have been given to Borrower or Lender when given as provided in this paragraph.

15. Governing Law; Severability. This Security Instrument shall be governed by federal law and the law of the jurisdiction in which the Property is located. In the event that any provision or clause of this Security Instrument or the Note conflicts with applicable law, such conflict shall not affect other provisions of this Security Instrument or the Note which can be given effect without the conflicting provision. To this end the provisions of this Security Instrument and the Note are declared to be severable.

16. Borrower's Copy. Borrower shall be given one conformed copy of the Note and of this Security Instrument.

17. Transfer of the Property or a Beneficial Interest in Borrower. If all or any part of the Property or any interest in it is sold or transferred (or if a beneficial interest in Borrower is sold or transferred and Borrower is not a natural person) without Lender's prior written consent, Lender may, at its option, require immediate payment in full of all sums secured by this Security Instrument. However, this option shall not be exercised by Lender if exercise is prohibited by federal law as of the date of this Security Instrument.

If Lender exercises this option, Lender shall give Borrower notice of acceleration. The notice shall provide a period of not less than 30 days from the date the notice is delivered or mailed within which Borrower must pay all sums secured by this Security Instrument. If Borrower fails to pay these sums prior to the expiration of this period, Lender may invoke any remedies permitted by this Security Instrument without further notice or demand on Borrower.

18. Borrower's Right to Reinstate. If Borrower meets certain conditions, Borrower shall have the right to have enforcement of this Security Instrument discontinued at any time prior to the earlier of: (a) 5 days (or such other period as applicable law may specify for reinstatement) before sale of the Property pursuant to any power of sale contained in this Security Instrument; or (b) entry of a judgment enforcing this Security Instrument. Those conditions are that Borrower: (a) pays Lender all sums which then would be due under this Security Instrument and the Note had no acceleration occurred; (b) cures any default of any other covenants or agreements; (c) pays all expenses incurred in enforcing this Security Instrument, including, but not limited to, reasonable attorneys' fees; and (d) takes such action as Lender may reasonably require to assure that the lien of this Security Instrument, Lender's rights in the Property and Borrower's obligation to pay the sums secured by this Security Instrument shall continue unchanged. Upon reinstatement by Borrower, this Security Instrument and the obligations secured hereby shall remain fully effective as if no acceleration had occurred. However, this right to reinstate shall not apply in the case of acceleration under paragraphs 13 or 17.

NON-UNIFORM COVENANTS. Borrower and Lender further covenant and agree as follows:

19. Acceleration; Remedies. Lender shall give notice to Borrower prior to acceleration following Borrower's breach of any covenant or agreement in this Security Instrument (but not prior to acceleration under paragraphs 13 and 17 unless applicable law provides otherwise). Lender shall notify Borrower of, among other things: (a) the default; (b) the action required to cure the default; (c) when the default must be cured; and (d) that failure to cure the default as specified may result in acceleration of the sums secured by this Security Instrument, foreclosure by judicial proceeding and sale of the Property. Lender shall further inform Borrower of the right to reinstate after acceleration and the right to assert in the foreclosure proceeding the non-existence of a default or any other defense of Borrower to acceleration and foreclosure. If the default is not cured as specified, Lender at its option may require immediate payment in full of all sums secured by this Security Instrument without further demand and may foreclose this Security Instrument by judicial proceeding. Lender shall be entitled to collect all expenses incurred in pursuing the remedies provided in this paragraph 19, including, but not limited to, attorneys' fees and costs of title evidence to the extent permitted by applicable law.

20. Lender in Possession. Upon acceleration under paragraph 19 or abandonment of the Property, Lender (in person, by agent or by judicially appointed receiver) shall be entitled to enter upon, take possession of and manage the Property and to collect the rents of the Property including those past due. Any rents collected by Lender or the receiver shall be applied first to payment of the costs of management of the Property and collection of rents, including, but not limited to, receiver's fees, premiums on receiver's bonds and reasonable attorneys' fees, and then to the sums secured by this Security Instrument.

21. Release. Upon payment of all sums secured by this Security Instrument, Lender shall discharge this Security Instrument without charge to Borrower. Borrower shall pay any recordation costs.

22. Reinstatement Period. Borrower's time to reinstate provided in paragraph 18 shall extend to one hour prior to the commencement of bidding at a sheriff's sale or other sale pursuant to this Security Instrument.

23. Purchase Money Mortgage. If any of the debt secured by this Security Instrument is lent to Borrower to acquire title to the Property, this Security Instrument shall be a purchase money mortgage.

24. Interest Rate After Judgment. Borrower agrees that the interest rate payable after a judgment is entered on the Note or in an action of mortgage foreclosure shall be the rate payable from time to time under the Note.

25. Riders to this Security Instrument. If one or more riders are executed by Borrower and recorded together with this Security Instrument, the covenants and agreements of each such rider shall be incorporated into and shall amend and supplement the covenants and agreements of this Security Instrument as if the rider(s) were a part of this Security Instrument. [Check applicable box(es)]

☐ Adjustable Rate Rider   ☐ Condominium Rider   ☐ 2–4 Family Rider

☐ Graduated Payment Rider   ☐ Planned Unit Development Rider

☐ Other(s) [specify]

BY SIGNING BELOW, Borrower accepts and agrees to the terms and covenants contained in this Security Instrument and in any rider(s) executed by Borrower and recorded with it.

Witnesses:

....(Seal)
—Borrower

....(Seal)
—Borrower

——————————————— [Space Below This Line For Acknowledgment] ———————————————

Part Seven
ASSIGNMENT, SATISFACTION, AND RELEASE OF MORTGAGES

I. ASSIGNMENT OF MORTGAGES

A mortgage note or bond is an instrument that can be sold, exchanged, donated, or otherwise traded, much like the bonds and stocks that are commonly traded on the stock exchanges. As a matter of law, a sale of the note entitles the purchaser to ownership of the mortgage. However, it is customary to transfer both the note and the mortgage, either in separate documents for each or in one document.

The mechanics for transferring a mortgage note are fairly simple. The seller may just endorse the note substantially as follows:

Pay to the order of [*name of buyer*] without recourse

The words "without recourse" mean that the seller makes no guaranty as to the credit of the borrower. If the note is not paid, the seller will have no responsibility. If, on the other hand, the buyer is bargaining for the credit of the seller as well as the credit of the borrower, the note may be endorsed "with recourse." If a note endorsed with recourse is not paid, the seller is obligated to repurchase the note from the buyer.

A note is sometimes assigned rather than merely endorsed. The buyer of the note will want to be sure (a) that the seller owns the note free and clear of any liens or charges or obligations in favor of third parties; (b) that it has not previously sold or assigned or agreed to sell or assign it to anyone else; and (c) that it has the right to sell the note to the buyer on the terms and conditions agreed on. The buyer will try to protect itself by obtaining warranties to this effect (if the seller is willing to give them) and by making a search of the public records to ascertain whether the mortgage has been previously assigned. The note or bond is not, of course, a public record, and there is no effective way of ascertaining whether it has been assigned except that it would be unusual for the seller to have assigned the note or bond and still retain possession of the original instrument. Moreover, it would be most unusual to assign the note or bond and not assign the mortgage.

The assignment of the mortgage instrument may be combined in the same document as the assignment of the note or may be in a separate document. Although the form of assignment will vary from state to state, a mortgage assignment will generally be in substantially the following form:

For value received, the undersigned [*name*], hereinafter called "Assignor," hereby assigns, transfers and sets over unto [*name of assignee*], hereinafter called "Assignee," all of the Assignor's right, title and interest in, to and under a certain mortgage between [*name of mortgagor*], as Mortgagor, and [*name of mortgagee*], as Mortgagee, dated _____ and recorded in the

Office of the Recorder of Deeds in _____ County on _____ [*date*] in Mortgage Book _____ Page _____, with reference to premises described as follows: [*description of premises*].

Together with the bond or note described in such mortgage and the money due and to become due thereon including interest. To have and to hold unto Assignee and its successors, legal representatives and assigns forever.

THIS assignment is made without recourse to and without covenant or warranty express or implied by Assignor in any event, or for any purpose whatsoever (if the Assignee has bargained for any warranties or the credit of the Assignor, this paragraph will be deleted and in lieu thereof any warranties the parties have agreed upon will be inserted here).

IN WITNESS WHEREOF, Assignor has executed this instrument the day of _____.

[*Signature of Assignor*]

The purchaser of a note may either pay the seller the amount owed on the note, or pay somewhat more (a "premium") or less (a "discount") than the amount owed. Whether or not a premium will be paid or a discount made will depend on the interest rate of the note as compared with the then prevailing interest rate and on the credit of the borrower. In any event the purchaser wants to be certain of the amount owed on the note at the time it buys the note. In order to be assured, the purchaser may require a warranty from the seller and a statement from the borrower acknowledging (a) the amount due and (b) that the borrower has no defenses against payments, and that there are no amounts owed the borrower that he or she is entitled to deduct or "set off." Such a statement from the borrower is commonly called a "Declaration of No Set-Off" or an "Estoppel Letter."

The undersigned, owner of the premises known as [*description of premises*] and covered by the mortgage in the amount of $_____ given by _____, as Mortgagor, to _____, as Mortgagee, dated _____, 19___ and recorded in the Office of the Recorder of Deeds on [*date*] in Mortgage Book _____, Page _____, hereby acknowledges that the principal amount due on such mortgage as of [*date*] is $_____; that interest thereon accrues at the rate of _____% per annum, the last such interest payment having been made on _____; that neither the mortgage nor the obligation which it secures have been modified, altered or amended in any way; and that there are no defenses, counterclaims or set-offs to the aforesaid mortgage or the bond or note secured thereby.

IN WITNESS WHEREOF, the undersigned has executed this Declaration this _____ day of _____, 19___.

[*Signature of borrower*]

II. SATISFACTION OF MORTGAGES

As already noted, a mortgage is recorded and becomes a public document. When the mortgage debt has finally been paid, the mortgagee will return to the borrower the mortgage note or bond marked "canceled" or "paid," and will mark the mortgage "satisfied of record." The procedure for causing the mortgage to be marked satisfied on the public records varies from location to location, but in general the original mortgage is required to be presented to the recorder's office together with a statement, either endorsed on the mortgage or on a separate document signed and acknowledged by the mortgagee, confirming that the debt has been paid and instructing the recorder to mark the mortgage satisfied on the public records.

III. RELEASE OF MORTGAGES

In some situations the borrower and lender may wish to release part of the property covered by the mortgage from the lien of the mortgage, without affecting the lien on the balance of the property, or to release all of the property from the lien of the mortgage without reciting that the underlying obligation has been satisfied. Such a need could arise when a builder or developer purchases land subject to a purchase money mortgage or creates a mortgage on vacant ground on which he or she wishes to build in stages. As the property is developed, the developer may have to create construction mortgages or obtain releases on completed buildings so that they can be conveyed to the ultimate purchaser. If a mortgagor contemplates obtaining partial releases prior to payment of the mortgage debt in full, the mortgage should contain the agreement of the mortgagor and mortgagee with reference to these releases.

The mortgagor wants to be sure that certain areas will be available when needed and that the mortgagee will join in (or release) easement areas required for streets, roads, electric lines, recreational facilities, and the like. The mortgagee, on the other hand, wants to be sure (a) that it obtains payment for each release commensurate with the value of the security lost by release of the portion being released; (b) that the areas to be released are of a certain minimum size; (c) that they are contiguous so that if the mortgagee is required to foreclose after some (but not all) of the property has been released, the mortgagee is not left with "islands" or landlocked areas at the rear of the tract that are much less valuable than road frontage; and (d) that the release will not otherwise affect the validity or priority of the mortgage. One example of a clause that deals with these requirements follows:

> Mortgagee agrees to release from the lien of the Mortgage such portions of the Mortgaged Premises as Mortgagor may require; provided (a) the portions to be released shall be at least one acre and shall be contiguous to the remainder of the premises not then subject to the Mortgage and shall be between lines perpendicular to Jones Road; and (b) Mortgagor pays Mortgagee $_____ per acre for each acre and a pro rata portion of said sum for any fractional acre to be released; and (c) when the last release is delivered the payment shall be sufficient, when added to all prior payments made by Mortgagor to Mortgagee, to comprise the total mortgage debt. All

costs incident to preparation of the releases, such as surveying, preparation of documents, and recording charges, shall be borne by Mortgagor.

Mortgagee will execute, acknowledge and deliver, without charge, any and all consents and subordinations that Mortgagor may require in connection with the installation of streets and public facilities such as water, storm drainage, gas and electricity.

After the mortgagor has ascertained which part of the property is to be released, a survey plan, together with a metes and bounds description, should be delivered to the mortgagee with a mortgage release document. The release document will vary from place to place, but will be in recordable form and will recite that the section described by the metes and bounds description is released from the lien of the referenced mortgage.

IV. SALES UNDER AND SUBJECT TO MORTGAGES

Many situations arise in which a mortgagor wishes to sell the property without paying off the mortgage loan. In such a case, the mortgagor will receive at settlement the difference between the total sales price and the amount outstanding on the mortgage.[30] Thereafter, the purchaser will make the mortgage loan payments. In Chapter Three we discussed the relative concerns of the parties and the different ways in which the situation is handled.

A. PURCHASER ASSUMES DEBT

The purchaser may specifically agree to assume and pay the mortgage debt personally. If the purchaser is to be personally liable for the debt, he or she will either sign a note or bond in favor of the mortgagee, commonly known as a "collateral bond," or the "under and subject" section of the deed from seller to purchaser will contain a clause stating that the purchaser "assumes and agrees to pay" the mortgage debt. If the purchaser is not to be personally liable on the mortgage, language to that effect should be inserted in the deed and the phrase "assumes and agrees to pay" should be deleted. In either case, the legal effect is to permit the mortgagee to sue the purchaser directly for repayment of the mortgage debt. The mortgagee is an intended beneficiary of such collateral bond or such "assumes and agrees to pay" provisions, and this creates the privity of contract between the purchaser and the mortgagee necessary for the mortgagee to sue the purchaser.

B. PURCHASER INDEMNIFIES SELLER

The purchaser may not agree to pay the mortgage debt personally but may expressly or by implication agree to indemnify the mortgagor against

---

30. The difference between the market value of a property and the principal balance of the outstanding mortgage loan is sometimes referred to as the owner's equity.

any loss suffered by the mortgagor by virtue of the purchaser's failure to pay the debt when it is due. Through an indemnification the purchaser is not made personally liable to the mortgagee, and therefore cannot be sued personally by the mortgagee[31] but is made liable to the seller in the event the seller suffers an actual loss. This might occur if the mortgagee elected to sue the seller on the note instead of foreclosing, or if the property had depreciated in value to such a point that the mortgagee did not satisfy the debt out of the property and subsequently sued the mortgagor personally. The obligation to indemnify is implied as a matter of law from an "under and subject" clause, which refers to the mortgage and does not contain the agreement to "assume and agree to pay." If this is not so in the particular state in which the real estate is located, the drafter may want to insert a clause specifically stating that the purchaser does not assume and agree to pay the mortgage, but does agree to indemnify the seller against any actual loss or damage the seller may suffer by reason of the purchaser's failure to make any payments thereunder.

C. NO LIABILITY ASSUMED BY PURCHASER

This is the best solution for the purchaser and the least desirable for the seller. The relative bargaining position of the parties will determine the extent of financial exposure in any given case. If the purchaser is to assume no personal liability and also wants to negate the implication of indemnification, the following language would be added to the under and subject clause that describes the mortgage:

> provided Grantee does not expressly or impliedly assume or agree to pay the aforesaid mortgage debt, nor does Grantee expressly or impliedly agree to indemnify Grantor or any other party in connection therewith.

★ V. SUBORDINATION OF MORTGAGES

Although mortgages generally take priority of right from the time they are recorded, it is possible to modify relative priorities by the agreement of the parties. For example, a developer may purchase a vacant tract of ground and give the seller a note and purchase money mortgage for part of the purchase price. Before the note and mortgage are due, the developer may want to improve the property with buildings and to do so a construction mortgage loan may be required. The construction lender will insist that its construction mortgage be a first mortgage on the property, with a priority over the existing purchase money mortgage. This requires the agreement of the purchase money mortgagee either to release the property or agree to subordinate the lien of the purchase money mortgage to

31. The purchaser cannot be sued personally because of a lack of privity of contract between the mortgagee and the purchaser.

the lien of the construction mortgage. In anticipation of this possibility, there may be a clause, such as the following provision, in the purchase money mortgage:

> This mortgage is hereby made subordinate in lien, operation and effect to the lien of any institutional mortgages now or hereafter placed upon the Mortgaged Premises (and any subsequent mortgages substituted therefor) provided such mortgage or mortgages are for the purpose of providing Mortgagor with funds for construction of improvements on or about the Mortgaged Premises. This subordination shall be effective without the need for any further act or writing by Mortgagor, Mortgagee, or any other party, but Mortgagee agrees, by its acceptance of this instrument, to execute, acknowledge and deliver any further instruments that any other Mortgagee may require to evidence and confirm this subordination. All costs incident to the preparation of the aforesaid easements and subordinations, such as surveying, preparation of documents and recording charges, shall be borne by Mortgagor.[32]

Subordination can also be accomplished by a separate agreement among the mortgagor and both mortgagees. This agreement should be in recordable form and should be recorded in the county in which the mortgages are recorded.

It should be stressed that a subordination does not affect the rights of other lien holders. Suppose Regina Stolz holds a $1,000,000 first mortgage on Greenacre, which is owned by Greenacre Associates. Continental Grading Co., Inc. may have obtained a $150,000 judgment against Greenacre Associates, which judgment has been properly recorded in the county in which Greenacre is located, but which judgment is clearly inferior in time and right to the $1,000,000 Stolz mortgage. Subsequently, Greenacre Associates has obtained a $4,700,000 mortgage loan from Colonial Bank, to which Stolz has agreed to subordinate. Stolz, by her subordination to Colonial, should not be able to grant Colonial superior rights over Continental for the full amount of the $4,700,000 Colonial loan. The most that Stolz should be able to grant is the right of Continental to get the first $1,000,000 plus the agreement of Stolz not to get paid anything until Colonial gets its entire $4,700,000.

Thus, one possible effect of the subordination is that the proceeds of a sheriff's sale would be distributed in the following order and priority:

1. $1,000,000 to Colonial
2. $150,000 to Continental
3. $3,700,000 to Colonial
4. $1,000,000 to Stolz

---

32. The quoted provision may not be acceptable to a purchase money mortgagor. There is no maximum amount to which the purchase money mortgagor agrees to be subordinate. There is no description of the sorts of improvements for which a construction mortgage may be obtained, and such improvements may be "about" the premises. Any improvements "about" the premises rather than "on" the premises should be limited to stated off-site improvements.

Thus, the effect if the above priority were determined by the courts[33] would be that Colonial does not have a first lien for its entire mortgage amount, even though it has received a subordination from the undisputed first lien mortgagee. For her part, Stolz assumed she was subordinating only $4,700,000. Instead, Stolz finds that she has ended up being inferior to the $150,000 Continental lien as well, to which she had been superior and to which she had never knowingly subordinated her first mortgage lien.

Part Eight
MORTGAGE FORECLOSURE

I. INTRODUCTION

The laws and rules that govern mortgage foreclosures are local in nature, and even neighboring states often have drastically different laws regarding foreclosures. This section, therefore, is only intended to familiarize the student with concerns inherent in the concept of a mortgage foreclosure. This section is not intended as a step-by-step guide to mortgage foreclosure.

II. ACTION ON NOTE OR ON MORTGAGE

Mortgage notes are evidence of a mortgagor's debt and of his or her obligation to pay interest. A mortgagee has two separate means for collecting the mortgage debt; the personal security, which is the note, and the real estate security, which is the mortgage. Traditionally, a bond or a note was usually accompanied by, or included, a warrant of attorney to confess judgment against the debtor, which offered a mortgagee a relatively quick and inexpensive means to collect the debt. The confession of judgment, which is now seldom used, gives the lender the right, on a default and sometimes before a default, to appear in court on behalf of the debtor and to plead that the debtor defaulted under the obligation.

Once judgment is secured, either by a confession of judgment or by a separate lawsuit to recover the debt on the note, the mortgagee could execute on the judgment by ordering the sheriff to seize the property (real or personal) of the debtor and sell it at sheriff's sale, generally without notice to the debtor.

Debtors were not always aware of the legal implications of signing a judgment note and even if they were, few people understood and could afford the procedures required to protect their property once a confession of judgment was wrongfully entered. Recognizing these realities, the courts have invalidated use of confessions of judgments in certain situations. Because of the possibility that these decisions might apply to a

---

33. State courts have been anything but consistent and logical in their application of subordination agreements in instances where there are intervening lienors.

given fact situation, most lawyers, at least with respect to individual debtors, do not use the confession of judgment contained in a bond or note accompanying a mortgage as a means of collecting a debt. The mortgagee can still bring an action on the bond or note in an independent lawsuit, obtain a judgment in an adversary proceeding, and execute and sell the property pursuant to that judgment. In some cases it will be better to bring a lawsuit on the note, especially when the mortgage accompanying the particular note is secured by real property less valuable than the amount of the debt or when there is substantial value in the debtor's personal property.[34] By obtaining a personal judgment in the suit brought on the note, the mortgagee will secure a lien on all the debtor's property in the county, not just the property encumbered by the mortgage that accompanied the mortgage note. Often, however, the better procedure for the mortgagee is to file a lawsuit on the mortgage.

III. THE DEFAULT

If the mortgagor is fulfilling his or her obligations under the bond or mortgage, the mortgagee has no right to compel the sale of the mortgaged property in order to satisfy the balance of the mortgage debt. The mortgagee's right to foreclose on the mortgage arises when the mortgagor fails to fulfill one or more of the obligations contained in the note or mortgage. For example, if the mortgage provides for repayment of the debt in monthly installments and the mortgagor fails to pay an installment in a particular month, the mortgagee may bring an action in mortgage foreclosure if the mortgage instrument so provides, which it generally does. The mortgagor's failure to make payments when due is the most common default leading to foreclosure. It is customary in installment mortgages to insert a provision in the note and the mortgage that accelerates the due date of principal, interest, taxes, and insurance, on a default in a monthly payment or in the event of other defaults in the mortgagor's obligations. The mortgagee may then institute an action to collect the debt, either by an action on the note or by mortgage foreclosure.

IV. THE COMPLAINT

A mortgage foreclosure proceeding is a kind of lawsuit and as such follows the general procedures for starting a legal action. The suit is generally instituted by filing a "complaint" with the state court in the county in which the land is located. The complaint constitutes the initial pleading of fact that the mortgagee intends to prove to the court, cites the relief requested by the mortgagee, and serves to bring the defendant within the power of the court. The original complaint is filed with the court, and a copy is served by the sheriff (or comparable official) on the de-

34. This assumes, of course, that the debtor's obligation is not limited to the land.

fendant. The normal method of serving a defendant is to leave a copy of the complaint at his or her residence, or, if the defendant's address is unknown but he or she can be located, to hand deliver a copy of the complaint.

A. PLAINTIFF

The plaintiff in a mortgage foreclosure is the mortgagee or mortgagees, or the heirs, executors, administrators, successors, or assigns of the mortgagee.

B. DEFENDANT

Generally, the plaintiff in an action of mortgage foreclosure must name as defendants in the complaint (a) the mortgagor and (b) the real owner of the property (if different from the mortgagor) or if the real owner is unknown, the grantee in the last recorded deed.

If the mortgagor is no longer the real owner of the property, and if the mortgagee is willing (assuming there is a choice) to absolve him or her of any personal responsibility and liability under the mortgage, then the mortgagor may not have to be made a party to the complaint. The rules in most states require that the plaintiff set forth in the complaint the fact that the mortgagor is released from liability on the debt secured by the mortgage.

Persons who are in possession of the property are not required to be joined as defendants to the action in mortgage foreclosure, although they may have to be served with a copy of the complaint. The law in many states is not clear as to the consequences of failing to serve a tenant with a copy of the complaint. It is possible, for example, that a tenant who has a lease that is subject to the mortgage and therefore subject to divestment as a result of a sheriff's sale on a foreclosure, may not be divested if he or she is not served with a copy of the complaint. In any event, prudent practice requires service of a copy of the complaint on all tenants. In New York the rules require that all parties whose interests in the land are claimed to be subordinate and subject to the mortgage must be made parties to the action. Accordingly, if a first mortgage is being foreclosed, all subordinate mortgages and all junior judgment creditors must be served and named as defendants. In California all persons having an interest of any sort in the property must be made parties.

Federal tax liens receive special treatment in a foreclosure sale. If the mortgage was recorded prior to the federal tax lien, it will be superior to the federal lien. However, the mortgagee must name the federal government as a party defendant in the foreclosure proceeding. If the mortgagee fails to name the federal government as a defendant, the federal tax lien will not be discharged by the foreclosure sale and the successful bidder at the sale will take the property subject to the federal lien.

C. DEFENSES AND COUNTERCLAIMS

Just as with any other lawsuit, there are many defenses or counterclaims that might be imposed by the defendant in a mortgage foreclosure action. We shall briefly review several possible defenses.

1. Performance and/or Waiver

The most obvious defense is that there was no default. More often, the defense will be either that the default has been cured within an acceptable time or that the mortgagee has by past forbearance waived its right to require strict adherence to all of the technical provisions of the mortgage. Most mortgages contain a provision stating that forebearance, even repeated forebearance, by a mortgagee shall not constitute a waiver by the mortgagee of its right to require strict performance. Such a provision may not be completely effective, and mortgagors are likely to attempt to impose a waiver defense notwithstanding the clause.

2. Invalidity of Mortgage

A mortgagor may claim that the mortgage itself was invalid for any number of technical reasons, such as failure of consideration (especially if the mortgagor was not the same party as the borrower), lack of authority of the signatories of the mortgage (where the mortgagor is a corporation or other entity), and failure to obtain the necessary signatories in their proper capacities. The mortgagee attempts to secure itself against this type of defense by requiring the mortgagor to obtain mortgagee title insurance from solvent title companies and by requiring mortgagor's counsel to supply opinion letters as to the validity of the mortgage.

3. Technical Defenses Regarding Foreclosures

The plaintiff in a mortgage foreclosure action must comply with certain requirements and rules of court. Failure to comply with those requirements and rules, such as notice provisions, may give rise to technical defenses. These may only delay the ultimate effect of the foreclosure action, but such delay may be significant.

4. Counterclaims and Offsets

In different jurisdictions, claims that the mortgagor may have against the mortgagee may be introduced into the foreclosure action. Almost certainly a mortgagor can interject a claim arising out of the mortgage relationship. This becomes significant with a combined construction loan and permanent loan. It is not at all unusual or difficult for a mortgagor to be able to work up some claim against the construction lender based on an alleged breach of the construction loan agreement. Since the loan agreement is referred to in the mortgage, the permanent lender, as assignee from the construction lender, would be susceptible to such counterclaims. This points out the importance to the permanent lender of the Declaration of No Set-Off signed by the mortgagor at the time of the permanent loan closing, which has the effect of estopping the mortgagor from interposing a counterclaim arising prior to the date of the permanent loan closing.

V. EXECUTION SALE

The first concept to be aware of is that the purchaser at the execution sale will take title to the mortgaged property free and clear of the mortgage. Even if there are insufficient funds to pay the mortgage in full, the mortgagee has no further rights in the property. The other important concept is that the mortgagee can bid at the execution sale without having to put up cash, except to the extent of the expenses of sale, any sums having a priority of payment to the mortgagee, and any amount above the total judgment that the mortgagee has obtained.

VI. CONCLUSION

The foreclosure action is the ultimate measurement of the effectiveness of a mortgage. If a mortgage is ineffective at the point of foreclosure, then it has failed to serve its basic purpose. However, foreclosure is just the strongest example of the tests that a mortgage should properly pass. Unlike an agreement of sale or a lease, a mortgage is a peculiarly negative document. Its only purpose is to take effect if something goes wrong, whether fire, condemnation, bankruptcy, or whatever. No drafter can anticipate all the adverse events that might occur. The decision for the drafter for the lender is to determine how much is enough, a determination that may differ from transaction to transaction.

Chapter 8

Settlements and Closings

I. GENERAL INFORMATION

The settlement or closing is the time at which the real estate transaction is consummated. The format of a closing varies markedly, as a matter of tradition, from one part of the country to another. In some areas it is common for all of the parties or their representatives to conduct settlement as a face-to-face meeting. In other jurisdictions, most settlements for the purchase of residential real estate take place without the presence of the parties. Instead, all of the necessary documents and consideration are forwarded to one person, normally an employee of a title company or bank, who acts as an escrow agent. When everything has been received, the escrow agent consummates the closing without the parties being present.

This chapter focuses on settlements or closings at which the parties are present, but the preparation for an escrow closing would be identical. Several kinds of settlements are considered, but the major emphasis is on purchases of residential property that involve a mortgage supplied by an institutional lender.

This chapter considers settlements as if they were being conducted by a title insurance company. This will not always be the case, and settlement may be conducted by an attorney or an agent. The principles remain the same, whoever actually conducts settlement.

II. PREPARATION FOR SETTLEMENT—PURCHASE— SALE OF PROPERTY

The closing itself is often anticlimactic. If the parties are well organized and prepared for closing, the event becomes a mere formality. It will make

271

a favorable impression on a client if the lawyer representing the client has anticipated everything needed for the settlement and has all of the documents in order.[1]

In order for an attorney or a paralegal to prepare for a closing concerning the sale or purchase of property, he or she must review the relevant documents, which usually include the agreement of sale, the title report or abstract, and, if a mortgage is being used by the purchaser, the mortgage commitment and any disclosure forms required by federal or state law. This review provides a list of things that must be done prior to settlement as well as the documents and consideration that must be produced at closing.

A. PREPARATION BY SELLER

There are a number of documents that must be produced by the seller at or before settlement.

1. Deed

The seller's basic obligation at settlement is to tender a deed to the buyer. The party responsible for the preparation of the deed will vary from one jurisdiction to another. In Pennsylvania, tradition dictates that a deed be prepared by the purchaser and delivered to the seller for review prior to settlement. In many states, such as New Jersey, preparation of the deed is the responsibility of the seller. The deed should be reviewed by both the seller and the purchaser in order to make certain that the legal description conforms to the property being sold.

If one or more of the grantors will not be present at closing, it is necessary to obtain the absent party's signature in advance, along with an acknowledgment of that signature. If all parties who will execute the deed will be present at closing, they can execute the deed at that time.

2. Objections and Exceptions in the Title Report

(a) Mortgage Pay-off Statement and Satisfaction Piece

If the property is subject to a mortgage that is to be removed at the time of settlement, it will be necessary to obtain from the mortgagee a statement of the exact amount of principal, interest, and other charges, if any, that will be due on the date of settlement in order to satisfy the mortgage.[2] This statement is referred to as a "pay-off statement," and it is normally in the form of a letter stating the aggregate amount owed on that date and indicating the daily interest that should be added to that figure in

---

1. It is especially impressive (and most useful) when each significant document has a separate file folder identifying the document, and the files are arranged in a logical sequence before closing.

2. If a mortgagee has been escrowing for the payment of real estate taxes, the payoff letter will show that funds currently held in escrow are being applied in reduction of principal.

the event settlement occurs a few days late. The party in charge of settlement will forward a check to the mortgagee who will return a satisfaction of mortgage in recordable form. In some instances the mortgagee will send an executed instrument in recordable form, stating that the mortgage debt has been satisfied (referred to as a "satisfaction piece"), to settlement with the understanding that it will be recorded only after the sum necessary to satisfy the mortgage has been sent to the mortgagee. (See *Examples 8-2* and *8-3* at the end of this chapter.)

(b) Real Estate Taxes

The agreement of sale will usually require that the property be conveyed free and clear of all liens for taxes. It will typically be necessary for the seller to produce at settlement, tax receipts for the prior two or three years.[3] If taxes for a current year have not been paid, the seller should produce the bill for those taxes if it has been received. Prior to settlement the receipts and bill referred to earlier should be obtained. If the receipts cannot be found, one can write to the taxing authority and request a letter acknowledging payment of the taxes. If taxes have been escrowed under the existing mortgage, the receipts may be held by the lender. Often the party conducting settlement will rely on the written statement of the mortgagee[4] that taxes have been paid without requiring production of receipts.

(c) Water and Sewer Rents

If water and sewer services are supplied by a municipality, and if the municipality has the power to impose a lien for unpaid charges, it will be necessary for the seller to produce receipts evidencing payment of these bills for several years prior to settlement. Again, any outstanding bill should be produced at settlement.

In many areas a minimum charge for water is made periodically. Less frequently the meter on the property is read and the owner is billed for any excess water usage. If possible, the seller should arrange to have the meter read near the date of settlement so that the seller can pay for any excess charges incurred to the date of closing. Otherwise, it will be necessary to make provisions for those charges at settlement as discussed later.

(d) Judgments

In the event that there are outstanding judgments against the premises, either the seller must arrange with the judgment creditor to have the

---

3. The exact number of years of tax receipts required will depend on the statute of limitations relating to tax sales for unpaid taxes, and will be listed on the title commitment under Schedule B, Section 1.

4. Title companies are often willing to rely on such statements from local institutional mortgage lenders but would be unlikely to do so if the mortgagee were a private individual or noninstitutional lender not familiar to them.

judgment satisfied of record prior to settlement, or the seller must deposit at settlement an amount of money sufficient to pay any such judgment so that it may be satisfied by the party in charge of settlement.

Often the title searcher picks up judgments against people whose names are similar to that of the seller. If, in fact, the judgments are not against the seller, they will normally be removed from the title report if the seller signs an affidavit to the title insurer stating that he or she is not the judgment debtor.

(e) Miscellaneous Title Objections

There may be any number of miscellaneous objections that will arise in a title report. Miscellaneous title objections are often removed by the title company in reliance on a sworn affidavit of the seller verifying the existence of facts that satisfy the objection.

For example, there may be a standard objection on a title report relating to the competency of the seller to sign the deed. That objection might be removed by an affidavit to the effect that the sellers are of legal age and have not been declared to be legally incompetent. An example of a seller's affidavit appears as *Example 8-4* at the end of this chapter. Other objections require more than an affidavit for removal. If, for example, the seller is presently unmarried but had been married and divorced, the seller might have to produce a copy of the divorce decree.

3. Documents Needed for Special Situations

The following documents are necessary for settlements in which the seller is not an individual or in which certain facts are present, such as the existence of leases.

(a) Corporation as Seller

If the seller is a corporation, the title company will require the seller to produce a certified copy of resolutions of the board of directors authorizing the sale of property.[5] In addition to corporate resolutions, it may be necessary to produce the articles of incorporation or the corporate charter at closing in order to prove the existence of the corporation. In the event that the corporation is a foreign corporation,[6] it may be necessary to obtain a certificate of authority from the state in which the property is located. That certificate should indicate that the seller is registered to do business and is in good standing in the state in which the property is located. Sometimes, when the seller is a corporation, the state may have a lien against the property for payment of state corporate taxes. Depending on

---

5. Often the title company will also require certified resolutions from a purchaser corporation, especially if the purchaser is obtaining a purchase money mortgage loan. A foreign corporation is simply one that is not incorporated under the laws of the state in question. If a settlement involves land in Alabama, then as far as that settlement is concerned, a Georgia corporation is a foreign corporation.

the procedures in the particular state, either such taxes may be paid at settlement or a certificate that allows the property to be transferred clear of state taxes may be obtained in advance. If the seller is a corporation, often the deed will have to be signed by two officers (usually the president or a vice-president and the secretary or an assistant secretary). The corporate seal normally is affixed to the deed.

(b) Leased Property

The agreement of sale must be reviewed in order to determine how occupancy leases for the property, if any, are to be handled.

i. Termination of Leases

If the leases are to be terminated prior to settlement, it is necessary to send the appropriate termination notices and take appropriate steps to free the premises for occupancy by the purchaser. Sometimes, because of the length of time by which notice must be given to an existing tenant, the property will not be vacated by tenants until after settlement. In such a case it is necessary to tender at settlement, proof that the seller has sent the proper termination notices.

ii. Assignment of Leases

If the existing leases are to be assigned to the purchaser, an instrument of assignment must be prepared and presented at closing. In addition, notice to each tenant that future rental payments are to be made to the purchaser must be signed by the seller and delivered at settlement. The question of which party actually prepares the assignment and the notices will vary from one jurisdiction to another and from one transaction to another.

(c) Purchaser Money Mortgage

In the event that the property is to be conveyed subject to a purchase money mortgage to be given by the purchaser to the seller, the note and the mortgage must be signed by the purchaser at closing. Again, these may be prepared by the seller or by the purchaser. In either event, the party preparing the documents should submit them to the other party well in advance of settlement for review and possible revision. The seller-lender may also have to make certain disclosures to the purchaser, as discussed in section VII of this chapter.

(d) New Construction

If the premises to be conveyed are newly constructed, several documents relating to the construction may have to be tendered at settlement.

i. Release of Liens and Proof of Payment from Contractors and Subcontractors

In order to satisfy provisions in the agreement of sale concerning conveyance of the property free and clear of liens, it may be necessary to produce a release of liens signed by all contractors, subcontractors, and material suppliers who were involved in work at the premises. In the event that the signature of any such party has not been obtained on a release, the seller may submit receipts or other proofs of payment, including affidavits.

ii. Subdivision Approval

If the property to be conveyed is part of a subdivision, the seller may have the responsibility of submitting proof that the subdivision plan has been approved by the appropriate local authorities.[7]

iii. Use and Occupancy Certificate

Often, in the case of new construction, it is the obligation of the seller to produce at closing a certificate from the appropriate local authorities indicating that the building has been inspected and that construction has been performed in compliance with the local building codes. Without such a certificate, often called a certificate of occupancy, it may be impossible for the purchaser to occupy and use the building.

(e) Conveyance When Record Owner Is Deceased

A variety of problems may arise if one of the record owners of the premises has died.

i. Joint Tenant Survives

In the event that the property is owned by a husband and wife as tenants by the entirety, or is owned by joint tenants with the right of survivorship, and one of the spouses or joint tenants dies, the property automatically passes to the other spouse or joint tenant. If this has happened, it will be necessary to produce at settlement proof of the death of the deceased spouse or joint tenant. Proof of death may be in the form of any actual death certificate or it may be sufficient for the remaining spouse or joint tenant to give an affidavit concerning the death of the deceased spouse or joint tenant.

ii. Property Now Owned by One Not Named in the Last Recorded Deed

---

7. In some circumstances the purchaser may have the responsibility of obtaining subdivision approval, especially in instances where the purchaser is acquiring land for development.

If the grantee named in the last deed is not the present owner, it will be necessary for the present owner to establish right of ownership at the time he or she sells the property. If the named grantee was an individual who has died, then in order to establish that right, the seller would normally have to produce a certified copy of the recorded will of the decedent. If there is no will, then proof of distribution of the property to the present owner must be submitted. In addition, proof of the death of the grantee named in the last deed would be necessary. If the prior grantee were a corporation that had dissolved, with the property passing by law to the shareholders, then the shareholders would have to show proof of such dissolution and of their status as shareholders.

If the property is being sold by the executor or administrator (also known as "personal representative") of the estate of the grantee named in the last deed, the personal representative would have to submit at closing proof of appointment as the personal representative of the decedent. That proof would typically take the form of a certified copy of the letters testamentary or letters of administration granted to the personal representative.

iii. Inheritance and/or Estate Tax Waivers

In the cases just discussed relating to a deceased prior owner, it will be necessary to obtain from the taxing authorities (state and federal) either documents indicating that the estate tax due by the estate of the grantee in the last deed has been paid, or documents waiving the right of the taxing authority to seek payment from the property to be conveyed.[8]

(f) Residential Property

An agreement of sale for residential property often provides for certain miscellaneous documents to be tendered to the purchaser at closing.

i. Termite Certificate

The residential agreement of sale may provide for the seller to tender at closing a certificate of a termite control company stating that the premises are free and clear of termites and other wood-boring and wood-destroying insects, and damage from such insects.

ii. Miscellaneous Certificates

Sometimes the agreement of sale requires the seller to have various systems within the premises, such as the heating, plumbing, air condi-

8. A title company may be willing to accept a letter from a party that it trusts, such as a local bank or law firm, stating either that the estate is not subject to inheritance or estate taxes or that the party writing the letter will make sure that the taxes are paid. The bank or law firm might be willing to give such a letter because it is executor of the estate or counsel to the estate.

tioning, and electrical systems, inspected prior to settlement, and to provide at settlement certifications respecting the satisfactory functioning of those systems. If the property is being sold to the purchaser receiving either an FHA or VA mortgage, the rules of those agencies will require many of these certifications.

(g) Commercial or Industrial Properties

Certain documents in addition to those already mentioned often must be obtained in connection with settlement of commercial or industrial properties.

i. Zoning Classification Certifications

Often the agreement of sale will provide that the seller must tender to the buyer at settlement a certification setting forth the zoning classification of the property and declaring that its present use is consistent with the zoning ordinance.

ii. Licenses

If the purchaser is purchasing the property in order to continue an existing business, it may be necessary for the seller to transfer to the purchaser at closing various licenses or permits relating to operation of the premises.

iii. Bill of Sale

If the property to be conveyed is a commercial or industrial site, there may be valuable personal property transferred in connection with the purchase and sale. In such a case it is often the custom to have a bill of sale executed by the seller transferring the personal property tendered at settlement.

iv. Inventory of Supplies at the Premises

If any supplies to be used in the operation of the property remain at the time of settlement, they must be valued just prior to settlement so that the seller can charge the purchaser for those items. An example of supplies would be heating fuel remaining in the tanks. The inventory process can be much more complicated if the sale of the real estate is in conjunction with the sale of a business, such as a grocery store.

B. PREPARATION BY THE PURCHASER

The following discussion outlines the purchaser's preparation for settlement. The purchaser must prepare certain documents and review others to ensure that he or she is receiving what has been promised. In addition, the purchaser must obtain the money to be tendered to the seller at settlement.

1. Title Report

The first step in preparing for settlement is normally to order a title search or a title report on the property. Once the title report has been received by the purchaser, a copy should be sent to the seller to inform the seller of the objections that must be removed to convey good title. The purchaser should also send a copy of the title report to the proposed mortgagee, if any. The title report will also be useful as the source of the legal description to be inserted in the deed.

2. Deed

The agreement of sale usually indicates which party is responsible for preparing the deed. If requested to do so, the preparer should send the deed to the other party for review in advance of settlement.

3. Survey

If the purchaser desires or is required to have a survey, it will be necessary to contact a surveyor or engineer and arrange for the preparation of the survey. The purchaser's counsel should make certain the survey includes all of the property described in the agreement of sale and that the legal description provided in the title report follows the boundary measurements on the survey.

4. Inspection of Property

If the agreement of sale grants the purchaser a right of inspection prior to settlement (known as a "presettlement inspection"), the purchaser should arrange for such an inspection with a reputable home inspection agency that is willing to provide a certification respecting the condition of the premises. At the presettlement inspection the purchaser should verify that all personal property listed in the agreement of sale is in fact present and in good working order.

5. Mortgage

When settlement has finally been scheduled, the purchaser must notify the mortgagee of the exact time and place of settlement several days in advance.[9] The mortgagee will either prepare the necessary mortgage documents or forward blank forms to the purchaser for preparation by his or her counsel. The mortgage commitment should be checked carefully for any other requirements imposed by the lender, which may include advance receipt of insurance policies, termite certificates, or the like. In any event the purchaser should receive the documents in advance of settlement to review them.

9. Often the mortgage commitment requires that such notice be received within a specified number of days.

The purchaser will also have to determine from the mortgagee the amount, if any, of prepaid interest, tax escrow, and fees that the purchaser will be required to pay at settlement. Calculation of prepaid interest and the various methods of disclosing the costs relating to closing and to the loan are discussed later in this chapter.

6. Fire Insurance

It is desirable to arrange in advance of settlement to obtain a fire insurance policy covering the premises to be purchased. A mortgagee will insist on insurance being in effect as of the time of settlement and will insist on receiving a copy of the policy at settlement. The policy must contain a clause acknowledging the interest of the mortgagee in the proceeds of the fire insurance. It is important for the purchaser's counsel to make certain that the purchaser has secured the necessary policy well in advance of settlement and brings a copy to settlement. If the risk of loss is on the purchaser as of the date of the acceptance of the agreement of sale, the purchaser should obtain a fire insurance binder effective as of that date to be protected in the event of a fire or casualty on the property prior to settlement. The amount of the fire insurance policy must be at least equal to the principal sum of the mortgage.

7. Public Utilities

The purchaser should notify the various public utilities whose services the purchaser will require of the date on which he or she will want the premises served. For example, it will be necessary to arrange in advance for electricity, gas, telephone, and water service to begin on a specific date.

8. Advance Calculation of Funds Needed to Complete Settlement

The purchaser's major obligation at closing is to tender the consideration for the premises. The purchaser's counsel must calculate the amount of money the purchaser will need to complete settlement, which will differ from the remainder of the purchase price. In doing so, real estate taxes and other apportionable expenses must be apportioned from the date of settlement unless another date is established in the agreement of sale. Each party imposing charges at settlement (such as the mortgagee and the title insurance company) should be requested to provide an itemization of those charges before settlement. Expenses such as transfer taxes, notary fees, and recording costs will also have to be calculated and apportioned, if local practice or the agreement of sale so provides. Some of these items will change if the date of settlement changes. The calculation of the apportionments and expenses will be discussed in detail later in this chapter.

When a determination of exactly how much the purchaser will need to complete settlement has been made, the purchaser's counsel should send a letter setting forth this amount.[10] The letter should specify the type of check (e.g., certified or cashier's) that the purchaser must bring to settlement and the exact day, time, and place of settlement.

9. Notice of Settlement

If the agreement of sale calls for either party to give notice of settlement to the other, such notice must be prepared and sent as specified in the agreement.

10. Special Situations

The discussion that follows relates to tasks that have to be performed if the purchaser is a corporation or if the property is subject to a lease.

(a) Purchaser as Corporation

If the purchaser is a corporation, the following documents may be needed for settlement:

i. Corporate Resolutions

The seller may require that the purchaser present at settlement a certified copy of resolutions of the board of directors authorizing the purchase of the premises. If there is to be a mortgage, the lender or the title company will almost certainly require such resolutions, which must include authorization for the creation of the mortgage.

ii. Corporate Charter

It may be necessary to produce the articles of incorporation or corporate charter at closing as evidence of the corporation's existence.

iii. Certificate of Authority

In the event the corporation purchasing the premises is a foreign corporation, it will often be necessary to present at settlement a certificate of authority to do business, as well as a "good standing" certificate evidencing the continued qualification of the corporation to do business in the state in which the property is located. Such certificates are available from the state's corporation bureau.

(b) Property Subject to Lease

If the property is subject to one or more leases, an assignment of lease and notice to tenants will be needed. Again, depending on the custom of

---

10. Often, a purchaser's counsel will add a certain sum to the calculation of the settlement costs in order to have a cushion in case there was some error in the calculations or in case there is some unexpected expense at settlement. Any excess will be reimbursed to the purchaser at settlement.

the jurisdiction in which you work, the assignment of lease and notices to tenants may be prepared by the purchaser or by the seller.

A settlement preparation checklist appears as *Example 8-5* at the end of this chapter. It is useful to review this checklist well in advance of closing to be sure that all closing items have been dealt with properly.

III. SETTLEMENT FOR THE PURCHASE AND SALE OF PROPERTY

This section focuses on the problems of the actual settlement. Most of the documents needed for settlement have already been referred to. In the event the preparation for settlement has been carefully carried out, settlement itself will be quite simple. If the transaction is complex, it may be wise to arrange for a rehearsal of closing (referred to as a "preclosing"). The purpose of a preclosing is to make certain that all documents that are necessary for settlement are complete and that there are no matters that must still be negotiated. In addition, all of the computations concerning the purchase price may be made in advance.

A. PLACE OF CLOSING

The place at which closing is held varies, depending on the practice in your locality. It is common to hold settlements for the purchase of real estate in the offices of title insurance companies, real estate brokers, and attorneys.

B. SETTLEMENT CLERK

In order to expedite settlement, it is normal for one person to act as a clerk in charge of settlement. That person is the recipient of all signed documents and money. It is the clerk's task to make certain that each party receives the appropriate documents, that all checks are drawn and forwarded to the appropriate recipients, and that any documents requiring recordation are in fact recorded and then returned to the appropriate parties. If the purchaser's title is being insured by a title insurance company, it is common for the title insurance company to provide a settlement clerk. It is also common for a real estate agent, attorney, or employee of a bank to perform the same duties.

C. MECHANICS OF THE SETTLEMENT

The following discussion is intended to familiarize the student with the various activities that take place at settlement.

1. Record of Parties Present

In order to obtain a complete record concerning closing, the attorneys for each party should prepare a list of all of the persons present.

2. Execution and Exchange of Documents

At settlement, all the documents discussed earlier in this chapter must be signed, acknowledged, and tendered to the settlement clerk or the party who is to receive the document. In many instances the settlement clerk is a notary public and will take any necessary acknowledgments.[11]

3. Conforming Copies of the Documents

In addition to the original documents that are tendered at the settlement, each party should retain several extra copies in order to maintain a complete record of the transaction. These may be conformed copies. A conformed copy is an unexecuted copy of an original document. The unexecuted copy is marked to indicate that the original has been executed. Typically this is done by printing the name of the person or persons who have signed the document on the signature line. In addition, the symbol "/s/" is printed prior to the name. An example of a conformed signature is set forth below:

/s/ John Seller
John Seller

4. Computation of the Amount to be Paid by Purchaser

As mentioned earlier, various adjustments, apportionments, and calculations must be made in order to determine how much money the purchaser needs to bring to complete settlement.

(a) Purchase Price

The purchaser must pay the purchase price to the seller at settlement. In calculating how much of the purchase price the purchaser needs to bring to settlement, you should credit toward the gross amount of the purchase price the sum of the following:

(1) any deposit the purchaser has already paid;
(2) the amount of any purchase money note the seller has agreed to accept; and
(3) the amount of any third-party mortgage financing.

---

11. If the settlement clerk is not a notary public, then the parties will have to make some advance arrangement for a notary public to be present, unless one of the other parties to be present is permitted to take acknowledgments in that jurisdiction. As you may recall, in many states an attorney of that state is permitted to take acknowledgments.

(b) Apportionments

The following are income and expense items relating to the property that are typically apportioned between the parties. Apportionment means that an expense (or an income item) is allocated so that each party bears a burden (or obtains a benefit) proportionate to his or her share of the time for which the expense accrued.

i. Real Estate Taxes

If the real estate taxes for the year of settlement have been paid by the seller, or are to be paid by the seller at closing, it will be necessary for the purchaser to pay the seller for the purchaser's proportionate share of taxes for the remainder of the tax year after the date of closing. On the other hand, if the tax bill will be paid by the purchaser, the seller must give the purchaser a credit for the seller's pro rata share of the bill.

Example: Suppose the real estate taxes are $3,600 and that they are assessed for the calendar year and paid in advance. If settlement is held on September 15, then the purchaser should reimburse the seller for three months and fifteen days worth of taxes. Each month's share is $300 and each day's share is $10. Thus, the purchaser must pay the seller an additional $1,050 for the apportionment of taxes (3 × $300 plus 15 × $10).

ii. Water and Sewer Rents

If minimum charges for water and sewer rent have been prepaid by the seller for periods extending beyond the date of closing, those minimum charges should be adjusted by requiring the purchaser to pay his or her pro rata share. If, on the other hand, the purchaser will receive a bill after closing, which would cover a period prior to closing, it will be necessary for the seller to make an adjustment in favor of the purchaser.

Example: Suppose minimum water rents are $45 for a three-month period, assessed every three months from January 15 of every year and paid in arrears. If settlement is on September 15, the seller must give the purchaser credit for the two-month period from July 15 to September 15, which would equal $30 ($45/3 × 2).

If the water meter has not been read immediately before closing, an adjustment will also have to be made for any excess water that may have been consumed by the seller since the last meter reading. That amount can be estimated based on previous bills that have been paid by the seller. Alternatively, the seller may be required to place a portion of the proceeds of sale in escrow to be applied to the excess water bill after the meter has been read.

iii. Rental Payments

If the premises being sold are subject to one or more leases, an adjustment will have to be made for rental payments. If the purchaser will or may receive rental payments from tenants covering periods prior to the date of settlement, the agreement of sale may provide that those payments will be apportioned and that the seller will receive his or her pro rata share of the payments only after they are actually paid by the tenant or it may provide that the rent will be apportioned at settlement as if they were already received.

Normally, rents are prepaid. Therefore, the only adjustments that will be made at settlement pertain to those rental payments that have already been paid to the seller and that cover periods after the date of settlement. The seller must credit the purchaser at the closing with the purchaser's pro rata share of such income. For example, if a tenant has paid $500 rent to the seller on the first day of the month, and settlement occurs on the fifteenth day of that month, the purchaser would be entitled to a $250 credit as his or her share of the rent for the remaining one-half of the month.

iv. Security Deposits

If tenants have made security deposits, it will be the obligation of the purchaser, as the new owner of the building, to return the deposits at the end of the lease terms. Therefore, the seller must either credit the purchaser with the total amount of such deposits, or assign the deposits to the purchaser.

v. Insurance

Often the seller assigns the existing fire insurance policy to the purchaser. In that event the purchaser will have to pay the seller a pro rata share of any premium already paid by the seller.

vi. Miscellaneous Apportionments

A variety of miscellaneous apportionments covering such matters as fuel and other supplies on the premises, salaries of employees at the premises, and related matters, may be made at settlement depending on the circumstances of the purchase and the provisions of the agreement of sale.

(c) *Expenses of Settlement*

The purchaser will also incur a variety of expenses relating to the purchase of the premises and the obtaining of mortgage financing for the purchase. These expenses are normally paid at or prior to settlement.

i. Title Insurance Charges

If the purchaser's title is to be insured by a title insurance company, the premium is normally paid by the purchaser at settlement. Each title insurance company publishes a schedule of its premiums. Normally, the premiums increase as the amount of title insurance increases.

ii. Recording Fees

The purchaser will incur recording fees in connection with the recordation of the deed and the mortgage.

iii. Brokerage Charges

In most transactions involving the purchase of real estate, brokerage commissions will be borne by the seller. However, the parties sometimes agree that some or all of the commission is to be borne by the purchaser. In that event the purchaser will pay a share of the commission at closing.

The broker may also perform certain extra services for the purchaser (such as preparing the deed) for which he or she will be compensated at closing.

iv. Attorney's Fees

Depending on the practice of a particular attorney and the custom of the community, the fee due the attorney for representation of the purchaser may be paid at settlement, or a bill may be rendered at a later date.

v. Extras

In the event the premises being purchased are being constructed by the builder/seller, the purchaser may have agreed to purchase certain extras from the builder. The cost of those items are added to the purchase price and paid either in advance or at settlement, as provided in the agreement of sale.

vi. Personal Property

In the event the purchaser has agreed to purchase items of personal property from the seller, the cost of such property must be added to the purchase price. In addition, if the personal property is unique or extensive and not specifically identified in the agreement of sale, a bill of sale for these items should be tendered at settlement.

vii. Payments to Mortgagee

(aa) Placement Fees and Service Charges

It may be necessary to make a variety of payments to the mortgagee at settlement. The mortgagee may impose a commitment fee and charge for credit reports, appraisals, preparation of documents, and other related matters. The charges that must be tendered at settlement will be set forth in the mortgagee's commitment letter. In addition, the mortgagee may require the purchaser to pay the fee of the attorney representing the mortgagee.

b) Prepaid Interest

Typically, the first mortgage payment of principal and interest will not be due until several weeks after closing. One must contact the mortgagee in advance of settlement in order to determine when the first payment of principal is due. In many instances the mortgagee will require the buyer to prepay at settlement the interest charges from the date of settlement to the date of the first principal payment, or to the date that is one month (or other regular interest period) prior to the date of the first principal payment. As discussed in Chapter Seven, the question of the date to which prepaid interest will be paid depends on whether interest is to be paid in arrears or in advance. If it is to be paid in advance, then interest must be prepaid to the date of the first payment of principal and interest. For example, if the buyer is borrowing $50,000 from the mortgagee at 8% interest (in advance) and if thirty-six days will elapse between the date of closing and the first mortgage payment, the prepaid interest is calculated as follows: 8% interest per annum on $50,000 equals $4,000. The interest for thirty-six days equals $4,000 $\times$ $^{36}/_{365}$, or approximately $395.[12]

viii. Mechanics' Lien Insurance

If the premises to be purchased are new or have undergone extensive repairs in the recent past, the mortgagee may require insurance against the possibility of a mechanics' lien being filed against the premises. Such insurance is normally issued as an endorsement to the title insurance policy. The cost of the endorsement is generally based on the amount of mortgage title insurance being purchased.

ix. Transfer or Recording Tax

If the state or local government levies a transfer or recording tax, the amount of that tax to be borne by the buyer is paid by the buyer at settlement.

Typically, all payments are made directly to the order of the bank, title company, or the law firm for whom the settlement clerk works. The settlement clerk then aggregates the sums paid, divides that sum into separate checks, and disburses the necessary payments to tax authorities, sellers, attorneys, brokers, mortgagees, recording offices, and real estate agents. The settlement clerk will also issue a check covering any overpayment made at settlement to the purchaser.

---

12. Many banks treat the year as consisting of only 360 days, with each month having thirty days. In such cases the calculation would be $\frac{4000}{360} \times 30 = \$400.$

5. Payments by the Seller

The apportionments between the purchaser and the seller affect the total sum the seller will take from settlement. From the proceeds, the seller must pay all of the expenses of sale, which might include commissions, payoffs of mortgages and judgments, attorney's fees, transfer taxes, payment for certification, and the like. The amount the seller takes from settlement is the net proceeds.

6. Settlement Sheet

Generally, it is the obligation of the settlement clerk to prepare a "settlement sheet" setting forth all of the payments and apportionments that must be made by both parties. If the Real Estate Settlement Procedures Act applies to this transaction, the Uniform Settlement Form must be used.

7. Escrow Accounts

If for any reason the seller has failed to complete any of the preclosing obligations, or if the payment of an unknown amount, such as for excess water assessments, must be made after closing, the seller may be required to place a portion of the proceeds in an escrow account to be used to discharge a specific obligation. For example, if the seller has not obtained the satisfaction of a $1,000 judgment, the parties may agree that the seller should place $1,500 in escrow. As a result of the money being placed in escrow, the title insurer will be willing to insure the purchaser's title free of the judgment.

8. Marked-Up Title Report

It is the duty of the settlement clerk to mark up the title report, indicating which objections will be removed and therefore not appear as exceptions to the title insurance policy to be issued to the purchaser. The purchaser's counsel should retain a copy of the marked-up title report because it constitutes the insurer's commitment to issue a policy based on its contents.

IV. POSTCLOSING—PURCHASE—SALE OF PROPERTY

After settlement, several matters must be attended to.

A. RECORDING

The settlement clerk typically takes the deed, mortgage, and any other documents to be recorded to the proper state, county, or local office for recordation. After the documents have been recorded and indexed, they will usually be forwarded to the settlement clerk. The settlement clerk will send the deed to the purchaser's counsel, who will usually forward the original directly to the client after making a copy for the counsel's files.

B. TITLE POLICY

Soon after the documents have been recorded, the title insurer will normally issue the actual title policy. The purchaser's or mortgagee's counsel should review the policy against the marked-up title report to ensure that the proper coverage (including endorsements) was issued and that objections that were removed from the title report were not listed as exceptions to the title policy. The original title policy is usually forwarded to the client, and a copy of the title policy is retained for the counsel's file.

C. ESCROW

As mentioned earlier, escrow accounts may have been created at settlement for payment of various sums. The items relating to the escrow accounts should be attended to, and any excess in the accounts should be returned to the seller promptly.

D. TENANT LETTER

If the premises are acquired subject to a lease, then the seller delivers at settlement letters to the various tenants indicating that rent should now be paid to the purchaser. The purchaser will send the letters to the various tenants after settlement.

E. BINDER

As discussed later in this chapter, many lawyers prepare a binder containing all of the important documents relating to the transaction. The binder should contain a table of contents listing the documents it contains and identifying the transaction, a closing report listing the parties present and reciting what occurred at closing, and a checklist of items that remain to be done after closing.

Binders, including closing reports and postclosing checklists, are often the responsibility of a paralegal to prepare. At the end of this chapter is an example of an index for a residential settlement binder in which the purchasers assumed a VA mortgage (Example 8-6).

In Chapter Seven the subject of mortgages was discussed in detail. The following sections of this chapter review the process of closing construction and permanent mortgages.

V. CONSTRUCTION LOAN CLOSING

A. PREPARATION FOR CLOSING

If the key to a closing is preparation, then the key to preparing for a construction loan closing is a close review of the commitment letter of the construction lender, the commitment letter of the permanent lender, and the title report. These documents set forth the items necessary to prepare for closing, and a closing checklist can be generated by reviewing these documents and other closing checklists in similar construction financings. The following documents are those that typically must be prepared for closing, by one party or another, and are discussed more fully in Chapter Seven.

1. Note and Mortgage

The note and mortgage will normally be prepared either by the borrower on forms supplied by the permanent lender or by counsel for the lender. The terms of the note will comply with the commitment letters.

2. Plans and Specifications

A complete set of plans and specifications usually have to be submitted to the permanent lender and the construction lender for their approval in advance of closing.

3. General Construction Contract

The general construction contract will be subject to the approval of (or on a form supplied by) the construction lender and will be assigned by the borrower to the construction lender at closing.

4. Corporate Resolutions

If the borrower is a corporation, a certified copy of corporate resolutions authorizing the borrower to incur the debt and create a mortgage should be prepared by the borrower for submission at closing. It is preferable to have the form of resolution approved by the permanent lender, construction lender, and title insurer before adoption by the borrower.

5. Survey

In addition to the plans and specifications, the construction and permanent lenders will normally want to review a survey of the property prior to the time of closing.

6. Insurance

The commitment letters will undoubtedly contain requirements for fire insurance and, in some cases, liability insurance. Such policies must be obtained well in advance of settlement and must set forth limits of liability consistent with the commitment letters. The commitment letters will require that the policies contain clauses recognizing the interest of the mortgagee.

7. Completion or Performance Bond

If a completion or performance bond is required by the construction loan commitment, it must be obtained by the prospective general contractor in order to be tendered at settlement.

8. Construction Loan Agreement

The construction loan agreement between the borrower and the construction lender may be prepared by the borrower's attorney or by the lender's attorney. In any event the document will have to be approved by the borrower and the construction lender in advance of settlement.

9. Building Permit

At closing, the commitment letter usually requires the developer to submit permits of the appropriate local authorities evidencing permission to build the proposed improvements. Such permits must be obtained in advance of closing.

10. Security Agreement and Financing Statements

If the commitment letter requires the borrower to execute a security agreement granting the lender a lien on personal property, then the security agreement, along with the requisite financing statements, would typically be prepared by the borrower's attorney and submitted to the lender's attorney for approval in advance of closing.

11. Declaration of Cross Easements or Declaration of Reciprocal Easements

As discussed in Chapter Seven, certain transactions require a reciprocal or cross easement agreement. Such an easement agreement is usually prepared for recording by the borrower's attorney and submitted to the lender's attorney for approval.

12. Buy-Sell Agreement

The buy-sell agreement is typically prepared by the construction or permanent lender and will be executed by both lenders and the owner at the construction loan closing.

13. Leases

If either or both of the commitment letters are conditioned on certain leases being in existence at the time of closing, then executed copies must be produced at or before closing. In addition, it may be necessary to present estoppel certificates at closing, evidencing the fact that the borrower (as landlord) is not in violation of any lease as of the date of closing.

14. Assignment of Lease

Any leases that are in existence at the time of closing will be assigned to the construction lender, who in turn will assign the assignment of leases to the permanent lender when the permanent lender purchases the note and mortgage.

15. Subordination Agreement

In the event an existing lease is superior to the construction mortgage and is to be subordinated, a subordination agreement must be prepared and tendered at closing.

16. Attornment/Nondisturbance Agreement

If there are to be leases on the premises subordinate to the mortgage, the lender and lessee may require the existence of an attornment/nondisturbance agreement at the time of closing. The lessee will probably not be present at the mortgage loan closing, and therefore, all documents to be signed by the lessee, such as the lease, estoppel certificate, and attornment/nondisturbance agreement must be signed by the lessee in advance of closing.

17. Waiver of Mechanics' Lien

If a waiver of mechanics' lien is to be filed at closing, the borrower must obtain the executed waiver from the general contractor prior to closing. In addition, the title company may require that photographs of the premises be taken prior to closing, evidencing that no work has begun.

18. Letter of Permanent Lender Approving Documents

The construction lender often requires that all of the documentation for closing be submitted to counsel for the permanent lender in advance of closing and that counsel for the permanent lender issue a letter to the borrower and the construction lender indicating that the permanent lender has reviewed and approved the documents.

19. Title Report

If the lenders require the issuance of a title policy certifying that their lien is a valid first lien, then the borrower must order the title report and distribute copies to the permanent and construction lenders. Often the title company will indicate, after consultation with the borrower, which of the objections on the title report it expects to remove at closing. The lenders may require that information in advance.

20. Letter Confirming Date of Closing

When all of the documents have been drafted, reviewed, and approved by the parties, one of the parties (usually the borrower) sends all the other parties a notice letter confirming the date, time, and place of closing.

21. Rehearsal for Closing

Because of the complexity of many construction loan closings, the parties to a particular transaction may conduct a dry closing, or a preclosing, in order to determine what remains to be done.

B. CLOSING

1. Place of Closing

As in the case of a purchase, closing might take place at a title company, a law firm, or a bank. In the event a title company will insure the title of the mortgagee, it is typical for an employee of the title company to act as the settlement clerk.

2. Closing Report

As in the case of the purchase of property, a list should be prepared setting forth information concerning the parties present at closing.

3. Mechanics of Closing

Closing itself is similar to the closing for the purchase of property. The parties execute and exchange various documents. Some documents, such as the mortgage, financing statements, and, possibly, a memorandum of lease, assignment of lease, or a reciprocal easement agreement, will be left with the settlement clerk for recording. Counsel should be certain to prepare conformed copies of all documents for their files. The borrower is required to make certain payments at settlement.

(a) Expenses of the Borrower

i. Placement Fees

If there are any placement fees, points, or similar charges to be paid by the borrower at the time of closing, such items may be deducted from the proceeds of the loan. If there is to be no disbursement on the loan at closing, or if any such fees may not be taken from the proceeds of the loan, the borrower must pay such expenses at closing.

ii. Tax Escrow

If the borrower is required to escrow $1/12$ of annual taxes monthly, it may be required to make payments into the escrow account at closing.

iii. Discharge of Liens

If there are objections to title based on taxes due, judgments against the borrower, or prior mortgages, these items must be discharged at closing by the borrower's depositing sufficient funds with the settlement clerk.

iv. Lender's Attorney's Fee

Often the commitment letter will provide that the borrower must pay the fee of the lender's attorney relating to the loan being closed. That payment is normally made at closing.

v. Title Insurance Premium

The borrower is required at closing to pay the premium for the policy insuring the lender's lien.

vi. Miscellaneous Expenses

The borrower may incur additional expenses for such items as recording costs, notary fees, and mortgage taxes, which can be either a minor or a substantial expense.

(b) Settlement Sheet

As in the case of a purchase of property, a settlement sheet is prepared by the settlement clerk. The settlement sheet evidences payment of the items just discussed.

(c) Marked-Up Title Report

The settlement clerk marks up one or more copies of the title report, indicating the state of title that will be insured to the mortgagee.

C. POST CLOSING

As in the case of the purchase of property, several steps must be taken after closing.

1. Recordation of the Mortgage and Other Documents

The mortgage must be recorded and forwarded to the lender by the settlement clerk after recordation. In addition, any financing statements, leases, and reciprocal easement agreements must be recorded.

2. Issuance of Title Policy

Typically, the title insurance company will not issue a policy until the loan is bought by the permanent lender, in order to avoid the payment of two full premiums. Instead, the commitment will be "kept open," and although the construction lender has a right to have a policy issued, it will normally not require the issuance of a policy unless a claim arises.

3. Binder

Because of the large number of documents involved, counsel usually prepares a binder similar to that for an acquisition settlement. An example of an index for a construction loan settlement appears at the end of this chapter (Example 8-7).

Some time after the construction loan closing, the construction on the premises presumably will be completed and conditions for closing the permanent loan will have been met.

VI. PERMANENT LOAN CLOSING

A. PREPARATION FOR CLOSING

When a permanent loan is not part of a package with a construction loan, preparation for closing is similar to preparation for a construction loan closing, except that there will be no buy-sell agreement, no construction loan agreement, and no construction contract. Settlement of a permanent loan pursuant to a buy-sell agreement involves some or all of the following:

1. Assignment of Mortgage

An assignment of the mortgage from the construction lender to the permanent lender must be prepared and executed by the construction lender.

2. Certificate of Occupancy

In many instances the permanent commitment letter requires as a condition of closing that the local governmental authorities issue a certificate acknowledging that the construction is sufficiently complete that the premises may be occupied for their intended purpose. Such a certificate must be obtained by the borrower for submission at closing.

3. As-Built Survey

Often the permanent lender's commitment letter requires that the borrower submit an as-built survey at the time of closing. The purpose of this survey is to ensure the lender that the buildings and on-site improvements are within the title line of the premises and that the buildings and improvements have been constructed in the locations shown by the plans and specifications, with the normal allowances for field conditions.

4. Rent Roll

If disbursement under the permanent loan commitment is contingent on achievement of a certain minimum rent roll, the borrower must submit to the lender a list of all leases in effect. In addition to the list, the lender may want to examine each of the leases.

5. Estoppel Certificates

If leases are to be assigned to the mortgagee, the permanent lender will require estoppel certificates from some or all tenants, evidencing that the owner is not in default in its obligations as landlord.

6. Declaration of No Set-Off

The declaration of no set-off assures the permanent lender, who takes the mortgage by assignment from the construction lender, that it is not accepting the mortgage subject to defenses of the borrower against the assignor.

7. Security Agreements and Financing Statements

Either a new set is prepared or the old set is assigned by the construction lender to the permanent lender.

8. Corporate Resolutions

A certified copy of corporate resolutions of the borrower, authorizing the permanent loan, must be prepared by counsel for the borrower and submitted at the permanent loan closing. These may already have been delivered as a part of the construction loan closing.

9. Advance Arrangements for Pay-Off of Construction Lender

At closing the permanent lender disburses the amount of its mortgage or a percentage of that amount if a rental achievement has not been met. The sum to be disbursed by the permanent lender is used to pay off the construction lender. If the mortgage is for a substantial sum, the borrower will desire to expedite the transfer of funds from the permanent lender to the construction lender in order to minimize interest payments. Interest will have to be paid to the permanent lender from the date of the permanent loan closing. Interest will be paid to the construction lender each day until the construction lender's account has been credited with repayment of the loan. If the parties merely tender checks at closing and put the checks through for normal deposit, the overlap could require the borrower to pay interest to both lenders for several days. In order to prevent that, the borrower will often arrange for the permanent lender to deposit its funds at the closing either by tendering at closing a check drawn directly on the Federal Reserve bank of the district in which closing takes place (and putting that check through for immediate deposit), or by wiring funds from the permanent lender's account directly into the account of the construction lender without a check being tendered at settlement. If you are working on a permanent loan closing, you should inquire of the lawyer for whom you are working whether special arrangements should be made to minimize interest charges to the borrower. Such arrangements must be made in advance.

10. Title Bring Down

Some time prior to settlement the title insurance company must be notified to undertake a bring down search from the date of the construction loan closing to the date of the proposed permanent loan closing.

11. Notice to Parties

The borrower normally notifies the lenders of the date, time, and place of settlement by letter.

B. CLOSING

Closing for the permanent loan is similar to other closings that have been considered.

1. Place of Closing

The closing will take place at a bank, title company, or law firm.

2. Parties Present

At a permanent loan closing the borrower and representatives of the permanent lender, construction lender, and title company are usually present. Again, a settlement clerk is needed to record documents and handle the exchange of funds. As in the case of all closings, a list of parties present should be prepared for inclusion in the closing report.

3. Mechanics of Closing

Permanent loan closings are relatively simple; the construction lender is paid off from the proceeds of the permanent loan, and only a limited number of documents are exchanged.

(a) Exchange of Money

i. Pay-Off of Construction Lender

The permanent lender purchases the construction loan note for the amount due on the note. If the permanent loan is to be advanced in stages, and if the first advance is insufficient to purchase the note, then the borrower must repay the excess principal balance of the note to the construction lender. If the permanent loan disbursement exceeds the sum due on the note, then the borrower receives the excess from the construction lender as a loan. In either case the new principal balance of the note is the amount disbursed by the permanent lender, whether the amount is equal to or more or less than the principal balance that had been due to the construction lender prior to settlement.

ii. Final Interest Payment to Construction Lender

The borrower must make a final interest payment to the construction lender covering the interest due from the date of the last interest payment to the date of closing (or later, if the funds paid to the construction lender at closing are not immediate funds).

iii. Return of Borrower's Stand-By Fee

Most permanent lenders require a prospective borrower to make a substantial deposit in order to secure the obligations of the borrower under the commitment. Such a deposit may be refundable at the time the permanent loan is closed.

iv. Escrows

In addition to normal tax escrows, the permanent lender may require other escrows, especially for work that has not been completed and for tenant-space finishing work that the borrower has contracted to perform in the various occupancy leases.

The discussions under construction loan closings relating to tax escrows, lender's attorney's fees, title insurance premiums, and miscellaneous expenses also apply to the permanent loan closing.

(b) Settlement Sheet

A settlement sheet is prepared by the settlement clerk setting forth all of the items referred to in *(a)*.

(c) Marked-Up Title Report

The title policy is marked up and assigned to the permanent lender. A copy of the marked-up report is given to each party.

C. POST CLOSING

After closing has taken place the settlement clerk records the assignment of the mortgage and any financing statements or assignments of financing statements. The assignment of mortgage and copies of the financing statements are returned to the lender.

If the full amount of the loan was not disbursed at closing because of failure to meet a rental achievement, further disbursement may take place as new leases are presented to the permanent lender. A closing may or may not be necessary for payment of those further sums, depending on whether the sums are already evidenced by the note, or whether another note will be required.

After the permanent loan closing, the title company issues a policy in favor of the permanent lender. The policy is usually forwarded to counsel for the permanent lender.

After closing, a binder of documents should be prepared.

VII. DISCLOSURE AND THE REAL ESTATE SETTLEMENT PROCEDURES ACT OF 1974

A. INTRODUCTION

Continuing a long tradition in Western civilization, the various American state governments have enacted a variety of laws to protect individuals with respect to the lending of money or extension of credit. The oldest tradition is of proscriptive statutes, and all the states still have some form of proscriptive statutes. The most familiar is a usury law, which in its strictest form sets a maximum interest rate above which no lender or borrower may legally go, no matter how well informed the borrower or how necessary it is for the borrower to borrow the money. American usury laws, as we have previously noted, are a patchwork and vary from states that now have no such limit to states that do not apply the limit to certain borrowers (such as corporations) or to certain loans (business loans over a certain amount or any loan over a larger amount), to states that apply the strict standard described to all loans and all lenders. Other forms of proscriptive laws carve out areas in which only certain regulated institutions are permitted to act, such as commercial banks, building and loan associations, savings banks or associations, and the like.

The second major kind of statute is the disclosure statute. The impulse behind the proscriptive statutes is that there are certain transactions that society will simply not permit. The impulse behind the disclosure statute is that the consumer needs certain information in order to operate effectively in the market and that the supplier will not provide such information unless forced to do so by competition or by law. Thus, the various disclosure acts are a requirement on lenders, particularly institutional lenders. Again, state disclosure acts vary tremendously, but there is a common thread of requiring disclosures for those thought to be least able to demand it. The laws that we would be concerned with most pertain to real estate mortgage loans, and the disclosure laws are generally applicable only to single-family or small multifamily residential mortgages. A sample of a disclosure statement in connection with a residential mortgage loan appears as *Example 8-8* at the end of this chapter.

State disclosure laws still exist in many states but have been in large measure superseded by the federal Real Estate Settlement Procedures Act of 1974, known as RESPA. RESPA was a hybrid in that it was also a proscriptive statute, prohibiting certain forms of kickbacks and referral fees, for example. But the major thrust was to provide uniform standards for disclosure of relevant information in a timely fashion. To that extent, RESPA represents a sharpening and extension in a limited field of the requirements of the federal Consumer Credit Protection Act of 1968, commonly known as the Truth-in-Lending Act, which governs disclosure respecting the lending of money and extension of credit much more generally, not just in the context of a residential mortgage loan. RESPA by no means supplants Truth-in-Lending; indeed, they are governed by different sets of regulations and even by different departments of the government.[13] Instead, RESPA supplements Truth-in-Lending.

This chapter is not designed to make the reader an expert on RESPA or Truth-in-Lending. If your future job is with a lender, you might be required to work closely with disclosure and regulatory laws, and in that case you will be trained in their use by your employer. We will, however,

---

13. RESPA is administered by the Department of Housing and Urban Development and the regulations relating to RESPA are generically known as Regulation X. Truth-in-Lending comes under the Treasury Department and the regulations are known as Regulation Z.

take the opportunity to review RESPA by examining a settlement sheet for a hypothetical settlement to familiarize you with the type of information disclosed, the form of settlement sheet presently required by RESPA, and the relationship between disclosure and the actual settlement costs.

B. SCOPE OF RESPA

1. Transactions Covered

RESPA covers real estate mortgage loans in connection with the purchase of residential real estate. Residential real estate includes condominiums, mobile homes, and cooperatives, as well as traditional residences, and includes the purchase of a duplex, triplex, or quadruplex. The loan must be made by a federal lender, as defined in the Act. The definition is so broad that almost any institutional lender falls within its definitions. The effect of the qualification is to exclude from RESPA only those residential purchase settlements in which either there is no mortgage involved, or the mortgage involved is a purchase money mortgage given to the seller or a regular mortgage loan from a relative or friend.

2. Prohibition Against Kickbacks and Unearned Fees

In many parts of the United States, lenders, brokers, and title insurance companies customarily paid referral fees to persons, such as brokers and lawyers, who directed a seller or purchaser/borrower to them. RESPA characterizes such referral fees and fee splitting as kickbacks and prohibits them in connection with a transaction covered by RESPA.

3. Limitations on Escrows

RESPA places limitations on the amounts that a lender can require to be escrowed for the payment of taxes and insurance premiums. The limitations have no effect on common practices and reach only to abuses.

4. Uniform Settlement Sheet

The Department of Housing and Urban Development (HUD) has devised a uniform settlement sheet that is intended for use nationwide, with only minor local variations permitted. The sheet must be used for all settlements to which RESPA applies. HUD believed that settlement sheets used in some areas were incomplete and failed to disclose all that transpired at settlement. You must become familiar with the sheet and be able to explain the sheet to a client and to use the sheet as a source of information after settlement. Part D of this section is devoted to a discussion of the RESPA sheet.

C. DISCLOSURES

RESPA has already undergone significant revisions since its enactment in 1974. Many of these revisions related to changes in the presettlement disclosure requirements of RESPA, which many found to be unworkable and unproductive, if not counterproductive. As of 1977, RESPA and Truth-in-Lending required between them the disclosure of certain items (discussed below) to the borrower, at various times during the transaction (but at latest at settlement). The lender is the party required to make the disclosures. Some of the disclosures required are of costs that are beyond the lender's control but that one can reasonably expect will be incurred. To the extent that the lender does not control such costs, it may make good faith estimates, clearly marked as such with an "(e)" after the estimated figure (a figure rather than a range must presently be given).

1. Booklet

Each lender must supply an applicant for a RESPA-covered loan with a booklet prepared by HUD explaining home loan financing, the settlement costs that might be expected, and the use of escrows for taxes.

2. Finance Charges and Annual Percentage Rate

At the time the lender issues its commitment letter, it must disclose to the borrower, on a form conforming with Regulation Z, the basics of the loan. (An example of the permissible form is shown as *Example 8-9* at the end of this chapter.) The basics include:

a. The amount of the loan, which is the purchase price less any downpayment.

b. Prepaid finance charges, which are charges paid to the lender at or prior to settlement, and which include any commitment fee (presently 1% of loan amount by custom in the Philadelphia area), any prepaid interest (usually from the day of settlement through the end of the month), mortgage guaranty insurance, and points (even if paid by the seller). This figure can be misleading to a borrower if the borrower thinks that these represent the total of his or her closing costs. Care must be taken to explain that the term "prepaid finance charges" is a term of art[14] used to define specific charges that are part of the computation of the annual percentage rate as defined by Truth-in-Lending.

c. The finance charge consists of the sum of prepaid finance charges, interest paid through the anticipated term of the loan, and any other finance charges that are not prepaid. The total finance charge is shown in the second box at the top of the form. This amount is treated as if it

---

14. "Term of art" is itself a term of art; that is, a phrase or word having a defined meaning within a trade, profession, or business.

were all interest and is calculated using as the base the amount financed, rather than using the principal amount, over the stated term of the loan. The result is the annual percentage rate. Whenever there are prepaid finance charges, then the annual percentage rate will be greater than the simple annual interest rate set forth in the note and as understood by home mortgage lenders and borrowers. As an example, a 1% service fee on a twenty-five year loan has the effect of making the annual percentage rate 8.25% on an 8% interest loan. You must be able to explain this difference to clients, as the result is often confusing to them.

d. The form also requires disclosure of the repayment terms (e.g., 300 equal and consecutive monthly payments), late charges, prepayment penalties, and the security being taken for the loan.

3. RESPA Disclosures

RESPA originally required certain disclosures to be made at least twelve days prior to settlement, which requirement had the effect of not permitting parties to meet deadlines because they had to wait twelve days after disclosure even if everyone wanted an earlier settlement. As of 1977, RESPA requires the following disclosures at or before settlement:

a. The cost of all settlement services charged to the borrower, which includes (among other things) title charges, document preparations, inspections and certifications, appraisals, services rendered by an attorney or broker, and surveys. Good-faith estimates must be made if not known. The reference to "services rendered by an attorney" does not apply to a fee to an attorney freely chosen by a borrower of their own volition and representing only the borrower and not the lender. Note that the total of settlement service charges of taxes and similar charges has many more components than prepaid finance charges.

b. The remainder of the purchase price, the apportionments between buyer and seller, and the amounts to be escrowed with the lender.

The sum of a. and b. should equal a good approximation of the total cash that the purchaser will have to pay before settlement, or bring to settlement to the extent not paid before settlement.

D. SETTLEMENT SHEET

The form of settlement sheet (also known as a "settlement statement") which is commonly used in a RESPA settlement is shown in *Example 8-1*. We will review the form of settlement sheet by showing how it would be filled in at a settlement based on the hypothetical situation which follows *Example 8-1*.

Example 8-1: **Settlement Sheet**

HUD— Rev. 5/76

| A. | U.S. DEPARTMENT OF HOUSING AND URBAN DEVELOPMENT |
| | **SETTLEMENT STATEMENT** |

Form Approved
OMB NO. 63 R 1501

| B. TYPE OF LOAN |
| 1. ☐ FHA   2. ☐ FMHA   3. ☐ CONV. UNINS. |
| 4. ☐ VA   5. ☐ CONV. INS. |
| 6. File Number :   7. Loan Number: |
| 8. Mortgage Insurance Case Number: |

NO. _____

C. NOTE: *This form is furnished to give you a statement of actual settlement costs. Amounts paid to and by the settlement agent are shown. Items marked "(p.o.c.)" were paid outside the closing; they are shown here for informational purposes and are not included in the totals.*

D. NAME OF BORROWER :	E. NAME OF SELLER :	F. NAME OF LENDER :
ALBERT BROWNE	ROSE SADOWSKI	UPPER DUBLIN BANK

G. PROPERTY LOCATION:	H. SETTLEMENT AGENT :	I. SETTLEMENT DATE:
49 W. LANDVIEW Dr. UPPER DUBLIN PENNSYLVANIA	PLACE OF SETTLEMENT:	10/10/85

	J. SUMMARY OF BORROWER'S TRANSACTION			K. SUMMARY OF SELLER'S TRANSACTION	
100.	GROSS AMOUNT DUE FROM BORROWER:		400.	GROSS AMOUNT DUE TO SELLER:	
101.	Contract sales price	100,000	401.	Contract sales price	100,000
102.	Personal Property		402.	Personal property	
103.	Settlement charges to borrower (line 1400)	5246.74	403.	Rent adjustment	
104.	Rent adjustment		404.	Acknowledgement of deed	
105.	Acknowledgement of deed		405.		
	Adjustments for items paid by seller in advance			Adjustments for items paid by seller in advance	
106.	City/town taxes 10/10 to 12/31	533.32	406.	City/town taxes 10/10 to 12/31	533.32
107.	County taxes to		407.	County taxes to	
108.	Assessments to		408.	Assessments to	
109.	Water/sewer rent 10/10 to 12/31	62.40	409.	Water/sewer rent 10/10 to 12/31	62.40
110.	School taxes to		410.	School taxes to	
111.			411.		
112.			412.		
120.	GROSS AMOUNT DUE FROM BORROWER	105,842.46	420.	GROSS AMOUNT DUE TO SELLER	100,595.72
200.	AMOUNTS PAID BY OR IN BEHALF OF BORROWER:		500.	REDUCTIONS IN AMOUNT DUE TO SELLER:	
201.	Deposit or earnest money	10,000	501.	Excess deposit (see instructions)	
202.	Principal amount of new loan(s)	80,000	502.	Settlement charges to seller (line 1400)	7,125
203.	Existing loan(s) taken subject to		503.	Existing loan(s) taken subject to	
204.			504.	Payoff of first mortgage loan	30,704.94
205.			505.	Payoff of second mortgage loan	
206.			506.		
207.			507.		
208.			508.		
209.			509.	Escrow	
	Adjustments for items unpaid by seller			Adjustments for items unpaid by seller	
210.	City/town taxes to		510.	City/town taxes to	
211.	County taxes to		511.	County taxes to	
212.	Assessments to		512.	Assessments to	
213.	Water/sewer rent 7/1 to 10/10	26.66	513.	Water/sewer rent 7/1 to 10/10	26.66
214.	School taxes to		514.	School taxes to	
215.			515.		
216.			516.		
217.			517.		
218.			518.		
219.			519.		
220.	TOTAL PAID BY/FOR BORROWER	90,026.66	520.	TOTAL REDUCTION AMOUNT DUE SELLER	37,856.60
300.	CASH AT SETTLEMENT FROM/TO BORROWER		600.	CASH AT SETTLEMENT TO/FROM SELLER	
301.	Gross amount due from borrower (line 120)	105,842.46	601.	Gross amount due to seller (line 420)	100,595.72
302.	Less amounts paid by/for borrower (line 220)	90,026.66	602.	Less reductions in amount due seller (line 520)	37,856.60
303.	CASH (☐ FROM) (☐ TO) BORROWER	15,815.80	603.	CASH (☐ TO) (☐ FROM) SELLER	62,739.12

Continued.

Example 8-1   Settlement Sheet *continued*

Page 2

	L. SETTLEMENT CHARGES		PAID FROM BORROWER'S FUNDS AT SETTLEMENT	PAID FROM SELLER'S FUNDS AT SETTLEMENT
700.	TOTAL SALES/BROKER'S COMMISSION based on price $ *100,000* @ = *6%*			
	Division of Commission (line 700) as follows:			
701.	$ *6,000* to *Hill 'N Dale Realty*			
702.	$ to			
703.	Commission paid at Settlement			*6,000*
704.				
800.	ITEMS PAYABLE IN CONNECTION WITH LOAN			
801.	Loan Origination Fee *1* % *($800 less $150 prepaid)*		*650*	
802.	Loan Discount %			
803.	Appraisal Fee to *Upper Dublin Bank*		*180*	
804.	Credit Report to			
805.	Lender's Inspection Fee			
806.	Mortgage Insurance Application Fee to			
807.	Assumption Fee			
808.				
809.				
810.				
811.				
900.	ITEMS REQUIRED BY LENDER TO BE PAID IN ADVANCE			
901.	Interest from *10/10* to *10/31* @ $ *26.67* /day		*586.74*	
902.	Mortgage Insurance Premium for months to			
903.	Hazard Insurance Premium for *1* years to		*280*	
904.	years to			
905.				
1000.	RESERVES DEPOSITED WITH LENDER			
1001.	Hazard Insurance months @ $ per month			
1002.	Mortgage Insurance months @ $ per month			
1003.	City property taxes *8* months @ $ *200* per month		*1,600*	
1004.	County property taxes months @ $ per month			
1005.	Annual assessments months @ $ per month			
1006.	School taxes months @ $ per month			
1007.	months @ $ per month			
1008.	months @ $ per month			
1100.	TITLE CHARGES			
1101.	Settlement or closing fee to			
1102.	Abstract or title search to			
1103.	Title Examination to			
1104.	Title insurance binder to			
1105.	Document preparation to *Seller*			*40*
1106.	Notary Fees to *Title Officer*		*10*	*10*
1107.	Attorney's fees to			
	(includes above items numbers:)			
1108.	Title insurance to		*680*	
	(includes above items numbers: 1101 to 1104)			
1109.	Lender's coverage $ *80,000*			
1110.	Owner's coverage $ *100,000*			
1111.	Disbursing fee:			
1112.	Endorsement fees to: *Endorsement (300)(100)*		*30*	
1113.				
1200.	GOVERNMENT RECORDING AND TRANSFER CHARGES			
1201.	Recording fees: Deed $ *15* ; Mortgage $ *15* ; Releases $ *15*		*30*	*15*
1202.	City/county tax/stamps: Deed $; Mortgage $		*500*	*500*
1203.	State tax/stamps: Deed $; Mortgage $		*500*	*500*
1204.				
1205.				
1300.	ADDITIONAL SETTLEMENT CHARGES			
1301.	Survey *XYZ Engineers*		*200*	
1302.	Pest inspection *Steve's Bug-OFF*			*60*
1303.				
1304.				
1305.				
1306.				
1307.				
1308.				
1400.	TOTAL SETTLEMENT CHARGES (enter on lines 103, Section J and 502, Section K)		*5,246.74*	*7,125*

The above settlement examined and approved, and a copy received, in consideration of which Title Insurance Company is directed and authorized to make distribution and payments in accordance herewith. Any funds held for the disposition of exceptions and/or for the protection of the Company, will be held without payment of interest and subject to the payment of an escrow service charge of $10.00 for the first six months and a like charge for each additional one year period. Any income arising from the fund shall be the property of Title Insurance Company. Seller specifically agrees with the disbursing charge as set forth above.

Seller's Signature	Purchaser's Signature
Seller's Signature	Purchaser's Signature
Address	Address

Example:

Albert Browne is purchasing a home at 49 W. Landview Drive from Rose Sadowski for $100,000. Browne is obtaining a loan from Upper Dublin Bank for $80,000 for a term of twenty-five years at 12% per annum simple interest. Settlement is to take place on October 10. Real estate taxes are paid on a calendar year basis (January 1–December 31) and are due on March 15 of each year. Presently, taxes are $2,400 per year. Water and sewer are paid on the same bill, quarterly in advance, with a reading for excess every six months. The quarterly minimum is $70, and the average six-month excess for this house is $48. The agreement of sale requires Sadowski to pay for a termite inspection and the 6% broker's commission to Hill'N Dale Realty. The mortgage commitment requires real estate tax escrows, a prepaid fire insurance policy, a survey, and Pennsylvania endorsements 100 and 300 to the title insurance coverage given to the mortgagee. The lender charges a 1% commitment fee (of which $150 has been paid with the application) and an appraisal fee of $180.

Based upon the foregoing information, it will be useful to walk through the settlement sheet. Blocks A through I are self-explanatory.

1. Block J. Summary of Borrower's Transaction

(a) Section 100

Section 100 relates to the gross amount due from the purchaser (who is characterized on the form as being the borrower) before credit apportionments, credit for deposit monies, and amount of the mortgage. It indicates the gross amount that the borrower will have to produce from all sources.

Line 101 is the purchase price, in this instance $100,000.

Line 102 is the price of any personal property being sold by the seller to the purchaser and not included in the purchase price. In our example, there is none.

Line 103 relates to the total settlement charges to be paid by the borrower, as calculated in Block L. As will be shown from the review of Block L below, this equals $5,246.74.

Lines 104 and 105 are for other direct charges that do not apply elsewhere.

Lines 106 through 112 are for items paid in advance by the seller for which the seller is entitled to some reimbursement. Lines 106 and 107 are used for different real estate taxes. Here there is only one real estate tax, the amount of which is shown on Line 106. The taxes are $2,400 per calendar year and have been paid for the year of settlement. The seller is entitled to be reimbursed from October 10 through December 31. Roughly, we can call this two months and twenty days using a thirty-day month, as is often done for ease of calculation. The total due the seller is $533.33, which is obtained by dividing $2,400 by 12 to get the monthly rate and then by 30 to get the daily rate, and by multiplying the monthly rate of $200 by 2 (for November and December) and the daily rate of $6.66 by 20. The space on Line 106 should indicate the period of apportionment as 10/10 to 12/31.

Line 109 can be used for the apportionment of prepaid sewer and water. Sadowski has paid the entire quarterly minimum charge of $70 for October, November, and December. Using artificial quarters of ninety days, this equals a per diem rate of $ .78, which should be multiplied by eighty days, for a total adjustment on line 109 of $62.40. Again the period of adjustment should be indicated.

Lines 110 through 112 remain vacant here. They could be used to apportion prepaid insurance, unpaid rent from a tenant, or similar items, where appropriate.

Line 120 is the sum of all the items completed in Section 100. In this case the sum of $105,842.46 should be entered on Line 120.

(b) Section 200

Section 200 indicates all amounts for which Browne will receive credit toward the amount due, or which will be paid by others on Browne's behalf.

Line 201 is for the deposit money, in this case 10%, which is $10,000.

Line 202 is for the amount of the mortgage loan, which is $80,000. Note that this is the actual amount of the loan, not the "amount financed" as defined by Truth-in-Lending.

Line 203 is vacant here, as there is no mortgage being assumed by Browne.

Lines 210 through 219 are the converse of Lines 106 through 112. They are items that Browne must pay, but for which Sadowski is at least in part responsible. In our case there are no unpaid taxes, so lines 210, 211, and 212 are vacant.

Line 213 contains an apportionment of estimated excess water and sewer. In our example the normal six-month excess is $48 and the period is from July 1 through December 31. Browne is entitled to reimbursement from July 1 through October 10, which is three months and ten days. The monthly rate is $8 and the daily rate is $.26, giving a total credit of $26.66 which is entered on Line 213.

Line 220 is the total of the items shown in Section 200, which in this case is $90,026.66.

(c) Section 300

Section 300 reconciles the information contained in Sections 100 and 200 by subtracting Line 220 from Line 120. This result, shown in Line 303, is the total cash that Browne must pay at settlement.

2. Block K. Summary of Seller's Transaction

(a) Section 400

Section 400 is fairly analogous to Section 100. The section calculates the total amounts due to Sadowski, before deductions for her various expenses.

Line 401 is the purchase price, again $100,000. As Line 102, Line 402 is blank.

Line 406 is $533.32, the same as Line 106, and Line 409 is $62.40, the same as line 109.

Line 420 is the sum of items in Section 400, in this case $100,595.72.

(b) Section 500

Section 500 includes the reductions in the gross amount that the seller is due to receive.

Line 502 relates to the total settlement charges to be paid by the seller, as calculated in Block L. As will be shown from the review of Block L below, this amount is $7,125.

Line 503 is blank, as there are no loans being assumed by Browne.

Line 504 is the amount needed to pay off any first mortgage with which the seller had encumbered the property. In our case the payoff (equal to unpaid principal, accrued interest, and any prepayment penalty) is $30,704.94. Line 505 is blank because there are no other mortgages or judgments.

Lines 510 through 514 are analogous to Lines 210 through 214. Again, the only entry is $26.66 for estimated sewer and water excess, which goes on Line 513.

Line 520 is the sum of items in Section 500, in this case $37,856.60.

(c) Section 600

Section 600 reconciles Sections 400 and 500, by subtracting Line 520 from Line 420. This result, shown in Line 603, is the total net proceeds of settlement to be paid to the seller.

3. Block L. Settlement Charges

(a) Section 700

Section 700 includes all brokers commissions to be paid by either party. Line 701 is for commissions paid by the seller. The sum of $6,000 ($100,000 × 6%) is entered on Line 703 under the column marked "Paid from Seller's Funds." (For purposes of our discussion, items placed under the column "Paid from Seller's Funds" will be referred to as under "Seller," and items placed under the column "Paid from Borrower's Funds" will be referred to as under "Borrower.")

Line 701 indicates that the entire $6,000 is being paid to Hill 'N Dale Realty. If the commission were being split, then some lesser amount would be paid to Hill 'N Dale and the remainder would go in Line 702 as being paid to the cooperating broker.

(b) Section 800

Section 800 includes items payable in connection with financing, whether paid to a lender or some other party.

Line 801 will read $800 (less $150 prepaid), for a total of $650 under Borrower.

There are no points being paid, so Line 802 is blank.

Line 803 is an appraisal fee of $180 payable by the borrower to Upper Dublin Bank.

In this case there are no further entries in Section 800.

(c) Section 900

Line 901 indicates interest payable for twenty-two days from 10/10 to 10/31 at $26.67 a day for a total of $586.74 under Borrower.

Because Browne is paying for his hazard insurance policy at settlement, the $280 premium is entered on Line 903 under Borrower.

(d) Section 1000

Section 1000 is for escrowed items. Because only real estate taxes are being escrowed, and there is only one real estate tax, the only entry is Line 1003. As noted earlier, Upper Dublin Bank requires a full year's taxes in escrow after receipt of the payment due on March 1. Because each monthly payment will be accompanied by an escrow payment of 1/12 of the taxes, Upper Dublin Bank will have received only 4/12 by March 1, being the payments for December (the first payment date), January, February, and March. In order to have 12/12 available on March 15, Upper Dublin Bank will require reserves paid at settlement by Browne of 8/12 of the year's taxes. Because the monthly rate is $200, Line 1003 will show $1,600 under Borrower.

(e) Section 1100

The first entry in Section 1100 is in Line 1105, where $40 is entered under Seller for preparation of the deed.

Line 1106 has entries of $10 each under Seller and under Borrower for notary fees.

Line 1107 is blank, either because none of the parties is represented or because the only attorneys are independent (i.e., they were not selected by Upper Dublin Bank) and do not elect to be paid at the settlement.

Line 1108 is $680 under Borrower, for the basic title company charge. Line 1109 indicates that the lender's coverage was $80,000. Line 1110 indicates that the borrower's coverage was $100,000. Line 1112 refers to Pa. Endorsements 100 and 300 for which $30 is entered under Borrower.

(f) Section 1200

Line 1201 shows recording fees of $15 each for the deed and the mortgage ($30 under Borrower) and $15 for the mortgage release (under Seller).

Lines 1202 and 1203 each indicate $500 under both Borrower and Seller, being a 1% transfer tax to the municipality and a 1% transfer tax to the state.[15]

---

15. The percentage amount of transfer tax charged varies from county to county. For example, the transfer tax in the City of Philadelphia is 3½% of the purchase price (2½% municipal, 1% state), whereas the transfer tax in Cape May County, New Jersey, is $3.50 per thousand.

(g) Section 1300

Line 1301 shows a $200 charge paid to XYZ Engineers for the survey, under Borrower.

Line 1302 shows a $60 charge paid to Steve's Bug-off for the termite certificate, under Seller.

(h) Section 1400

Section 1400 simply represents the sum of items under each of the columns. The Line 1400 total under Borrower is inserted into Line 103 in Block J. The Line 1400 total under Seller is inserted into Line 502 in Block K.

PROBLEM

Please prepare the settlement sheet in the back of this chapter *(Example 8-10)* based on the following information, and identify items that should be reflected on the settlement sheet which are not identified below.

Date of Closing: November 10, 1983
Seller: Edward I. Macartney
Buyer: Christopher and Karen Sullivan
Property: 928 Dorchester Avenue, City of Chicago,
        Cook County, Illinois
Mortgage: Highrate Savings Bank

Consideration:	$120,000.00
Deposit:	$ 12,000.00
Mortgage:	$108,000.00
Property Assessment:	$ 42,000.00
Tax Milage:	
School—18	
County and Township—8	
Water/Sewer Rent (quarterly bill flat rate $35.00, excess usage $7.39):	$ 42.89
Township Garbage Removal (annual bill):	$ 50.00
Real Estate Commission:	.06%
Hazard Insurance Premium:	$ 343.00
Escrow by Mortgagee:	
School Tax: 2 months	
County and Township Tax: 7 months	
Hazard Insurance: 2 months	
Mortgagee Charges:	
Loan Origination Fee:	.01%
Appraisal:	$ 125.00
Credit Report ($15 already paid):	$ 25.00
Mortgage Payoff (as of 10/31/83):	$ 73,231.19
Annual Interest Rate (on mortgage to be paid off):	.09%
Title Insurance:	$ 784.00

VIII. SUMMARY

A. CLOSING AGENDA

The preparation for any closing is greatly facilitated by the use of some form of checklist. One helpful form of checklist is an agenda that can be revised as the closing nears and can be used as an actual agenda for conducting the closing itself. The elements of a good closing agenda are as follows:

1. Personae

The agenda should contain a list of the full and correct names of all the persons and entities involved, their respective roles in the transaction and their addresses and telephone numbers. Listing all of these in one place simplifies matters for secretaries and typists and serves as a reminder of the parties who should receive drafts of documents, copies of notices, and the like.

2. Documents

The agenda should contain a listing of all the documents that are involved in closing, including the basic documents (such as the agreement of sale or the commitment letter) and all documents, instruments, certificates, and other items that must be produced or tendered at settlement. This list can be produced initially by a review of the basic documents, the title report, and binders of past similar transactions to see what documentation is specifically required to be produced or which may be expected to be part of the transaction. There should be a separate file folder for every document listed in the agenda, and drafts should be maintained in these folders.

3. Status and Responsibility

As each document is listed, there should be an indication of which party is responsible for drafting or otherwise producing the document and which parties have rights of approval. There should be a status report indicating from time to time what stage the document is in at that time (e.g., first draft out for review by permanent lender; comments received from construction lender on March 3).

4. Disposition

The expected disposition of each document should also be listed, including the parties who will be receiving executed or conformed copies and the number of copies they are to receive. Indicating whether or not the document is to be recorded will also provide a checklist of which documents need to be acknowledged by a notary.

The agenda is not intended to be a fixed document. In addition to status changes, there will likely be revisions in the list of documents, and there may even be revisions in the parties to the transaction. As settlement approaches, the agenda should change less, except in terms of status, but it is common for additional documents to be prepared and executed at settlement itself to deal with a specific, unanticipated problem or situation. New documents at settlement should be included on the agenda so that they are not overlooked.

Normally, in a large transaction each party begins with its own agenda. However, the parties often exchange their agendas, and ultimately, they may agree on a common agenda. This is particularly important with regard to disposition of documents and the list of documents itself. There are certain items which some lenders and title insurance companies will require and which others will not, and whether or not such items will be required is not always obvious from the face of the commitment letter or title report. For this and other reasons the copies of agendas that are first exchanged will often be edited versions of the actual agenda then under consideration by a party, especially by a borrower.

The agenda acts as a checklist at settlement of all the documents that need to be produced, exchanged, executed, acknowledged, and delivered for recording. At the end of settlement the parties can review their own agendas, or the common agenda if one agenda is being used by all parties, to determine whether they have received all the documents to which they are entitled.

The agenda serves two other functions. If the attorney working on the matter should become indisposed or unavailable for any reason, the agenda will provide crucial information to the attorney who takes over the matter. The agenda also serves as the basis for the creation of a binder after completion of the transaction.

B. CLOSING REPORT AND BINDER

Human memory being what it is, fallible and selective, the attorney or paralegal should immediately after settlement write a closing report. The closing report should summarize the transaction, which can be understood in detail from the underlying documents, and should provide a more detailed account of any problems or other situations that arose at settlement, and any concessions, compromises, promises, or representations that were made at settlement. The closing report essentially serves three functions. The first is to provide a narrative account of the transaction for persons not directly involved with the mechanics of the transaction but having some interest in it, such as accountants, corporate officers, and other attorneys in the office. The second purpose is to memorialize the events of settlement, especially concessions and the like mentioned above, for assistance in settling later disputes. The third is to serve as an introduction to the documents themselves in the event that someone five or ten years hence has to review the file for any reason, such as a dispute. Even the closing attorney may forget the basics of the transaction in the interim, and an attorney or paralegal who was a stranger to the transaction would certainly appreciate an introduction before plunging into a binder of documents.

The document binder should contain copies of all documents relevant to the transaction, which may be as few as fifteen documents or may exceed 100. The documents should be arranged in some sensible order, probably culminating in a settlement sheet and a closing report. As recorded copies are returned from the recorder, they should be inserted in place of the photocopies of those documents.

Many binders are made in the office, using fasteners. Some binders are literally bound, as hard-cover books. The method used will depend on cost and custom. In any event a determination will have to be made as to how many copies to produce and who will retain which original documents.

Occasionally, as an aid to interpreting what a document really means, a court will want to review prior drafts of the document. For this reason, prior drafts are often maintained, at least for a number of years, for major transactions. To reduce the bulk of the main file, the prior drafts may be placed in an ancillary file.

The binder and the correspondence folder, with an occasional assist from the prior draft file, should serve as complete records of a transaction. An attorney picking up the file years later should be able to trace the entire transaction from these sources alone.

Example 8-2 **Mortgage Pay-Off Statement**

SURETY FEDERAL BANK
1407 Bridge Street
Yardley, PA 19067
(215)555-1213

July 5, 1985

Surveyors Title Insurance Company   Premises: 420 Rugby Avenue
935 Broad Street   Our Files: 47-901B
Philadelphia, PA 19107   Your No.   BG2270-44B
                                           Settlement Date: 7/31/85

Dear Mr. DePersia:

The following is a statement of the amount which we will require for satisfaction of our mortgage on the indicated premises, which is recorded in Mortgage Book 795, Page 402.

Principal of mortgage as of 7/5/85	$ 22,768.49		
Interest to 7/31/85	$ 164.50		
Prepayment charge ____ Days on ____	Waived		
Credit for Escrow	-0-	Sub. Tot.	$ 22,932.99
Credit for Disability Insurance	-0-	Sub. Tot.	-0-
Charge for Life Insurance	-0-	Sub. Tot.	-0-
Satisfaction Fee	$ 15.00	Balance	$ 22, 947.99

Upon receipt of the foregoing sum on or before July 31, 1985, we shall be pleased to cause our mortgage to be

satisfied of record   ~~endorsed for cancellation~~

Receipts for taxes and other charges for prior years, if paid by this Bank, were sent to mortgagors at the close of each year. Current receipts in our files are: None.

Very truly yours,

Example 8-3 **Mortgage Satisfaction Piece**

Mortgage Satisfaction Piece — Corporation - Phila. - 845   Copyright 1977 Printed and Sold by John C. Clark Co., 1326 Walnut St., Phila., Pa.

Mortgage Satisfaction Piece

TO

Prems: ....

Know all Men by these Presents, That

do   hereby certify that a Certain Indenture

of Mortgage bearing date the   day of   , Nineteen Hundred and
(19   ) made and executed by

TO

to secure the payment of the principal
Dollars and duly recorded
sum of
in the Department of Records of the City of Philadelphia in Mortgage Book   No.
Page   &c., on the   day of   , Nineteen Hundred and
(19   ), and secured upon

has been paid and that upon the recording of this instrument the said Mortgage shall be and is hereby
forever discharged. The Mortgage has not been assigned except as follows:

In Witness Whereof, the said Corporation has caused its common or corporate seal to be hereunto
affixed the   day of   A. D., 19
Signed, Sealed and Delivered
in the presence of:

....
                                                              President

ATTEST: ....
                                                              Secretary

....
Address of Mortgagee or Assignee

COMMONWEALTH OF PENNSYLVANIA
                                                   SS:
COUNTY OF

On the   day of   , A. D. 19   , before me, the undersigned officer,
personally appeared   , who acknowledged
himself to be the   of
a corporation, and that he as such   , being authorized to do so, executed the foregoing instrument for the purposes therein contained by signing the name of the Corporation by himself
as

In Witness Whereof. I have hereunto set my hand   Seal.

....

Example 8-4   Seller's Affidavit

All Questions in this Affidavit must be answered.

APPLICATION No.

PREMISES_____ DATE: _____ 19_

On the above date before me, a Notary Public for the Commonwealth of Pennsylvania, personally appeared

_____

who, being duly sworn according to law, and intending to be legally bound, deposes and says that the answers and statements are true.

(1) Has a bill been received or notice served for additional taxes assessed for new construction or major improvements? _____

_____

(2) Are water, sewer services or electricity supplied by Municipality or Municipal Authority? _____

_____

(specify)

(3) Has any building construction, alterations, additions been done on the above premises within the four month period preceding the above date?_____

(4) Has any work for sewer construction, water pipe, paving of street, driveway, curb or sidewalk been done or ordered to be done abutting or upon the premises?_____

(5) Are there any mortgages, judgments or pending court suits affecting the said premises other than those shown on above numbered Title Report? _____

(6) Who is in possession of the premises? _____

(7) Are there any Agreements of Sale outstanding other than relating to the present transaction? _____

_____

(8) Are all taxes, water and sewer rents assessed against above premises up to and including the year of 19_____ fully paid?_____

_____

FURTHER that the Grantor(s) Mortgagor(s) in the present transaction are of full age, and under no legal disability to execute the proposed conveyance-mortgage.

FURTHER that the deponent(s) named herein is (are) the same person(s) as the person(s) so named in the Recital set forth in the above numbered title report, and that the facts of identity relating to any other person(s) named in the said Recital are true and correct.

FURTHER that the Grantees in the last deed of record as set forth in said Recital, if shown to be husband and wife, have not been divorced after the acquisition of title on the date set forth herein.

Deponent(s) make this affidavit for the purpose of inducing the Commonwealth Land Title Insurance Company to hold settlement for the above premises, and to issue its Title Insurance Policy insuring the title thereto.

Sworn and subscribed before me the
day and year aforesaid.

_____   _____ (SEAL)
            Notary Public

                                                         _____ (SEAL)

810-35-589

Example 8-5 Settlement Preparation Checklist

The following is a checklist of responsibilities to be completed by the seller and purchaser prior to settlement:

1. Seller

    (a) Review Title Report.

    (b) Procure pay-off figures necessary to remove the liens of any mortgage or judgment.

    (c) Procure required real estate tax and water and sewer rental bills and receipts or tax certificates.

    (d) Procure documents, receipts, or other papers necessary to remove any other title objections.

    (e) Make escrow arrangements with the title insurance company, if necessary.

    (f) Order and procure necessary zoning and notice certificates. *

    (g) Order and procure necessary use and occupancy certificates. *

    (h) Order and procure a 3407 Certificate for condominium units from the management office of the condominium association. †

    (i) Satisfy all of purchaser's conditions to the agreement of sale; deliver timely notice of fulfillment or nonfulfillment of all of seller's conditions.

    (j) Prepare or review proposed deed and submit to purchaser's counsel for review and approval, if necessary.

    (k) Prepare or review proposed purchase money note and mortgage, if necessary.

---

* This requirement varies from county to county. Check with the municipal authorities for each county's specific requirements.

† A 3407 Certificate sets forth the amount of the monthly common expense assessment, any unpaid common expenses or special assessment charges currently due and payable from seller of the units, and additional general information and documents concerning the organization and the management of the condominium. An example of a 3407 Certificate appears at the end of Chapter Eleven.

(l) Have utility meters read and final bills rendered.

(m) Procure termite report and termite certificate at settlement if the agreement of sale so requires.

(n) Procure evidence of corporate, partnership, or other authority, if necessary.

(o) Procure necessary signatures (notarized where applicable) on seller's documents (e.g., deed and seller's affidavit from the title company) in advance of settlement if seller will not attend settlement.

(p) If property is tenant occupied, cancel the lease or instruct the tenant to make rental payments to purchaser, and arrange for an assignment of the security deposits, as may be required by the agreement of sale.

(q) Confirm the date, time, and place for settlement.

(r) Advise an individual seller to bring spouse to settlement, if necessary, and corporate seller to have present an executive officer, the secretary or an assistant secretary, and the corporate seal.

(s) Bring to settlement all keys to property and garage-door openers, if applicable.

2. Purchaser

(a) Procure fire insurance coverage (in the form of an insurance binder) at the time the agreement of sale is executed and order a fire insurance policy effective as of the date of settlement.

(b) Order title insurance and deliver copies of the title report to seller, seller's counsel or seller's broker (if the seller has not obtained legal services), and mortgagee (if necessary).

(c) Apply for and fully complete all applications necessary for mortgage financing, if any, within any applicable time periods. Review mortgage commitment letter.

(d) Advise seller of the papers and other materials he or she will be required to produce at settlement.

(e) Satisfy all of seller's conditions to the agreement of sale; deliver a timely notice of fulfillment or nonfulfillment of all of purchaser's conditions.

Continued.

Example 8-5 **Settlement Preparation Checklist** *continued*

(f)   Prepare or review proposed deed and submit to seller's counsel and title company for review and approval, if necessary.

(g)   Prepare or review proposed note, mortgage, and other loan documents.

(h)   Determine whether seller will arrange to have the utility meters read and final bills rendered at or immediately prior to the date of settlement.

(i)   Advise seller, seller's counsel, title insurance representative, proposed mortgagee, and broker of the date, time, and place of settlement.

(j)   Advise individual purchaser to bring spouse to settlement (if necessary), and corporate purchaser to have present an executive officer, the secretary or an assistant secretary, and the corporate seal.

(k)   Prepare an estimated settlement sheet considering the following costs: (1) balance of the purchase price; (2) apportionment of real estate tax, water and sewer rental, and prepaid insurance premiums (if policy is transferred to purchaser); (3) title insurance premiums (including mechanics' lien coverage and mortgagee endorsements); (4) recording and notary fees; (5) realty transfer taxes; (6) commitment, processing, appraisal, credit report, attorneys' and other fees, and charges payable to mortgagee; (7) real estate tax and insurance premium escrows; (8) mortgage interest payments due at settlement; (9) insurance premiums; (10) rental income apportionment and credit for security deposits; and (11) any special charges contemplated by the agreement of sale.

(l)   Advise purchaser of the estimated settlement costs and the amount of the certified or cashier's check he or she will be required to produce at settlement. Advise purchaser to bring a personal check to settlement to be used as a cushion, if necessary.

(m)   Arrange for inspection of the property prior to settlement.

(n)   Procure evidence of corporate, partnership, or other authority, if necessary.

(o)   Prepare a bill of sale, if necessary, for any items the purchaser is buying that are not included in the purchase price or that are unique items not identified in the agreement of sale as part of the property.

(p)   Procure necessary signatures (notarized where applicable) on purchaser's documents in advance of settlement if purchaser will not attend settlement.

At Settlement

1.   Seller

(a)   Produce required documents.

(b)   Review and procure necessary signatures for seller's affidavit, deed, and settlement sheet.

2.   Purchaser

(a)   Review documents and other papers deliverd by seller if not required prior to settlement:

(1)   zoning and notice certificate,

(2)   use and occupancy certificate,

(3)   termite report and certification, and

(4)   leases, if necessary.

(b)   Review deed, note, mortgage, and other loan documents (even if reviewed prior to settlement); verify names, signatures, and acknowledgments where necessary.

(c)   Procure necessary signatures for note, mortgage, and other loan documents.

(d)   Review marked-up title report or title policy.

(e)   Review and procure necessary signatures for purchaser's affidavit and settlement sheet.

(f)   Collect copies of all papers and keys to the property; advise the title company where to deliver the deed following its recording and the title policy if not issued at settlement.

Example 8-6 **Sample Residential Settlement Index**

KARIN B. BAYB and JOHN M. BAYB
Purchase of 4 Boat House Road
Lower Merion Township,
Montgomery County, Pennsylvania

October 31, 1985

1.   Agreement of Sale (the "Agreement") dated August 5,
        1984, between Karin B. Bayb and John M. Bayb ("Buyers")
        and Terrence R. Allgier ("Seller").

2.   Amendment dated September 10, 1984, to the Agreement.

3.   Deed dated October 31, 1985, from Seller to Buyers.

4.   Mortgage (the "Mortgage") dated August 5, 1978, from
        Seller to Lenders Mortgage Corporation ("Lenders").

5.   Miscellaneous forms submitted to Veterans Administration
        in connection with Buyer's assumption of the
        Mortgage.

6.   Letter dated September 27, 1985, from Veterans
        Administration regarding confirmation of Buyers'
        assumption of the Mortgage.

7.   Loan Assumption Statement issued October 6, 1975, by
        Lenders.

8.   Promissory Note (the "Note") dated October 31, 1985, in
        the principal amount of $20,000.00 issued by Buyers and
        payable to the order of Seller.

9.   Mortgage dated October 31, 1985, issued by Buyers and
        securing the Note.

10.   Amortization Schedule.

11.   Termite Report, Certification, and Service Warranty
        dated October 30, 1985.

12.   Urea-Formaldehyde Foam Insulation Certificate dated
        October 30, 1985, together with documentation in
        connection therewith.

13.   Marked-up Title Report (No. 00011-A) dated September 10,
        1985, issued by Landmark Title Insurance Company
        ("Landmark").

14.   Settlement Sheet dated October 31, 1985.

15.   Policy of Title Insurance (No. 00011-B) issued by Landmark.

16.   Closing Report.

17.   Postclosing Checklist.

Example 8-7 Index for a Construction Loan Settlement

TRIUMPHS, LTD.

$5,000,000 Construction Loan
from Peoples Federal Bank for the
Construction of a Remanufacturing Plant
on Silver Spring, Maryland

BACKGROUND

Pursuant to a Loan Commitment Letter dated October 31, 1984, Peoples Federal Bank (the "Bank") agreed to loan $5,000,000 (the "Loan") to Triumphs, Ltd., a Pennsylvania limited partnership (the "Borrower"), in connection with the construction of a remanufacturing plant (the "Project") on a tract of land located in Silver Spring, Montgomery County, Maryland (the "Premises"), which will constitute Phase I to a two-phase development, Phase II of which will be constructed on a tract of land adjacent to the Premises (the "Additional Premises").

Morgan, Rover & Austin ("Morgan") acted as counsel to the Bank; Martin & Jaguar ("Martin") acted as general counsel to the Borrower; and Maserati, Alfa & Romeo ("Maserati") acted as local counsel to the Borrower in the State of Maryland.

The Closing occurred on April 15, 1985, at 10:00 A.M. at the offices of Martin.

CLOSING AGENDA

PRECLOSING MATTERS

1.   Loan Commitment Letter dated October 31, 1984, from the Bank was accepted by the Borrower on November 20, 1984.

2.   Conditional Acceptance Letter dated November 21, 1984, from the Borrower was accepted by the Bank.

3.   Real Estate Appraisal of the Premises and the Additional Premises dated December 15, 1984, and prepared by Pils, Stout & Ale was delivered to the Bank.

4.   Letter from World Wide Velocipedes ("WWV") dated December 16, 1984, pursuant to which WWV committed to invest not less than an additional $3,000,000 in the Borrower as paid-in capital on or before June 30, 1985, was delivered to the Bank.

CLOSING MATTERS

5.   Certificate of Limited Partnership of the Borrower dated as of April 1, 1985, was delivered to the Bank.

6.   Certified copy of the Agreement of Limited Partnership of the Borrower dated as of October 31, 1984, was delivered to the Bank.

Continued.

Example 8-7   **Index for a Construction Loan Settlement** *continued*

7.   Certified copy of resolutions adopted by the Board of
     Directors of WWV on November 30, 1984, was delivered to the Bank.

8.   Certified copy of financial statements of the Borrower as of
     April 1, 1985, was delivered to the Bank.

9.   Certified copy of consolidated financial statements of WWV
     as of April 1, 1985, was delivered to the Bank.

10. Architect's Contract dated January 5, 1985, between the
     Borrower and Yuengling & Associates (the "Architect") was
     delivered to the Bank.

11. Construction Contract dated as of February 5, 1985, between
     the Borrower and Olde Frothingslosh CC, Inc., (the
     "Contractor") was delivered to the Bank.

12. Architect's Certification dated March 15, 1985, and prepared
     by the Architect was delivered to the Bank.

13. Engineering Certification dated March 15, 1985, and prepared
     by Anchor Steam & Cooling, Inc. was delivered to the Bank.

14. The following miscellaneous documents were delivered to the Bank:

     a.   Letter dated March 30, 1985, from Pinto Power
          Company regarding the availability of gas service.

     b.   Letter dated March 24, 1985, from Franklin Key
          Electric regarding the availability of electric
          services.

     c.   Letter dated February 6, 1985, from the Municipality
          of Silver Spring regarding zoning, site plan, and
          landscaping approval.

     d.   Letter dated February 2, 1985, from Wild Water
          Adventurers, Inc., regarding the location of the
          Premises and the Additional Premises outside the
          flood plain boundary.

     e.   Letter dated February 2, 1985, from the County of
          Montgomery regarding the availability of water and
          sanitary sewer.

     f.   Letter dated January 14, 1985, from Mason & Dixon
          Associates regarding survey certification.

15. Uniform Commercial Code and Tax Lien Certifications
     regarding the Borrower and WWV were delivered to the Bank.

16. Marked-up Title Commitment dated March 15, 1985, issued
     by Surveyors Title Insurance Company ("Surveyors") was
     delivered to the Bank.

17. Notice of Commencement dated March 22, 1985, as filed with
     the Register of Deed Office in Montgomery County, Maryland
     was delivered to Surveyors.

18.   Settlement Sheet was prepared by Surveyors and executed by
        the Borrower.

CLOSING DOCUMENTS

19.   Construction Loan Agreement dated April 1, 1985, was
        executed by the Borrower and the Bank.

20.   Note dated April 1, 1985, in the maximum principal amount
        of $5,000,000 was issued by the Borrower to the Bank.

21.   Mortgage dated April 1, 1985, covering the Premises was
        granted by the Borrower to the Bank.

22.   UCC Financing Statements were executed by the Borrower, as
        debtor, and the Bank, as secured party.

23.   Guaranty dated April 1, 1985, was executed by WWV and
        delivered to the Bank.

24.   Pledge Agreement dated April 1, 1985, was executed by WWV
        and delivered to the Bank.

25.   Collateral Assignment of Land Contract dated April 1,
        1985, was executed by the Borrower and delivered to the
        Bank.

26.   Completion Bond dated April 1, 1985, was executed by WWV
        and delivered to the Bank.

27.   Letter Agreement dated April 1, 1985, setting forth con-
        ditions of funding the Loan was executed by the Borrower
        and the Bank.

28.   Opinion of Maserati dated April 1, 1985, was delivered to
        the Bank.

29.   Opinion of Martin dated April 1, 1985, was delivered to
        the Bank.

30.   Opinion of Morgan dated April 1, 1985, was delivered to
        the Borrower.

POSTCLOSING MATTERS

31.   Certificates of Insurance issued by Hambrose Agency and
        Insurance Binder issued by Investment Associates Co. were
        delivered to the Bank.

32.   Final building permits for the Project were delivered to
        the Bank.

33.   Final Cost Breakdown of the Borrower was certified by the
        Architect and the Contractor and delivered to the Bank.

34.   Title Policy dated April 1, 1985, issued by Surveyor was
        delivered to the Bank.

Example 8-8 **Disclosure Statement**

```
                    SURETY FEDERAL BANK
                    1407 Bridge Street
                    Yardley, PA 19067
                    (215)555-1213


                    August 20, 1985

Mortgage Department

        Re:  795 Fairmount Lane, Yardley, PA  19067
        Borrowers:  William Foss and Kathlyn Foss
        Loan:  $40,000
```

DISCLOSURE STATEMENT REQUIRED BY PENNSYLVANIA ACT NO. 6 of 1974

    In compliance with the aforesaid Act, an estimate of your settlement costs is outlined below. These costs, exclusive of any adjustments between Buyer and Seller, are predicated on a settlement taking place in the month of September.

```
    Transfer Tax                          $    600.00
    Title Insurance                       $    450.00
    Mechanics' Lien Insurance             $    ------
    Title Company Endorsements            $     13.50
    Recording Fees                        $     20.00
    Notary Fees and Affidavits            $      7.50
    Preparation of Deed                   $    ------
    Preparation of Debt Instrument        $    ------
    Fire Insurance Premium                $    175.00
    Flood Insurance Premium               $    ------
    Private Mortgage Insurance Premium    $    ------
    Service Charge                        $    350.00
    Certifications                        $    ------
    Tax Escrow                            $    ------
        School    (7 mo.)  at $68.24      $    477.68
        Township  (10 mo.) at $ 9.79      $     97.90
        County    (11 mo.) at $10.28      $    113.08
    Other (Specify)                       $    ------
                                            _____

                            Total         $ 2,304.66
```

    The loan shall be prepared in 300 equal monthly installments of $349.48 interest and principal, due and payable on the first day of each month. If the loan continues to maturity, the total payments of interest and principal to be made by you over the life of the loan are outlined below.

```
Total monthly payments of interest and principal    $104,844
Less principal amount of the loan                   $ 40,000
Amount of interest                                  $ 64,844
```

Example 8-9 **Federal Truth-In-Lending Disclosure Statement**

Borrower _____

Loan Number _____

Date _____

ANNUAL PERCENTAGE RATE The cost of your credit at a yearly rate.	FINANCE CHARGE The dollar amount the credit will cost you.	AMOUNT FINANCED The amount of credit provided to you or on your behalf.	TOTAL OF PAYMENTS The amount you will have paid after you have made all payments as scheduled.
_____%	$_____	$_____	$_____

Payments: Your payment schedule will be:

Number of Payments	Amount of Payments	When Payments Are Due
	$	
	$	
	$	
	$	
	$	
	$	

Demand Feature: ☐ This obligation has a demand feature.

Late Charge: If a payment is more than _____ days late, you will be charged _____%. of the payment.

Prepayment: If you pay off early you:

☐ may ☐ will not have to pay a penalty.

☐ may ☐ will not be entitled to a refund of part of the finance charge.

Security: You are giving a security interest in:

☐ The property being purchased.

☐ _____

Filing Fees: $_____

Assumption: Complete 1 or 2

☐ Someone buying your house may, subject to conditions, be allowed to assume the remainder of the mortgage on the original terms.

☐ Someone buying your house may not assume the remainder of the mortgage on the original terms.

See your contract documents for any additional information about non-payment, default and any required prepayment in full before the scheduled date and prepayment refunds and penalties.

_____

(e) means an estimate ☐ All dates and numeral disclosures except the late payment disclosures are estimates.

Insurance: Homeowner's Insurance or fire and extended coverage is required as a condition of the loan. In addition, if the property securing this loan is located in a flood hazard area, you will be required to purchase available flood insurance. You may obtain property insurance from anyone you want, provided the insurer is acceptable to us.

I understand that this disclosure statement is neither a contract nor a commitment to lend. Please acknowledge receipt of the above information by signing below:

I acknowledge receipt of a copy of the foregoing disclosure statements with all blanks appropriately filled in on this _____ day of _____ 19 _____.

Borrower _____

Borrower _____

If mailed: Mailed By _____ Date: _____

Example 8-10 **Settlement Sheet**

HUD— Rev.5/76

Form Approved
OMB NO. 63-R-1501

A.	U.S. DEPARTMENT OF HOUSING AND URBAN DEVELOPMENT	B. TYPE OF LOAN
	SETTLEMENT STATEMENT	1. ☐ FHA 2. ☐ FMHA 3. ☐ CONV. UNINS. 4. ☐ VA 5. ☐ CONV. INS.

6. File Number :

7. Loan Number:

8. Mortgage Insurance Case Number:

NO. _____

C. NOTE: *This form is furnished to give you a statement of actual settlement costs. Amounts paid to and by the settlement agent are shown. Items marked "(p.o.c.)" were paid outside the closing; they are shown here for informational purposes and are not included in the totals.*

D. NAME OF BORROWER :	E. NAME OF SELLER :	F. NAME OF LENDER :

G. PROPERTY LOCATION:	H. SETTLEMENT AGENT :	I. SETTLEMENT DATE:
	PLACE OF SETTLEMENT:	

J. SUMMARY OF BORROWER'S TRANSACTION		K. SUMMARY OF SELLER'S TRANSACTION	
100. GROSS AMOUNT DUE FROM BORROWER:		**400. GROSS AMOUNT DUE TO SELLER:**	
101. Contract sales price		401. Contract sales price	
102. Personal Property		402. Personal property	
103. Settlement charges to borrower (line 1400)		403. Rent adjustment	
104. Rent adjustment		404. Acknowledgement of deed	
105. Acknowledgement of deed		405.	
Adjustments for items paid by seller in advance		*Adjustments for items paid by seller in advance*	
106. City/town taxes to		406. City/town taxes to	
107. County taxes to		407. County taxes to	
108. Assessments to		408. Assessments to	
109. Water/sewer rent to		409. Water/sewer rent to	
110. School taxes to		410. School taxes to	
111.		411.	
112.		412.	
120. GROSS AMOUNT DUE FROM BORROWER		**420. GROSS AMOUNT DUE TO SELLER**	
200. AMOUNTS PAID BY OR IN BEHALF OF BORROWER:		**500. REDUCTIONS IN AMOUNT DUE TO SELLER:**	
201. Deposit or earnest money		501. Excess deposit (see instructions)	
202. Principal amount of new loan(s)		502. Settlement charges to seller (line 1400)	
203. Existing loan(s) taken subject to		503. Existing loan(s) taken subject to	
204.		504. Payoff of first mortgage loan	
205.		505. Payoff of second mortgage loan	
206.		506.	
207.		507.	
208.		508.	
209.		509. Escrow	
Adjustments for items unpaid by seller		*Adjustments for items unpaid by seller*	
210. City/town taxes to		510. City/town taxes to	
211. County taxes to		511. County taxes to	
212. Assessments to		512. Assessments to	
213. Water/sewer rent to		513. Water/sewer rent to	
214. School taxes to		514. School taxes to	
215.		515.	
216.		516.	
217.		517.	
218.		518.	
219.		519.	
220. TOTAL PAID BY/FOR BORROWER		**520. TOTAL REDUCTION AMOUNT DUE SELLER**	
300. CASH AT SETTLEMENT FROM/TO BORROWER		**600. CASH AT SETTLEMENT TO/FROM SELLER**	
301. Gross amount due from borrower (line 120)		601. Gross amount due to seller (line 120)	
302. Less amounts paid by/for borrower (line 220)	(	602. Less reductions in amount due seller (line 520)	(
303. CASH (☐FROM) (☐TO) BORROWER		**603. CASH (☐TO) (☐FROM) SELLER**	

Page 2

L. SETTLEMENT CHARGES		PAID FROM BORROWER'S FUNDS AT SETTLEMENT	PAID FROM SELLER'S FUNDS AT SETTLEMENT
700.	**TOTAL SALES/BROKER'S COMMISSION** based on price $ @ =		
	Division of Commission (line 700) as follows:		
701.	$ to		
702.	$ to		
703.	Commission paid at Settlement		
704.			
800.	**ITEMS PAYABLE IN CONNECTION WITH LOAN**		
801.	Loan Origination Fee %		
802.	Loan Discount %		
803.	Appraisal Fee to		
804.	Credit Report to		
805.	Lender's Inspection Fee		
806.	Mortgage Insurance Application Fee to		
807.	Assumption Fee		
808.			
809.			
810.			
811.			
900.	**ITEMS REQUIRED BY LENDER TO BE PAID IN ADVANCE**		
901.	Interest from to @ $ /day		
902.	Mortgage Insurance Premium for months to		
903.	Hazard Insurance Premium for years to		
904.	years to		
905.			
1000.	**RESERVES DEPOSITED WITH LENDER**		
1001.	Hazard Insurance months @ $ per month		
1002.	Mortgage Insurance months @ $ per month		
1003.	City property taxes months @ $ per month		
1004.	County property taxes months @ $ per month		
1005.	Annual assessments months @ $ per month		
1006.	School taxes months @ $ per month		
1007.	months @ $ per month		
1008.	months @ $ per month		
1100.	**TITLE CHARGES**		
1101.	Settlement or closing fee to		
1102.	Abstract or title search to		
1103.	Title Examination to		
1104.	Title insurance binder to		
1105.	Document preparation to		
1106.	Notary Fees to		
1107.	Attorney's fees to		
	(includes above items numbers:)		
1108.	Title insurance to		
	(includes above items numbers: 1101 to 1104)		
1109.	Lender's coverage $		
1110.	Owner's coverage $		
1111.	Disbursing fee:		
1112.	Endorsement fees to: Endorsement 300, 100		
1113.			
1200.	**GOVERNMENT RECORDING AND TRANSFER CHARGES**		
1201.	Recording fees: Deed $; Mortgage $; Releases $		
1202.	City/county tax/stamps: Deed $; Mortgage $		
1203.	State tax/stamps: Deed $; Mortgage $		
1204.			
1205.			
1300.	**ADDITIONAL SETTLEMENT CHARGES**		
1301.	Survey		
1302.	Pest inspection		
1303.			
1304.			
1305.			
1306.			
1307.			
1308.			
1400.	**TOTAL SETTLEMENT CHARGES** (enter on lines 103, Section J and 502, Section K)		

The above settlement examined and approved, and a copy received, in consideration of which Title Insurance Company is directed and authorized to make distribution and payments in accordance herewith. Any funds held for the disposition of exceptions and/or for the protection of the Company, will be held without payment of interest and subject to the payment of an escrow service charge of $10.00 for the first six months and a like charge for each additional one year period. Any income arising from the fund shall be the property of Title Insurance Company. Seller specifically agrees with the disbursing charge as set forth above.

Seller's Signature		Purchaser's Signature	
Seller's Signature		Purchaser's Signature	
Address		Address	

HUD-1 Rev.5/76

Chapter 9

Recording Statutes

I. INTRODUCTION

In the United States the methods of proving ownership of land and of conveying interests in land are based on a system of recording in a public place all deeds and other written documents that evidence ownership of, or some other interest in, any parcel of land. This recording system provides accessible, reliable, and predictable information about various interests in land, affording interested persons the ability to make informed decisions with respect to buying, selling, taking mortgages on, and using real property. To that end, each state has enacted a recording statute that penalizes those who fail to record interests and that protects those who comply with the statute.

There are variations from state to state with respect to (a) which instruments are recordable, (b) what the recording requirements are, and (c) which persons and interests are protected by the statutes. All of the states, however, attempt to establish rules for determining the priority[1] of rights among competing claims to a parcel of land, based on a variety of considerations, including the time the claim was first established, the time the claim was first recorded, the nature of the claim, whether or not

---

1. A claim that is given precedence over another claim is said to be superior, and the lesser claim is said to be subordinate. The word "priority" is sometimes used to mean superior, but at other times is simply used to mean that the prior claim was established before the claim to which it is being compared. Although a claim that is "prior in time" is sometimes also "prior in right," this is not always the case. For purposes of this chapter, assume that the word "prior" refers to priority of time, unless the text specifically refers to priority of rights.

something of value was given for the claim, and the "innocence" of each claimant.

Several states, in addition to recording statutes, have adopted the "Torrens System" of land registration. Under the Torrens System each interest in a parcel of land is registered. Whereas the recording system does not make judgments as to the merits of the documents recorded, the Torrens System involves an evaluation by a court of each interest claimed.

The following discussion is intended to familiarize the student with the fundamentals of recording interests in real estate under the various recording statutes and under the Torrens System.

II. RECORDING STATUTES

The recording statutes provide evidence of an interest of a person or entity in a particular parcel of real estate. Although the statutes themselves vary among the states, the basic theory behind each of them is similar. A place for public recording and a system for recording and retrieving information are provided. Their use is encouraged by granting certain protections to those who use them and by withholding protections from those who fail to use them.

The recording statutes vary in terms of the priority of rights given to instruments recorded and unrecorded and in terms of the penalities for not recording. There are three general types of recording statutes: "race" statutes, "notice" statutes, and "race-notice" statutes.

A. TYPES OF STATUTES

1. "Race" Statutes

Race statutes provide that interests in real estate receive their priority of right based solely on the time of recording. The actual date on which an interest was obtained is irrelevant. The race statute puts a premium on adherence to the system. The use of the word "race" in connection with such statutes refers to the possibility that there might be a race to the recording office to record a document when there are two parties with competing interests. The first person to record his or her interest will receive priority of right, notwithstanding that he or she may actually know of the interest another party has in the land.

Because of the unfair results often caused by the application of race statutes, they are rarely used today with respect to deeds, although several states have race statutes that apply to mortgages. An example is the Pennsylvania law governing the priority of mortgages:

> From and after the passage of this act, all mortgages, or defeasible deeds in the nature of mortgages, made or to be made or executed for any lands, tenements, or hereditaments within this Commonwealth, shall have priority according to the date of recording the same, without regard to the time

of making or executing such deeds; and it shall be the duty of the recorder to endorse the time upon the mortgages or defeasible deeds and on the record thereof, when left for record, and if two or more are left upon the same day, they shall have priority according to the time they are left at the office for record. No mortgage, or defeasible deed in the nature of a mortgage, shall be a lien, until such mortgage or defeasible deed shall have been left for record, as aforesaid.
[Act of April 27, 1927, P.L. 440, § 1; Act of April 28, 1978, P.L. 202, No. 53, §10(96)]

The Pennsylvania mortgage race statute has a significant feature that is common to mortgage race statutes. Mortgages taken by the seller of a property to secure payment of the purchase price ("purchase money mortgages"), and mortgages created to pay the purchase price that are expressly stated to be purchase money mortgages receive special treatment under the Pennsylvania race statute. So long as such mortgages are recorded within ten days of their delivery, the lien dates back to the date of creation. Therefore, these types of mortgages are not really subject to the race effect of the statute until ten days have elapsed.

Example:

Purchaser purchased land from Seller on July 15 and financed the purchase with a mortgage loan from First National Bank. On July 20, Purchaser borrowed money from Friendly Finance Co. and secured the loan by granting to Friendly Finance a mortgage on the same piece of real property. If First National records its mortgage by the 25th of July it will have the superior lien even if Friendly Finance has previously recorded its mortgage. After the expiration of the 10-day period on July 25, the priority of right of these mortgages will depend on the first to record. Friendly Finance is in a very unfavorable position. Notwithstanding its ignorance of First National's mortgage, even after checking the records, the lien of its mortgage will be subordinate to the lien of the First National mortgage if First National records by July 25.

2. "Notice" Statutes

The theory of a notice statute is that a person who records his or her interest should be protected from later claimants, whereas one who fails to record his or her interest should lose priority of right to another party whose interest is subsequently created, *provided* the latter party has no knowledge of the unrecorded interest. The theory is implemented by creating the legal presumption that the recording of a document in the proper place of public record is tantamount to giving actual notice of the contents of the document to every person who might later claim an interest in the property in question. Every such person is presumed to have checked the public records before acquiring any such interest. Whether or not the person has done so, the later claimant is said to have "constructive notice" of any such recorded documents. If the original claimant in a notice state, however, fails to record an instrument, he or she cannot retain priority just by beating the owner of a subsequently created interest to the recorder's office. The original claimant loses his or her unrecorded priority once the subsequent interest is *created*.

A purchaser who is without actual or constructive notice of a prior deed is called an "innocent" purchaser. An innocent purchaser who receives a deed is immediately protected against a prior deed that is unrecorded on that date. It makes no difference whether the prior purchaser records its deed after the subsequent transfer but before the recording of the subsequent deed. To illustrate the operation of a notice statute, assume Appley conveys to Bendix, who does not record the deed. Thereafter, Appley conveys to Cutter, who is without actual or constructive notice of the deed to Bendix, and who has paid money to Appley in exchange for the conveyance.[2] Cutter's right is superior to Bendix's, even if Bendix records before Cutter does, and whether or not Cutter ever records. Bendix is penalized for not recording and for not recording immediately.

Approximately two-thirds of the states have "notice" recording statutes similar to the Massachusetts statute reprinted below:

> A conveyance of an estate in fee simple, fee tail or for life, or a lease for more than seven years, . . . shall not be valid as against any person, except the grantor or lessor, his or her heirs and devisees and persons having actual notice of it, unless it . . . is recorded in the registry of deeds for the county or district in which the land to which it relates lies.
> [Massachusetts General Laws Annotated Ch. 183, § 4 (1977)]

3. "Race-Notice" Statutes

The race-notice statute is similar to, and far more common than, the race statute. Bascially, it works like a race statute except when the party trying to claim priority of interest had actual or constructive notice of the prior unrecorded interest. A pure race statute disregards actual or constructive notice, whereas a race-notice statute grants no priority of right to the owner of the subsequent interest if such subsequent owner had actual or constructive knowledge of the prior interest, no matter which party records first.

The race-notice statute, unlike the typical notice statute, protects the subsequent bona fide purchaser for value without notice only in the event he or she records the deed before the prior unrecorded deed is recorded. To illustrate, assume Appley conveys property to Bendix. Subsequently, Appley also conveys the same property to Cutter who searches the record

---

2. It is not necessary for a grantee or assignee of an interest in property to pay money in order to achieve a favored status, but if money is not paid, then some legal equivalent must be given, such as a promise to do something, the forgiveness of a debt or the payment of some property other than money. The favored status is referred to as a "purchaser for value," and excludes the recipient of a gift. If the transfer was not a sham or a fraud, then the purchaser attains the most favored status of a "bona fide purchaser for value," which is often referred to just as a "bona fide purchaser" or "b.f.p."

and, because Bendix has yet to record his deed, finds nothing inconsistent on the record with Appley's title. Bendix then records his interest. Subsequently, Cutter records his deed. Title belongs to Bendix under the above statute. Although Cutter had no record notice, he is penalized for not recording immediately.

An example of a race-notice statute is the recording act of Pennsylvania concerning deeds and other conveyances (but not mortgages), reprinted below:

> All deeds, conveyances, contracts, and other instruments of writing wherein it shall be the intention of the parties executing the same to grant, bargain, sell, and convey any lands, tenements, or hereditaments situate in this Commonwealth, upon being acknowledged by the parties executing the same or proved in the manner provided by the laws of this Commonwealth, shall be recorded in the office for the recording of deeds in the county where such lands, tenements, and hereditaments are situate. Every such deed, conveyance, contract, or other instrument of writing which shall not be acknowledged or proved and recorded, as aforesaid, shall be adjudged fraudulent and void as to any subsequent bona fide purchaser[3] or mortgagee or holder of any judgment, duly entered in the prothonotary's[4] office of the county in which the lands, tenements, or hereditaments are situate, without actual or constructive notice unless such deed, conveyance, contract, or instrument of writing shall be recorded, as aforesaid, before the recording of the deed or conveyance or the entry of the judgment under which such subsequent purchaser, mortgagee, or judgment creditor shall claim. Nothing contained in this act shall be construed to repeal or modify any law providing for the lien of purchase money mortgages.
>
> [Act of May 12, 1925, P.L. 613 § 1; June 12, 1931, P.L. 588, No. 191, § 1]

B. OTHER TIME LIMITS UNDER RECORDING STATUTES

Many states have provisions in their recording statutes that make certain recordable interests void against all third parties if these interests are not recorded within a specified period.

In Pennsylvania, for example, deeds and other instruments of conveyance executed within the Commonwealth must be recorded within ninety days of their delivery. Those executed outside the Commonwealth must be recorded within six months of their execution. Failure to record deeds in accordance with the stated time limits makes the deed or conveyance fraudulent and void against subsequent purchasers or mortgagees for a valuable consideration, and against creditors of the grantor, whether or not the subsequent purchaser records the deed, the mortgagee records the mortgage, or the creditor enters the judgment.

Similarly, a mortgage that encumbers Pennsylvania real estate will be effective between the parties but will not be a valid security instrument

---

3. See footnote 2 regarding bona fide purchasers.

4. In Pennsylvania the chief clerk of a trial-level court is called a *prothonotary*.

on the real property unless recorded within six months from the date of execution.

PROBLEM

1. Is your state a race, notice, or race-notice jurisdiction as to deeds? As to mortgages? What time restrictions are there on effective recording of deeds? Of mortgages?

2. A conveys a parcel of land called "Blackacre" to B. A thereafter conveys Blackacre to C who takes without notice of the prior conveyance. A thereafter conveys Blackacre to D who takes with notice only of the prior conveyance from A to B. D records his deed first, B records his deed second, and C records his deed third. Who has title to Blackacre in a race jurisdiction? In a notice jurisdiction? In a race-notice jurisdiction?

C. WHAT CLASSES OF PERSONS ARE PROTECTED BY RECORDING STATUTES

In a few states the priorities established through recording benefit all third parties (i.e., anyone other than the original owner and the party whose interest is evidenced by a recordable instrument). In other states only purchasers and mortgagees are benefited. In still other states certain creditors of the grantor of an unrecorded deed are benefited.

Whether a purchaser or creditor is protected from an unrecorded instrument in some states may depend on whether he or she has notice. A party may have actual knowledge of the unrecorded instrument or constructive notice. Constructive notice may be, for example, the presence of a party in possession of the land in question. The theory of constructive notice is that certain facts should alert a reasonable person to the possibility that there may be an adverse claim to the property and lead that person to make further inquiry as to the state of the title.

In general, the recording statutes attempt to protect a party if he or she is a bona fide purchaser, mortgagee, or creditor without actual or constructive notice of the prior unrecorded instrument.

D. WHAT INSTRUMENTS MAY BE RECORDED

The modern recording statutes embrace practically all instruments that may affect legal or equitable title to land, including, in some cases, leases. The following are instruments that may be recorded in one or more states:

1. Deeds
2. Mortgages
3. Agreements of Sale or Memoranda of Agreements of Sale
4. Assignments of Mortgage

5. Certificates of Bankruptcy
6. Conveyances of Permanent Rights or Privileges
7. Decrees of a Court
8. Judgments
9. Leases or Memoranda of Leases
10. Maps or Plans of Subdivision
11. Powers of Attorney Relating to Real Property
12. Purchase-Money Mortgages
13. Releases or Satisfactions of Mortgage Liens
14. Sheriff or Marshal's Deeds
15. Trust Deeds
16. Condominium Documents
17. Homeowners' Association Documents
18. Options or Memoranda of Options
19. Assignments of Leases
20. Assignments of other Interests in Real Property
21. Security Agreements
22. Financing Statements
23. Trust Agreements

The following sections are intended to familiarize you with the recording of various instruments other than deeds and mortgages, some of which will be covered in detail in various chapters of this text.

1. Judgments and Judgment Notes

A judgment is a decision by a judge or jury or a written admission (in recordable form) that one party owes a particular sum of money to another. Judgments are recorded in an index generally referred to as the "judgment index." Once it is entered in the appropriate index, a judgment creates a lien on all real property of the judgment debtor in the jurisdiction (usually the county) in which the judgment is recorded. A judgment obtained in states that use counties as the basis for court jurisdiction may be transferred from the county in which it is obtained to other counties in the same state or may even be transferable to other states. Once transferred, the judgment will create a lien on all property of the debtor in the county to which the judgment is transferred as well as the county from which it was transferred.

Prior to execution on a judgment, however, the judgment holder possesses a lien (as of the date of recording) that attaches to all the debtor's real property in the county in which the judgment is recorded. Thereafter, if the debtor conveys a portion of the debtor's real property to a third party, the third party will take the property subject to the lien of the judgment, so that when the judgment holder executes on the judgment, he or she may order the sheriff to sell the third party's land formerly owned by the debtor. The third party will have record (constructive) notice of the judgment lien from the fact that the judgment is recorded against the debtor in the judgment index. Thus, the lien of a judgment is similar to the lien of a mortgage.

2. Lis Pendens

A complaint, which is a document used to initiate a lawsuit, may be recorded in certain instances. When there is a dispute between parties affecting title to land, the party asserting the claim to ownership will want the asserted interest recorded so that the record owner cannot sell or transfer the property to an innocent third party. This situation might arise, for example, if a seller refuses to transfer title to a purchaser because the seller believes that the purchaser breached the terms of the agreement of sale. If the purchaser is not in breach, the purchaser may bring a lawsuit in a court of equity to compel the seller to convey the property to the purchaser. This action does not, however, prevent the seller from conveying good title to a third party if the agreement of sale is not recorded. In order to protect his or her interest in the land, the purchaser can have the pendency of the lawsuit noted in the office of the prothonotary or court clerk in the judgment index. This entry of a "lis pendens" (pending lawsuit) constitutes constructive notice to the public of the claims contained in the pleadings of the purchaser's lawsuit. If another puchaser purchases the land in question after the lis pendens is recorded, he or she takes title subject to the outcome of the lawsuit. If the plaintiff-purchaser wins the lawsuit, he or she will have the right to purchase the property in preference to whatever rights the second purchaser has in the property. The lis pendens is available only when the lawsuit affects title to the land.

3. Agreements of Sale

An agreement of sale need not be recorded in order to make it effective between the parties. However, unless the purchaser is in possession of the premises (thereby giving constructive notice to third persons of the purchaser's interest), the purchaser is exposed to the risk that third parties, such as bona fide purchasers and lienors of the seller, may acquire rights superior to the purchaser's. Therefore, it would appear to be in the purchaser's best interest to record the agreement of sale. However, in most areas agreements of sale are customarily not recorded and the seller typically requires that the agreement of sale not be recorded. The reason that sellers take this attitude is that if the purchaser should default under the agreement of sale, the seller would be unable to convey title to another purchaser unless the agreement is canceled or in some way stricken from the record. Unless the defaulting purchaser cooperates, the process for accomplishing either result is expensive and time-consuming. In addition, the seller may be unwilling to state as a matter of public record the terms of the agreement of sale, particularly the purchase price. If the initial purchaser under a recorded agreement of sale defaults, the seller might find it difficult to negotiate with a subsequent purchaser a higher purchase price or more favorable terms.

4. Leases and Memoranda of Leases

A lease of real property grants to a tenant rights of possession in the tenant, as well as other rights. Under certain circumstances they should be recorded. For example, if the owner has agreed to lease a store that is not yet built, the tenant will not have immediate possession. The tenant can establish a priority for his or her rights under the lease by recording the lease or, more typically, a memorandum of the lease.[5] Similarly, if the tenant is not taking immediate possession and a mortgage will be created before the tenant takes possession, it is sometimes desired by all the parties (tenant, mortgagee, and owner) that the lease be prior to the mortgage. This can be accomplished by recording the lease before the mortgage. The desirability of the prior recorded lease is discussed in greater detail in Chapter Ten. Additionally, a lease that grants the tenant special rights in the property, such as an option to purchase the property, should be recorded. This would protect the tenant from bona fide purchasers who, while they might have had constructive notice (due to the tenant's possession) of the tenant's possessory rights under the lease, would not have had notice of the tenant's right to purchase.

In some circumstances it will not be desirable to record the entire lease, usually either because of its length or because the lease contains certain matters that the parties do not wish to be of public knowledge. The law in many states recognizes this possibility and permits the recording of a memorandum of lease, which has the same effect as if the lease were recorded. The content of the memorandum of lease is dictated by the recording statute and the desires of the parties. Generally, however, the memorandum must at least set forth (a) the names of the parties, (b) a description of the premises, and (c) the term of the lease. The Pennsylvania statute requires at least the following information to be contained in a memorandum of lease:

(1) The name of the lessor in such lease, sublease or agreement;
(2) The name of the lessee therein;
(3) The addresses, if any, set forth therein as addresses of such parties;
(4) A reference to the date thereof;
(5) The description of the demised premises in the form set forth therein;
(6) The date of commencement of the term of the lease, if a fixed date, and, if not, the full provision or provisions thereof pursuant to which such date of commencement is to be fixed;
(7) The term of the lease;
(8) If the lessee has a right of extension or renewal, the date of expiration of the final period for which such right is given;

5. Most states (but not all) permit the recording of memoranda or short forms of agreements in lieu of recording the entire agreement.

(9) If the lessee has a right of purchase of or refusal on the demised premises or any part thereof, a statement of the term during which such right is exercisable.
[Act of June 2, 1959, P.L. 454, § 2]

Leases, subleases, and memoranda of leases are indexed by the recording officer in the grantor index against the lessor and in the grantee index against the lessee.

5. Assignments of Mortgages

Often the holder of a mortgage wishes to sell his or her interest to another in order to recover all or a portion of the debt owed him or her without waiting for the full term of the mortgage to expire.[6] This is accomplished by assigning the mortgage to the purchaser of the original mortgagee's interest. Such assignments of mortgages are recorded in order to protect the interest of the assignee. If the assignee's interest was not recorded, a satisfaction or release of the mortgage given by the original mortgagee would be binding on the assignee with respect to any party or prospective claimant without actual knowledge of the assignment. Assignments are recorded in a separate assignment of mortgage book. In addition, the assignment will be noted on the margin of the mortgagor–mortgagee index where the original is set out, together with the book and page where the assignment of mortgage is recorded and the date of the assignment.

6. Satisfaction of Mortgages

After a mortgage debt has been paid, the mortgagee must execute a "satisfaction piece" indicating that the terms of the mortgage have been fulfilled and the mortgagee has no further interest in the property. The mortgagee, at the request of the mortgagor or owner of the mortgaged premises, must enter the satisfaction piece of record in the office where the mortgage is recorded.[7] The satisfaction piece constitutes a discharge of the mortgage debt and a release of the lien of the mortgage, and its recording is essential to clear the title to the land from the mortgage encumbrance.

The recording officer indexes the satisfaction piece against the name of the mortgagee or the last assignee of the mortgage and indicates the recording of the satisfaction piece beside the original mortgage record.

---

6. This has been especially true from the time that the government commenced efforts to develop a secondary market in mortgages by the creation of the Federal National Mortgage Association (FNMA), the Government National Mortgage Association (GNMA), and the Federal Home Loan Mortgage Corporation (FHLMC), all of which are discussed in Chapter Seven.

7. Some jurisdictions impose penalties on a mortgagee who, having been fully repaid, refuses to execute a proper mortgage satisfaction.

E. HOW TO RECORD DOCUMENTS

Having reviewed the common types of recording systems and some of the documents that may be recorded, we shall briefly discuss the mechanics of recording an instrument.

Recording is effected by taking the document, in an approved form, properly executed and acknowledged, and presenting it to the office of the public official charged with the responsibility of recording such instruments in the county in which the real estate involved is located.[8] The public official usually immediately stamps the document with a time-date stamp to indicate the time and date deposited.

An instrument is deemed to be recorded at the time and date it is deposited with the proper official. Subsequently, the instrument is entered into the appropriate record book either by photocopy or by microfilming. The original instrument is then returned to the owner of the instrument.

1. The Index

The recording system would be unmanageable and ineffective without an index to title records. Two methods of indexing are generally used.

(a) Tract Indices

If a state has instituted a system in which all the land has been officially surveyed and the parcels or tracts assigned numerical designations,[9] the index is subdivided numerically to coincide with the tract designations. A portion of such an index is set aside for each tract of land and contains recording references to the books and pages of the records that have documents relating to that tract. Indices may, in addition, provide information describing the character of the instruments listed and noting date, date of recording, and the names of the parties. Such indices are known as "abstract books." In several states, tract indices or abstract books are part of the recording system and are matters of public record. In other states they are not part of the recording system and either do not exist or are privately maintained.

(b) Name Indices

Name indices are based on the names of the parties to the instrument. The names of the parties granting an interest in real estate, as grantor, mortgagor, vendor, lessor, optionor, or assignor, are entered in pages of the record books or in separate books used for indexing purposes only. As each instrument is recorded, the name of the grantor is written in the page or book corresponding to the alphabetical index of the grantor's

---

8. If the real estate is located in more than one county, the document must be recorded in each of the counties involved.

9. The process is generally known as "platting" and the surveys are known as "plats."

name, together with the name of the other party to the instrument, the book and page in which the instrument is recorded, relevant dates, and a description of the property. At the same time, in either the same index or in a separate index maintained for this purpose, the name of the party receiving the interest, as grantee, mortgagee, vendee, lessee, optionee, or assignee, is recorded alphabetically, together with same sort of relevant information concerning the instrument.

We speak of these indices as the "grantor index" and the "grantee index," respectively. In some states, mortgage information is separately indexed in a "mortgagor index" and a "mortgagee index." These indices also may be divided into separate sheets or books for different years. There may also be separate indices for judgments, liens, and miscellaneous documents.

The value of the name indices is that they permit a title "searcher" to search the prior title history from the present owner, whose name may be found in the grantee index, by finding his or her immediate grantor, tracing back that grantor's grantor from the grantee index, and so on, until the original conveyance from the sovereign, such as the English king, Spanish king, or federal or state government.

Then, in order to ascertain the existence of mortgages or other encumbrances on the property, the relevant indices (e.g., mortgage or judgment) must be examined. To be reliable, the examination must cover the period during which a particular grantor and all predecessors in title owned the property. Use of the indices are discussed in detail in Chapter Six.

2. Acknowledgments

Any instrument presented for recording must be acknowledged. An acknowledgment is an affidavit by an authorized state or local official that the person whose signature appears on the instrument personally appeared before the official and "acknowledged" executing the instrument with full knowledge of its contents and purpose. The Uniform Acknowledgment Act provides that acknowledgments may be taken by the following individuals:

a. Judge of a court of record
b. Clerk or deputy clerk of a court having a seal
c. Commissioner or register (or recorder) of deeds
d. Notary public
e. Justice of the Peace

An instrument executed by a corporation is signed by both an authorized officer of the corporation (usually the president or a vice-president) and the secretary or assistant secretary, who attests to the seal of the corporation. The authorized officer then appears before the appropriate official and acknowledges that he or she is in fact the officer whose name appears as an officer in the instrument.

An acknowledgment taken in the United States, but not in the state in which the instrument is being offered for recording, must generally, in accordance with the Uniform Acknowledgment Act, be authenticated by a certificate that verifies the authority of the state or local official who made the acknowledgment. If the acknowledgment is taken by the clerk or deputy clerk of a court, the presiding judge of the court must execute the authentication. If the acknowledgment is taken by a notary public, or any other authorized person, the authentication must be made by a clerk of any court of record of the county in which the acknowledgment is taken.

Laws and local practices regarding acknowledgments vary widely from jurisdiction to jurisdiction. Some states do not accept acknowledgments made by an attorney. Some states accept a rubber stamp of the acknowledging official, whereas other states require a seal that is embossed on the document, leaving a permanent impression. The language of the form of acknowledgment varies. Also, local laws or practices may dictate that the signatory actually sign the document while the party taking the acknowledgment looks on. In such areas an attempt by a signatory to have a previously made signature acknowledged will be unsuccessful. The best practice, especially when the document concerned is to be recorded outside your usual locale, is to consult a local attorney or the public official who will be receiving the document for recording and to inquire as to the local requirements.

3. Recording Costs

In all states and counties a person who submits a document to a local official for recording must pay certain fees and charges.

(a) Filing Fees

Generally, the filing fee is collected by the official who accepts instruments for recording. This fee is normally computed from a published schedule and is usually based on the type of document presented for recording and the number of pages that the document contains. The filing fee can be viewed as a type of handling charge collected by the local recorder to help defray the costs of maintaining an index system.

(b) Transfer, Recording, and Intangible Taxes

In addition to filing fees, most state or local governments impose a tax on certain transactions or on the documents effecting the transaction. Such taxes are usually assessed on a transfer of title or a mortgage but may include other transactions.

It is important to know whether the recording of a particular deed or any other particular instrument is taxable under state or local law or ordinance.[10] Realty transfer taxes and recording taxes are quite popular sources of revenue because they are easily administered and cannot be avoided except at the risk of losing the benefits of the recording system. Evidence that the taxes have been paid is generally a condition to acceptance of an instrument for recording. The taxes are often substantial and in some states can represent one of the major costs of settlement for the seller or the purchaser, or both.

Usually the amount of the tax is based on the dollar amount of the transaction. If the document does not set forth the true consideration for the transaction, or if the transfer is claimed to be exempt from tax,[11] it is usually necessary to insert at the end of the deed, or to attach to the deed, an affidavit stating the true consideration or reason for exemption.

III. THE TORRENS SYSTEM

Under the recording statutes system, the evidence of ownership or title is made public for the prudent purchaser or creditor to examine and to draw his or her own conclusions.

In the midnineteenth century an alternative recording system was developed by an Australian, Sir Robert Torrens, and bears his name, the Torrens System. Torrens suggested a system whereby a purchaser of property could go to a court and have his or her title officially determined. As a result of the proceeding, the purchaser would receive a certificate declaring his or her ownership, and a duplicate of the certificate would be registered in the Torrens section of the public land records. The certificate would have noted on it any mortgages, liens, or other interests in the property. When the owner subsequently sold the land, it would not be necessary to search the chain of title because the certificate of title would serve as conclusive proof of ownership. The Torrens registration officer would simply search the records to confirm that the seller has not already conveyed the property and that no liens exist other than those noted on the owner's certificate. In due course the registration officer would then issue a new owner's Torren registration certificate to the buyer. By using the Torrens System, the need for title insurance (discussed in Chapter Six) is theoretically obviated. In practice, many banks and other mortgagees are unwilling to rely on the Torrens certificate alone and require either title insurance or other proof of title.

In each state that has a Torrens registration statute, the system is voluntary and exists side by side with a recording system. Because of the expense of the court proceeding required for initial registration, the Torrens system is not widely used in any state.

10. In prior years the federal government imposed a stamp tax on such transfers. That tax is no longer in effect.

11. Intrafamily transfers are an example of a class of transactions that might be exempted from a transfer tax.

IV. SUMMARY

A legal assistant needs to know how to use the recording system, both in terms of getting documents recorded and retrieving information. A legal assistant should also be aware of the theory behind the local system. This understanding is useful in many aspects of real estate and is especially useful in working with title abstracts and title insurance reports, which are the subjects of Chapter Six.

Chapter 10

Leasing

Part One
BASIC ELEMENTS OF A LEASE

I. INTRODUCTION

The relationship of landlord and tenant is created by an agreement (either oral or written) called a lease.[1] A lease is a contract whereby one party (the landlord or lessor) grants to another party (the tenant or lessee) the right to possess real or personal property for a period of time that may or may not be fixed, usually, but not always, in return for the payment of rent. This chapter focuses on the leasing of real property. There is a great deal of common law and statutory law that govern the landlord-tenant relationship. However, almost all of the provisions of the laws governing the landlord-tenant relationship are subject to change by the parties in their written or oral agreement. Thus, the drafter of a lease must be aware of the relevant landlord-tenant law in order to judge the effect of a lease that does not address specific aspects of the landlord-tenant relationship.

This chapter is devoted to a discussion of the components of lease agreements. Those elements that are common to virtually all leases will be considered first. A standard form of lease, which contains most of these elements, is reprinted as *Example 10-1* at the end of this chapter. Later parts of the chapter deal with matters that are unique to special types

---

1. Note that the word "lease" is used both as a noun and as a verb. You may recall from Chapter One that the tenant's interest cre- ated by a lease is referred to as a leasehold interest.

343

of leases, such as leases of undeveloped ground (a "ground lease") and leases for shopping centers and office buildings.

Before proceeding further, the reader should be aware of the importance of printed form leases to lawyers and landlords. Lawyers in most communities will have available to them standard leases covering the rental of office space, homes, apartments, and retail and commercial space. Often these standard printed forms provide the basis for the lease executed between the landlord and tenant, with minor changes or deletions being made on the printed form and additional clauses being added on separate pages attached to the printed form of the lease (often called a "rider" to the lease).

II. ESSENTIAL ELEMENTS OF A LEASE

Several requisite elements are included in virtually every lease. They are set forth below in the usual order in which they appear in the simplest form of written lease.

A. DATE

The date on which the agreement is executed should be included.

B. PARTIES

The lease must adequately identify the parties and should contain the correct names and addresses of the landlord and tenant. After each party's name, his or her capacity (i.e., landlord or tenant) should be stated.

1. Landlord

The landlord's name should conform exactly with the name of the party or parties holding record title (or, in the case of a sublease, with a party having the right of possession) to the property. If the landlord is not an individual, the type of entity should be mentioned. Additional considerations that vary with the type of landlord in a particular situation are set forth below:

(a) Individual as Landlord

An individual landlord's spouse who does not have any ownership interest in the property need not join in signing the lease unless the lease gives the tenant an option to purchase the property.

(b) Partnership as Landlord

It is good practice for all partners of a partnership to be named as well as the name of the partnership itself. For example, "A, B, and C, co-partners trading as ABC Company."

(c) Corporation as Landlord

Following the name of a corporation, include its state of incorporation. For example, "XYZ Corporation, an Illinois corporation." The authority of the officers of the corporation to lease a particular property should be ascertained. To determine whether the officers of a corporation have the authority to lease a particular property, the tenant should ask the landlord to produce a certified copy of resolutions of the landlord's board of directors, authorizing execution of the lease by the officers who propose to sign it.

(d) Fiduciaries

The name of the fiduciary and a description of his or her role should be included. For example, "John Smith, executor under the will of Betsy Jones, Deceased." The authority of a fiduciary to lease the property should be ascertained by the tenant. To determine the authority of the executor or administrator of an estate, the tenant should request the landlord to give the tenant a copy of the letters testamentary (in the case of an executor) or letters of administration (in the case of an administrator), evidencing appointment as a personal representative and certified as accurate by an appropriate official of the court that granted the letters.

In the case of a trustee-landlord, the tenant may ascertain the trustee's power to lease the property by reviewing a copy of the instrument creating the trust.

(e) Agents

If the lease is to be executed by an agent of either party, the lease should clearly indicate that the party signing the lease is acting as an agent (e.g., George Jackson, agent). The authority of the agent to lease the property should be investigated by the tenant. It is best to have the lease approved in writing by the principal for whom the agent is acting.

2. Tenant

The landlord should check the status and authority of the prospective tenant to enter into an enforceable lease. The rules stated earlier for describing the landlord also apply to the tenant.

C. STATEMENT OF DEMISE

The lease should use the historical words for granting a leasehold estate, such as "landlord does hereby let and demise" or "landlord does hereby lease." These words have been construed by the courts in many cases and have a fixed meaning.

D. DESCRIPTION OF PREMISES

The leased ("demised") premises should be clearly identified. If the premises are an apartment or small office, the street address of the building and the number of the individual apartment or office is usually considered sufficient. If part of a building comprising less than an entire floor is demised, a plan showing the space demised should be attached to the lease as an exhibit. If dimensions are set forth, they should be clearly designated as approximate dimensions, or the landlord may be deemed to have warranted that the exact dimensions set forth are accurate. If an entire building is leased, a full legal description of the property is necessary.

If the leased premises are not yet built, a reference is usually made to the location of the premises on a site plan. In addition, the plans and specifications for the erection of the building should be included as an exhibit to the lease.

If the tenant is to have use of personal property located on the leased premises, that fact should be stated and the lease should contain an exhibit setting forth the items of personal property included in the lease.

If a tenant is leasing space in a multitenant building that contains common or public areas, the lease should contain a specific grant of the right to use those areas in common with other tenants. If certain areas outside the space actually being leased are to be for the tenant's exclusive use (e.g., assigned parking or storage), then such rights of exclusive use should be set forth.

E. TERM OF LEASE

In leases for a fixed term, the term of the lease, together with the commencement and expiration dates,[2] must be set forth. An example of such a provision follows:

> This lease shall be for a term of five (5) years beginning the 1st day of January 1986 and ending the 31st day of December 1991.

The date of the lease, the date of the commencement of the term, and the date of the commencement of the obligation to pay rent may be different. A lease may be signed well in advance of the intended commencement of the term. The obligation to pay rent may not commence until a substantial period has expired after commencement of the term; for example, the tenant may have use of the property without rent for a period of time

---

2. The date set for the end of a lease is called the expiration date. If for some reason the term actually ends prior to the expiration date (e.g., because the tenant defaults), then the lease term is said to terminate. In current legal jargon "expiration" is the natural end of a lease term, whereas "termination" refers to any end of the term, but especially a premature end.

so that the tenant has the opportunity to alter and furnish the premises for the tenant's own purposes.

Not all leases are for a fixed term. Some leases are simply silent as to term. Such a lease is considered to be a "tenancy at will" and to be terminable by either party with reasonable notice (thirty days in most jurisdictions). There are also leases that will terminate on a given event, often the death of the tenant (such a tenant is said to have a "life estate" or a "tenancy for life") or of some other party (a life estate *pur autre vie*).

F. RENTAL

If the lease is one that provides for rent, then the rental is usually expressed in a fixed dollar sum. Often the total rental for the entire term is also stated, followed by a provision as to the time and amount of each installment. For example, in a one-year lease, the following rental provision might appear:

> Tenant shall pay, without demand and without set-off or deduction, a minimum annual rental of Twelve Hundred Dollars ($1,200) payable in equal monthly installments of One Hundred Dollars ($100) each, and a pro-rata portion thereof for any part of a month, on the first day of each month in advance, beginning the 1st day of January 1986 and on the first day of each month thereafter.

The phrase "in advance" is essential because the common law provides that without that phrase, the entire rent will be paid at the end of the term. The words "minimum rental" are used because other sums due the landlord may be classified as rent (see below). The rent clause includes the words "without demand" because in the absence of those words the landlord may not be able to take advantage of all of the remedies available to the landlord unless a prior demand for payment of the rent has first been made. The rental clause should also include the words "without set-off or deduction" or the tenant may withhold rent if the tenant feels the landlord owes him or her money (whether for sufficient or insufficient reason), thereby prejudicing the landlord's or the mortgagee's financial position.

The place of payment of the rent should be stated because otherwise, rent is payable on the premises. The usual clauses direct payment to be made at the landlord's office, with his or her address given, or at such other place as the landlord may from time to time designate.

Often a lease requires the tenant to pay certain expenses, such as real estate taxes and water and sewer rents. If the tenant is required to make additional payments, the lease should specifically provide that all such additional payments are collectible as rent. This would attempt to ensure that all remedies applicable to the collection of rent and priorities in bankruptcy and insolvency proceedings would be available with respect to the additional payments.

G. EXECUTION

If a written lease is required by the Statute of Frauds (which requirement is discussed later), then all parties must sign the lease. Corporate signatures should be in the corporate name by a principal officer, such as the president or vice-president, attested by a secretary or assistant secretary, and the corporate seal affixed. If a lease is to be recorded, the proper acknowledgments must be completed.

In addition to the basic elements set forth above, there are many provisions that are common to most leases. Such provisions are the subject of section IV of Part One of this chapter.

III. THE NEED FOR A WRITTEN LEASE

In section I, B of Chapter Three we discussed the Statute of Frauds, a variation of which has been adopted by nearly every jurisdiction. The Statute of Frauds for a particular state will usually require that leases for longer than a specified term must be in writing, or must otherwise qualify as having satisfied the Statute of Frauds, in order to be enforceable against either the landlord or the tenant.

The landlord-tenant relationship is one that may continue over an extended period. During that period the parties may modify the relationship by increasing or reducing the term of the lease or the rent or by amending the terms of the lease in any number of ways. The question of which amendments and modifications to a lease must be in writing and be signed by the parties is a difficult and controversial one, and many jurisdictions have not settled even some of the more obvious of the issues, such as whether an extension or reduction of the term of the lease must be evidenced by a written and signed agreement. Consider also whether a lease that otherwise need not be in writing should be incorporated into a written agreement if it contains an option to purchase the demised premises.

PROBLEM

Determine what leases must be in writing in order to be enforceable in your jurisdiction.

IV. ADDITIONAL PROVISIONS COMMON TO ALL TYPES OF LEASES

The basic requirements of a lease establish the relationship of landlord and tenant, ensure the tenant possession for a specified term, and, as a matter of law, afford the landlord certain minimum benefits, including the right to collect the rent and the right to exercise the remedies provided by law for the collection of rent and for the recovery of possession of the demised premises at the termination of the lease. In addition, every lease should include specific provisions dealing with the issues discussed below. Otherwise, the common law and the statutory provisions of landlord and tenant law dictate terms that are often contrary to the actual intent of the parties.

A. USE CLAUSE

If no provision as to the use of the premises is set forth, the tenant is entitled to use the premises without restriction, except that he or she may not commit "waste," i.e., destroy the premises or let the property fall into an unreasonable state of disrepair. If the landlord does not wish the tenant to be free to use the property for any purpose, he or she must provide in the lease for restrictions on the use of the property to limit the tenant's use to the actual intended purpose. For example, in a dwelling or apartment house, the tenant might be limited to use of the premises as "a private dwelling and no other," or to use of the premises as a "single-family dwelling and no other."

The tenant will desire the broadest possible use clause, and the landlord, especially in a multitenant building or a shopping center, will generally want to limit the use strictly.

In commercial properties a restriction limiting the use of the demised premises to a particular business may be desired by the landlord to limit competition with other property in the vicinity owned or acquired by the landlord. In shopping centers, particular care must be taken to limit the type of business and to avoid infringement of exclusive use clauses in the leases of other tenants.

There are many other reasons for a landlord to restrict use. Heavy or inflammable material, machines causing vibration, noxious odors, and the like endanger the building and annoy other tenants. Some uses impair the image of the building and either increase insurance costs or make it impossible to procure insurance.

In drafting a use provision it is important that the actual intent or agreement of the parties with respect to the use be ascertained. The drafter should be as specific as possible in describing the use. Although desirable, it is usually not possible to list all the items that may be sold at the premises. However, it may be possible, for example, to limit the use to "sales at retail" and further limit such sales to "retail sales of shoes" or even more explicitly, "retail sales of men's shoes." An example of a simple use provision is set forth below:

> The premises may be used only as a restaurant for the sale of fast-food items and the incidental sale of nonalcoholic beverages for consumption on or off the premises. The premises shall not be used for any other purpose.

A tenant should know in advance whether there are any legal impediments to the use of the premises for the intended purpose. The existence of governmental restrictions can be checked by obtaining a permit from the municipality in which the premises are located, stating that the intended use is permissible. There may also exist private restrictions contained in an agreement or in a clause of a deed restricting the use of the premises. Restrictions imposed in private agreements or deeds will not affect third parties (including tenants) unless they are recorded. The information needed by a prospective tenant concerning private restrictions, therefore, can be obtained by searching the title to the property to be leased.

If the tenant is concerned about the legality of the use, and has not had an opportunity to check with the appropriate governmental authorities, a provision conditioning the validity of the lease on obtaining the appropriate use permit may be inserted.

PROBLEM

Draft a clause making a lease contingent on the tenant obtaining a use registration permit from the local municipal authorities on or before June 10, 1985, for use of the premises as a retail shoe store.

B. REPAIRS

1. Generally

At common law, in the absence of any provision in the agreement, the landlord has no obligation to repair or rebuild damaged premises except for common areas of a multitenant building. Therefore, if the parties intend that the landlord will perform certain repairs, the obligations of the landlord should be set forth.

In the absence of an agreement to the contrary, the common law imposes an obligation on the tenant to make ordinary repairs. The obligation of the tenant does not extend to major repairs and does not include repairs resulting from acts of third parties or destruction by fire, wind, or other act of God. Written leases often require the tenant to keep the leased premises clean and in good repair and at the termination of the lease to return the premises in the same condition as when it was leased, reasonable wear and tear and damage by accidental casualty excepted.

There are alternative approaches in leasing to the obligation of each party to repair. The tenant of an entire building, for example, is often responsible for all repairs, interior and exterior, structural or otherwise. Sometimes a landlord will agree to make repairs to the roof and exterior walls, while requiring the tenant to make all interior repairs. Another alternative is for the landlord to agree to make all structural repairs, while requiring the tenant to make all nonstructural repairs. There is no precise definition of these terms, but in most states there are numerous cases in which the courts have decided whether a particular repair is structural or nonstructural.

A lease should state specifically who is responsible for repairs to the electrical, plumbing, heating, and air conditioning or ventilating systems. It is also good drafting policy to indicate the party who is responsible for replacement of plate glass windows, as they are subject to a high rate of breakage and are expensive to repair.

2. Areas Outside Building

A tenant who leases an entire building or the first floor tenant in a multitenant building is often responsible for maintenance of the grounds and walks adjoining the building. A general provision to that effect follows:

> Tenant shall be responsible for the condition of the pavement, curb, cellar doors, awnings and other erections in the pavement during the term of this lease, shall keep the pavement free from snow and ice, and hereby agrees to release and relieve Landlord and save Landlord harmless from any liability for any accidents, due or alleged to be due to their defective condition or to any accumulations of snow and ice.

3. Compliance with Requirements of Public Authorities

In addition to repair requirements occasioned by deterioration of the structure, repairs or alterations may be required by local authorities in order for the structure to comply with various safety codes. Therefore, the lease may include a provision, in addition to the general repair provision, obligating the landlord or tenant to make repairs or changes to the premises that are required by the authorities. For example, a provision requiring the tenant to comply with local ordinances might render the tenant responsible for installing or repairing a fire alarm system. The tenant should be certain that his or her responsibility is limited to requirements imposed by the authorities that relate to the particular use and occupancy of the tenant.

C. ALTERATIONS AND IMPROVEMENTS

A tenant may wish to make alterations to the premises. For example, in a retail store a tenant may wish to move the partition between the sales and storage areas. However, absent a provision in the lease or permission of the landlord, a tenant may not alter the premises. A landlord ordinarily will want to prohibit alterations unless he or she approves them in advance. An example of a provision to that effect follows:

> Tenant covenants and agrees that he or she will not, without the consent in writing of Landlord first had and obtained, make any alterations, improvements or additions to the demised premises. All alterations, improvements, additions or fixtures, whether installed before or after the execution of this lease, shall remain upon the premises at the expiration or sooner termination of this lease and become the property of Landlord, unless Landlord shall, prior to the termination of this lease, have given written notice to Tenant to remove the same, in which event Tenant will remove such alterations, improvements and additions, and restore the premises to the same good order and condition in which they now are. Should Tenant fail to do so, Landlord may do so and collect the cost and expense thereof from Tenant as additional rent.

The above provision gives the landlord the option to keep the alterations or improvements at the termination of the lease or to require the tenant to remove them.

A professional or commercial tenant should always add a provision to the effect that the tenant will be permitted to remove trade fixtures and equipment, provided the tenant repairs any and all damage caused to the demised premises by reason of the removal. Trade fixtures and equipment may include display cases, furniture, shelves, office equipment, and many kinds of machinery and equipment. Whether or not other alterations and improvements that do not fall into the category of trade fixtures may be removed by the tenant is a matter that may be negotiated by the parties.

Often the parties agree that before the tenant occupies the premises the landlord or tenant is to make certain alterations or renovations to the premises in order to make the premises suitable for the tenant. The work should be described, and if possible, plans and specifications for the work should be attached to the lease and initialed by the parties.

If the landlord is performing the work, he or she should be obligated to complete the work by a specified time, with reasonable allowance for delays beyond the landlord's control. The landlord should also provide a warranty for the work performed. The tenant will want a clause permitting the tenant to cancel the lease should the landlord fail to complete alterations within the specified period. If such a clause is not inserted and the work runs beyond the specified time, state law may limit the tenant's remedies to a suit for damages. In certain cases the lease will provide that the term of the lease or the obligation to pay rent shall not commence until the landlord's work is completed.

Improvements made by the tenant may be the basis of mechanics' liens filed against the real estate. To protect itself, the landlord should include a provision requiring the tenant to pay for all work promptly, so that no liens are filed, and obligating the tenant to remove promptly any lien that may be filed. It is common to have language in the lease to the effect that the landlord will not be liable for work done by contractors for the tenant and that no liens shall affect the landlord's interest in the premises. It is unlikely, however, that such a provision will effectively prevent the filing or enforcement of mechanics' liens. In jurisdictions where the right to file a mechanics' lien may be waived by individual contractors and material suppliers, or by the general contractor on behalf of all subcontractors and material suppliers, then the lease might require the tenant to have the necessary waivers filed in a timely manner in the appropriate location.

D. FIRE

A lease should deal with three issues that arise in the event of a fire that causes damage to the demised property and equipment of the tenant: (1) whether the tenant will be entitled to stop paying rent if there is damage to the demised premises; (2) which party, if either, will be obligated to repair the damage to the demised premises; and (3) whether the landlord is legally responsible for any damage to the tenant's property if the fire is the fault of the landlord or his or her employees, and whether the tenant is legally responsible for any damage to the demised property if the fire is the fault of the tenant or his or her employees.

1. Obligation to Pay Rent and Make Repairs

Every lease should state which party is to make repairs and restore the premises in the event of a fire. Typically, that is the obligation of the landlord. In addition, the lease should establish whether the tenant must pay rent during the period of repairs or restoration. Generally, if the premises are totally destroyed, rent abates and the tenant is not required to pay any rent. If the premises are partially destroyed and the tenant can still use a portion of the premises, the lease sometimes provides for an adjustment (or partial abatement) to the rent. A typical provision is set forth below:

> In the event that the demised premises are totally destroyed or so damaged by fire or other casualty that the same cannot be repaired or restored within a reasonable time, this lease shall absolutely cease and determine, and the rent shall abate for the balance of the term.
>
> If the damage caused as above be only partial and such that the premises can be restored to their then condition within a reasonable time, the Landlord may, at his or her option, restore the same with reasonable promptness, reserving the right to enter upon the demised premises for that purpose. The Landlord also reserves the right to enter upon the demised premises whenever necessary to repair damage caused by fire or other casualty to the building of which the demised premises are a part, even though the effect of such entry be to render the demised premises or a part thereof untenantable. In either event, the rent shall be apportioned and suspended during the time the Landlord is in possession, taking into account the proportion of the demised premises rendered untenantable and the duration of the Landlord's possession.

In the sample provision above, the use of the phrase "reasonable time" lacks precision, and a tenant may wish to specify a period within which the premises must be restored. The tenant often tries to negotiate for a provision that terminates the lease if fire or casualty damage is extensive and cannot be repaired or restored within a specified period.

2. Liability for Damage Caused by Fire

Typically, the landlord carries fire insurance on the building[3] and the tenant carries fire insurance on the equipment and property located within the building. Such insurance is intended to cover any loss irrespective of who may have caused the fire.

Under general principles of tort law, one whose negligent action causes a fire may be held liable for damages resulting from the fire. This tort liability is unconnected with the issues of the obligation to make repairs or pay rent. However, tort liability may be waived by the parties to a lease, and this is often the case. In doing so, one must consider the impact of such a waiver or release on the insurance coverage.

The insurance company, if it is required to pay a claim of its insured for damages caused by fire, acquires the legal right (referred to as the right of "subrogation") to take over any tort claims of its insured against any person whose acts caused the damage. Therefore, the landlord's insurance company, after paying a claim for fire damage, can succeed to the landlord's right to obtain recovery from the person causing the fire, such as the tenant or his or her employee or agent.

If the landlord or tenant agrees not to hold the other party to a lease responsible for its negligent act in causing a fire, this will nullify the insurance company's right of subrogation. Unless the insurance company has agreed to such a provision, it may jeopardize the landlord's or tenant's insurance coverage. A solution to this problem is to request from the appropriate insurance company a "waiver of subrogation" by which the insurance company agrees to forfeit its right of subrogation without prejudice to the insured. Some insurance companies will issue such waivers only if an additional insurance premium is charged, and the lease should deal with this possibility.

The following sample clause deals with obtaining waivers of subrogation and waiving any right of recovery, as between landlord and tenant, to the extent that insurance coverage exists. The parties will not waive any claim beyond that covered by insurance, as that would result in the loss being borne by the party who was innocent of any responsibility in causing the damage.

> Landlord and Tenant hereby release each other from any and all liability or responsibility to the other or anyone claiming through or under them by

---

3. Certain types of leases require the tenant to carry insurance. In that case the same discussion applies, but it is the landlord who needs protection in the event his or her negligent act causes a fire.

way of subrogation or otherwise for any loss or damage to property covered by any insurance then in force, even if such loss or damage shall have been caused by the fault or negligence of the other party, or anyone for whom such party may be responsible, provided, however, that this release shall be applicable and in force and effect only with respect to any loss or damage occurring during such time as the policy or policies of insurance covering said loss shall contain a clause or endorsement to the effect that this release shall not adversely affect or impair said insurance or prejudice the right of the insured to recover thereunder. Any liability, fire, and extended coverage insurance policies covering the Premises shall contain such a clause if available without extra charge. If there be a charge, the party bearing the expense of the particular policy shall notify the other party and, in such event, shall have the clause added to that policy if the other party agrees to pay such extra charge.

E. OTHER CASUALTY

Fire is the usual but not the only cause of damage or destruction. Some casualties, such as flood, are either noninsurable or seldom insured against. If the tenant is obligated to repair, and no exceptions are spelled out in the lease, the tenant will be required to repair or rebuild after a flood. The tenant is protected if damage by "casualty" is excepted from the obligation to repair. If the parties intend the lease to terminate in the event of destruction, the fire clause should provide for termination in the event of destruction "by fire or other casualty."

F. CONDEMNATION

A taking of the entire premises by eminent domain obviously terminates a lease. A taking of only a part of the premises will not terminate a lease in the absence of a specific agreement by the parties. In either case, eminent domain law in most jurisdictions provides that the tenant will have a right to participate in the eminent domain award. The landlord will not want the tenant to participate because the value of the tenant's lease may take a substantial part of the award otherwise payable to the landlord. The standard lease provision states that the tenant is not to be compensated for the value of the tenant's leasehold interest. A sample provision is set forth below:

> In the event that the premises demised or any part thereof is taken or condemned for a public or quasi-public use, this lease shall, as to the part so taken, terminate as of the date title shall vest in the condemnor, and rent shall abate in proportion to the square feet of leased space taken or condemned or shall cease if the entire premises be so taken. In either event the Tenant waives all claims against the Landlord and the condemning authority by reason of the complete or partial taking of the demised premises, and it is agreed that the Tenant shall not be entitled to any notice whatsoever of the partial or complete termination of this lease by reason of the aforesaid. Notwithstanding the foregoing, Tenant may obtain an

award from the condemning authority as reimbursement of Tenant's moving expenses.

The consequences that flow from partial condemnation should be set forth in the lease. If the part taken is such that the remainder will be insufficient for the tenant's business, the tenant will want the right to cancel the lease. Of course, it would be advantageous to set forth in the lease guidelines for determining when the premises are no longer satisfactory for tenant use. If the parties agree to use space as a criteria, a formula could be expressed based on the amount of space taken by the condemning authority that will render the premises unsuitable for the tenant. For example, the lease could provide that it will terminate if "more than 2,000 square feet of the premises is taken." Another provision might terminate the lease if "more than 20% of the floor area of the store on the demised premises, or more than 15% of the parking area is taken."

If the lease is not terminated after a partial condemnation, normally the rent is reduced, because the tenant will be occupying less space. Again, it is difficult to provide a formula that will precisely account for the reduced value of the premises to the tenant. An adjustment based solely on the percentage of space taken does not take into account the different value of different areas of the premises. For example, the showroom or sales space in a store is more valuable than the storage space. One solution is to adjust the rent by applying to it the ratio that the value of the premises after the taking bears to the value before the taking. If such a provision is used, a method for fixing the value of the premises will have to be set forth.

Often the lease will provide that in the event of a partial condemnation, the premises will be restored to a condition as near as possible to that which existed before the condemnation unless such restoration is physically impossible or economically impractical. For example, if part of the parking area is taken, there might be room on the remainder of the premises to create new parking areas. Responsibility for the expense of restoration should rest with the party who receives the condemnation award, which is normally the landlord. A sample provision requiring the landlord to reconstruct follows:

> If, after a partial taking of the premises as a result of the exercise of the power of eminent domain, this lease is not terminated, Landlord shall do such work as may be reasonably necessary to restore what may remain of the premises to tenantable condition for Tenant's use; provided, however, that Landlord shall not be required to expend more than the net award Landlord reasonably expects to receive as a result of the taking.

In this example, failure of the landlord to restore the property would effect a termination of the lease.

G. ASSIGNMENT AND SUBLETTING

Unless the lease provides otherwise, either party may assign his or her interest in the lease to another. An assignment is a transfer of the entire term or entire remaining term of the lease on the same provisions as the original lease. The tenant may also sublet the premises unless the lease provides to the contrary. A sublease is a transfer of a part of the term or the entire term but with at least one new or different provision.

For a variety of reasons, in most leasehold situations, the landlord will prohibit any assignment or subletting without prior written consent.

The tenant should request that the landlord's consent shall not be unreasonably withheld. If the tenant is a corporation, the lease may provide that subletting or assignment is permitted to a parent, subsidiary, or affiliated corporation or to a surviving corporation in a merger. A consent to an assignment or subletting should not relieve the original tenant from liability under the lease, and the assignee or sublessee should assume liability in writing directly to the landlord.

The standard restrictions against assignment and subletting are viewed by the courts as restraints on the right of an individual to transfer his or her property freely. Accordingly, such restrictions are interpreted narrowly by the courts. For example, if the lease contains a covenant barring only assignment, the court will allow subletting.

The ordinary restriction against a transfer by the tenant of his or her leasehold interest may be circumvented, in the case of a corporate tenant, by a transfer of the corporate stock. The transfer of stock will not cause a change in the identity of the entity holding the leasehold estate, and is, therefore, not an assignment of the leasehold itself. Recognizing this means of circumventing restrictions against subletting and assignment, the landlord might include a provision stating that a sale or transfer of the majority of a corporation's stock is deemed an assignment of the lease.

PROBLEM

Prepare a lease provision prohibiting a corporate tenant from assigning or subletting without the landlord's consent, taking into account the considerations set forth in the preceding paragraphs.

H. ENTRY AND INSPECTION

The landlord often reserves a right to enter the premises from time to time during the term of a lease so that he or she may inspect and make the repairs and changes the landlord has agreed, or is otherwise required, to make. The landlord also often reserves the right to effect repairs and changes that are the responsibility of the tenant, but which the tenant has failed to make. In the latter case the landlord should be entitled to charge the tenant the cost of any such work. The landlord should also retain the right to exhibit the premises to prospective purchasers and tenants.

I. DEFAULT PROVISIONS

1. Default by Tenant

The lease must spell out precisely what acts or omissions of the tenant will constitute a default under the lease. The most obvious event of default is failure to pay rent when due. Generally, the lease will also provide that the tenant is in default if he or she fails to meet any obligation under the lease. Default provisions are generally combined with provisions setting forth the remedies that a landlord can pursue if the tenant is in default.

(a) Landlord's Remedies

Remedies are tied to local laws and procedures that vary from state to state. However, the basic remedies sought by landlords are similar in all jurisdictions.

i. Acceleration of Rent

The landlord will want the right to accelerate the rent for the balance of the term, thereby making it all due at once. Without this remedy, the landlord would be required to bring suit against the tenant each month as the rent came due.

ii. Landlord's Right to Reenter and Relet

The landlord will want the right to reenter and relet the demised premises for the balance of the term of the lease. In order to make clear that this does not relieve the tenant of responsibility for any loss or deficiency in rent suffered by the landlord, the landlord will relet the premises as agent for the tenant. The tenant will remain liable for the difference between the lease rental and that collected by reletting. Furthermore, any expenses (including alterations) that the landlord incurs in reletting the premises will be deducted from the rent being collected from the new tenant.

iii. Termination of the Lease

Alternatively, the landlord will want the right to terminate the lease and cut off any further right of the tenant to possession of the premises.

(b) Landlord's Enforcement of Remedies

In addition to setting forth the events of default and the remedies available to the landlord, the lease should specify how the landlord may enforce his or her remedies. The following means of enforcement are common to most leases, although some, such as confessions of judgment, are available only in certain states.

i. Distraint

The landlord will generally seek the right to distrain on the personal property of the tenant located on or within the demised premises. In effect, this means that the landlord may obtain a lien on the personal property of the tenant, which will give the landlord an interest in such personal property. This lien is prior to any rights of the tenant's unsecured creditors. The amount of the lien will be the unpaid amount due the landlord under the lease.

ii. Judgment for Rent and Other Money Damages

The landlord, whether or not granted power by the lease, has the power to sue the tenant in a court of law and obtain a judgment for all sums due under the lease, including amounts that become due as a result of the acceleration of rent. The landlord can then enforce that judgment by executing against the property of the tenant, causing it to be sold to satisfy the judgment.

iii. Confession of Judgment

In Pennsylvania and a few other states, leases often contain a "confession of judgment" clause that permits the landlord to appear as attorney for the tenant in court, on the basis of the authority granted by the lease, and obtain a judgment against the tenant. The enforceability of confessions of judgment is questionable in light of recent court decisions. However, in states where confessions of judgment have traditionally been used, they are still included in most leases.

iv. Action of Ejectment

If the landlord wishes to pursue his or her right to remove a tenant in default from the premises, the landlord must bring a court action known as an action of ejectment. Leases in those states in which confessions of judgment for money are used often contain a provision allowing the landlord to confess judgment in ejectment. The problems of enforcement of this provision are the same as in the case of confessions of judgment for money damages.

Set forth below is a comprehensive lease provision dealing with a tenant's default and the landlord's remedies:

> In the event Tenant (a) Does not pay in full when due any and all installments of rent or any other charge or payment whether or not herein included as rent; or (b) Violates or fails to perform or otherwise breaks any covenant or condition herein contained or any other obligation imposed upon lessee; or (c) Abandons the demised premises or removes or attempts to remove Tenant's goods or property therefrom other than in the ordinary course of business without having first paid to Landlord in full all rent and other charges that may become due as well as all which will become thereafter; or (d) Becomes insolvent in any sense or makes an assignment for

the benefit of creditors or offers a composition or settlement to creditors or calls a meeting of creditors for any such purpose, or if a petition in bankruptcy or for reorganization or for an arrangement with creditors under any federal or state act is filed by or against Tenant, or if a bill in equity or other proceeding is filed in any court for the appointment of a receiver, trustee, liquidator, custodian, conservator, or similar official for any of Tenant's assets, or if any of the real or personal property of Tenant's shall be levied upon by any sheriff, marshal, or constable,

Then, and in any such event, at the sole option of Landlord, (1) the whole balance of rent and charges, whether or not payable as rent, for the entire balance of the term herein reserved and any renewal or extension thereof, or any part of such rent and charges, and also all or any costs and sheriff's, marshal's or constable's commissions, whether chargeable to Landlord or Tenant, including watchman's wages, shall be taken to be due and payable and in arrears as if by the terms of this lease said balance of rent and such other charges and expenses were on that date payable in advance; or (2) the term created by this lease shall terminate and become absolutely void, without notice and without any right on the part of Tenant to save the forfeiture by payment of any sums due or by other performance of any condition, term, or covenant broken, and upon such termination, or also if there be no termination, Landlord may, without notice or demand, enter the demised premises breaking open locked doors, if necessary, to effect entrance, without liability for damages for such entry or for the manner thereof, for the purpose of distraint or execution or to take possession of the premises to minimize the loss by reason of Tenant's default, and to take possession of and sell under distraint the goods or chattels found upon the premises. Whether or not any rent due or unpaid, should Tenant at any time remove, or attempt or indicate an intention to remove, the goods or chattels from the premises other than in the ordinary course of business, Tenant authorizes Landlord to follow the same for a period of ninety days after such removal or attempted or intended removal and to take possession of and cause to be sold sufficient of such goods and chattels to meet the rent and charges in arrears, as well as payable for the balance of the full term then remaining or any part thereof.

Tenant expressly agrees that any judgment, order or decree entered in favor of Landlord by any court or magistrate shall be final, and that Tenant will not take or file an appeal, certiorari, writ of error, exception, or objection to the same, or file a motion or rule to strike off or open the same or to stay any execution under the same, and Tenant releases to Landlord, all errors in the said proceedings, and all liability therefor. Tenant expressly waives the benefits of all laws, now or hereafter in force, exempting any goods within the demised premises or elsewhere from distraint, levy or sale.

After reentry or retaking or recovering the premises, whether by way of termination of this lease or not, Landlord may lease said premises or any part or parts thereof to such person or persons upon such terms as may in Landlord's discretion seem best and for a term within or beyond the term of this lease, and Tenant shall be liable for any loss of rent for the balance of the term plus the costs and expenses of reletting and of making repairs and alterations to the premises.

In addition to the extensive provisions above, the lease will provide that any remedies set forth in the lease are in addition to those the landlord is granted by law.

All remedies available to Landlord hereunder and at law and in equity shall be cumulative and concurrent. No termination of this lease nor taking or recovering possession of the premises shall deprive Landlord of any remedies or actions against lessee for rent, for charges or for damages for the breach of any covenant or condition herein contained, nor shall the bringing of any such action for rent, charges or breach of covenant or condition, nor the resort to any other remedy or right for the recovery of rent, charges or damages for such breach, be construed as a wavier or release of the right to insist upon the forfeiture and to obtain possession.

Although the lease provides for cumulative remedies, no court of law will permit a landlord to recover more than actual damages. Therefore, although the landlord has the right to accelerate all the rent due under a lease, to terminate the lease, and to relet the property to another tenant, the landlord cannot expect to receive more than his or her actual damages, which will include past due rent and the difference between the rent that would have been received from the defaulting tenant and the rent that actually is received, during the remaining term of the lease, from any new tenant. A lease provides for cumulative remedies in order to permit the landlord to have the greatest flexibility in proceeding against a defaulting tenant.

(c) Tenant's Right to Cure Default

The tenant's greatest concern is that the tenant may inadvertently be in default of a lease. For example, the tenant or an employee of the tenant may simply forget to send the check for payment of rent. An even greater problem exists with regard to the tenant's obligation to maintain the premises in good condition. A defect may exist in the premises without the tenant's knowledge. In either of the above cases the tenant can be protected from being in default by providing that the tenant will not be in default unless when notified of the default by the landlord the tenant fails to remedy it (cure it) within a specified period. Generally, a short period[4] will be allowed to cure defaults due to failure to pay rent or other money due and a longer period will be allowed to cure other defaults, such as repairing part of the premises. The following is a provision for a grace period during which the tenant can cure a default:

Tenant shall not be in default hereunder unless and until Landlord gives written notice thereof to Tenant and Tenant fails to cure such default within (a) ten days if said default consists of the nonpayment of rent or any other sums required to be paid by Tenant hereunder, or (b) thirty days if such default relates to something other than the payment of money; provided, however, in the event a default other than the failure to pay money reasonably takes in excess of thirty days to cure, Tenant shall not be in default if Tenant commences to cure said default within said thirty-day period and proceeds diligently thereafter to complete the same.

---

4. Lawyers refer to the time during which a party may cure a default as a "grace period."

2. Default by Landlord

Most leases contain little in the way of protection for the tenant if the landlord is in default of his or her obligations under the lease. The tenant generally has no recourse except to sue the landlord for any damages incurred. However, if the tenant has substantial bargaining power, the tenant may obtain remedies for certain types of defaults by the landlord. For example, if the landlord is unable to deliver possession of the premises to the tenant by a specified date, the tenant may reserve a right of cancellation or a right to collect damages from the landlord for each day during which the landlord is unable to deliver possession. If the landlord fails to make certain repairs, the tenant may have the right to withhold rent or to make the repairs and deduct (off-set) the cost of the repairs from the rental due. Rights of deduction and set-off are strongly resisted by landlords and by lending institutions making mortgage loans to the landlord.

J. RENEWALS

Whenever possible, a tenant will want to have the right to renew a lease beyond its fixed term. This is especially true when a tenant has spent substantial sums of money in preparing premises for use or has built up a great deal of good will with respect to a particular business location. In order to capitalize fully on good will and improvements, a tenant will request the right, at the tenant's option, to extend the lease beyond the original term for one or more renewal periods. Renewals may be on the same basic terms as contained in the lease for the original term, or may provide for an increase in rent during each successive renewal term, as well as other modifications. A sample renewal clause is as follows:

> Provided that the Tenant at the time of exercise of the option herein contained is not in default of any of the terms, covenants, and conditions or agreements provided for in this lease, Tenant shall have the right, option, and privilege of renewing and extending the term of this lease for two additional periods of five years each. The said option periods may be exercised by Tenant upon six months written notice to Landlord prior to the expiration of the original term hereof, or any renewal or extension terms hereof. All of the terms, covenants, and conditions of this lease pertaining to the original term hereof shall equally pertain in all respects to all renewals and extensions of this lease.

If a tenant is not granted an option to renew the term of the lease, the lease often provides that at the end of the initial term the lease will continue in effect on a month-to-month or year-to-year basis until terminated by either party giving notice of termination on or before a fixed period before expiration of the then current term.

> It is hereby mutually agreed that either party hereto may terminate this lease at the end of the term by giving to the other party written notice thereof, at least sixty days prior thereto, but in default of such notice this

lease shall continue upon the same terms and conditions in force immediately prior to the expiration of the term hereof for a further period of one year and so on from year to year unless or until terminated by either party's giving the other sixty days' written notice of termination previous to the expiration of the then current term.

K. NOTICES

Every lease should provide for the manner and place for giving notice to the other party wherever required in the lease. The notice provision should state that either party may from time to time designate a different address for service of notice, and may generally be in the same format as the notice provisions in an agreement of sale, as discussed in Chapter Three.

L. RECORDING OF LEASES; ACKNOWLEDGMENTS

As discussed in Chapter Nine, recording statutes operate to impose notice of the interests that exist in real property. If a person fails to record his or her interest in real property, that interest may be lost to a third party who has no actual notice of such interest.

In many states the recording statutes do not penalize a person who is in possession of real property and fails to record that interest because the very fact of possession imposes notice on third parties. In such states it is unnecessary for a tenant who is in possession to record the lease. However, some states require the recording of leases that have a term of at least a certain number of years.

PROBLEM

Does your jurisdiction require the recording of leases? If so, of what term? What is the result of failure to record?

Even in those jurisdictions in which a tenant in possession is not in jeopardy by reason of failure to record the lease, various circumstances may require recording or make recording desirable:

(1) If the lease is executed but the tenant is not yet in possession of the premises, recording is necessary to protect the tenant's rights during the period prior to possession;

(2) If the lease contains an option to purchase or a right of first refusal, recording the lease will notify third parties of the tenant's rights;

(3) If the lease is to be superior to a mortgage, the lease may have to be recorded even if the tenant is in possession when the mortgage is recorded; and

(4) If a lease for a portion of a multi-occupancy building or shopping center provides that the landlord will not lease other parts of the building or shopping center for competing uses, the tenant can put other tenants and third parties on legal notice of that provision by recording all or part of the lease.

It should be observed that landlords frequently prefer to avoid recording. If the lease is prematurely terminated by agreement or by court action following a default, the landlord may have certain practical difficulties in clearing record title to the property subject to the lease.

As discussed in Chapter Nine, many states permit recording of a short form or memorandum of lease instead of the complete lease. The memorandum usually must state the names of the parties, a description of the premises, and the term of the lease. Unless recordation is being effected simply to notify third parties of the tenant's right to possession, the memorandum should contain those provisions of the lease that the parties want to make matters of record, such as an option on the part of tenant to purchase the premises. The advantage of recording a memorandum or short form of lease, rather than the whole lease, is that it permits the parties to keep private those parts of the lease that they do not want to be matters of public record, such as the amount of rent.

Any document that is to be recorded must be acknowledged. If the parties intend to record a memorandum of lease, only the memorandum need be acknowledged.

M. INABILITY TO GIVE POSSESSION

A landlord may be unable to deliver possession of the premises at the commencement of the term. Therefore, a lease usually provides for release of the landlord from liability by reason of the holding over of an existing tenant, or delay in completing a new structure or alterations or repairs. The tenant may wish to add a provision giving him or her the right to cancel the lease if the tenant is not given possession on or before a specified date.

N. ADDITIONAL RENT

It is common in a lease for the tenant to be obligated to make certain payments to the landlord in addition to periodic rent. Such payments are designed to shift to the tenant certain costs related to the ownership and operation of the premises being rented and thereby relieve the landlord of the risk of financial loss resulting from increases in such costs during the term of the lease.

In the lease agreement, payments other than periodic rent are referred to and treated as "rent." If the tenant defaults in his or her obligation to make such additional payments, the landlord wants to have the same rights and remedies as exist on a default in the payment of periodic rent. A typical additional rent provision respecting increases in real estate taxes is set forth below:

Tenant further agrees to pay as rent in addition to the minimum rental herein reserved, Tenant's pro rata share of all taxes assessed or imposed upon the building of which the demised premises are a part during the term of this lease, in excess of and over and above those assessed or imposed at the time of making this lease. The amount due hereunder on account of such taxes shall be apportioned for that part of the first and last calendar years covered by the term hereof. The same shall be paid by Tenant to Landlord on or before the first day of July of each and every year. Tenant's pro rata share shall be 22.3% of any such increase.

The specific items of additional rent vary from lease to lease, depending on the business arrangement between the landlord and the tenant.

In most municipalities that supply water and sewers, there is a standard minimum charge for those services. In addition, with regard to water, there is a charge for water actually consumed in excess of a minimum quantity. Meters are installed to measure consumption, and in multitenant buildings, separate meters may be installed for each rental unit. The "additional rent" clause, in addition to imposing the obligation on the tenant to pay all or part of such water charges, should state which party has the responsibility of installing and maintaining these meters. In some leases the tenant will be required to pay the entire bill for taxes and water and sewer rents, and in other leases the tenant will have to pay only the excess over the minimum.

Often the landlord is concerned that the activities of the tenant on the premises may cause an increase in the landlord's fire and/or liability insurance rates. As a result, the "additional rent" clause may provide that the tenant shall pay for any increase in the landlord's insurance premiums if the increase is caused by any act or neglect of the tenant or by the nature of the tenant's use of the premises. The tenant should take care to ascertain in advance whether its intended use of the premises will cause an increase in the lessor's fire insurance and, if so, to what extent.

A tenant leasing a large space with an obligation to pay a pro rata share of real estate tax increases may want to include a provision allowing the tenant to dispute any tax increases.

O. SERVICES AND UTILITIES

If the tenant is to receive any services or utilities from the landlord, the facts must be expressly set forth in the lease. In many apartment leases the landlord supplies water, gas, and electricity. In an office building lease the description of the services to be supplied by the landlord is especially important. Unlike the case of an apartment building, the services of an office building may be supplied only during certain hours and on certain days. For example, the lease may provide that elevator service, heat, and air conditioning will be provided only on weekdays between the hours of 9:00 AM and 6:00 PM The lease may or may not obligate the landlord to provide cleaning service for the offices. The tenant must determine whether the services to be provided are satisfactory for the tenant's purpose. If, for example, the tenant has a night office shift, the lease must allow the tenant access to the building, and perhaps heat and air conditioning, during the hours of work of that shift.

If the landlord has covenanted to supply services such as air conditioning, heat, and elevators, the landlord will normally request a "breakdown" clause eliminating any liability that the landlord might incur because of the interruption of any service caused by the need for inspection or repair or any cause beyond the landlord's control. A tenant, on the other hand, may insist on abatement of rent if the discontinued service is not restored within a specified period.

P. LIABILITY AND INDEMNIFICATION PROVISIONS

The terms of a lease may allocate, as between the landlord and the tenant, the responsibility for losses and damages caused to the landlord, to the tenant, or to third persons that occur on or about the demised premises. Some allocations of such responsibility are discussed below.

1. Injury to Tenant or Damage to Tenant's Property

If the lease is silent and the tenant is injured, or the tenant's property is damaged as a result of negligent conduct by the landlord or the landlord's servants or agents, the landlord will be responsible to the tenant for any such injury or damage. Landlords often insist, however, that the tenant release the landlord and the landlord's servants or agents from any liability that may arise as a result of the negligence or misconduct of such persons. In a lease the tenant's agreement releasing the landlord is referred to as an "exculpatory" clause, an example of which follows:

> Landlord shall not be held responsible for, and is hereby expressly relieved from, any and all liability by reason of any injury, loss, or damage to Tenant or Tenant's property in or about the demised premises or the building due to any cause whatever, and whether the loss, injury, or damage is due to any oversight, neglect, or negligence of Landlord, occurring before or after the execution of this lease.

Although exculpatory clauses are enforceable in most states, courts construe such clauses strictly against the landlord. This means that if there is any doubt as to whether the tenant has released the landlord from liability in a particular situation, the doubt will be resolved in favor of the tenant.

2. Injury to Third Persons or Damage to Their Property

A person may be injured, or property damaged, on or about the leased premises because of the negligence of a tenant. Even if the tenant is clearly responsible, the injured party might choose to sue the landlord as well as the negligent tenant. Clearly, the landlord would want the lease to contain a provision, referred to as an "indemnification clause," that imposes on the negligent tenant the responsibility of protecting the landlord from any liability, including any costs incident to defending a lawsuit, that arises because of the tenant's negligence. An example of such a provision, which may also be referred to as a "hold harmless" clause, follows:

> Tenant will indemnify Landlord and save it harmless from and against any and all claims, actions, damages, liability, and expense in connection with loss of life, personal injury, and/or damage to property occurring in or about, or arising out of, the demised premises and adjacent sidewalks and loading platforms or areas occasioned wholly or in part by any act or omission of Tenant, his agents, contractors, customers, or employees.

Going a step further, the landlord may insist on indemnification by the tenant from any liability arising from injuries to third persons or damages to the property of third persons arising from an act occurring or conditions existing on the demised premises, irrespective of who is responsible for such injury or damage. An example of such a broad clause follows:

> Tenant agrees to be responsible for and to relieve and hereby relieves Landlord from all liability by reason of any injury or damage to any person or property in the demised premises or any part or portion of the building of which the demised premises is a part, caused by any fire, breakage or leakage in any part or portion of the demised premises, or from water, rain, or snow that may leak into, issue, or flow from any part of said premises, or of the building of which the demised premises is a part, whether such breakage, leakage, injury, or damage be caused by or result from the negligence of Landlord or his or her servants or agents or any person or persons whatsoever.

Such a provision is unpalatable to a tenant. One way to minimize the burden of such a clause is for the tenant to obtain insurance protection against the extra risk that he or she is undertaking. A second approach is to make the indemnification inoperative if the injury or damage is attributable to the negligence of the landlord or his or her servants or agents.

Q. SUBORDINATION

The landlord's mortgagee may require the tenant to agree that the lease will be subordinate to its mortgage, or the landlord may require that the lease be subordinate to any future mortgages or replacements thereof that the landlord may place on the leased premises. In addition, if the landlord does not own the premises, the lease should be subordinate to any other lease or arrangement under which the landlord is in control of the premises. In either of the above cases the lease should contain a waiver of any damages by reason of termination of the tenant's lease caused by the termination or forfeiture of the landlord's right of possession. The clause should also include an agreement by the tenant to execute any documents required by a mortgagee to confirm the lease provisions.

Without a subordination clause the landlord may be unable to effect satisfactory refinancing because many lenders insist that their mortgage have a first priority.[5] If the lease is subordinate to a mortgage, a strong tenant may request a "nondisturbance" agreement stating that so long as the tenant fulfills his or her obligations under the lease, the mortgagee or purchaser at a foreclosure sale will recognize the lease. The tenant will, in return, be expected to execute an "attornment" agreement providing that in the event of foreclosure, the lease will not be discharged and the tenant will recognize the mortgagee or the purchaser at the foreclosure sale as its new landlord.

A provision dealing with subordination, attornment, and nondisturbance is set forth below:

> Tenant hereby subordinates this Lease to any mortgage created by Landlord on the Premises and will execute any and all documents which Landlord may desire to confirm such subordination, provided that the mortgagee under any such mortgage shall furnish Tenant with a written agreement in recordable form and binding upon the mortgagee's successors and assigns, satisfactory to Tenant providing that so long as Tenant, its assigns, successors, or subtenants are not in default under this Lease, Tenant's possession of the Premises and its rights under this Lease shall not be interfered with by the Mortgagee (whether or not the mortgage is in default and notwithstanding any foreclosure action), any insurance proceeds and any condemnation award shall be applied as provided in the Lease, and the lien of the mortgage shall not cover any equipment used in Tenant's business on the Premises.
>
> Tenant, at the request of any mortgagee, or anyone acquiring title to the Landlord's estate or the Premises by foreclosure, deed in lieu of foreclosure, or otherwise, shall attorn to the then owner and recognize such owner as landlord for the balance of the term of this lease subject to all the terms and provisions hereof. Such mortgagee or purchaser at such foreclosure sale shall not be (a) liable for any act or omission of the Landlord, (b) subject to any offsets or defenses which Tenant may have against the Landlord, (c) bound by any rent or additional rent which the Tenant may have paid to the Landlord for more than the current month, or (d) bound by any amendment or modification of the lease made without its consent.

R. SECURITY DEPOSITS

In most leases the landlord requires the tenant to grant some form of security deposit or advance rental payment at the time the lease is signed. A security deposit is not treated the same as advance rent. The security deposit is a fund that may be used by the landlord to discharge any unfulfilled obligation of the tenant, such as unpaid rent or unrepaired damage to the premises. It is generally provided that resort to the security

5. Cf. Chapter Seven. Some lenders want the leases to be superior to the mortgages.

deposit is optional for the landlord, thus preserving all other remedies. In the event that all of the tenant's obligations under the lease are discharged, the landlord is obligated to return the security deposit to the tenant at the end of the term of the lease. Additionally, many jurisdictions have enacted legislation governing security deposits for residential leases.

PROBLEM

Draft a simple lease provision providing for a two months' security deposit.

S. OPTION TO PURCHASE

A tenant of an entire building often attempts to obtain an option to purchase the premises during the term or at the end of the lease. The same considerations that arise in negotiating and drafting an agreement of sale must be covered when including an option to purchase in a lease. The option provisions in the lease in and of themselves must be a complete agreement of sale, or must refer to and incorporate an agreement of sale that is attached to the lease as an exhibit.

1. Purchase Price

The purchase price should be stated in a fixed or determinable sum (such as by appraisal or by a per acre price), and the method of payment should be set forth. For example:

> The option price shall be $100,000 payable as follows:
> (i) $10,000 shall be payable to lessor in cash or certified check and shall accompany the document exercising the option;
> (ii) the balance, being $90,000, shall be paid in full in cash or by certified check at the settlement for the purchase of the premises.

2. Manner of Exercising Option and Time of Exercise

The time within which the option must be exercised and the manner of exercise, for example, by written notice accompanied by a predetermined deposit, must be clearly specified.

PROBLEM

Draft a provision requiring written notice by December 31, 1986, for exercise of the option, exercise to be by submission of signed agreements of sale together with a 10% deposit.

---

3. Time of Settlement

A specific provision regarding the time and place for settlement on the purchase of the premises should be included.

4. Condition of Title

The usual clauses in an agreement of sale dealing with the condition of title should be included.

5. Other Provisions

The lease should state whether the option is to be terminated in the event of a condemnation, destruction of the building, or death of either party. Provision should also be made for the application of fire insurance proceeds to the purchase price if the option is exercised after fire damage and before restoration. The landlord usually will want to condition the option on the tenant having made no default under the terms of the lease. The tenant, in turn, may request that if a default is waived or cured, it will not forfeit the option.

A lease with an option to purchase, or a memorandum of such a lease, should be recorded in order to notify potential purchasers of the tenant's interest. If the option were not recorded, most recording statutes would provide that a purchaser from the landlord, who had no notice of the option, would not have to recognize the tenant's option.

T. RIGHTS OF FIRST REFUSAL

A landlord may be unwilling to grant an option to purchase the premises because the value of the property may exceed the option price at the time the option may be exercised. If a tenant cannot obtain an option, he or she may seek a "right of first purchase" or "right of first refusal." This device does not commit the landlord to sell at any time or at any price. It merely provides that if the landlord receives a bona fide offer to purchase the property and the landlord does decide to sell pursuant to that offer, the landlord will give the tenant an opportunity to buy at the same price and on the same terms that the landlord is willing to accept from the third party who has made the offer.

The lease provision should require the landlord to communicate the exact terms of the offer the landlord is willing to accept and should provide that the tenant must accept the offer within a specified period or the landlord may sell to another party. A sample provision follows:

> In the event Landlord shall receive a bona fide offer for the purchase of the property or any part thereof, whether or not in conjunction with any other property, which Landlord desires to accept, Landlord shall give written notice thereof (hereinafter called "Offering Notice") to Tenant. Said Offering Notice shall contain:

(a) The name and address of the proposed purchaser;

(b) An exact copy of the terms and conditions of said offer; and

(c) An offer to sell the property involved to Tenant upon the same terms and conditions of the aforesaid offer made by the proposed purchaser.

Tenant shall be entitled to purchase such property offered by giving written notice thereof to Landlord within fifteen (15) days after receipt of the Offering Notice. If Tenant fails to agree to purchase such property within the time aforesaid, Landlord shall have the right to complete the sale to the proposed purchaser who shall then hold said property subject to the provisions of this Lease Agreement.

In the event of any change in the identity of the proposed purchaser or of the terms and conditions of the Offering Notice, notice thereof and opportunity to purchase shall again be given by Landlord to Tenant in accordance with the terms hereof.

The landlord must be careful to reserve the right to effect certain transfers of the property without triggering the tenant's right of first refusal. The situations for which the landlord's right of transfer should be reserved will vary, depending on the fact situation. If the landlord is a corporation, it may want to retain the right to transfer the property to any parent, subsidiary, affiliate, or successor by merger without having to first offer the premises to the tenant. If the landlord is an individual, he or she may want to reserve the right to transfer the premises to certain relatives, or trust for them, without having to first offer it to the tenant.

If the landlord who has granted a right of first refusal owns land in addition to the demised premises (and especially if such other land is on an adjoining parcel), the right of first refusal should deal with the possibility that the landlord will receive an offer to purchase a package comprising the demised premises and the adjacent land, eliminating the right of first refusal in such a case.

U. RULES AND REGULATIONS

It is customary for the landlord in a lease for a multitenant building to prescribe certain rules and regulations that each tenant must adhere to and that may be changed from time to time so long as the changes apply equally to all tenants. The initial rules and regulations must be drafted to cover the particular building or buildings involved, as no single set can apply in all situations. A set of rules and regulations is likely to be concerned with subjects of general interest to all tenants, such as hours of access to the building, days on which the building is closed, excessive noise and nuisances.

In order to bind a tenant to comply with the rules and regulations, the lease must contain a provision giving the landlord the right to prescribe rules and regulations and requiring the tenant to comply with the same. A provision granting the landlord the right to prescribe rules and regulations follows:

The Rules and Regulations regarding the building wherein the said demised premises are located, printed upon the fourth page of this lease and marked Schedule "A," and such alterations, additions, and modifications thereof as may from time to time be made by Landlord shall be considered a part of this lease with the same effect as though written herein; and Tenant covenants and agrees that said Rules and Regulations and all alterations, additions and modifications thereof shall be faithfully observed by Tenant, the employees of Tenant, and all persons invited by Tenant into such building.

V. AFFIRMATIVE COVENANTS

Most leases contain a provision that, in general terms, obligates the tenant to perform a variety of acts. Examples of affirmative covenants on the part of a tenant might be to pay the rent promptly, to keep the premises clean, to take all necessary precautions against fire, and to keep the premises open for business.

W. NEGATIVE COVENANTS

The provision relating to negative covenants differs from the provision relating to affirmative covenants only in that the items listed are things that the tenant is not to do without the prior written consent of the landlord.

Most landlords include a provision to the effect that the tenant will not remove the tenant's goods or property from the demised premises otherwise than in the usual course of business, without having first paid and satisfied the landlord for all rent that may become due during the entire term of the lease. The landlord may also add that the tenant shall not vacate or desert the premises during the term of the lease. These provisions are added to protect the landlord against tenants moving in the middle of the night without paying their rent. The landlord in many states has a right of "distraint" that gives the landlord a special lien against the tenant's personal property on the premises, and the landlord will lose the advantage of the power to distrain if the tenants remove their goods. Furthermore, the landlord may want the premises occupied because in many urban areas it is difficult or even impossible to obtain fire insurance on vacant buildings.

X. MISCELLANEOUS PROVISIONS

Most leases contain the following or similar standard provisions:

1. Waiver of Custom

The landlord will wish to make clear that although he or she may choose not to exercise rights against the tenant at any given time, any such waiver shall not prevent the landlord from exercising rights when the same or a different fact situation occurs in the future. For example, the landlord may allow the tenant to pay the rent ten days late one month. The landlord is not thereby giving the tenant permission to pay the rent ten days late in the future.

> It is hereby covenanted and agreed, any law, usage, or custom to the contrary notwithstanding, that Landlord shall have the right at all times to enforce the covenants and provisions of this lease in strict accordance with the terms hereof, notwithstanding any conduct or custom on the part of Landlord in refraining from so doing at any time or times, and further that the failure of Landlord at any time or times to enforce his or her rights under said covenants and provisions strictly in accordance with the same shall not be construed as having created a custom in any way or manner contrary to the specific terms, provisions, and covenants of this lease or as having in any way or manner modified the same.

2. Integration Clause

The parties will desire to make clear that the written lease contains all of the provisions that govern their relationship. This provision would be substantially similar to integration clauses discussed in previous chapters.

3. Heirs and Assigns

Generally, the parties will expressly provide that the lease will be binding on their respective heirs (in the case of an individual party), successors (in the case of a corporate party), and assigns. Furthermore, if there are several landlords or tenants acting jointly, the lease will provide that they are jointly and severally responsible. This means that each is required to perform his or her share of the obligations, and each is required to perform the obligations of his or her fellow tenants or fellow landlords, as the case may be.

PROBLEM

Prepare an "heirs and assigns" clause for a lease between a corporation as landlord and an individual as tenant.

---

4. Captions

The drafter of a lease may include captions or titles preceding various provisions for ease of reference. The lease should state that the captions are for reference purposes and are not to affect the interpretation of any provision.

PROBLEM

Big Foot, a company selling high-styled shoes for large women, is interested in leasing space in the Gallery II Mall. Big Foot is a relatively small tenant with not much ability to negotiate a favorable lease, but the Landlord has already agreed in principal to the following:

(a) Big Foot may remove trade fixtures at the expiration of the term of the lease.

(b) Landlord will restrict other tenants in the mall from competing with Big Foot.

(c) Landlord will waive tort liability against Big Foot in the event that Big Foot's negligence causes a fire in the leased premises.

(d) Landlord will provide air conditioning between the hours of 8:00 AM and 6:30 PM

(e) Big Foot (which is responsible for the payment of its pro rata share of taxes) may contest any increase in taxes.

1. You represent the landlord. Draft provisions that reflect the terms agreed to above in a posture most favorable to the landlord.

2. You represent Big Foot. Draft a provision that deals with all of the issues involved with the commencement of the term of the lease and the commencement of rent payments.

Part Two
SPECIAL TYPES OF LEASES

The preceding discussions in this chapter have been applicable to almost all leases. In the remainder of this chapter the focus will be on lease clauses that are unique to the following types of leases: commercial and shopping center leases, office building leases, and net or ground leases. Each type of lease is discussed in detail below.

I. COMMERCIAL AND SHOPPING CENTER LEASES

Leases covering space that will be used for clothing stores, food stores, restaurants, and other business activities in which goods or services are sold directly to customers at the location of the business are commonly referred to as "commercial or shopping center" leases. Significant variations exist among commercial and shopping center leases. The lease for space in a shopping center is typically more complicated than the lease of the corner drugstore because of the need to deal with the existence of adjacent stores also owned by the landlord and shared common areas and facilities. Moreover, shopping center leases often reflect the interests of institutional lenders who have financed the construction of the shopping center and who depend on the leases as security for the repayment of loans. Let us consider various individual provisions of commercial and shopping center leases.

A. TRADE FIXTURES

As previously discussed, a standard lease provides that fixtures, alterations, and additions remain on the premises at the termination of the lease and become the property of the landlord unless the landlord gives notice to the tenant that the landlord wants the items removed. Such a provision may be unacceptable to a commercial tenant who has made a substantial investment in display cases and other fixtures that can easily be removed and transferred to a new store. In addition, the commercial tenant may want the option to remove alterations or additions made to the leased space. A sample of a clause incorporating a tenant's wishes concerning trade fixtures and improvements and alterations follows:

> Any trade fixtures, equipment, and other property installed in or attached to the demised premises by and at the expense of Tenant shall remain the property of Tenant, and Tenant shall have the right at any time and from time to time, so long as Tenant is not in default hereunder, to remove any of the same so installed or attached in the demised premises, including, but not limited to counters, shelving, showcases, chairs, and movable machinery. If Tenant shall not remove such property at the termination of this Lease, then the same shall be deemed to be abandoned by Tenant, but the failure to remove such property shall not be deemed to be a holding over by Tenant or a ground for claiming a renewal or extension of this Lease. Tenant shall repair all damage to the demised premises caused by the removal by Tenant of such property, except for necessary holes and other openings and unavoidable damage to plaster and painted surfaces resulting therefrom.

B. PERCENTAGE RENT

Percentage rent generally means that the tenant pays a basic annual rent plus an amount of rent calculated by reference to the volume of business transacted by the tenant at the premises. Often the percentage rent applies only when the volume of business exceeds a specific amount set forth in the lease. Percentage rent is common in leases for retail stores in prime commercial locations and for stores in most shopping centers. The advantage to the landlord is to ensure rental income commensurate with the economic value of the location (which is measured in part by the volume of business conducted at the location). The advantage to the tenant is the possibility of a low-base rent that will be increased only if the tenants' volume of business at the premises is good. In addition, in an inflationary period, the landlord will be more willing to grant a lease for a long term if the rent will increase as the dollar volume of the tenant's business increases. A percentage rent gives to the landlord reasonable assurance that the rent will increase to keep pace with inflation.

There are several possible percentage rent provisions:

1. Straight Percentage Rent

It is possible to write a lease in which there is no basic rent. Instead, rent is merely a percentage of the tenant's volume of business at the premises. Obviously, such a lease is risky from the landlord's standpoint because the landlord cannot, with any degree of certainty, predict the volume of business and therefore the amount of rent that will be received. Generally, in order to finance a shopping center, the landlord must show the prospective lender that the leases for the project will provide for a sufficient amount of fixed rent to cover debt service, real estate taxes, and basic operating expenses. Thus, it is rare that a straight percentage rent will be aggreed to. In addition to being risky for a landlord, such a lease is unlikely to be acceptable to a mortgage lender.

2. Minimum or Basic Rent Plus a Percentage

The most commonly used percentage rental provision calls for the tenant to pay a basic fixed minimum rent plus a percentage of the volume of business at the premises. Generally, the percentage rent is based on the amount of sales in excess of a minimum amount. For example, a lease might provide that the tenant pays basic rent equal to $20,000 a year plus 2% of the tenant's sales (which term must be carefully defined) at the premises in excess of $1,000,000. Since $20,000 is 2% of $1,000,000, this example suggests that the tenant is simply paying a rent equal to 2% of sales and is bearing the risk that sales will at least equal $1,000,000. It is common for the percentage rent calculation to be based on a minimum amount that when multiplied by the percentage factor will equal the minimum rent. However, this need not be the case. For example, the rent could be a minimum of $10,000 a year plus 5% of sales in excess of $800,000. In most cases the amount of "basic rent" will reflect a judgment of the volume of business that could be expected if the tenant's business is moderately successful.

PROBLEM

In the example above, if the tenant has sales in a year of $1,500,000, what would be the total rent the tenant would pay?

A lease may provide that there are circumstances, such as fire damage, that cause a suspension of the payment of basic rent. If this is the case, then the lease must provide for the consequence of such abatement on the amount of percentage rent that is payable. For example, if there is an abatement in basic rent, there may be a corresponding reduction in the minimum volume of sales above which the percentage rent is computed.

3. Definition of "Sales"

Percentage rent is generally based on the tenant's "gross sales" or "gross receipts" at the premises. These terms must be defined in each lease since they have no commonly accepted definitions. From the landlord's perspective, the definition should include all sales of merchandise, or charges for services, made in, on, or from the leased premises, whether by cash or credit, and, if on credit, irrespective of whether the sales price is actually collected or not. Furthermore, the definition should include orders received at the demised premises regardless of the place from which delivery is made. Sales by concessionaires[6] should be included as sales by the tenant, or rental received by the tenant from concessionaires, multiplied by a factor to approximate the amount of sales of concessionaires, should be included as sales by the tenant. The tenant will seek to have excluded from the definition of sales all sales to employees, all sales on credit where payment is never received, income derived from services (such as repair work), the sale of trade fixtures, and transfers of merchandise to other stores of the tenant. Certain items, such as returns, exchanges, sales taxes, or their equivalent, are typically excluded from the definition.

4. Record of Gross Sales

The lease should require the tenant to keep records of all sales, and such records must be in a permanent form and in accordance with accepted accounting procedures. The tenant should be required to make periodic reports of gross sales (monthly or quarterly); to furnish an annual report certified by a certified public accountant or the proprietor, partner, or chief officer; to retain copies of sales slips or cash register tapes for inspection by the landlord; and to permit the landlord or a representative of the landlord to examine all books and records of the tenant relating to purchases and sales, as well as copies of tax returns.

5. Time for Payment of Percentage Rent

If a tenant's volume of business creates the obligation to pay percentage rent, the landlord will typically want to receive all or a portion of such percentage rent on a regular monthly or quarterly basis, and not wait until the end of each year before any percentage rent is paid. Because the exact amount of percentage rent payable under a lease cannot be ascertained until after the end of each year, the tenant would make periodic payments based on advance estimates of the percentage rent, with an annual adjustment when the actual amount is determined. Many

---

6. Many commercial tenants devote part of their space to a concession that pays the tenant for the right to operate on the tenant's premises. For example, the shoe department of a clothing store may be operated as a concession rather than being directly operated by the tenant.

tenants, especially those whose sales are particularly seasonal, will successfully resist the requirement for interim estimated payments.

PROBLEM

Why would tenants having a seasonal business object most strongly to interim estimated payments?

---

6. No Partnership

Often the landlord will require a provision stating that payments based on a percentage of sales are rent only and that the landlord has not become a partner in the tenant's business and is not responsible for the tenant's debts.

A sample percentage rent provision incorporating many of the considerations discussed above follows:

In addition to the minimum rent, Tenant shall pay to Landlord a percentage rental for each lease year (as herein defined) during the term hereof equal to the amount by which six percent (6%) of the gross sales (as herein defined) made by Tenant on or from the Premises exceeds the minimum rent actually paid. A lease year is hereby defined as the yearly period beginning with the first day of the calendar month succeeding the commencement of the term of this Lease and thereafter the lease years hereunder shall begin on the same day of each succeeding year during the term.

The term "gross sales" as used herein is hereby defined to mean the selling price of all merchandise whatsoever sold and charges for all services rendered by Tenant, or any licensee or concessionaire of Tenant, on or from the Premises, whether such sales or services be for cash or credit, less refunds or allowances made for returned or defective merchandise or improperly performed services. The term "gross sales" shall not include the amount of any sales or gross receipts tax or other imposts upon sales levied directly on sales by City, County, State, or Federal authorities, and collected from customers, provided, however, that specific record is made at the time of each sale of the amount of such sales or gross receipts tax and the amount thereof is charged separately to the customer.

Within thirty (30) days after the end of each lease year, commencing with the first lease year, Tenant shall deliver to Landlord a complete statement signed and certified by Tenant or by a duly authorized officer or representative of Tenant acting on Tenant's behalf, showing accurately and in reasonable detail, on a monthly basis, the full amount of Tenant's gross sales in the Premises during the immediately preceding lease year and the percentage rent computed for that lease year. At the same time, Tenant shall pay to Landlord the full percentage rent payable for that lease year, if any. Each lease year during the term of this Lease shall be deemed a different and distinct accounting year, and there shall be no adjustment from one lease year to another. Tenant agrees to keep at its principal offices, a complete record of all gross sales in accordance with its regular system of accounting now in effect or hereafter adopted and in accordance with generally accepted accounting principles. Landlord shall at reasonable times during business hours of Tenant, but not more often than four times during each lease year, have the right of access to the sales records pertaining to the business upon the Premises, and the right to have such sales records examined for the purpose of verifying the gross sales or Tenant's statements concerning them, or audited by a Certified Public Accountant chosen by Landlord at Landlord's expense; but no examination of the sales records of any other stores or premises shall be permitted.

If it is determined that the actual gross sales for any period covered by the statement required pursuant to this Paragraph shall exceed by five percent (5%) or more the amount of gross sales shown in that statement, Tenant shall pay all the reasonable expenses incurred by Landlord in determining the actual gross sales for that period.

Tenant further agrees that in the event that Tenant shall at any time during the term hereof enter into a sublease with a sublessee for all or a portion of the premises hereby demised, as hereinafter provided, or a license or concession agreement with a licensee or concessionaire, such sublease or agreement will contain provisions that such sublessee, licensee, or concessionaire shall submit to Landlord annual statements of gross receipts of the sublessee, licensee, or concessionaire, shall maintain records and books of account at the Premises, and shall give to Landlord the right to make examinations of such books and records, all in the same manner as is herein provided with respect to Tenant.

Nothing contained in this Lease shall be deemed or construed to create a partnership or joint venture between Tenant and Landlord or confer upon Landlord any interest in the business of Tenant, or cause Landlord to be responsible in any way for the debts or obligations of Tenant.

7. Other Considerations Applicable to Percentage Rent

In addition to the part of the lease that describes percentage rent, the following sections of the lease relate directly to percentage rent:

(a) Active Operation

Because the percentage rent depends on the volume of the business done, the landlord will want to include as an express covenant that the tenant will actively and continuously operate his or her business throughout the lease term. The provision may simply state that or may be expanded to include (a) the obligation to staff the store with adequate personnel and merchandise to produce the maximum possible amount of gross sales in and from the demised premises; (b) the obligation to keep the store open every day excepting Sundays (if local law or custom so dictates) and legal holidays usually observed in the area; (c) the obligation to open the store daily for the minimum hours customary for the area and type of business; and (d) a statement that temporary closing because of strikes or similar circumstances beyond the tenant's reasonable control shall not constitute a breach of the tenant's obligation to be open for business. The above provisions are usually found in the affirmative covenants section of the lease.

(b) Diversion of Sales

Because the landlord is depending on the tenant's sales at the premises to produce percentage rent, the landlord should be protected against diversion of sales by the tenant to a nearby branch store. This may be done by a covenant in the lease that the tenant will not directly or indirectly[7] operate a business from any other location within a specified radius or distance from the demised premises during the term of the lease. If the tenant has an existing store that violates the noncompetition provision and that store is to remain open, the noncompetition provision must be phrased so as to except the existing store from its coverage.

C. COMMON AREAS

1. Use, Location, and Control

A shopping center has extensive facilities, called "common areas," that are for the use of the customers of all the tenants, including parking lots, walkways, and enclosed areas. The lease normally grants the tenant and the tenant's customers the nonexclusive right to use the common areas along with other tenants and their customers.

A prospective tenant of a shopping center is vitally interested in the number of persons walking past the store or business. This volume of traffic is determined in part by the relationship of the tenant's space to the shopping center's common areas. In a completed and operating center, the tenant can ascertain by physical inspection the relationship of the tenant's space to the common areas and can be reasonably certain that the relationship will not change in the future. If the shopping center is not complete, the architectural plan of the center, showing the common areas and the tenant's space, may be incorporated into the lease so as to assure the tenant of the location of common areas. The landlord will want to maintain control of the common areas and to reserve the right to change the location of common areas. The differing interests of landlord and tenant become the subject of negotiation.

2. Common Area Maintenance Expenses

In most shopping center leases the landlord is obligated to maintain the common areas. However, the tenant is generally required to pay part of the cost of operating and maintaining the common areas and facilities. Such expenses are referred to in the trade as common area maintenance

---

7. Indirect control could result from the use of related parties or entities to operate the business under joint or common control.

expenses. The specific common area for which a tenant is making contribution payments should be clearly defined in the lease. The amount of the tenant's payment is usually based on the ratio of the square footage of the demised premises to the square footage of all of the gross rentable area in the shopping center. Sometimes a landlord will insist that the tenant's contribution be based on the ratio of the square footage of the demised premises to the square footage of all of the occupied space in the shopping center. The latter formula is more favorable to the landlord because he or she does not absorb the contribution relating to any unoccupied store space. When the tenant is required to contribute to maintenance and operation of common area, it is advisable to specify the items of expense for which the tenant is responsible, such as cleaning, fire protection, snow removal, lighting, rubbish removal, landscape maintenance and supplies, liability and other insurance premiums, fire insurance premiums, wages for those employed in maintenance, and workmen's compensation. Sometimes depreciation on maintenance equipment and personal property taxes are included.

Some shopping center leases specify a flat sum for each tenant to pay toward common area maintenance costs based on the area leased by the tenant, without regard to the actual costs of maintenance. Such a provision is normally coupled with an escalation clause, which computes increases in the common area maintenance charge by reference to increases in a cost of living index. A provision of this sort eases the accounting burden of the landlord and is often an acceptable alternative.

3. Heating, Ventilation, and Air Conditioning

If the lease is for space in an enclosed mall, the obligation on the part of the landlord to supply heating, ventilation, and air conditioning (commonly referred to as "HVAC") for the mall should be clearly set forth in the section of the lease dealing with common areas. The tenant usually shares the cost for such services either by including such costs under a common area and facility provision such as that above or by including a separate provision.

4. Merchants' Association

In order to promote the business of the shopping center, most landlords require the formation of a merchants' association. Generally, the leases require all tenants to join and contribute toward the advertising and public relations expenses of the association. Sometimes, however, large food and department store tenants who do their own advertising are not required to join the merchants' association. Merchants' associations are usually formed as associations or as nonprofit corporations. It is customary for the landlord to contribute between 20% and 30% of the budget adopted by the association. The leases of the individual tenants will set forth contributions applicable to each tenant. Many tenants will covenant that they will join a merchants' association only if a specified percentage (by number or square footage) of tenants in the shopping center, other than department store tenants, are similarly required to join.

D. COMMENCEMENT OF THE TERM AND RENT

1. If the Shopping Center Is in Existence

If the shopping center is in existence, the commencement of the term of the lease and the payment of rent will be specified in the lease.

2. If the Shopping Center Is Not Completed

Even though the shopping center is not yet completed, some leases are written to provide that the term of the lease shall start immediately on signing. In such cases the tenant is subject to the obligations of the lease immediately on execution, with certain exceptions:

(a) Payment of Rent

The commencement date for the payment of rent might be keyed to the earlier of (1) the date of opening the business by the tenant or (2) a specific number of days after notice from the landlord that the store is ready for occupancy by the tenant, which in many cases means only that the landlord's work is completed and not that the premises are ready to be opened for business. Occasionally, a landlord will agree that it will install all fixtures for the tenant and will deliver the store in "turn-key" condition.

(b) Fixturing Period

The provision outlined in (a) above allows the tenant a rent-free period to "fixture" the store by installing display cases and making improvements and alterations and to stock the store prior to the opening for business. Often a lease will provide that the tenant's work may be carried on while some of the landlord's finishing work is being completed, if the tenant's work does not interfere with the landlord's work. From the time the tenant starts fixturing and stocking the premises, the tenant should be obligated by all of the lease terms other than the payment of rent.

(c) Indemnification

In the event that the lease term commences immediately on execution of the lease, the tenant should not be obligated under any tort indemnification provision in favor of the landlord until such time as the tenant actually enters the premises.

(d) Store Openings

The prospective tenants in a shopping center are vitally interested in the time their stores will open, and each desire to time his or her own opening to coincide with a joint opening of several tenants. The lease may require each tenant to defer opening, at the landlord's request, to make possible a joint opening.

Another approach, which is desirable from the standpoint of an individual tenant, is to condition the tenant's obligation to open (and pay rent) on the prior opening of a specified percentage of tenants or square footage of store space of the shopping center. The small tenant can expect only to condition his or her opening on the prior or coincident opening of one or more major tenants, who are recognized as the most important draw of any shopping center. A major tenant, on the other hand, may condition its opening on (1) a certain percentage of the gross rentable area of the center also being open for business; (2) the shopping center being substantially completed; (3) the parking being minimally adequate, even if not 100% completed; and (4) certificates of occupancy being issued for the building and the particular premises. A fair compromise might be that a tenant would be required to open before all such conditions are met, but would pay only a percentage of gross sales and no fixed minimum rent until all conditions were met by the landlord.

Some tenants will request a deferment of the requirement of opening for business during certain periods of the year. For example, a department store that does a large volume of its annual business during the Christmas season may request a provision in the lease that if occupancy is not available by October 1, they will not accept occupancy prior to February 1 of the following year. It is not unusual for landlords to acquiesce to such requests when they are based on a sound business reason.

E. INSURANCE

1. Fire and Extended Coverage Insurance

The buildings comprising the shopping center must be insured against fire and extended coverage risks. It is customary that the landlord carry the fire and extended coverage insurance on all or the major portion of the shopping center. However, a major tenant, such as a department store, sometimes pays for and carries the fire insurance on its own building, especially in those circumstances in which the department store tenant has the concomitant obligation of fully repairing or restoring the building in the event of fire damage.

If the landlord carries the insurance, the tenant usually covenants to pay any increases in the landlord's fire insurance premiums if they are caused by the nature of the use or occupancy of the tenant or any act of negligence or violation of the insurance policy provisions by the tenant. The lease customarily prohibits the tenant from bringing combustibles onto the premises and requires the tenant to follow insurance company or underwriting bureau recommendations for lowering premium rates, such as installing fire extinguishers.

2. Liability Insurance

In addition to insuring against damage to the premises from fire and other casualty, it is customary to insure against damage to persons or property caused by the negligence of the landlord, the tenant, or the servants, agents, or employees of either. An insurance policy granting this coverage is referred to as a general liability and property damage policy. In the normal shopping center or office building leasing situation, the tenant is obligated to carry his or her own general liability and property damage insurance. If the tenant has indemnified the landlord, then the policy must insure against acts of the landlord as well as the tenant. The dollar limits of coverage of the insurance policies must be set for each particular leasing situation. Required limits have been increasing because of the magnitude of verdicts in personal injury cases. The standard provision usually requires that the tenant be the insured and that the landlord (and often the managing agent and the mortgagee) be named as an additional insured. Generally, the tenant is required to deliver a certificate from the insurer to the landlord. The certificate sets forth the general terms of the coverage as well as the dates of commencement and termination of the insurance. The landlord should require that no termination or amendment of the insurance coverage can occur unless the landlord has received ten days' prior written notice thereof from the insurer. Therefore, if the tenant has failed to pay for a renewal of the policy, the landlord will be notified and will have ten days in which to make the payment in order to continue the coverage, or to get the tenant to do so.

F. WORK TO BE DONE BY THE LANDLORD

The lease must describe in detail the obligations of the landlord regarding construction of the building and the store premises. It may be that the landlord is to produce a "turn key" job, which means finishing the building sufficiently that the tenant needs only to move in stock before opening for business. Alternatively, the landlord may be obligated only to build the shell of the store and the common facilities. In the latter situation the lease will likely specify that it is tenant's obligation to finish the interior work in accordance with plans and specifications approved by the landlord. In such a case a landlord would sometimes agree to pay the tenant a certain amount of money (called the "tenant allowance") as reimbursement for finishing the premises. If a tenant allowance is payable, the lease should state when and on what conditions it is to be paid. The lease should identify the party responsible for insuring the premises while work is in progress and should require that suitable workmen's compensation and protection against mechanics' liens are procured.

G. EXCLUSIVES[8]

A tenant who opens a particular type of store in a shopping center may want assurance that he or she will not have competition from other similar stores in the shopping center. In order to gain that assurance, a tenant who is to open a bakery will request that his or her lease contain a provision granting him or her the "exclusive" right to operate a bakery in the shopping center. The landlord tries to avoid granting exclusive use provisions to specific tenants, since they reduce flexibility in leasing space. Furthermore, with the tendency of larger stores to sell diversified lines of goods and services, tremendous overlappings occur. For example, a department store might have a baked goods department. Therefore, lease provisions such as "landlord covenants not to permit any other tenant to sell . . ." should be avoided. Such a clause should instead be drawn in terms of an agreement by the landlord not to "lease any space in the shopping center to a tenant whose primary or main business is . . ." The use of such language will permit some overlapping of the sale of similar merchandise. The exclusive might not cover the department stores, whose leases sometimes permit any lawful use, or any tenants who have already been granted or to whom the landlord anticipates granting a similar use. Also, a landlord will want to draft the exclusive narrowly. For example, the exclusive may be in terms of "high-fashion women's shoes" rather than just "shoes."

Holders of mortgages on shopping centers dislike exclusives. Mortgagees are especially concerned about the possibility of a tenant's being able to terminate a lease because of a violation of the exclusive use provision. Therefore, in granting an exclusive, the landlord should limit the tenant's remedies for breach of such an obligation, as the following example illustrates:

> In the event Landlord violates the provisions of this section, Tenant's remedies shall be limited to injunctive relief and/or the recovery of money damages, but in no event shall Tenant be entitled to any other remedy, including but not limited to cancellation of this Lease, recision of the term of this lease, or withholding of rent or set off against rent, all of which latter remedies Tenant hereby expressly waives.

H. TAX ESCALATION

Shopping center leases typically have a lease term of five, ten, or fifteen years. In setting the rent, a shopping center landlord must strike a balance between making sure that the rent is currently competitive with alternate locations and making sure that he or she is not stuck with

---

8. Exclusives and their counterpart, radius restrictions, are becoming much less common because of the application of antitrust laws establishing that such provisions are, at least in certain circumstances, illegal restraints on trade.

rental income that is insufficient to pay increased expenses, including real estate taxes, during the term of the lease. To aid in striking this balance, shopping center leases almost always contain a "tax escalation" provision that requires a tenant to pay a pro rata share of increased taxes on the shopping center over the real estate taxes imposed in a base year, which is usually the initial year of the lease term.[9] Even if the landlord were willing to forego such a provision, the mortgagee would probably insist on a tax escalation clause to insure that the landlord's expenses in future years did not exceed rental income. Similarly, most leases require the tenants to share assessments for public improvements that benefit the shopping center as a whole, such as sewer lines, widened streets, and sidewalk installation.

1. Tenant's Share of Escalation

The usual escalation provisions require the tenant to pay a proportionate share (as defined in the lease and usually based on the amount of space leased) of the increase in real estate taxes on the shopping center over the taxes in a designated base year. One of the problems inherent in a provision requiring the tenant to bear a "proportionate share" is the question of whether the landlord or the tenant bears the burden of the vacant space. If the landlord is to bear that burden, the tenant's share would be computed by a formula based on the tenant's space divided by the space in the center that can be rented (the rentable space). If, on the other hand, the tenants are to bear the burden of the escalation attributable to vacant space, the formula would be based on the tenant's space divided by the space in the center actually rented to other tenants.

2. Base Year

Escalation of taxes, or of any other expense, must have reference to a base year. In an established, fully assessed shopping center any year could be used. In a new center, however, taxes will increase for the first few years because of the increased value of the center as new stores are completed. The tenant will not want to pay for any increases that are due solely to new construction. The parties therefore often agree that the base year shall be the year during which the shopping center was first assessed as a fully completed shopping center.

A sample provision for a new shopping center is as follows:

> Commencing with the calendar year next following the calendar year in which the total real estate tax assessment (whether based upon a fiscal or calendar year) upon Landlord's property in the Shopping Center shall reflect

---

9. An escalation provision that requires a tenant to pay a share of some expense over some base (whether the base is the cost in a year or a set figure not tied to a year) is known in the shopping center industry as a "stop," and such a provision relating to real estate taxes is called a tax stop. If a tenant agrees that it will pay for such increases, but not beyond a certain maximum, then the maximum is referred to as a "cap."

the completion of the building of which the demised premises are a part, Tenant shall pay to Landlord each year on demand, as additional rent, "Tenant's share of excess real estate taxes," if any, as hereinafter described. Tenant's share of excess real estate taxes for any such calendar year shall be an amount equal to the product obtained by multiplying the number of square feet of gross floor area leased by Tenant by the excess, if any, of the "current tax per square foot" in such year over the "basic tax per square foot." The "basic tax per square foot" shall be computed by dividing the amount of the total real estate taxes levied on the Shopping Center in the first year for which the assessment thereof reflects the completion of the building of which the demised premises are a part, by the total number of square feet in rentable floor area in the Shopping Center reflected in such assessment. The "current tax per square foot" for any year shall be computed by dividing the amount of the total real estate taxes levied on the Shopping Center for such year by the total number of square feet of rentable floor area in the Shopping Center reflected in the real estate tax assessment thereof for such year.

3. Deduction of Tax Escalation from Percentage Rental

Tenants often take the position that they should be able to deduct real estate tax and other escalation payments from any percentage rental due. A landlord would not want such an off-set right to be cumulative; that is, he or she would want to make sure that the tenant would only off-set against percentage rent due during any year the escalations paid during that year. Many business compromises are possible in this area.

PROBLEM

Prepare a lease clause providing that the tenant may offset against 50% of percentage rent, noncumulatively, the amount by which the aggregate escalations for real estate taxes and common area maintenance charges that the tenant pays in any year exceeds $1.00 per square foot of rentable space in the demised premises.

---

4. Tenant's Right to Contest Increased Taxes

If a tenant leases a substantial amount of space and its share of tax increases amounts to a significant sum of money, the tenant may request the right to contest tax increases. A sample provision follows:

> If Landlord shall fail or refuse, on demand of Tenants of the Shopping Center whose stores aggregate at least 75% of the leasable store area of the Shopping Center, to take any necessary steps to contest the validity or amount of the assessed valuation or of the real estate tax for any tax escalation year, then such tenants at their own cost and expense, may undertake, by appropriate proceedings, in their own name, to review the validity or amount

of the assessed valuation or of the real estate tax for any tax escalation year. Any documents required to enable Tenant to prosecute any such proceeding shall be executed and delivered by Landlord within a reasonable time after demand therefore.

5. Tax Escalation Due to Additional Construction

Escalation due to increased construction is not an unforeseen expense of the landlord. In addition, if the new space produces new rent, the tenants of that space will bear the expense of those taxes. Therefore, the tenant should try to protect against tax escalation due to additional construction. An appropriate provision follows:

> In the event of any increase in rentable space, or any increase in land area comprising the shopping center site, or any additional improvements made to the shopping center over and above those upon the shopping center site at the time of the base tax year, the real estate taxes resulting therefrom shall not be considered for Landlord's tax increase, nor shall the gross square foot area of such increased area of space improvements be included within the computation of the gross square foot area in all of the buildings of the shopping center.

6. Caps

A strong tenant may be able to set a maximum on the potential liability under an escalation clause. Such a maximum is known as a "cap." The cap may be an absolute maximum, usually expressed as a dollar figure, or it may be the maximum amount by which the charge may be increased in any year, with no absolute maximum.

7. Tenants Pay All Taxes and Operating Costs

The discussion in this section has been concerned with tax escalation provisions. In such situations the landlord has set the initial fixed minimum rent at a figure the landlord believes will be sufficient to enable him or her to pay landlord debt service and all initial operational costs of the shopping center, including real estate taxes. Thus, the minimum rent has a real estate tax factor in it, as well as factors for common area maintenance and HVAC, which are other operating costs for which escalation provisions are common. However, the factors are just a guess on the part of the landlord, and if the guess is on the low side of actual expenses, he or she will never recover the difference. Thus, if the real estate tax factor in the minimum rent is $1.00 per square foot and the actual real estate taxes assessed during the base year works out to $1.50 per square foot, the tax stop provision will require the tenant to pay only increases from $1.50. In a year in which the actual taxes are $2.00 per square foot, the landlord will be receiving only $1.50 per square foot from the tenant (1.00 as built into the minimum rent and $.50 from the tax stop), and the remaining $.50 per square foot will come out of and reduce the profit factor built into the minimum rent.

Some landlords have found that the guesses of what taxes and other operating costs will be in the base year are too difficult to make and that the consequences of a wrong guess are too serious. Therefore, some landlords have taken the usual operating cost factors out of the minimum rent and have provided in their leases that the tenant shall share in the entire costs of real estate taxes and other operating costs without regard to any base year. The relevant provisions are not escalation provisions or stops, but are a pro rata share in such expenses "from the first dollar."

PROBLEM

Using the tax stop provision as a guide, prepare a clause requiring the tenant to pay its pro rata share of all real estate taxes imposed on the shopping center.

I. PARKING

The amount and the ease of parking is a major item of concern for the tenant at a shopping center. Major tenants often require the landlord to covenant that there will be a given number of parking spaces available in the shopping center and that the landlord will stripe, clean, light, maintain, and, in some instances, police the parking areas. The expenses of doing so will usually be borne by the tenants ultimately to the extent that they pay a share of common area maintenance and operating expenses.

A major tenant will generally require a landlord to provide a minimum number (often five) of parking spaces for each 1,000 square feet of gross rentable area in the shopping center. The landlord generally tries to avoid guaranties as to the number of car spaces that will be provided for each 1,000 square feet of rentable space, and in lieu thereof, the landlord will try to guarantee a gross number of spaces regardless of the gross rentable area in the shopping center. The landlord may want to expand the store area at the expense of parking area if the center turns out to be highly successful. If there are non-shopping center retail spaces, different minimum parking requirements will apply to such spaces.

The landlord will normally restrict the tenant and employee parking to certain areas of the parking lot, although it is difficult to enforce such a provision.

J. ESTOPPEL CERTIFICATES

At various times it may be necessary for the landlord to be able to prove that all of the leases are effective and that he or she is not in breach of any lease. For example, a prospective buyer of the shopping center or a prospective mortgage lender will want to know whether there are un-fulfilled obligations of the landlord for which the buyer will be responsible. The best evidence of the facts would be a document signed by each tenant certifying that the lease is in good standing; that the tenant has accepted possession of the premises; that there are no defaults on the part of either party; that the tenant has no claims against the landlord; and confirming the basic data of the leases, such as the rent, term, and expiration date. Such a certificate is referred to as an "estoppel certificate." The landlord will want a provision in the lease obligating the tenant to tender such a certificate (to the extent the facts are true) on request.

K. CLAUSES OF CONCERN TO MORTGAGEE

During negotiations with the tenant, the landlord must consider the mort-gagee's requirements. Indeed, usually all leases are subject to the ap-proval of the mortgagee. In the event of default under the mortgage, the mortgagee must be able to sell the shopping center at a foreclosure sale or take over the operation as owner of the center. The following are some of the clauses that are of particular interest to the mortgagee:

(1) Self-help clauses giving the tenant the right to cure the landlord's defaults and recoup the cost out of rent will be acceptable to the mortgagee only if the deduction comes out of percentage rent and not out of minimum rent.

(2) Any clause giving the tenant the right to cancel a lease or sur-render the premises or abate the payment of rent, except in the event of destruction or eminent domain, might be unacceptable to a mortgagee.

(3) Clauses giving tenants exclusive rights that generally limit com-petition and that, if breached, might in some circumstances give rise to cancellation of the lease by the tenant, might be unac-ceptable to a mortgagee.

(4) Clauses restricting competition on land owned by the landlord outside of the shopping center are often unacceptable to mort-gagees, unless such provisions exclude application to a mortgagee.

(5) Clauses requiring or giving the tenant the right to make im-provements for which the tenant is to be reimbursed by the land-lord, or that require the landlord to do the work, such as future expansion of the store, may trouble a mortgagee. Because the mortgagee may have to step into the landlord's position vis-à-vis a tenant, the mortgagee is alert to any circumstances that would permit the tenant, on failure by the landlord to act, to do work at the landlord's expense and to recoup the cost of such work by offsetting the cost against the rent or by acquiring a lien on the land. Furthermore, these provisions will alarm a mortgagee be-cause any default by the landlord may give rise to a right by the tenant to cancel the lease.

(6) An option to purchase the store premises or the center may be unacceptable to the mortgagee. In some states an option is considered an encumbrance that prevents a regulated lender, such as an insurance company, from making a first mortgage loan. Because a shopping center usually contains many tenants, it is unusual for a shopping center developer to grant an option to any one tenant, but the department store tenant in a one-major-tenant center might demand and receive such an option.

(7) Clauses committing the landlord to make repairs after fire, regardless of the adequacy of insurance proceeds, are generally unacceptable to a mortgagee.

(8) Provisions allowing a tenant to share in any condemnation award, without first applying the award to pay off the mortgage in full, are unacceptable to a mortgagee.

(9) Regardless of the law of any particular state, some mortgagees, as a matter of policy, prefer their mortgage to be subordinate to the major leases so as not to run the chance of the lease being terminated automatically by reason of a mortgage foreclosure. In most cases an attornment provision will cure the problem of a lease that is subordinate.

Part Three
OFFICE BUILDING LEASES

Some of these provisions also appear in shopping center and other commercial leases. The following discussion considers those provisions that tend to be found in office building leases.

I. IN GENERAL

A. SERVICES

As mentioned previously, an office building landlord usually furnishes heat, water, electricity, air conditioning, elevator service, and janitor service. However, some or all of these services are usually provided only during certain hours and on certain days of the week. The tenant should require enumeration of the services to be furnished and the periods during which they are furnished in order to make certain that the space will serve the tenant's purposes. The landlord should be careful to include a release of liability for interruption of services due to causes beyond the landlord's control. An example of a provision imposing requirements on the landlord is set forth below:

So long as Tenant is not in default under any of the provisions of this lease, Landlord shall

(a) provide elevator facilities on business days from 8 AM to 6 PM and on Saturdays from 8 AM to 1 PM and have an elevator subject to call at all other times;

(b) furnish heat to the demised premises, when necessary, on business days from 8 AM to 6 PM and on Saturdays from 8 AM to 1 PM;

(c) furnish air conditioning to the demised premises, when necessary, on business days from 8 AM to 6 PM and on Saturdays from 8 AM to 1 PM;

(d) clean or cause the demised premises to be kept clean, provided the same are kept in order by Tenant;

(e) furnish a reasonable amount of electricity, as Landlord may determine, for normal office use in the demised premises during business hours;

(f) furnish a directory with names of tenants of the building on the first floor or lobby of the building.

B. CONSUMER PRICE INDEX ESCALATION

For a number of years the steady inflation has caused a continual increase in the cost of operating rental property. Rental rates that are reasonable one year are too low the next because of increases in real estate taxes, wages of building personnel, and the cost of gas and electricity. One method for the landlord to protect against inflation is to include the standard additional rent provisions covering, among other expense items, real estate taxes, water and sewer rents, and insurance. However, such provisions merely reimburse the landlord for excess costs and do not give the landlord the benefit of increased rental values or any compensation for the lower purchasing power of his or her profit. A common method for assuring the landlord of increases in rent during the term of the lease, and therefore making the landlord more receptive to accepting a longer term lease, is to provide for rental adjustments on a regular basis in accordance with increases in the cost of living. These rental adjustments might be in addition to increased real estate and operating expenses escalation provisions. Such provisions can be found in all types of commercial leases and, recently, can even be found in some apartment leases.

A. As used herein:

(1) "Index" shall mean the "Consumer Price Index (New Series) for Urban Wage Earners and Clerical Workers (1967 = 100) for all Items for Philadelphia, Pennsylvania, issued by the Bureau of Labor Statistics of the United States Department of Labor";

(2) "Lease Date" shall mean the date of this lease;

(3) "Anniversary Date" shall mean the date which is one year after the Lease Date and each successive such date thereafter;

(4) "Percentage Increase" shall mean the percentage of increase in the Index on each Anniversary Date equal to a fraction the numerator of which shall be the Index on the Anniversary Date and the denominator of which shall be the Index on the Lease Date.

B. The minimum annual rent shall be adjusted on each Anniversary Date such that the rent from that Anniversary Date to the next succeeding Anniversary Date shall be the greater of:

(i) the minimum annual rent reserved pursuant to § 501 hereof; and

(ii) the product of the minimum annual rent reserved pursuant to § 501 hereof multiplied by the Percentage Increase.

C. In the event the Index shall hereafter be converted to a different standard reference base or otherwise revised, the determination of the Percentage Increase shall be made with the use of such conversion factor, formula or table for converting the Index as may be published by the Bureau of Labor Statistics.

C. ACTUAL COST ESCALATION

We have already mentioned cost escalation as a device whereby the landlord can be protected from increases in the cost of operating rental property. In lieu of, or in addition to, an adjustment in minimum rent based on an increase in a price index, office leases may contain cost escalation provisions whereby the tenant pays its share of the actual increases in operating costs. Such a provision may be similar to the real estate tax and common area maintenance escalation provisions used in shopping center leases, except that the description of what constitutes operating expenses will differ considerably due to the different categories of cost encountered in the different commercial settings.

A common variation of the actual increased operating cost provision is an escalation provision keyed to increases in one or more specific areas, such as a porter's wage and the cost of fuel. This method is less accurate, but greatly reduces the paper work needed to document the requested increases.

D. LANDLORD'S WORK

The owner of a new office building will generally agree to perform certain work on the space to be leased to each tenant. Typically, the landlord agrees to provide certain standard lighting fixtures in the ceiling, to partition the space into offices, to paint the walls of the space, and to provide other minor services for the new tenant. Many tenants find the landlord's work to be inadequate for their particular needs and will want to make changes in the work performed by the landlord along with additional improvements to the space. It is customary for a work letter to be signed by the landlord and the tenant specifying exactly what work each is obligated to perform in order to put the space into the condition desired by the tenant. The letter should state the specifications of the landlord's standard work and indicate substitutions that may be made. If the tenant requests the landlord to perform work beyond that which the landlord normally provides, the extra cost to the tenant and the method of payment should be described. If, on the other hand, the tenant wants to employ his or her own contractors to do work that the landlord would otherwise do, the amount of credit allowed the tenant by the landlord should be specified.

II. NET AND GROUND LEASES

Businesses often find that capital can most profitably be invested in machinery and inventory rather than in real estate needed for plants, offices, or stores. A long-term lease gives the industrial or chain store tenant most of the advantages of ownership without the permanent investment of a large amount of capital. Moreover, tax considerations make leasing attractive to the tenant, since the entire amount of rental payments is deductible in computing federal income taxes, whereas for an owner of a building, that portion of the mortgage payment that is applied to reduce the principal of the mortgage is not so deductible. In addition, the tenant will be able to ensure its use of the property through a long-term lease with renewal options.

For a landlord, a long-term lease to a single tenant of a plant or store can be more like a passive investment than the traditional active landlord's position. To ensure that the landlord-investor will realize a fixed return on the investment, the "net lease" is used. Under a net lease the tenant bears all operating costs, utilities, taxes, insurance, and other expenses and risks that are normally incident to ownership of the property. The tenant also pays the landlord-investor an amount of rent sufficient to pay the debt service on any mortgaged loans secured by the property and to provide a satisfactory return on the investment in the property. The term of the lease is normally computed so as to coincide with or exceed the length of any mortgages on the property.

A. INTENT CLAUSE

Although there are many variations, a completely net lease contemplates the landlord's receiving the rent free and clear of any expenses relating to the property except debt service on any preexisting mortgage loans and with no obligations to incur any expenses respecting the property whatsoever. This intent is expressed in a general provision that is supplemented by specific provisions dealing with specific costs and expenses:

> It is the purpose and intent of Landlord and Tenant that the rent shall be absolutely net to the Landlord, so that this Lease shall yield, net to the Landlord, the minimum net rent specified herein in each year during the term of this Lease and that all costs, operating expenses, impositions, premiums, fees, interest, charges, expenses, reimbursements, and obligations of every kind and nature whatsoever relating to the demised premises, excepting only certain taxes of Landlord, which may arise or become due during or out of the term of this Lease, shall be paid or discharged by Tenant as additional rent, and that Landlord shall be indemnified and saved harmless by Tenant from and against such costs, operating expenses, impositions, premiums, fees, interests, charges, expenses, reimbursements, and obligations.

B. IMPOSITIONS

In a completely net lease situation the tenant pays all taxes and assessments on the real estate:

As additional rent, Tenant shall pay throughout the term hereof, at least ten (10) days before any fine, penalty, interest, or cost may be added thereto for the nonpayment thereof (or sooner if elsewhere herein required): (a) all levies, assessments, water and sewer rents and charges, liens, license and permit fees, charges for public utilities (including, without limitation, charges for electricity, gas, light, heat, steam, power, and telephone service), and all other charges, imposts, or burdens of whatsoever kind and nature, whether or not particularized by name, and whether general or special, ordinary or extraordinary, foreseen or unforeseen, which at any time prior to or during the term of this Lease may have been or may be created, levied, assessed, confirmed, adjudged, imposed, or charged upon or with respect to the Premises or any improvements made thereto; (b) all real estate taxes levied or imposed against the Premises in excess of those levied for the calendar year in which the term hereof commences.

Provided, however, that if any imposition shall be created, levied, assessed, adjudged, imposed, charged, or become a lien with respect to a period of time which commences before or ends after the commencement and expiration dates of the term of this Lease respectively (other than by reason of breach of the terms hereof by Tenant), then Tenant shall only be required to pay that proportion of such imposition which is equal to the proportion of said period which falls within the term of this Lease. Nothing herein contained shall require Tenant to pay any income or excess profits taxes assessed against Landlord, or any corporation capital stock and franchise taxes imposed by Landlord. Tenant shall furnish Landlord, no later than ten (10) days prior to the last day upon which they may be paid without any fine, penalty or interest, evidence satisfactory to Landlord of the payment of all impositions.

C. INSURANCE

Under a net lease, the tenant usually pays for and maintains the fire insurance, boiler insurance and public liability and property damage insurance. A provision to that effect is set forth below:

(a) During the term of this Lease or any extension thereof, Tenant, at its expense and for the respective interests of Landlord and Tenant, shall keep the buildings and improvements on the Premises insured against loss or damage by fire and the hazards included in the standard extended coverage endorsement, in an amount equal to one hundred percent (100%) of the replacement value. Said policy shall provide for at least ten (10) days' notice to Landlord before cancellation and shall be issued by a responsible insurance company authorized to do business in the state in which the Premises are located and approved by Landlord, which approval shall not be withheld unreasonably. If there is a mortgage on the Premises, such policy shall have attached standard noncontributory mortgagee clauses making losses payable to the mortgagee. Tenant shall pay all premiums or assessments on such insurance to the insurer and from time to time shall furnish Landlord (and the mortgagee of the Premises, if any) with a memorandum of such insurance.

(b) Tenant shall also at its expense provide and keep in force general liability insurance in which Landlord shall be named as an additional assured, said policy to contain minimum limits of liability in respect to bodily injury (including death) of Five Hundred Thousand Dollars ($500,000) for each person, One Million Dollars ($1,000,000) for each occurrence and property damage of One Hundred Thousand Dollars ($100,000). Such policy shall cover the entire Premises including the sidewalks and streets abutting thereon, and shall provide for at least ten (10) days' notice to Landlord before cancellation. Tenant shall, from time to time, furnish to Landlord at its request a memorandum of such insurance.

(c) Upon Tenant's failure to supply and/or maintain any of the policies of insurance referred to in subparagraphs (a) and (b) above, Landlord shall have the right to purchase such insurance or any part thereof, and the cost of such insurance shall become due and payable as additional rental hereunder, to be collectible by Landlord in the same manner as herein provided for the collection of rent.

D. REPAIRS

In a net lease the tenant usually makes and bears the expense of all repairs and improvements, ordinary and extraordinary, including rebuilding in the event of destruction. A sample provision to that effect follows:

> Tenant covenants throughout the term of this Lease, at Tenant's sole cost and expense, to take good care of the Premises, and, subject to the provisions of this Lease elsewhere set forth, to keep the same in good order and condition, and promptly at Tenant's own cost and expense to make all necessary nonstructural repairs to the interior of the Premises, ordinary as well as extraordinary, foreseen as well as unforeseen. When used in this Article, the term "repairs" shall include replacements and renewals, and all such repairs made by Tenant shall be at least equal in quality and usefulness to the original improvements and equipment.

Sometimes the landlord is responsible for repairs to the exterior and/or structural portions of the premises. That obligation would be undertaken as a result of negotiation between the parties and would constitute a deviation from a completely net lease.

E. GROUND LEASES AND LEASEHOLD MORTGAGES

It is common for a tenant to decide to lease vacant property for a long term (often as long as 100 years), in order to contruct on the property an office building, hotel, shopping center, or industrial plant. For the tenant-developer of the property, the use of a lease permits the avoidance of an outlay of funds necessary to purchase the property. In such a case the rental paid for the property will reflect the value of the undeveloped property and not the value of the property and improvements that are ultimately to be constructed on it. At the end of the lease term (or any renewals), the property will revert back to the owner of the property, who will also at that time receive title to the improvements.

The developer will usually seek financing for the construction of the improvement on the leased property. As security for its loan, the lender will want a "leasehold mortgage," which is a security interest in the tenant's rights under the lease, and which gives to the mortgagee the right to take over the tenant's position under the lease. The tenant's interest in the lease (often referred to as a "leasehold interest") is valuable because the tenant has the right to use the property for a long time, during which the rental payments under the lease relate only to the value of the unimproved land, while the earning power of the tenant is directly related to the value of the improvements constructed on the land. For example, Mr. Smith, a developer, may have entered into a lease for the unimproved property requiring rental payments of $10,000 a year. Mr. Smith then constructed an industrial plant that he leased to a major corporation under a "net lease" at a rental of $100,000 a year. Mr. Smith, as the owner of the leasehold interest, receives $90,000 per annum (the difference between the rent received from the tenant of the plant and the rent payable to the owner of the land). The net amount received by Mr. Smith is intended to reflect a rate of return for the investment made by Mr. Smith in constructing the leasehold improvements. Mr. Smith is in a position to give his leasehold as security for any loan incurred to construct the leasehold improvements, and that leasehold interest has a value measured by the annual excess of the rent received from the corporation above the rent payable to the owner of the unimproved property.

If there is to be a leasehold mortgage, the lease with the owner of the unimproved property should contain certain provisions that one would expect the mortgagee to require. Because the mortgagee's security is the leasehold interest, the mortgagee will want to protect itself against a premature termination of the lease caused by the default of the tenant by being able to cure any such defaults. In addition, the mortgagee will want a voice as to whether a renewal option will be exercised. The mortgagee will also want to establish its rights to the proceeds of any condemnation award to fire insurance policy applicable to the leasehold improvements. In effect, the leasehold mortgagee wants to have rights in the leasehold improvement that are in many ways prior to the rights of the landlord. The leasehold mortgagee is concerned about two types of possible tenant defaults under the lease:

1. Defaults That May Be Cured by Payment of Money

A default caused by failure to pay rent, real estate taxes, water and sewer rents, insurance obligations, and the like can be cured by the mortgagee's paying the requisite amount. The leasehold mortgagee will want the lease to require that it receive notice of such defaults and an opportunity to cure them before the lease may be terminated.

2. Defaults Consisting of a Failure to Repair

If a default is due to the failure of the tenant to make repairs or perform work necessary to make the premises comply with the law, the leasehold mortgagee cannot cure the default unless it can obtain entry to the premises. The only sure way for the mortgagee to gain entry is by obtaining possession of the premises. Therefore, the leasehold mortgagee can be protected against this type of default if it is given enough time to acquire the leasehold interest of the tenant by foreclosure or other similar procedure. However, if the default relates to noncompliance with the law, the landlord may be exposed to fines or other penalties because of the delay. An improper assignment of the lease by tenant, insolvency, and other breaches of the lease cannot be prevented or cured by the mortgagee. Again, the only real protection for the mortgagee is time to acquire the tenant's rights by foreclosure or otherwise.

The leasehold mortgagee can obtain effective protection if the lease provides that in the event of breach by the tenant, the landlord will enter into a new lease, identical to the old one, with the mortgagee as tenant. The mortgagee would be obligated to cure any defaults of the tenant as a condition to obtaining the new lease.

The danger to the mortgagee arising from an unexercised renewal option can be avoided by giving the leasehold mortgagee the right to exercise any renewal right that the tenant fails to exercise. If the mortgagee exercise such a renewal right, it would become the tenant.

Before granting a mortgage, a prospective leasehold mortgagee can be expected to require an estoppel certificate stating that the lease is in good standing and that all obligations of the tenant to date have been met.

F. ALTERATIONS

A long-term net lease often permits the tenant not only to make alterations, but also to demolish completely an existing building and build a new one. The landlord usually requires prior approval of plans and specifications and adequate assurance against mechanics' liens that might be placed on the landlord's interest in the property.

G. CASUALTY

In a net lease the tenant usually carries the fire insurance and agrees to restore the premises with no abatement of rent during the period of restoration. The landlord will generally specify the amount of insurance to be carried. The replacement value of the building should be appraised from time to time and the insurance coverage adjusted if inadequate.

H. CONDEMNATION

For many purposes the tenant of a long-term ground lease can be considered as the real owner of the property, subject to an agreement to turn the property over to another party someday. Condemnation poses an especially difficult problem because state law regarding entitlement to proceeds of condemnation might have more to do with strict legal questions of title than with economic reality. Therefore, it is not unusual for the landlord and tenant to include elaborate condemnation provisions that attempt to divide condemnation proceeds along the lines of economic reality. Such clauses often resort to formulae and appraisals in an attempt to describe what the value of the respective parties will be at any time during the lease term that condemnation might occur.

I. SALE AND LEASEBACK TRANSACTIONS

Ground or net leases have often been used in sale and leaseback transactions. A ground lease is often more of a financing transaction than a typical lease transaction. The financing aspect is even clearer in the sale and leaseback situation.

Traditionally, the owner of a property who wants to develop or substantially renovate the property, or who has a developed property but needs cash, will obtain a loan and will grant a mortgage encumbering the property. The loan is often relatively long term (twenty-five to thirty-five years) and self-amortizing, in whole or in part. However, a variety of factors, including lending limits and criteria, accounting practices, and tax considerations, sometimes dictate that some other financing technique is more attractive than a mortgage in a particular situation. The "other financing technique" is often a sale and leaseback. A sale and leaseback involves a sale by the user of the property to the financial institution for a cash purchase price (the economic analog of the principal amount of the loan) and a simultaneous net lease from the financial institution to the user for a long term (the analog of the term of a mortgage) and at a specified minimum rent (the economic analog of the debt service on a mortgage). The concerns of the institutional investor in a sale and leaseback transaction are directly analogous to the concerns of a permanent lender secured by a mortgage, and the documents will be similar in many respects. In preparing documents for a sale and leaseback transaction, a legal assistant shall therefore consider the mortgagee's typical concerns, as discussed in Chapter Seven.

J. CLOSE CORPORATION/PARTNERSHIP NET LEASE

One task that you may have as a legal assistant is to prepare net leases from an individual or partnership that owns the property to a corporation closely held by that individual or partnership. The occasion for such a lease would arise as a result of tax and business planning considerations. It might be advantageous for persons who want to own property out of which they plan to operate a business to acquire the real estate in a partnership but to incorporate for the actual operation of the business. In such situations the parties usually intend to let the corporation bear all economic risks and shield themselves and the property from the economic risks of the operation of the business. Thus, a net lease is usually appropriate. However, the net lease may not be a completely net lease in the sense that we have described a completely net lease. For example, the parties may not want to require the corporation as tenant to reconstruct the property after a fire or other casualty if the damage is such that the corporation will be forced to cease operations for a substantial period. An analysis should be done in preparing a net lease in this situation to determine the appropriateness of the typical net lease provisions. The conceptual difficulty in doing so is that at the start, the ultimate parties in interest are identical. This identity of interest may not continue to exist, due to deaths,[10] bankruptcy of either the partnership or the corporation, or changes in personnel resulting from public sale of corporate stock, stock options to key employees, or the like. The drafter must try to consider all of the possibilities and arrive at some reasonable determination.

PROBLEM

Using a common printed form of commercial lease available in your area, prepare a net lease between Hardy and Wilkins, Co-Partners as the owner of 14 King Street and H and W, Inc. as the tenant, for a term of ten years at $12,000.00 a year. Presumably, this assignment will require you to delete certain provisions of the lease, to modify others (either by interlineation or by rider), and to add other provisions entirely, presumably by a rider.

III. SURETY OR GUARANTY AGREEMENT

If the tenant's credit is not established or not adequate, and especially if the tenant is a newly formed corporation, it is not unusual for the landlord to obtain a guaranty of the lease from a person or entity having substantial assets. In order to serve its intended purpose, the guaranty must make clear that the guarantor's obligations will not be affected by (a) the release or discharge of the tenant in any type of bankruptcy proceeding; (b) the impairment, limitation, or modification of the liability of the tenant

---

10. The partnership agreement and the stockholder's agreement may vary as to the consequences of the death of a partner/shareholder.

or its estate in bankruptcy, or any remedy for the enforcement of the tenant's liability under the lease, resulting from the operation of any present or future provision of the Bankruptcy Code or other such statutes; (c) the rejection of the lease in any such proceedings; (d) the assignment or transfer of the lease by the tenant; (e) any disability or other defense of the tenant; or (f) the cessation from any cause whatsoever of the liability of the tenant. The guarantor often requires that he or she receive adequate notice of any default and have an opportunity to cure it.

IV. ASSIGNMENT OR SUBLETTING

Generally, a tenant may assign or sublet all or part of the premises that he or she is leasing. However, virtually all printed leases, such as apartment leases, office leases, and leases for small stores, prohibit assignment and subletting without the consent of the landlord. Because the landlord is usually in a strong bargaining position, often the only concessions a tenant can obtain are an agreement by the landlord not to withhold consent unreasonably and an agreement to permit assignment to an identified category of persons or entities (e.g., wholly owned subsidiaries).

According to proper legal terminology, a transfer of part of the tenant's interest in all or part of the premises is a sublease, whereas a transfer of all of the tenant's interest in all or part of the premises is an assignment. It is often important to determine whether a sublease or an assignment has occurred. One reason is that a landlord may not directly sue a subtenant for breach of a subtenant's lease (since the landlord is not a party to that lease). However, the landlord may sue an assignee to enforce the lease that has been assigned. In either case, the original tenant remains liable to the landlord for fulfillment of the original tenant's obligations under the lease if the assignee or subtenant fails to meet those obligations. Generally, it is difficult for a tenant who has assigned his or her rights to regain possession of the premises if the assignee defaults. Therefore, the tenant may end up performing under the lease while not having possession of the premises. On the other hand, it is possible for a sublessor to regain possession if the sublessee defaults under the sublease.

A subtenant incurs several risks over and above those incurred by an ordinary tenant. First of all, the prime lease must permit subletting, or the prime landlord must have consented, in order for the sublease to be valid. Since the sublease derives its entire interest from the prime lease, the subtenant can retain possession only so long as the tenant under the prime lease (the subtenant's landlord) retains his or her right of possession under the prime lease. If the prime lease ends either by normal termination, due to breach, or otherwise, the subtenant will lose his or her right to possession of the premises. In order to be assured of continued possession, the sublessee needs an agreement with the prime landlord stating that the sublease will not be terminated by reason of a default by the prime tenant (the sublessor) without first giving the subtenant notice of the default and an opportunity to cure the same.

When the landlord's consent to an assignment is requested, most landlords of shopping centers or office buildings require a three-party agreement to be entered into between the landlord, tenant, and the assignee. This agreement includes language to effect the actual assignment. It also includes a consent to the assignment by the landlord. Such agreements will reiterate that the original tenant's liability continues in full force and effect after the assignment. Finally, the assignee assumes the obligations under the lease and submits to the special remedies provided in the jurisdiction in the event of a default under the lease.

A sublease usually looks exactly the same as the prime lease with the exception of the term and the rent. The use of the sublease has recently become common in office buildings. A tenant may lease a certain amount of space that is adequate for its present needs. However, the tenant may want the ability to expand to additional space as the tenant grows through the years. Landlords are reluctant to agree to hold space available for the tenant in the future. Therefore, the tenant may lease the expansion space right from the beginning of the lease. The extra space is then either subleased by the tenant to a third party or leased back to the landlord for a relatively short term.

Example 10-1 Standard Lease

LEASE FOR REAL ESTATE
PART ONE OF A TWO PART AGREEMENT

L-1969
REV. 1/78

This form recommended and approved for, but not restricted to
use by members of the Pennsylvania Association of Realtors when
used with an approved addendum attached hereto.
— **Agent For The Lessor** —

PRINCIPALS
(1-78)

𝕿𝖍𝖎𝖘 𝕬𝖌𝖗𝖊𝖊𝖒𝖊𝖓𝖙, made this...........................day of ........................A.D. 19........

Between ....
....hereinafter called Lessor, and
....
....hereinafter called Lessee,

PROPERTY
(11-74)

1. (a) WITNESSETH: Lessor agrees to let unto the Lessee premises being known as........................
....
.... of .... , County of .... , State of Penna.

with improvements consisting of ....

....

upon the following terms and conditions to wit:

(b)	Total rental for entire term payable to Lessor	$...............
(c)	Payments in advance ☐Monthly ☐ .... in the amount of:	$...............
(d)	Cash or check to be paid before possession by Lessee which is to be applied on account as follows:	

Advance rent.................... 19.....to.............19..... Paid $ .... Due $ ....
On account of final payment of rent.................... Paid $ .... Due $ ....
Security deposit (see par. 1 (f)).................... Paid $ .... Due $ ....
Credit report.................... Paid $ .... Due $ ....
.... Paid $ _____ Due $ _____
Totals – Paid to date .... Paid $...........
Balance due before possession............... Due $ ....

(e)	Adjusted payment of rent until regular due date, if any	$...............
(f)	Security deposit	$...............
(g)	Late charge if rent not paid within grace period	$...............
(h)	Due date for each payment...	
(i)	Term of this lease...	
(j)	Commencement of lease...................................... day of ..................A.D. 19.....	
(k)	Expiration date of lease...................................... day of ..................A.D. 19.....	
(l)	Required written notice to terminate this lease.	
(m)	Renewal term if not terminated by either party.	
(n)	Lessee will occupy premises ONLY as	
(o)	Maximum number of occupants under this lease	
(p)	Payments to be made promptly when due in lawful money of the United States of America to: ☐ Lessor ☐ Agent	
(q)	Utilities & services to be supplied as follows:	

Lessor will supply: ☐ cold water,   ☐ hot water ,   ☐ gas,   ☐ heat,   ☐ electric,   ☐ lawn care,
☐ snow removal,   ☐ janitor service,   ☐ yearly oil burner cleaning,   ☐ cesspool cleaning,   ☐ ....
☐ Lawn & Shrubbery care.   ☐ ....
Lessee will supply: ☐ cold water,   ☐ hot water   ☐ gas,   ☐ heat,   ☐ electric,   ☐ lawn care,
☐ snow removal,   ☐ water in excess of yearly minimum charge,   ☐ yearly oil burner cleaning,
☐ cesspool cleaning,   ☐ Lawn & Shrubbery care.   ☐ ....

(r)	Notwithstanding anything herein to the contrary, Lessee will pay cost of any or all repairs of any kind whatsoever, occurring after commencement of this lease where the individual cost of each repair is less than $ ....
(s)	No pets or animals of any kind whatsoever will be permitted on or within the herein described premises excepting ....

SPECIAL
CLAUSES

2.

ADDENDUM

3. The Lessor and Lessee agree for themselves, their respective heirs and successors and assigns to the herein described terms and also to those set forth in the addendum attached hereto entitled "TERMS AND CONDITIONS," (PART TWO) all of which are to be regarded as binding and as strict legal conditions.

LESSEE............... LESSEE................. LESSEE.............. LESSOR................. LESSOR............... AGENT.............

INITIALS

Continued.

Example 10-1 **Standard Lease** *continued*

PART TWO OF A TWO PART AGREEMENT
APARTMENT LEASE
TERMS AND CONDITIONS

FORM L-1A
(REV. 1-78)

This form recommended and approved for, but not restricted to,
use by members of the Pennsylvania Association of REALTORS®

Copyright Pennsylvania Association of REALTORS® 1973

Rules and Regulations

4. The Rules and Regulations in regard to the building wherein the said demised premises are located, and to such alterations, additions and modifications thereof as may from time to time be made by the Lessor shall be considered a part of this lease, and the Lessee covenants and agrees that said Rules and Regulations and all alterations, additions and modifications thereof shall be faithfully observed by the Lessee, the employees of Lessee and all persons invited by Lessee into said building.

(a) The public halls and stairways shall not be obstructed or used for any other purpose than for ingress to and egress from the apartments.

(b) No Lessee shall make or permit any disturbing noises to be made in the building by himself, members of his family, guests, his agents, servants or licensees; nor do or permit anything to be done that will interfere with the rights, comforts or convenience of other tenants. No Lessee shall play or suffer to be played any musical instruments, television or radio, in the demised premises between the hours of ten-thirty o'clock, P.M. and the following eight-thirty o'clock, A.M., if the same shall disturb or annoy other occupants of the building. All cooking equipment must be used in such a way as to prevent noxious odors from permeating the building.

(c) The Lessee shall not throw or permit to be thrown anything whatever out of the windows or doors, or into the halls of the building.

(d) The delivery of kitchen supplies, market goods, towels. ice, water, newspapers, or other supplies and packages of every kind will be permitted only at the entrance provided therefor, and under the direction, control and supervision of the Lessor, and the Lessor will not be held responsible for the loss or damage of any such property, notwithstanding such loss or damage may occur through the carelessness or negligence of the employees of the building. The Lessor will not be responsible for any article left with any employee or in any part of the building.

(e) No baby carriages, velocipedes, bicycles or other large articles will be allowed in passenger elevators, or in the halls, passageways, areas or courts of the building.

(f) The Lessee shall keep the premises leased in good state of preservation and cleanliness, and shall not sweep or throw or permit to be swept or thrown from the premises leased, any dirt or other substance into any of the corridors or halls, elevators or stairways of said building.

(g) The fire escape shall not be obstructed.

(h) No ash can, garbage can, woodbox, kitchen supplies, ice or other articles shall be placed in the halls or on the staircase landings, nor shall anything be hung from the windows, balconies or placed upon the window sills. Neither shall any tablecloths, clothing, curtains, rugs or other articles, be shaken or hung from any of the windows or doors.

(i) The water-closets and other water apparatus shall not be used for any other purpose than that for which they were constructed, nor shall any sweepings, rubbish, rags or any other improper articles be thrown into the same; and any damage resulting from misuse thereof shall be borne by the tenant by whom or upon whose premises it shall have been caused.

(j) Children shall not play in the public halls, entrances, stairways or elevators.

(k) Each tenant shall use the laundry and drying apparatus, if any, only on such days and hours as the Lessor shall designate.

(l) No animals shall be carried on the elevators or kept in or about the premises, except on written consent of the Lessor.

(m) No window shades or awnings shall be placed on any of the windows excepting those approved by Lessor or the manager of the building, and no awning shall be placed on any window prior to May 1st or allowed to remain on any window after October 1st in any year.

(n) The Lessor reserves the right to rescind any of these rules and to make such other and further rules and regulations as, in Lessor's judgment, may from time to time be needful for the safety, care, maintenance, operation and cleanliness of the building and for the preservation of good order therein, which, when so made and notice thereof is given to the Lessee, shall have the same force and effect as if originally made a part of the foregoing lease. However, such other and further rules shall not be inconsistent with the proper and rightful enjoyment by the Lessee under the foregoing lease of the premises therein referred to.

Security Deposit (9-75)

5. The "security deposit" specified in Par. #1. (f) shall be held by Agent as security for the performance of all the terms, covenants and conditions of this lease and for the cost of any trash removal, housecleaning and for the correction of damage (which is, in the opinion of the Lessor and/or Agent, in excess of normal wear and tear); otherwise, the "security deposit" or any balance thereof shall be returned after the Lessee has vacated and left the premises in an acceptable condition (following a personal inspection by Lessor and/or Agent) and surrendered all keys to Agent. If the Lessor determines that any loss, damage or injury chargeable to the Lessee hereunder, exceeds the security deposit, the Lessor at his option, may retain the said sum as liquidated damages or may apply the sum against any actual loss, damage or injury and the balance thereof will be the responsibility of the Lessee. Lessor's determination of the amount, if any, to be returned to the Lessee shall be final. It is further understood and agreed that the said security deposit is not to be considered as the last payment under the lease, however the rights of the Lessor shall not be hindered to retain the security deposit, or a portion therefrom as payment on account of uncollected rents, if any.

The aforementioned "security deposit" shall be paid to the Agent who will deposit same in a separate custodial type account. Agent shall keep records of all funds so deposited as required in accordance with the Act of July 9, 1957, P.L. 608, Section 4. Said account will be clearly identified as required indicating the date and from whom he received money, the date deposited, the date of withdrawals and other pertinent information concerning this transaction. It is understood and agreed that should the property herein mentioned be sold, exchanged, transferred or conveyed to a new owner, that at the time of settlement, any money held as a security deposit shall be transferred to the new owner or his agent, to be continued to be held as a security deposit.

Affirmative Covenants of Lessor

6. (a) If the terms in paragraph #1. (q) provide for the Lessor to supply heat to Lessee, the Lessor agrees to furnish a reasonable amount of heat commencing not before the first day of October, and continuing not later than the first day of May following, in each year. In consideration that no extra charge is made therefor, should Lessor fail to supply same for any reason, Lessor shall not be liable for any damage caused by any such failure not due to gross negligence on the part of the Lessor, not for any damage to property of Lessee caused in any manner by fire, water or stream, or the lack thereof.

(b) If the Lessee so desires, Lessor, if possible, may make available to Lessee, without charge, a space in the building for the storage of goods and effects of Lessee. In consideration of the fact that no extra charge is made for the furnishing of such space by the Lessor, it is understood that Lessor shall not be liable for loss or damage to any stored goods through fire or theft or any cause whatever, and Lessee expressly releases Lessor as bailee or otherwise from all claims for any such loss or damage. It is further understood that the use of storage space by the Lessee shall be limited to the time of the Lessee's occupancy, and that goods left over thirty days after the expiration of Lessee's occupancy may be sold for storage charges at public or private sale without further notice to Lessee.

(c) The Lessor may furnish additional service not herein provided for but any such service shall be gratuitous unless otherwise agreed and shall not be an obligation of the Lessor or part of the consideration for the rent.

Place of Payment

7. All rent shall be payable without prior notice or demand at the office of Lessor or Agent as specified in paragraph #1. (p).

8. Lessee covenants and agrees that he will without demand:

Affirmative Covenants of Lessee (11-74)

Payment of Rent

(a) Pay the rent and all other charges herein reserved as rent on the days and times and at the place that the same are made payable, without fail, and if Lessor shall at any time or times accept said rent or rent charges after the same shall have become due and payable, such acceptance shall not excuse delay upon subsequent occasions, or constitute or be construed as a waiver of any of Lessor's rights. Lessee agrees that any charge or payment herein reserved, included, or agreed to be treated or collected as rent and/or any charges, expenses, or costs herein agreed to be paid by the Lessee may be proceeded for and recovered by the Lessor by legal process in the same manner as rent due and in arrears.

Late Charges (11-74)

(b) All rental payments are due and payable on the due date as specified in paragraph #1. (h) of this agreement or within five days thereafter (grace period) without penalty. However, after 5:00 PM on the fifth day after due date as aforementioned, any rental payment not paid in full will be subject to a late charge. Payments not made on or before 5:00 PM on the tenth day after due date, together with late charge, may be referred to Magistrate or Justice of the Peace for the collection and/or ejectment.

Cleaning, Repairing, etc.

(c) Keep the demised premises clean and free from all ashes, dirt and other refuse matter; replace all broken glass windows, doors, etc.; keep all waste and drain pipes open; repair all damages to plumbing and to the demised premises; in general, keep the same in as good order and repair as they are at the beginning of the term of this lease, reasonable wear and tear and damage by accidental fire or other casualty not occurring through negligence of Lessee or those employed by or acting for Lessee alone excepted. The Lessee agrees to surrender the demised premises in the same condition in which Lessee has herein agreed to keep the same during the continuance of this lease.

Requirements of Public Authorities

(d) Comply with any requirements of any of the constituted public authorities, and with the terms of any State or Federal statute or local ordinance or regulation applicable to Lessee or his use of the demised premises, and save Lessor harmless from penalties, fines, costs or damages resulting from failure to do so.

Fire

(e) Use every reasonable precaution against fire.

Surrender of Possession (11-74)

(f) Peaceably deliver up and surrender possession of the demised premises to the Lessor at the expiration or sooner termination of this lease, promptly delivering to Lessor at his office, all keys for the demised premises, with all trash and personal belongings removed and building(s) broom-swept clean.

Notice of Fire, etc.

(g) Give to Lessor prompt written notice of any accident, fire or damage occurring on or to the demised premises.

Pay for Gas and Electricity

(h) Promptly pay for all gas and electricity, water, heat, lawn care and services consumed in the herein demised premises during the continuance of this lease if so specified in paragraph #1 (q); and should Lessee fail to make these payments when due, Lessor shall have the right to settle therefor, such sums to be considered additional rent and collectible from Lessee, as such, by distress or other process, and to have all the priorities given by law to claims for rent.

Indemnification

(i) Indemnify and save Lessor harmless from any and all loss occasioned by Lessee's breach of any of the covenants, terms and conditions of this lease, or caused by his family, guests, visitors, agents and employees.

Negative Covenants of Lessee

9. Lessee covenants and agrees that he will do none of the following things without the consent in writing of Lessor:

Use of Premises

(a) Occupy the demised premises in any other manner or for any other purpose than as above set forth in paragraph #1 (n).

Assignment and Subletting

(b) Assign, mortgage or pledge this lease or under-let or sub-lease the demised premises, or any part thereof, or permit any other person, firm or corporation to occupy the demised premises, or any part thereof; nor shall any assignee or sub-lessee assign, mortgage or pledge this lease or such sub-lease, without an additional written consent by the Lessor, and without such consent no such assignment, mortgage or pledge shall be valid. If the Lessee becomes embarrassed or insolvent, or makes an assignment for the benefit of creditors, or if a petition in bankruptcy is filed by or against the Lessee or a bill in equity or other proceeding for the appointment of a receiver for the Lessee is filed, or if the real or personal property of the Lessee shall be sold or levied upon by any Sheriff, Marshal or Constable, the same shall be a violation of this covenant.

Signs (c) Place or allow to be placed any stand, booth, sign or show case upon the doorsteps, vestibules or outside walls or pavements of said premises, or paint, place, erect or cause to be painted, placed or erected any sign, projection or device on or in any part of the premises. Lessee shall remove any sign, projection or device painted, placed or erected, if permission has been granted and restore the walls, etc., to their former conditions, at or prior to the expiration of this lease. In case of the breach of this covenant (in addition to all other remedies given to Lessor in case of the breach of any conditions or covenants of this lease) Lessor shall have the privilege of removing said stand, booth, sign, show case, projection or device, and restoring said walls, etc., to their former condition, and Lessee, at Lessor's option, shall be liable to Lessor for any and all expenses so incurred by Lessor.

Alterations Improvements (d) Make any alterations, improvements, or additions to the demised premises. All alterations, improvements, additions or fixtures, whether installed before or after the execution of this lease, shall remain upon the premises at the expiration or sooner determination of this lease and become the property of Lessor, unless Lessor shall, prior to the determination of this lease, have given written notice to Lessee to remove the same, in which event Lessee will remove such alterations, improvements and additions and restore the premises to the same good order and condition in which they now are. Should Lessee fail to do so, Lessor may do so, collecting, at Lessor's option, the cost and expense thereof from Lessee as additional rent.

Machinery (e) Use or operate any machinery that, in Lessor's opinion, is harmful to the building or disturbing to other tenants occupying other parts thereof.

Weights (f) Place any weights in any portion of the demised premises beyond the safe carrying capacity of the structure.

Fire Insurance (g) Do or suffer to be done, any act, matter or thing objectionable to the fire insurance companies, whereby the fire insurance or any other insurance now in force or hereafter to be placed on the demised premises, or any part thereof, or on the building of which the demised premises may be a part, shall become void or suspended, or whereby the same shall be rated as a more hazardous risk than at the date of execution of this lease, or employ any person or persons objectionable to the fire insurance companies or carry or have any benzine or explosive matter of any kind in and about the demised premises. In case of a breach of this covenant (in addition to all other remedies given to Lessor in case of the breach of any of the conditions of covenants of this lease) Lessee agrees to pay to Lessor as additional rent any and all increase or increases of premiums on insurance carried by Lessor on the demised premises, or any part thereof, or on the building of which the demised premises may be a part, caused in any way by the occupancy of Lessee.

Removal of Goods (h) Remove, attempt to remove or manifest an intention to remove Lessee's goods or property from or out of the demised premises otherwise than in the ordinary and usual course of business, without having first paid and satisfied Lessor for all rent which may become due during the entire term of this lease.

Vacate Premises (i) Vacate or desert said premises during the term of this lease, or permit the same to be empty and unoccupied.

Agency on Removal 10. The Lessee agrees that if, with the permission in writing of Lessor, Lessee shall vacate or decide at any time during the term of this lease, or any renewal thereof, to vacate the herein demised premises, prior to the expiration of this lease, or any renewal hereof, Lessee will not cause or allow any agent to represent Lessee in any sub-letting or reletting of the demised premises other than an agent approved by the Lessor, and that should Lessee do so, or attempt to do so, that Lessor may remove any signs that may be placed on or about the demised premises by such other agent without any liability to Lessee or to said agent, the Lessee assuming all responsibility for such action.

Lessor's Rights 11. Lessee covenants and agrees that Lessor shall have the right to do the following things and matters in and about the demised premises:

Inspection of Premises (a) At all reasonable times by himself or his duly authorized agents to go upon and inspect the demised premises and every part thereof, and/or at his option to make repairs, alterations and additions to the demised premises or the building of which the demised premises is a part.

Rules and Regulations (b) At any time or times and from time to time to make such rules and regulations as in his judgment may from time to time be necessary for the safety, care and cleanliness of the premises, and for the preservation of good order therein. Such rules and regulations shall, when notice thereof is given to Lessee, form a part of this lease.

Sale, Rent, Signs and Prospects (11-74) (c) To display a "For Sale" sign at any time, and also, after notice from either party of intention to determine this lease, or at any time within six months prior to the expiration of his lease, a "For Rent" sign, or both "For Rent" and "For Sale" signs; and all of said signs shall be placed upon such part of the premises as Lessor may elect and may contain such matter as Lessor shall require. Prospective purchasers or tenants authorized by Lessor may inspect the premises Monday thru Saturday between the hours of 11:00 AM and 8:00 PM.

Discontinue Service, etc. (d) The Lessor may discontinue all facilities furnished and services rendered by Lessor or any of them, not expressly covenanted for herein, it being understood that they constitute no part of the consideration for this lease.

12. (a) In the event that the demised premises is totally destroyed or so damaged by fire or other casualty not occurring through fault or negligence of the Lessee or those employed by or acting for him, that the same cannot be repaired or restored within a reasonable time, this lease shall absolutely cease and determine, and the rent shall abate for the balance of the term.

(b) If the damage caused as above be only partial and such that the premises can be restored to their former condition within a reasonable time, the Lessor may, at his option, restore the same with reasonable promptness, reserving the right to enter upon the demised premises for that purpose. The Lessor also reserves the right to enter upon the demised premises whenever necessary to repair damage caused by fire or other casualty to the building of which the demised premises is a part, even though the effect of such entry be to render the demised premises or a part thereof untenantable. In either event the rent shall be apportioned and suspended during the time the Lessor is in possession, taking into account the proportion of the demised premises rendered untenantable and the duration of the Lessor's possession. If a dispute arises as to the amount of rent due under this clause, Lessee agrees to pay the full amount claimed by Lessor. Lessee shall, however, have the right to proceed by law to recover the excess payment, if any.

Damage for Interrupted Use (c) Lessor shall not be liable for any damage, compensation or claim by reason of inconvenience or annoyance arising from the necessity of repairing any portion of the building, the interruption in the use of the premises, or the termination of this lease by reason of the destruction of the premises.

Representation of Condition 13. The Lessor has let the demised premises in their present condition and without any representations on the part of the Lessor, his officers, employees, servants and/or agents. It is understood and agreed that Lessor is under no duty to make repairs or alterations at the time of letting or at any time thereafter.

Miscellaneous Agreements and Conditions

Effect of Repairs or Rentals 14. (a) No contract entered into or that may be subsequently entered into by Lessor with Lessee, relative to any alterations, additions, improvements or repairs, nor the failure of Lessor to make such alterations, additions, improvements or repairs as required by any such contract, nor the making by Lessor or his agents or contractors of such alterations, additions, improvements or repairs shall in any way affect the payment of the rent or said other charges at the time specified in this lease.

Waiver of Custom (b) It is hereby covenanted and agreed, any law, usage or custom to the contrary notwithstanding, that Lessor shall have the right at all times to enforce the covenants and provisions of this lease in strict accordance with the terms hereof, notwithstanding any conduct or custom on the part of the Lessor in refraining from so doing at any time or times; and further, that the failure of Lessor at any time or times to enforce its rights under said covenants and provisions strictly in accordance with the same shall not be construed as having created a custom in any way or manner contrary to the specific terms, provisions and covenants of this lease or as having in any way or manner modified the same.

Conduct of Lessee (c) This lease is granted upon the express condition that Lessee and/or the occupants of the premises herein leased, shall not conduct themselves in a manner which the Lessor in his sole opinion may deem improper or objectionable, and that if at any time during the term of this lease or any extension or continuation thereof, Lessee or any occupier of the said premises shall have conducted himself, herself or themselves in a manner which Lessor in his sole opinion deems improper or objectionable, Lessee shall be taken to have broken the covenants and conditions of this lease, and Lessor will be entitled to all of the rights and remedies granted and reserved herein, for the Lessee's failure to observe any of the covenants and conditions of this lease.

Failure of Lessee to Repair (d) In the event of the failure of Lessee promptly to perform the covenants of Par. #8. (c) hereof, Lessor may go upon the demised premises and perform such covenants, the cost thereof, at the sole option of Lessor, to be charged to Lessee as additional and delinquent rent.

Remedies of Lessor (11-74) 15. If the Lessee

(a) Does not pay in full when due any and all installments of rent and/or any other charge or payment herein reserved, included, or agreed to be treated or collected as rent and/or any other charge, expense, or cost herein agreed to be paid by the Lessee; or

(b) Violates or fails to perform or otherwise breaks any covenant or agreement herein contained; or

(c) Vacates the demised premises or removes or attempts to remove or manifests an intention to remove any goods or property therefrom otherwise than in the ordinary and usual course of business without having first paid and satisfied the Lessor in full for all rent and other charges then due or that may thereafter become due until the expiration of the then current term, above mentioned; or

(d) Becomes embarrassed or insolvent, or makes an assignment for the benefit of creditors, or if a petition in bankruptcy is filed by or against the Lessee or a bill in equity or other proceeding for the appointment of a receiver for the Lessee is filed, or if proceedings for reorganization or for composition with creditors under any State or Federal law be instituted by or against Lessee, or if the real or personal property of the Lessee shall be sold or levied upon by any due process of law, then and in any or either of said events, there shall be deemed to be a breach of this lease, and thereupon ipso facto and without entry or other action by Lessor;

(d1) The rent for the entire unexpired balance of the term of this lease, as well as all other charges, payments, costs and expenses herein agreed to be paid by the Lessee, or at the option of Lessor any part thereof, and also all costs and officers' commissions including watchmen's wages and further including the five percent chargeable by Act of Assembly to the Lessor, shall, in addition to any and all installments of rent already due and payable and in arrears and/or any other charge or payment herein reserved, included or agreed to be treated or collected as rent, and/or any other charge, expense or cost herein agreed to be paid by the Lessee which may be due and payable and in arrears, be taken to be due and payable and in arrears as if by the terms and provisions of this lease, the whole balance of unpaid rent and other charges, payments, taxes, costs and expenses were on that date payable in advance; and if this lease or any part thereof is assigned, or if the premises or any part thereof is sub-let, Lessee hereby irrevocably constitutes and appoints Lessor Lessee's agent to collect the rents due by such assignee or sub-leasee and apply the same to the rent due hereunder without in any way affecting Lessee's obligation to pay any unpaid balance of rent due hereunder; or in the event of any of the foregoing at any time at the option of Lessor;

(d2) This lease and the term hereby created shall determine and become absolutely void without any right on the part of the Lessee to save the forfeiture by payment of any sum due or by other performance of any condition; term or covenant broken; whereupon, Lessor shall be entitled to recover damages for such breach in an amount equal to the amount of rent reserved for the balance of the term of this lease, less the fair rental value of the said demised premises, for the residue of said term.

16. In the event of any default as aforesaid, the Lessor, or anyone acting on Lessor's behalf, at Lessor's option:

Further Remedies of Lessor (a) May without notice or demand enter the demised premises, breaking open locked doors if necessary to effect entrance, without liability to action for prosecution or damages for such entry or for the matter thereof, for the purpose of distraining or levying and for any other purposes, and take possession of and sell all goods and chattels at auction, on three days notice served in person on the Lessee, or left on the premises, and pay the said Lessor out of the proceeds, and even if the rent be not due and unpaid, should the Lessee at any time remove or attempt to remove goods and chattels from the premises without leaving enough thereon to meet the next periodical payment, Lessee authorizes the Lessor to follow for a period of ninety days after such removal, take possession of and sell at auction, upon like notice, sufficient of such goods to meet the proportion of rent accrued at the time of such removal; and the Lessee hereby releases and discharges the Lessor, and

Continued.

Example 10-1 Standard Lease *continued*

his agents from all claims, actions, suits, damages and penalties, for or by reason or on account of any entry, distraint, levy, appraisement or sale; and/or

(b) May enter the premises, and without demand proceed by distress and sale of the goods there found to levy the rent and/or other charges herein payable as rent, and all costs and officers' commissions, including watchmen's wages and sums chargeable to Lessor, and further including a sum equal to 5% of the amount of the levy as commissions to the constable or other person making the levy, shall be paid by the Lessee, and in such case all costs, officers' commission and other charges shall immediately attach and become part of the claim of Lessor for rent, and any tender of rent without said costs commission and charges made after the issue of a warrant of distress shall not be sufficient to satisfy the claim of the Lessor. Lessee hereby expressly waivers in favor of Lessor the benefit of all laws now made or which may hereafter be made regarding any limitation as to the goods upon which, or the time within which, distress is to be made after removal of goods, and further relieves the Lessor of the obligations of proving or identifying such goods, it being the purpose and intent of this provision that all goods of Lessee, whether upon the demised premises or not, shall be liable to distress for rent. Lessee waives in favor of Lessor all rights under the Act of Assembly of April 6, 1951, P.L. 69, and all supplements and amendments thereto that have been or may hereafter be passed, and authorizes the sale of any goods distrained for rent at any time after five days from said distraint without any appraisement and/or condemnation thereof. The Lessee further waives the right to issue a Writ of Replevin under the Pennsylvania Rules of Civil Procedure, No. 1071 &c. and Laws of the Commonwealth of Pennsylvania, or under any other law previously enacted and now in force, or which may be hereafter enacted, for the recovery of any articles, household goods, furniture, etc., seized under a distress for rent or levy upon an execution for rent, damages or otherwise; all waivers hereinbefore mentioned are hereby extended to apply to any such action; and/or

(c) May lease said premises or any part or parts thereof to such person or persons as may in Lessor's discretion seem best and the Lessee shall be liable for any loss of rent for the balance of the then current term.

(d) Any re-entry or re-letting by Lessor under the terms hereof shall be without prejudice to Lessor's claim for damages and shall under no circumstances release Lessee from liability for such damages arising out of the breach of any of the covenants, terms and conditions of this lease.

Zoning

17. It is understood and agreed that the Lessor hereof does not warrant or undertake that the Lessee shall be able to obtain a permit under any Zoning Ordinance or Regulation for such use as Lessee intends to make of the said premises, and nothing in this lease contained shall obligate the Lessor to assist Lessee in obtaining said permit; the Lessee further agrees that in the event a permit cannot be obtained by Lessee under any Zoning Ordinance, or Regulation, this lease shall not terminate without Lessor's consent, and the Lessee shall use the premises only in a manner permitted under such Zoning Ordinance or Regulation.

Responsibility of Lessee (11-74)

18. Lessee agrees to be responsible for and to relieve and hereby relieves the Lessor from all liability by reason of any injury or damage to any person or property in the demised premises, whether belonging to the Lessee or any other person, caused by any fire, breakage or leakage in any part or portion of the demised premises, or any part or portion of the building of which the demised premises is a part, or from water, rain or snow that may leak into, issue or flow from any part of the said premises, or of the building of which the demised premises is a part, from the drains, pipes, or plumbing work of the same, or from any place or quarter, whether such breakage, leakage, injury or damage be caused by or result from the negligence of Lessor or his servants or agents or any person or persons whatsoever.

Additional Responsibility of Lessee (11-74)

19. Lessee also agrees to be responsible for and to relieve and hereby relieves Lessor from all liability by reason of any damage or injury to any person or thing which may arise from or be due to the use, misuse or abuse of all or any of the elevators, hatches, openings, stairways, hallways of any kind whatsoever which may exist or hereafter be erected or constructed on the said premises, or from any kind of injury which may arise from any other cause whatsoever on the said premises or the building of which the demised premises is a part, whether such damage, injury, use, misuse or abuse be caused by or result from the negligence of Lessor, his servants or agents or any other person or persons whatsoever.

Confession of Judgment

20. If rent and/or charges hereby reserved as rent shall remain unpaid on any day when the same should be paid Lessee hereby empowers any Prothonotary or attorney of any Court of Record to appear for Lessee in any and all actions which may be brought for rent and/or the charges, payments, costs and expenses reserved as rent, or agreed to be paid by the Lessee and/or to sign for Lessee an agreement for entering in any competent Court an amicable action or actions for the recovery of rent or other charges or expenses, and in said suits or in said amicable action or actions to confess judgment against Lessee for all or any part of the rent specified in this lease and then unpaid including, at Lessor's option, the rent for the entire unexpired balance of the term of this lease, and/or other charges, payments, costs and expenses reserved as rent or agreed to be paid by the Lessee, and for interest and costs together with an attorney's commission of 15%. Such authority shall not be exhausted by one exercise thereof, but judgment may be confessed as aforesaid from time to time as often as any of said rent and/or other charges reserved as rent shall fall due or be in arrears, and such powers may be exercised as well after the expiration of the original term and/or during any extension or renewal of this lease.

Ejectment

21. When this lease shall be determined by condition broken, either during the original term of this lease or any renewal or extension thereof, and also when and as soon as the term hereby created or any extension thereof shall have expired, it shall be lawful for any attorney as attorney for Lessee to file an agreement for entering in any competent Court an amicable action and judgment in ejection against Lessee and all persons claiming under Lessee for the recovery by Lessor of possession of the herein demised premises, for which this lease shall be his sufficient warrant, whereupon, if Lessor so desires, a writ of habere facias possessionem may issue forthwith, without any prior writ or proceedings whatsoever, and provided that if for any reason after such action shall have been commenced the same shall be determined and the possession of the premises hereby demised remain in or be restored to Lessee. Lessor shall have the right upon any subsequent default or defaults, or upon the termination of this lease as hereinbefore set forth, to bring one or more amicable action or actions as hereinbefore set forth to recover possession of the said premises.

Affidavit of Default

22. In any amicable action of ejectment and/or for rent in arrears, Lessor shall first cause to be filed in such action an affidavit made by him or someone acting for him setting forth the facts necessary to authorize the entry of judgment, of which facts such affidavit shall be conclusive evidence, and if a true copy of this lease (and of the truth of the copy such affidavit shall be sufficient evidence) be filed in such action, it shall not be necessary to file the original as a warrant of attorney, any rule of Court, custom or practice to the contrary notwithstanding.

Waivers by Lessee of Errors, Right of Appeal, Stay, Exemption Inquisition

23. Lessee expressly agrees that any judgment, order or decree entered against him by or in any Court or Magistrate by virtue of the powers of attorney contained in this lease, or otherwise, shall be final, and that he will not take an appeal, certiorari, writ of error, exception or objection to the same, or file a motion or rule to strike off or open or to stay execution of the same, and releases to Lessor and to any and all attorneys who may appear for Lessee all errors in the said proceedings, and all liability therefor. Lessee expressly waives the benefits of all laws, now or hereafter in force, exempting any goods on the demised premises, or elsewhere from distraint, levy or sale in any legal proceedings taken by the Lessor to enforce any rights under this lease. Lessee further waives the right of inquisition on any real estate that may be levied upon to collect any amount which may become due under the terms and conditions of this lease, and does hereby voluntarily condemn the same and authorizes the Prothonotary to enter a fieri facias or other process upon Lessee's voluntary condemnation, and further agrees that the said real estate may be sold on a fieri facias or other process. If proceedings shall be commenced by Lessor to recover possession under the Acts of Assembly, either at the end of the term or sooner termination of this lease, or for nonpayment of rent or any other reason, Lessee specifically waives the right to the three months notice and/or the fifteen or thirty days notice required by the Act of April 6, 1951, P.L. 69, and agrees that five days notice shall be sufficient in either or any such case.

Right of Assignee of Lessor

24. The right to enter judgment against Lessee and to enforce all of the other provisions of this lease hereinabove provided for may, at the option of any assignee of this lease, be exercised by any assignee of the Lessor's right, title and interest in this lease in his, her or their own name, notwithstanding the fact that any of all assignments of the said right, title and interest may not be executed and/or witnessed in accordance with the Act of Assembly of May 28, 1715, I Sm. L. 99, and all supplements and amendments thereto that have been or may hereafter be passed and Lessee hereby expressly waives the requirements of said Act of Assembly and any and all laws regulating the manner and/or form in which such assignments shall be executed and witnessed.

Remedies Cumulative

25. All of the remedies hereinbefore given to Lessor and all rights and remedies given to it by law and equity shall be cumulative and concurrent. No determination of this lease or the taking or recovering of the premises shall deprive Lessor of any of its remedies or action against the Lessee for rent due at the time or which, under the terms hereof, would in the future become due as if there has been no determination, or for sums due at the time or which, under the terms hereof, would in the future become due as if there had been no determination, nor shall the bringing of any action for rent or breach of covenant, or the resort to any other remedy herein provided for the recovery of rent be construed as a waiver of the right to obtain possession of the premises.

Subordination

26. This Agreement of Lease and all of its terms, covenants, and provisions are and each of them is subject and subordinate to any lease or other arrangement or right to possession, under which the Lessor is in control of the demised premises, to the rights of the owner or owners of the demised premises and of the land or buildings of which the demised premises are a part to all rights of the Lessor's landlord and to any and all mortgages and other encumbrances now or hereafter placed upon the demised premises or upon the land and/or the buildings containing the same; and Lessee expressly agrees that if Lessor's tenancy, control, or right to possession shall terminate either by expiration, forfeiture or otherwise, then this lease shall thereupon immediately terminate and the Lessee shall, thereupon, give immediate possession and Lessee hereby waives any and all claims for damages or otherwise by reason of such termination as aforesaid.

Condemnation

27. In the event that the premises demised or any part thereof is taken or condemned for a public or quasi-public use, this lease shall, as to the part so taken, terminate as of the date title shall vest in the condemnor, and rent shall abate in proportion to the square feet of leased space taken or condemned or shall cease if the entire premises be so taken. In either event the Lessee waives all claims against the Lessor by reason of the complete or partial taking of the demised premises, and it is agreed that the Lessee shall not be entitled to any notice whatsoever of the partial or complete termination of this lease by reason of the aforesaid.

Termination of Lease

28. It is hereby mutually agreed that either party hereto may determine this lease at the end of said term by giving to the other party prior written notice thereof in accordance with paragraph #1 (l), but in default of such notice, this lease shall continue upon the same terms and conditions in force immediately prior to the expiration or the term hereof as are herein contained for a further period as specified in paragraph #1 (m), and so on from renewal term to renewal term unless or until terminated by either party hereto, giving the other the aforementioned written notice for removal previous to expiration of the then current term; PROVIDED, however, that should this lease be continued for a further period under the terms hereinabove mentioned, any allowance given Lessee on the rent during the original term should not extend beyond such original term, and further provided, however, that if Lessor shall have given such written notice prior to the expiration of any term hereby created, of its intention to change the terms and conditions of this lease, and Lessee shall not within thirty days from such notice notify Lessor of Lessee's intention to vacate the demised premises at the end of the then current term, Lessee shall be considered as Lessee under the terms and conditions mentioned in such notice for a further term as above provided, or for such further term as may be stated in such notice. In the event that Lessee shall give notice, as stipulated in this lease, of intention to vacate the demised premises at the end of the present term, or any renewal or extension thereof, and shall fail or refuse so to vacate the same on the date designated by such notice, then it is expressly agreed that Lessor shall have the option either (a) to disregard the notice so given as having no effect, in which case all the terms and conditions of this lease shall continue thereafter with full force precisely as if such notice had not been given, or (b) Lessor may, at any time within thirty days after the present term or any renewal or extension thereof, as aforesaid, give the said Lessee ten days written

notice of his intention to terminate the said lease; whereupon the Lessee expressly agrees to vacate said premises at the expiration of the said period of ten days specified in said notice. All powers granted to Lessor by this lease may be exercised and all obligations imposed upon Lessee by this lease shall be performed by Lessee as well during any extension of the original term of this lease as during the original term itself.

Inability to give Possession

29. If Lessor is unable to give Lessee possession of the demised premises, as herein provided, by reason of the holding over of a previous occupant, or by reason of any cause beyond the control of the Lessor, the Lessor shall not be liable in damages to the Lessee therefor, and during the period that the Lessor is unable to give possession, all rights and remedies of both parties hereunder shall be suspended.

Additional Rent

30. Lessee agrees to pay as additional rent any and all sums which may become due by reason of the failure of Lessee to comply with any of the covenants of this lease and any and all damages, costs and expenses which the Lessor may suffer or incur by reason of any default of the Lessee or failure on his part to comply with the covenants of this lease, and also any and all damages to the demised premises caused by any act or neglect of the Lessee, his guests, agents, employees or other occupants of the demised premises.

Notices

31. All notices required to be given by Lessor to Lessee shall be sufficiently given by leaving the same upon the demised premises, but notices given by Lessee to Lessor must be given by certified mail, and as against Lessor the only admissable evidence that notice has been given by Lessee shall be a certified return receipt signed by Lessor or his agent.

Right to Enforce

32. The Lessor shall have the right, at all times, to enforce any or all the covenants and provisions of this lease, notwithstanding the failure of the Lessor at any previous time, or times, to enforce his rights under any of the covenants and provisions of this lease.

Definition of Lessor and Lessee

33. The word "Lessor" as used herein, shall include the Owner and the Landlord, whether Person, Firm or Corporation, as well as the Heirs, Executors, Administrators, Successors and Assigns each of whom shall have the same rights, remedies, powers, privileges and obligations as though he, she, it or they had originally signed this lease as Lessor, including the right to proceed in his, her, its, or their own name to enter judgment by confession, or otherwise. The word "Lessee" as used herein, shall include the Tenant, whether Person, Firm or Corporation, as well as the Heirs, Executors, Administrators, Successors and Assigns, each of whom shall have the same rights, remedies, powers, privileges, and shall have no other liabilities, rights, privileges or powers than he, she, it or they would have been under or possessed had he, she, it or they originally signed this lease as Lessee.

Agent

34. It is expressly understood and agreed between the parties hereto that the herein named agent, his salesmen and employees or any officer or partner of agent and any cooperating broker and his salesmen and employees and any officer or partner of the cooperating broker are acting as agent only and will in no case whatsoever be held liable either jointly or severally to either party for the performance of any term of covenant of this agreement or for damages for the nonperformance thereof.

Heirs and Assignees

35. All rights and liabilities herein given to, or imposed upon, or waivers of the respective parties hereto shall extend to and bind the several and respective heirs, executors, administrators, successors and assigns of said parties; and if there shall be more than one Lessee, they shall all be bound jointly and severally by the terms, covenants and agreements herein, and the word "Lessee" shall be deemed and taken to mean each and every person or party mentioned as a Lessee herein, be the same one or more; and if there shall be more than one Lessee, any notice required or permitted by the terms of this lease may be given by or to any one thereof, and shall have the same force and effect as if given by or to all thereof. No rights, however, shall inure to the benefit of any assignee of Lessee unless the assignment of such assignee has been approved by Lessor in writing as aforesaid.

Lease Contains Entire Agreement

36. The Lessor and Lessee hereby agree that this lease sets forth all the promises, agreements, conditions and understandings between the Lessor, or his Agent, and the Lessee relative to the demised premises, and that there are no promises, agreements, conditions or understandings, either oral or written, between them other than as are herein set forth, and any subsequent alteration, amendment, change or addition to this lease shall not be binding upon the Lessor or Lessee unless reduced to writing and signed by them.

Severability (11-74)

37. If any section, subsection, sentence, clause phrase or requirement of this lease is contrary to law or laws subsequently enacted, or should be found contrary to laws during the term or any renewal or extension thereof, the validity of the remaining portions shall not be affected thereby. The parties hereby agree that they would have agreed to each section, subsection, clause sentence, phrase or requirement herein irrespective of the fact that one or more section, subsection sentence, clause, phrase or requirement was contrary to law or during the term or any renewal or extension thereof or are found to be contrary to the law.

Descriptive Heading

38. The descriptive headings used herein are for convenience only and they are not intended to indicate all of the matter in the sections which follow them. Accordingly, they shall have no effect whatsoever in determing the rights or obligations of the parties.

Approval (1-78)

IN WITNESS WHEREOF, the parties hereto, including to be legally bound hereby, have hereunder set their hands and seals the day and year first above written.

WITNESS AS
TO LESSEE .... LESSEE .... (SEAL)

WITNESS AS
TO LESSEE .... LESSEE .... (SEAL)

LESSEE .... (SEAL)

The Lessor hereby approves this contract on this .... day of .... 19 .... and in consideration of the services rendered in procuring the herein named Lessee and/or collection of rents as agreed and specified in part one of this lease, the Lessor agrees to pay the herein named agent a fee and/or commission in the amount of $ .... for obtaining Lessee together with a commission of ....% for the collection of rents during the term, renewal or extention of this lease or additional lease with the herein named Lessee. Should the Lessee purchase the demised premises from the Lessor during the term of this lease, or during a renewal, extention or any additional lease between said parties for the demised premises, or within a reasonable period of time after the expiration of any such lease, the Lessor agrees to pay to the agent, at the time of settlement, a sales commission of ....% based on the purchase price.

WITNESS AS
TO LESSOR .... LESSOR .... (SEAL)

WITNESS AS
TO LESSOR .... LESSOR .... (SEAL)

AGENT BY ....

Chapter 11

Condominiums, Planned-Unit Developments, and Cooperatives

I. INTRODUCTION

Since the 1960s, the United States has witnessed the growth of residential, commercial, office, and industrial development projects that have combined, often in creative ways, traditional forms of ownership. These development projects usually involve the exclusive ownership of those portions of the project that benefit individual owners (such as an apartment, a store, or an office) along with joint ownership of other portions of the project that benefit the entire project (such as recreational facilities, parking lots, and open areas). Some of the more predominant methods of creative development include the use of condominiums, planned-unit developments, and cooperatives, or a combination of some or all of these methods. Each of these methods has its own unique structure and set of legal documents creating the structure. The discussion that follows is intended to familiarize the real estate legal assistant with these differing structures and documents.

II. CONDOMINIUMS

The term "condominium" is derived from Latin and means "owning together." In a condominium the owner of a unit (referred to as a "unit owner") is the sole owner of that portion of the building that encloses his or her unit. At the same time the unit owner is one of many co-owners or tenants-in-common of the common facilities that service all units and the common areas that may be used and enjoyed by all unit owners. It is this coupling of exclusive ownership of a unit with shared ownership of the common elements that distinguishes condominium ownership from other forms of property ownership.

Common facilities and common areas that are not part of a unit are known as "common elements." In certain cases such common facilities and common areas benefit less than all of the unit owners, and are known as "limited common elements." Common elements may include the land, structural components of the building, utility systems, lobbies, and halls; limited common elements may include individual parking spaces, storage spaces, balconies, porches, and gardens. Limited common elements entitle a particular unit owner to the exclusive right to use each limited common element that is appurtenant to such owner's unit. In the event that a limited common element is appurtenant to more than one unit, each owner of a unit to which that limited common element is appurtenant has the right to use that limited common element jointly with the other owners of those units, but to the exclusion of all other unit owners.

The undivided ownership interest of each individual unit owner in the common elements is referred to as a "percentage interest" and is expressed in the form of a percentage or decimal. The ownership of this percentage interest gives each unit owner the right to use the common elements and to participate in the control of the common elements through membership in an association of all unit owners (usually referred to as a "condominium association" or a "unit owners' association"). The ownership of this percentage interest also imposes on each unit owner the obligation to pay a percentage of the expenses of operating and maintaining the common elements.

For simplicity and ease of reference, we will discuss primarily residential condominiums, which are by far the most common form of condominiums in the United States at this time. It is important to realize, however, that most of the discussion in this chapter is equally applicable to commercial, office, and industrial condominiums, such as shopping centers, office buildings, and factories.

A. THE LEGAL BASIS OF CONDOMINIUM OWNERSHIP

The condominium concept is an ancient one, originating in Rome and commonly used for many years in Europe. When the concept was imported to the United States in the early 1960s, many lawyers believed that the common law provided the necessary tools to organize and govern condominiums and that no additional legislation was required. There were, however, substantial areas of doubt that caused various state legislatures to pass statutes authorizing the creation of condominiums and setting forth the requirements, rights, and obligations of condominium ownership. There is little uniformity among these statutes, and in analyzing the legal aspects of any condominium project one must consult the statute of the state in which the condominium is located. The Uniform Condominium Act, however, which was approved by the National Conference of Commissioners on Uniform State Laws in 1977, has been adopted by several states to date and probably will be adopted by many other states in the near future. The Uniform Condominium Act contains certain provisions that are common to virtually all state condominium laws and therefore will serve as the basis for our discussion of condominiums.

A number of documents create and govern the operation of a condominium. Under the Uniform Condominium Act, these documents include the declaration, the bylaws, the rules and regulations, and the public offering statement, which are commonly referred to collectively as the "condominium documents." There is also a deed to each unit and various agreements affecting the day-to-day operations of the condominium. The following is a summary of the principal documents relating to a condominium.

1. Declaration

The declaration of condominium (also known as a "master deed") is the document that creates the condominium. It is executed by the owner of the property on which the condominium is to be created, which in most cases is the developer of the condominium (commonly referred to as the "declarant"). The declaration sets forth the basic rights and obligations of the unit owners, as well as their tenants and mortgagees. Because the declaration is recorded in a place of public record, each unit owner, and each tenant and mortgagee of a unit, is charged with knowledge of the contents of the recorded declaration (even if it has not been read by such party) and each is bound to comply with its terms to the extent applicable. The declaration usually includes the following:

(a) General Information

The declaration usually begins with a description of the property. This will include not only a metes and bounds description such as one would expect to find in a deed, but also a rather full description of any building on the property, including permanent fixtures such as heating and cooling systems, elevators, and the like. The declaration will also set forth the various unit designations (e.g., Unit 101, 201, etc.) and will contain any restrictions placed on the use of units, common elements, and limited common elements (e.g., a specified type of window covering might be required in each unit).

(b) Description of Units

The declaration will provide a definition of what constitutes a unit and what constitutes the common elements and limited common elements. The definition is usually precise. A unit may include, for example, only the interior space from the unit-side surface of walls and ceilings. Anything that is near the boundaries of the unit (such as windows, door frames, subfloors, plumbing, and the like) must be defined as either a part of the unit, a common element, or a limited common element. The title lines of a unit establish that all portions of the unit contained within those lines are owned by the unit owner. The unit owner has sole responsibility for the maintenance, repair, and replacement of all portions of his or her unit, and for the payment of real estate taxes assessed against such unit.

(c) Common Expenses and Limited Common Expenses

The declaration will specify the percentage interest in the common elements that is allocable to each unit and, if different, the percentage share of common expenses that must be borne by the owner of that unit (referred to as the unit owner's "common expense liability"). Common expenses are defined in the declaration to include the cost of operating and maintaining the common elements and the administrative costs of the unit owners' association. Common expenses also include real estate taxes on the condominium property, and each unit owner (as a tenant-in-common of such property) may take a tax deduction for that portion of the unit owner's common expense liability attributable to the payment of real estate taxes. The declaration usually provides for a special assessment of common expense liability in the event that there are additional common expenses not provided for in the annual budget of the unit owners' association.[1] Limited common expenses are also defined in the declaration and are usually broken down into the cost of operating and maintaining each limited common element. Limited common expenses are allocated to a unit in proportion to such unit's interest in a particular limited common element.

(d) Managing Body

The declaration also provides for the establishment of a managing body. Under the Uniform Condominium Act, the managing body is an executive board elected by a unit owners' association composed of all unit owners. Other managing bodies include condominium councils, boards of managers, and boards of directors, each selected in the manner set forth in applicable statutes and in the bylaws of the respective condominiums. Some functions of the executive board include the preparation and adoption of a budget and the assessment of common expenses against individual owners. Although the executive board is responsible for the overall management and operation of the condominium, as a practical matter the condominium association usually engages a professional managing agent to assume the day-to-day managerial responsibilities of the condominium.

---

1. An unanticipated capital repair, such as replacing the elevator system, is one example of what might necessitate a special assessment of common expense liability. Another example is the occurrence of an accident on any of the common elements. Because the common elements are owned by all unit owners as tenants-in-common, each unit owner is liable for such owner's pro rata share of any uninsured liability with respect to the common elements.

(e) Plans

Generally, a set of plans prepared by an architect or engineer either accompanies or is included in the declaration. The plans depict the perimeter of the property and the layout of each floor and each unit and of the common elements and limited common elements. These plans are similar to a survey; they are a graphic two-dimensional representation of the verbal description of the units, common elements, and limited common elements.

2. Articles of Incorporation

If the unit owners' association is a corporation, articles of incorporation meeting the particular state's corporation laws must be properly filed and the corporation must be duly organized.

3. Bylaws or Code of Regulations

The bylaws of the unit owners' association set forth procedures for the administration of its affairs in the same manner as do the bylaws of a business corporation. Some of the items normally covered in the bylaws include the following:

(a) the membership rights of all unit owners in the unit owners' association;

(b) the time and place of regular meetings of the unit owners, and quorum and voting procedures at such meetings;

(c) the number and qualifications of members of the executive board, their terms of office, and the time and place of their meetings;

(d) the election of officers, their qualifications, and terms of office;

(e) the method of determining and assessing common expenses and limited common expenses;

(f) procedures for the collection of delinquent assessments;

(g) restrictions on the use of the units, common elements, and limited common elements;

(h) procedures for the maintenance and repair of the common elements;

(i) restrictions, if any, on additions, alterations, and improvements to a unit;

(j) the type and amount of insurance and the application of insurance proceeds;

(k) restrictions, if any, on the sale, leasing, and mortgaging of units; and

(l) books and records and other managerial matters.

4. Rules and Regulations

The board may from time to time promulgate rules and regulations governing the details of the use and operation of the units, the common elements, and the limited common elements. The rules and regulations are normally kept at the office of the unit owners' association at the condominium.

5. Public Offering Statement

Under the Uniform Condominium Act, the public offering statement must be furnished by the declarant to all prospective purchasers of condominium units. The public offering statement is intended to disclose to the prospective purchaser all significant features of the condominium, including:

(a) the name and principal address of the declarant;

(b) a general description of the condominium;

(c) the purchase price and common expense liability of each unit;

(d) information concerning the management of the condominium;

(e) the events on which the declarant must relinquish control of the executive board to the unit owners (discussed in the next section of this chapter);

(f) any encumbrances on title to and any litigation involving the condominium property;

(g) the amount of any payment required to be made by the initial purchase of each unit to provide working capital for the unit owners' association (usually a nonrefundable payment in the amount of two times the unit's common expense liability); and

(h) warranties provided by the declarant respecting the units, common elements, and limited common elements (the declarant is required to provide certain minimum warranties under the Uniform Condominium Act).

The public offering statement consists of several parts. The first part is a narrative that summarizes the significant features of the condominium and presents additional information of interest to prospective purchasers. The other parts contain the proposed declaration, the proposed bylaws, the form of agreement of sale for the individual units, the projected budget for the first year of operation of the condominium, a schedule of each unit's monthly assessment of common expense liability, and an architect's report describing the condition, useful life, and replacement cost of the structural components of the building comprising the condominium.

In the event that the declarant failed to deliver a public offering statement to a purchaser before the execution of an agreement of sale, the Uniform Condominium Act grants a right of recision for fifteen days after the purchaser has received the public offering statement. Purchasers who have gone to settlement without having received a public offering statement are permitted damages in an amount equal to 5% of the sales price of the unit up to a maximum of $2,000 or actual damages, whichever is greater.

The Uniform Condominium Act has different disclosure requirements with respect to different types of condominiums, including a flexible condominium (which allows the declarant to add property to, or withdraw property from, the condominium), a time-share estate (which is an interest in a unit for a particular period of each year, such as the first two weeks of April, in which title to the unit rotates among the time-share owners of the unit according to their respective periods of ownership), and a conversion condominium (which is created by converting an existing rental apartment building into a condominium).

6. Management Contract

In order to ensure the success of the condominium, and in some cases to earn management fees, the declarant often desires to remain in charge of management until all units are sold and for some time thereafter. The Uniform Condominium Act, however, requires that the declarant relinquish some control over the executive board upon the sale of a specified number of units,[2] and total control over the executive board upon the sale of 75% of the units (but in any event within seven years of the recording of the declaration).

On the other hand, purchasers are generally eager to have the declarant remain with the condominium at least for a limited amount of time to ensure the continuity of mangement. This is particularly true in the case of conversion condominiums. In such cases the unit owners' association will normally enter into a contract with the declarant pursuant to which the declarant will agree to perform normal management functions, such as billing and collecting the monthly assession of common expense liability, hiring and supervising employees, and overseeing maintenance and repairs. The contract should be for a specific period of time[3] and should stipulate the amount payable to the manager, the time or times at which payments are to be made, and the management functions to be performed.

B. FIRE INSURANCE

Fire insurance presents an unusual problem that merits special attention. In a condominium each owner has an interest in seeing that all portions of the building are covered by insurance and that the insurance proceeds will be available for repair or reconstruction in the event of damage or destruction. As a result, many high-rise condominiums obtain a single

---

2. Twenty-five percent of the executive board members must be elected by unit owners other than the declarant upon the sale of 25% of the units; 33⅓% of the executive board members must be elected by unit owners other than the declarant upon the sale of 50% of the units.

3. Under the Uniform Condominium Act the management agreement and any other agreement entered into by the unit owners' association during the period of declarant control must be terminable on ninety days' notice.

insurance policy naming all of the unit owners as insureds, with mortgagee clauses in favor of their respective mortgagees. The policy is held by the unit owners' association and the premiums are paid as a common expense. Insurance obtained for the whole building will not normally cover the contents of a unit against loss by fire or theft. Therefore, each unit owner will have to maintain insurance on the contents of his or her unit, and may also want to be insured separately for any major improvements made to the unit.

Many statutes and condominium documents provide that in the event the property is destroyed, the unit owners will decide collectively whether or not to rebuild the condominium. The Uniform Condominium Act specifies that the insurance proceeds must be used for reconstruction unless 80% of the unit owners vote not to rebuild. If the unit owners vote not to rebuild, the land and the remains of the building, if any, will be sold, and the proceeds of the sale plus the insurance proceeds will be allocated among the unit owners in accordance with their percentage interests in the common elements. The unit owners will then apply their share of the proceeds to the repayment of mortgages and other liens on their units and will retain any balance for their own use.

C. ASSISTING A CONDOMINIUM PURCHASER

In assisting a prospective purchaser of a unit in a condominium, there are several areas of concern to the purchaser's attorney and legal assistant.

1. The Condominium Documents

The condominium documents must be read with care to ascertain whether they will provide a practical, as well as a legally correct, set of procedures for the operation of the condominium. Particular attention should be paid to the voting rights of the unit owners (especially with respect to approval of the budget) and procedures for electing and removing the managing body. Procedures for establishing the budget and assessing and collecting common expense liability must be carefully considered to be sure that they are responsible and fair to the prospective purchaser and, at the same time, provide adequate means for assessing and collecting common expenses from all of the unit owners. Matters involving the relinquishment of declarant control over the unit owners' association, proposed management arrangements, and fire insurance issues should also be examined thoroughly.

The seller of a condominium unit should make copies of the currently effective condominium documents available to a prospective purchaser. In the event that the seller does not do so, the legal assistant should be able to obtain access to the currently effective condominium documents through the secretary of the unit owners' association. It is important to be sure that, if any of the condominium documents have been amended, all amendments and any other modifications or revisions have been reviewed.

PROBLEM

The seller of a condominium unit has misplaced her copy of the condominium documents and the secretary of the unit owners' association will not return your calls. How would you proceed to obtain a copy of the condominium documents for a prospective purchaser?

---

2. Common Expenses and Percentage Interests

In connection with common expenses, the purchaser will want to know what the estimated expenses will be, how and by whom the estimates have been prepared, and on what experience the estimates are based. The purchaser will also want to known on what basis the percentage interests in the common elements have been allocated; for example, whether all apartments of the same size and type have the same percentage interest in the common elements, whether percentage interests have been allocated on the basis of square footage, on the basis of the value of amenities within the apartment, or on some combination of these items. The purchaser will also want to know what guarantees, if any, the seller is prepared to make with respect to the common expenses. In some instances, the seller will agree to make good the difference between estimated common expenses and actual common expenses if actual expenses are higher than estimated. In other cases, as part of the seller's guarantee with respect to expenses, the seller will agree to buy back the apartment within a specified period (usually one or two years) at the same price as the original sale. Without such guarantees, or some reasonable assurance that the estimates are correct, the purchaser may find that the monthly charges are far in excess of what was originally anticipated. As previously discussed, the Uniform Condominium Act requires the declarant to disclose in the public offering statement the common expense liability of each unit, and the declarant is liable for any misrepresentation of this information.

According to the Uniform Condominium Act, the purchaser of a condominium unit is entitled to a certificate (entitled a "3407 Certificate") wherein the unit owners' association certifies, among other things, that all assessments imposed against the unit have been paid. A form of a 3407 certificate is reprinted at the end of this chapter.

3. Reserved Rights of the Declarant

The purchaser's counsel should also scrutinize the documents (especially the proposed agreement of sale) to be sure that the declarant has not reserved the right to amend the condominium documents after the purchaser has signed an agreement of sale, except for minor amendments that do not increase the liability or obligation of the purchaser or in any way adversely affect the purchaser or the unit to be purchased. Under no circumstances should the seller have the right to change the percentage interests in the common elements, because this could result in a substantial increase in the purchaser's common expense liability. Conversely, a reduction in the percentage interest could adversely affect the purchaser in the event of total destruction by fire because a unit owner's share of the insurance proceeds is based on such unit owner's percentage interest.

If the declarant has reserved the right to expand the condominium, the purchaser should be informed as to whether the declaration requires additional buildings to be architecturally and aesthetically similar to the existing condominium. The method for reallocation of the percentage interests on the expansion of the condominium must be examined to ensure that the prospective purchaser's percentage interest will not be disproportionately diluted. In addition, if the declarant has reserved the right to withdraw property or improvements from the condominium, the purchaser's counsel should ensure that such withdrawal will not affect the prospective purchaser's enjoyment of the condominium or the value of the unit to be purchased.

III. PLANNED-UNIT DEVELOPMENTS

Planned-unit developments ("PUDs") are often known by other names, such as "Planned Residential Developments," "Cluster Developments," "Subdivisions with Home Associations," and "Planned Communities." PUDs can take many different forms but in general consist of individual lots owned in fee by individual lot owners, and common areas owned either by a homeowners' association organized as a nonprofit corporation or an unincorporated association, or by a trustee in trust for the lot owners. Alternatively, the common areas may be retained by the developer and operated for profit.

If a development contemplates different uses of the property (such as residential, office, and commercial uses), the form of PUD development is usually structured in what are called "multiple tiers." Under such a scheme the highest tier imposes restrictions on the entire development and provides for the common ownership and administration of the "most common" of the common areas, such as roadways, storm water and sewer drainage systems, and open areas. The second or lower tiers may consist of various PUDs, condominiums, or cooperatives, each organized to own and administer the "less common" of the common areas, and each serving one neighborhood within the development.

The way in which the common areas are owned is the major factor that distinguishes a PUD from a condominium. Whereas the common areas of a condominium are owned by all of the lot owners as tenants-in-common, the common areas of a PUD are owned by a legal entity.

Consequently, the lot owners in a PUD are generally not liable for injuries occurring in the common areas (as are the unit owners in a condominium), except injuries resulting from a lot owner's individual negligence. Because the lot owners do not own the common areas, however, they do not recognize any tax advantages from the payment of real estate taxes for the common areas, as do the unit owners in a condominium.

A. THE LEGAL BASIS OF PUD OWNERSHIP

There is no uniform law controlling the formation and operation of PUDs. In fact, most states have not yet adopted comprehensive PUD statutes regulating the field in a manner comparable to the Uniform Condominium Act's regulation of its field. In one state, for example, the legislature has adopted enabling legislation permitting the governing body of each municipality to enact, amend, and repeal ordinances fixing standards and conditions for PUDs.

Although not statutorily prescribed, the legal documents that are used to form and govern PUDs are often similar to those used to form and govern condominiums, and typically include the following:

1. Declaration of Covenants, Restrictions, and Easements

A declaration of covenants, restrictions, and easements is a recorded document that creates a PUD with respect to a development. This document is characterized as a "covenant running with the land," which means that the rights and obligations contained in this document will continue to benefit and bind future owners of the property even though such future owners did not execute the document. The declaration of covenants, restrictions, and easements performs the same function as a declaration of condominium, and usually contains fairly similar provisions respecting the identification of individual lots and common areas, the allocation of costs in connection with the operation, maintenance and repair of the common areas and facilities, the establishment of a homeowners' association, and restrictions on the use of the lots and the common areas and facilities.

In a PUD declaration, easements over the common areas owned by the homeowners' association are granted to the lot owners for purposes of use and enjoyment. These easements are appurtenant to each lot, and therefore pass with title to each lot. In cases in which easements are granted over recreational facilities, such easements are often subject to the payment of reasonable admission and other fees. Similar easements are contained in a declaration of condominium, only those easements run to the benefit of the unit owners' association because title to the common elements is vested in the unit owners.

The declaration of covenants, easements, and restrictions for PUD projects involving new construction will usually establish an architectural control committee to oversee the development of individual lots and the common areas. The purpose of this committee is generally to ensure the harmonious and efficient development and maintenance of the PUD by requiring that certain improvements made to any lot or common area be subject to the prior approval of the architectural control committee.

2. Articles of Incorporation

If the homeowners' association that owns the common areas is a corporation, the corporation must be properly incorporated and duly organized, as in the case of a condominium unit owners' association formed as a corporation.

3. Bylaws

The bylaws of a homeowners' association govern the management and administration of the affairs of the homeowners' association and generally contain the same provisions as the bylaws of a condominium association.

4. Book of Resolutions

The book of resolutions contains the rules and regulations governing the PUD, as adopted from time to time by the board of directors of the homeowners' association. The book of resolutions is customarily kept on file at the PUD premises and, if the homeowners' association is a corporation, in the minute book of the homeowners' association.

B. ASSISTING A PUD PURCHASER

The same matters discussed in the previous section on condominiums should serve as the focus of attention when dealing with a prospective purchase of a lot in a PUD. Because there is often no disclosure material similar to the public offering statement, however, the PUD documents should be read with particular care.

IV. COOPERATIVE APARTMENTS

The concept of cooperative apartments ("co-ops") had its beginning in eighteenth-century France and made its way to England at the turn of the next century. The cooperative concept was introduced to the United States in New York City in the midnineteenth century but was not widely accepted until after World War II. Co-ops have become popular in certain cities (such as New York and Chicago) and are virtually nonexistent in others.

A co-op is distinguishable from both a condominium and a PUD. Unlike a unit owner in a condominium or a lot owner in a PUD, a person residing in a co-op holds stock in the cooperative corporation that owns the building, and leases an apartment from the corporation. A cooperative participant does not own the apartment because no fee interest is ever conveyed; the entire building is owned in fee by a corporation whose shareholders are made up of all residents in the building. The corporation leases to its shareholders apartments in the building under long-term leases (referred to as "proprietary leases" or "occupancy agreements"), and therefore each resident in a cooperative building is both a shareholder and a tenant of the cooperative corporation.

In a condominium or a PUD, real estate taxes are assessed directly against the individual unit or lot, and mortgages and other liens created by an owner encumber the individual unit or lot. When a unit owner or lot owner fails to make mortgage payments, the lending institution will foreclose on the unit or lot encumbered by the mortgage. This foreclosure does not affect other units or lots, nor does it affect the common elements in the condominium or PUD. In a co-op, however, real estate taxes are assessed against, and mortgages and other liens created by the cooperative corporation encumber, the entire cooperative building. Therefore, the failure of one cooperative member to pay such member's share of common expenses could cause the cooperative corporation to default under its mortgage, in which event the mortgagee would foreclose on the entire cooperative building. A co-op member might be forced to pay a portion or all of a delinquent co-op member's share of common expenses to avoid such foreclosure. This causes prospective co-op members to be fairly concerned about the track record and financial capabilities of existing members of the cooperative, and it also causes existing co-op members to select prospective members with care. Almost invariably the prospective co-op member is subject to approval by the board of directors, and frequently one of the qualifications for approval is that the prospective co-op member not finance the purchase of stock in the cooperative corporation.

A. THE LEGAL BASIS OF COOPERATIVE OWNERSHIP

A developer forms a cooperative by conveying to a cooperative corporation title to a newly constructed or existing building and to the land on which it is built. The right to lease a particular apartment in the co-op requires the purchase of a designated number of shares. Apartments are allocated differing numbers of shares, depending on the size, location, and desirability of the apartment, and the purchase price of such shares is usually tied to the fair market value of the apartment.

Under the proprietary lease or occupancy agreement, the cooperative member must pay a monthly charge that is similar to the common expense liability in a condominium or PUD. This amount is fixed each year by the board of directors of the corporation and reflects each cooperative member's pro rata share, based on the number of shares held, of the corporation's expenditures for the operation, maintenance, and repair of the cooperative building. This amount also covers the corporation's mortgage payments, real property taxes, and, if the corporation is incorporated for profit, corporate taxes.

Except with respect to the initial offering of stock of the cooperative corporation (which is usually regulated by specific statutory provisions) and certain tax matters (which are controlled by state and federal tax laws and regulations), the formation of a co-op is governed by the general corporate law of the state in which it is created.

The documents necessary in most states to form a cooperative include:

(1) the plan of organization of the cooperative;

(2) the prospectus (or "black book"), which is normally a full disclosure document similar to that required by state by federal securities laws prior to the issuance of certain stock;

(3) the stock subscription agreement, pursuant to which the prospective purchaser subscribes for the appropriate number of shares, makes representations respecting the purchaser's financial status, and agrees to allow the cooperative developer to withdraw its offer if a certain amount of stock is not subscribed for by a certain date;

(4) the proprietary lease or occupancy agreement, which dictates the contractual relationship between the cooperative corporation and a co-op member;

(5) the articles of incorporation and bylaws of the corporation; and

(6) the rules and regulations of the cooperative.

B. ASSISTING A PROSPECTIVE CO-OP MEMBER

The concept of cooperative ownership should be explained to a prospective co-op member and the significant provisions of the pertinent documents should be discussed. When assisting a prospective member of a newly formed co-op, all of the documents identified above are pertinent. When assisting a prospective member of a cooperative that has been in existence for a while, however, the original plan of organization, the prospectus, and the subscription agreement are of less (and often little) significance because the information contained in these documents is either outdated or no longer relevant.

A prospective member of an existing co-op has the advantage of inspecting the cooperative corporation's books and records. The legal assistant should request from the managing agent of the co-op access to (and, if permitted, copies of) the minute book and financial statements covering the three immediately preceding years of operation of the corporation. The financial statements should be analyzed to ascertain the financial strength or weakness of the corporation; to determine whether there have been any deferred items of maintenance, repair, or replacement; and to ascertain the amount of the corporation's reserve funds. By a careful review of the minute book the legal assistant should be able to determine the condition of the structural components and the mechanical and electrical systems in the cooperative building, any potential liability of the cooperative corporation, and any anticipated capital expenditures. For instance, if the minute book reveals a series of repair authorizations for a significant component of the building (such as the roof or the elevator system), it is likely that the component will require major repair or replacement in the near future. A review of the minute book will also disclose whether any "flip tax" has been authorized by the board of directors. The flip tax, which is assessed against a prospective seller usually in the amount of 2% or 3% of the sales price of the cooperative stock, is a popular device by which the cooperative corporation shares in the appreciation of the cooperative building.

PROBLEM

Draw a chart comparing a condominium, a PUD, and a cooperative with respect to the following matters:

  (a) type of governing legal structure,
  (b) form of ownership of the units and the common elements,
  (c) method of assessing liability for the payment of common expenses,
  (d) advantages and disadvantages of each form of ownership, and
  (e) significant matters a prospective purchaser should be made aware of with respect to each form of ownership.

3407 CERTIFICATE

This Certificate and accompanying attachments have been prepared on _____ on behalf of _____ , owner of Unit # _____ at _____ , hereinafter called The Association, in accordance with the Pennsylvania Uniform Condominium Act, Act No. 1980-82, July 2, 1980.

1. The Association: ☐ Does ☐ Does not have the right of first refusal on the sale of all units.
                ☐ Does ☐ Does Not have the right to approve all mortgages.
                ☐ Does ☐ Does Not require exact copies of all executed mortgages.
   Request for waiver of the right of first refusal and mortgage approvals may be applied for through the Management office or _____
   Such requests must be accompanied by a fully executed agreement of sale.

2. The monthly common expense assessment for the subject unit for the current fiscal year is $ _____ . This assessment is subject to change, either higher or lower, effective on the first day of the next fiscal year which is _____ There is $ _____ common expense and/or special assessment currently due and payable by the selling unit owner. A prospective purchaser is advised that this amount is subject to change by additional monthly assessments, special assessments or payments made prior to the date of settlements.

3. In addition to the regular monthly common expense free the subject unit is also responsible for the following fees:
   ☐ NONE
   ☐ Monthly Capital Assessment $ _____
   ☐ Special Assessment $ _____
   ☐ _____ $ _____
   ☐ _____ $ _____

4. The current amount of Reserves for Capital Expenditures is $ _____ If amounts have been allocated for specific capital projects, they are listed below:

PROJECTS	AMOUNT
_____	_____
_____	_____

5. There are no alterations or improvements to the unit or the limited common elements assigned thereto violating any provisions of the declaration known to the Council or Board of Directors, except as follows:

_____
_____

6. There are no violations of the health or building codes with respect to the unit, limited common elements assigned thereto, or any other portion of the condominium known to the Council or Board of Directors, except as follows:

_____
_____

7. There are no Leasehold Estates affecting the Association.

8. The following documents are attached hereto:
   ☐ A copy of the most recently available Balance Sheet and Income and Expense Statement of the Association.
   ☐ The current Operating Budget of the Association.
   ☐ A statement of proposed Capital Expenditures for the current and two next succeeding years.
   ☐ A statement of any judgments against the Association and the status of all pending suits, if any.
   ☐ A schedule of the Association's insurance.

Validation of this Certificate requires receipts of $ _____ for processing expenses and signatures of the unit owner(s) or the owner's agent and an authorized agent of the Association.

_____   _____

      Signature   **Owner/Agent**   **Date**

_____   _____

    Signature of Association Agent   **Date**

* Provided by Community Association Management Co., Inc., 511 West Chester Pike, Havertown, PA 19083

Glossary

Abatement   The suspension or cessation, in whole or in part, of a continuing charge, such as rent.

Adverse Possession   One may gain title to or a right to use over real property by adverse possession. Adverse possession is open, continuous (for a specified period of time), adverse (in such a manner as is contrary to ownership being in another) use and without right (the owner has not consented).

Agency   The legal relationship between a person (the agent) who is acting on behalf of another person (the principal). Most of the law respecting the agency relationship deals with the duties and responsibilities of an agent to his principal, and the responsibilities of the principal to third parties for the acts of his agent.

Amortization   The payment or repayment of a principal amount over a period of time in installments. A self-amortizing mortgage is one in which the entire principal amount will be repaid by the regularly scheduled payments, with the result that no large portion of the loan is due upon the maturity of the loan. A standing loan is one in which the principal is not repaid or reduced during the term of the loan, but is due in full at maturity.

Apportionment   The allocation of a charge or cost such as real estate taxes between two parties, often in the same ratio as the respective times that the parties are in possession or ownership of property during the fiscal period for which the charge is made or assessed.

425

Assignment The transfer by a party of all of its rights to some kind of property, usually intangible property such as rights in a lease, mortgage, agreement of sale or a partnership. Tangible property is more often transferred by possession and by instruments conveying title such as a deed or a bill of sale.

Assumption The agreement of a party to be responsible and liable for performance of the obligations of another party. A person to whom intangible property is assigned, such as the rights of a tenant under a lease, often agrees to assume the obligations of the assigning party under the contract being assigned.

Attornment The agreement of a person to recognize a third party as a permissible successor party to a contract; most often, the agreement of a tenant to pay rent to a new landlord, especially a mortgagee who has foreclosed.

Beneficial Owner One who does not have title to property but has rights in the property which are the normal incident of owning the property. The persons for whom a trustee holds title to property are the beneficial owners of the property, and the trustee has a fiduciary responsibility to them.

Capital Contribution The money or other property which a partner invests in a partnership. Normally, personal services are not considered property that may be contributed to a partnership as capital.

Completion Bond A form of surety or guaranty agreement which contains the promise of a third party, usually a bonding company, to complete or pay for the cost of completion of a construction contract if the construction contractor defaults.

Condition Precedent In a contract or other document, a specified event which must occur before all or part of the contract or document takes effect. This is to be distinguished from a condition subsequent, which is an event the occurrence of which will have the effect of rescinding or supervening some or all of the document or agreement which otherwise is in effect.

Condominium A form of ownership of real property which includes exclusive ownership and use of some portion, such as an apartment in a high-rise building, and joint and commmon use of the non-exclusive areas. The condominium concept was not rooted in English common law and most condominiums in the United States are formed in accordance with specific state enabling statutes.

Consideration   That which is given in return for the agreement or act of another person. The consideration for most contracts is the mutuality of the promises set forth in the contract.

Convey   Transfer; usually the transfer of legal title to property by deed or bill of sale.

Corporation   An organization established in accordance with a state or federal enabling law and having the legal status of a person. A corporation's identity is considered to be separate and distinct from its shareholders, officers, and directors.

Covenant   A promise, in a deed or contract, either to do something (an affirmative covenant) or to refrain from doing something (a negative covenant or a restrictive covenant). Normally the covenant specifically affects the property which is the subject of the deed or contract.

Creditor   One to whom a debtor is obligated to pay money.

Debt Service   The periodic payments that must be made in payment of a debt, including interest and principal.

Debtor   One who has an obligation to pay money.

Declaration   A document by the owner of property which is recorded in order to establish a legal order upon the property, such as a condominium (by a declaration of condominium or master deed), a system of cross-easements (by a declaration of easements) or a homeowners' association (by declaration of covenants, restrictions, and easements).

Default   A failure to perform a contractual obligation in a timely manner.

Defeasible Deed   A deed containing a condition subsequent the happening of which will cause title to the property to revert to the grantor or to go to some third party.

Demised Premises   That property, or portion of a property, which is leased to a tenant.

Depreciation   A tax accounting concept which may be applied to investment properties. The assumption is that physical structure and equipment, such as a building or an airplane (but not land) diminishes in value over time due to physical deterioration or obsolescence. Therefore, income to the taxpayer from the investment property (or from other sources) should not be taxed to the extent that the property itself has diminished (depreciated) during a tax year. The reduction in taxable income is called depreciation. Claiming depreciation on an investment property results in an equivalent reduction in the taxpayer's tax basis in the property. If property is eventually sold above the tax basis, then the taxpayer will recognize income from the sale, so that the claiming of depreciation may result in taxable income being realized at the time of sale.

Devise   To leave real property by a specific provision in a will. Real property is "devised," while personal property is "bequeathed."

Dissolution   The winding up and conclusion of a corporation (but not necessarily a partnership) as a business.

Distraint   The inchoate right and interest which a landlord has in the property of a tenant located on the demised premises. Upon a tenant's default, a landlord may in some jurisdictions distrain upon the tenant's property, generally by changing the locks and giving notice, and the landlord will then have a lien upon the goods. The priority of the lien will depend on local law.

Easement   A right of use over the property of another. Traditionally the permitted kinds of uses were limited, the most important being rights of way and rights concerning flowing waters. The easement was normally for the benefit of adjoining lands, no matter who the owner was (an easement appurtenant), rather than for the benefit of a specific individual (easement in gross). The land having the right of use as an appurtenance is known as the dominant tenement and the land which is subject to the easement is known as the servient tenement.

Eminent Domain   The paramount right of the government to take the property located within the state. In the United States, the power of eminent domain is found in both the federal and state governments. However, the constitution limits the power to taking for a public purpose and prohibits the exercise of the power of eminent domain without just compensation to the owners of the property which is taken. The process of exercising the power of eminent domain is referred to as "condemnation."

Encumbrance   Any continuing restriction or obligation upon real property, which may include a lease, mortgage, easement, ground rent, license and the like.

Equity   The difference between market value of property and the aggregate of the current outstanding balances of all mortgages upon and other liens against the property is often referred to as the owner's equity. The term came from the development in English courts of equity of the right of an owner of property to redeem his property even after a foreclosure, a right which came to be known as the equity of redemption. The existence of the right was predicated on the property being of far greater value than the debt owed to the party that foreclosed.

Escrow   The holding in safekeeping by a third party (the escrowee) of certain property, documents or money which is the subject of a dispute, or which the parties simply wish to be held pending the occurrence of specified events. Deposit money for an agreement of sale is often held in escrow by an attorney or agent pending settlement.

Estoppel Certificate   A signed statement by a party, such as a tenant or a mortgagee, certifying for the benefit of another party that a certain statement of facts is correct as of the date of the statement, such as that a lease exists, that there are no defaults and that rent is paid to a certain date. Delivery of the statement by the tenant prevents (estops) the tenant from later claiming a different state of facts.

Exclusive   A right granted to a tenant in a shopping center to be the only tenant in that center (with perhaps some specified exception) permitted to sell certain items.

Execution   (a) Execution of an agreement or document by a party is the valid signing and sealing of the agreement with all of the formalities required by law and by all of the persons necessary to bind that party. (b) Execution upon a judgment is the legal process of enforcing the judgment, usually by seizing and selling property of the debtor.

Fee Title and Fee Simple Absolute   Fee title is any kind of present ownership of real property. The fee estate is distinct from other interest, such as a leasehold estate (a tenant's interest) or an easement. Fee simple absolute is the most common kind of fee interest in the United States, and represents full ownership without any restrictions or limitations in the quality of title itself.

Fiduciary   A person who holds, controls, or manages money or property for the benefit of others in a situation such that the beneficiary has the right to expect a high degree of trust and confidence. The status of being a fiduciary gives rise to certain legal incidents and obligations, including the prohibition against investing the money or property in investments which are speculative or otherwise imprudent.

Financing Statements   A form of public notice of the existence of a security interest in personal property.

Fixtures   Items of personal property which are affixed to land or to a building in such a way that they become part of the real estate itself.

Habendum The "to have and to hold" section of a deed. When quality of title is to be limited to something less than fee simple absolute, the limitation is likely to be set forth in the habendum.

Hereditament Something which can be inherited. Some interests in real estate are potential interests rather than present interests. Some of these potential interests are hereditaments and some are not.

Indemnification The promise of one party to vouchsafe another party from financial harm with respect to a particular property or transaction.

Interest (a) A right in something; one having some right in particular real property is said to have an interest in the property, which may be a leasehold interest, fee interest, security interest, or other right (b) payments made for the loan of money, in addition to repayment of the loan, are called interest, interest being normally expressed as an annual percentage of the principal amount of the loan.

Intestate Dying without leaving a valid will. The intestacy laws of the various states control how property is to be distributed when a person dies intestate.

Joinder The consent to an agreement or document by a party who has an interest in the subject matter of the agreement or document, but who is not himself an active party to the agreement or document.

Judgment Note A form of note (a promise to pay money) which contains a warrant of attorney authorizing the holder of the note to enter (confess) judgment against the debtor without first having any legal proceeding in which the debtor can take part.

Lease The grant by the owner of real property of the right to use the property for a period of time, usually for the payment of rent. The tenant under a lease has a leasehold interest in the property, which is a form of non-fee interest in the land.

Liquidated Damages An agreed sum of money which will serve as the full payment of damages to be paid to a party to a contract upon the default of the other party.

Lis Pendens A notice entered on the public records indicating that there is a suit pending, the outcome of which could affect title to specified real property.

Mechanics' Lien Various states have a statute giving to persons who work on constructing or improving real property a right to impose a lien upon the real property, and in some cases to obtain special priorities, if they are not paid for their work.

Metes and Bounds   A way of describing land by listing the compass directions and distances of the boundaries.

Mortgage   A document granting an interest in real property as security for the payment of a note or performance of some other obligation.

Non-Disturbance Agreement   Usually part of an attornment agreement, it is an agreement by a mortgagee that it will not cancel a non-defaulting tenant's lease if it forecloses on the property.

Note   A document evidencing the obligation to pay money.

Option   The contractual right to purchase property, but with no obligation to purchase. Options to purchase are sometimes included in leases for real property.

Partnership   A form of business organization consisting of two or more persons. The traditional form of partnership is a general partnership, in which all of the partners take part in the business and have personal liability for partnership obligations. A limited partnership is a statutory hybrid between a general partnership and a corporation, and includes passive investors who do not have personal liability for partnership obligations.

Personal Liability   A kind of responsibility for the payment or performance of an obligation which exposes the personal assets of the responsible person to payment of the obligation.

Personalty or Personal Property   Any form of property whether tangible (a necklace) or intangible (a loan evidenced by a note), which is not real property. The distinction is not always an easy one to make, for example, the interest of a partner in a partnership is considered to be personalty even if the only asset of the partnership is real property.

Points   Usually, one percent. Often, in loan transactions the borrower is charged a loan fee which is expressed as a percentage of the principal loan amount or as points. The term is also used in setting interest rates. If the prime rate of interest is 7% per annum, then an interest rate of two points over prime would be 9% per annum.

Precedent   Courts attempt to decide cases on the basis of principles established in prior cases. Prior cases which are close in facts or legal principles to the case under consideration are called precedents.

Prime Rate of Interest   Usually defined as the lowest rate of interest from time to time charged by a specific lender to its best customers for short term unsecured loans. Prime is often used as the measuring rod for interest rates on other loans.

Priority The order in which claims may be satisfied out of the sale of real property.

Privity of Contract Persons who are either parties to a contract or are intended beneficiaries of the contract are said to have privity of contract. Only parties having privity of contract may sue for enforcement of the contract.

Profit (a) Most commonly, the gross proceeds of a business transaction less the costs of the transaction. (b) In English common law, a *profit à prendre* was a kind of property right which included the right to remove certain items (such as wood or specified minerals) from the land.

Purchase Money Mortgage (a) Generally, any mortgage given to secure a loan made for the purpose of acquiring the land on which the mortgage is given, (b) more particularly, a mortgage given to the seller of land to secure payment of a portion of the purchase price.

Purchaser Buyer, vendee; one who has contracted to purchase property.

Recission A remedy at law, the right of recission is the right to cancel (rescind) a contract upon the occurrence of certain kinds of default by the other contracting party. Not every default in a contract will give rise to a right of recission.

Remedies The rights given to a party by law or by contract which that party may exercise upon a default by the other contracting party, or upon the commission of a wrong (a tort) by another party.

Restriction A limitation, often imposed in a deed or lease respecting the use to which the property may be put.

Security Agreement An agreement granting a creditor a security interest in personal property, which security interest is normally perfected either by the creditor taking possession of the collateral or by filing financing statements in the proper public records.

Security Interest A form of interest in property which provides that the property may be sold in order to satisfy the obligation for which the security interest is given. A mortgage is used to grant a security interest in real property.

Seller Vendor; one who has contracted to sell property.

Settlement Closing; the culmination of a particular transaction involving real property, such as the purchase and sale of the property, the execution of a lease or the making of a mortgage loan.

Straw Party   Nominee; one who acts as an agent for another for the purpose of taking title to real property and executing whatever documents and instruments the principal may direct respecting the property.

Subordination Agreement   An agreement by which the subordinating party agrees that its interest in real property should have a lower priority than the interest to which it is being subordinated.

Subrogation   The lawful substitution of a third party in place of a party having a claim against another party. Insurance companies, guarantors and bonding companies generally have the right to step into the shoes of the party whom they compensate and sue any party whom the compensated party could have sued.

Tender   To offer; at a settlement under an agreement of sale the seller tenders the executed deed to the purchaser, who tenders the remainder of the purchase price to the seller. Although the requirement for tender may be waived in the agreement of sale, in instances of default by either party, the non-defaulting party will often go to the place of settlement at the appointed time, even though the other party is not there, and make tender.

Termination   (a) Of a lease or contract, an ending, usually before the end of the anticipated term of the lease or contract, which termination may be by mutual agreement or may be by exercise of one party of one of his remedies due to the default of the other party. (b) Of a partnership, a winding up and cessation of the business as opposed to only a technical ending (as upon the death of a partner) which is a dissolution. A dissolved partnership may terminate or may be continued by a partnership of the remaining partners, including perhaps the estate or heirs of the deceased partner.

Torrens System   A system of registering titles to lands that presumes an adjudication of title each time a deed or claim is filed.

Usury   Collectively, the laws of a jurisdiction regulating the charging of interest rates. A usurious loan is one whose interest rates are determined to be in excess of those permitted by the usury laws.

Warranty   A promise that certain facts are truly as they are represented to be and that they will remain so, subject to any specified limitations. In certain circumstances the courts will presume a warranty, known as an implied warranty.

Index

Abstract of title, 161, 166
Acceleration, 239, 358
Acceptance, 149
Acknowledgment, 146, 254, 339, 363
Acreage, 39
Advance money obligation, 239
Adverse possession, 6
Affidavit, 315
Agent, 66, 97, 345
Agreement of purchase, 234, 335
Agreement of sale, 30, 62, 80, 335
Air rights, 4
ALTA, 170
Alterations, 351, 398
American Land Title Association, 170
Amortization, 190
Annual percentage rate, 301
Application, loan, 193, 203
Apportionments, 51, 96, 102, 284
Appurtenances, 139
Arc, 115
Articles of Incorporation, 412, 419
"As is" clause, 74
Assessments, 102
Assignment, 37, 63, 260, 275, 291, 295, 337, 356, 401
Assumption of debt, 263

Attorney fees, 286, 293
Attorney in fact, 129, 145
Attornment, 207, 292

Balloon payment, 189
Base line, 108
Base year, 386
Basis, 20
Bearing, 107
Beneficial ownership, 32
Binder, 289, 294
Boilerplate, 61
Bond, 220, 290
Book of resolutions, 419
Boundaries, 117
Bounds, 107
Brokers, 61, 97
Building permits, 91, 220, 291
Buy-sell agreement, 220, 291
Bylaws, 419

Captions, 63, 171
Cash flow, 202
Casualty, 72, 355, 398
Certificate of authority, 281
Certificate of occupancy, 295
Chain of title, 167

Chord, 115
Close corporation, 399
Closing, 198, 209, 227, 271, 293
Cloud on title, 163
Coal, 150
Commercial lease, 374
Commerical mortgage, 201
Commercial real estate, 14, 104
Commitment letter, 195, 205, 215
Common areas, 380
Compass, 107
Complaint, 267
Completion bond, 220, 290
Condemnation, 39, 55, 247, 355, 399
Condemnation award, 39
Condominium, 138, 150, 408
Confession of judgment clause, 359
Consideration, 124, 135
Construction, 103, 252, 275, 289
Construction lender, 296
Construction loan settlement, 322
Construction mortgage, 210, 252, 289
Consumer Credit Protection Act, 299
Conveyance, 120
Consumer price index, 392
Cooperatives, 408
Corporate nominee, 27
Corporate taxes, 23, 27
Corporation, 18, 23, 27, 35, 66, 129, 274, 281, 345
Co-tenants, 11
Counterclaim, 269
Covenant, 8, 141, 372
Covenant running with the land, 132
Credit, 299
Cross-default provision, 239
Cross easements, 223
Curtesy, 7, 12

Damages, 56
Date, 34, 89, 122
Declaration of covenants and easements, 138
Declaration of cross easements, 223, 291
Declaration of no set-off, 228, 261, 295
Declaration of reciprocal easements, 291

Declaration of trust, 26
Deductions, tax, 20
Deed, 44, 120, 272
Deed of grant, 137
Deed pool, 121
Default, 56, 239, 248, 267, 358, 397
Delivery, 149
Demise, 345
Depletion, 20
Deposit, 41, 89, 368
Depreciation, 20
Description, 37, 78, 89, 100, 105, 127, 173, 242, 346, 410
Disclosure, 301, 324
Distraint, 359
Dower, 7, 12

Easements, 5, 44, 136, 209, 223, 291, 418
Ejectment, 359
Eminent domain, 39, 55, 247, 355, 399
Encumbrance clause, 130, 144
Endorsements, 173
England, 2
Entry of leased premises, 357
Equitable ownership, 32
Equity, 230
Equity of redemption, 187
Escrow account, 41, 288
Escrow agent, 66
Escrow delivery, 149
Escrow funds, 199, 244
Estoppel certificates, 229, 295, 389
Estoppel letter, 261
Exclusives, 385
Execution clause, 144
Execution sale, 270
Expenses, 95

Fanny Mae, 192
Federal Home Loan Mortgage Corporation, 192, 337
Federal Housing Administration, 192, 229
Federal National Mortgage Association, 192, 337
Fee, 4, 286, 300, 340
Fee simple absolute, 4

Fee simple deed, 151
FHA, 192, 229
Fiduciary, 345
Fiduciary's warranty, 143
Filing fees, 340
Finance charges, 301
Finance statement, 223, 247, 291
Fire, 72, 280, 353, 383, 414
First refusal, right of, 370
Fixture, 39, 75, 91, 375
Foreclosure sale, 68, 187, 266
Freddy Mac, 192
Future interest, 5

General warranty, 142
Gift, 6
Good title, 46
Government survey system, 108
Grantee, 121
Granting clause, 124
Grantor, 121
Grantor-grantee index, 165, 339
Gross sales, 377
Ground lease, 394, 396
Guaranty, 400

Habendum, 122, 140, 243
Have and to hold, 140
Heirs and assigns clause, 374
HUD, 231
Husband. *See* Curtesy, Spouse, Tenancy by the entirety.

Implied warranty, 125
Improvements, 352
Income, 95
Income taxes, 19
    See also Taxes.
Indemnification, 135, 263, 366, 382
Indenture, 121, 151
Index, 165, 338
Industrial development authority loan, 233
Industrial mortgage, 201
Inheritance, 6, 125
Inheritance taxes, 14, 277
Inspection, 60, 73, 80, 279, 357
Installment sale, 98

Insurable title, 47
Insurance, 73, 161, 198, 205, 230, 245, 280, 290, 383, 395, 414
Insurance, mortgage, 230
Integration, 64
Integration clause, 373
Interest, 4, 188, 232, 287
Interest subsidy, 232
Intestacy, 6, 12, 33

Joinder, 66
Joint names, 11
Joint tenants, 12, 126, 276
Joint venture, 15, 17
Judgments, 168, 273, 334

Kickbacks, 300

Land use, 7
Landlord. *See* Lease.
Lease, 4, 93, 206, 275, 291, 336, 343 ff.
Leaseback, 99, 399
Leasehold mortgage, 396
Legal description. *See* Description.
Level payment loan, 189
Liability insurance, 384.
    See also Insurance.
License, 92
Lien, 8, 44, 79, 133, 168
Life estate, 5
Limited partnership, 16, 24
Lis pendens, 335
Loan, 189, 212, 230, 233
Loan, industrial development, 233
Loss of bargain, 57

Magnuson-Moss Act, 79
Maintenance, 246, 380
Maker, 235
Management contract, 414
Managing agent, 97
Map file, 128
Marked-up title report, 288, 298
Marketable title, 46, 162
Mechanics' liens, 79, 171, 226, 287, 292

Memorandum of lease, 336
Merchants' Association, 381
Merger, 50, 61
Meridians, 108
Metes and bounds, 107
Mineral rights, 4
Mineral severance clause, 150
Monuments, 111
Mortgage, 8, 25, 67, 71, 133, 168, 172, 186ff., 229, 241, 256, 279
Mortgage assignment, 260, 337
Mortgage contingency, 71, 83
Mortgage, construction, 252
Mortgage defenses, 269
Mortgage, drafting, 241
Mortgage foreclosure, 266
Mortgage insurance, 230
Mortgage lien, 8
Mortgage loan, 234
Mortgage pay-off, 313
Mortgage release, 262
Mortgage satisfaction, 261, 314, 337
Mortgage, second, 252
Mortgage, subordination of, 264
Municipal lien, 171

Name index, 338
Negative covenants, 372
Net and ground leases, 394, 399
Non-disturbance agreement, 208, 292
Note, 219, 235, 254
Notice, 62
Notice statute, 330
Nuisance, 8

Objections, 172, 274
Obligor, 235
Office building lease, 391
Offset, 269
Option agreement, 98
Option to purchase, 369
Ownership, 3
Ownership, determination of, 9
Parking, 389
Payment, 40, 124, 189, 237, 288, 296
Parties, 34, 99, 123, 235, 242, 344
Partnership, 15, 22, 34, 65, 378, 399
Partnership taxation, 22

Percentage rent, 96, 375, 387
Performance bond, 296
Personal liability, 68, 134
Personal property, 2, 8, 75, 91, 286
Personalty. See Personal property.
Plain language, 9
Plan, 37, 112
Planned-unit developments, 408
Platting, 338
Plot, 112
Points, 71, 200
Possession, 49, 92, 364
Premises, 122
Prepaid interest, 287
Prepayment privilege, 238
Prescription, 139
Price, 40, 100, 283
Principal, 189
Profit à pendre, 4
Public offering statement, 413
Public streets, 39
Public utilities, 280
PUD, 408
Punch list, 80
Purchase, 6
Purchase money mortgage, 67, 70, 275
Purchaser, 37

Quitclaim deed, 44, 55, 144, 155

Race-notice statute, 331
Race statute, 329
Radius, 115
Raw land, 103
Real property, defined, 2
Real estate as bundle of rights, 3
Real estate broker, 61
Real estate, defined, 2
Real Estate Settlement Procedures Act, 47, 298
Real estate taxes, 53, 199, 273, 284
Real estate transfer taxes, 53
Receipt, 146
Recital, 128
Reciprocal easement agreement, 138
Recording, 62, 164, 286, 288, 294, 328, 363

Recording tax, 287
Rectangular survey system, 108
Regulation Z, 301
Release of mortgage, 260
Remedies, 56, 102, 248, 358
Renewals, 362
Rent, 285, 364, 375
Rental, 347
Rent roll, 295
Rent supplement, 233
Repairs, 350, 396
Representations, 64, 82
Residential mortgage, 188
Residential property, 76
RESPA, 47, 298
Right of first refusal, 370
Right of way, 5
Risk of loss, 33, 72, 102
Running with land, 132

Sale leaseback, 99
Sales, 377
Satisfaction of mortgage, 260, 337
Satisfaction piece, 272
Search title, 164, 197
Second mortgage, 252
Security agreement, 223, 250, 291
Security deposit, 285, 368
Section 236 program, 232
Self-amortizing loan, 189
Self-liquidating loan, 189
Seller, 36
Selling real estate, 29
Service contract, 96
Services, 365
Set-off, 228, 261, 295
Settlement, 48, 89, 101, 198, 271, 302
Settlement checklist, 316
Settlement clerk, 282
Settlement index, 320
Settlement sheet, 302
Sewer, 78, 80, 171, 273, 284
Shelter, tax, 21
Sheriff's sale, 68, 129, 149, 158
Shopping center lease, 374
Shrubbery, 82
Signature and signature lines, 35, 65, 145

Single-family residence, 66, 77
Special warranty, 142
Specific performance, 56
Spouse, 13, 36
Statute of frauds, 31, 40, 165, 348
Stockholder, 18
Straw parties, 24, 202
Streets, public, 39
Subdivision, 78, 90, 112, 276
Subordination of lease, 367
Subordination of mortgage, 264, 292
Subletting, 356, 401
Subsidy, 232
Surety, 400
Survey, 3, 105, 220, 279, 290
Survivorship, 12, 276

Tax escalation, 385
Tax lien, 168
Taxes, 14, 18, 19, 52, 199, 244, 273, 284, 287, 340
Tax shelter, 21
Tenant. *See* Lease.
Tenants by the entirety, 13, 126
Tenants in common, 11, 126
Tender, 48
Termites, 73, 198, 277
Time, 48
Title abstracting, 161
Title checklist, 101
Title, condition of, 46
Title, construction loan, 214
Titleholders, 10
Title index, 166
Title insurance, 161, 205, 289, 294
Title, methods of acquiring, 6
Title policy, 177
Title report, 162, 169, 177, 279, 288, 292
Title search, 9, 164, 197
Torrens system, 163, 341
Township, 109
Tract index, 338
Trade fixture, 375
Transfer of title, 251
Transfer tax, 53, 287, 340
Transit, 107
Trust, declaration of, 26
Truth in lending, 299, 325

Under and subject clause, 131
Undivided interest, 4
Uniform Condominium Act, 411
Use clause, 349
Utilities, 365

Variance, 59
Veterans Administration (VA), 192

Waiver, 269, 277, 292, 372
Warranty, 62, 78, 95, 125, 141, 250
Warranty deed, 55
Water, 78, 171, 273, 284
Widow, widower, 7
Wife. *See* Dower, Spouse.

Zoning, 7, 8, 58, 78, 92, 278